Maine
AN EXPLORER'S GUIDE

Looking north from Little Beach to Main Beach in Ogunquit

Maine
AN EXPLORER'S GUIDE

CHRISTINA TREE & ELIZABETH ROUNDY

Seventh Edition

The Countryman Press
Woodstock, Vermont

Dedications

To Timothy Alfred Davis
— C.T.

To the memory of Nancy Gilles
— E.R.

Library of Congress Cataloging-in-Publication Data
Tree, Christina.
Maine : an explorer's guide / Christina Tree and Elizabeth Roundy. — 7th ed.
p. cm.
Includes index.
ISBN 0-88150-328-2
1. Maine—Guidebooks. I. Roundy, Elizabeth. II. Title.
F17.3.T73 1995
917.4104'43—dc20
95-2275
CIP

Published by Countryman Press
P.O. Box 748
Woodstock, Vermont 05091

Distributed by W.W. Norton & Company, Inc.
500 Fifth Avenue
New York, New York 10110

Text design by Glenn Suokko

Maps by Alex Wallach

Cover design by Georganna Towne

Cover a detail of painting, *Houses Overlooking Stonington Harbor, June,* by Jill Anise Hoy

Text composition by Bud Swanson

Printed in the United States of America
10 9 8 7 6 5

Explore With Us!

We have been fine-tuning *Maine: An Explorer's Guide* for the past 13 years, a period in which lodging, dining, and shopping opportunities have more than quadrupled in the state. As we have expanded our guide, we have also been increasingly selective, making recommendations based on years of conscientious research and personal experience. What makes us truly unique is that we describe the state by locally defined regions, giving you Maine's communities, not simply her most popular destinations. With this guide you'll feel confident to venture beyond the tourist towns, along roads less traveled, to places of special hospitality and charm.

WHAT'S WHERE

In the beginning of the book you'll find an alphabetical listing of special highlights and important information that you may want to reference quickly. You'll find advice on everything from where to buy the best local lobster to where to write or call for camping reservations and park information.

LODGING

We've selected lodging places for mention in this book based on their merit alone; **we do not charge innkeepers for inclusion.** We're the only travel guide that tries personally to check every bed & breakfast, farm, sporting lodge, and inn in Maine, and one of the few that does not charge for inclusion.

Prices: Please don't hold us or the respective innkeepers responsible for the rates listed as of press time in 1995. Some changes are inevitable. The 7-percent state rooms and meals tax should be added to all prices unless we specifically state that it's included in a price. We've tried to note when a gratuity is added but it's always wise to check before booking.

Smoking: Many B&Bs are now smoke-free and many inns and restaurants feature smoke-free rooms. If this is important to you, be sure to ask when making reservations.

RESTAURANTS

In most sections, please note a distinction between *Dining Out* and *Eating Out*. By their nature, restaurants included in the *Eating Out* group are generally inexpensive.

KEY TO SYMBOLS

☞ The special-value symbol appears next to selected lodging and restaurants that combine quality and moderate prices.

✐ The kids-alert symbol appears next to lodging, restaurants, activities, and shops of special interest or appeal to youngsters.

We would appreciate any comments or corrections. Please address your correspondence to Explorer's Guide Editor, The Countryman Press, PO Box 748, Woodstock, Vermont 05091-0175.

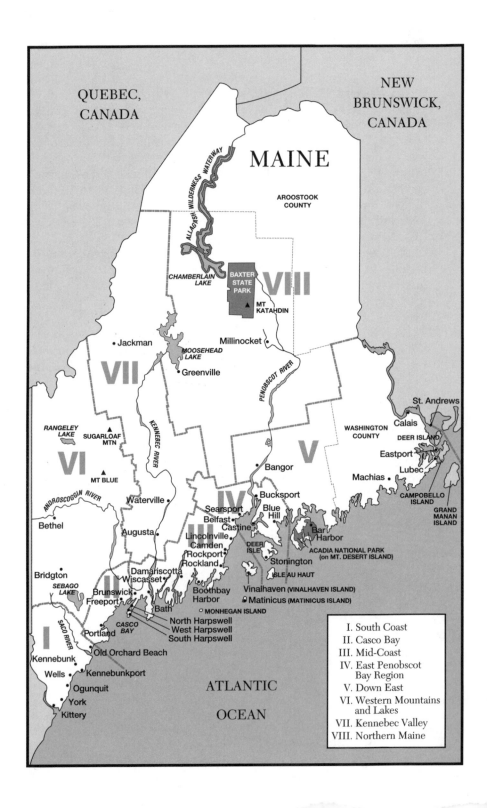

QUEBEC, CANADA

NEW BRUNSWICK, CANADA

MAINE

AROOSTOOK COUNTY

ALLAGASH WILDERNESS WATERWAY

CHAMBERLAIN LAKE

BAXTER STATE PARK

VIII

▲ MT KATAHDIN

• Jackman

MOOSEHEAD LAKE

• Millinocket

• Greenville

PENOBSCOT RIVER

VII

RANGELEY LAKE

SUGARLOAF MTN

KENNEBEC RIVER

St. Andrews

Calais

WASHINGTON COUNTY

DEER ISLAND

VI

▲ MT BLUE

Eastport

Lubec

• Bangor

ANDROSCOGGIN RIVER

Waterville

Machias

CAMPOBELLO ISLAND

GRAND MANAN ISLAND

• Bucksport

Searsport• Blue Hill
Belfast•

Bethel

IV

Castine

Bar Harbor

Augusta

Lincolnville
Camden
Rockport
Rockland•

III

DEER ISLE

ACADIA NATIONAL PARK (on MT. DESERT ISLAND)

Bridgton

SEBAGO LAKE

Damariscotta
•Wiscasset

Stonington

ISLE AU HAUT

SACO RIVER

Boothbay Harbor

Vinalhaven (VINALHAVEN ISLAND)

Brunswick
Freeport•

Bath

Matinicus (MATINICUS ISLAND)

II

CASCO BAY

North Harpswell
West Harpswell
South Harpswell

○ MONHEGAN ISLAND

Portland

Old Orchard Beach

I

Kennebunk

ATLANTIC

Wells

Kennebunkport

Ogunquit

York

OCEAN

Kittery

I.	South Coast
II.	Casco Bay
III.	Mid-Coast
IV.	East Penobscot Bay Region
V.	Down East
VI.	Western Mountains and Lakes
VII.	Kennebec Valley
VIII.	Northern Maine

Contents

9   Introduction
13   What's Where in Maine

I. SOUTH COAST
37   *Kittery and the Yorks*
55   *Ogunquit and Wells*
73   *The Kennebunks*
92   *Old Orchard Beach Area*

II. CASCO BAY
103 *Portland Area*
125 *Freeport*

III. MID-COAST AND THE ISLANDS
139 *Mid-Coast Area*
141 *Brunswick and The Harpswells*
153 *Bath Area*
167 *Wiscasset*
175 *Boothbay Harbor Region*
189 *Damariscotta/Newcastle and Pemaquid Area*
209 *Rockland/Thomaston Area*
225   The Islands
235 *Rockport, Camden, and Lincolnville*

IV. EAST PENOBSCOT BAY REGION
261 *Belfast, Searsport, Stockton Springs, and Bucksport*
272 *Castine*
277 *The Blue Hill Area*
288 *Deer Isle, Stonington, and Isle au Haut*

V. DOWN EAST
299 *Bar Harbor and Acadia Area*
332 *Bangor Area*
339 *Washington County, Campobello, and St. Andrews*
342   The Atlantic Coast: Milbridge to Campobello
357   Eastport and Cobscook Bay
362   Calais and the St. Croix Valley
366   New Brunswick: St. Andrews

VI. WESTERN MOUNTAINS AND LAKES REGION

373   *Sebago and Long Lakes Region*
391   *Bethel Area*
409   *Rangeley Lakes Region*
421   *Sugarloaf and the Carrabassett Valley*

VII. THE KENNEBEC VALLEY

435   *Augusta and Mid-Maine*
446   *The Upper Kennebec Valley and Jackman*

VIII. NORTHERN MAINE

457   *The North Woods*
459   *Moosehead Lake Area Including Lower Piscataquis*
474   *Katahdin Region*
483   *Aroostook County*

495   General Index
506   Lodging Index

Introduction

He who rides and keeps the beaten track studies the fences chiefly.

—*Henry David Thoreau,* The Maine Woods, *1853*

Back in the 1920s "motor touring" was hailed as a big improvement over train and steamer travel because it meant you no longer had to go where everyone else did—over routes prescribed by railroad tracks and steamboat schedules.

Ironically, though, in Maine cars have had precisely the opposite effect. Now 90 percent of the state's visitors follow the coastal tourist route as faithfully as though their wheels were grooved to Route 1.

Worse still, it's as though many tourists are on a train making only express stops—at rush hour. At least half of those who follow Route 1 stop, stay, and eat in all the same places (such as Kennebunkport, Boothbay or Camden, and Bar Harbor)—in August. Although this book should help visitors and Maine residents alike enjoy the state's resort towns, it is particularly useful for those who explore less frequented places.

When *Maine: An Explorer's Guide* first appeared in 1982, it was the first 20th-century guidebook to describe New England's largest state region by region rather than by tourist towns listed alphabetically. From the start it critiqued places to stay and to eat as well as everything to see and to do—based on merit rather than money (we don't charge anyone to be included).

In the beginning it didn't seem like a tall order; but over the years—which coincided with a proliferation of inns, B&Bs, and other lodging options—we've been including more and more of Maine from Matinicus to Madawaska and from the White Mountains to Campobello, not to mention all of Route 1 from Kittery to Fort Kent. In this edition we have added Aroostook, Maine's largest, most remote, and least visited county.

In all, we now describe more than 500 places to stay, ranging from campgrounds to grand old resorts and including farms as well as B&Bs and inns—in all corners of the state and in all price ranges. We have also checked out many hundreds of places to dine and to eat (we make a distinction between dining and eating); and, since shopping is an important part of everyone's travels, we include exceptional stores we've discovered while browsing along the coast and inland. We have opinions about everything we've found, and we don't hesitate to share them. In every category, we record exactly what we see, again because we charge no business to be included in the book.

Guidebooks either atrophy and die after an edition or two, or they take on a life of their own. We are relieved to report that by now *Maine: An Explorer's Guide* has introduced so many people to so many parts of Maine that it has become a phenomenon in its own right.

Chris is a Bay Stater addicted to many Maines. As a toddler she learned to swim in the Ogunquit River and later watched her three sons do the same in Monhegan's icy waters—and then learn to sail at summer camp in Raymond and paddle canoes on the Saco River and down the St. John's. Before beginning this book, she thought she "knew" Maine, having already spent a dozen years exploring it for the *Boston Globe,* describing the charm of coastal villages and the quiet of inland mountains and lakes. For the *Globe,* she continues to write about a variety of things to do, from skiing at Sugarloaf and Sunday River and llama trekking in Bethel to sea kayaking off Portland and windjamming on Penobscot Bay. But after 14 years, some 70,000 miles, and seven editions of the book, Chris no longer claims to "know" Maine. What she does know are the state's lodging places (she also co-authors *Best Places to Stay in New England*), restaurants, and shops, from Kittery to Calais and from Matinicus to Kokadjo and Grand Lake Stream.

Elizabeth was born and raised in the Bangor area, and she took Maine for granted, never appreciating its beauty and uniqueness until she returned after moving out of state for a few years. She has lived in the Bangor area, Augusta, Bar Harbor, and the Portland area and has spent time in "camps" on lakes with her family as a child; one of her favorite spots remains a large lodge overlooking the ocean on Sandy Point, where she spent many special summers. She too thought she knew Maine but, in the course of this research, realized that she was wrong, that there are many less traveled areas that even a native can overlook, places she had avoided with misconceived notions of how they would be, only to be pleasantly surprised. She also discovered some amazing history she had been missing but won't soon forget.

Maine's history continues to fascinate both of us. We are intrigued by the traces of ancient Native American habitations and pre-Pilgrim settlements, by colorful tales of 17th-century heroes like Baron de St. Castin (scion of a noble French family who married a Penobscot Indian princess), and by the state's legendary seafaring history, well told in the Maine Maritime Museum in Bath (where a total of 5000 vessels have been launched over the years) and at the Penobscot Marine Museum (in Searsport, a small village that once boasted of being home to a full 10 percent of all American sea captains). And, of course, there is the heady saga of the lumbering era (dramatized in the Lumberman's Museum in Patten), which finally ensured Maine's admission to the Union in 1820, but not until Massachusetts had sold off all unsettled land, the privately owned "Unorganized Townships" that add up to nearly half of inland Maine.

We are also fascinated by the ways in which 150 years of tourism, as much as any industry, have helped shape Maine's current landscape: by the fact, for instance, that long-vanished trains and steamboats still determine where you stay in Maine. With the exception of Sugarloaf/ USA (one of New England's largest ski resorts), all resort villages date from the time when visitors from Boston, New York, and Philadelphia were ferried directly to the tips of peninsulas and coastal islands or deposited at inland train depots, frequently to board boats bound for lakeside hotels.

Cars have altered this picture only to a degree, narrowing the number of towns geared to accommodating any volume of visitors. Nineteenth-century resorts like Stonington, Castine, Pemaquid Point, and Christmas Cove, all of them too far off Route 1 to attract much traffic today, contentedly cater to yachtsmen and inn lovers. And of all the inland villages that once welcomed summer "rusticators," only Bridgton, Bethel, Rangeley, and the Moosehead area still serve non-cottage owners in any number.

This book's introductory section, "What's Where in Maine," is a quick reference directory to a vast variety of activities available within the state. The remainder of the book describes Maine region by region. The basic criterion for including an area is the availability of lodging.

Note that "off-season" prices are often substantially less than those in July and August. September is dependably sparkling and frequently warm. Early October in Maine is just as spectacular as it is in New Hampshire and Vermont, with magnificent mountains rising from inland lakes as well as the golds and reds set against coastal blue. It's also well worth noting that the inland resorts of Bethel and the Sugarloaf area are "off-season" all summer as well as fall.

Maine is almost as big as the other five New England states combined, but her residents add up to fewer than half the population of Greater Boston. That means there is plenty of room for all who look to her for renewal—both residents and out-of-staters.

We would like to thank Christopher Lloyd and Helen Whybrow of The Countryman Press for shepherding our manuscript through the many stages to publication of this, the seventh, edition. Chris owes thanks to John Johnson and Nathaniel Bowditch of the State Tourism Office, to Virginia Fieldman of Jonesport, David Potter and Julia Bayly of Fort Kent, Linda Pagels of Milbridge, Joan Yeaton of Addison,

Sailboats in Bar Harbor

Wende Gray of Bethel, Mark Hodesh of Castine, Sue Antal of York, and to her son and fellow Maine-sleuth, Tim Davis, and her ever-helpful husband, William Davis. Elizabeth thanks her family for their tremendous support, and Todd Lyons for weathering her absences, her mutterings at the computer, and her bouts of anxiety. She also owes thanks to John Johnson and Marjory Wright at the Maine Office of Tourism.

We would also like to thank all the people who took the time to write in response to our plea for reader input in our last edition. We welcome your comments and appreciate all your thoughtful suggestions for future editions of *Maine: An Explorer's Guide.*

What's Where in Maine

AGRICULTURAL FAIRS

The season opens with the small, family-geared **Pittston Fair** in late June (pig scrambles all 3 days!) and culminates with the big, colorful **Fryeburg Fair** during the first week of October. Among the best traditional fairs are the **Union Fair** (late August) and the **Blue Hill Fair** (Labor Day weekend). The **Common Ground Country Fair** (late September at the fairgrounds in Windsor) draws Maine's back-to-the-earth and organic gardeners from all corners of the state, and the **Full Circle Summer Fair** in Blue Hill (mid-July) is a smaller, even less "commercial" gathering. Request a pamphlet listing all the fairs from the Maine Department of Agriculture (287-3221), State House Station 28, Augusta 04333.

AIRPORTS AND AIRLINES

Portland, with connections to most American and Canadian cities, is an increasingly important gateway to northern New England. Bangor International is also served by major carriers. Bar Harbor/Hancock County Regional, Rockland/Knox County Regional, and Northern Maine Regional (Presque Isle) are served by smaller planes from Portland and Boston.

AIR SERVICES

Also called flying services, these are useful links with wilderness camps and coastal islands. Greenville, prime jump-off point for the North Woods, claims to be New England's largest seaplane base. In this book, flying services are also listed in the Rangeley and Katahdin chapters. From Rockland, air taxis also serve some islands.

AMUSEMENT PARKS

Funtown in Saco, which includes Cascade Water Park, is Maine's biggest, and **Aquaboggan** (pools and slides) is also on Route 1 in Saco. **Palace Playland** in Old Orchard Beach is a classic with a 1906 carousel, a Ferris wheel, rides, and a 60-foot water slide. **York's Wild Kingdom** at York Beach and **Funland** in Caribou are small areas offering kiddy rides and arcades.

ANTIQUARIAN BOOKS

Maine is well known among book buffs as a browsing mecca. Within this book we have noted antiquarian bookstores where they cluster along Route 1 in Wells and in Portland. More than 75 are described in a directory available from all the antiquarian dealers mentioned in this guide.

ANTIQUES

A member directory listing more than 100 dealers is produced by the Maine Antiques Dealers' Association, Inc., also available from the Maine Publicity Bureau (MPB) (623-0363). Other useful resources are the monthly *Maine Antiques Digest,* available in many bookstores, and Ed Welch's *Maine Antiques Dealers Directory* listing over 200 dealers by area, available for $1.00 at many dealers or for $1.50 from Edward M. Welch, Jr., RFD 3, Box 1290, Winslow 04901.

APPLES

Fall brings plenty of pick-your-own opportunities across the state, and many orchards also sell apples and cider. For a list of orchards, contact the Department of Agriculture (287-3491) for their brochure "Maine Apples."

AQUARIUMS

The **Maine Aquarium** in Saco is open daily year-round, exhibiting seals, penguins, sharks, and tide pool animals. The **Mount Desert Oceanarium** has three locations: Southwest Harbor has 20 tanks exhibiting sea life; Bar Harbor features everything you ever wanted to know about lobsters; and the working lobster hatchery in downtown Bar Harbor is where thousands of lobsters are raised for later release.

AREA CODE

The area code for Maine is 207. You are now required to dial the area code in-state when calling outside the local calling area.

ART GALLERIES

Commercial galleries selling work by local artists have proliferated so in recent years that the Maine Publicity Bureau (623-0363) has compiled a partial list of more than 75. Within this book, look for detailed listings in **Ogunquit, Portland, Brunswick,** the **Blue Hill** area, **Bar Harbor and Acadia,** and **Eastport.**

ART MUSEUMS

Portland Museum of Art (775-6148), 111 High Street, Portland, has an outstanding collection of American paintings. The **Farnsworth Museum** in Rockland and the **Bowdoin College Museum of Art** in Brunswick are both worth a trip for lovers of 19th- and 20th-century Maine artists. Among seasonal galleries, the **Ogunquit Museum and Barn Gallery** (Ogunquit), the **Maine Art Gallery** in Wiscasset (also open weekends in winter), and the **Maine Coast Artists Gallery** in Rockport (closed in winter) stand out.

BALLOONING

Hot-air rides are available across the state. Some places offering rides are: in the Portland area, **Balloon Rides** (1-800-952-2076), **Balloon Sports** (772-4401), **Hot Fun** (799-0193), and **Freeport Balloon Co.** (865-1712); in Augusta, **Balloon Drifters, Inc.** (622-1211); in Hollis, **Fantasy Ballooning Co.** (929-3200); in Lyman, **Lovell Balloon Works** (1-800-788-5562); in Auburn, **Rosebud Balloon Co.** (784-2257); and in Brewer, **Damn Yankee Balloons, Inc.** (989-7673).

BEACHES

Just 2 percent of the Maine coast is public, and not all of that is beach. Given the summer temperature of the water (from 59 degrees in Ogunquit to 54 degrees at Bar Harbor), swimming isn't the primary reason you come to Maine. But Maine beaches can be splendid walking, sunning, and kite-flying places (see York, Ogunquit, Wells, the Kennebunks, Portland, Reid State Park, Popham, and Pemaquid). At **Ogunquit** and in **Reid State Park,** there are also warmer

NANCY G. HORTON

backwater areas in which small children can paddle, but families tend to take advantage of the reasonably priced cottages available on lakes, many of them just a few miles from the seashore (see *Lakes*). Other outstanding beaches include 7-mile-long **Old Orchard** and, nearby, state-maintained **Crescent Beach** on Cape Elizabeth, **Scarborough Beach** in Scarborough, and **Ferry Beach** in Saco. The big, state-maintained freshwater beaches are on **Lake Damariscotta, St. George, Sebec, Rangeley, Sebago,** and **Moosehead;** also on **Pleasant Pond** in Richmond. All state beach facilities include changing facilities, rest rooms, and showers; many have snack bars. The town of Bridgton has several fine little lakeside beaches. In 1994, state beaches charged $2.00 per person entrance; $2.50 at Crescent Beach, Montpelier, Range Ponds, and Sebago Lake.

BED & BREAKFASTS

We visited hundreds of B&Bs and were impressed by what we saw. They range from elegant town houses and country mansions to farms and a fisherman's home. Prices vary from $30 to $385 (in Bar Harbor in August) for a double and average $85 in high season on the coast. With few exceptions, they offer a friendly entrée to their communities. Hosts are usually delighted to advise guests on places to explore, dine, and shop. The "Maine Guide to Inns and Bed & Breakfasts," available from the Maine Publicity Bureau (623-0363), includes more than 275 descriptive listings for 1994. The largest statewide reservation service, Bed & Breakfast Down East Ltd., includes many homes that advertise no other way (a $3 directory describing more than 100 homes is available from Box 547, Eastbrook 04634). If you are particularly impressed or disappointed in a B&B you find listed in this book, please let us know. (Also see *Farm B&Bs*.)

BICYCLING

Mountain biking has become a widely popular sport and is often the best way to explore islands, trails, and country roads. The carriage roads in **Acadia National Park** are particularly well suited for mountain biking. Routes are outlined in local handouts, and rentals are available. **Sunday River's Mountain Bike Park** offers high-altitude trails and a bike school (see Bethel); **Sugarloaf/USA** also rents bikes and suggests trails. A few Maine islands are best toured by bike: see Casco Bay Islands, Vinalhaven, Islesboro, and Swans Island. Bicycle and moped rentals are available in Bar Harbor, Kennebunkport, Ogunquit, and Windham. Five-day inn-to-inn tours are offered by **Maine Coast Cyclers,** based in Camden. **American Youth Hostels** maintains nominally priced, bicyclist-geared hostels in Portland, Carmel, and Bar Harbor; contact AYH, Greater Boston Council, 1020 Commonwealth Avenue, Boston, MA 02215 (617-731-5430). Another good resource for bikers is *25 Bicycle Tours in Maine* by Howard Stone (Backcountry Publications).

BIRDING

The **Maine Audubon Society** (781-2330), based at Gilsland Farm in Falmouth, maintains a number of birding sites and sponsors nature programs and field trips, which include cruises to Matinicus Rock and to Eagle Island. (For details about the **National Audubon Ecology Camp** on Hog Island, see Damariscotta area.) The most popular coastal birding spots are the **national wildlife sanctuaries** between Kittery and Cape Elizabeth, especially the area now preserved as **Laudholm Farm** in Wells. **Biddeford Pool, Scarborough Marsh, Merrymeeting Bay,** and **Mount Desert** are the other top birding sites. **Monhegan** is the island to visit. The

Moosehorn National Wildlife Refuge (454-3521) in Washington County represents the northeastern terminus of the East Coast chain of wildlife refuges and is particularly rich in bird life. We recommend *A Birder's Guide to the Coast of Maine* by Elizabeth Cary Pierson and Jan Erik Pierson (Down East Books). (Also see *Puffin-Watching* and *Nature Preserves.*)

BLUEBERRYING

Maine grows 98 percent of America's lowbush blueberries. More than 40 million pounds are harvested annually from an estimated 25,000 acres. Because of pruning practices, only half the acreage produces berries in a given year, and there are absolutely no human-planted wild blueberry fields. Lowbush blueberry plants spread naturally in the present commercial fields after the forests are cleared or by natural establishment in abandoned pastures. Unfortunately, very few berries are sold fresh (most are quick-frozen), and few growers allow U-pick, at least not until the commercial harvest is over. Then the public is invited to go "stumping" for leftovers. On the other hand, berrying along roads and hiking paths, under power lines, and on hilltops is a rite of summer for all who happen to be in southern Maine in late July or farther Down East in early August. For a look at the **blueberry barrens**—thousands of blueberry-covered acres—you must drive up to Cherryfield, Columbia, and Machias (site of the state's most colorful blueberry festival in August) in Washington County. For more about Maine's most famous fruit, write: Wild Blueberry Association of North America, 142 Kelley Road, Orono 04473.

BOAT BUILDING

Wooden Boat School (359-4651) in Brooklin (see "The Blue Hill Area") offers more than 75 warm-weather courses, including more than 24 on various aspects of boat building. The **Maine Maritime Museum** in Bath offers an apprenticeship program; the **Landing School of Boatbuilding & Design** in Kennebunk offers summer courses in building sailboats; the **Rockport Apprenticeshop** (236-6071) in Rockport offers 2-year apprenticeships, 6-week internships, and 6-week volunteer stints; and the **Washington County Vocational-Tech Inst. Marine Trades Center** at Deep Cove attracts many out-of-staters.

BOAT EXCURSIONS

You don't need to own your own yacht to enjoy the salt spray and views, and you really won't know what Maine is about until you stand off at sea to appreciate the beauty of the cliffs and island-dotted bays. For the greatest concentrations of boat excursions, see Boothbay Harbor, Rockland, and Mount Desert; there are also excursions from Ogunquit, Kennebunkport, Camden, and Stonington. (Also see *Coastal Cruises, Ferries, Sailing,* and *Windjammers.*) See "Western Mountains and Lakes Region" and "Augusta and Mid-Maine" for lake excursions.) A partial list of 85 "Maine Boat Cruises/Ferries" is published in Maine Publicity Bureau's annual free magazine, *Maine Invites You.*

BOAT RENTALS

Readily available in the Belgrade Lakes, the Sebago Lake area, in Rangeley, Jackman, Rockwood, and all other inland lake areas. (Also see *Canoe Rentals* and *Sailing.*)

CAMPING

Almost half of Maine lies within "unorganized townships": wooded, privately owned lands, most of which are open to the public on condition that basic rules be observed. These rules vary with the owners. See the North Woods chapters for details about camping within these vast fiefdoms, also for camping in **Baxter State Park** and in the **Allagash Wilderness.** For camping within **Acadia National Park,** see Mount Desert. For the same within the **White Mountain National Forest,** see Bethel. For private campgrounds, the booklet "Maine Camping Guide," published by the Maine Campground Owners Association, lists most privately operated camping and tenting areas in the state and is available from the Maine Publicity Bureau (623-0363). Reservations are advised for the state's 13 parks that offer camping; phone 287-3821. We have attempted to describe the state parks in detail wherever they appear in this book (see Camden, Damariscotta, Mount Desert, Greenville, Rangeley, and Sebago). Note that though campsites can accommodate average-sized campers and trailers, there are no trailer hookups. Warren Island off Lincoln offers organized camping, and primitive camping is permitted on a number of islands through the Island Institute (see *Islands*). (Also see *Parks, State.*)

CAMPS, FOR ADULTS

The **Appalachian Mountain Club** maintains a number of summer lodges and campsites for adults and families seeking a hiking and/or canoeing vacation. Intended primarily for members, they are technically open to all who reserve space, available only after April 1. The full-service camps in Maine (offering three daily meals, organized hikes, evening programs) are at **Echo Lake** and **Cold River Camp** in Evans Notch (near the New Hampshire border within the White Mountain National Forest). For details about all facilities and membership, contact the AMC (617-523-0636). **Outward Bound** (594-5548) in Rockland and Bethel offers a variety of adult-geared outdoors adventures. **Audubon Ecology Camp** on Hog Island off Bremen offers a series of

week-long courses; contact the Registrar (203-869-2017). The **University of Maine at Machias** (255-3313) is a summer center for ornithology workshops, summer field courses, and Elderhostel. **Maine Folk Dance Camp** (647-3424) in Bridgton has been a center for international dance and customs since 1950. Nine weekly sessions start the last week in June; before then phone 516-661-3866. Photographers should check out the **Maine Photographic Workshop** (see Camden); also check boat-building schools (**Wooden Boat** offers much more than boat building) and **Elderhostel** (617-426-7788), which offers a variety of programs throughout Maine for everyone over age 60.

CAMPS, FOR CHILDREN

More than 200 summer camps are listed in the exceptional booklet published annually by the Maine Youth Camping Association, PO Box 455, Orono 04473 (581-1350); also available from the Maine Publicity Bureau (623-0363).

CAMPS, RENTAL

In Maine, "camp" is the word for a second home or cottage. See *Cottage Rentals* for inexpensive vacation rentals.

CANOEING, GUIDED TRIPS

Saco Bound, just over the New Hampshire line (Box 1, Conway, NH 03813; 603-447-2177), offers guided tours on the calm (great for beginners) Saco River as well as white–water canoeing and rafting. A number of "outfitters" specializing in Allagash Waterway and other wilderness trips are listed in the "Outdoor Guide to Maine" published by the Maine Professional Guides Association and available from the Maine Publicity Bureau (623-0363), which also publishes a list of whitewater rafting outfitters in M*aine Invites You.* **Sunrise County Canoe**

Expeditions (454-7708), Cathance Lake, Grove Post Office 04638, offers week-long tours on most northern Maine waterways.

CANOEING THE ALLAGASH

The ultimate canoe trip in Maine (and on the entire East Coast for that matter) is the 7- to 10-day expedition up the Allagash Wilderness Waterway, a 92-mile ribbon of lakes, ponds, rivers, and streams through the heart of northern Maine's vast commercial forests. Since 1966 the land flanking the waterway has been owned (500 feet back on either side of the waterway) by the state of Maine. A map pinpointing the 65 authorized campsites within the zone (and supplying other crucial information) is available free from the Bureau of Parks and Recreation (287-3821), State House Station 22, Augusta 04333. A more detailed map, backed with historical and a variety of other handy information, is DeLorme's "Map and Guide to the Allagash and St. John." Anybody contemplating the trip should be aware of black flies in June and the "no-seeums" when warm weather finally comes. For further information, check *Camping* and *Guide Services*.

CANOE RENTALS
Rentals are under *To Do* within this book.

CHILDREN, ESPECIALLY FOR

The Maine Publicity Bureau publishes a list of over 80 activities entitled "Fun For the Whole Family" in its guide, *Exploring Maine*. Within this book, note that we have marked a number of sites and activities that have special child appeal with a "✐."

CLAMMING

Maine state law permits the harvesting of shellfish for personal use only, unless you have a commercial license. Individuals can take up to ½ bushel of shellfish or 3 bushels of hen or surf clams (the big ones out in the flats) in 1 day, unless municipal ordinances further limit "the taking of shellfish." Be sure to check locally at the town clerk's office (source of licenses) before you dig and make sure there's no red tide. Some towns do prohibit clamming, and in certain places, there is a temporary stay on harvesting while the beds are being seeded. In a few places clamming has been banned because of pollution.

COASTAL CRUISES

"Cruise" is a much used (and abused) term along the Maine coast, used chiefly to mean a boat ride. *Maine Invites You* (see *Information*) lists over 85 "Boat Cruises and Ferries," most of them described in the appropriate chapters of this book. We have also tried to list the charter sailing yachts that will take passengers on multiday cruises and have described each of the windjammers that sail for 3 and 6 days at a time (see *Windjammers*). The **M/V Pauline** (1-800-999-7352), based in Rockland, is an 83-foot, former Maine sardine carrier that has been rebuilt as a luxurious motor vessel and takes up to 12 guests at a time on multiday and weekly cruises throughout the summer.

COTTAGE RENTALS

Cottage rentals are the only reasonably priced way to go for families who wish to stay in one Maine spot for more than a week (unless you go for camping). Request the booklet "Maine Guide to Camp & Cottage Rentals" from the Maine Publicity Bureau (623-0363). The 1994 booklet's weekly rates for coastal cottages in July and August began at $250. Each spring we browse through this book when it comes out and then shoot off postcards to a half-dozen places. We always receive pleasant letters back, and if cottages are already filled for the time we request, their owners frequently refer us to others. If you have your heart set on one particular area and cannot get satisfaction through the booklet, we recommend obtaining a printout of realtors just for that county, then sending notes off to agents in the precise area in which you are interested. The printouts are available for a small fee by writing to the Maine Department of Business Regulation, Central Licensing Division, State House Station 35, Augusta 04333 (287-2217).

COVERED BRIDGES

Of the 120 covered bridges that once spanned Maine rivers, just 9 survive. A leaflet guide is available from the Maine Publicity Bureau (623-0363). The most famous, and certainly as picturesque as a covered bridge can be, is the **Artist's Covered Bridge** (1872) over the Sunday River in Newry, northwest of Bethel. The others are: **Porter Bridge** (1876) over the Ossipee River, .5 miles south of Porter; **Babb's Bridge,** recently rebuilt, over the Presumpscot River between Gorham and Windham; **Hemlock Bridge** (1857), 3 miles northwest of East Fryeburg; **Lovejoy Bridge** (1883) in South Andover; **Bennett Bridge** (1901) over the Magalloway River, 1.5 miles south of the Wilson's Mills Post Office; **Robyville Bridge** (1876), Maine's only completely shingled covered bridge, in the town of Corinth; and the **Watson Settlement Bridge** (1911) between Woodstock and Littleton. Carefully reconstructed **Low's Bridge** (1857) across the Piscataquis River between Guilford and Sangerville was added in 1990.

CRAFTS

"Maine Cultural Guide," published by the Maine Crafts Association, is available by writing Box 288, Deer Isle 04627, or phoning 348-9943. The free, 80-page booklet describes hundreds of studios, galleries, and museums in Maine. For a shorter listing of craftspeople and juried crafts shows, write Directions, PO Box 10832, Portland 04104. United Maine Craftsmen Inc. (621-2818) also sponsors several large shows each year.

CRAFTS CENTERS

Haystack Mountain School of Crafts (see Deer Isle) is a nationally respected summer school in a variety of crafts, offering 3-week courses beginning mid-June and continuing through mid-September. Applicants must be more than 18 years old; enrollment is limited to 65. Work by students is displayed in the visitors center, which also serves as a forum for frequent evening presentations. The surrounding area (Blue Hill to Stonington) contains the largest concentration of Maine craftspeople, many of whom invite visitors to their studios.

DEEP-SEA FISHING

"Maine Deep Sea Fishing Charter & Head Boats," available from the Maine Publicity Bureau (623-0363), describes boats based in Kittery, York Harbor, Ogunquit, Kennebunkport, Biddeford, Saco, Portland, South Freeport, South Harpswell, Harpswell,

Bailey Island, Boothbay Harbor, Rockland, Camden, Bar Harbor, Northeast Harbor, Milbridge, Jonesport, Lubec, and Eastport. We have described specific boats within each chapter.

DIVE SHOPS

The Maine Publicity Bureau keeps a state-wide list (see *Information*).

DOGSLEDDING

Although racing is a long-established winter spectator sport, the chance actually to ride on a dogsled is relatively recent and growing in popularity. Tim Diehl at **Sugarloaf/USA** offers half-hour rides throughout the day during ski season (you ride behind a team of friendly, frisky Samoyeds), **Bethel Outdoor Adventures** (1-800-533-3607) offers dogsled workshops and tours, and in Newry, Polly Mahoney and Kevin Slater (**Mahoosuc Mountain Adventures**) offer multiday treks with their huskies. Diehl also offers summer rides. See the Sugarloaf and Bethel chapters for details.

EVENTS

We have listed outstanding annual events within each chapter of this book, and leaflet guides to events are published by the state four times a year. Check with the Maine Publicity Bureau (623-0363).

FACTORY OUTLETS

See the "Kittery" and "Freeport" chapters.

FACTORY TOURS

Tours range from Tom's of Maine (toothpaste) to Rackliffe and Rowantrees Pottery-makers (Blue Hill), and include Blueberry Processors & Growers (Cherryfield) and Maine Wild Blueberry Company (Machias).

FALL FOLIAGE

Autumn is extremely pleasant along the coast; days tend to be clear, and the changing leaves against the blue sea can be spectacular. Many inns remain open through foliage season, and the resort towns of Ogunquit, Kennebunkport, Boothbay Harbor, and Camden all offer excellent dining, shopping, and lodging through Columbus Day weekend. Off-season prices prevail, in contrast with the rest of New England at this time of year. *Maine Invites You* outlines some particularly beautiful tours, as does *Maine Fall Foliage Tours* published by Down East Enterprise, Inc., and available at Maine Publicity Bureau information centers.

FARM B&BS

In 1994, 15 farms are described in a brochure available from the Maine Farm Vacation B&B Association, RR 1, Box 1145, Outlet Road, Hallowell 04347. Note that this is a promotional association, not an officially approved and inspected group. Properties vary widely. Some are just what you might expect: plenty of space, animals, big breakfasts, friendly, informal atmosphere, and reasonable prices. Others are more formal. Some are not farms. The properties are scattered widely across Maine. Though we haven't made it to all of those listed yet, the ones we have seen are recommended in their regions. We wish there were more in Aroostook County.

FARMERS' MARKETS

The Maine Federation of Farmers' Markets, RFD 1, Box 234 Hebron 04238, publishes a pamphlet listing over 25 farmers' markets statewide.

FERRIES, TO CANADA

Portland to Yarmouth, Nova Scotia: **Prince of Fundy Cruises** offers nightly sailings (departing 9:30 PM), late April through the Columbus Day weekend. The ferry itself is a car-carrying cruise ship with gambling, restaurants, and cabins aboard (1-800-482-0955 in Maine; 1-800-341-7540 in the US). The **Canadian National Marine Line** (1-800-341-7981 for the continental United States) also offers overnight car and passenger service year-round aboard its *Bluenose* between Bar Harbor and Yarmouth, Nova Scotia. Note that it's very possible to use these ferries as part of a loop: going on one and returning on the other. Mid-June to mid-September **East Coast Ferries Ltd.** (506-747-2159), a small car ferry based on Deer Island, serves Eastport (30 minutes) and Campobello (45 minutes), and another small provincial (free) **Deer Island-L'Etete Ferry** (506-453-2600) connects the island with the New Brunswick mainland. The 65-car **Coastal Transport Ltd. Ferry** (506-662-3724) runs year-round from Black Harbor, not far east of L'Etete to the island of Grand Manan.

FERRIES, IN MAINE

Maine State Ferry Service (1-800-521-3939 in-state, 207-596-2202 outside of Maine), Rockland 04841, operates year-round service from Rockland to Vinalhaven and North Haven, from Lincolnville to Islesboro, and from Bass Harbor to Swan's Island and Long Island. For private ferry services to Monhegan, see Port Clyde and Boothbay Harbor; for the Casco Bay Islands, see Portland; for Matinicus, see Rockland; and for Isle au Haut, see Stonington.

FIRE PERMITS

Maine law dictates that no person shall kindle or use outdoor fires without a permit, except at authorized campsites or picnic grounds. Fire permits in the organized towns are obtained from the local town warden; in the unorganized towns, from the nearest forest ranger. Portable stoves fueled by propane gas, gasoline, or sterno are exempt from the rule.

FISHING

"The Maine Guide to Hunting and Fishing," published by the Maine Publicity Bureau (see *Information*), is a handy overview of rules, license fees, and other matters of interest to fishermen. (Also see *Deep-Sea Fishing*.) Detailed descriptions of camps and rustic resorts catering to fishermen can be found in the Rangeley Lakes and North Woods chapters. A 1-day fishing license cost nonresidents $7 in 1994; 3-, 7-, and 15-day licenses are also available at most general stores and sporting goods outlets or by writing the Maine Department of Inland Fisheries and Wildlife, State House Station #41, Augusta 04333 (287-3371).

FLYING SCHOOLS

The Maine Publicity Bureau keeps a list (see *Information*).

FORTS

To be married to a fort freak is to realize that there are people in this world who will detour 50 miles to see an 18th-century earthworks. Maine's forts are actually a fascinating lot, monuments to the state's own unique and largely forgotten history. Examples: **Fort William Henry** at Pemaquid, **Fort Edgecomb** in Edgecomb, **Fort George** in Castine, **Fort Kent** and **Fort Knox** near Bucksport, **Fort McClary** in Kittery, **Fort O'Brien** near Machias, **Fort Popham** near Bath, and **Fort Pownall** at Stockton Springs.

GOLF

The Maine Publicity Bureau publishes a statewide list of golf courses in *Maine Invites You*. Within this book, we list golf courses for each area. The major resorts catering to golfers are the **Samoset** in Rockland, the **Bethel Inn** in Bethel, **Sebasco Estates** near Bath, the **Country**

Club Inn in Rangeley, the **Cliff House** in Ogunquit, and **Sugarloaf/USA** in the Carrabassett Valley.

GORGES

Maine has the lion's share of the Northeast's gorges. There are four biggies. The widest is the **Upper Sebois River Gorge** north of Patten, and the most dramatic, "Maine's Miniature Grand Canyon," is **Gulf Hagas** near the Katahdin Iron Works (see the "Katahdin Region"). Both **Kennebec Gorge** and **Ripogenus Gorge** are now popular whitewater rafting routes.

GUIDEBOOKS

Among guidebooks to Maine, the following have proved helpful to us: *The Coast of Maine: An Informal History* by Louise Dickinson Rich (Thomas Y. Crowell Company); *The Maine Coast: A Nature Lover's Guide* by Dorcas Miller (The East Woods Press); *The Maine Atlas and Gazetteer* (David DeLorme and Company, PO Box 298, Freeport 04032); and *Fifty Hikes in Southern Maine* by John Gibson and *Fifty Hikes in Northern Maine* by Cloe Caputo (Backcountry Publications). Down East Books (PO Box 679, Camden 04843) offers: *A Birder's Guide to the Coast of Maine* by Elizabeth Cary Pierson and Jan Erik Pierson, *Walking the Maine Coast* by John Gibson, and *Islands in Time: A Natural and Human History of the Islands of Maine* by Philip W. Conkling. Serious hikers should secure the *AMC Maine Mountain Guide*, and all lovers of the Maine woods should take a look at *The Wildest Country: A Guide to Thoreau's Maine* by J. Parker Huber; both books are available from the AMC Books Division, Dept. B, 5 Joy Street, Boston, MA 02108. We also enjoy the books by retired *Portland Press Herald* columnist Bill Caldwell: *Enjoying Maine, Maine Coast, Maine Magic*, and *Islands of Maine*, all pub-

lished by Guy Gannett Publishing Company of Portland. We also recommend two photography books on Maine: *My Maine Thing*, photos by Tony King, and *A Maine Deeper In*, photography and text by Martin Brown, published by Down East Books. *Island Hopping in New England* by Mary Maynard (a *Yankee Magazine* guidebook); *Maine Off the Beaten Path* by Wayne Curtis (The Globe Pequot Press); *Maine Forever, Guide to Nature Conservancy Preserves in Maine* (available from the Maine Chapter of The Nature Conservancy, PO Box 338, 122 Main Street, Topsham 04086); and *Maine*, by Charles C. Calhoun (Compass American Guides), with its superb illustrations and well-written background text, are also recommended.

GUIDE SERVICES

There are more than 1000 registered Maine guides—men and women who have passed a qualifying test. Finding the guide to suit your needs, be it fishing, hunting, or canoeing the Allagash Waterway, can be a confusing business. A list of guides is available from the Maine Professional Guides Association, 18 White Street, Topsham 04086 (785-2061).

HIKING

For organized trips, contact the Appalachian Mountain Club's Boston office (617-523-0636). In addition to the *AMC Maine Mountain Guide* and the AMC map guide to trails on Mount Desert, we recommend investing in *Fifty Hikes in Southern Maine* by John Gibson and *Fifty Hikes in Northern Maine* by Cloe Caputo (both from Backcountry Publications), which offer clear, inviting treks up hills of every size throughout the state. *The Maine Atlas and Gazetteer* (DeLorme Publishing Company) also outlines a number of rewarding hikes.

HISTORIC HOUSES

The Maine Publicity Bureau's outstanding booklet, "Maine Guide to Museums and Historic Houses," is worth requesting (623-0363). Within this book, dozens of historic houses open to the public are listed by town.

HORSE RACING

Harness racing can be found at **Scarborough Downs:** US 1, or Exit 6 off the Maine Turnpike, April through November, Tuesday through Sunday. For Downs Club dining call 883-2020. The **Bangor Raceway** is open late May through late July, Wednesday, and Friday through Sunday. **County Raceways** has several scheduled dates in June, July, and August. The leaflet guide, "Maine Agricultural Fairs," also lists harness racing dates at all agricultural fairs of the current season and is available from the Maine Department of Agriculture (287-3221).

HORSEBACK RIDING

Pleasant River Pack Trips (see The North Woods) offers entire days as well as shorter stints in the saddle. For trail riding, check the Old Orchard Area, Boothbay Harbor, Union, the Upper Kennebec Valley, and the Moosehead Lake Region.

HUNTING

Hunters should obtain a summary of Maine hunting and trapping laws from the Maine Department of Inland Fisheries and Wildlife, State House Station #41, Augusta 04333 (287-3371). For leads on registered Maine guides who specialize in organized expeditions (complete with meals and lodging), contact the sources we list under *Fishing, Guide Services, Canoeing,* and *Camping.* You might also try the Moosehead Region Chamber of Commerce (695-2702). A handy "Maine Guide to Hunting and Fishing" booklet, published annually by the Maine Publicity Bureau (623-0363), is filled with information and ads for hunting lodges, guides, and the like.

INFORMATION

The Maine Publicity Bureau (623-0363 or 1-800-533-9595 outside of Maine), PO Box 2300, Hallowell 04347, publishes *Maine Invites You,* as well as "Exploring Maine," "Maine Guide to Hunting and Fishing," "Maine Guide to Winter," and a variety of other guides noted here under specific headings. Write or phone the bureau's office if you have a special query, or stop by one of the MPB year-round information centers: on I-95 in Kittery (439-1319); just off coastal Route 1 and I-95 in Yarmouth (846-0833); both northbound and southbound on I-95 in Hampden near Bangor (862-6628/6638); in Calais (454-2211); and in Houlton (532-6346). There is also a seasonal information center on the New Hampshire line on Route 302 in Fryeburg (935-3639). (Also see *Guidebooks.*)

INNS

In this book, we have been more selective than in earlier editions because there are simply so many more new inns and B&Bs out there. While researching this book, we personally inspected more than 400 inns and B&Bs. Realizing that "inn books" tend to focus on the higher end of the price spectrum, we have tried to include more reasonably priced, equally appealing options in the same area. The booklet guide "Inns and Bed & Breakfasts" is also useful and is free from the Maine Publicity Bureau (623-0363). *Best Places to Stay in New England* by Christina Tree and Kimberly Grant (Houghton Mifflin) also includes a wide spectrum of places to stay in Maine.

ISLANDS

In all there are said to be over 3000 islands, most uninhabited, ranging from oversized rocks to several thousand acres. The state owns some 1500 of these islands, totaling 800 acres (the average size is a half acre), and 45 are open to the public; so are 15 privately owned islands. Access is through the **Maine Island Trail Association,** part of the Island Institute (594-9209; 60 Ocean Street, Rockland 04841). For $35 you receive a map guide to the 74 islands, scattered over 325 miles from Casco Bay to Machias Bay. For details about camping on state-owned islands, contact the **Bureau of Public Lands** in Augusta (287-3061) and request the brochure "Your Islands on the Coast." The islands that offer overnight accommodations are Chebeague and Peaks Islands in Casco Bay (see Portland), Monhegan, Vinalhaven and Islesboro, North Haven, Isle au Haut, Islesford, and Matinicus.

NEAL PARENT

LAKES

Maine boasts some 6000 lakes and ponds, and every natural body of water over 10 acres—which accounts for most of them—is, theoretically at least, available to the public for "fishing and fowling." Access is, of course, limited by the property owners around the lakes. Because so much acreage in Maine is owned by paper companies and other land management concerns that permit public use provided the public obeys their rules (see *Camping*), there is ample opportunity to canoe or fish in unpeopled waters. Powerboat owners should note that most states have reciprocal license privileges with Maine; the big exception is New Hampshire. For more about the most popular resort lakes in the state, see Bridgton, Rangeley, Greenville, and the Belgrade Lakes in the Kennebec Valley. The state parks on lakes are **Aroostook** (camping, fishing, swimming; Route 1 south of Presque Isle), **Damariscotta Lake State Park** (Route 32 in Jefferson), **Lake St. George**

State Park (swimming, picnicking, fishing; Route 3 in Liberty), **Lily Bay State Park** (8 miles north of Greenville), **Peacock Beach State Park** (swimming, picnicking; Richmond), **Peaks-Kenny State Park** (Sebec Lake in Dover-Foxcroft), **Rangeley Lake State Park** (swimming, camping; Rangeley), **Range Ponds State Park** (Poland), **Sebago Lake State Park** (swimming, picnicking, camping; near Bridgton), **Mt. Blue Lake State Park** (Weld), and **Swan Lake State Park** (Swanville). Families with small children should be aware of the many coastal lakes surrounded by reasonably priced cottages (see *Cottages, Rental*).

LIGHTHOUSES

Maine takes pride in its 63 lighthouses. The most popular to visit are **Portland Head Light** (completed in 1790, automated in 1990, now a delightful museum featuring the history of lighthouses) on Cape Elizabeth; **Cape Neddick Light** in York; **Marshall Point Light** at Port Clyde; **Fort Point Light** at Stockton Springs; **Pemaquid**

Point (the lighthouse keeper's house is now a museum, there's an art gallery, and the rocks below are peerless for scrambling); **Owl's Head** (built 1826); **Bass Harbor Head Light** at Bass Harbor; and **West Quoddy Head,** start of a beautiful shore path. On **Monhegan,** the lighthouse keeper's house is a seasonal museum, and at **Grindle Point** on Islesboro, there is also an adjacent seasonal museum. True lighthouse buffs also make the pilgrimage to **Matinicus Rock,** the setting for children's books. Lighthouse aficionados tell us that **East Quoddy Head Lighthouse** on the island of Campobello, accessible at low tide, is the ultimate adventure to get to; it is also a prime whale-watching post. Captain Barna Norton (497-5933) runs charters from Jonesport to lighthouses on Libby Island, Moose Peak, Nash Island, and Petit Manan, as well as to Machias Seal (see *Puffin-Watching*).

LITTER
Littering in Maine is punishable by a $100 fine; this applies to dumping from boats as well as other vehicles. Most cans and bottles are redeemable.

LLAMA TREKKING
The principle is appealingly simple: The llama carries your gear; you lead the llama. At the **Telemark Inn** (836-2703), surrounded by semi-wilderness west of Bethel, Steve Crone's herd of these shaggy, nimble, and amiable beasts has grown to more than a dozen. Day treks are available, but outings can also last several days and include canoeing on nearby lakes. **Pleasant Bay Bed & Breakfast** in Addison (483-4490) is a working llama farm; guests are encouraged to meander the property's waterside trails with the llamas.

LOBSTER POUNDS
A lobster pound is usually a no-frills seaside

MAINE OFFICE OF TOURISM

restaurant that specializes in serving lobsters and clams steamed in seawater. The most basic and reasonably priced pounds are frequently fishermen's co-ops such as that in New Harbor. Expect good value but no china plates and salads at **Chauncey Creek Lobster Pound** in Kittery, **Harraseeket** in South Freeport, **Beal's Lobster Pound** in Southwest Harbor, and the **Fisherman's Landing** in Bar Harbor. The **Ogunquit Lobster Pound** in Ogunquit is the state's priciest pound; other lobster-eating landmarks include **Nunan's Lobster Hut** in Cape Porpoise, **Eaton's** on Deer Isle, **Robinson's Wharf** at Townsend Gut near Boothbay, the **Lobster Shack** on Cape Elizabeth, the **Lobster Pound** in Lincolnville Beach, the **Lobster Shack** in Searsport, **Trenton Bridge Lobster Pound** on Route 3 at the entrance to Mount Desert, and (the ultimate) **Tidal Falls Lobster Pound** in Hancock.

LOBSTERS TO GO
The Maine Publicity Bureau (see *Information*) keeps a list of firms that will ship lobsters anywhere in the world.

THE MAINE FESTIVAL
Maine's biggest, splashiest cultural happening of the year, the festival is held for 4 days around the second weekend in August at Thomas Point Beach in Brunswick. Performing artists are from everywhere, but the Maine folk artists and performers are defi-

nitely local as are the artists and craftspeople; children's entertainment, a food garden, and plenty of outdoor sculpture are also part of the scene. Sponsored by Maine Arts: 772-9012 or 1-800-639-4212.

MAINE TURNPIKE TRAVEL CONDITIONS
(1-800-675-PIKE)

MAPLE SUGARING
Maine produces roughly 8000 gallons of syrup a year, and the Maine Department of Agriculture publishes a list of producers who welcome visitors on **Maine Maple Sunday** (also known as Sap Sunday) in late March.

MOOSE-WATCHING
Moose have made a comeback from their near-extinct status in the 1930s and now number more than 20,000. Your chances of spotting one are best in early morning or at dusk on a wooded pond or lake or along logging roads. If you are driving through moose country at night, go slowly because moose typically freeze rather than retreat from oncoming headlights. For details about commercial moose-watching expeditions, check the Rangeley and Moosehead Lake chapters. The Moosehead Lake Region Chamber of Commerce sponsors **"Moosemainea,"** mid-May through mid-June, with special events and a huge moose locator map. Suspicious that this promotion coincided with Moosehead's low tourist season, we queried

BILL SILLIKER JR.

the state's moose expert who agreed that moose are most visible in late spring. Last season 5200 moose were spotted.

MUSEUM VILLAGES
What variety! Open seasonally as a commercial attraction, **Willowbrook** at Newfield is a 19th-century village center consisting of 31 buildings that have been restored by one man. Other attractions include the old village center of **Searsport,** restored as a fine maritime museum; **Sabbathday Lake Shaker Museum,** still a functioning religious community; **York Village** with its Old Gaol, school, tavern, church, and scattering of historic houses open to the public that add up to a picture of late 18th-century life in coastal Maine; **Norlands,** a former estate with a neo-Gothic library, school, and farm buildings, as well as a mansion that invites you to come and live for a weekend as if you were in this particular place (Livermore) in the 1870s.

MUSEUMS
"Maine Guide to Museums and Historic Houses," a booklet guide published by the Maine Publicity Bureau (623-0363), is an exceptional free guide to the state's museums—big and small, historical, art, or whatever. Our own favorites are the **Peary-MacMillan Arctic Museum** at Bowdoin College in Brunswick, the **Seashore Trolley Museum** in Kennebunkport, the **Portland Museum of Art,** the **Owl's Head Transportation Museum** near Rockland, the **Robert Abbe Museum** in Acadia National Park (outstanding for its regional Native American artifacts), the **Wilson Museum** in Castine, the **Patten Lumberman's Museum** in Patten (which surprises you with the extent and quality of its exhibits), and the **Colonial Pemaquid Restoration** in Pemaquid (which presents fascinating archaeological finds from the

adjacent, early 17th-century settlement). The **Maine Maritime Museum** in Bath stands in a class by itself and should not be missed. Easily the most under-visited in the state, the **Maine State Museum** has outstanding exhibits on the varied Maine landscape and historical exhibits ranging from traces of the area's earliest people to rifles used by State of Mainers in Korea; you can also see exhibits on fishing, agriculture, lumbering, quarrying, and shipbuilding. (Also see *Art Museums*.)

MUSIC CONCERT SERIES

Among the most famous summer concert series are the **Bar Harbor Festival** (288-5744) and the **Mount Desert Festival of Chamber Music** (276-5039); the **Sebago Long Lake Region Chamber Music Festival** in North Bridgton (627-4939); the **Bay Chamber Concerts** presented in the Rockport Opera House (236-4731), which offers concerts year-round; the Kneisel Hall chamber concerts in Blue Hill and **Bowdoin College Summer Concerts** in Brunswick (725-8731, ext. 321); and **Machias Bay Chamber Concerts** in Machias (255-8685). There is, of course, the **Portland Symphony Orchestra** (773-8191), which also has a summertime pops series, and the **Bangor Symphony Orchestra** (945-6408).

MUSIC SCHOOLS

Notable are **Bowdoin College Summer School** (see *Music Concert Series*), Kneisel Hall in Blue Hill (call 725-8731 only after June 24; prior inquiries should be addressed to Kneisel Hall, Blue Hill 04614); the **Pierre Monteux Memorial Domaine School** in Hancock (442-6251); **Salzedo Summer Harp Colony** in Camden (236-2289); **New England Music Camp** in Oakland (465-3025); **Maine Summer Youth Music** at the University of Maine, Orono (581-1960); and

Maine Music Camp at the University of Maine, Farmington (778-3501).

NATURE PRESERVES, COASTAL

Rachel Carson National Wildlife Refuge is a total of nine separate preserves salted between Kittery and Cape Elizabeth along the Atlantic Flyway. Request a leaflet guide from the Parker River National Wildlife Refuge, Newbury, MA 01950. **Gilsland Farm** (open year-round) has 70 acres with nature trails through woodlands, meadows, and marshes. The **Maine Audubon Society** maintains a nature center at **Scarborough Marsh** and offers canoe tours, bird walks, and a variety of other summer programs (883-5100). There are also nature trails to follow at the Audubon Society headquarters at Gilsland Farm in Falmouth. The society also maintains self-guiding nature trails (cross-country ski trails in winter) and facilities for picnicking and tenting at the 150-acre **Mast Landing Sanctuary** in Freeport. **Birdsacre,** a 40-acre preserve in Ellsworth, harbors 109 species of birds in and around a network of nature trails and maintains a museum that honors pioneer ornithologist Cordelia Stanwood, open June 15 through October 15 and other times by appointment (667-8683). **Acadia National Park,** with its miles of hiking trails and extensive naturalist-led programs, is the state's busiest preserve (see "Bar Harbor and Acadia Area"). Some 30 miles east of Ellsworth is **Petit Manan National Wildlife Refuge** (1999 acres), a peninsula offering two hiking trails. At the extreme eastern end of Maine, the **Moosehorn National Wildlife Refuge** in Calais (454-3521) consists of two units, roughly 20 miles apart. The bigger (16,065 acres) is partially bounded by the St. Croix River, and the 6600-acre Edmunds Unit overlooks Cobscook Bay; a visitors center is open May through September, and there are hiking trails. The largest private landowner of preservation land in Maine is the **Nature Conservancy,** protecting 71 preserves adding up to more than 25,000 acres throughout the state. For details, request "Maine Forever, A Guide to Nature Conservancy Preserves in Maine," available through the Maine chapter of the Nature Conservancy, PO Box 338, 122 Main Street, Topsham 04086. (Also see *Islands* and *Birding*.) Recently acquired preserves are detailed in "Land for Maine's Future," a brochure worth requesting from the Maine State Planning Office (287-3261), State House Station 38, 184 State Street, Augusta 04333.

NATURE PRESERVES, INLAND

Steve Powell Wildlife Management Area, described in a booklet available from the Maine Department of Inland Fisheries and Wildlife, 284 State Street, Augusta 04333 (289-3651), consists of two islands and several hundred acres of intervening tidal flats at the head of Merrymeeting Bay. Southeast of Fryeburg, the **Brownfield Bog Wildlife Management Areas** (5454 acres) are a mix of marshland, floodplain, and upland that invites exploration by canoe; a campsite at Walker's Falls is maintained by the Appalachian Mountain Club (see *Hiking*). In the Bridgton area there is the **Hiram Nature Study Area** maintained by the Central Maine Power Company (647-3391), some 60 acres of woodland in Baldwin with a trail along the Saco River and picnic facilities. **Vaughan Woods,** a 250-acre state park, offers a few fine miles of wooded hiking trails along the Salmon Falls River, good for cross-country skiing and birding as well as hiking and picnicking (from Kittery take Route 236 north more than 9 miles; turn west on Route 91, and take a left at the "T"). Free. The greatest inland preserve is **Baxter**

State Park in Maine's North Woods. (Also see *Camping, Fishing, Hiking,* and *Hunting,* and The Nature Conservancy and "Land for Maine's Future" under *Nature Preserves, Coastal*.)

PARKS AND FORESTS, NATIONAL

Acadia National Park (288-5262), which occupies roughly half of Mount Desert, plus scattered areas on Isle au Haut, Little Cranberry Island, Baker Island, Little Moose Island, and Schoodic Point, adds up to a 44,000-acre preserve offering hiking, touring, swimming, horseback riding, canoeing, and a variety of guided nature tours and programs as well as a scenic 56-mile driving tour. Note that an entry fee is now charged to drive the Loop Road on Mount Desert and that camping is by reservation only. See "Bar Harbor and Acadia Area" for details. The **White Mountain National Forest** encompasses 41,943 acres in Maine, including five campgrounds under the jurisdiction of the Evans Notch Ranger District, Bridge Street, Bethel 04217 (824-2134). For details see "Bethel Area."

PARKS, STATE

The Bureau of Parks and Recreation (287-3821), Station 22, Augusta 04333, can send a packet of information describing each of the parks and hiking and camping. In the text, we have described parks as they appear geographically. In 1995 day-use fees are between $1.00 and $2.50 per person, and camping fees are $10.50–12.00 per site for residents, $14.00–16.00 for nonresidents. There is also a $2.00 per night reservation fee for camping. Phone (Monday through Friday) at least 14 days in advance to make a campground reservation. (Also see *Lakes*.)

POPULATION

Approximately 1.2 million.

PUFFIN-WATCHING

Atlantic puffins are smaller than you might expect. They lay just one egg a year and were heading for extinction around the turn of the century when the only surviving birds nested either on Matinicus Rock or Machias Seal Island. Since 1973 the Audubon Society has had nesting areas on Eastern Egg Rock in Muscongus Bay, 6 miles off Pemaquid Point. Since 1984 there has been a similar puffin restoration project on Seal Island in outer Penobscot Bay, 6 miles from Matinicus Rock. The best months for viewing puffins are June and July or the first few days of August. The only place from which you are permitted to view the birds on land is at Machias Seal Island, where visitors are permitted in limited numbers. Contact **Barna Norton** in Jonesport (497-5933) and **Bold Coast Charter** in Cutler (259-4484). With the help of binoculars (a must) you can also view the birds from the water via tours offered by **Atlantic Expeditions** in St. George (372-8621), **Lively Lady Enterprises** based on Vinalhaven (863-4461), **Offshore Passenger & Freight** in Rockland (366-3700), **Cap'n Fish Boat Trips** in Boothbay Harbor (633-3244), **Northeast Whalewatch** (276-5803) in Seal Harbor, the **Hardy III Tours** (677-2026) out of New Harbor, and the **Maine Audubon Society** (781-2330).

RAILROAD RIDES & MUSEUMS

Boothbay Railway Village delights small children and offers railroad exhibits in its depot. For rail fans there are other sites to see: the **Sandy River Railroad** in Phillips, the **Belfast & Moosehead Lake Railroad Company** in Belfast (daily excursion runs Memorial Day through Labor Day), the **Maine Coast Railroad** in Wiscasset, and the new **Maine Narrow Gauge Railroad Co. & Museum,** Portland.

RATES

Please regard any prices listed for *Lodging, Dining Out,* and *Eating Out,* as well as for museums and attractions, as benchmarks in the rising tide of inflation. Call ahead to confirm them. MAP stands for Modified American Plan: breakfast and dinner included in rate. AP stands for American Plan: three meals included in rate. EP stands for European Plan: breakfast included in rate. B&B stands for bed and breakfast: continental breakfast included in rate.

ROCKHOUNDING

Perham's Maine Mineral Store at Trap Corner in West Paris, which claims to attract an annual 90,000 visitors, displays Maine minerals and offers access to its four quarries. The store also offers information about other quarries and sells its own guidebooks to gem hunting in Oxford County and throughout the state. Open year-round 9–5 daily except Thanksgiving and Christmas. For other rockhounding meccas, check the Bethel chapter. Thanks to the high price of gold, prospectors are back-panning Maine streambeds; a list of likely spots is available from the Maine Geological Survey, Department of Conservation, State House Station 22, Augusta 04333 (289-2801). A helpful pamphlet, "Maine Mineral Collecting," lists annual gem shows and gem shops as well as quarries and is available from the Maine Publicity Bureau (582-9300).

SAILING

Windjammers and yacht charter brokers aside, there are a limited number of places that will rent small sailing craft, fewer that will offer lessons to adults and children alike. **Blue Seas Adventure Co.** in Camden rents sailboats by the day or longer, as does **Mansell Boat Company,** Southwest Harbor. Learn-to-sail programs are offered by **Wooden Boat School** in Brooklin and in

NINA KENNEDY

Camden by both the **Camden Yacht Club** and **Bay Island Sailing School. Linekin Bay Resort** in Boothbay Harbor features sailing lessons and races for its guests of all ages. Sailboat rentals and day trips are listed throughout the book. (Also see *Windjammers*.)

SEA KAYAKING

Sea kayaking is the fastest growing sport along the coast of Maine, and outfitters are responding to the demand, offering guided half-day and full-day trips, also overnight and multiday expeditions with camping on Maine islands. Paddling a kayak is a comfortable way to sit—not crouching, as in a canoe, or arched over, as in a rowboat. You're also low, so low that you can stare down a duck or a cormorant, or study the surface of the water and its kaleidoscopic patterns. Maneuverable in as little as 6 inches of water, kayaks are ideal craft for "gunkholing" (poking in and out of coves) around the rocky edges of Maine islands. The leading outfitters are **Maine Island Kayak Company**

(766-2373), on Peaks Island off Portland, and **Maine Sport Outfitters** (236-8797) in Rockport, both of which specialize in multiday camping trips as well as offering introductory lessons. Others include **H2Outfitters** (833-5357) on Orrs Island near Brunswick, **Tidal Transit** (633-7140) in Boothbay Harbor, **Indian Island Kayak Co.** (236-4088) in Camden, **Outward Bound School** (1-800-341-1744), **The Phoenix Center** (374-2113) in Blue Hill Falls, **Coastal Kayaking Tours** (288-9605) in Bar Harbor, **Schoodic Kayak Tours** (963-7958) in Corea, and **Norumbega Outfitters** (773-0910) in Portland. **L.L. Bean Sea Kayak Symposium,** held in early July at the Maine Maritime Academy in Castine (by reservation only), is New England's oldest and still its biggest annual kayaking event: a 2-day program geared to neophytes and all levels of ability, with lessons and equipment demonstrations. **L.L. Bean's Coastal Kayaking Workshop,** held the beginning of August at the University of New England, Biddeford, is a smaller, more skills-oriented event. For details and reservations call 1-800-341-4341, ext. 2509. *Sea Kayaking Along the New England Coast* by Tamsin Venn (Appalachian Mountain Club, 1991) includes detailed guidance to kayaking routes from Portland to Cobscook Bay; it also offers tips on local lodging and dining as well as an overall introduction to the sport. *Atlantic Coastal Kayaker* (508-774-0906), a monthly magazine ($2) based

TAMSIN VENN

in Wenham, Massachusetts, is a source of outfitting information and equipment buys.

SKIING, CROSS-COUNTRY

Carrabassett Valley Touring Center at Sugarloaf is the largest commercial Nordic network in the state. Bethel, with four trail networks (**Sunday River Inn, the Bethel Inn, Carter's X-C Ski Center,** and **Telemark Inn & Llama Treks**), offers varied terrain. The trails at **Saddleback Mountain** in Rangeley are the highest in Maine and may, in fact, be snow-covered when no place else is. The most adventurous touring is found in the Katahdin/ Moosehead area in Maine's North Woods. **The Birches** in Rockwood and **Little Lyford Camps** near Brownville Junction offer guided wilderness tours. **Mahoosuc Mountain Adventures** in the Bethel area

also offers guided trips with dogsleds toting gear for overnight camping. The "Maine Guide to Winter," published by the Maine Publicity Bureau (see *Information*), lists most Nordic areas, and the Maine Nordic Ski Council (PO Box 645, Bethel 04217) publishes its own guide and maintains a snow phone: 1-800-754-9263.

SKIING, DOWNHILL

Sugarloaf/USA in the Carrabassett Valley and **Sunday River Ski Area** in the Bethel area vie for the title of Maine's number one ski resort. The two are very different and actually complement each other well. Sugarloaf is a high, relatively remote mountain with New England's only lift-serviced snowfields on its summit and a classy, self-contained condo-village at its base. Sunday River, just 1 hour north of Portland (from which it's accessible by train), consists of six adjoining (relatively low altitude) mountains; snowmaking is a big point of pride, and facilities include a variety of slope-side condo lodging. **Saddleback Mountain** (in the

Rangeley area) is a big mountain with a small, enthusiastic following. **Mount Abram** (also in the Bethel area) is a true family area with a strong ski school and some fine runs. **Shawnee Peak** in Bridgton is a medium-sized, family-geared area that offers night as well as day skiing. **Moosehead Resort and Ski Area** (alias Squaw Mountain) in Greenville is another medium-sized area. Locally geared ski hills include **Lost Valley** in Auburn, **Mt. Jefferson** in Lee, **Camden Snow Bowl** in Camden, **Titcomb Mountain** in Farmington, and **Eaton Mountain** in Skowhegan. At this writing, Maine offers toll-free ski reports: out-of-state callers dial 1-800-533-9595; in-state, 773-SNOW. The annual magazine *Maine Guide to Winter*, profiling all ski areas, is available from the Maine Publicity Bureau (see *Information*).

SNOWMOBILING

Maine has reciprocal agreements with nearly all states and provinces; for licensing and rules contact the Fish and Game Department. The **Maine Snowmobile Association** (MSA) represents 270 clubs and maintains some 10,500 miles of an ever-expanding, cross-state trail network. Aroostook County, given its reliable snow conditions, is a particularly popular destination, geared to handling visitors and in the Upper Kennebec Valley, Jackman is a snowmobiling mecca; for details contact the MSA (622-6983), Box 77, Augusta 04330. For maps and further information, write to the Snowmobile Program, Bureau of Parks and Recreation, State House Station 22, Augusta 04333; MSA maintains a trail condition hotline: 1-800-880-SNOW.

SPA

Northern Pines in Raymond is the only fully developed spa program of which we are aware in Maine.

SPORTING CAMPS

The Maine sporting camp is a distinctly Maine phenomenon that began appearing in the 1860s—a gathering of log cabins around a log lodge by a lake, frequently many miles from the nearest road. In the 19th century, access was usually via Rangeley or Greenville, where "sports" (urbanites who wanted to hunt wild game) would be met by a guide and paddled up lakes and rivers to a camp. With the advent of float planes, many of these camps became more accessible (see *Air Services*), and the proliferation of private logging roads has put most within reach of sturdy vehicles. True sporting camps still cater primarily to fishermen in spring and hunters in fall, but since August is neither hunting nor a prime fishing season, they are increasingly hosting families who just want to be in the woods by a lake in summer. True sporting camps (as opposed to "rental camps") include a central lodge in which guests are served all three meals; boats and guide service are available.

The Maine Sporting Camp Association (PO Box 89, Jay 04239) publishes a brochure and list of its more than 40 members. One of our favorites not on this list is **West Branch Ponds Camps** near Kokadjo, a vintage 1930s complex that's been in the same family for three generations (see "Moosehead Lake Area").

THEATER, SUMMER

The **Ogunquit Playhouse** (646-5511) is among the oldest and most prestigious summer theaters in the country. The **Hackmatack Playhouse** in Berwick (698-1807) and **Biddeford City Theater** (282-0849) are other south coast options. The **Maine State Music Theater** and **Children's Theatre Program** on the Bowdoin Campus (725-8769) and the **Theater Project** (729-8584) are in Brunswick. Farther along the coast, look for the **Camden Civic Theatre** based in the newly refurbished Opera House in Camden (236-7595), **The Belfast Maskers** (338-4427), **Cold Comfort Summer Theatre** (326-8830) in Castine, the **Surry Opera Company** in Surry (667-2629), the **Acadia Repertory Theatre** (244-7260) in Somesville, and **Down River Theater Company** (255-4997) in Machias. Inland, **The Theater at Monmouth** is housed in the fine old Customs Hall (933-2952). **Lakewood Theater** (474-7176) is in Madison, **Deertrees Theater** (583-6747) is in Harrison, and **Celebration Barn Theater** (743-8452) is in South Paris.

THEATER, YEAR-ROUND

Acadia Repertory Theater in winter performs in Bangor (942-3333). Other companies are the **Performing Arts Center** in Bath (442-8455), the **Camden Civic Theatre** in Camden (236-4885), and the **Kennebec Performing Arts Center** in Gardiner (582-1325). **Portland Performing Arts Center** is at 25A Forest Avenue,

Portland 04112 (774-0465). Also, the **Portland Players** (799-7337) present a winter season of productions, as does the **Maine Acting Company** (784-1616) in Lewiston.

WATERFALLS

The following are all easily accessible to families with small children: **Snow Falls Gorge** off Route 26 in West Paris offers a beautiful cascade (ask for directions at Perham's Gem Store); **Smalls Falls** on the Sandy River, off Route 4 between Rangeley and Phillips, has a picnic spot with a trail beside the falls; **Step Falls** is on Wight Brook in Newry off Route 26; and just a ways farther up the road in Grafton Notch State Park is **Screw Auger Falls** with its natural gorge. Another Screw Auger Falls is in Gulf Hagas (see *Gorges*), off the Appalachian Trail near the Katahdin Iron Works Road north of Brownville Junction. **Kezar Falls,** on the Kezar River, is best reached via Lovell Road from Route 35 at North Waterford. An extensive list of "scenic waterfalls" is detailed in *The Maine Atlas and Gazetteer* (DeLorme Publishing Company). Check out 90-foot **Moxie Falls** at The Forks.

WHALE-WATCHING

Each spring humpback, finback, and minke whales migrate to New England waters where they remain until fall, cavorting, it sometimes seems, for the pleasure of excursion boats. One prime gathering spot is **Jeffries Ledge,** about 20 miles off Kennebunkport, and another is the **Bay of Fundy.** For listings of whalewatch cruises see the Kennebunks, Portland, Bar Harbor, Cutler, Eastport and Campobello. The East Quoddy (Campobello) and West Quoddy (Lubec) lighthouses are also prime viewing spots.

WHITEWATER RAFTING

Whitewater rafting is such a spring through fall phenomenon in Maine today it's diffi-
cult to believe it only began in 1976, coincidentally the year of the last log drive on the Kennebec River. Logs were actually still hurtling through Kennebec Gorge on that day in the spring of 1976 when fishing guide Wayne Hockmeyer (and eight bear hunters from New Jersey he had talked into coming along) plunged through it in a rubber raft. At the time, Hockmeyer's rafting know-how stemmed solely from having seen *River of No Return* in which Robert Mitchum steers Marilyn Monroe down the Salmon River. Needless to say, Hockmeyer's **Northern Outdoors** and the more than a dozen other major outfitters now positioned around the tiny village of The Forks, near the confluence of the Kennebec and Dead Rivers, are all well skilled in negotiating the rapids through nearby 12-mile-long Kennebec Gorge. Numbers on the river are now strictly limited, and rafts line up to take their turns riding the releases—which gush up to 8000 cubic feet of water per second—from the Harris Hydroelectric Station above the gorge. Several rafting companies—notably **Northern Outdoors, New England Whitewater Center, Crab Apple White Water,** and **Unicorn Rafting Expeditions**—now have fairly elaborate base facilities in and around The Forks, while **Wilderness Expeditions** offers facilities both here and at The Birches, a family-geared resort on nearby Moosehead Lake. **Eastern River Expeditions** uses its Greenville base to bus patrons either to the Kennebec or to Ripogenus Gorge (on the Penobscot River); several outfitters—including **Northern Outdoors, Wilderness Expeditions,** and **Unicorn**—have established food and lodging facilities for patrons who want to raft the Penobscot near Baxter State Park. Some 60,000 rafters a year now run either the Kennebec, Penobscot, or Dead Rivers. For information about most outfitters, call Raft Maine at 1-800-723-8633.

WINDJAMMERS

In 1935 a young artist named Frank Swift fitted a few former fishing and cargo schooners to carry passengers around the islands of Penobscot Bay. At the time, there were plenty of these old vessels moored in every harbor and cove, casualties of progress. Swift called his business **Maine Windjammer Cruises,** and during the next 2 decades it grew to include more than a dozen vessels. Competitors also prospered through the fifties, but the entire windjammer fleet almost faded away with the advent of rigorous Coast Guard licensing requirements in the sixties and the increased cost of building and rebuilding schooners. The seventies and eighties have, however, seen the rise of a new breed of windjammer captain. Almost every one of those now sailing has built or restored the vessel he or she commands. Members of the current Maine windjammer fleet range from the *Stephen Taber* and the *Lewis French*, both originally launched in 1871, to the *Heritage*, launched in 1983.

Taber co-captain Ellen Barnes recalls her own joy upon first discovering the windjammers as a passenger: "No museums had gobbled up these vessels; no cities had purchased them to sit at piers as public-relations gimmicks. These vessels were the real thing, plying their trade as they had in the past with one exception: the present-day cargo was people instead of pulpwood, bricks, coal, limestone, and granite."

Windjammers offer a sense of what the Maine coast and islands are all about. Most sail with the tide on Monday mornings with no set itinerary; where they go depends on the wind and the tide. Clad in old jeans and sneakers, passengers help haul a line and then lounge around the decks, gradually succumbing to the luxury of steeping in life on the face of Penobscot Bay. As the wind and sun drop, the schooner eases into a harbor. Supper is hearty Yankee fare, maybe fish chowder and beef stew with plenty of fresh corn bread. Before or after supper, passengers can board the vessel's yawl for a foray into the nearest village or onto the nearest road (most landlubbers feel the need to walk a bit each day). By Wednesday, the days begin to blur. Cradled in a favorite corner of the deck, you sun and find yourself seeing more: flocks of cormorants and an occasional seal or minke whale, eagles circling over island nests. The sky itself seems closer, and you are mesmerized by the ever-changing surface of the sea.

Choosing which vessel to sail on, in retrospect, turns out to be the most difficult part of a windjammer vacation. All have ship-to-shore radios and sophisticated radar, and some offer more in the way of creature comforts (hot showers and lounges) than others; some are known for their food or a captain with great jokes or songs. Within the section "Rockport, Camden, and Lincolnville" we have described each vessel in the kind of detail we devote to individual inns. Windjammers accommodate between 20 and 44 passengers, and the cost of 3- to 6-day cruises ranges from $300–700. Excessive drinking is discouraged on all the vessels, and guests are invited to bring their musical instruments. Children under 14 are permitted only on some vessels. See the "Rockland" and "Rockport, Camden" chapters for details and toll-free numbers for the various vessels.

WORKSHOPS

See Camps, For Adults.

I. SOUTH COAST

Kittery and the Yorks
Ogunquit and Wells
The Kennebunks
Old Orchard Beach Area

The beach at Ogunquit

TOM JONES

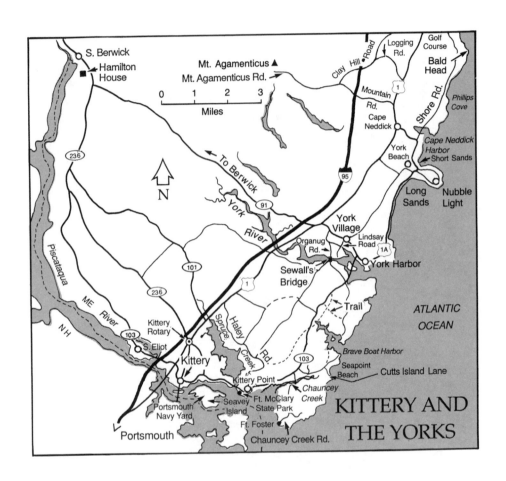

S. Berwick
Hamilton House
Mt. Agamenticus ▲
Mt. Agamenticus Rd.

0   1   2   3
Miles

Clay Hill Road
Logging Rd.
Golf Course
Bald Head
Mountain Rd.
Phillips Cove
Cape Neddick
Cape Neddick Harbor
Short Sands
York Beach
Long Sands
Nubble Light
236
To Berwick
York River
95
91
York Village
Lindsay Road
Organug Rd.
1A
York Harbor
Sewall's Bridge
Piscataqua
101
236
ME River
1
NH
103
S. Eliot
Kittery Rotary
Kittery
Spruce Creek
Haley Creek Rd.
Trail
ATLANTIC OCEAN
103
Brave Boat Harbor
Seapoint Beach
Cutts Island Lane
Kittery Point
Chauncey Creek
Ft. McClary State Park
Seavey Island
Portsmouth Navy Yard
Ft. Foster
Chauncey Creek Rd.
Portsmouth

N

Shore Rd.

KITTERY AND THE YORKS

Kittery and the Yorks

The moment you cross the Piscataqua River you know you are in Maine. You have to go a long way Down East to find any deeper coves, finer lobster pounds, rockier ocean paths, or sandier beaches than those in Kittery and York.

Both towns claim to be Maine's oldest community. Technically Kittery wins, but York looks older . . . depending, of course, on which Kittery and which York you are talking about.

Kittery Point, an 18th-century settlement overlooking Portsmouth Harbor, boasts Maine's oldest church, some of the state's finest mansions, and "America's oldest family store," Frisbees. The village of Kittery itself, however, has been shattered by so many bridges and rotaries that it seems to exist only as a gateway, on one hand for workers at the Portsmouth Naval Shipyard and on the other for patrons of the outlet malls on Route 1.

The Kittery Historical Naval Museum is well worth searching out, as are the dining, strolling, and swimming spots along coastal Route 103.

In the late 19th century, artists and literati gathered at Kittery Point. Novelist William Dean Howells, who summered here, became keenly interested in preserving the area's Colonial-era buildings. Howells and his friend Sam Clemens (otherwise known as Mark Twain) were part of a group of wealthy summer people who began buying up splendid Colonial-era buildings. They appreciated the fact that the old jail, the school, the church, the burial ground, and the abundance of 1740s homes in York Village comprised the oldest surviving Maine community.

In 1900 Howells suggested turning the "old gaol" in York Village into a museum. At the time, you could count the country's historic house museums on your fingers. In the Old Gaol of today, you learn about the village's bizarre history, including its origins as a Native American settlement called Agamenticus, one of many settlements wiped out by a plague in 1616. In 1630 it was settled by colonists, and in 1642 it became Gorgeana, America's first chartered city. It was then demoted to the town of York, part of Massachusetts, in 1670. Fierce Native American raids followed, but by the middle of the 18th century the present Colonial village was established, a crucial way station between Portsmouth and points east.

York is divided into so many distinct villages that Clemens once observed, "It is difficult to throw a brick . . . in any one direction without danger of disabling a postmaster." Not counting Scotland and York Corners, York includes York Village, York Harbor, York Beach, and Cape Neddick—such varied communities that locals can't bring themselves to speak of them as one town; they refer instead to "the Yorks."

The rocky shore beyond York Village was Lower Town until the Marshall House was opened near the small, gray sand beach in 1871 and its address was changed to York Harbor. Soon the hotel had 300 rooms, and other mammoth frame hotels appeared at intervals along the shore. All the old hotels are gone. All, that is, except the 162-room Cliff House, which, although physically in York, has long since changed its address and phone to Ogunquit, better known now as a resort town.

Still, York Harbor remains a delightful, low-key retreat. The Marshall House has been replaced by the modern Stage Neck Inn, and several dignified old summer "cottages" are now inns and B&Bs. The accommodations are handy to a narrow, mile-or-so path along the shore that was first traced by fishermen and later smoothed and graced with small touches such as the "Wiggly Bridge," a graceful little suspension bridge across the river and through Steedman Woods.

Landscaping and public spaces were among the consuming interests of the 19th-century summer residents, who around the turn of the century also became interested in zoning. In *Trending into Maine* (1935), Kenneth Roberts noted York Harbor's "determination to be free of billboards, tourist camps, dance halls and other cheapening manifestations of the herd instinct and Vacationland civilization."

A York Harbor corporation was formed to impose its own taxes and keep out unwanted development. The corporation's biggest fight, wrote Roberts, was against the Libby Camps, a tent-and-trailer campground on the eastern edge of York Harbor that "had spread with such fungus-like rapidity that York Harbor was in danger of being almost completely swamped by young ladies in shorts, young men in soiled undershirts, and fat ladies in knickerbockers."

Libby's Oceanside Camp still sits on Roaring Rock Point, its trailers neatly angled along the shore. Across from it is matching Camp Eaton, established in 1923. No other village boundary within a New England town remains more clearly defined than this one between York Harbor and York Beach.

Beyond the campgrounds stretches 2-mile Long Sands Beach, lined with a simpler breed of summer cottage than anything in York Village or York Harbor. There is a real charm to the strip and to the village of York Beach, with its Victorian-style shops, restaurants, and boardwalk amusements.

Whatever the day or weather, a group is sure to be standing spell-bound in front of the Goldenrod's big plate-glass windows, watching taffy being stirred, pulled, and neatly packaged into "Goldenrod kisses." It is still owned by the same family that opened it in 1896, about the time the electric streetcar put York Beach within reach of "the working class."

During this "Trolley Era," a half-dozen big hotels accommodated 3000 summer visitors, and 2000 more patronized boardinghouses in York Beach. Today's lodgings are a mix of motels, cottages, and B&Bs. There are beaches (with free or metered parking), Fun-O-Rama games and bowling, and York's Wild Kingdom with exotic animals and carnival rides.

York Beach, too, has now gained "historic" status, and the Old York Historical Society, keeper of the half-dozen, Colonial-era buildings open to the public in York Village, now sponsors York Beach walking tours.

GUIDANCE

The Kittery Information Center (439-1319), Maine's gatehouse in a real sense, is on I-95 northbound in Kittery, a source of advice on local as well as statewide lodging, dining, and attractions. It's open daily except Christmas and Thanksgiving, 8 AM–9 PM in summer months, otherwise 9–5 (bathrooms open 24 hours daily). We usually stop by the center for information and a weather update (press a button outside the men's room to get a full report).

The Kittery-Eliot Chamber of Commerce (439-7545 or 1-800-639-9645), just north of the Route 1 rotary (across from the Kittery Historical and Naval Museum), publishes a guide to lodging, dining, and sights.

York Chamber of Commerce (363-4422), PO Box 417, York 03909. On Route 1 just off Exit 4 (York), a handsome, new information center modeled on a 19th-century York Harbor "cottage" is open year-round, 9–5 (later on Friday and Saturday) in summer; shorter hours off-season.

GETTING THERE

Trailways and **Greyhound** serve Portsmouth, NH, some 12 miles south. **Little Brook Airport** in Eliot serves private and charter planes. **Coastal Connection** (282-5408) offers van service for points between Kittery and Kennebunkport.

GETTING AROUND

From late June to Labor Day, 10 AM–8 PM, an open-sided trolley links York Village, Harbor, and Beach with Cape Neddick and Route 1. Narrated tours are offered every hour. For details check with the chambers of commerce.

MEDICAL EMERGENCY

York Hospital 24-Hour Emergency Services (363-4321), Lindsay Road, York Village.

TO SEE

In Kittery

Kittery Historical and Naval Museum (439-3080), Route 1, just north of the Route 236 rotary. Open daily May through October, Monday through Friday 10–4. $3.00 adults, $1.50 ages 7–15; senior, family, and group rates. A fine little museum filled with ship models, naval relics from the Portsmouth Naval Yard, and exhibits about the early history of this stretch of the South Coast. Displays include archaeological finds, ship models, early shipbuilding tools, navigational instruments, trade documents, and mariner's folk art, including samples of work by Kittery master ships' carver John Haley Bellamy (1836–1914).

Portsmouth Naval Shipyard (open one day a week and by appointment: 438-3550), sited on Seavey Island at the mouth of the Piscataqua River. Also known as the Kittery Navy Yard, it is very visible from downtown Kittery. Established in 1806, it was the site of the treaty ending the Russo-Japanese War in 1905 and was responsible for building half of all American submarines during World War II. Today the navy yard remains an important submarine maintenance point. The PNS Command Museum has exhibits from the yard's past.

Fort McClary, Route 103 (south of Pepperrell Cove). A state park open seasonally, grounds accessible year-round. A hexagonal, 1846 block-house on a granite base, it was the site of fortifications in 1715, 1776, and 1808. The site was first fortified in the early 18th century to protect Massachusetts's vessels from being taxed by the New Hampshire colony. There is a fine view of Portsmouth Harbor, but the formal picnicking area across the road has no view.

In York

Old York Historical Society Homes (363-4974), Box 312, York 03909. The society maintains an outstanding local historical research library and archives in its headquarters, a former bank building at 207 York Street in the middle of York Village. Administrative offices are open year-round, 9–5, Monday through Friday; the library is open Monday through Friday, 10–2 and by appointment. In addition, seven other buildings are open to the public from mid-June through September. $6.00 adults, $2.50 children ($16.00 maximum per family) includes admission to all buildings; admission to individual buildings also available. The society also sponsors walking tours and special events.

Jefferds Tavern Visitors Center, Route 1A. Begin your tour here: A 1759 building moved from Wells in 1939. See the orientation video for Old York here and purchase tickets to other museum buildings and tours. Exhibits change, and food is frequently cooking on the hearth at the Tavern Kitchen.

The Old School House next door, an original, mid-18th-century York school, houses an exhibit on education of the period.

Old Gaol, York Village center. Dating from 1719 and billed as the oldest remaining public building of the English colonies, it once served the whole province of Maine and continued to house York County prisoners until 1860. You can inspect the cells and jailer's quarters and learn about York's early miscreants.

Emerson-Wilcox House, Route 1A. Dating in part from 1742 and expanded over the years, period rooms and gallery space trace the development of domestic interiors and decorative arts in York from the Revolutionary period to the 1930s. Exhibits include furniture, ceramics, glass, and a complete set of bed hangings embroidered by Mary Bulman in 1745.

Elizabeth Perkins House, Lindsay Road (at Sewall Bridge—a replica of the first pile bridge in America, built on this spot in 1761). Our favorite building, this 1730 farmhouse is down by the York River. It is still filled with Colonial-era antiques and the spirit of the real powerhouse behind York's original Historic Landmarks Society. It was Miss Perkins who saved the Jefferds Tavern. She's buried under the simple plaque in a boulder at the edge of the lawn overlooking the river.

John Hancock Warehouse and Wharf, Lindsay Road. An 18th-century warehouse with exhibits of 18th-century life and industry on and around the York River.

George Marshall Store (a former chandlery at which large schooners once docked), 140 Lindsay Road, houses exhibits relating to the maritime history of the region.

First Parish Church, York Village. An outstanding, mid-18th-century meetinghouse with a fine old cemetery full of old stones with death's heads and Old English spelling.

Civil War Monument, York Village. Look closely at the monument in the middle of the village. The soldier is wearing a rebel uniform. The statue commissioned for York stands in a South Carolina town because the sculptor made a mistake. At the time, both towns agreed that freight rates were too high to make the switch, a consensus that continues to prevail every time a swap is seriously considered.

In York Harbor and York Beach

Sayward-Wheeler House (363-2709), 79 Barrell Lane, York Harbor. Open June to October 15, Wednesday through Sunday 12–5; $4, maintained by the Society for the Preservation of New England Antiquities (SPNEA). A fine, early 18th-century house built by Jonathan Sayward—merchant, ship owner, judge, and representative to the Massachusetts General Court—who retained the respect of the community despite his Tory leanings. It remained in the same family for 200 years and retains its Queen Anne and Chippendale furnishings, family portraits, and china brought back as booty from the expedition against the French at Louisburg in 1745. It overlooks the river and is accessible from York's Shore Path, near the Wiggly Bridge (see *Walks*).

Nubble Light, York Beach. From Shore Road take Nubble Road out through the Nubble (a cottage-covered peninsula) to Sohier Park at the tip of the peninsula. It includes a parking area, rest rooms, and a seasonal information center and overlooks an 1879 lighthouse perched on a small island of its own. Note the sign: "No Diving on Sunday."

York's Wild Kingdom (363-4911 or 1-800-456-4911), York Beach. Rides open daily, noon–10 PM, June through Labor Day weekend (weekends only in June, September, and October); zoo is open 10–5 May through Columbus Day. This is a combination amusement area and zoo with paddleboats, midway rides, and over 500 animals including some real exotica and acrobatic goats. There are also miniature golf and both pony and elephant rides (but the performing goats, long a trademark, are gone). It's expensive: $11.50 per adult, $9.50 per child 10 and under for zoo/ride admission.

SCENIC DRIVES

Kittery Point. From Route 1, find your way to Route 103 (see map) and follow its twists and turns along the harbor until you come to a simple, old, white wooden church and small Green across from a striking, privately owned Georgian-style house. An old graveyard overlooking the harbor completes the scene. Park at the church (built in 1730, Maine's oldest), notice the parsonage (1729), and walk across to the old graveyard. The magnificent house was built in 1760 for the widow of Sir William Pepperrell, the French and Indian War hero who captured the fortress at Louisburg from the French. Knighted for his feat, Pepperrell went on to become the richest man in New England. Sir William's own handsome house still stands in Pepperrell Cove, but today everyone in the cove seems to be named Frisbee. Five generations of Frisbees have operated the store here; they also own Cap'n Simeon's Galley (see *Dining Out*) and the neighboring B&B.

South Berwick. A short ride north of the Route 1 outlets and clutter transports you to a bend in the Salmon Falls River that is capped by a splendid, 1780s Georgian mansion, restored through the efforts of local author Sarah Orne Jewett; a formal garden and riverside trails through the woods add to the unusual appeal of this place. From Kittery take either Route 236 north from the I-95 Eliot exit or Route 101 north from Route 1 (through high farmland to join Route 236). From York take Route 91 north. Hamilton House and Vaughan Woods are the first left after the junction of Routes 236 and 91 (Brattle Street); follow signs. **Hamilton House** (384-5269) is open June to October 15, Tuesday, Thursday, Saturday, and Sunday 12–4, with tours on the hour ($4); grounds open every day dawn to dusk, Sunday afternoon garden concerts in-season. The foursquare Georgian mansion built in 1785 on a promontory above the river had fallen into disrepair by the time Sarah Orne Jewitt was growing up in nearby South Berwick; she used it as the setting for her novel, *The Tory Lover,* and persuaded wealthy friends Emily and Elizabeth Tyson to restore it in 1898 (the same period that William Dean Howells was involved in restoring nearby York Village). What the Tyson ladies did to the interior of the house is well worth seeing; they also added the splendid formal garden and eventually donated the property to SPNEA, which also maintains the **Sarah Orne Jewett Birthplace** (384-5269) farther up Route 236, smack in the middle of the village of South Berwick. This is another fine 1774 Georgian house that has been preserved to look much as the author knew it. She actually grew up in the house next door that's now the town library.

TO DO

BOAT EXCURSIONS

Port City Lady (439-5070 or 1-800-688-5070), Badger's Island, Kittery. A 57-foot motor yacht offers excursions and charters.

Lobstering Trips (call between 5 and 6 PM: 363-3234), Town Dock #2, York Harbor. When he's not teaching science at the local school, Tom Farnum offers 1-hour lobstering trips around York Harbor in his 22-foot, wooden lobster skiff. $6.50 per person.

Isles of Shoals Steamship Co. (603-431-5000) in Portsmouth offers daily cruises in-season to the Isles of Shoals.

(Also see "Ogunquit and Wells" for excursions from Perkins Cove.)

FISHING

Check with the York Chamber of Commerce about the half-dozen deep-sea fishing boats operating from York Harbor. Surf casting is also popular along Long Sands and Short Sands in York Beach.

GOLF

York Corner Golf (363-5439), Route 1, York. Nine holes, par 3.

HORSEBACK RIDING

Mount Agamenticus Riding Stables (361-2840), summit of Mount Agamenticus (turn off Route 1 at Flo's Hot Dogs). Open daily late June through October, 8–8: 1-hour trail rides, extended rides, corral rides, private lessons.

MOUNTAIN BIKING

The **Mount Agamenticus base lodge** is a source of rental bikes to use on the mountain's trails. For details phone 363-1040.

SCUBA DIVING

York Beach Scuba (363-3330), Railroad Avenue, York Beach. Guided dives around Nubble Light, boat dives, rental equipment, and instruction are all offered.

GREEN SPACE

BEACHES

Long Sands is a 2-mile expanse of coarse, gray sand stretching from York Harbor to the Nubble, backed by Route 1A and summer cottages.

Short Sands is a shorter stretch of coarse, gray sand with a parking lot (meters), toilets, and the Victorian-era village of York Beach just behind it.

York Harbor Beach is small and pebbly, but pleasant. Limited parking. This is the western terminus of the Cliff Walk.

York Beach

Cape Neddick Beach, Shore Road just east of Route 1A, is smallest of all, at the river's mouth, sheltered, and a good choice for children.

Seapoint Beach, Kittery, is long with silky soft sand. Parking only for residents right at the sand, but limited public parking .5 mile back.

PARKS

Fort Foster Park. Beyond Pepperrell Cove, look for Gerrish Island Lane and turn right at the "T" on Pocahontas Road, which leads, eventually, to this 92-acre town park. It incorporates a World War I coastal defense site and fills the whole point of land at the entrance to Portsmouth (NH) Harbor. The fortifications are ugly, but there is a choice of small beaches with different exposures, one very popular with wind surfers. There are extensive walking trails and picnic facilities. Entrance fee.

Mount Agamenticus (363-1040), open weekdays 8:30–4:30. Just 580 feet high but billed as the highest hill on the Atlantic seaboard between York and Florida. A defunct ski area now owned by the town of York, it can be reached by an access road from Mountain Road off Route 1 (turn at Flo's Hot Dogs). The summit is cluttered by radio and TV towers, but the view is of lowland to the north and out to sea on the west. A pile of rocks marks the grave of St. Aspinquid, a Native American medicine man who died at age 94 in 1682; according to the plaque, 6723 wild animals were sacrificed here at the wise man's funeral. See *To Do* for details about mountain biking and horseback riding. Inquire about the pleasant, ⅘-mile hiking trail to the summit.

Vaughan Woods, South Berwick. A 250-acre preserve on the banks of the Salmon Falls River; picnic facilities and nature trails. The first cows in

Maine are said to have been landed here at "Cow Cove" in 1634. See directions under *Scenic Drives*.

WALKS

Shore Path, York Harbor. For more than a mile you can pick your way along the town's most pleasant piece of shorefront. Begin at the George Marshall Store (see *To See*) and walk east along the river and through the shady Steedman Woods. Go across the Wiggly Bridge (a mini-suspension bridge), then continue across Route 103, past the Sayward House, along the harbor, down the beach, and along the top of the rocks.

Cliff Walk, from York Harbor Beach west along the dramatic rocks and open ocean, below the most elaborate of York Harbor's "cottages." The path is eroded in sections, recommended only if you're in good shape and well shod.

Brave Boat Harbor Trail. The Kittery Land Trust maintains a 43-acre conservation area with a 2-mile trail. Note the pullout on Route 103.

The Old York Historical Society offers seasonal, guided tours of both York Village and York Beach.

LODGING

In Kittery

Gundalow Inn (439-4040), 6 Water Street, Kittery 03904. Open year-round. Cevia and George Rosol have turned an 1890s brick village house into an exceptional B&B. Situated just off the Kittery Village Green, across from the Piscataqua River, this makes a good hub for exploring both Portsmouth and Maine's South Coast. The six guest rooms have each been carefully, imaginatively furnished; our favorite is the dainty third-floor room with a queen-sized bed and a water view, but really it's difficult to choose. All rooms have private baths (some claw-foot tubs). The inn has a gracious living room with a baby grand piano and plenty of books, a cozy tiled breakfast room with a fireplace and patio. $80–105 double, including a full breakfast. No smoking. No children under age 16.

Whaleback Inn (439-9570), Box 162, Kittery Point 03905. Open Memorial Day through October. Part of the Frisbee compound (see the introduction), this roadside house offers three upstairs bedrooms, each with a theme. The front room is filled with images and mementos, even a few things that once belonged to Queen Victoria. The room with small windows overlooking the harbor is dedicated to the fact and fiction of the Native American, and the smaller room is decorated with antique toys. All have double beds, and the Native American room ($65) has its own bath and TV. The other two ($55) share a bath, and all share a cheery kitchen/breakfast room as their sole common space. Your collector/hosts are Frank Frisbee and Ron Ames; rates include breakfast. Small pets and children over 12 years welcome.

☞ **High Meadows Bed & Breakfast** (439-0590), Route 101, Eliot 03903. Technically in Eliot, this pleasant retreat is really just a few miles off Route 1 in Kittery. Open April through October. A 1736 house with five nicely furnished rooms, all with private baths. Our favorite is the Wedgewood Room with its canopy bed and highboy. There's a comfortable common room with a wood stove and a formal living room with a fireplace, also a wicker-furnished porch overlooking the landscaped grounds. Walking trails lead through the surrounding 30 acres. No children under 14. All rooms are $70, $60 off-season, full breakfast and afternoon snack included.

☞ **The Moses Paul Inn** (437-1861 or 1-800-552-6058), 270 Goodwin Road (Route 101), Eliot 03903. Open year-round. Just 5.5 miles from Kittery's outlets stands this red 1780 house with five guest rooms: two downstairs with private baths, three upstairs that share. "Moses," a friendly combination greyhound and black Lab, meets you at the door and follows you through the open kitchen and dining area overlooking a mowed meadow; the common room is low beamed and attractive with a fireplace. Your hosts are Joanne Weiss, an interpreter for the deaf, and her husband, Larry James, a merchant seaman. Interestingly, this is one of only two Maine B&Bs we know of that preserve the old tradition of a wife taking in guests while her husband is away at sea, and both houses have ghosts (ask about "Henry"). $70 private, $60 shared bath; $10 less off-season.

In York Village and York Harbor

INNS

Dockside Guest Quarters (363-2868), PO Box 205, Harris Island Road, York 03909. Open daily May through October, weekends the rest of the year. Two generations of the Lusty family imbue this fine little island hideaway with a warmth that few inns this size possess. On Harris Island in York Harbor (connected to Route 103 by a short causeway), Dockside is a 7-acre compound with six buildings: the gracious, 19th-century Maine House, four newer, multiunit cottages, and the Restaurant at Dockside Guest Quarters. In all there are 22 guest rooms—including 7 apartment/suites with kitchenettes—all with water views. Breakfast is served buffet style in the Maine House. It's a nominally priced, "Continental Plus" (fruit compote, baked goods, etc.), muffins-and-juice breakfast, laid out on the dining room table—a morning gathering place for guests who check the blackboard weather forecast and plan their day. Guests can use a canoe or Boston whaler or take advantage of regularly scheduled harbor and river cruises. Special lodging and cruise packages are offered June through October. Two-night minimum stay during July and August. May through early June and the last half of October: $59–98 for double rooms, $98–138 for cottage units. Off-season from $40 (shared bath) to $75 for an apartment suite, breakfast included. Inquire about off-season packages.

Stage Neck Inn (363-3850 or 1-800-222-3238), York Harbor 03911. Open year-round. An attractive 1970s complex of 58 rooms built on the site of the 19th-century Marshall House. Sited on its own peninsula, the inn offers water views (by request), a formal dining room, a less formal Sand Pipers Grill (see *Dining Out*), tennis courts, an outdoor pool, a small indoor pool, and a Jacuzzi. The lobby, sitting room, and main dining room are formal. $135–194 double in summer, less off-season and through packages.

York Harbor Inn (363-5119 or 1-800-343-3869), PO Box 573, York Street, York Harbor 03911. Open year-round. The inn sits right on Route 1A across from the harbor. The beamed lobby, built in 1637, is said to have served as a fisherman's hut on the Isles of Shoals. By the 19th century, the building was elegant enough to serve for a spell as an exclusive men's club, and it is now a popular dining spot. Its Cellar Lounge, which is graced with an elaborately carved bar, is a local gathering place. There are 24 rooms upstairs in the inn itself; request one with a working fireplace or ocean view. Next door in the Yorkshire Building, eight more rooms have been fitted with private baths and furnished with antiques; three have Jacuzzis and sitting areas. All rooms have phones and air-conditioning. $65–119 double, $149.95 per couple includes dinner for two, continental breakfast, taxes, and gratuities.

BED & BREAKFASTS

☞ **Inn at Harmon Park** (363-2031), PO Box 495, York Harbor 03911. Open year-round. A shingled Victorian, this B&B has been Sue Antal's home for more than 20 years. It's attractive and airy, with a living room and upstairs den/TV room; in the middle of the village of York Harbor, within walking distance of the beach and Shore Path. The five guest rooms are all nicely furnished. $69–79 for large rooms with private baths (one has a working fireplace), $49–69 for a smaller room with shared bath; a full, healthy breakfast on the sun porch included. The room diaries are filled with thanks to Sue for her unusual hospitality and sound suggestions for enjoying the immediate area.

Hutchins House (363-3058), 209 Organug Road, York 03909. Closed November through April. This is a spacious, gracious house overlooking the York River. Linda Hutchins has raised her six children here and now offers three unusually pleasant rooms, all with private bath. Common rooms range from formal (there's a player grand piano in the parlor) to an inviting sun porch furnished in wicker. An outdoor Jacuzzi overlooks the York River, and there's a canoe for guest use. $89 in-season, full breakfast included; less in spring/fall.

Edwards' Harborside Inn (363-3037 or 1-800-273-2686), PO Box 866, York Harbor 03911. Open year-round. Nicely sited near York Harbor Beach, this solidly built summer mansion is owned by Jay Edwards, managed by innkeeper Tracy Piquette. Breakfast is served in one of the pleasantest rooms in the area: a sun porch with an unbeatable view of the harbor. You can enjoy the view all day from a lawn chair. Many of the 10 guest rooms also have water views, and you can walk in either direction along the water for miles. Guests have access to the Stage Neck Inn tennis courts across the road and to cruises on the inn's own motor yacht. $85 (shared bath) to $190 (for a suite) in July and August, $50–140 off-season.

Canterbury House Bed & Breakfast (363-3505), Route 1A, York Harbor 03911. Open year-round. James Pappas has refurbished a white-clapboard home in the center of York Harbor, within walking distance of beach and paths. There is a gracious living room, a dining room with formally set tables, and eight carefully furnished rooms with shared baths. $59–75 double includes continental breakfast and afternoon tea; $69–85 with a full breakfast; a suite is $100–110. No children under 12.

The **Bell Buoy B&B** (363-7264), 570 York Street, Box 445, York Harbor 03911. Open year-round. A spacious, 19th-century "summer cottage" converted to a B&B by Iowans Wes and Kathie Cook. $70 double, $85 for an efficiency suite (includes a full breakfast); $10 less off-season.

In York Beach 03910

☞ The **Katahdin Inn** (363-1824), 11 Ocean Avenue Extension. Open mid-May to mid-October. The photo of York Beach in this chapter could have been taken from the front porch of this 1890s guest house overlooking Short Sands Beach and the ocean. Eight of the eleven guest rooms have water views. Number 9 on the third floor is small and white with a window and a skylight that seem to suspend it above the water. Most rooms have a small fridge. More water views fill the living room and two porches (one enclosed), which are equipped with games for poor weather. From $65 for shared to $85 for a large room, private bath; less off-season. Your affable hosts are Bob and Rae LeBlanc. No breakfast.

The **Union Bluff Hotel** (363-1333), 8 Beach Street. Open year-round. The old hotel burned a few years ago, but the new one is almost an exact replica with 40 rooms. The view down the beach is great, and you are right in the middle of things; but there's a price: $95–135 per room in summer, more for suites; almost half price in winter. Inquire about package plans.

The **Willows B&B** (363-9900), 3 Long Beach Avenue. A spacious, turn-of-the-century house on Route 1A within walking distance of Short Sands Beach; four rooms with private baths, four with shared; request a water view. $59–69.

View Point (363-2661), 229 Nubble Road, PO Box 1980. Office open daily in summer, selected days off-season. A nicely designed, condominium-style complex overlooking the Nubble Lighthouse. All suites have a living room, kitchen, porch or patio, gas fireplace, phone, cable TV, CD stereo, VCR, washer/dryer. $180 for one bedroom to $300 for three-bedroom unit in-season; half that in winter. Weekly rates available.

✐ The **Anchorage Inn** (363-5112), Route 1A, Long Beach Avenue. A total of 178 motel-style rooms, most with water views across from Long Sands

Beach. For families, this is a good choice; facilities include indoor and outdoor pools, rooms that sleep four, TV, small fridge. $95–140 per room in high season, $220 per suite; half that in winter; off-season bargain packages.

Cutty Sark Motel (363-5131), Long Beach Avenue. Minimum 3-night stays in high season. A three-story, 27-room motel right on the beach, and five guest rooms in the neighboring house with a lawn overlooking the water; $95–130 in-season, half that otherwise.

Cape Neddick

Cape Neddick House (363-2500), Box 70, Route 1, Cape Neddick 03902. Open year-round. Although it is right on Route 1, this Victorian house (in the Goodwin family for more than 100 years) offers an away-from-it-all feel and genuine hospitality. There are five guest rooms with private baths, two with working fireplaces, all furnished with antiques. Breakfast is an event—maybe strawberry scones and ham with apple biscuits—served on the back deck (overlooking garden and woods), in the dining room, or in the homey kitchen. A six-course dinner—from stuffed mushrooms to raspberry cheesecake, all cooked on the 80-year-old Glenwood wood stove—can be reserved in advance. $55–75 double, $75–90 for a suite, depending on season.

The Riverbed (363-3630), 154 Route 1A, PO Box 730, York Beach 03910. Open Memorial Day through Columbus Day. Built in 1761, this classic old house is nicely sited with views of the Cape Neddick River. Cassandra and Steve Ewing offer three rooms, two with shared baths and two with decks overlooking the water. A canoe and outdoor hot tub add to the appeal of this place, and a path leads to Cape Neddick Beach and the lobster pound. $75–85 includes breakfast.

Wooden Goose Inn (363-5673), Route 1, Cape Neddick 03902. Open year-round except January. The six guest rooms—and six bathrooms—are fussily exquisite, and the gardens are beautiful. Hosts Tony and Jerry pride themselves on pampering guests, preparing breakfasts such as poached salmon. $110 includes afternoon tea as well as breakfast. No children.

WHERE TO EAT

DINING OUT

☞✐ **Cap'n Simeon's Galley** (439-3655), Route 103, Pepperrell Cove. Open year-round for lunch and dinner; closed Tuesdays from mid-October to Memorial Day. A very special place with one of the best water views of any Maine restaurant. You enter through the original Frisbee Store (the building is said to date back to 1680; the store opened in 1828) to a spacious dining area with picture windows overlooking the cove and beyond to Portsmouth Harbor. Seafood is the specialty, but you can get anything from a grilled cheese ($2.50) to a New York choice sirloin steak ($12.50), from a quiche and salad ($5.75) to a fisherman's fried seafood platter ($11.95); lobster is priced daily.

Warren's Lobster House (439-1630), 1 Water Street, Kittery. Open year-round; lunch, dinner, and Sunday brunch; docking facilities. A low-ceilinged, knotty-pine dining room overlooking the Piscataqua River and Portsmouth, NH, beyond. An old dining landmark with 1940s decor. The salad bar features over 50 selections ($6.95 as a meal in itself), and the specialty is seafood, fried and broiled. Dinner entrées average $13.

Cape Neddick Inn and Gallery (363-2899), Route 1, Cape Neddick. Open year-round for dinner and Sunday brunch; closed Monday and Tuesday from Columbus Day to mid-June. When a fire damaged this dining landmark, the chef/owners rebuilt it beautifully, keeping the old facade and atmosphere but redesigning the dining area—the better to display quality artwork. The menu changes every six weeks, although roast duckling remains a year-round staple along with fish and pasta *du jour*. Lamb loin with Dijon mustard and Swiss-chard sauce baked in phyllo, and broiled haddock with sesame-oyster hollandaise are examples. The desserts are spectacular. Reservations suggested. Entrées: $9–28.

The York Harbor Inn (363-5119), Route 1A, York Harbor. Open year-round for lunch and dinner; also Sunday brunch. Four pleasant dining rooms, most with views of water. The menu is large. The seafood chowder is studded with shrimp, scallops, and crabmeat as well as haddock ($3.95 a cup); milk-fed veal, fresh seafood, and pastas are the specialties. The dinner entrées range from pasta primavera to Yorkshire Lobster Supreme (lobster stuffed with scallop and shrimp filling: $21.95). Sunday brunch is big. For dinner, plan to spend $60 per couple, excluding wine, tax, and tip. The Cellar Pub menu runs to burgers, soups, sandwiches, and salads.

Clay Hill Farm (361-2272), corner of Agamenticus and Logging Roads, York. Open for dinner only, year-round; reservations. This is a special occasion favorite, worth finding a few miles from Route 1. The rambling farmhouse, dating in part from 1780, houses a large restaurant on outstanding grounds. You dine by candlelight and might begin with Thai scallops ($6.75) or smoked Maine mussels ($4.75); entrées range from Caesar salad with shrimp ($12.95) to Mediterranean scampi ($20.95).

The Restaurant at Dockside Guest Quarters (363-2628), Harris Island, York Harbor. Open for lunch and dinner late May through Columbus Day except Mondays. Docking facilities, glass-walled and porch dining overlooking York Harbor. Specializes in seafood (from $6.95 for broiled scrod or fish and chips at lunch to $17.95 for a fisherman's platter at dinner). Roast-stuffed duckling is also featured (from $10.95). Dinners include "The Salad Deck" as well as breads and veggies. Children get a Dockside Vacation coloring book to use while waiting.

☞✐**Fazio's** (363-7019), 38 Woodbridge Road, York Village. This popular trattoria is decorated with original murals and photos of Annette Fazio's mother. The menu is traditional—fettuccine carbonara (pancetta, cheese, cream, cracked pepper, and egg) for $8.95 ($7.50 until 5:30), chicken Francese (white wine and lemon sauce served with cheese pasta: $10.95), etc. The pasta is made daily. Patrons would not complain at twice the price. There's also a children's menu. (Also see *Eating Out*.)

Cape Neddick Lobster Pound (363-5471), Route 1A (Shore Road), Cape Neddick. Open April through December for dinner only. Situated at the mouth of a tidal river, this modern, shingled building has the look of always having been there. Besides lobster and clams, there are tempters such as bouillabaisse or baked sole with Maine shrimp, crab, cheddar, and lemon stuffing, or smoked trout with herb mayonnaise. Moderate to expensive. Live music, dancing after 9 PM.

Stage Neck Inn (363-3850), Stage Neck Road, York Harbor. Open year-round for breakfast, lunch, and dinner. We find the crystal chandeliers and linen napery a bit too formal (jackets are not required), but the view of rocks and sea is splendid. The à la carte menu includes pâté *de campagne* ($5.50) and a large choice of entrées ranging in price from seafood-stuffed chicken ($16.95) to veal Oscar ($18.95). Reservations required. The inn's less formal **Sand Pipers Cafe,** overlooking the beach, has a strong local following. Try the "blackened Maine crab cakes" ($11.95).

Mimmo's (363-3807), Long Sands, York Beach. Open for breakfast and dinner June through September and for dinner only the rest of the year, closed only on Christmas and Thanksgiving. Named for its colorful chef Mimmo Basileo, this trattoria is a hot spot in summer (reservations necessary). Tables are close packed, the water view is limited to the front dining room, and the menu ranges from eggplant parmigiana ($13.95) through a variety of pastas to seafood "coastazurro" (mussels, shrimp, haddock, calamari, sautéed with garlic, etc.; $17.95). BYOB.

The Lobster Barn (363-4721), Route 1, York. Open year-round for lunch and dinner. A pubby, informal, popular dining room with wooden booths and a full menu. Specialties such as scallop and shrimp pie earn this place top marks from locals. In summer, lobster dinners (in the rough) are served under a tent out back. Most of the seafood casseroles are $11.95; lobster is priced daily.

Fox's Lobster House (363-2643), Nubble Point, York Beach. Open daily in-season 11:45–9. A large, tourist-geared place with a great water view and good food ranging from hot dogs ($2.95) to shore dinners ($18.95–20.95).

EATING OUT

The Goldenrod (363-2621), York Beach. Open Memorial Day to Columbus Day for breakfast, lunch, and dinner. In business since 1896, one of the best family restaurants in New England; same menu all day from 8 AM–10:30 PM, served up at time-polished, wooden tables in the big dining room with a fieldstone fireplace as well as at the old-style soda fountain.

Famous saltwater taffy kisses cooked and pulled in the windows. A wide selection of homemade ice creams and yogurts, good sandwiches (cream cheese and olive or nuts is still $1.75), daily specials.

Cap'n Simeon's Galley (see *Dining Out*) is also the best bet in Kittery for a fried scallop roll or burger at lunch.

Chauncey Creek Lobster Pound (439-1030), Chauncey Creek Road, Kittery Point. Open during summer only. Lobster in rolls and in the rough; steamed clams and mussels are the specialty. There is also a raw bar. An average dinner with steamers cost $12.00, but don't expect any extras. The locals bring their own salad, bread, and wine. The setting is great, but service can be slow.

Bob's Clam Hut (439-4233), Route 1, Kittery. Open year-round. The best fried clams on the strip. Here since 1956 and now, finally, with indoor seating.

Rick's All Season Restaurant (363-5584), 240 York Street, York (next to Cumberland Farms, middle of York Village). Open from early morning to 2:30 in the afternoon, except Wednesday and Thursday when it's open for dinner. A find. Cheap, good, friendly. The breakfast special is $1.75, the chowder is homemade, the beer-batter haddock dinner is $5.95, the chili burger comes in a bowl (it's hot), and the cheesecake is delicious. There's also a pub side.

The Line House (439-3401), Route 1 on the Kittery/York line. Open year-round for breakfast (with an amazing variety of egg dishes), lunch, and dinner; family run and geared, a favorite with the local police force. You can dine on lazy lobster pie or a seafood platter, but this is also one of the few places around featuring smothered liver and onions ($5.45) and baked ziti ($5.95). Children's portions and specials.

SNACKS

Brown's Ice Cream (363-4077), Nubble Road, a quarter mile beyond the lighthouse, York Beach. Seasonal. All ice cream is made on the premises, exotic flavors.

Pie in the Sky Bakery (363-2656), Route 1, Cape Neddick, York Beach. Open Monday through Saturday except January; hours vary off-season. The purple house at the corner of River Road is filled with delicious smells and irresistible muffins, pies, tortes, and breads, all baked here by John and Nancy Stern.

ENTERTAINMENT

Hackmatack Playhouse (698-1807), in Berwick, presents summer-stock performances most evenings; Thursday matinees.

Seacoast Repertory Theatre (603-433-4472), 125 Bow Street, Portsmouth. Professional theater productions.

(Also see "Ogunquit and Wells.")

York Beach Cinema (363-2074), 6 Beach Street, York. First-run movies.

SELECTIVE SHOPPING

ART GALLERIES
Firehouse Gallery (363-5452), Kittery. Open noon–5 daily except Mondays. **York Art Association Gallery** (363-4049 or 363-2918), Route 1A, York Harbor. Annual July art show, films, and workshops.

CRAFTS SHOPS
York Village Crafts (363-4830), 211 York Street, York Village. Open daily 9–5. Housed in the vintage 1834 church in the center of York Village, more than 100 displays of crafts, art, books, and antiques. **York Handcrafters Association** (363-7616), Route 1 at Cape Neddick House. Open daily in summer, weekends in spring and fall. A nonprofit outlet for area craftspeople.

OUTLET MALLS
Note: For the Kittery shopping strip, take I-95, Exit 3.
   At this writing, there are 115 discount stores within a 1.3-mile strip of Route 1 in Kittery. They represent a mix of clothing, household furnishings, gifts, and basics. All purport to offer savings of at least 20 percent on retail prices, many up to 70 percent. Note that the Kittery Trading Post (described above) is the original anchor store of this strip. In summer most outlets are generally open 10–9, except Sunday when hours are 10–6; Labor Day through Memorial Day, Sunday through Wednesday 10–6, Thursday through Saturday 10–8.

Maine Outlet Mall, Route 1. Largest of the outlet malls with 28 shops, including Samuel Roberts (tailored, top-drawer clothing for men and women), Timberland (men's and women's shoes and hiking boots), and Mikasa (china, glassware, and gifts).

Tidewater Outlet Mall, Route 1 (north of the Maine Outlet Mall). This is a small but quality shopping center, worth the stop for Lenox china and crystal; also for North Country Leather (luggage, wallets, belts, and briefcases—quality stuff made nearby in East Rochester, NH) and Boston Traders (sportswear).

Kittery Outlet Center, Route 1 (across from the Maine Outlet Mall). Stores include Royal Doulton (fine china and toby mugs), Van Heusen (shirts for men and women), and Le Sportsac (own-brand lightweight luggage, totes, and accessories).

Dansk Square, Route 1 (south of the Maine Outlet Mall). Dansk is the anchor store here and a great place to shop for gifts: kitchenware, china, bowls, and plasticware.

Maine Gate Outlets, Route 1. Eddie Bauer is the big name here (men and women's sportswear). There are also the Kitchen Collection and the Leather Loft (handbags, belts, and briefcases).

Other outlets in the strip include Dexter Shoe (Maine-made footwear; note that Dexter has another shoebox-shaped log cabin farther north on Route 1 in York), Dunham (also quality boots and shoes), Polo, Ralph Lauren, J. Crew, Crate & Barrel, FAO Schwarz, and Bass Shoe.

SPECIAL SHOPS

Kittery Trading Post (439-2700), Route 1, Kittery. A local institution since 1926. The sprawling store is always jammed with shoppers in search of sportswear, shoes, children's clothing, firearms, outdoors books, and fishing or camping gear. The summer-end sales are legendary, and many items are routinely discounted.

Books Plus (363-1450), York Village Shopping Center. A full-service bookstore that welcomes browsers; also good for music, greeting cards, and magazines.

SPECIAL EVENTS

Note: Be sure to pick up the area's unusually lively "Summer Social Calendar" at the York Chamber of Commerce (see *Guidance*).

June: **Strawberry Festival,** South Berwick.

July: **Independence Day celebrations,** York—parades, cannon salutes, militia encampment, crafts and food fair, picnic, and dinner. Kittery— **Seaside Festival** at Fort Foster's Park. **Band concerts,** Wednesday evenings at Short Sands Pavilion, York Beach. **Old York Designers' Show House** sponsored by the Old York Historical Society. **York Days Celebration** (last days of month, see August)—raffle, puppet shows, and skits.

August: **York Days Celebration** (beginning of the month)—flower show, church supper, concerts, square dances, parade, and sand castle contest. **Seacoast Crafts Fair** (late in the month).

September: **House Tours. Eliot Festival Days** (late September).

October: **Harvest Fest,** York Village (third weekend)—an oxen roast, oxcart races, hay and horse rides, militia encampment, music, and live entertainment.

December: **Christmas Open-House Tours. Kittery Christmas Parade and Tree Lighting** and **York Festival of Lights Parade.**

Ogunquit and Wells

Ogunquit and Wells are beach towns, between which lie more than 7 scarcely interrupted miles of sand from the entrance to Ogunquit Beach to the eastern end of Wells Beach.

Named for the English cathedral town, Wells was incorporated in 1653. Ogunquit was technically part of Wells until 1980 but seceded in spirit long before that, establishing itself as a summer magnet for top artists and actors in the 1920s. During that decade, both the community's 3-mile tongue of beach and dune and the mile-long Marginal Way (an exceptional seaside path) were declared public. Ogunquit and Wells together continue to satisfy an amazing mix of visitors: Canadians and New Yorkers, yuppies and families, retirees and young singles.

Hotels in both towns began to appear in the 1880s. The first guests from New York and Philadelphia arrived by the Boston & Maine Railroad, and residents of nearer cities began coming by the Atlantic Shore Line trolleys in 1907. Some very grand hotels and many splendid shingled cottages appeared along the shore in Ogunquit, and more modest cottages soon lined the beachside streets in Wells.

"Motor courts" mushroomed along Route 1 in the 1920s, and some of the best survive among the many resort motels and condo complexes that now line the Route 1 Ogunquit/Wells "strip." This lineup still holds great appeal for families. Thanks to the lay of the land, most of the lodgings on the water side of Route 1 actually have water views.

In the village of Ogunquit, most of the old wooden hotels were razed during the 1960s and replaced by luxury motels. With the 1980s came condos, more motels, high-priced restaurants, an abundance of art galleries, and boutiques. Luckily, it also brought trolleys-on-wheels to ease the traffic crunch at Perkins Cove and the beaches.

In summer, the towns' open-sided trolleys in Ogunquit carry as many as 12,000 people per day, shuttling constantly between the beaches, Perkins Cove, and lodging places to connect with the trolleys shuttling up and down between the Route 1 shops and restaurants and the Wells waterfront.

Natural beauty remains surprisingly accessible in both Ogunquit and Wells. Given the vast expanse of sand, you can always find an uncrowded spot, and Wells harbors more than 4000 acres of conservation

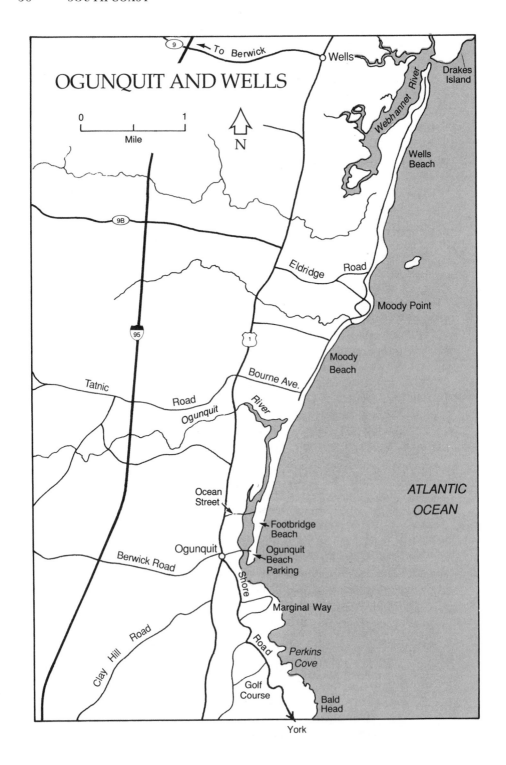

OGUNQUIT AND WELLS

9 ← To Berwick

Wells

Webhannet River

Drakes Island

Wells Beach

0   1
Mile

N

9B

95

Eldridge   Road

Moody Point

Tatnic

1

Bourne Ave.

Moody Beach

Road

Ogunquit   River

ATLANTIC OCEAN

Ocean Street

Footbridge Beach

Ogunquit Beach Parking

Ogunquit

Berwick Road

Shore

Marginal Way

Clay Hill   Road

Road

Perkins Cove

Golf Course

Bald Head

York

land, much of it webbed with trails (see *Nature Preserves*).

Ogunquit Beach offers surf, soft sand, and space for kite flying, as well as a sheltered strip along the mouth of the Ogunquit River for toddlers. On weekends a tidal wave of day-tripping Bostonians spreads over the beach and eddies through Perkins Cove, but it recedes on Sunday evenings. Both Ogunquit and Wells are relatively peaceful midweek in summer and especially delightful in September and October.

GUIDANCE

Chamber of Commerce (646-2939), Box 2289, Ogunquit 03907. The information center (646-5533) on Route 1, just south of Ogunquit Village, is open Memorial Day through Labor Day, Monday to Saturday 9–5, Sunday 10–2; then until Columbus Day, Friday to Sunday. It's the place to check for vacancies, menus, excursions, and events; it even has rest rooms. During the off-season, phone the town office: 646-5139.

Wells Chamber of Commerce (646-2451), PO Box 356, Wells 04090. Open daily 9–5, until 9 on Friday, June through fall foliage. Also open 10–5 the rest of the year, Tuesday through Saturday. Look for the information center on Route 1 in Moody.

GETTING THERE

By car: Coming north on I-95, take Exit 1 (York) and drive up Route 1 to the village of Ogunquit. Coming south on I-95, take Exit 2 (Wells).

By taxi: Since you can hop the trolley to almost anywhere in the Ogunquit area, it makes sense to take **All Season Taxi** (646-1126) from the Portsmouth, New Hampshire, bus stop (the nearest dropping-off point), or from the airport in Portland, rather than rent a car.

By bus: **Coastal Connection** (282-5408) is a seasonal bus line that transports passengers between York and Kennebunkport, with eight stops along the way, including Oqunquit and Wells. A good way to get from one coastal spot to the next without driving. Maps and schedules are available from the chambers of commerce.

GETTING AROUND

During summer months, **open-sided trolleys** make frequent stops throughout the village of Ogunquit, Perkins Cove, at the beach, and along Route 1. They connect with the trolleys that circulate up and down Route 1 and through the beach and lodging areas in Wells. Fare is nominal. Trolley maps are available from the chambers of commerce.

PARKING

Park and walk or take the trolley. In summer this is no place to drive. There are at least seven public lots; rates range from $4–6 per day. There is also free parking (2-hour limit) on Route 1 across from the Leavitt Theatre just north of Ogunquit Square or adjacent to Cumberland Farms. Parking at the main entrance to Ogunquit Beach itself is $2 per hour. (For more on beach parking, see *Beaches*.) In Wells, parking at the five public lots is $6 per day, and monthly permits are available from the town office.

MEDICAL EMERGENCY
  Ambulance/Rescue Squad (646-5111), town of Ogunquit.
  York Hospital (363-4321), 24-hour emergency, 15 Hospital Drive, York Village.
  Wells Ambulance (646-9911). In Wells, you may be nearer to **Southern Maine Medical Center** (283-3663), 1 Mountain Road, Biddeford.

VILLAGES

Perkins Cove. This is probably Maine's most painted fishing cove with some 40 restaurants and shops, now housed in weathered fish shacks. It is the departure point for the area's excursion and fishing boats, based beside the famous draw-footbridge. Parking is nearly impossible in the summer, but there are public lots nearby, and the trolley stops here regularly. The cove can also be reached on foot via the Marginal Way (see *Walks*).

TO SEE

MUSEUMS
Ogunquit's two most prominent art galleries qualify as museums. (For more galleries, see *Selective Shopping*.)
Ogunquit Museum of American Art (646-4909), Shore Road, Ogunquit. Open July to late September, 10:30–5 daily, Sunday 2–5; $3 adults/$2 seniors, free to members and children under 12. Built superbly of local stone and wood with enough glass to let in the beauty of the cove it faces, the museum displays selected paintings from its permanent collection, which includes the strong, bright oils of Henry Strater and other one-time locals such as Reginald Marsh. Special exhibitions feature nationally recognized artists.
The Barn Gallery (646-5370), Shore Road and Bourne Lane, Ogunquit. Open June through Columbus Day weekend, Monday to Saturday 10–5 and Sunday 2–5. The gallery showcases work by members of the Ogunquit Art Association; also stages frequent workshops, lectures, films, and concerts.
✐ **Wells Auto Museum** (646-9064), Wells. Open daily mid-June to mid-September, 10–5. More than 70 cars dating from 1900 to 1963, plus nickelodeons, toys, and bicycles.

TO DO

BICYCLING
Bikes are an ideal mode of transportation in Ogunquit and Wells. Touring bikes and bike tours are available from **Classic Bike** (646-7909) in Ogunquit. **Wheels & Waves, Inc.** (646-5774) in Wells also rents mountain bikes.

BOAT EXCURSIONS

From Perkins Cove

Finestkind (646-5227). Scenic cruises to Nubble Light, cocktail cruises, and "lobstering trips" (watch lobster traps hauled, hear about lobstering).

Ugly Anne (646-7202). Half- and full-day, deep-sea fishing trips with Captain Ken Young Sr.

The Bunny Clark (646-2214). Half- and full-day, deep-sea fishing trips with Captain Tim Tower.

FISHING

Tackle and bait can be rented at Wells Harbor. The obvious fishing spots are the municipal dock and harbor jetties. There is surf casting near the mouth of the Mousam River.

MINI-GOLF

⬦ **Wells Beach Mini-Golf,** next to Big Daddy's Ice Cream, Route 1, Wells. Open daily in-season, 10–10.

⬦ **Wonder Mountain,** Route 1, Wells. A mini-golf mountain, complete with waterfalls; adjoins Outdoor World.

⬦ **Sea-Vu Mini Golf** is another Route 1 option in Wells.

SAILING

The Silverlining (361-3800), a 42-foot, wooden Hinckley sloop, sails out of Perkins Cove on regularly scheduled, 2-hour cruises. Minimum six people, $28; also available for half- and full-day charters.

SWIMMING

See *Beaches.*

TENNIS

Three public courts in Ogunquit. Inquire at **Dunaway Center** (646-9361).

Wells Recreation Area, Route 9A, Wells. Four courts.

THEATER

Ogunquit Playhouse (646-5511), Route 1 (just south of Ogunquit Village). Open late June through August. Billing itself as "America's Foremost Summer Theater," this grand old summer-stock theater (now air-conditioned) opened for its first season in 1933 and continues to feature top stars in productions staged every evening during the season except Sunday. Matinees are Wednesday and Thursday. Usually we describe summer stock under *Entertainment* near the end of a chapter, but in this case the Playhouse is one of the major things to do.

GREEN SPACE

BEACHES

Three-mile-long **Ogunquit Beach** can be approached three ways: (1) The most popular way is from the foot of Beach Street. There are boardwalk snacks, changing facilities, and toilets, and it is here that the beach forms a tongue between the ocean and the Ogunquit River (parking in the lot here is $2 per hour). (2) The **Footbridge Beach** access (take Ocean

Beach on Marginal Way in Ogunquit

NANCY C. HORTON

Street off Route 1 north of the village) offers rest rooms and is less crowded (parking is $6 per day). (3) The **Moody Beach** entrance is off Route 1 at Eldridge Street in Wells (parking is $6 per day). Be sure to park in the lot provided and to walk west onto Ogunquit Beach; Moody Beach is now private above the high-water mark.

Wells Beach. Limited free parking right in the middle of the village of Wells Beach, also parking ($6) at east end by the Jetty station. Wooden casino and boardwalk, clam shacks, clean public toilets, a cluster of motels, concrete benches—a gathering point for older people who sit while enjoying the view of the wide, smooth beach.

Drakes Island. Take Drakes Island Road off Route 1. There are three small parking areas on this land spit lined with private cottages.

NATURE PRESERVES

Wells National Estuarine Research Reserve at Laudholm Farm (646-1555), Laudholm Road (off Route 1, just south of junction with Route 9), managed by the Laudholm Trust. The reserve consists of 1,600 acres of estaurine habitat for the area's wildlife. *Estuarine,* by the way, means whatever is formed by an estuary (the area where ocean tides meet freshwater currents). The reserve is divided into two parts, each with its own access point. Grounds include meadows and two barrier beaches at the mouth of the Little River. Laudholm Farm is a former estate, owned by the Lord family from 1881 until 1986 (George C. Lord was president of the Boston & Maine). It is now a visitors center with a slide show, exhibits, rest rooms, and parking ($5 in July and August). Seven miles of trails meander through fields, woods, and wetlands (bring a bathing suit if you want to swim at the beach). The Laudholm Trust grounds are open year-round (gates open daily 8–5), and guided trail walks are offered daily in summer, weekends in spring and fall. This is a birder's mecca.

Rachel Carson National Wildlife Refuge (operated by United States Fish and Wildlife Service), off Route 9, subtly marked. Open sunrise to sunset. The nature trail is 1 mile long—a loop through a white pine forest and along the Little River through a salt marsh area. Maps and guides are available from the resident manager's office (646-9226) near the entrance to the refuge along Route 9.

WALKS

Marginal Way. In 1923 Josiah Chase gave Ogunquit this windy path along the ocean. A farmer from the town of York just south of here, Chase had driven his cattle around rocky Israel's Head each summer to pasture on the marsh grass in Wells, just to the north. Over the years, he bought land here and there until, eventually, he owned the whole promontory. He then sold off sea-view lots at a tidy profit and donated the actual ocean frontage to the town, thus preserving his own right-of-way. There is very limited parking at the mini-lighthouse on Israel's Head.

Wells Harbor. Here is a pleasant walk along a granite jetty and a good fishing spot. There is also a recently expanded recreation area, with playground and gazebo where concerts are held.

Old Trolley Trail, an interesting nature walk and cross-country ski trail; begins on Pine Hill Road North, Ogunquit.

Mount Agamenticus is a defunct ski area and the highest hill on the Atlantic between Florida and Bar Harbor. Take the Big A access road off Agamenticus Road, Ogunquit.

LODGING

RESORT

The Cliff House (361-1000), PO Box 2274, Ogunquit 03907. Open late March to mid-December. The tower-topped, mansard-roofed Cliffscape Building, opened in 1990, is now the centerpiece of this 162-room, 70-acre resort. The new building's multitiered lobby and dining rooms make the most of the oceanside roost atop Bald Head Cliff, and the atmosphere is a rare blend of new amenities (including an indoor lap pool) and family antiques. It's all the work of Kathryn Weare, a great-granddaughter worthy of Elsie Jane Weare, the indomitable lady who opened the The Cliff House in 1872.

The news that the Boston & Maine Railroad would be adding a spur line to York was what prompted Elsie Jane to persuade her sea-captain husband to invest all their money in buying Bald Hill Cliff. Her brother built the hotel with wood from the family lots, milled in their own sawmill. The clean rooms, fine food (provided from the adjacent Weare Farm), fresh air, and dramatic location—all for $6 a week, including three meals a day—soon lured the Biddles of Philadelphia, the Havermeyers of New York, and the Cabots and Lodges of Boston.

The family-run resort continued to maintain its status throughout the Roaring Twenties and shaky thirties, but World War II about did it in. The resort was literally drafted—as a radar station, keeping a 24-hour vigil for Nazi submarines. When the Weares were finally permitted back on their property, they found it in shambles. Discouraged, Charles Weare placed an ad in a 1946 edition of the *Wall Street Journal:* "For sale. 144 rooms. 90 acres, over 2500 feet ocean frontage for just $50,000."

There were no takers. Charles turned the property over to his son Maurice, who went with the times, shaving off the top two floors and transforming it into a "resort motel"—which is what it was until 1990. High-season summer rates range from $125 for a motel-like unit with a limited view to $315 for a one-bedroom suite; off-season rates run $90–185. These rates do not include meals, but a variety of packages bring the rack rate way down. Facilities include outdoor and indoor pools, a sauna and Jacuzzi, exercise room, a game room, tennis courts, and a summertime trolley into the village and to the beach.

RESORT MOTOR INNS

Our usual format places inns before motels, but in the 1960s, some of Ogunquit's leading resorts replaced their old hotel buildings with fancy "motor inns."

Sparhawk (646-5562), Shore Road, Box 936, Ogunquit 03907. Open early April to late October. The 50 prime units in this complex, each with a balcony, overlook the entrance to the Ogunquit River and down the length of Ogunquit Beach. The 20 units in neighboring Ireland House (with balconies canted toward the beach) are combination living room/ bedroom suites, and the Barbara Dean, a spacious old village house, has seven suites and three apartments. The Sparhawk Apartment, a three-room house with fireplace and private deck overlooking the ocean, is rented by the week. Guests register and gather in Sparhawk Hall; a continental breakfast is served here, and there are books and comfortable spaces to read and to study local menus. Recreation options include a pool, shuffleboard, croquet, and tennis. One-week minimum stay, June 30 to mid-August; $135–210 in high summer, $65–140 in spring and fall.

Aspinquid (646-7072), Box 2408, Beach Street, Ogunquit 03907. Open mid-March through mid-October. A picture of the old Aspinquid hangs above the check-in counter of this condo-style complex just across the bridge from Ogunquit Beach. Built in 1971 by the owners of the old hotel, the two-story clusters still look modern. They are nicely designed and range in size from motel units to two-room apartments; all have two double beds, phones, and TVs; most have kitchenettes. Facilities include a pool, a lighted tennis court, a sauna, a spa, and a fish pond with waterfall ideal for peaceful reading and relaxation. $105–120 for a motel room, $125–130 for an efficiency unit, $180–200 for a two-room apartment in high-season; $55–110 off-season.

INNS AND BED & BREAKFASTS

All inn listings are for Ogunquit 03907 unless otherwise indicated.

Beachmere (646-2021 or 1-800-336-3983), Box 2340. Open late March to mid-December. Sited on the Marginal Way with water views, this fine old mansion has a motel annex; there are also rooms in Mayfair and Bullfrog cottages a half-mile away on Israel's Head Road. Three of the rooms in the old mansion have working fireplaces, and many have decks; all have kitchenettes and cable TV. The large, inviting grounds overlook Ogunquit Beach, and smaller beaches are a few minutes' walk. Rates range from $75 per day for a third-floor efficiency accommodating two to $160 for a suite with fireplace in high-season; $60–125 in shoulder season, $50–85 off-season.

☞ **Ye Olde Perkins Place** (361-1119), 749 Shore Road (south of Perkins Cove), Cape Neddick 03902. Open late June to Labor Day. Overlooking the ocean, this 1717 homestead has six rooms, three in a more modern annex. The location is great, away from the village but within walking distance of a pebble beach. $55–65 per room; coffee, juice, and muffins included. No credit cards.

Marginal Way House and Motel (646-8801; 363-6566 in winter), Box 697, 8 Wharf Lane. Open late April through October. Ed and Brenda Blake have owned this delightful complex for more than 25 years. Just a short walk from the beach and really in the middle of the village, it is hidden down a back, waterside lane. There are old-fashioned guest rooms with private baths in the inn itself; and six standard motel rooms in a small, shingled, waterside building, as well as seven efficiency apartments (one or two bedrooms). The landscaped grounds have an unbeatable ocean view. From $40 per room off-season; $72–108 during high-season in the inn; $118 in the motel and $896–1,050 per week for an apartment.

The Pine Hill Inn (361-1004), PO Box 2336. Open mid-May to mid-October. A Victorian summer house set in a rock garden, high above a quiet residential road but within walking distance of Perkins Cove and handy to everywhere by trolley. Walls throughout the house are all tongue-in-groove paneling, and the four tastefully furnished guest rooms have private baths. A large living room and screened-in porch are inviting spots. There is also a two-bedroom cottage adjacent to the inn. Diana Schmidt is a welcoming host. Children over age 12 please; younger allowed in cottage. $75–85 per room includes breakfast. Three-night minimum for cottage, $300 ($600 for a week).

The Hayes Guest House (646-2277), 133 Shore Road. Open June through

October. Elinor Hayes has been renting rooms in her country home at the entrance to Perkins Cove since 1950. The house is furnished with antiques, and Mrs. Hayes's collections of 500 dolls (many of which she has made) and 1000 salt dishes and spoons are on display for all to enjoy. There is an outdoor pool, and Marginal Way footpath is close by. The guest rooms in the main house all have air conditioners and private baths ($70–75 per night); there is also a small "semi-efficiency" ($80 per day, $500 per week), and a two-bedroom apartment with a sun porch ($130 per day, $800 per week).

Rose Cottage (646-6552), PO Box 2092, 7 Bourne Lane. This charming house was once part of the Dunelawn estate (since made into condos) by the Ogunquit River, where it hosted famous Playhouse performers such as Rita Hayworth, Mickey Rooney, and Bette Davis. In 1986 the classic, shingle-style house was moved to the other side of the village, within walking distance of the Marginal Way and Perkins Cove. It offers five rooms, ranging from $40.00 (for a single with shared bath) to $85.50 for a large double with private bath. Rates include breakfast. Innkeepers Larry and Marcia Smith also own Ogunquit's Camera Shop.

Seafair Inn (646-2181), PO Box 1221. Open mid-April through October. A spacious, 1890 Victorian home in the middle of the village with an elegant living room and 18 rooms, 14 of which have private baths; efficiency units are tucked away in back. A continental breakfast is included and served in the dining room or on the sun porch. $40 with shared bath off-season, $99 for efficiency units in-season; $65 shared bath and $90 for a room with private bath in-season.

The Admiral's Inn (646-7093), PO Box 2241, 70 South Main Street. Open year-round. A large Colonial house on Route 1 just south of the village of Ogunquit (there's a trolley stop nearby). There are eight old-fashioned guest rooms with shared baths ($28–75 depending on room and season); also four motel-style units ($35–59), four efficiencies ($45–98), and one studio apartment ($52–98). There's an outdoor pool in back. Breakfast is included in-season, and children are welcome.

Morning Dove (646-3891), PO Box 1940, 30 Bourne Lane. Open late June through Labor Day, weekends in spring and fall. On a quiet side street off Shore Road, within walking distance of everything, is this carefully restored 1860s farmhouse originally owned by one of Ogunquit's first families. The six rooms have been uniquely decorated by host and interior decorator Eeta Sachon. Our favorite is "Grandma's Attic" with a king bed, private bath, spinning wheel, butter churn, and Palladian window with European lace curtains. Pete Sachon keeps the gardens flourishing beautifully. Wine on arrival. $60–110 (depending on season) per room includes breakfast.

The Grey Gull (646-7601), 321 Webhannet Drive, RR 4, Box 1978, Wells 04090. Open year-round. Primarily a restaurant, but there are five rooms upstairs in the 1890s summer hotel; nicely furnished, shared baths, water views, walk to the beach. $55–65 in high season, from $35 per room in spring.

Beach Farm Inn (646-7970), Eldredge Road, Wells 04090. A 19th-century farmhouse, tastefully restored by Don and Sandy Conant. Cozy rooms simply furnished with iron beds, antiques, some private baths. We like the large third-floor room with lacy curtains and a comfortable wicker chair. Set back from the main road, a peaceful setting with a country feel and a pool, handy to Moody Beach and on the trolley line. $50–60 per couple, including breakfast; less off-season and for long stays.

COTTAGES

We have noted just a few of the dozens of cottage, condominium, and motel complexes that line Route 1. The unusually helpful Wells Chamber of Commerce keeps track of vacancies in these and in many private cottages along the ocean.

Dunes (646-2612), Box 917, Route 1, Ogunquit 03907. Open mid-May to mid-October. Set way back from the highway and fronting on the Ogunquit River, the complex offers direct access to Ogunquit Beach by rowboat at high tide and on foot at low tide. The 36 units include 19 old-style Maine classics—cottages with white-and-green trim—scattered over 12 spacious, well-kept acres. Most have fireplaces. Refrigerators and color TVs in all rooms. Cottages are $65–88 off-season, $85–128 in-season (June 24 to Labor Day). Two-week minimum stay in July and August. Rooms are $56–75 double off-season, $75–120 in-season.

Cottage in the Lane Motor Lodge (646-7903), Drakes Island Road, Wells 04090. There are 11 housekeeping cottages all facing landscaped grounds under the pines (an artistic play structure forms the centerpiece); salt marsh beyond. It's a 0.75-mile walk or bike ride to the beach. The quiet setting borders the Rachel Carson Wildlife Preserve and Laudholm Farm (see *Nature Preserves*). $420–445 per week for a three-room cottage accommodating four, and $495–575 for a four-room cottage good for five people; from $42 per night off-season.

MOTELS

Riverside Motel (646-2741), PO Box 2244, Shore Road, Ogunquit 03907. Open late April through late October. Just across the foot-drawbridge and overlooking Perkins Cove is this trim, friendly place with 41 units; also four rooms in the 1874 house. The property has been in Harold Staples's family for more than 100 years. All rooms have color TVs and full baths, and all overlook the cove; continental breakfast is included and served in the lobby around the fireplace or on the sun deck. $50–115, depending on season and location of room. Three-day minimum July 1 through August 20.

Seagull Motor Inn (646-5164), Route 1, Wells 04090. Open late June to mid-October. Facilities include 24 motel units, twenty-four cottages, a pool, a playground, and lawn games on 23 acres. Having spent four summer vacations here as a child (40 years ago), Chris Tree is happy to report that the place is still essentially the same solid value, with a loyal following. Rentals are nightly or by the week, moderate.

Wonderview Motor Village (646-2304), Route 1, Wells 04090. Open May through October. Twelve units (eight cottages and four motel units) are scattered on 2 acres; screened porches, playground, shuffleboard and other lawn games. Cottages are $55–100 per night high season, and $38 and up in May and after mid-September.

WHERE TO EAT

DINING OUT

Arrow's (361-1100), Berwick Road, Ogunquit. Dinner 6–10, late April through October. Considered one of the best restaurants—possibly *the* best—in Maine with an emphasis on fresh local ingredients. A 1765 farmhouse is the setting for nouvelle-inspired dishes such as bamboo-steamed Maine lobster with a vegetable roll, sugar snap peas, and red curry sauce; and red flannel hash cake with smoked duck cracklings, crème fraîche, and warm chard salad. The chef-owners are Mark Gaier, former executive chef at Ogunquit's once famous (now sadly defunct) Whistling Oyster in Perkins Cove, and Clark Frasier, a Californian who studied cooking in China. Entrées begin at $19.95.

Clay Hill Farm (646-2272), Agamenticus Road (north of Ogunquit Village). Open year-round for dinner but closed Monday and Tuesday in winter. A gracious old farmhouse with valet parking and an elegant Victorian setting. Specialties include grilled chicken with pineapple salsa, scallops frangelico, and prime rib au jus. Entrées range from $12.95–22.95.

Poor Richard's Tavern (646-4722), Shore Road and Pine Hill, Ogunquit. This local dining landmark is back where it began 30 years ago, in a charming old house near Perkins Cove. Chef-owner Richard Perkins prides himself on his lobster stew ($4.95 a cup) and Infamous Lobster Pie ($16.95), and offers a large menu ranging from Richard's Gourmet Meatloaf ($10.95) and Julia Perkins's Boarding House Chicken ($12.95) to charbroiled filet of salmon ($17.95).

Jonathan's (646-4777), 2 Bourne Lane, Ogunquit. Open for dinner nightly year-round, for breakfast daily in summer; otherwise just on weekends and for lunch Sunday through Friday. Entertainment nightly in the summer, from Maine humor to concerts to murder-mystery theater. This inviting place—composed of a half-dozen different dining rooms—offers something for everyone. Dishes range from seafood specialties to Jaeger Schnitzel—thin, breaded tenderloin of pork, pan fried with mushrooms, with a lemon bordelaise sauce ($13.75). Entrées start at $8.95.

Cliff House (361-1000), Bald Hill Cliff, Shore Road, Ogunquit. Open for breakfast and dinner most of the year, for lunch in July and August. The dining room is in the Cliffscape Building, with dramatic ocean views. Unique creations like the chicken Hyannis, a boneless breast sautéed and served in creamy cranberry chutney sauce with cashews ($13.95), await you; and where else can you try lobster tails lightly breaded in hazelnuts and sautéed in lemon wine butter ($20.95).

Dianne's Fine Food & Spirits (646-9703), 111 Shore Road, Ogunquit. Open early May through mid-October for dinner, lunch daily during July and August and on weekends in spring and fall. Chef-owner Scott Walker, ably assisted by wife Dianne, has created a very pleasant setting for dining on chicken béarnaise ($14.95) or lobster sautéed in sherry cream sauce, served in puff pastry ($16.95). Light lunches also served.

Ogunquit Lobster Pound (646-2516), Route 1 (north of Ogunquit Village). Open Mother's Day through Columbus Day weekend for dinner. After more than 40 years of ownership by the Hancock family, this pound is one of the few where you can still pick out your own lobster and watch as it's plunged into the big stone pit. Dine either in the rustic log building or outside on swinging, wood-canopied tables. Beer and wine are available along with cheeseburgers and steak, but lobsters and clams are what the place is about. Try the lobster stew and deep-dish blueberry pie.

Gypsy Sweethearts (646-7021), 18 Shore Road, Ogunquit Village. Open May to October. Breakfast all morning, dinner until 10. Fine dining in a charming old house. A great place for a leisurely breakfast on a rainy morning. The menu ranges through a variety of imaginative egg dishes and usually includes blueberry crêpes with sour cream. Dinner appetizers can be made into a light meal (with vegetable and potato) for $3.50. The linguini with scallops and shrimp was quite nice. $11.95–17.00.

The Old Village Inn (646-7088), 30 Main Street (Route 1 north of Ogunquit Square). Open for dinner most of the year; also breakfast 7:30–11:30 on weekends and Monday holidays. Five Victorian-style dining rooms, an English pub-style bar; specialties include roast duckling and a range of pasta dishes like scampi-style vegetable primavera and Atlantic linguine with shrimp, scallops, and lobster meat. Entrées: $13.95–21.95.

Hurricane Restaurant (646-6348), Perkins Cove. Year-round for lunch and dinner except Tuesday. An attractive, trendy place that maximizes its ocean view; grilled seafood, chowders, bar burgers, and lobster-stuffed pasta shells. Jazz on Sunday; hip, young crowd. Entrées: $13.95–19.95.

Valerie's (646-2476), Route 1, Ogunquit Square. Open mid-May through mid-October for lunch and dinner. More than 45 years in the same family. Sandwiches and omelets for lunch; seafood such as crabmeat-stuffed sole for dinner, but always some Greek specialties like spanakopita. Moderate.

Roberto's Italian Cuisine (646-8130), 82 Shore Road, Ogunquit. Ogunquit's chef-owned trattoria. Chef-owner Roberto specializes in no-nonsense southern Italian dishes like veal parmigiana, chicken Marsala, and seafood lasagna. Entrées: $7.95–15.95.

Blue Water Inn (646-5559), Beach Street, Ogunquit. The water view is hard to beat, and the specialty is fish—mako shark as well as mackerel and haddock. The haddock almondine is $12.95. Entrées run $10.95–17.95.

Grey Gull Inn (646-7501), 321 Webhannet Drive, Moody Point (Wells). Open year-round for dinner. Dining rooms maximize the water view. Good for stuffed prime rib ($15.95) or broiled haddock flavored with soy and ginger ($15.50). Pastas begin at $9.95, other entrées range from $12.95–17.95.

Litchfield's (646-5711), Route 1, Wells. Open daily, year-round, for lunch and dinner. This is a favorite spot among local aficionados: reliable food and good value. Even the lobster is fairly priced, served baked and stuffed as well as straight. Specialties include Aztec chicken and prime rib as well as seafood dishes. A wide variety of lunch sandwiches are outstanding. Dinner entrées run $8.95–17.95.

EATING OUT

Einstein's Deli Restaurant (646-5262), 2 Shore Road, Ogunquit. Open year-round for breakfast, lunch, and dinner. On the corner in Ogunquit Square, an art deco–style eatery with a curvy counter, booths, downstairs rest rooms, and Albert's Café, your friendly neighborhood bar. Open 4 PM to closing. The fish-and-chips daily special hits the spot.

Charlie's Restaurant (646-2632), Ogunquit Beach. Seasonal, now serving breakfast and lunch only. Easy to overlook since it's in the pavilion at the beach. The decor is simple but pleasant and very casual. A sign reads "bathing suits and sandy toes welcome, shirts not required." Now in its 60th season. Sandwiches, chowder, homemade pies.

Barnacle Billy's (646-5575), Perkins Cove. Open May through mid-October, 11–10 daily. Dining room with fireplaces and deck-dining overlooking boats. Order lobster at the counter and wait for your number; beer and wine. Mobbed during summer. Dinners run $9–18.

☞ **Lobster Shack** (646-2941), end of Perkins Cove. Open May through Columbus Day weekend. A genuine old-style, serious lobster-eating place since the 1940s (when it was known as Maxwell and Perkins); oilcloth-covered tables, outstanding chowder, apple pie à la mode, wine and beer. Possibly the most reasonably priced and satisfying place in town to feast on lobster.

Oarweed Cove Restaurant (646-4022), at the entrance to the Marginal Way in Perkins Cove. Open daily mid-May through mid-October for lunch and dinner. Large, rustic dining room with water view. Same menu all day; specialties include baked stuffed potato, chowder, seafood (none fried).

Lord's Harborside Restaurant (646-2651), Wells Harbor. Open April to November for lunch and dinner, closed Tuesdays in spring and fall. A big, ungarnished dining room with an unbeatable harbor view and a reputation for fresh fish and seafood. Lobster (fried, boiled, and baked) is the big draw.

Billy's Chowder House (646-7588), Mile Road, Wells. Open daily year-round, closed for lunch on Thursday in winter. A knotty-pine and shamrock atmosphere with views of salt marsh and water out the windows. Frequently a long line in-season for seafood like baked stuffed jumbo shrimp or grilled swordfish, as well as lobsters and clams.

Jake's Seafood (646-6771), Route 1, Bourne Avenue, Moody. Open for all three meals year-round. Specializes in good American cooking, fresh seafood, homemade ice cream.

Congdon's Donuts Family Restaurant, Route 1, Wells. Open from 6:30 AM–2 PM year-round, seasonal at Wells Beach. Fresh muffins, breads, pastries, and doughnuts; also ice cream made on premises.

Maine Diner (656-4441), Route 1, Wells. Open year-round 7 AM–9 PM, near the junction of Routes 1 and 9. A classic diner with a large menu for all three meals, plus beer, wine, takeout; breakfast all day, great corned beef hash, and outstanding clam chowder. The homemade chicken pie takes a few minutes longer, but it's worth the wait.

COFFEE BARS

S.W. Swan, 117 Shore Road, Ogunquit, is a delightful coffee- and teahouse carrying on the tradition of "Aunt Eliza," a sea captain's widow who opened her parlor to guests for afternoon refreshments in order to earn a living. Also a gourmet gift shop with a helpful and enthusiastic staff.

SNACKS

Bread & Roses Bakery (646-4227), 28A Main Street (up an alley), Ogunquit. A pleasant source of muffins, coffee, and delectable pastries.

Big Daddy's (646-5454), Route 1, just south of the Route 9 intersection, Wells. Open mid-March to late November, 11–11 in-season. *The* best ice cream around, made on the spot in tempting flavors like chocolate peanut-butter chip. Steamed hot dogs, too.

ENTERTAINMENT

THEATER

Hackmatack Playhouse (698-1807), Route 9, Berwick. Stages live performances throughout the year.

Leavitt Fine Arts Theatre (646-3123), Route 1, Ogunquit Village. Open early spring through fall. An old-time theater with new screen and sound; first-run films.

Ogunquit Square Theatre (646-5151), Shore Road, Ogunquit Village. Another old-time theater with all the latest movies.

(See also Ogunquit Playhouse under *To Do—Theater.*)

SELECTIVE SHOPPING

ANTIQUARIAN BOOKS

Boston book lovers drive to Wells to browse in this cluster of exceptional bookstores along Route 1. **Douglas N. Harding Map & Print Gallery** (646-8785) is huge and excellent: 4500 square feet of old and rare books, maps, and prints, plus some 100,000 general titles. **The Arringtons** (646-4124) specializes in prints, postcards, maps, ephemera, military Americana, and world history. **The Book Barn** (646-4926) specializes in old paperbacks, comic books, baseball cards, and collectors' supplies. **East Coast Books** (646-3584), Depot Street at Route 109, has a large general collection, autographs, prints, drawings, paintings, and historical paperbacks. **Austin's Antiquarian Books** (646-4883) specializes in Americana and the West, fine bindings, antique prints, and maps.

ANTIQUES SHOPS

Route 1 from York through Wells and the Kennebunks is studded with antiques shops. **MacDougall-Gionet** (646-3531), open 9–5 Tuesday through Sunday, is a particularly rich trove of country furniture in a barn; 60 dealers are represented. **The Wells Union Antique Center** (646-6612) is a complex of nine shops representing 15 dealers. **R. Jorgensen Antiques** (646-9444) has nine rooms filled with antique furniture, including fine formal pieces from a number of countries.

ART GALLERIES

In addition to the **Museum of Art of Ogunquit** and **The Barn Gallery** (under *To See*), there are more than a dozen galleries and studios in Ogunquit, all seasonal. A sampling:

The Ogunquit Photography School (646-7055), 28 Agamenticus Road. Seminars and workshops conducted by well-known photographers and photography teachers. **Hoyt's Lane Art Gallery** (646-9964), Route 1 and Hoyt's Lane (just north of the village); open daily, 10–5. Recently renovated under new ownership, a wide variety of fine art, handcrafted jewelry, ceramics, and sculpture. **Main Street Art Gallery** (646-5246), Main Street at Berwick Road in the middle of the village. Exhibits work by 48 artists. **June Weare Fine Arts** (646-8200), Shore Road; open mid-May to mid-October, 10–4. Original prints, paintings, and sculpture. **George Carpenter Gallery** (646-5106), Perkins Cove. Watercolors, oils, and pastel portraits by Virginia Carpenter. **Heartstone at Stonecrop Gallery** (361-1678), Shore Road at Juniper Lane, three doors south of the Ogunquit Museum. Landscape paintings and handsome stoneware by a husband and wife, displayed in their unusual gallery/home. **Scully Gallery** (646-2850), Perkins Cove (also studio/gallery on Route 1). Watercolors, original graphics, and acrylics. **Left Bank Gallery** (646-3524), Perkins Cove. Oils, watercolors, and prints by Frances Borofsky. **Shore Road Gallery** (646-5046), 112 Shore Road; open Memorial Day through Columbus Day weekend, daily. Fine arts, jewelry, and fine crafts by nationally known artists. **Bartok Studio/Gallery** (646-7815), 104 Shore Road. Watercolors by John Bartok. **PS Galleries** (361-1900), Route 1 South; open June to September, daily. Works by nationally recognized artists from throughout the country and by established New England artists.

FACTORY OUTLETS

Bass Shoe, Dexter, and **Quoddy Crafted Footwear** all have footwear outlets on Route 1. **Down East Company** factory outlet in Moody is open year-round: blankets, pot holders, hearth mats, and vests. **Hathaway Factory Outlet** is open year-round and features brand-name sportswear. **Cannon** offers sheets and towels, and across the street an outlet features Champion and other brand name activewear.

SPECIAL SHOPS

Ogunquit Camera (646-2261), at the corner of Shore Road and Wharf Lane in Ogunquit Village. Open year-round, and features 1-hour film developing. A great little shop that's been here since 1952. It's also a trove of toys, towels, windsocks, beach supplies, and sunglasses.

Chris Davis Stoneware Pottery, Perkins Cove. May through mid-December. A range of Maine-made stoneware and porcelain.

Harbor Candy Shop, 26 Main Street, Ogunquit. Seasonal. Chocolates and specialty candies are made on the spot; also a selection of imported candies.

SPECIAL EVENTS

April: **Big Patriot's Day celebration** at Ogunquit Beach.

June: **Wells Week** in Wells (end of the month)—a week-long celebration centering around **Harbor Park Day;** events include launching of new boats built by the Arundel Boat School, a big chicken barbecue, sand sculpture contest.

July: **Independence Day Fireworks** at Ogunquit Beach. **Sand Building Contest,** middle of the month.

August: **Sidewalk Art Show. Great Inner Tube Race. Kite Day.**

September: **Open Homes Day** sponsored by the Wells Historical Society. **Nature Crafts Festival** at Laudholm Farm (second weekend). **Capriccio,** a celebration of the performing arts.

December: **Christmas Parade** in Wells; **Christmas by the Sea** in Ogunquit.

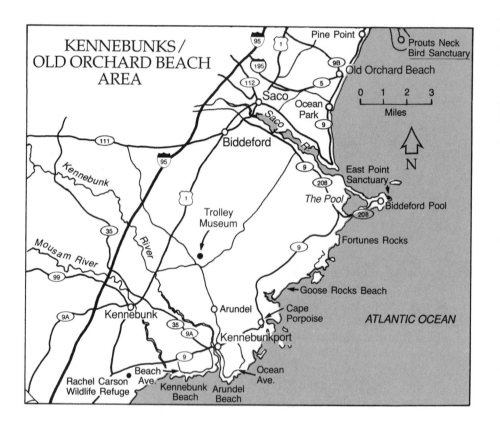

KENNEBUNKS /
OLD ORCHARD BEACH
AREA

Pine Point
Prouts Neck
Bird Sanctuary
95
1
9B
195
Old Orchard Beach
112
5
Saco
Ocean
Park
Saco
9
111
Biddeford
9
Kennebunk
East Point
Sanctuary
208
1
The Pool
Biddeford Pool
Trolley
Museum
208
35
Fortunes Rocks
Mousam River
River
9
99
Goose Rocks Beach
9A
Arundel
Cape
Porpoise
ATLANTIC OCEAN
Kennebunk
35
9A
Kennebunkport
9
Beach
Ave.
Ocean
Ave.
Rachel Carson
Wildlife Refuge
Kennebunk
Beach
Arundel
Beach

0 1 2 3
Miles

N

The Kennebunks

The Kennebunks have been around under one name or another since the 1620s. They began as a fishing stage near Cape Porpoise, which was repeatedly destroyed by Native American raids. In 1719 the present "port" was incorporated as Arundel, a name that stuck through its peak shipbuilding and seafaring years until 1821, when the name was changed to Kennebunkport. Later, when the novel *Arundel* by Kenneth Roberts (born in Kennebunk) had run through 32 printings, residents attempted to reclaim the old name and succeeded in doing so in 1957, at least for North Kennebunkport. Geographically, the Kennebunks are confusing. Kennebunk is a busy commercial center that straddles the strip of Route 1 between the Mousam and Kennebunk Rivers. A 10-minute ride down Summer Street brings you to Kennebunkport. Then there is Kennebunk Beach, Cape Porpoise, Goose Rocks Beach, Cape Arundel, and Kennebunk Lower Village. Luckily, free, detailed maps are readily available, and all that many visitors care about finding are Dock Square and the former summer White House, Walker Point.

Former President Bush's summer estate fills a private, 11-acre peninsula off Ocean Avenue (mansion row). Built by the president's grandfather George Herbert Walker in 1903, its position was uncannily ideal for use as a president's summer home, moated by water on three sides, yet clearly visible from the pull-out places along the avenue and perfectly positioned for picture-taking.

In the 1870s, this entire, spectacular 5-mile stretch of coast—from Lord's Point at the western end of Kennebunk Beach all the way to Cape Porpoise on the east—was acquired by a Massachusetts group, the Boston and Kennebunkport Sea Shore Company.

No fewer than 30 grand hotels and dozens of summer mansions (including Walker Point) sprung up in the area to accommodate the wave of summer visitors the easy train service brought. The Kennebunks shared the 1940s to 1960s decline suffered by all Maine coastal resorts, losing all but a sparse scattering of old hotels. Their comeback, visible during the 1970s, accelerated into a boom through the 1980s. Some of the surviving hotels were converted into condominiums, inns were rehabbed, and dozens of new B&Bs opened.

Unfortunately, the 1990s have brought a headache the 1890s boom didn't—traffic. Back in the Golden Era, you could come by train from Boston to Dock Square or Kennebunk Beach. If you didn't mind changing umpteen times, you could even get there by trolley.

The Kennebunks happen to be one of Maine's most convenient resorts. Downtown Kennebunk is just off I-95, and a 10-minute ride down Summer Street brings you to Kennebunkport. Although traffic has receded now that George Bush is no longer president and the bridge is no longer a drawbridge, the Kennebunks are still better suited to extended visits than day trips. You should stay for at least 2 days, renting a bicycle or using the trackless trolley to get around.

Try to stay within walking distance of Dock Square. Described in Booth Tarkington's 1930 novel *Mirthful Haven* as "Cargo Square," this spot is one of the liveliest summer places on the New England coast. Clustered around the classic monument "to our soldiers and sailors," the weathered, waterside buildings house an assortment of shops and restaurants. You can spend hours sipping, munching, and browsing— eventually to stroll down Ocean Avenue, along the river, to the rocks and sea. You pass the dock where Tarkington used to summer, writing on his schooner. The River Club across the way is a very private gathering point for families who have been summering here in roomy "cottages" for generations.

Even with all the activity in Dock Square, the Kennebunks have retained a certain quaint charm. The shops lining the streets offer top-quality merchandise rather than cheap, tourist-oriented gifts. Just a block or two from the center, you can experience the serene feel of an elegant residential neighborhood.

Old inns still line Ocean Avenue, and a number of former captains' homes on neighboring streets also take in guests. The Kennebunks may just offer Maine's widest selection of accommodations. You can stay in an old-style resort hotel, a waterside cottage, or any number of bed & breakfasts and inns.

Summer and fall are the peak seasons in the Kennebunks, but most inns and shops in Cape Porpoise, Goose Rocks Beach, and Kennebunkport remain open for Christmas Prelude in early December. Many also remain open year-round.

GUIDANCE

Kennebunk–Kennebunkport Chamber of Commerce (967-0857), PO Box 740, Kennebunk 04043. Open year-round; information booth open Memorial Day to Columbus Day at 173 Port Road (Route 35) just before Lower Village, 9–5 daily. The chamber publishes a pamphlet with a map and keeps track of vacancies.

Kennebunkport Information and Hospitality Center (967-8600), open Memorial Day to Columbus Day, rest rooms and information in Dock Square next to Ben & Jerry's. Open 10–9 daily in July and August, shorter hours during shoulder months.

GETTING THERE

You can fly your own plane into **Sanford Airport;** otherwise, drive up I-95 to Exit 3. **Munroe's Limousine Service** (646-9067) serves the Portland airport as well as most destinations. **Coastal Connection** (282-5408) transports passengers seasonally to eight points from York to Kennebunkport. Maps and schedules are available from the chamber.

GETTING AROUND

Intown Trolley Co. (967-3686) offers narrated sight-seeing tours with tickets good for the day, so you can also use them to shuttle between Dock Square and Kennebunk Beach. They leave Dock Square every half hour, daily, late May through October. $5 adults, $2 children.

PARKING

A **municipal parking lot** is hidden just off Dock Square behind Allison's restaurant. There are two free nearby lots: one at St. Martha's Catholic Church on North Street, the other at the Consolidated School, Route 9.

MEDICAL EMERGENCY

Southern Maine Medical Center (283-7000), Medical Center Drive (off Route 111), Biddeford.

Kennebunk Walk-in Clinic (985-6027), Route 1 North, Kennebunk.

VILLAGES

Cape Porpoise. Here is where the original 1600s settlement was, and the attractive cove is still an authentic Maine fishing village, with a busy pier and lobster and commercial fishing boats dominating the harbor. This area also has some good places for seafood and top-quality galleries and shops worth browsing through.

Goose Rocks Beach. A small, waterfront village on a terrific beach. This neighborhood is a place of quiet solitude amid private summer homes, some available for rental.

TO SEE

MUSEUMS

The Brick Store Museum (985-4802), 117 Main Street, Kennebunk. Open year-round, Tuesday through Saturday, 10–4:30. Admission is $3 per adult ($4 with Taylor-Barry House), $2 per child. A block of early 19th-century commercial buildings, including William Lord's Brick Store (1825), a space used for changing exhibits of fine and decorative arts and marine collections. Architectural walking tours are offered of **Kennebunk's National Register District** in summer.

Seashore Trolley Museum (967-2800), Log Cabin Road, located 3.2 miles up North Street from Kennebunkport or 2.8 miles north on Route 1 from Kennebunk then right at the yellow blinker. Open daily late May to mid-October, varying hours (phone to check on special events, which include a Halloween ghost trolley and New Year's Eve celebration). Admission is $6 for adults; senior, children, and family rates. Though only a roadside marker notes the location of the headquarters of the Atlantic Shore Line Railroad, this nonprofit museum has preserved the history of that era, displaying more than 200 vehicles from the world over. The impressive collection began in 1939, when the last open-sided, Biddeford–Old Orchard Beach trolley was retired to an open field straddling the old Atlantic Shore Line rail bed. The museum now owns 300 acres as well as cars shipped here from London, Budapest, Rome, and Nagasaki, among other places. A 4-mile, round-trip excursion on a trolley takes visitors out through woods and fields, along a route once traveled by summer travelers en route to Old Orchard Beach.

HISTORIC SITES

Taylor-Barry House, 24 Summer Street, Kennebunk. Operated by the Brick Store Museum. Guided tours are offered June through September, Tuesday through Friday 1–4, and by appointment; $2 per adult. A Federal-period sea captain's home with a stenciled hallway and period furnishings. Also a 20th-century artist's studio.

Kennebunkport Historical Society (967-2751). Based in the Town House School on North Street. Open year-round Wednesday through Friday, 1–4. Displays local memorabilia; also maritime exhibits housed next door in the former office of the Clark Shipyard.

White Columns, also known as the **Nott House** (967-2513), Maine Street, Kennebunkport. Also maintained by the Kennebunkport Historical Society. Open June to Columbus Day, Wednesday through Friday, 1–4. A Greek Revival house with a Doric colonnade; also with original wallpapers, carpets, and furnishings. $2 per adult. Inquire about walking tours.

St. Anthony Monastery and Shrine (967-2011), Kennebunkport. A Tudor-style mansion set on 200 acres of peaceful, riverside fields and forests on Beach Road, now maintained by Lithuanian Franciscans as a shrine and retreat center. Visitors are welcome; gift shop. Inquire about lodging in the Guest House.

Wedding Cake House, Summer Street (Route 35), Kennebunk. Ann Burnett's studio, featuring artwork on furniture and clothing, is open to the public. The house itself is private. This 1826 house is laced up and down with white wooden latticework. The tale is that a local sea captain had to rush off to sea before a proper wedding cake could be baked, but he more than made up for it later.

South Congregational Church, Temple Street, Kennebunkport. Just off Dock Square, built in 1824 with a Christopher Wren–style cupola and belfry; Doric columns added in 1912.

Louis T. Graves Memorial Library (967-2778), Maine Street, Kennebunkport. Built in 1813 as a bank, which went bust, it later served as a customs house. It was subsequently donated to the library association

Wedding Cake House: Kennebunk

by artist Abbott Graves, whose pictures alone make it worth a visit. You can still see the bank vault and the sign from the customs collector's office. Upstairs, the book sale room is full of bargains.

First Parish Unitarian Church, Main Street, Kennebunk. Built in 1772–1773 with an Asher Benjamin–style steeple added in 1803–1804, along with a Paul Revere bell. In 1838 the interior was divided into two levels, with the church proper elevated to the second floor.

SCENIC DRIVES

Ocean Avenue. The road winds past many magnificent summer homes, including Walker's Point. The ocean views are spectacular, and you don't have to worry about driving too slowly, because everyone else is, too. Follow the road to Cape Porpoise, the area's commercial fishing center.

TO DO

BICYCLING

The lay of this land lends itself to exploration by bike, a far more satisfying way to go in summer than by car since you can stop and park wherever the view and urge hit you. Rental bikes are available from **Cape-Able Bike Shop** (967-4382), Townhouse Corners (off Log Cabin Road), Kennebunkport.

BLUEBERRYING

The Nature Conservancy (729-5181) maintains 1500 acres of blueberry plains in West Kennebunk; take Route 99 toward Sanford.

BOAT-BUILDING SCHOOL
The Landing School of Boat Building and Design (985-7976), River Road, Kennebunk, offers a September-to-June program in building sailing craft. Visitors welcome if you call ahead.

BOAT EXCURSION
Elizabeth 2 (967-5595), May through October, offers 1½-hour narrated tours of the Kennebunk River and northeast along the Atlantic to Cape Porpoise Harbor. Departs behind the Mobil station next to the bridge on Route 9, Kennebunkport. This excursion is good to take when you first arrive, because it familiarizes you with the area, and Cap'n Showalter's narration is studded with information as well as puns and jokes.

DEEP-SEA FISHING
A variety of boats offer trips; check with the chamber of commerce.

GOLF
Cape Arundel Golf Club (967-3494), Kennebunkport, 18 holes. These are the local links former President Bush frequents. Open to the public except from 11 to 2:30. **Webhannet Golf Club** (967-2061), Kennebunk Beach, 18 holes. We've read that Edmund Muskie prefers this slightly more challenging course. Open to the public except from 11:30 to 1. **Dutch Elm Golf Course** (282-9850), Arundel, 18 holes; cart and club rental, lessons, pro shop, snack bar, putting greens.

HORSEBACK RIDING AND HAYRIDES
Bush Brook Stables (284-7721 or 284-8311), 463 West Street, Biddeford. Hayrides and trail rides offered. **Maplebrook Farm** (384-8108) Berwick, offers horse-drawn trolley rides in Lower Village. Friday through Sunday 3–7 PM, May 31 through October 12.

SAILING
Maine Sail School (967-5043), Ocean Avenue, Kennebunkport. Sailing lessons (private or in scheduled sessions), coastal cruises, sunset sails, half- and full-day charters. For other current day sailers, check with the chamber of commerce.

WHALE-WATCHING
This is Maine's prime departure point for sighting the whales who feed on Jeffrey's Ledge, about 20 miles offshore. If you have any tendencies toward seasickness, be sure to choose a calm day. Chances are you will see more than a dozen whales. Frequently sighted species include finbacks, minkes, rights, and humpbacks.

Nautilus (967-0707), a 65-foot boat carrying up to 100 passengers, offers narrated trips daily from May to October. Departs from behind the Mobil station next to the bridge on Route 9, Kennebunkport. Free parking, but you'll have to leave your keys.

Indian Whale Watch (967-5912), July through October from the Arundel Wharf, Ocean Avenue. This 75-foot boat holding 72 passengers is slower and takes longer to reach the whales than some but features narration by a mammalogist; sunset cruises.

CROSS-COUNTRY SKIING
Harris Farm (499-2678), Buzzell Road, Dayton. A 500-acre dairy farm with more than 20 miles of trails. Equipment rentals available. Located 1.5 miles from the Route 5 and Route 35 intersection.

GREEN SPACE

BEACHES
The Kennebunks avoid an overabundance of weekend day-trippers by requiring a permit to park at its major beaches. Day and seasonal passes must be secured from either the Kennebunk or Kennebunkport town halls (open weekdays only), depending on which beach you want to use. Passes are, of course, also available from local lodging places. You can park in one of the town lots and walk, bike, or take a trolley to the beach.

Kennebunk and **Gooch's Beaches** in Kennebunk are both long, wide strips of firm sand backed by Beach Avenue, divided by Oak's Neck. Beyond Gooch's Beach, take Great Hill Road along the water to Strawberry Island, a great place to walk and examine tidal pools. Please don't picnic.

Parson's Beach, south of Kennebunk Beach on Route 9, requires no permit, but in-season you will probably be able to stop only long enough to drop someone off; off-season you have a chance at one of the half-dozen parking spaces. You can always park along the road on the other side of Route 9 and walk down the grand avenue of sugar maples to the sand. It's a splendid place for an early morning or evening walk.

Goose Rocks Beach, a few miles north of Kennebunkport Village on Route 9, is another wide, smooth stretch of sand backed by the road. You can also walk down Ocean Avenue to tiny **Arundel Beach** near the Colony Hotel at the mouth of the Kennebunk River. It offers nice rocks for climbing.

NATURE PRESERVES
Biddeford Pool East Sanctuary, Route 9 (north of Kennebunkport), is a place to observe shorebirds.

Rachel Carson National Wildlife Refuge encompasses 1600 acres with a mile-long nature trail and is an excellent spot for birding (see *Nature Preserves* in "Ogunquit and Wells").

Vaughns Island Preserve offers nature trails on a wooded island separated from the mainland by two tidal creeks. Cellar holes of historic houses are accessible by foot 3 hours before and 3 hours after high tide.

(Also see Laudholm Farm described under *Nature Preserves* in "Ogunquit and Wells.")

WALKS
Henry Parsons Park, Ocean Avenue, is a path along the rocks leading to Spouting Rock and Blowing Cave, both sights to see at midtide. A great way to view the beautiful homes along Ocean Avenue.

LODGING

RESORT HOTELS

The Colony (967-3331), Ocean Avenue and King's Highway, Kennebunkport 04046. Open May through October. With 133 rooms in four buildings, this is one of the last of New England's coastal resorts that's still maintained in the grand, three-meals-a-day style. It's set on a rise, overlooking the point at which the Kennebunk River meets the Atlantic. It's been owned by the Boughton family since 1948; many guests have been coming for generations. Amenities include a saltwater pool, tennis, beach, social program, nightly entertainment, and dancing. A 2-night minimum is required for advance weekend reservations during July and August. $165–305 double per day includes all three meals; $50 per extra person (children under 2, $25) plus $12 for service. Worth it.

The Shawmut Inn (967-3931 or 1-800-876-3931), PO Box 431, Kennebunkport 04046. Open mid-May to January 1. The inn is away from the village on 22 oceanfront acres with spectacular views. Major renovations and expansions began at the end of the 1994 season on the 96 units in the Main Inn and other buildings. The Main Inn contains a large, low-slung lobby and large dining room with ocean views from every table; facilities include a rocky shore, a tidal pool perfect for exploring, a pool, and lawn games. Per person double occupancy rates range from $59 for a back room off-season to $159 for an ocean-view room in high season; full breakfast included.

INNS AND BED & BREAKFASTS

All inn listings are for Kennebunkport 04046 unless otherwise indicated.

The Captain Jefferds Inn (967-2311), Pearl Street, Box 691. Closed November and January to March. This is a strikingly handsome, Federal-era mansion, elegantly furnished with an eclectic mix of art and antiques (it has been featured as a *House Beautiful* cover story) by innkeeper Warren Fitzimmons. There are 12 rooms, all with private baths, many with canopy beds and chaises, all furnished with such flair that it's difficult to choose. We especially like the "Blue Room," with its deep-blue flowered paper and a big brass bed, and the attic retreat with its rooftop view and Hobo art. The three efficiency units in the carriage house are furnished in a more casual country style but with no less care and pizzazz. Breakfast is a production (maybe eggs Benedict or blueberry crêpes), usually served in the formal dining room or on the terrace at umbrellaed tables of four. Afternoon tea is offered in cooler months in the yellow living room that's walled in original Al art. Guests are encouraged to tickle the keys of the Steinway grand. $85–135 for double occupancy rooms, $145–165 for suites in the Carriage House; rates include a full breakfast.

Captain Lord Mansion (967-3141), PO Box 800. Open year-round at the corner of Pleasant and Green Streets. One of the most splendid mansions in New England is now one of the most romantic inns around. The three-story, Federal-era home is topped with a widow's walk from which guests can contemplate the town and sea beyond. Other architectural features include a three-story, suspended elliptical staircase and pine doors that have been painted trompe l'oeil style to simulate inlaid mahogany. There are 16 meticulously decorated rooms, 11 with working fireplaces, some with high four-posters and canopy beds—and all with antiques and private baths. The gathering room is also very elegant, but the full breakfast is an informal affair, served in the large country kitchen. Now in their 17th season, hosts Bev Davis and Rick Litchfield emphasize warmth and go out of their way to make each guest feel special. Phebe's Fantasy, a separate building, has four more rooms with fireplaces, and two rooms in the Captain's Hideaway have both fireplaces and whirlpool tubs. $135–199 per room in high season, breakfast and tea included; $89–159 off-season.

Old Fort Inn (967-5353 or 1-800-828-FORT), PO Box M. Open mid-April to mid-December. An unusual combination of things, but it works. The reception area is in an antiques store in the former barn. This is also where you'll find a spacious sitting room in which guests enjoy a morning buffet breakfast and are otherwise drawn to relax. Grounds and buildings represent the remnants of an 1880s resort, nicely converted to serve 1990s families, with a pool, tennis court, horseshoes, and shuffleboard. The sturdy stone and brick carriage house now offers 16 guest rooms with stenciled walls, antiques, color TV, phones, and wet bars. Two suites available. A path leads down to the ocean. Unsuitable for children under 12. Two-night minimum during high season. $125–230 in high-season, $89–170 off-season, breakfast included.

Bufflehead Cove (967-3879), Box 499, off Route 35. Open year-round except March. This is a hidden gem, sequestered on 6 acres at the end of a dirt road, overlooking an 8-foot tidal cove, but less than a mile from the village of Kennebunkport. It's a Dutch Colonial–style home in which Harriet and Jim Gott raised their children. Harriet is a native of nearby Cape Porpoise, and Jim is a commercial fisherman. There are six pretty guest rooms, some with hand-painted or stenciled wall designs. We are particularly enchanted with the Hideaway, a romantic room with a fireplace that opens into the bedroom on one side and into the sitting area on the other. Other features are a living room with a hearth and deep window seats, an inviting veranda, and woods and orchard to explore. $85–170 includes a full breakfast and afternoon wine and cheese.

Inn on South Street (967-5151), South Street, PO Box 478A. A Greek Revival home on a quiet street preserves a sense of the era in which it was built. Innkeeper Jack Downs is a college professor with a keen interest in the China trade, and the living room furnishings include the kind of Chinese furniture and furnishings a Kennebunkport sea captain might well have brought back. There are three guest rooms and a suite. Our favorite, named for "Mrs. Perkins," has a fireplace, a pine four-poster bed with a canopy, Oriental rugs, and a portrait of its namesake tucked in the closet. The less expensive, third-floor "Romantic Room" is also appealing. The first-floor suite has its own sitting room, a four-poster bed and wood-burning stove, a bath with Jacuzzi, a kitchen, and a porch overlooking the herb garden. Eva Down's amazing breakfasts are delivered to this kitchen, also served upstairs in the dining room to other guests; afternoon tea is also served, and is included in rates that run $85–135 for a double room, $155–185 for the suite.

Kennebunkport Inn (967-2621), Dock Square. Open year-round; dining room closed November to April. Originally an 1890s mansion, but serving as an inn since 1926. Although just a skip from Dock Square, it is set back from the hubbub. The personalized feel is retained despite the size: 34 rooms, one with a fireplace. The inn has three sections—the main house; a 1980s Federal-style addition; and a 1930s river house, with smaller rooms and stenciled walls. Each room is individually decorated with antiques, and all have TVs and private baths; many have water views. In summer, a small pool on the terrace is available to guests. The cocktail lounge is dark and friendly with a huge old bar and green-hooded lights, evening piano music. Special packages include meals and a lobster cruise. High-season rates run $79–189 per room or $94–119 per person MAP. From $62 off-season.

The Inn at Harbor Head (967-5564), 41 Pier Road, Cape Porpoise. Open year-round. Joan and Dave Sutter offer five rooms with private baths in their rambling, shingled home overlooking Cape Porpoise harbor. The Summer Suite (available May through the first week in December) has a view of the picturesque Cape Porpoise harbor from the bath as well as the bed. Most rooms have water views and Joan's beautifully detailed, hand-painted seascapes on walls; all are decorated with florals and antiques, and guests' first names are placed on the door. Guests have access to the inn's dock, terrace, and sitting rooms, with an inviting fireplace in the library. Joan, who unabashedly claims to coddle lodgers, whips up fresh-baked goods to top off her large breakfasts and prepares afternoon snacks (tea or wine and cheese, as tastes dictate). Beach passes and towels provided for nearby Goose Rocks Beach. No smoking. No TV. $130–195 per room in-season, $95–160 in winter.

Lake Brook B&B Guest House (967-4069), 57 Western Avenue, Lower Village, Kennebunk 04043. Year-round accommodations in a turn-of-the-century farmhouse. Large, wrap-around porch overlooks a salt marsh and tidal brook. One-half mile from Dock Square, but feels like much farther away. The three, second-floor guest rooms are decorated with matching comforters and curtains, and one has a queen brass bed and very large bath. Hostess Carolyn McAdams serves a full breakfast, maybe baked French toast with sausage, and she sits down to eat with her guests. $80–90 in-season. Suite available in July and August, perfect for families.

White Barn Inn (967-2321), PO Box 560C, Beach Street. Open year-round. The barn is now an elegant dining room (see *Dining Out*) attached to the old inn. The inn was built in 1865 as a farmhouse, later enlarged as the Forest Hills Hotel. Guests choose from antiques-furnished rooms in three sections: inn rooms in the original farmhouse; deluxe suites in the carriage house, with four-poster king beds, fireplaces, and marble baths with whirlpool tubs; or the smaller gatehouse rooms with sleigh beds, fireplaces, and whirlpool tubs. Elegant living rooms and a large front porch with wicker chairs. $130–285 per couple, including breakfast, afternoon tea, and use of touring bikes. You can walk both to Dock Square and the beach. Cheaper off-season. Inquire about special packages.

The Breakwater Inn (967-3118), Ocean Avenue. Inn and restaurant are open April to late October; rooms in the annex are closed January to mid-February. Parts of two 19th-century guest houses merged to form this restored inn. The Breakwater itself, which also houses a popular public restaurant, holds eight pleasant rooms (private baths). The adjacent Riverside holds a dozen rooms with hand-stenciled walls and period furnishings. All have water views, and many have a sliding door opening onto a porch. Each has double beds, a small refrigerator, and bar sink as well as private bath and TV. $95–140 includes a full breakfast; cheaper off-season.

☞ **The Green Heron** (967-3315), PO Box 2578, Ocean Avenue. Open daily mid-May to late October, Thursday through Sunday during the rest of the year, closed in January. Within walking distance of both village and shore, this old house has just 10 guest rooms that are attractive, clean, and bright, individually decorated and filled with the spirit of a friendlier, simpler day. There is also a coveside cottage perfect for a family. The famous breakfast is included in the guest rates; it's also available to the public. Ownership passed from one brother to another in 1988, but it remains in the Reid family, retaining its special atmosphere. The front porch is an inviting evening gathering place, and the paved path overlooking the creek leads to steps to a tiny gravel beach. $72–90 for a double in-season, $62–82 off-season; $15 for an extra person, $10 ages 12 and under. This is one place where both children and pets are welcome.

Welby Inn (967-4655), PO Box 774, Ocean Avenue. Open daily May to October, then most weekends. A fine, old, gambrel-roofed home with a spacious living room sporting bright pillows, fresh flowers, oak furniture, wing chairs, a large fireplace, and a sunny, welcoming window seat. Coffee is available after 7:30, and at 8:30 (promptly), innkeepers Betsy and David Knox serve a fairly elaborate breakfast in the dining room and adjoining sun porch. There are seven guest rooms, one with a working fireplace, all with private baths, Betsy's hand-painted tiles, stenciling (some matches the 1800s furniture), and old bedsteads with handmade quilts. $80–95 per night in summer; $60–110 (for a fireplace) off-season.

Maine Stay Inn and Cottages (967-2117, 1-800-950-2117), Box 500A, Maine Street. Open year-round. The 1860 house, listed on the National Historic Register, is big, white, and distinctive with a large cupola. It offers six guest rooms, each with private bath, and two suites, one with a working fireplace. There are also 11 cottages of varying sizes, four with fireplaces, all but one with efficiency kitchens. A full breakfast is served and might include blueberry blintzes, apricot scones, fresh strawberries, and homemade granola (cottage guests have the option of breakfast delivered in a basket). All guests can enjoy a full afternoon tea in the attractive living room or on the wraparound porch. Carol and Lindsay Copeland are warm hosts, eager to help you make the most of your stay. $125–185 per night; winter, $75–145.

Chetwynd House Inn (967-2235), PO Box 130TN, Chestnut Street. Open year-round. This was Kennebunkport's first B&B, a gracious 1840s home near Dock Square. Susan Chetwynd offers five antiques-furnished guest rooms with private baths. Our favorite is the gable room with its slanted ceilings and double beds. This room can open into a two-room suite. Extraordinary breakfasts—maybe ham and cheese omelets and a quarter melon with peaches, blueberries, and bananas— are served family style at the dining room table; afternoon refreshments are also served in the sitting room/library. High-season rates are $100– 160; $75–140 off-season.

Kylemere House "Crosstrees" (967-2780), 6 South Street. Open May through early December. A graceful, Federal-era house with four spacious guest rooms, one with a working fireplace. All are furnished with period furniture and antiques and have private baths and sitting areas. The downstairs living room shelves are well stocked with books and this is where mother and daughter hosts, Ruth and Helen Toohey, serve afternoon refreshments. A full breakfast is served in the formal dining room overlooking the gardens. $95–135 in-season, $80–125 in the shoulder months.

The Captain Fairfield Inn (967-4454; 1-800-322-1928), corner of Pleasant and Green Streets. Bonnie and Dennis Tallagon put a Vermont inn on the hospitality map and then sold it, but they say they missed innkeeping too much not to give it another try. They found this Federal-era captain's home and lovingly restored it to its present grandeur. There are nine bedrooms, all individually decorated with antiques and wicker, four poster and canopy beds. Each has a private bath, one handicapped accessible, three with fireplaces. Those in the front part of the house are more elegant, while those in the rear wing are newer and equipped with air-conditioning. The enthusiasm of the hosts makes this a truly special place. Dennis is an accomplished chef and offers a choice for breakfast. On a typical day it might be between crêpes, blueberry pancakes, and eggs Benedict. $85–160; $20 per extra person.

Cape Arundel Inn (967-2125), PO Box 530-A. Open late May to mid-October. Nicely sited overlooking the Atlantic between Spouting Rock and Blowing Cave. This is a grand old summer cottage with 14 units—8 are in the house, 6 in the motel—and a carriage house apartment. All rooms have private baths and ocean views. There is also a comfortable living room and porch overlooking the ocean. The dining room is open to the public. $95–145 in the house and motel units, $115–155 for a motel efficiency, 2-day minimum in the Carriage House apartment, $570–780 per week.

☞ **Cove House Bed & Breakfast** (967-3704), RR 3, Box 1615. Kathy Jones has lived in Kennebunkport most of her life and offers a warm welcome to her guests. The 18th-century Colonial house is down by Chick's Cove on the Kennebunk River, within walking distance of a beach and easy bicycling distance of Dock Square. The three pleasant guest rooms have private baths. There's a book-lined living room with a wood stove. $70; $15 per extra person, includes breakfast. A nearby cottage is $350–450 per week.

The 1802 House (967-5632, 1-800-932-5632), PO Box 646-A, 15 Locke Street. Open year-round. Recently remodeled and updated, this country home offers six guest rooms, each with private bath. One has a two-person whirlpool tub, some have working fireplaces. The house is away from town on the edge of the Cape Arundel Golf Club with an out-in-the-country feel, shaded by two large pine trees; in winter you can step right off into the fields for cross-country skiing. A ship's bell calls guests to breakfast, which is served in a cozy breakfast room with a wood stove. Comfortable guest parlor and small "made in Maine" gift area. $65–145 for a room with fireplace/whirlpool.

On the Beach

The Ocean View (967-2750), 72 Beach Avenue, Kennebunk Beach 04043. Open spring through fall, and Christmas Prelude. A cheerful, colorful, painted lady right on Kennebunk Beach. The main house has five guest rooms, a comfortable TV room, and living room with fireplace. A separate building houses four pretty suites with sitting areas, color TVs, and private terraces. Breakfast includes your own heated carafe of tea or coffee, maybe a brioche with cheese, fruit, and jams, topped off with fresh strawberries and cream. "Breakfast in bed" is served to guests in suites. High-season rates run $130–170.

Sundial Inn (967-3850), 48 Beach Street, PO Box 1147, Kennebunk 04043. Open year-round; right on Kennebunk Beach. Built in 1891, virtually rebuilt and substantially enlarged several years ago, now has 34 antiques-furnished rooms with brass and iron beds. Most have ocean views. In high-season $101–151, breakfast included; less off-season.

Tides Inn By-the-Sea (967-3757), RR 2, Box 737, Goose Rocks Beach. Open May to October. Away from Kennebunkport Village but right across from a great beach. Twenty-two Victorian rooms in the original inn and Tides Too next door. Rooms in the main house are furnished with antiques, and there are some interesting paintings on hallway walls. The Henriksens have owned the inn since 1972 and have created a casual family spot with character. The attractive, informal dining room and pub are open to the public, geared to singles and young couples. $60–95 per room; inquire about special packages.

The Inn at Goose Rocks (967-5425), Dyke Road. Open year-round. Surrounded by 10 wooded acres near the saltwater marshes, also within walking distance of the beach on the marshes. A gracious old home with modern, traditionally decorated rooms (each with phone, cable TV, private bath) added on. A total of 32 rooms with an upstairs lounge and rooftop deck, outdoor pool, dining room, and meeting space. $95–125 per room in high season.

Seaside Inn & Cottages (967-4461), PO Box 631, Gooch's Beach. Rooms in the 1756 inn are rented just from July through Labor Day, cottages are rented May through October, motor inn is year-round. An attractive complex formed by a 1720s homestead, a 1756 inn, a modern 22-room motor inn, and 10 housekeeping cottages—all on a private beach next to one of Maine's best public strands. This property has been in the Severance family for 13 generations. The old homestead is rented as a cottage, and there are still four antiques-furnished guest rooms in the old inn. A buffet breakfast is included in the rates. Cottages are per month in July and August, per week the rest of the season. One-week minimum in oceanfront rooms and two-day minimum in terraceside rooms in high season. $140–160 per night for motel rooms, $95–130 for rooms in the 1756 house; less off-season.

MOTELS

All motel listings are for Kennebunkport 04046 unless otherwise indicated.

Yachtsman Motor Inn and Marina (967-2511 or 1-800-9-YACHTS), PO Box 2609, Ocean Avenue. Open early May through late October. This is a beautifully positioned property, right on the Kennebunk River, a short walk from Dock Square. Units are tastefully decorated with private riverside patios. Slip space for boats available at the marina. $79–129.

Village Cove Inn (967-3993), Box 650, Chick's Cove. Open year-round. A resort motel with a dining room (open to the public) and meeting space, sited on a tidal cove with indoor and outdoor pools; 33 large, motel-style rooms with two double beds; color cable TVs and phones. There is a guest lounge with fireplace off the lobby. Entertainment in the lounge weekends year-round. A housekeeping cottage sleeps six. Special weekend and midweek packages. $89–98, in high season; cottage rented by the week.

✐ **Idlease Guest Resort** (985-4460), PO Box 3086, Route 9. A terrific family find. A traditional motel and cottage complex, recently renovated. Some cathedral ceilings with skylights were added, giving the cottages a more spacious appearance. Within walking distance of Parson's Beach (one of the most beautiful, least commercial beaches on the south coast). The establishment caters to large families and family reunions. Diversions include outdoor pool, yard games, horseshoes, basketball, and more. Motel and cottage rooms $58 for a double; $73 for four people; house-keeping cottages $73–175 (accommodating up to eight), $442–895 per week. Additional two-bedroom, two-bath cottage with living room available (sleeps 6–10).

OTHER LODGING

Franciscan Guest House (967-2011), Beach Avenue, Kennebunkport 04046. The Franciscan monastery has extensive grounds and a modern facility with 70 air-conditioned rooms and suites. Amenities include color cable TV, a swimming pool, and meals. Walk to the beach. Moderate.

Cabot Cove Cottages (967-5424), PO Box 1082, South Main Street, Kennebunkport 04046. Open mid-June through mid-September. Fifteen old-style, knotty-pine walled, brightly furnished cottages on 2 acres bordering a tidal cove. One- and two-bedroom units, all with new kitchen facilities. Within walking distance of both Dock Square and a sandy beach. $695–895 per week.

Schooners Wharf (967-5333), PO Box 709, Ocean Avenue, Kennebunkport 04046. Open seasonally. Every room in this elegant facility has a water view, is named after a schooner, and is furnished with Thomas Moser furniture. Modern amenities include private bath, cable TV, phones; the master suite has a raised sitting area, whirlpool bath, and private deck. $115–225 per night in high season, substantially less off-season.

Clover Hill Farm (490-1105), RR 1, Box 24A, Alfred 04002. Alfred is a 20-minute drive from the coast, and it's a beautiful old village, with the kind of good places to eat you would expect in the York County seat (see *Eating Out*). Clover Hill Farm is a classic white farmhouse 5 miles from the village, with 100 acres of rolling hills and woodland. The clean, simply furnished guest rooms share two baths and cost $65 for a double ($55 single, $10–15 for a third person), with a breakfast that may include freshly laid eggs and pasta garnished with just-picked chives and strawberries. Margit Lassen and her gardeners sell their organic produce and raise sheep, goats, and a couple of pigs.

WHERE TO EAT

DINING OUT

White Barn Inn (967-2321), Kennebunk Beach. Open for dinner year-round (closed Mondays in winter); also for Sunday brunch. One of New England's most luxurious barns, still attached to the 19th-century inn for which it was built but with its face now glassed; nicely decorated to create a warm, candlelit atmosphere. This is the most elegant and expensive (but worth it) restaurant in the Kennebunks. Presentation is formal from beginning to end. A beginning morsel (perhaps a paté) starts off a fantastic meal. Your appetizer may be a lobster spring roll or mix of young lettuces, followed by a chilled cherry soup. Your entrée choices might include veal chops and tenderloin of beef. The menu changes frequently, but the specialty remains steamed lobster on fettuccine with carrots and ginger (priced daily). Finally, you will be given delectable dessert choices like chocolate marquis torte. The soft piano music, elegant ambience and attentive service encourages lingering. $52 per person prix fixe. Cocktails and extensive wine list.

Cape Arundel Inn (967-2125), Ocean Avenue, Kennebunkport. Open May to mid-October for breakfast and dinner (closed Sunday evenings). The dining room overlooks the ocean, and the dinner menu is Continental. You might start with lobster ravioli with seafood mousseline and then try roast salmon fillet in a lemon grass broth or baked halibut in a pine-nut crust with a basil cream sauce. Breakfasts also get rave reviews. Entrées: $16.50–22.95.

Kennebunkport Inn (967-2621), Dock Square, Kennebunkport. Open April through December. Breakfast and dinner daily May through October. Elegant dining in two lacy dining rooms. This is a local favorite, with entrées ranging from the daily pasta special to constants like bouillabaisse (lobster, shrimp, scallops, swordfish, mussels, and clams in a tomato-fennel broth, served with hot pepper sauce on the side; $22.95). $5–23.

Windows on the Water (967-3313), Chase Hill, Kennebunkport. Open for lunch, dinner, and Sunday brunch. A dining room with views of the port through arched windows, screened terrace or alfresco dining, and live entertainment on Friday and Saturday. Seafood is the specialty. Lobster-stuffed potato is popular at lunch. Lightfare selection for smaller appetites. Reservations are a must for dinner. Dinner entrées: $9.95–20.95

☞ **Breakwater Restaurant and Inn** (967-3118), Ocean Avenue, Kennebunkport. Open May through December for breakfast and dinner. Casual, attractive dining room. Menu selections range from a chef's vegetarian platter to shrimp and lobster crêpes with lobster sauce. Specialties include a stuffed boneless breast of chicken wrapped in phyllo dough. Children's prices available. Dinner entrées: $10.95–17.95.

The Colony (967-3331), Ocean Avenue, Kennebunkport. The elegant dining room at this resort is open to the public for all three meals. Dinners include a relish tray and rolls, appetizer, soup, main dish, vegetables, salad, beverage, and dessert for $21.95. Menu selections change each night and might include Citrus Shrimp and Scallops on herbed fettuccine, and baked, maple-cured ham with cider sauce. Sunday brunch is served from 11–2, with a different theme (such as Christmas in July) each week.

Seascapes (967-8500), Pier Road, Cape Porpoise. Open for lunch and dinner daily in-season, varying days April through December. Seascapes combines a great location (on a working fishing pier) with well-known local management (Angela LeBlanc has put her Kennebunk Inn on the south coast dining map). Specialties include Maine bouillabaisse and roasted Maine lobster on vegetable fettuccine. Entrées: $13.95–24.95.

Topher's Restaurant (967-5009), Routes 35 and 9, Lower Village, Kennebunk. Open for lunch and dinner (piano bar) most of the year. We like the atmosphere and the varied menu here. Dinner entrées: $8–15.

☞ **Bartley's Dockside** (967-5050), Kennebunkport (by the bridge). Open 8 AM–9 PM daily. There is candlelight dining by the fire and a water view. Known for its chowder. Dinner entrées start at $10.95.

Mabel's Lobster Claw (967-2562), Ocean Avenue, Kennebunkport. April to mid-October, open for lunch and dinner. A favorite with locals, including George Bush. The specialty is lobster, pure or richly dressed with scallops, shrimp, and fresh mushrooms in a creamy Newburg sauce, topped with Parmesan cheese. The lunch special is a lobster roll with Russian dressing and lettuce in a buttery, grilled hot-dog roll. Entrées: $11.95–16.95.

Alisson's (967-4841), 5 Dock Square, Kennebunkport. Open at 6:30 for breakfast; also serves lunch and dinner. The bar here is the local hangout for various old salts. Soups and sandwiches, or you can dine on fried seafood. Given its atmosphere, convenience, and prices, this place is so popular in high season that you'd better plan on coming early or late. Entrées run $12.95–17.95.

EATING OUT

Note: This area offers an unusual number of first-rate alternatives to expensive dining.

☞ **The Wayfarer** (967-8961), One Pier Road, Cape Porpoise. Open at 6:30 for breakfast, lunch, and dinner. Closed Monday off-season. The atmosphere is upscale coffee shop with a counter and booths, and the food is superb: haddock chowder ($4.50 bowl), scallop and shrimp linguini finished with garlic and parsley ($12.50), or the night's roast (maybe turkey or Yankee pot roast). Basic burger ($3.95) or hot dog ($1.95) and smaller portions on some meals available for kids. All meals include salad, starch, and hot rolls. BYOB from the general store across the road.

The Green Heron (967-3315), Ocean Avenue, Kennebunkport. *The* place for breakfast, a long-standing tradition, served on a glassed-in, waterside porch. The menu is vast and varied.

Nunan's Lobster Hut (967-4362), Route 9, Cape Porpoise. Open for dinner May through October. This low, shedlike landmark packs them in and charges, too. This is the place for a classic lobster feed—there are sinks with paper towels to wipe off the melted butter. Lobster, clams, and pies are the fare. No credit cards.

Satellite Grill (967-0202), Dock Square, Kennebunkport. Open mid-April through fall, daily 11–11. Same menu throughout the day, served upstairs in a Federal-era building in the middle of Dock Square. In addition to inside tables, a terrace counter and patio tables offer the best dining view going of the busy square. Big salads and vegetarian chili in bread bowls are the lunch standouts, and for dinner, four-cheese lasagna, seafood kabobs, or seafood chowder in a bread bowl. Full bar.

Federal Jack's/Kennebunkport Brewery (967-4322), 8 Western Avenue, Lower Village, Kennebunk. Open for lunch and dinner, offering a variety of hand-crafted ales. Standard pub fare.

The Impastable Dream (985-4290), 17 Main Street, Kennebunk. Open daily except Sunday, 11–8. An old house set back from the main drag with a deli take-out side and a delightful dining room, with stenciled walls and pine floors, featuring Italian dishes. So locally popular that you may have to wait at peak dining times; come early or late. Specialties include steamed mussels at lunch, eggplant Parmesan, and vegetable lasagna at dinner. Extremely satisfying portions.

Tilly's Shanty (283-1548), Route 1 North, Arundel. Open for lunch and dinner. Formerly on the wharf at Cape Porpoise, this beloved local landmark has survived its move to Route 1 and expanded its menu to include every kind of fried seafood, in addition to its famous $9.95, 1-pound lobster dinner.

SEAFOOD MARKETS

Preble Fish (967-4620), Cape Porpoise, where the locals get their fish, and you can get steamed lobster-to-go.

Port Lobster (967-2081), Ocean Avenue, Kennebunkport. Live or cooked lobsters packed to travel or ship, and lobster, shrimp and crab rolls to go (several obvious waterside picnic spots are within walking distance).

The Clam Shack (967-3321 or 967-2560), Kennebunkport (at the bridge). Clams, lobsters, and fresh fish. Look for their seasonal take-out stand at the bridge.

Leedy's Restaurant (324-5856), Alfred Square, Alfred. Closed Tuesday, otherwise open for all three meals. This is the kind of place you walk into and know everything is going to taste good. Straight-shooting, all-American cooking specializing in seafood and prime rib. $3.95–15.95.

SNACKS

Chase Hill Bakery (967-2283), Chase Hill, Kennebunkport. Open year-round. Delectable cookies, brownies, and cakes such as "lemon cloud." Everything is made from scratch. Soups and sandwiches. A few tables and fresh-ground Green Mountain Coffee for those who like to linger.

ENTERTAINMENT

Hackmatack Playhouse (698-1807), Route 9, Beaver Dam, Berwick. Local actors, rave reviews.

(Also see *Entertainment* in "Ogunquit and Wells.")

SELECTIVE SHOPPING

ANTIQUES SHOPS
The Kennebunks are known as an antiques center with a half dozen shops, representing a number of dealers, most on Route 1.

ART GALLERIES
More than 60 galleries, most of them seasonal, are now listed in the annual Art Guild of the Kennebunks map/guide. Notable is **Mast Cove Galleries** (967-3453) on Maine Street, touted as the "largest group gallery in the area."

SPECIAL SHOPS
Kennebunk Book Port, 10 Dock Square, Kennebunkport. Open year-round. The oldest commercial building in the port (1775) is one of the most pleasant bookstores in New England. Climb an outside staircase into this inviting mecca, which is dedicated to reading as well as to buying. Helpful, handwritten notes with recommendations from staff make browsing even easier. Books about Maine and the sea are specialties.

Lafayette Center, Storer and Main Streets, Kennebunk. Open daily year-round. A former shoe factory has been recycled as a complex of upscale shops.

Brick Store Exchange, 4 Dane Street, Kennebunk. Open year-round 10–4; closed Sunday, also Monday in winter. A sweet-smelling, volunteer-run outlet for locally crafted gifts.

Port Canvas (967-2717), Dock Square, Kennebunkport. Open year-round. Canvas totes, suitcases, and hats all made in Kennebunkport.

Carla's Corner (967-2206), Ocean Avenue, Kennebunkport. A long-established upscale women's clothing boutique with a wide and enthusiastic following.

The Good Earth, Dock Square, Kennebunkport. Open daily May through October, varying hours; closed from January to March. Stoneware in unusual designs—mugs, vases, and bowls. Great browsing in the loft showroom.

Goose Rocks Pottery (967-2105), Wharf Lane (just off Dock Square), Kennebunkport. Great painted tiles, to-go and customized orders.

SPECIAL EVENTS

February: **Winter Carnival Weekend** (first weekend).
June: **Bed & Breakfast Inn and Garden Tour.**
July: Old-fashioned **picnic and band concert** on the 2nd.
August: **Riverfest** (first Saturday). **Kennebearport Teddy Bear Show** (second Saturday).
September: **Old Time Fiddlers Contest** (second Saturday).
December: **Christmas Prelude** (first and second weekends). Dock Square is decked out for Yuletide, and there are church suppers, concerts, and carols.

Old Orchard Beach Area

When Thomas Rogers was granted 12 acres of land in 1657 and planted a fruit orchard on it, he undoubtedly had no idea it would one day become a resort area so popular that its year-round population would multiply by ten in the summer.

In 1837, E.C. Staples first recognized the area's potential as a summer playground. From taking in boarders on his farm for $1.50 a week, he moved to building the first "Old Orchard House." His instincts proved right, for rail travel brought a wave of tourists to the beach from both the United States and Canada.

The Grand Trunk Railroad did away with the long carriage ride from Montreal, and Canadians discovered that the Maine shore was a great place to vacation. The area is still a popular destination for French Canadian visitors, and you are likely to hear French being spoken almost anywhere you go.

When the first pier at Old Orchard Beach was built in 1898, it stood 20 feet above and 1800 feet out over the water and was constructed entirely of steel. The pavillions housed animals, a casino, and a restaurant. In the decades that followed, the original pier was rebuilt many times following damage by fire and storms, until in 1980 a new, wider, and shorter pier of wood was built. The pier continues to be a focal point in the community and a hub of activity.

An amusement area first appeared in 1902 and grew after World War I. The 1920s brought big-name bands such as Guy Lombardo and Duke Ellington to the Pier Casino, and thousands danced under a revolving crystal ball.

Fire, hard economic times, the decline of the railroad and steamboat industries—all took their toll on Old Orchard Beach over the years. Though the 7 miles of sandy beach and the amusement park near the pier have endured, the 1980s saw the area deteriorate and succumb to a younger, wilder crowd.

In the early 1990s, the citizens decided to take their town back. A major revitalization plan widened sidewalks, added benches and street lights, and passed and enforced ordinances. The result is a cleaner, more appealing, yet still lively and fun vacation spot.

Historically diverse, the area is also well known for the camp meetings held beginning in the late 1800s, first by Methodists, then by the Salvation Army. These meetings continue in the Ocean Park area today.

Biddeford and Saco are often called the "twin cities," and no two Maine towns are more different or more closely linked. Saco is a classic Yankee town with white-clapboard mansions lining its main street, and Biddeford is a classic mill town with a strong French Canadian heritage and mammoth, 19th-century brick textile mills that have stood idle since the 1950s. A few years back, the largest mills were renamed Saco Island and slated for redevelopment as a combination hotel, office, shop, and condo complex. At present the project is still on hold. Still, Biddeford is worth visiting, especially for *La Kermesse,* the colorful Franco-American festival in late June. Saco's Route 1 strip of family-oriented amusement parks is a big draw for those with children.

Parts of Scarborough's 49 square miles belong more in Casco Bay descriptions, but Pine Point and its surrounding area is the easternmost tip of Old Orchard Beach, and is often a less crowded, quieter spot to visit. A large saltwater marsh in Scarborough also makes for quiet relaxation and exploring.

GUIDANCE
Old Orchard Beach Chamber of Commerce (934-2500), PO Box 600 (First Street), Old Orchard Beach 04064, maintains a seasonal walk-in information center; offers help with reservations.

Biddeford–Saco Chamber of Commerce (282-1567), 170 Main Street, Biddeford 04005.

GETTING THERE
By air: **Portland International Jetport** is 13 miles north, and rental cars are available at the airport. You can also fly your own plane into **Sanford Airport.**

By car: Exits 5 and 6 off the Maine Turnpike (I-95) take you easily to the center of Old Orchard Beach. You can also find the town from Route 1 (turn by the large flea market).

GETTING AROUND
From many accommodations in Old Orchard Beach, you are close enough to walk to the pier, the town's center of activity. The **Biddeford-Saco-OOB Transit** also takes you right to the center of town. Call 282-5408 for schedules.

PARKING
An abundance of privately operated lots can be found in the center of Old Orchard Beach. Most charge $2–3 for any length of time—10 minutes or all day. There are meters on the street if you don't mind circling a few times to catch a free one.

MEDICAL EMERGENCY
Southern Maine Medical Center (283-7000), Biddeford.

VILLAGES

Ocean Park is a historic community founded by Free Will Baptists and well known for its outstanding religious, educational, and cultural programs. There is a neighborhood association that sponsors lectures, concerts, and other events throughout the summer.

Pine Point. This quiet and less crowded end of the beach offers a selection of gift shops, restaurants, lobster pounds, and places to stay.

TO SEE AND DO

MUSEUMS

York Institute Museum (282-3031), 371 Main Street, Saco. Open Tuesday through Friday 1–4, May to October; also Saturday (same hours) in July and August. November to April it's open Tuesday and Wednesday 1–4, and year-round it's open Thursday 1–8. Admission is $2 per adult, $1 under 16 and over 60 (free under 6). Original paintings, furniture, decorative arts, and tools; also natural history specimens. Trace the history of southern Maine; inquire about frequent lectures, tours, and special exhibits. The Institute's **Dyer Library** next door has an outstanding Maine history collection.

HISTORIC SITES

The Old Orchard Beach Historical Society, 4 Portland Avenue, is open from 1–4 Tuesday through Saturday, June through October 1, and by appointment. The building is full of exhibits from Old Orchard's past. Each year, in addition to the regular school, fire, and aviation exhibits, there is a special exhibit on display. Pick up the timeline of the area's history and the walking map of historic sites.

FOR FAMILIES

The Route 1 strip in Saco and nearby Orchard Beach makes up Maine's biggest concentration of kid-geared "attractions." Be prepared to pay.

Maine Aquarium (284-4511), Route 1, Saco. Open daily, year-round. Marine life exhibits include seals, penguins, sharks, tidepool animals. Also nature trails, and picnic grounds. Handicapped accessible. $6 per adult, less for seniors and kids. Interesting, but the price is too high.

Funtown USA/Cascade Water Park (284-5139 or 287-6231), Route 1 just south of Route 195 in Saco. Open daily mid-June to Labor Day, weekends in spring and fall. Water activities and a large amusement park: bumper cars, New England's largest log flume, canoe ride down "Adventure River," kiddie rides, antique cars.

Aquaboggan Water Park (282-3112), Route 1, Saco. Open June through Labor Day. Water slides, swimming pool, bumper boats, mini-golf, arcade, shuffleboard, toddler area.

Pirate's Cove Adventure Golf (934-5086), 70 First Street, Old Orchard

Beach. Thirty-six up-and-down miniature golf holes, waterfalls, ponds.
Palace Playland (934-2001), Old Orchard Street, Old Orchard Beach.
Open late June through Labor Day. For more than 60 years, fun-seek-
ers have been wheeled, lifted, shaken, spun, and bumped in Palace
Playland rides; there's also a 1906 carousel with hand-painted, wooden
horses and sleighs, a Ferris wheel, and a 60-foot-high water slide.
Charge is by the ride or $16 for an afternoon pass.

GOLF
Old Orchard Beach Country Club (934-4513), 49 Ross Road, Old Or-
chard. Nine-hole course. **Biddeford-Saco Country Club** (282-5883),
Old Orchard Road, Saco. Eighteen-hole course.

HORSEBACK RIDING
Long Horn Stables (934-9578), 93 Ross Road, Old Orchard Beach. Trail
rides, hayrides, sleigh rides. A bridle path follows the Mousam River.
Bush Brook Stables (284-7721), 463 West Street, Biddeford. Trail
rides and hayrides. **Horseback Riding Plus** (883-6400), 338 Broad-
turn Street, Scarborough. Guided trail rides for adults; kiddie and pony
rides available.

RACING
Scarborough Downs (883-4331), off I-95, Exit 6 in Scarborough. The largest harness racing facility in New England. Live harness racing, post
time: Wednesday, Friday, and Saturday 7:30 PM, Sunday 1:30 PM. Thor-
oughbred and harness racing via simulcast Tuesday through Sunday 1–
10 PM. Downs Club Restaurant (883-3022) is open for dinner and Sunday brunch.
Beech Ridge Motor Speedway (883-5227), Holmes Road, Scarborough.
Summer stock-car racing.

TENNIS
The Ocean Park Association (934-9325) maintains public tennis courts,
open in July and August.

CROSS-COUNTRY SKIING
Beech Ridge Farm Cross Country Ski Center (839-4098), 193 Beech
Ridge Road, Scarborough. One hundred fifty acres of fields and woods
with 15 km of groomed tracks. Warming hut, rentals, lessons.

GREEN SPACE

BEACHES
Obviously, **Old Orchard Beach** is the big draw in this area, with 7 miles of
sand and plenty of space for sunbathing, swimming, volleyball, and
other recreation.
Ferry Beach State Park is marked from Route 9 between Old Orchard
Beach and Camp Ellis, in Saco. The 100-acre preserve includes 70 yards
of sand; also a boardwalk through the dunes, nature trails, picnic area
with grills, lifeguards, changing rooms. $1 per person, free under age 12.

Attractions at Old Orchard Beach

Bay View Beach, at the end of Bay View Road near Ferry Beach, is 200 yards of mostly sandy beach; lifeguards, free parking.

Camp Ellis Beach, Route 9, Saco. Some 2000 feet of beach backed by cottages; also a long fishing pier. Commercial parking lots.

Scarborough Town Beach, farther down Route 207 and overlooking Pine Point, usually has parking space because the entrance fee is $8. Great for off-season walking.

Pine Point, Route 9, the easternmost stretch of Old Orchard, usually offers space and parking.

NATURE PRESERVES

Scarborough Marsh Nature Center (883-5100, seasonal), Pine Point Road. Open daily mid-June to Labor Day, 9:30–5:30. The largest salt marsh (3000 acres) in Maine. This Maine Audubon Nature Center offers canoe rentals, exhibits, a nature store, guided walking tours, and canoe tours throughout the summer.

LODGING

INNS AND BED & BREAKFASTS

The Carriage House (934-2141), 24 Portland Avenue, Old Orchard Beach 04064. Just off the main drag, this Victorian home and carriage house offers a welcome alternative to the abundance of motels and condominiums lining the beach. There are eight pretty rooms furnished in period antiques in the main house, all with shared bath. A downstairs room has a beautiful antique brass bed. The carriage house suite is large and private, with a kitchen and TV. Also available is a five-room apartment with a deck.

The Atlantic Birches Inn (934-5295), 20 Portland Avenue, Old Orchard Beach 04064. Just around the corner from the center of activity is this lovely Victorian, shingle-style home, built in the area's heyday. Six rooms ranging from accommodations for two to a two-room, third-floor suite that can accommodate five. Decorated with a mix of old and new furnishings; living room and large front porch shaded by white birches. $39–75 (for suite) off-season, $59–120 in high season.

☞ **Crown 'n' Anchor Inn** (282-3829), PO Box 228, Saco 04072-0228. This is a rare find: a Greek Revival, pillared mansion built in 1827 by a local lawyer, sold in 1841 to Stephen Goodale, in whose family it remained until 1925. Obviously, these were all well-to-do folk, and Stephen's son George became a Harvard professor of botany, involved with the planning and execution of the university's botanical museum (he was the man who commissioned those famous "glass flowers"). Host John Barclay fell in love with the house several years ago while searching for an inn to buy but was deterred by its dilapidated state—which only increased in ensuing years as it continued to stand empty. We won't attempt to tell the story of why he is here and how the inn came to look the way it does. Suffice it to say, the common space includes a double living room, the front room restored to its traditional look as a "receiving parlor," and all six rooms are painstakingly restored, each with an elegant bathroom. The Normandy Suite with its two working fireplaces and Jacuzzi bath is a steal at $85 per night double occupancy. The inn is just up the street from the York Institute and a 10-minute drive from Saco's relatively uncrowded sands (see *Beaches*). A candlelight breakfast is served on fine china in the small but formal dining room. $65–85.

☞✐**Country Farm** (282-0208), 139 Louden Road, Saco 04072. Open year-round. Nothing fancy, just a 150-acre working farm (cattle, goats, several kittens, and a horse) that's been in the same family for several generations with two clean, comfortable guest rooms (shared bath) and plenty of space to wander—down to the shore of the Saco River. Arlene and Norman Gonneville seem to enjoy their guests, children included. $45 for a double includes a big breakfast; $10 per additional guest.

MOTELS, COTTAGES, AND CONDOMINIUMS

Old Orchard Beach offers an overwhelming number of motel, cottage, and condominium complexes along the beach and main roads. The chamber of commerce publishes a helpful "Old Orchard Beach Vacation Planner" that lists many of your choices. A word of caution—some of these establishments have been around for years, with no renovations and poor upkeep. It's a good idea, if possible, to check out a room before making reservations. Generally, condominiums on the beach are better kept, and many have reasonable rates.

The Brunswick (934-2171), 39 West Grand Avenue, Old Orchard Beach 04064. A large condominium building on the beach with a lively dining room, lounge, and patio bar with live entertainment. Condominium living with the amenities of a hotel. One- and two-bedroom oceanfront suites with patios and fully equipped kitchens. Motel rooms also available. $95–185 motel in-season, $147–205 condominium in peak season, 3-day minimum stay.

Beachfront Condotel (934-7434), One Walnut Street, Old Orchard Beach 04064. Offers range from standard studio to two-bedroom suites. All units have full-service kitchenettes and can be rented by the night, week, or month (two-month minimum). The beach is steps from the front door; some units have fireplaces. $80–175 depending on room and season; $560–1051 weekly.

Grand View (934-4837), 189 East Grand Avenue, Old Orchard Beach 04064. Twenty-six units with efficiency, one-, two-, and three-bedroom condominiums. The building is right smack on the beach, with an outdoor pool and Jacuzzi for added fun. $65–195 in-season; $45–95 off-season; weekly rentals range from $400–1100 in-season.

The Dunes (883-5829), 95 East Grand Avenue, Pine Point, Scarborough. On the quieter end of the beach, just across the street from Grand Beach. Offers motel rooms, cottages, and one house (weekly) that can sleep up to six. $55–70 per night for motel in-season; cottages $275–500 weekly (small cottages available for nightly rental in shoulder seasons).

CAMPGROUNDS

Camping is a budget-minded family's best bet in this area. There are at least a dozen campgrounds here, many geared to families and offering games, recreational activities, and trolley service to the beach in-season. Following are a couple of recommendations; check with the chamber for a full listing.

Bayley's Camping Resort (883-6043), 27 Ross Road, West Scarborough. Just down the road from Pine Point, you hardly have to leave the grounds to have a terrific vacation. In 1993, Bayley's was named Campground of the Year by the National Association of RV Parks/Campgrounds, and it's easy to see why with all it has to offer. Paddleboats, swimming pool, Jacuzzi, horseback riding, fishing, game room, special programs for children and adults—the list goes on and on. Rates range from $27.50–36.50 depending on hook-ups; lower in spring and fall.

Powder Horn (934-4733), PO Box 366, Old Orchard Beach 04064. A 450-site campground with much to offer. Playgrounds, shuffleboard, horseshoes, volleyball, rec hall and game room, miniature golf, trolley service to the beach.

WHERE TO EAT

DINING OUT

Cornforth House (284-2006), 893 Route 1, Saco. Open for breakfast and dinner year-round. A large, red house transformed into a fantastic restaurant. A series of small dining rooms creates an intimate but casual atmosphere. Meals are prepared with an emphasis on fresh, local ingredients. Appetizers might include champagne lobster, sautéed and served with a saffron-champagne cream sauce over puff pastry ($6.95). Entrées may include steak dianne and veal captiva (scaloppine of veal sautéed with lobster meat, garnished with béarnaise). Save room for the delicious homemade desserts. $12.95–15.95.

Village Inn (934-7370), 213 Saco Avenue, Old Orchard Beach. Open for lunch and dinner, with a large and varied menu. Lunch specials include fried seafood, pastas, and chicken cordon bleu. At dinner, there is everything from a large, fried, seafood combo ($14.95) to eggplant Parmesan ($6.95) to baked chicken stuffed with broccoli, rice, and cheese and topped with a creamy broccoli sauce ($7.95).

Joseph's by the Sea (934-5044), 55 West Grand Avenue, Old Orchard Beach. A fine dining tradition in the area since 1968. Dine on creative seafood specialties (maybe baked stuffed lobster), beef or pasta dishes in a romantic setting in two dining rooms overlooking the water. $12.95–20.00.

EATING OUT

Note: Near the pier and on the main drag of Old Orchard Beach is an abundance of take-out stands and informal restaurants serving pizza, burgers, hot dogs, fried seafood, and almost anything you could want.

Danton's Family Restaurant (934-7701), Old Orchard Beach Street. Easy to overlook on the main drag amid all the souvenir shops and take-out stands, but don't. Established in 1946, this little place is still going strong. Home-cooked meals for breakfast, lunch, and dinner at very reasonable prices. Daily lunch specials might include baked macaroni and cheese, fish and chips. Try the homemade pies.

Bill's Pizza (934-1949), 12 Old Orchard Street. For pizza, this is the place to go.

Chowderheads (883-8333), Oak Hill Plaza, Route 114, Scarborough. A few minutes away from the center of activity, but just off Route 1. A good seafood place with a loyal following. Excellent chowder, good specials, and generous portions.

Hattie's (282-3435), Biddeford Pool. The local gathering spot for breakfast and lunch. *The* place (the only place) to eat in Biddeford Pool, and it's a find. Former President Bush knows it well.

Wormwoods (282-9679), Camp Ellis Beach, Saco. Open year-round, daily for lunch and dinner. A large, friendly, old-fashioned place that you can count on for a good chowder and family-geared dining if you are exploring this quiet corner of the south coast.

LOBSTER POUNDS

Bayley's Lobster Pound (883-4571), Pine Point, Scarborough. A popular place for lobster and seafood.

Lobster Claw (282-0040) Route 5, Ocean Park Road, Saco. Lobsters cooked outside in giant kettles, stews and chowders, cozy dining room, and takeout available. Twin lobster specials, also steamers, fried seafood. Lobster packed to travel.

SNACKS

The pier and surrounding area is the place to go for munchies from french fries and fried dough to ice cream treats and everything in between.

ENTERTAINMENT

The Ballpark (934-1124), Old Orchard Beach. Once a professional baseball stadium, the park now features a mix of entertainment throughout the summer including sporting events, concerts, fairs, festivals, and family shows. Seating capacity of 12,500, and parking for 2000 cars.

THEATER

City Theater (282-0849), Main Street, Biddeford. A 660-seat, 1890s theater, recently restored, now offering a series of live performances.

SPECIAL EVENTS

Summer: **Fireworks** on the beach every Thursday night through Labor Day.
May: **Apple Blossom Festival.**
Late June: Annual *La Kermesse* **Franco-American Festival,** Biddeford. Parade, public suppers, dancing, entertainment, sand-castle competition.
July: **Canada/USA Days,** Ocean Park, festival and children's parade.
August: Ocean Park **Festival of Lights. Beach Olympics. Chowdafest.**
September: **Classic car weekend,** Old Orchard Beach.
October: Columbus Day weekend **Jamboree & Harvestfest.**
December: **Tree lighting ceremony.**

II. CASCO BAY

Portland waterfront

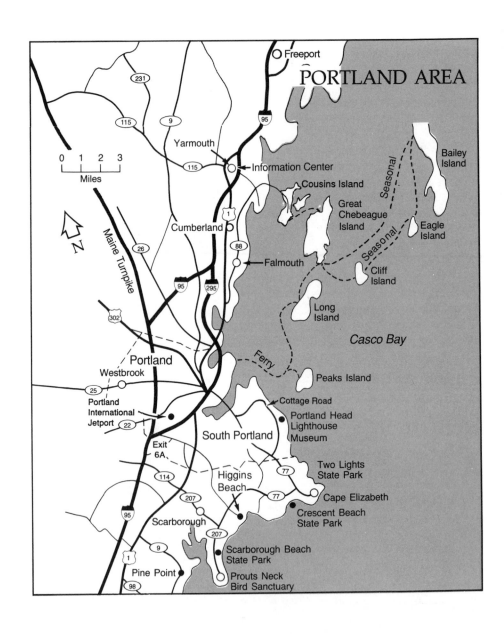

Portland Area

In Portland, sea gulls perch on skyscrapers and a smell and sense of the sea prevails. Northern New England's most sophisticated and one of its most important cities since the 1820s, it is blessed with distinguished buildings from every era. Portland provides a showcase for resident painters, musicians, actors, dancers, and craftspeople.

Portland is Maine's largest city, yet it still has a small-town feel. The total population still hovers around 64,000, and downtown is invitingly walkable. Hundreds of shops and galleries and dozens of restaurants are packed into ornate Victorian buildings in one, five-block waterfront neighborhood. Known as the Old Port Exchange, this area was a canker at the city's heart until the 1970s, when it was first slated for urban renewal.

Portland's motto, *resurgam* ("I shall rise again"), could not be more appropriate. First, the 17th-century settlement was wiped out twice by Native Americans, then once by the British. It was not until after the American Revolution that the community really began to prosper—as is evidenced by the Federal-era mansions and commercial buildings like the granite and glass Mariner's Church, built in 1820 to be the largest building in the capital of a brand new state.

This port is the one that was loved by a small boy named Henry Wadsworth Longfellow, who later wrote:

> *I remember the black wharves and the ships*
> *And the sea-tides tossing free*
> *And the Spanish sailors with bearded lips*
> *And the beauty and mystery of the ships*
> *And the magic of the sea.*

Portland continued to thrive as a lumbering port and railroad terminus through the Civil War and until the Independence Day at that war's end. Then disaster struck again. On July 4, 1866, a firecracker flamed up in a Commercial Street boatyard and quickly destroyed most of downtown Portland. The city rose like the legendary phoenix, rebuilding yet again, this time in sturdy brick. The buildings were replete with the kind of flourishes you would expect of the Gilded Age, years during which these city blocks were the core of northern New England's shipping, rail, and manufacturing businesses.

These very buildings, a century later, were "going for peanuts," in the words of a realtor who began buying them up in the late 1960s. The city's prominence as a port had been eclipsed by the opening of the St. Lawrence Seaway in 1959, and its handsome Grand Trunk Station was torn down in 1966. Decent folk did their shopping at the department and chain stores up on Congress Street, itself threatened by the Maine Mall out by the interstate highway.

Down by the harbor, artists and craftspeople were renting shop fronts for $50 per month. They formed the Old Port Association, hoping to entice people to stroll through the no-man's-land that separated the shops on Congress Street from the few famous fish restaurants and the ferry dock on Commercial Street. That first winter they strung lights through upper floors to convey a sense of security, and they shoveled their own streets, a service the city had long ago ceased to provide to that area. At the end of the winter, they celebrated their survival by holding the first Old Port Festival, an exuberant street fair that is still held each June.

Portland's Old Port Exchange continues to thrive, and on its fringes, new semi-high-rise, red-brick buildings blend with the old and link Old Port with the Congress Street shops and offices.

Condominiums now line a wharf or two, but Portland remains a working port. It's also a departure point for the ferry to Yarmouth, Nova Scotia, and for the fleet of Casco Bay Liners that regularly transport people, mail, and supplies between Casco Bay's Calendar Islands. These islands range from Peaks Island—accessible in just 20 minutes by commuter ferry, and offering rental bikes, guided sea kayaking, lodging, and dining—to Cliff Island, more than an hour's ride, offering sandy roads and the feel of islands usually found farther Down East. In summer, these ferries bill their longer runs as "Casco Bay Cruises" and add "Music Cruises" and a lazy circuit to Bailey Island. Two excursion lines (one from south Freeport) also service Eagle Island, preserved as a memorial to Arctic explorer Admiral Peary. The waterfront is, moreover, the departure point for deep-sea fishing, harbor cruises, and daysailing.

Art lovers can easily spend a day among Portland's museums and galleries. The Portland Museum of Art quintupled in the 1980s and exhibits American painters like John Singer Sargent, Winslow Homer, George Bellows, and Jamie Wyeth. Next door, the Children's Museum of Maine is sure to please both adults and children with its interactive, educational displays.

Visitors can find a variety of food, from Thai and Afghan to seafood and burgers in the more than 40 restaurants Portland offers. Downtown boasts some appealing bed & breakfasts, as well as a few good

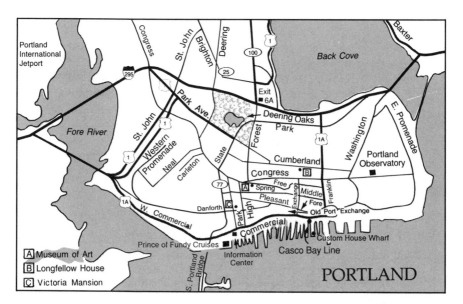

hotels. Cape Elizabeth, just south of Portland, offers beaches and birding, and both Falmouth and Yarmouth, just east of the city, are worth exploring.

GUIDANCE

The Convention and Visitors Bureau of Greater Portland (772-4994) publishes *Greater Portland Visitors Guide,* listing restaurants, sights, museums, and accommodations. Its helpful walk-in information center at 305 Commercial Street is well stocked with menus and pamphlets, and courtesy phones connect with lodging places and services.

The **Maine Publicity Bureau** (846-0833) staffs a major state information center on Route 1 in Yarmouth, just off I-95, Exit 17.

For details about guided walking tours of the city, contact **Greater Portland Landmarks** (774-5561), 165 State Street, Portland 04101. Be sure to request their self-guided walking tour leaflets (also available from the visitors bureau) that outline walking tours of Congress Street, the Old Port Exchange, State Street, and the Western Promenade.

GETTING THERE

By air: **Portland International Jetport** (774-7301) is served by Delta Air Lines (1-800-221-1212), Continental Airlines (1-800-525-0280), United (1-800-241-6522), USAir (1-800-428-4322), and Northwest Airlink (1-800-241-2525), connecting with Boston, New York, Atlanta, Cincinnati, Philadelphia, Chicago, Washington DC, and Newark. Car rentals at the airport include National Inter-rent, Avis, Hertz, and Budget.

By bus: **Vermont Transit** (772-6587) stops in Portland daily en route from Boston to points farther up the coast and to inland points north. But the terminal is dingy, inconvenient to Congress Street, the Old Port, or ferries, and it closes early, forcing passengers to stand out in the cold and rain. **Concord Trailways** (828-1151) stops in Portland daily en route from Boston to Bangor or coastal points. They offer movies and music on the way and sometimes a small snack.

By ferry: Canadians may cruise to Portland aboard the **Prince of Fundy Company's** ferry, *Scotia Prince,* out of Yarmouth, Nova Scotia (775-5616 or, seasonally, 1-800-482-0955 in Maine; 1-800-341-7540 outside Maine). Overnight cruises are offered early May through October. Prices vary, depending on the season, cabin, or a variety of special packages. Restaurants, shops, live entertainment, and a casino are some of the features passengers enjoy aboard. The luxury cruise vessel accommodates 1500 passengers in 800 cabins plus 250 cars.

GETTING AROUND

The **Metro** (774-0351) bus transfer system serves Greater Portland. The Metro city buses connect airport and city.

PARKING

Portland meters are limited to 2 hours, hard to come by, and checked often. The city urges visitors to use its many parking garages. The **Fore Street Garage** (439 Fore Street) puts you at one end of the Old Port, and the **Custom House Square Garage** (25 Pearl Street), at the other. The **Casco Bay Garage** (Maine State Pier) and **Free Street Parking** (130 Free Street, just up from the art museum) are also handy.

MEDICAL EMERGENCY

Portland Ambulance Service (dial 911). **Maine Medical Center** (871-0111), 22 Bramhall Street, Portland.

VILLAGES

Cape Elizabeth is a peaceful residential area. The main village of **Pond Cove** is a refuge for many Portland commuters, who live in homes overlooking the Atlantic ocean. Two Lights State Park and a large, popular beach are also part of this community.

Falmouth is a suburb of Portland. The village, known as **Falmouth Foreside,** has tremendous old houses in the original section of town. A popular marina and restaurant (see *Dining Out*) offer terrific views and water access.

Yarmouth has carried the charm of a Colonial village into the 19th century with style. Commercial and tourist-aimed businesses are relegated to Route 1, leaving the inner village lined with 18th- and 19th-century homes mixed with quaint stores and antiques shops. North Yarmouth Academy's original Greek Revival brick buildings, the 18th-century meetinghouse, and many fine old churches are must-sees for architecture buffs. Several parks are open to the public, including the village Green with its historic, round railroad station and Royal River Park, offering recreation in all seasons. In July, Yarmouth really comes alive with the clam festival.

TO SEE

MUSEUMS

Portland Museum of Art (775-6148 or, for a weekly schedule of events and information, 773-ARTS, 1-800-639-4067), 7 Congress Square, Portland 04101. Tuesday through Saturday 10–5, Thursday 10–9, and Sunday noon–5; closed New Year's Day, July 4th, Thanksgiving, and Christmas. $3.50 per adult, $2.50 per student or senior citizen, and $1.00 per child 16 or under. Maine's largest art museum houses an extensive collection of American artists, featuring Maine-based masters such as Winslow Homer, Edward Hopper, and Andrew Wyeth. The adjoining museum buildings include the splendid, Federal-style McLellan-Sweat mansion, built for Portland's biggest shipowner in 1800. The museum itself was founded in 1882. In 1991, Joan Whitney Payson's collection was also absorbed into the museum. It includes works by Renoir, Degas, Prendergast, and Picasso as well as Homer and Wyeth.

Children's Museum of Maine (828-1234), 142 Free Street, Portland. Next door to the Museum of Art, this elaborate new museum offers three levels of interactive, hands-on exhibits, designed to help the young and old learn together. Permanent exhibits include Maine Street USA (with toddler park, cave, farm, supermarket, bank, and fire department), a space shuttle, a news center, and much, much more. Enough to keep kids and their parents entertained for an entire afternoon.

The Museum at Portland Head Light (799-2661), 1000 Shore Road in Fort Williams Park. Open June through October 10–4, and November, December, April, and May, weekends 10–4. $2 per adult, $1 children 6–18. This is the oldest lighthouse in Maine, first illuminated in 1791 per order of George Washington. It has been recently automated, and the former keeper's house has been transformed into an exceptional museum with exhibits about the world history of lighthouses, the lighthouses in Maine, and the evolution of this particular light and of the local shipping industry. This is a great spot to come just for the view. Bring a picnic; there are tables with water views in the surrounding **Fort Williams Park,** just 4 miles from downtown Portland: Take State Street (Route 77) south across the bridge to South Portland, then left on Broadway and right on Cottage Street, which turns into Shore Road. On the way back, you might want to check out the **Spring Point Museum** (799-6337) on Fort Road, marked from Route 77 in South Portland. Open Memorial Day weekend through October, Thursday to Sunday 1–4; $2 per adult, $1 children. Sited in a brick repair shop that was part of Fort Preble and is now part of Southern Maine Technical College, it mounts changing exhibits on local maritime history and features an ongoing restoration of the pieces of the *Snow Squall,* an 1850s Portland clipper ship wrecked in the Falkland

CONVENTION & VISITORS BUREAU

Portland Head Light

Islands. The **Spring Point Lighthouse,** at the end of a breakwater, is another good vantage point on the harbor.

Portland Fire Museum, 157 Spring Street. Open mid-June to mid-September, Monday and Thursday 7–9 PM. Donations requested. Given Portland's unusual fire-fighting history, this collection of artifacts and photos is something to see. Housed in a granite Greek Revival firehouse.

Maine Narrow Gauge Railroad Co. & Museum (828-0814), 58 Fore Street, Portland. Open daily 10–4. Hard to spot if you aren't looking for it—but you should. From the 1870s to the 1940s, Maine had a unique, smaller-than-standard railroad system, with rails spaced just 2 feet apart. The "2-footers" were more economically viable, and five lines carried visitors to the more remote parts of the state. After the lines went out of business, a millionaire cranberry grower who loved the 2-footers bought as much of the equipment and rail cars as he could. His collection evolved into Edaville, a major tourist attraction until its closing in 1991 due to lease disputes. Phineas Sprague Jr. and a group of railroad enthusiasts brought the cars and equipment back to Portland and set up this great little museum. Displays include the world's only 2-foot parlor car, the "Rangeley," locomotives, a railbus, a model-T inspection car, and a caboose. There is also a short video on 2-footer history, and well-informed, enthusiastic guides show you around.

Baxter Gallery of Portland School of Art (775-5152), 619 Congress Street. Art lovers shouldn't miss the photo and primary gallery in this beautiful old building, just south up Congress Street from the Portland Museum of Art.

HISTORIC SITES

Wadsworth-Longfellow House, 485 Congress Street. Maintained by the
Maine Historical Society (879-0427), which also offers the Maine History Gallery and an extensive research library next door. Open June to
October, Tuesday through Sunday 10–4 (closed July 4th and Labor
Day; gallery and library open in winter, Wednesday through Saturday
12–4). $3 per adult, $1 per child under 18. Allow 45 minutes for a
guided tour. Built by the poet's grandfather, this was the home of an
important Portland family. Peleg Wadsworth was a Revolutionary War
hero, and the entire clan of Wadsworths and Longfellows was prominent in the city. The house, in which Henry spent his childhood, is a
good example of how such families lived in the 19th century. The garden behind the house has been adapted from gardens of the era, and
most furnishings are original. At Christmastime, the Wadsworth-
Longfellow House has a popular open house, with decorations and
festivities of the season.

Portland Observatory (772-5547), 138 Congress Street. Open Memorial
Day to Halloween whenever the flag is flying. In June, September, and
October, it is generally open Friday through Sunday 1–5, and during July
and August, Wednesday, Thursday, and Sunday 1–5, Friday and Saturday
10–5. $1.50 admission, children $.50. Built in 1807, this octagonal,
shingled landmark is the last surviving 19th-century signal tower on the
Atlantic. Climb the 102 steps for a surprisingly rewarding view at the top
and a sense of what it must have been like to scan the horizon for your
husband's returning ship in the 1800s.

Victoria Mansion, the Morse-Libby House (772-4841), 109 Danforth Street
(at the corner of Park Street). Open Memorial Day to Labor Day, Tuesday through Saturday 10–4, Sunday 1–5 (closed July 4th and Labor Day).
Weekends from Labor Day to Columbus Day. $4 per adult, $1.50 per
child 6–18. About as Victorian as can be, this brownstone Italianate home
was built in 1859 for a Maine native who had made his fortune in the
New Orleans hotel business. The interior is extremely ornate: frescoed
walls and ceilings, a flying staircase with 377 hand-carved balusters of
Santo Domingo mahogany, giant gold-leaf mirrors, marble mantels, ornate chandeliers, stained glass, and much more. The Victoria Mansion
reopens during the Christmas season for special programs.

First Parish Church, 425 Congress Street. Open June to August, Tuesday
11:30–1, free. If you happen to be walking down Congress Street on a
summer Tuesday afternoon, step into the vintage 1826 meetinghouse
in which the pews are tipped forward—so that dozing parishioners
would fall onto the floor.

Neal Dow Memorial (773-7773), 714 Congress Street. Open year-round,
Monday through Friday 9–4. A handsome Greek Revival house built
in 1829 by the man responsible for an 1851 law that made Maine the first
state to prohibit the manufacture and sale of alcoholic beverages. Cur-

rently the headquarters of the Maine Women's Christian Temperance Union, the mansion is a memorial to Neal Dow.

George Tate House (774-9781), 1270 Westbrook Street (follow Congress Street west across the Fore River to Westbrook). Open July 1 to September 15, Tuesday through Saturday 10–4, Sunday 1–4. $3 per adult, $1 per child. George Tate, mast agent for the Royal Navy, built this Georgian house in 1755 to reflect his important position. Both inside and outside are unusual, distinguished by fine windows, a gambrel roof, wood paneling, and elegant furniture. An 18th-century herb garden is part of the historic landscape.

TO DO

BICYCLING

Hundreds of acres of undeveloped land offer some great bicycling. Call **Portland Recreation** (874-8793) for designated trails. **Forest City Mountain Bike Tours** (780-8155) offers 2- to 6-hour guided rides of the city and off-road areas. Rentals available, reservations required.

BOAT EXCURSIONS

Casco Bay Lines (774-7871), Casco Bay Ferry Terminal, 56 Commercial Street at Franklin. Founded in 1845, this business was said to be the oldest continuously operating ferry company in the country when it went bankrupt in 1980. The present, quasi-municipal Casco Bay Island Transit District looks and functions much the way the old line did. Its brightly painted ferries are still lifelines to six islands, carrying groceries and lumber as well as mail.

No one seems sure how many islands there are in Casco Bay. Printed descriptions range from 136 to 222. Seventeenth-century explorer John Smith dubbed them the "Calendar Islands," saying there was one for every day of the year.

Of the six islands accessible via Casco Bay Lines, five invite exploring. There's a state-owned beach on **Long Island** (also a general store and restaurant) and a classic summer hotel (at the other end of the island from where the ferry docks) on **Great Chebeague.** On **Peaks Island,** a 20-minute ferry ride from Portland, you can spend the night, learn to paddle a sea kayak (see *Sea Kayaking*), dine with a great view of Portland (see Will's under *Dining Out*), or rent a bike at Peaks Island Mercantile (766-5631) and tour the rocky promontories of the undeveloped Back Shore. Peaks is about 1 mile square (5 miles around).

You can also lunch or dine and sleep on neighboring **Great Diamond Island** (see The Diamond's Edge restaurant under *Dining Out* and McKinley Estates under *Bed & Breakfasts*). On **Cliff Island,** a full 1½-hour ferry ride from the rest of the city (though technically a part of Portland), you can walk the dirt road to sandy beaches. Each island retains its own rarefied world of 19th-century summer cottages and fishermen's homes, of wildflowers and quiet inlets.

    Casco Bay excursions include the year-round, daily mail boat run (2 hours, 45 minutes), putting into all the islands in the morning and again in the afternoon ($9.25 per adult, $4.00 per child), and a variety of seasonal, special excursions including a 5½-hour Bailey Island Cruise ($13.50 per adult, $6.00 per child) (see "Brunswick and The Harpswells"). Also year-round, frequent, daily car-ferry service to Peaks Island.

Eagle Tours, Inc. (774-6498 or 799-2872), Long Wharf, Portland. Runs late June through Labor Day, some trips through September. The *Kristy K* takes you out to Eagle Island, the former home of Admiral Peary, now maintained by the state as an historic site and nature preserve (see the "Brunswick" and "Freeport" chapters); the 49-passenger *Fish Hawk* is used for a harbor and island cruise and for seal-watching. Group charters available.

Bay View Cruises (761-0496), Fisherman's Wharf, Portland. Daily mid-May to October, weekends from April. Narrated harbor cruises aboard the *Bay View Lady;* harbor lunch cruise (bring your own sandwich) from 12:10–12:50; just $3. Otherwise $8 per adult, $7 per child for a 1½-hour cruise; Sunday brunch cruise June through August.

The ultimate cruise out of Portland is the overnight run (early May to late October) to Yarmouth, Nova Scotia (see *Getting There*).

CANOEING

(See Scarborough Marsh Nature Center under *Green Space*.)

DEEP-SEA FISHING AND SAILING

Several deep-sea fishing boats and sailing yachts are based in Portland every summer. Check with the Convention and Visitors Bureau (772-5800) for current listings. Also see *Sea Kayaking* for details about self-propelled cruising through Casco Bay.

HOT-AIR BALLOONING

Hot Fun (799-0193), Box 2825, South Portland. Hot-air balloons carry up to six passengers.

SEA KAYAKING

Maine Island Kayak Co. (766-2373, 1-800-796-2373), 70 Luther Street, Peaks Island. Late May through October. One of the state's leading kayaking outfitters, offering 1- to 10-day (camping) tours as far Down East as Machias; also weekend overnights on Jewell Island—on the outer fringe of Casco Bay—and 7-day expeditions through the islands of the bay. Introductory paddling sessions available. Casco Bay is a great place to learn to sea kayak, given its easy access both to a wide variety of islands and to open ocean.

GREEN SPACE

BEACHES

Crescent Beach State Park (8 miles from Portland on Route 77) is a mile of sand complete with changing facilities, playground, picnic tables, and snack bar. $2.50 adults, $.50 ages 5–11.

Higgins Beach, farther down Route 77 in Scarborough, is an extensive strand within walking distance of lodging but with no parking.

Scarborough Beach State Park (Route 207, 3 miles south of Route 1 on Prouts Neck) is a superb beach, but only a 65-foot stretch is technically public. Thanks to limited parking, however, the crowd is rarely excessive. $1.50 per person.

PARKS

Deering Oaks, a 51-acre city park designed by Frederick Law Olmstead, has a pond, swans, paddleboats, fountains, a playground, and a fine grove of oak trees. A farmer's market is held here every Saturday morning throughout the summer and into November. Ice skating on the pond in winter.

Two Lights State Park is open April 15 through November. No swimming, but 40 acres of shore for picnicking and fishing. $1.50 per person. (Also see Fort Williams Park and Spring Point Lighthouse under *To See*.)

NATURE PRESERVES

Gilsland Farm Sanctuary (781-2330), 118 Route 1, Falmouth Foreside (3 miles east of Portland). The headquarters of the **Maine Audubon Society** are located here. The sanctuary is open sunrise to sunset, year-round. The nature-oriented shop is open Monday through Saturday 9–5, Sunday 2–5. Sixty acres of trails, rolling fields, river frontage, and salt marsh. There is also a solar-heated education center with exhibits; special programs and field trips are year-round.

Prouts Neck Cliff Path and Wildlife Sanctuary. Winslow Homer painted many of his seascapes in the small studio attached to the summer home, which was—and still is—part of the exclusive community on Prouts Neck, beyond the Black Point Inn. It's not a long walk from the inn to Winslow Homer Road where the Cliff Walk (unmarked) begins. It's a beautiful walk along the rocks, around Eastern Point, and back almost to the inn. You can also walk through the sanctuary between Winslow Homer Road (just east of St. James Episcopal Church) and Library Lane, donated by Winslow's brother Charles. The studio itself is open July and August 10–4, marked only by a "Studio" sign on the shedlike room attached to a private house.

Scarborough Marsh Nature Center (883-5100, seasonal), Pine Point Road (10 miles south of Portland). Open daily mid-June to Labor Day, 9:30–5:30. The largest salt marsh (3000 acres) in Maine. This Maine Audubon Nature Center offers canoe rentals, exhibits, a nature store, guided walking tours, and canoe tours throughout the summer.

Fore River Sanctuary (781-2330), near Exit 8, off Brighton Avenue. A 76-acre preserve owned by Maine Audubon Society. Hidden behind a suburban neighborhood where explorers may not think to look, the 2.5 miles of hiking trails offer access to Portland's only waterfall, Jewell

Falls. A set of railroad tracks (be careful—they are active) marks the beginning of the trail that then leads you through woods and marshland.

WALKS

Eastern Cemetery, Congress Street and Washington Avenue (near the Portland Observatory on Munjoy Hill). More than 4000 souls are interred in these 9 acres, and the headstones, dating back to the mid-17th century, are embellished with angels' and death's heads. Despite its derelict state, this is an utterly fascinating place.

Fort Allen Park dates from 1814 and is on a blustery point on Casco Bay, a sure bet for a fresh breeze on the hottest day, as is the adjacent, 68-acre **Eastern Promenade,** part of the turn-of-the-century park system designed by the famous, Boston-based landscape architects, the Olmsteads. (The Olmsteads also designed Boston's Emerald Necklace and New York's Central Park.) The **Western Promenade,** first laid out in 1836, is another part of this grand plan. Sited on the edge of a 175-foot-high plateau, it commands a long view to the west (theoretically you can see Mt. Washington on a clear day) and serves as the front porch for Portland's poshest and most architecturally interesting residential neighborhood. You might want to pick up a copy of the Portland landmarks leaflet, "Guide to the Western Promenade" ($1) from the visitors bureau (see *Guidance*).

LODGING

HOTELS

There are 2000 hotel and motel rooms in and around Portland. Right downtown, within walking distance of the Portland Museum of Art and the Old Port, you can choose from the following hotels, all in Portland 04101.

The Eastland Plaza Hotel (775-5411 or 1-800-777-6246), 157 High Street. A 12-story landmark built in 1927, the hotel reclaimed its original name in January 1995. In the mid-1980s it fell to bankruptcy, and the bank owned the property for 10 years. In 1992 the building was purchased, and major renovations were done to bring back the character of the place. Its refurbished lobby and rooms now reflect the elegance of that long ago era. There are 204 guest rooms, many with harbor views. Geared to business travelers but a distinct cut above most small city hotels, the Plaza boasts attractive rooms, unusually friendly service (including elevator operators), original art in the hallways, Portland's only rooftop lounge, two restaurants, and van service to Freeport shops. $80–135 for a double, depending on season; includes breakfast. Ask about weekend packages.

Portland Regency (774-4200 or 1-800-727-3436), 20 Milk Street. The 95-room hotel, housed in a century-old armory in the middle of the Old Port Exchange, offers rooms decorated with reproduction antiques and equipped with amenities such as TV, two phones, and an honor bar. There is a formal dining room, attractive lounge, and a full health spa. Complimentary coffee with your wake-up call. $115–140 in high season, otherwise $95–130; no meals included.

Holiday Inn by the Bay (775-2311 or 1-800-HOLIDAY), 88 Spring Street. It is a high-rise, 236-room hotel. $44–87, slightly more in high season.

Hotel Everett (773-7882), 51A Oak Street. Describing itself as an "informal, European-style hotel with a homelike atmosphere," this is a welcoming, inexpensive place to stay that's a step up from the Y. There's a browsing library next to the front desk, and many of the patrons are young job hunters. $35–49.

Portland Hall (874-3281), 645 Congress Street, is a summer (June through August) AYH hostel with comfortable dorm-style lodging right across from the Portland Museum of Art. Under $20 per person.

Note: Portland does have the major chains, but they are mainly located by I-95 at Exit 8 in Westbrook, or in South Portland by the mall.

INNS AND BED & BREAKFASTS

Pomegranate Inn (772-1006 or 1-800-356-0408), 49 Neal Street, Portland 04102. This is an extraordinary place to stay. Isabel and Alan Smiles have turned an 1880s Western Promenade house into a work of art. Nothing stiff, just one surprise for the eye after another. An interior designer and former antiques dealer, Isabel has created eight amazing rooms furnished in a mix of antiques and "objets," most with hand-painted walls (not wallpapered) in bold, original designs. Downstairs, the walls of the wide entryway are a hand-mottled tangerine, and the mantel and four columns in the living room are marbelized. Guest rooms have phones, discreet TVs, and private baths, and the living room is well stocked with art books. Breakfast is exquisite. Frankly, we're glad we stayed here before its fame spread, because what has since been described as the Pomegranate's "high style" came as a complete surprise. Still, repeat visits have been as good as the first. $95–150 per room in-season, $85–125 off-season, includes breakfast.

The Inn on Carleton Street (775-1910), Portland 04102. An attractive town house in the Western Promenade area offers seven rooms equipped with marble-topped sinks and furnished with Victorian-era antiques. We like the feel of this place. Proprietor Sue Cox makes guests feel welcome, and they tend to form a congenial group around the breakfast table. No smoking. From $49 for a single, off-season, with shared bath, to $95 for a double in summer with private bath.

The Inn at Park Spring (774-1059), 135 Spring Street, Portland 04101. An 1835 three-story town house very near the Portland Museum of Art and Congress Street shops and restaurants. Innkeeper Judi Riley welcomes guests to one of seven elegant guest rooms, some with fireplaces and decks or terraces. Breakfast is brought to your room or served in the kitchen, living room, or courtyard. $75–95, includes tea and brandy as well as breakfast.

Interior of Pomegranate Inn

On Casco Bay Islands
(See the island descriptions under *Boat Excursions.*)

The Chebeague Inn By-the-Sea (864-5155), Chebeague Island 04017. Open Memorial Day through September. A three-story, flat-roofed summer hotel set high on a knoll. What we like about this place is the large, open-beamed living room with its massive stone fireplace, brightly upholstered chairs, and rainy-day board games. The 21 guest rooms (15 with private bath) have a nice, sea-washed feel and are decorated simply but with taste. All three meals are served in July and August. On sunny days you can play golf (the nine-hole public course is just below the hotel), swim at Hamilton Beach, or explore the island by bike, and on rainy days you can take the 15-minute ferry to Cousins Island not far from Freeport's shops. Casco Bay Line service to Portland leaves from the other end of the island (shuttle service is available from the hotel). $70–130 for a double in high season includes a full breakfast; less in May and June. Warning: Be sure to get detailed directions to the Cousins Island ferry and inquire about parking options.

Diamond Cove (772-2992, 766-5804 for reservations), PO Box 3572, Portland 04104 (on Great Diamond Island, served by regular Casco Bay Line service from Portland). Nineteenth-century Fort McKinley on Great Diamond Island has been turned into an exclusive resort area offering townhouse rentals and sales. Amenities include health club, beaches, a restaurant, tennis courts, a heated pool, and walking path and woodland area for hiking, biking, and cross-country skiing. In-season there's a 2-night minimum at $160–200 per couple per night; all units have fully equipped kitchens; weekly rates run $1000–1890; 15 percent discount off season.

Keller's (766-2441), Box 8, Peaks Island 04108. Open year-round. Just up from the ferry landing, a former general store and restaurant is now a home with four guest rooms, all with water views and full baths. Innkeeper Carolyn Parker provides guests with a map of the island, marked with points of interest. Beach on the property. $60 single, $75 double, includes a full breakfast with Belgian waffles, pastries, fresh fruit, and beverages. No credit cards (personal checks accepted).

Beyond Portland

Inn by the Sea (799-3134), Route 77, Cape Elizabeth 04107. Just a 10-minute drive from downtown Portland (Cape Elizabeth is a residential neighborhood of the city), this luxurious resort is sited on a rise above Crescent Beach (part of the state park), facing the ocean. The marble lobby is hung with Audubon prints, and accommodations include one- and two-bedroom garden and loft suites, cottages, and a beach house. Furnishings include reproduction antiques, down comforters, TVs, VCRs; all units have kitchens, a living/dining area, patios, and water view. The landscaping is superb, and there is a boardwalk to the beach. Amenities include an outdoor pool, tennis courts, and croquet. The dining room specializes in creative American with a Pacific Coast flair. July and August, $195–310 per night; May and June, September and October, $160–250; November to March, $75–180. No meals included.

Black Point Inn Resort (883-4126), Prouts Neck 04074. Open early May to late October. Easily one of the most elegant inns in the state; a vintage 1878 summer hotel that is so much a part of its exclusive community that guests are permitted to use the Prouts Neck Country Club's 18-hole golf course and 14 tennis courts. Guests may also rent boats or moor their own at the local Yacht Club. Public rooms are extensive and elegant with views of the south coast on one side and of the open ocean on the other. Facilities include two sandy beaches, indoor and outdoor pools, two Jacuzzis, a sauna, and a manned elevator. There are 80 rooms, poolside buffets with a pianist, afternoon tea, evening cocktails, and dancing. No children under age eight. A London taxi serves as a shuttle to the airport and into Portland. $260–360 for double MAP per night plus 15 percent gratuity. A $10 noon buffet is offered. See Prouts Neck under *Green Space*.

Higgins Beach Inn (883-6684), 34 Ocean Avenue, Scarborough 04074 (7 miles south of Portland). Open Memorial Day to Columbus Day. An 1890s, three-story, wooden summer hotel near sandy Higgins Beach. The pleasant dining room, open July and August, features home cooking prepared with Gram's secret "receipts." There is also a cocktail lounge, homey TV room, and a sun porch. Upstairs, the 24 guest rooms are basic but clean and airy, 14 with private bath. Continental breakfast is available after Labor Day. Owners Jack and Carlene Harrison have been improving this old place steadily over the past 27 years and take pride in the fact (as they should) that their rates haven't risen in three years. $60–75 for a double per day or $364–455 per week in-season; an even better bargain at $588–679 for a double MAP. Cheaper in shoulder months.

COTTAGES

South of Portland, cottages in the Higgins Beach and Pine Point areas can be found through the Scarborough Chamber of Commerce (772-2811), 142 Free Street, Portland 04101. Seasonal rentals are also listed in the *Maine Sunday Telegram.* For listings on summer cottages in the Casco Bay Islands, contact Casco Bay Development Association, Peaks Island 04108.

Also check the "Maine Guide to Camp & Cottage Rentals" available from the Maine Publicity Bureau (623-0363).

WHERE TO EAT

The claim is that Portland has more restaurants per capita than any other city in America. Take a look at the following partial list, and you will begin to believe it. The quality of the dining is as exceptional as the quantity. People from all over Maine look forward to a reason for dining in Portland. Enjoy!

DINING OUT

In and around the Old Port Exchange

Walter's Cafe (871-9258), 15 Exchange Street. Open for lunch and dinner daily. A very popular storefront space that's been deftly transformed into a bistro. Lunch includes unusual soups and salads, with hot entrées ranging from burgers to pasta dishes like sausage and capiccola with olive oil and seasonings on spinach penne. At dinner there are nightly specials; usually also grilled lamb and fish dishes. $8.95–13.95.

Cafe Always (774-9399), 47 Middle Street. Open for dinner except Sunday, Monday. A small, strikingly decorated (in yellow and black), Old Port standout. Though not right in the middle of all the activity, it's worth finding. The menu changes daily and might include lobster sautéed with Jamaican butter sauce and grilled venison with sun-dried cherry sauce. Save room for the outstanding desserts, maybe chocolate shortcake with native berries and sweet cream. $15–20.

David's (773-4340), 164 Middle Street. Open for lunch and dinner, this new popular spot features casual cafe dining with raw bar upstairs, candlelight dining downstairs. Features unique creations by the chef, possibly seared salmon with lobster *beurre rouge,* basil, and sherry, or breast of duck with maple-and-ginger-baked acorn squash. $7–19.

Street & Company (775-0887), 33 Wharf Street. Open for lunch and dinner year-round. A small, informal, incredibly popular (make reservations) seafood place. Seafood grilled, broiled, pan-blackened, and steamed, much of it served right in the pan it's been cooked in. A specialty is lobster diavolo for two, served over linguine. Entrées: $15–20.

☞ **The Afghan Restaurant** (773-3431), 90 Exchange Street. Open for lunch and dinner except Sunday. Authentic Afghan food at reasonable prices. This storefront restaurant is hung with scenes of Afghanistan painted by the owner. Try the combination plate. Bring your own wine. Entrée and dessert are less than $10.

The Pepperclub (772-0531), 78 Middle Street. Open for dinner nightly. Vegetarian heaven: soups, rice and bean dishes, some fish, chicken, organic beef, zany decor, imported beers. Under $10, no credit cards.

Hugo's Portland Bistro (774-8538), 88 Middle Street. Dinner Tuesday through Saturday. Eclectic, mismatched antiques decor and a varied menu. Specialties include Maine crabcakes, fresh fruit sherry trifle, and Irish coffee. Check out the imported beer list. $10–15.

The Seamen's Club (772-7311), 375 Fore Street. Open 11–11 daily. Try to get a table upstairs in the library by the Gothic window so you can watch shoppers hustling along the brick sidewalks below. Very pleasant service and atmosphere. Best at lunch, but also offering candlelight dining. Often has bands in the bar on weekends. Entrées: $3.95–11.95.

Baker's Table (775-0303 or 773-3333), 434 Fore Street (also an entrance on Wharf Street). Open daily, 10–10. The lunchtime specials are chowders, sandwiches, and bistro fare. Dinner is full-service dining with candlelight. Diverse European and New England fare, fresh-baked desserts. Dinner entrées: $10.95–18.95.

DiMillo's Floating Restaurant (772-2216), Long Wharf. Open for lunch and dinner. Maine's only floating restaurant, this converted car ferry serves seafood, steaks, and Italian cuisine to customers who come as much for the old nautical atmosphere and the views of the waterfront as they do for the food. Entrées run $8.95–24.95 (shore dinner with chowder, salad, lobster, steamed clams, vegetable, potato, ice cream and beverage).

F. Parker Reidy's (773-4731), 83 Exchange Street. Open for lunch, dinner, late supper. One of the first restaurants to open (in the former Portland Savings Bank) when the Old Port was coming back to life. This is the traditional place to go after a Pirates' hockey game at the nearby Cumberland County Civic Center (see *Entertainment*). Victorian atmosphere, very cheery bar. Steaks, seafood, and fashionable fare. Entrées: $10.95–15.95.

Boone's Restaurant (774-5725), 6 Custom House Wharf. Open for lunch and dinner year-round. Still going strong since it opened in 1896, serving lobster and seafood specialties at competitive prices. A real slice of the waterfront's long history. $4.95–12.95.

Beyond the Old Port

The Diamond's Edge (766-5708 or 797-6241), Great Diamond Island. Open in summer for lunch and dinner. Reservations a must. A short

The Seamen's Club in Portland

ride on the Casco Bay Line brings you to this fairly formal restaurant in a century-old warehouse overlooking Diamond Cove. Daily specials, local fish featured. Dinner entrées: $11–17.

West Side (773-8223), 58 Pine Street. Serving breakfast, lunch, and dinner; brunch Sunday. A find. A delightful café near the Western Promenade with an informal, friendly atmosphere featuring rotating paintings by local artists. With new owners, the style of cuisine changed significantly, but the fare is still delicious. New menus biweekly, with fresh game, Maine seafood, and organic produce. A recent menu included delectable mahogany clams over pasta with sun-dried tomatoes, and venison medallions with cracked pepper and Merlot sauce. $10.95–18.95.

☞ **Will's** (766-3322), Island Avenue, Peaks Island. Since there is limited inside-seating, the time to lunch or dine at Will's is on a summer day when you can sit on the deck and enjoy the view of Portland's waterfront across the harbor. Burgers are always a possibility, but there are also some great seafood specials. Wine by the glass. Under $10 for an entire dinner.

Madd Apple Café (774-9698), 23 Forest Street. Open for dinner Tuesday through Saturday at 5:30; adjacent to the Portland Performing Arts Center. The accent is southern here, and the menu includes Caribbean and Creole dishes and reliables like barbecued lamb ribs, pan-fried trout, and red beans and rice. Dinner entrées: $8.95–15.95.

Back Bay Grill (772-8833), 65 Portland Street. Open for dinner nightly. The 20-foot mural of Portland is by Steve Quattruci, a professional artist and former maître d' at Boston's Ritz Café. The menu changes daily but consistently includes some memorable soups, grilled pizza appetizers, pastas, and grilled (yes, grilled) lobster. Entrées: $15.00–21.75.

Snow Squall Restaurant (799-2232 or 1-800-568-3260), 18 Ocean Street, South Portland waterfront (on Route 77 en route to Portland Head Light). Lunch weekdays, dinner nightly, Sunday brunch. Try the crabcakes or clam chowder for lunch, grilled salmon fillets or lobster fettuccine for dinner. Entrées: $9.95–17.50.

South of Portland

Black Point Inn (883-4126), Prouts Neck. Dining by reservation in a formal dining room with water views. The menu changes nightly; varies from basics like Yankee pot roast and boiled lobster to Cajun-style sautéed shrimp on angelhair; extravagant desserts. $30 prix fixe plus tax and gratuity.

North of Portland

The Galley Restaurant (781-4262), 215 Foreside Road, Falmouth. Lunch and dinner daily. One of Maine's dining landmarks, overlooking a working marina. Specialties include seafood linguini and five different haddock dishes. Entrées: $12.95–17.95.

The Cannery Restaurant at Lower Falls Landing (846-1226), Yarmouth. Open daily for lunch and dinner, Sunday brunch. Built in 1913 as a herring factory; then served as a sardine-packing plant from the 1920s right up until 1980. The building, now part of a complex that includes a marina and some interesting shops, makes an attractive restaurant space with a waterside terrace. Prices are reasonable, but portions can be small. $7.95–15.95.

Moose Crossing Fish 'n' Steak House (781-4771), Route 1, Falmouth. Open for dinner. The atmosphere is "Maine cabin" with tongue-and-groove paneling, old camping gear, antlers, and old photos of the Moosehead Lake Region. Specialties are mesquite-grilled fish and poultry. There is a wide selection of fish specials nightly. Entrées: $7.50–15.95.

EATING OUT

In the Old Port

Note: Most of the restaurants described under *Dining Out* also serve a reasonably priced lunch.

The Porthole (774-3448), 32 Customs Wharf. Open early for breakfast, also lunch and dinner. Great chowder; breakfast dishes at unbeatable prices. Cheerful service at both counter and tables. Great all-you-can-eat fish fry ($3.95 at lunch, $5.95 at dinner). If you stick your head in and don't like what you see, this isn't for you. What you see is what you get. This is the last holdout on the funky former Casco Bay wharf.

Dock Fore (772-8619), 336 Fore Street. Open for lunch and dinner. A sunny, casual pub (most seating is at the bar or sidebar) serving hearty fare and homelike specialties. Large portions at good prices.

Village Café (772-5320), 112 Newbury Street. Open for lunch and dinner except Sunday. This is an old family favorite that pre-dates the Old Port renaissance (it's just east of the Old Port). The third generation of the Realis family is now welcoming patrons to the same comfortable place. A large, often crowded space with pasta specialties but standard American fare, too.

Anthony's Italian Kitchen (774-8668), 151 Middle Street. This is a great little place, always crowded at lunch time. It smells like a real Italian kitchen, and the aromas are not misleading. Terrific pizza and specials, service that makes you feel like an old friend.

Gritty McDuff's (772-2739), 396 Fore Street. A brew pub specializing in its own ales, stouts, and bitters, with such pub fare as fish and chips and shepherd's pie. Predictable wood and rugby decor.

Carbur's (772-7794), 123 Middle Street. Serves lunch and dinner daily. Be prepared to choose the first menu item on which your eye falls or to study the 20-page menu carefully to select the one thing that appeals to you the very most. This is a fun place, where all the sandwiches (their specialty) are big enough for a meal and come with outrageous names.

Near the Portland Museum of Art

Note: The museum has its own garden café in summer.

Ruby's Choice (773-9099), 116 Free Street. Burgers, burgers, and more burgers—but very fancy ones, with toppings such as humus, cilantro salsa, garlic dressing, pickled vegetables, lettuce, onions, and tomatoes that you put on yourself at a toppings bar. Other specialties include burritos and deep-fried scrod on a bun. The burgers come in two sizes: half pounders and one-third pounders. A great place to entertain the kids while you get a good meal into them.

Beyond Portland

The Lobster Shack (799-1677), Cape Elizabeth (off Route 77 at the tip of the cape, near Two Lights State Park). Open for lunch and dinner April to mid-October. A local landmark since the 1920s, set below the lighthouse and next to the fog horn. Dine inside or out. This is the place to pick a lobster out of the tank and watch it being boiled—then eat it "in the rough." Herb and Martha Porch are also known for their chowder and lobster stew, fried Maine shrimp, scallops and clams, lobster, and crabmeat rolls.

Spurwink Country Kitchen (799-1177), 150 Spurwink Road (near Scarborough Beach), Scarborough. Open mid-April to mid-October, 11:30–9. Part of this place's beauty is that it's here at all, right where you wouldn't expect to find a place to eat. Then you discover it's a special place, looking much the same and serving much the same food as when Hope Sargent opened it in 1955. Specials vary with the day and include soup, potato, vegetable or rolls, tea or coffee. Tuesday is homemade meatloaf or grilled liver and onion, Wednesday is homemade chicken pie ($6.95) or angelhair pasta. On Sunday you can choose from roast pork or roast lamb (each $8.95). Great homemade pies.

COFFEE BARS

Green Mountain Coffee Roasters/Bagel Works (773-4475), 15 Temple Street, Portland. A shop that sells all sorts of coffee beans and teas as well as elaborate equipment for preparing the perfect cup of either at home. Coffees and teas on one side, numerous varieties of bagels and juices on the other.

Portland Coffee Roasting, Co. (761-9525), 111 Commercial Street, Portland. A cozy little place offering baked goods and gourmet coffee. Also a selection of gift items.

Java Joes (761-5637), 13 Exchange Street, Portland. A good place to go for late-night coffee and conversation.

ENTERTAINMENT

Cumberland County Civic Center (775-3481; hot line: 775-3825), 1 Civic Center Square, Portland. A modern, 9000-seat arena, the site of year-round concerts, special presentations, ice-skating spectaculars, winter hockey games, and other events. Pick up a free monthly calendar of events.

State Theater (879-1112), 609 Congress Street, Portland. This 1729 vaudeville/movie house is the only one of seven that still survives. Rescued from its declining state and completely restored in 1993, the theater is elegant, with a fountain, murals, and gilded proscenium arch. It now hosts a variety of activities, including concerts, theater, movies, and private functions.

MUSIC

Portland Symphony Orchestra (773-8191), City Hall Auditorium, 389 Congress Street, Portland. The winter series runs October to April, Tuesdays at 7:45 PM. In the summertime, the symphony delights audiences throughout the state at outdoor pops concerts in some of the most beautiful settings, such as overlooking Casco Bay or by Camden Harbor.

LARK Society for Chamber Music/Portland String Quartet (761-1522). This distinguished chamber group grows in stature every year; performances are in a variety of Portland locations as well as around the state.

Portland Concert Association (772-8630). Sponsors orchestra, jazz, opera, musical theater in various locations; throughout Maine in the summer.

PROFESSIONAL SPORTS

In the 1993–94 season, Portland welcomed three new professional sports teams. The **Portland Pirates** (828-4665) brought ice hockey back to the city with a bang, winning the Calder cup, the highest honor in their division. Home games are played at the Cumberland County Civic Center. The **Portland Sea Dogs,** a double-A baseball team, play in newly constructed Hadlock Stadium on Park Avenue (next to the Expo). Finally, the **New England Stingers** brought a unique sport, roller hockey (played on in-line skates) to Portland in the summer of 1994.

THEATER

Portland Performing Arts Center, 25A Forest Avenue (just off Congress Street), Portland. The city's old Odd Fellows Hall now houses an elegant, intimate, 290-seat theater that serves as home base for the **Portland Stage Company** (774-0465 for tickets), which performs September to April, and for the **Ram Island Dance Company** (773-2562), which stages weekend performances year-round.

Portland Players (799-7337), Thaxter Theater, 420 Cottage Road, South Portland, also stages productions September to June.

Portland Lyric Theater (799-1421), Cedric Thomas Playhouse, 176 Sawyer Street, South Portland. This community theater presents four musicals each winter.

Oak Street Theatre (775-5103), 92 Oak Street. Newly renovated with 90 seats, its performances range from comedy to jazz and classic drama.

SELECTIVE SHOPPING

The Old Port Exchange has become the center for shopping and is filled with handicrafts, imported clothing, art, home furnishings, jewelry, books, and much, much more. Most Old Port shops are owner-operated and have been restored individually. We have returned home from Portland laden with purchases ranging from an egg separator to a dining room table. Even when you are not shopping, it is always pleasant to stroll along the Old Port's brick sidewalks, pausing at a bench beneath a gas lamp to watch the shoppers. At Christmas time, with all of the decorations and fairy lights, it resembles an old English town.

The Old Port hosts a half-dozen noteworthy galleries. Other favorite stores include the **Whip & Spoon,** a fascinating Commercial Street emporium that sells every imaginable piece of cookware plus gourmet foods and wines, and **Maine Potters Market,** a 14-member crafts cooperative in the Mariner's Church, Fore Street. **Nancy Margolis Gallery** (367 Fore Street) reserves half its space for special museum-quality shows, the remainder for selling unusual crafts pieces. **Abacus/ Handcrafters Gallery** (44 Exchange Street) offers two floors full of crafted items, from jewelry to furniture. **The Stein Glass Gallery** (20

Milk Street) displays stunning pieces by 40 artists. The clothiers in the Old Port are **A.H. Benoit,** an old Portland institution moved from Congress to Middle Street, and **Joseph's** (410 Fore Street), featuring well-tailored clothing for both men and women.

There are stores dedicated to selling records, posters, ballet outfits, tobacco, wood stoves, canvas bags, cheese, woodenware, paper products, art materials, stencil equipment, games, potting supplies, herbs, children's toys and clothing, and more.

Beyond Portland proper is the **Maine Mall** (Exit 7 off I-95), whose immediate complex of more than 100 stores is supplemented by large shopping centers and chain stores that ring it for several miles.

BOOKSTORES

In the past couple of years, Portland has become a mecca for book lovers. **Books Etc.** (38 Exchange Street) is a very inviting store. **Bookland's** in-town store at One Monument Way stocks a full range of books and has a great children's section and bargain table. **Raffle's Cafe Bookstore** (55 Congress Street) caters to browsers and serves breakfast, lunch, and dinner. **Harbour Books** (846-6306), at Lower Falls Landing, Yarmouth, is part of the same rehabbed sardine cannery complex that includes the Cannery Restaurant. This is a very special independent bookstore, the kind book lovers will feel completely comfortable in and probably walk out of with something they never intended to buy. Soft music, views of the harbor, and bargain tables. Open daily 9–6, Friday until 8 PM, Sunday 12–5. Visible from I-95; take Exit 17.

SPECIAL EVENTS

First Sunday in June: **Old Port Festival**—special sales and a special performance in the streets that make up the Old Port.

Mid-July: **Family Festival**—something for every age; formerly held in Deering Oaks Park, but a new location will be found beginning in 1995. Also the **Yarmouth Clam Festival** in downtown Yarmouth.

August: **Cumberland Crafts Fair,** Cumberland Fair Grounds. **Sidewalk Art Festival,** Congress Street.

December 31: **Portland New Year's Celebration**—modeled after the First Night begun in Boston, with performances throughout the city from afternoon through midnight.

Freeport

Think of Freeport, and you think of shopping; but hidden behind the discounts and bargain stores is a history more than 200 years old. The area was granted a charter separating itself from North Yarmouth in 1789. With the War of 1812, shipbuilding became an important industry, with one famous ship inspiring Whittier's poem, "The Dead Ship of Harpswell." The town is particularly proud of the fact that in 1820 the papers separating Maine from Massachusetts were signed in the historical Jameson Tavern (see *Dining Out*).

These days, shopping is high on visitors' lists. Each year as many as 15,000 cars per day squeeze up and down the mile of Main Street (Route 1) that is lined on both sides with upscale, off-price shops. L.L. Bean, ranked not only as Maine's number-one emporium but also as its number-one man-made attraction, has been a shopping landmark for over 75 years. The establishment of more than 100 neighboring outlet stores, however, didn't begin until the early 1980s.

Although the shops are the major draw for most travelers, the village has retained the appearance of older days—even McDonalds has been confined to a gracious old Colonial house, with no golden arches in sight. Some come to the area simply to stroll wooded paths in Wolfe's Neck Woods State Park and the Maine Audubon's Mast Landing Sanctuary. The Desert of Maine is also an interesting sight. The quiet countryside and waterside retreats away from the crowds are enjoyed by many.

GUIDANCE

The **Freeport Merchants Association** (865-1212), PO Box 452, Freeport 04032, does not have a visitors center, but they gladly respond to telephone and mail requests for information. Among the materials they send out is their excellent, free visitor's guide containing maps and a list of all the stores, restaurants, accommodations, and other services. Be sure to get one in advance or pick one up as soon as you arrive in town—almost all the merchants have them.

The **Maine Publicity Bureau's** welcome center in Kittery stocks some Freeport brochures, and there is a state information center on Route 1 just south of Freeport, in Yarmouth, at Exit 17 off I-95. In Freeport itself, you'll find a limited selection of brochures at L.L. Bean's information desk and in a small building on Depot Street, which also houses public rest rooms.

GETTING THERE

Bus service to Freeport from Boston and Portland is available via **Greyhound. Mid Coast Limo** runs to and from the Portland Jetport (1-800-834-5500 within Maine, or 1-800-937-2424 outside Maine). A number of **bus tour companies** also offer shopping trips to Freeport from Boston and beyond. Most people drive, which means there's often a shortage of parking spaces, especially in peak season. The best solution to this problem is to stay at an inn or B&B within walking distance and leave your car there.

MEDICAL EMERGENCY

Mid Coast Hospital (729-0181), 58 Baribeau Drive, Brunswick.

VILLAGES

South Freeport has been a fishing center from the start. Between 1825 and 1830 up to 12,000 barrels of mackerel were packed and shipped from here each year. Later, the area specialty became crabmeat packing. A very different feel from the chaotic shopping frenzy of downtown Freeport, the harbor is still bustling with activity and offers some great seafood. From here you can take a cruise to explore Eagle Island in the summer.

Porter's Landing. Once the center of commercial activity, this is now a quiet residential neighborhood, amid rolling hills, woods, and streams. The village is part of the Harraseeket Historic District in the National Register of Historic Places.

TO SEE AND DO

Desert of Maine (865-6962), Desert Road, Freeport (3 miles from L.L. Bean). Open daily, mid-May to mid-October, 9 AM to dusk. Narrated coach tours ($4.75 adults, $2.75 children, $4.25 senior citizens) and self-guided walks through 40 acres of sand that was once the Tuttle Farm. Heavily farmed, then extensively logged to feed the railroad, the topsoil eventually gave way to the glacial sand deposit beneath it, which spread . . . and spread until entire trees sank below the surface. It is an unusual sand, rich in mineral deposits that make it unsuited for commercial use but interesting to rock hounds. Children love it. There's also a sand museum and a 1783 barn museum here, plus gift and souvenir shops; 2½ miles from downtown Freeport. Overnight camping available.

Freeport Balloon Company (865-1712), Bob Scheurer, RR 4, Box 4392, Freeport. Year-round hot-air balloon flights, weather permitting, just after sunrise and a few hours before sunset. Most trips last a little over an hour and cover from 5 to 12 miles; there's a champagne toast after touchdown. Rates start at $125 per person (the balloon accommodates up to three plus pilot). Reservation with deposit required.

BOAT EXCURSIONS

Anjin-San (772-7168), near town landing, South Freeport. A 34-foot sportfishing boat custom-built for Captain Greg Walts. Day trips for mackerel, bluefish, and shark. Also sightseeing and diving trips, and charters.

Atlantic Seal (865-6112), Town Wharf, South Freeport. Memorial Day through mid-October. Daily trips aboard this 40-footer out into Casco Bay include three-hour cruises to Eagle Island, former summer home of Admiral Robert E. Peary, the first man to reach the North Pole. Seal- and osprey-sighting trips and fall foliage cruises after Labor Day. Lobstering demonstrations are usually included, except Sunday when lobstering is prohibited by Maine law.

CANOEING

The **Harraseeket River** in Freeport is particularly nice for canoeing. Start at Mast Landing, the northeastern end of the waterway; there are also launching sites at Winslow Memorial Park on Staples Point Road and at South Freeport Harbor. Phone the **Maine Audubon Society** in Falmouth (781-2330) for details about periodic, scheduled guided trips through the area. Nearby lake canoeing can be found at **Run Around Pond** in North Pownal (the parking lot is off Lawrence Road, 1 mile north of the intersection with Fickett Road).

GOLF

Freeport Country Club (865-4922), Old Country Road, Freeport. Nine holes.

CROSS-COUNTRY SKIING

The areas listed under *Green Space* are good cross-country skiing spots; rent or purchase equipment from L.L. Bean, which also offers classes in cross-country skiing (see *Special Learning Program*).

SPECIAL LEARNING PROGRAM

L.L. Bean Outdoor Discovery Program (865-3111), Route 1, Freeport. An interesting series of lectures and lessons that cover everything from cross-country ski lessons (on weekends beginning in January) and golf to survival in the Maine woods, making soap, tanning hides, paddling sea kayaks, building fly rods, cooking small game, and fishing for Atlantic salmon. Call 1-800-341-4341, ext. 6666 for free program guide.

GREEN SPACE

Winslow Memorial Park (865-4198), Staples Point Road, South Freeport. Open Memorial Day through September. A 90-acre municipal park with a sandy beach and large, grassy picnicking area; also boating and camping. Facilities include rest rooms with showers. Admission fee.

✐ **Wolfe's Neck Woods State Park** (865-4465), Wolfe's Neck Road (take Bow Street, across from L.L. Bean), Freeport. Open Memorial Day weekend to Labor Day weekend. Day-use fee. A 244-acre park with shoreline hiking along Casco Bay, the Harraseeket River, and salt marshes. Guided nature walks are available; picnic tables and grills are scattered about.

Mast Landing Sanctuary, Upper Mast Landing Road (take Bow Street south), Freeport. Maintained by the Maine Audubon Society, this 100-acre sanctuary offers trails through apple orchards, woods, and meadows and along a mill stream. Several paths radiate from a 1-mile loop trail.

✐ **Bradbury Mountain State Park** (688-4712), Route 9, Hallowell Road, Pownal (just 6 miles from Freeport: from I-95 take Exit 20 and follow signs). Open May 15 through October 15. $2.50 per adult, $.50 children ages 5–11, under age 5 free. The summit, accessible by an easy hike (even for young children), yields a splendid view of Casco Bay and New Hampshire's White Mountains. Facilities in the 297-acre park include a small playground, a softball field, hiking trails, toilets, and a small overnight camping area.

Pettengill Farm (phone the Freeport Historical Society at 865-3170), Freeport. Open for periodic guided tours. A saltwater farm with 140 acres of open fields and woodland that overlook the Harraseeket Estuary, with a totally unmodernized, vintage 1810 saltbox house.

LODGING

All entries are for Freeport 04032 unless otherwise indicated.

INN

Harraseeket Inn (865-9377 or 1-800-342-6423), 162 Main Street. Just two blocks north of L.L. Bean, this luxury hotel is the largest in the area, with 54 rooms and 6 suites. It has maintained the elegant atmosphere of the 1850 Greek Revival house next door, where this operation first began as a five-room B&B. Nancy and Paul Gray are native Mainers, but their family also owns the Inn at Mystic, Connecticut, and they definitely know how to make the most of their location. Twenty-three of the rooms are decorated with antiques and reproductions and feature canopy beds and Jacuzzis or steam baths; 20 have fireplaces. The inn has its formal dining rooms and the casual Broad Arrow Tavern downstairs (see *Dining Out*). Other public rooms include a drawing room, library, and ballroom. Rates in-season are $145–225; full breakfast and afternoon tea are included. Two-night minimum stay required on some holiday weekends. Package plans available.

BED & BREAKFASTS

The **Freeport Area Bed & Breakfast Association** lists about a dozen members, all of which must meet certain standards established by the association. You can get a copy of their brochure by writing to PO Box

267, Freeport 04032. The majority of Freeport's B&Bs have opened in the past decade, since the shopping craze began. Many are in the handsome, old, white-clapboard Capes and Federal-style houses that stand side by side flanking Main Street just north of the shopping district.

The Isaac Randall House (865-9295), 5 Independence Drive. Open year-round. Historically, this property has been a dairy farm, dance hall, and tourist court. The handsome farmhouse became the first bed & breakfast in Freeport in 1984. There are eight air-conditioned rooms with antiques, oriental rugs, and lovely old quilts. Two have working fireplaces. The Loft, furnished all in wicker (including the king bed), is nice. A full breakfast is served in the beam-ceilinged country kitchen; a playground out back can keep children (who are welcome) entertained. Pets are also welcome. On a small street off Route 1, but within walking distance of downtown shopping area. Doubles are $70–105, breakfast and snacks included.

One-Eighty-One Main Street (865-1226), 181 Main Street. Open year-round. This 1840s grey Cape with white trim and black shutters has been featured in *Country Home,* and it's easy to see why. The seven guest rooms, all with private baths, are attractive and cozy. Furnishings include American primitive antiques from hosts David Cates's and Ed Hassett's collections, oriental rugs, and quilts made by David's mother. There are two parlors with books and games, gardens, and a swimming pool. Full breakfast, served at individual tables in the dining room, is included in the $95 room rate.

White Cedar Inn (865-9099), 178 Main Street. Open year-round. This restored, white-clapboard Victorian house was once the home of Arctic explorer Donald B. MacMillan, who went to the North Pole with Admiral Peary. There are six bedrooms with private baths and simple, but pretty, furnishings. Three have a single bed in addition to a double or queen. Our favorite room, up under the eaves, offers more privacy with its own staircase. Full breakfast, included, is served at small tables in the sun room, adjacent to the country kitchen. Innkeepers Carla and Phil Kerber live in the remodeled ell and barn that extend from the back of the inn. Doubles, $80–100.

Kendall Tavern Bed & Breakfast (865-1338), 213 Main Street. Open year-round. Slightly farther up Main Street than the others, but still just a half mile from the shopping district. This big, yellow-clapboard house with attached barn offers an indoor spa in addition to rooms with private baths and a choice of queen or twin beds. The two downstairs parlors have glowing wide-board floors and fireplaces. No smoking. Doubles in-season are $100–110 (for a room with a sitting area).

Holbrook Inn (865-6693), 7 Holbrook Street. Open year-round. Just a block from Main Street and all its shops (turn off at the Mikasa store), this very pleasant, century-old Victorian is operated by welcoming Freeport natives, Ralph and Bea Routhier. The rooms all have queen-sized beds, private baths, color TVs, air-conditioning, and antique furnishings. Double rooms are $75, including full breakfast.

Nicholson Inn (865-6404), 25 Main Street, at the corner of Holbrook Street. A small B&B with a long-standing tradition in hospitality. In the forties and fifties, the Nicholson family built a reputation for being warm hosts. Their granddaughter, Jane Grant, and her husband, Alden, have renovated the property and are carrying on the tradition with style. Rooms have queen beds, period furnishings, individual heat control, and private baths. The location, in the middle of town, makes shopping extremely convenient. Doubles are $90, including a full breakfast.

Maple Hill B&B (865-3730), 18 Maple Avenue. Open year-round. A short drive off Main Street just north of the shopping district, this hilltop farmhouse offers three guest rooms. The two upstairs with a shared bath are good for families (one has twin beds). The three-room suite downstairs has a private bath (the painted sink from Italy is fascinating) and living room. Guests can enjoy the fireplace in the sitting room. Hostess Barbara McGivaren's attention to detail ensures a pleasant stay. Rates are $75–90, including a full breakfast with choices like eggs Dijon or baked fondue.

Porter's Landing B&B (865-4488), 70 South Street. Open April through December. Peter and Barbara Guffin offer three guest rooms in the 1800s post-and-beam carriage house adjacent to their elegant home in the Historic District. Quiet country setting about a mile from L.L. Bean. The rooms, built to preserve the historic architectural details, have private baths and are furnished with antiques and handmade quilts. The large common room has a Count Rumford fireplace; the sunny, airy loft, with sky windows and books lining the walls, is a perfect place to read. Doubles are $95, including full breakfast that might feature Belgian waffles or the special Porter's Landing omelet.

Atlantic Seal B&B (865-6112), Main Street, Box 146, South Freeport 04078. Open year-round except for Christmas. Just 5 minutes away from downtown Freeport but eons away from the bustle, this 1850 Cape in the village of South Freeport boasts views of the harbor from each of its three guest rooms. Owned and operated by the owners of the *Atlantic Seal* tour boat, it is furnished with antiques and nautical collections. Rates, including "hearty sailor's breakfast," range from $65 for a double bed and shared bath to $85 for a queen bed with shared bath to $125 for a queen bed and a double with private shower. Resident dog. Guests also receive a discount on *Atlantic Seal* morning cruises. Van service from the Portland airport can be prearranged.

The Bagley House Bed and Breakfast (865-6566), RR 3, Box 269C; 10 minutes from downtown Freeport. This 1772 house was built as an inn. It also housed the first worship service in town and operated as a schoolhouse until one could be built. Susan Backhouse and Susan O'Connor fulfilled a lifelong dream when they purchased Bagley House in 1993.

Five guest rooms are furnished in antiques or custom-made pieces. Special touches include handsewn quilts and stenciled rugs. Two rooms have queen beds, the other doubles, and all have a private bath. No smoking. $95 double in-season, including full breakfast.

Country at Heart (865-0512), 37 Bow Street. Open year-round except Thanksgiving and Christmas. This circa 1870 house is brimming with country collectibles and cute accents. Each of the three guest rooms has a private bath and a theme: Shaker, Quilt, or Teddy Bear, with appropriate collections on display and antique and reproduction furnishings. The Dubays's little Lhasa Apso, Precious, enjoys welcoming guests. Full breakfast included in the $75–85 summer rates ($65–75 in winter). A gift shop, featuring counted cross-stitch and rug hooking kits and patterns, is off the dining room.

MOTELS

The Village Inn (865-3236), 186 Main Street. Eight units to the rear of an old house, each with color cable TV and air-conditioning. Walking distance to all the shops. Owned and operated by Freeport natives.

On Route 1, south of Freeport near the Yarmouth town line, there are a number of modern motels. Among these is the **Freeport Inn** (865-3106 or 1-800-99-VALUE), Route 1, Freeport. Set on 25 acres of lawns and nature trails, all rooms have wall-to-wall carpeting, cable TV, air-conditioning, and in-room phones. Doubles are $69–99 in-season. There's also a swimming pool and a pond where you can ice skate in winter. Canoes are available for paddling on the Cousins River. The inn's café and bakery serves breakfast and lunch and operates the Muddy Rudder (see *Eating Out*) just down the road.

CAMPGROUNDS

Sandy Cedar Haven Campground (865-6254), Baker Road, Freeport. Forty-five mostly wooded sites, each with fireplace and picnic table. Water and electricity hook-ups. Five tent sites. Store with wood, ice, and groceries. Two miles from Route 1 and downtown Freeport.

Desert of Maine Campgrounds (865-6962), 95 Desert Road, Freeport. Wooded and open sites adjacent to this natural glacial sand deposit (see *To See and Do*). Hook-ups, hot showers, laundry, convenience store, propane, fire rings and picnic tables, horseshoe pits, nature trails. Campsites are $15–18 per night.

WHERE TO EAT

DINING OUT

Fiddlehead Farm and Country Café (865-0466), Independence Drive and Lower Main Street, Freeport. Open year-round. This exceptional restaurant in a restored 1800s Greek Revival farmhouse continues to please diners with attentive but unpretentious service and an imaginative menu. Highlights include scaloppine done several ways, plus lamb chops, unusual pasta combinations, and lovely fresh seafood with simple but special sauces. Most entrées are under $20. A fireplace adds warmth to the decor—wide-pine floors, flowered wallpaper, simply swagged curtains. The Country Café offers casual, moderately priced, home-style meals. There's also a bakery on the premises.

Harraseeket Inn (865-9377), 162 Main Street, Freeport. Open year-round. Continental cuisine and elegant service in three formal dining rooms. The chef uses fresh ingredients from local gardeners and farm-ers in-season and creates such delicacies as grilled mushroom risotto, Maine lobster clambake (a complete dinner with dessert) two-texture duckling, and three dishes for two (one is châteaubriand, $50 for two) prepared at the table. Desserts are sure to please here, too. In addition to dinner, the Harraseeket is known for its outstanding Sunday brunch, which often features such delicacies as caviar, oysters on the halfshell, and even venison. The inn also serves lunch, high tea, and a breakfast buffet. $14.95–22.95. Proper attire is required; reservations suggested.

Jameson Tavern (865-4195), 115 Main Street, Freeport. Lunch and din-ner are served in several inviting dining rooms in the tavern where the papers separating Maine from Massachusetts were signed in 1820. Spe-cialties include chicken Provençal and tavern scampi. $13.50–17.95.

EATING OUT

The Broad Arrow Tavern (865-9377), Harraseeket Inn, 162 Main Street, Freeport. Downstairs in this elegant inn, the atmosphere is relaxed and pubby. The menu is appropriate to the setting.

Crickets Restaurant (865-4005), Lower Main Street, Freeport. Open daily for breakfast, lunch, and dinner, plus Sunday brunch. The almost over-whelming lunch/dinner menu offers something for just about everyone, from generous specialty sandwiches ($6–8), to fajitas, to six pasta dishes, to heavier steak and seafood entrées (most entrées between $9 and $15). We're particularly intrigued with the crumb-coated, deep-fried lobster tails.

Tap Room (865-4195), Jameson Tavern, 115 Main Street, Freeport. This informal tavern to the rear of the building serves inexpensive snacks and sandwiches until late in the evening.

Blue Onion (865-9396), Lower Main Street, Freeport. Open for lunch and dinner except Monday. A charming dining room in an old, blue road-side house located south of Freeport's downtown traffic squeeze. Soups, salads, quiche for lunch; baked and broiled fish, lobster pie, and other fish, veal, and chicken dishes for supper. No liquor.

Muddy Rudder (846-3082), Route 1, Freeport. Operated by the nearby Freeport Inn, this newly renovated, popular restaurant serves a wide selection of seafood dishes plus steaks, sandwiches, and salads; you can also have a full clambake on the deck. The atmosphere is relaxed, with piano music in the evening. Overlooking the water.

Harraseeket Lunch & Lobster Co. (865-4888), South Freeport (turn off

Route 1 at the giant wooden Indian outside Levinsky's, then turn right at a stop sign a few miles down). Open May through October. In the middle of the Harraseeket boatyard, this dockside pound is where you order lobsters and clams on one side, fried food on the other, and eat at picnic tables (of which there are never enough at peak hours) overlooking a boat-filled harbor. There is also a small, inside dining room. Worth seeking out.

Ocean Farms Market Restaurant (865-3101), 23 Main Street, Freeport. Breakfast, lunch, and dinner. Offers moderately priced seafood dishes, homemade chowder, and live boiled lobsters. Lobsters also packed to travel.

The Corsican (865-9421), 9 Mechanic Street, Freeport. Seafood, chicken, and vegetarian entrées. Takeout menu, too.

The Lobster Cooker (865-4349), 39 Main Street, Freeport. Steamed lobster, sandwiches, chowders; dining on the outdoor patio. Beer and wine.

China Rose (865-6886), 10 School Street, Freeport. Good and reasonably priced, specializing in Szechuan-Mandarin and Hunan food.

SELECTIVE SHOPPING

☞ FREEPORT FACTORY OUTLETS

As noted in the introduction to this chapter, Freeport's 125-plus factory outlets constitute what has probably become Maine's mightiest tourist magnet. *Boston Globe* writer Nathan Cobb described it well: "A shoppers' theme park spread out at the foot of L.L. Bean, the high church of country chic." Cobb quoted a local landlord: "The great American pastime now is shopping, not hiking."

Although hiking and hunting put L.L. Bean on the tourist map in the first place, tourists in Freeport are intently studying the map of shops these days. L.L. Bean has kept step by selling fashionable, sporty clothing and an incredible range of sporting equipment, books, gourmet products and gifts, as well as its golden boot.

L.L. Bean contends that it attracts at least 2.5 million customers annually—roughly twice the population of Maine. In the early 1980s, neighboring property owners began to claim a portion of this traffic. Instead of relegating the outlets to malls (see "Kittery and the Yorks"), they have deftly draped them in brick and clapboard, actually improving on the town's old looks (although longtime shopkeepers who were forced to move because of skyrocketing real estate prices might well disagree). Ample parking lots are sequestered behind the Main Street facade (it's still sometimes tough to find a space). In summer there is a festive atmosphere, with hot-dog and ice-cream vendors on key corners. But it is the quality of the shops that ensures a year-round crowd. Just about any well-known clothing, accessory, and home furnishing line has a factory store here. The following is a selected list of some of the more unique outlets offered. Many stores claim 20–70 percent off suggested retail prices, and even L.L. Bean has a separate outlet store.

L.L. Bean (1-800-221-4221 for orders; 1-800-341-4341 for customer service), 95 Main Street. Open 24 hours a day, 365 days a year. More than a store—for millions it is the gateway to Maine. Most shoppers arrive having already studied the mail-order catalog (which accounts for 85–91 percent of sales) and are buying purposefully. The store has been expanded several times in recent years to the point where it's hard to find the old boot factory—built by Leon Leonwood Bean—that is at its heart. With its outdoor waterfall, indoor trout pond, and thousands of square feet of retail space, the building now resembles a fancy shopping mall more than it does a single store. It was back in 1912 that Mr. Bean developed his boot, a unique combination of rubber bottom and leather top. He originally sold it by mail order but gradually began catering to the hunters and fishermen who tended to pass through his town in the middle of the night. L.L. Bean himself died in 1967, but grandson Leon Gorman continues to sell nearly a quarter of a million pairs of the family boots each year. Gorman's leadership, together with an excellent marketing staff, has seen Bean grow substantially in the last few decades. Current stock ranges from canoes to weatherproof cameras to climbing gear. There is a wide variety of clothing as well as every conceivable gadget designed to keep you warm. It is the anchor store for all the outlets in town.

L.L. Bean Factory Store (1-800-341-4341), Depot Street (in the middle of the parking lot across Main Street from the retail store). Seconds, samples, and irregular merchandise are offered here. You never know what you'll find, but it's always worth a look. Unlike the main store, the outlet is not open 24 hours a day.

Dooney & Bourke (865-1366), 52 Main Street (in back). Stylish pocketbooks, shoulder bags, belts, wallets, and portfolios in water-repellent, coarse-grained leather.

Totes/Sunglass World (865-9404), 42 Main Street. Men's and women's rain gear, umbrellas, hats, luggage, national brand-name sunglasses.

Cuddledown of Maine Factory Store (865-1713), Route 1 South. Comforters, pillows, gift items, all filled with goose down. "Only European down-filling room in the country that we know of."

Bed & Bath Outlet (865-4820), 140 Main Street. Two floors of comforters, towels, pillows, and much more.

Maine Wreath & Flower Factory Outlet (865-3019), 13 Bow Street. Quality Maine dried flowers and wreaths at discount prices.

The Ribbon Outlet (865-4150), 22 Main Street. Ribbons and trims of every imaginable description. Some are as inexpensive as 6 yards to the dollar.

Buttons and Things Factory Outlet (865-4480), 24 Main Street (next to the Ribbon Outlet). A warren of rooms chock-full of buttons, beads, bead books, and findings.

Casey's Wood Products (865-3244), 15½ School Street. Bins full of wood turnings, craft materials, and toys. Free catalog.

The old L.L. Bean Store in the 1930s

Mainely Bags (865-3734), 32 Main Street. Finely crafted leather bags.

Dansk Factory Outlet (865-6125), 92 Main Street (across from Bean's). Scandinavian-design tableware, cookware, and gifts.

Mikasa Factory Store (865-9441), 31 Main Street. Dinnerware, bone china, crystal, linens, and gifts. Three floors offering a large inventory.

Freeport Crossing, 200 Lower Main Street (Route 1 south of the center of town). A complex housing outlets for **Calvin Klein** (865-1051), **Polly Flinders** (865-6223), **Leslie Fay** (865-1052), **Reebok/Rockport** (865-1228), **Oneida,** and others.

SPECIAL SHOPS

Harrington House Museum Store (865-0477), 45 Main Street, Freeport. This charming house, right in the middle of all the outlet shops, is owned by the Freeport Historical Society. Faced with escalating property taxes, the preservationists came up with a unique way to hold onto their house and keep up with the times. Every room is furnished with 1830- to 1900-era reproductions, all of which are for sale. Pieces, all documented, range from handsome furniture and weavings to artwork, crafts, Shaker baskets, kitchen utensils, and toys. The historical society mounts changing exhibits in the newly renovated barn.

Edgecomb Potters/Hand in Hand Gallery (865-1705), 8 School Street, Freeport. Fine contemporary crafts. Displays colorful porcelain, jewelry, blown glass, and iron.

Brown Goldsmiths (865-4126), 1 Mechanic Street, Freeport. Open Monday through Saturday. Original designs in rings, earrings, and bracelets.

DeLorme's Map Store (865-4171), Route 1 (south of downtown Freeport). The publishing company's own maps, atlases, and pamphlets; also guidebooks and maps of the United States and the world.

Bridgham & Cook, Ltd. (865-1040), 8A Bow Street (behind Polo-Ralph Lauren). Packaged British foods, toiletries, gifts—a must for the Anglophile.

Good Earth Farm (865-9544), 55 Pleasant Hill Road, Freeport. Dried flowers and herbs are sold in the drying barn, and vegetables are sold in-season at the farm stand. There are farm animals to visit, and sometimes hayrides to take.

Just Ship It (865-0421), 15 Bow Street, Freeport. If you've bought something you just can't fit into your suitcase, into the car, or onto the airplane, they'll ship it home for you. And if you forget to buy something while you're in Freeport, give them a call and they'll buy it and ship it for you!

Maine Street Books (865-4682), 148 Main Street, Freeport. One block north of L.L. Bean. A small, charming general bookstore.

SPECIAL EVENTS

All-night Christmas shopping. Not just L.L. Bean, but all the shops stay open throughout the night the weekend before Christmas to accommodate late shoppers. Adding to the atmosphere are costumed carolers and hot refreshments.

III. MID-COAST AND THE ISLANDS

Brunswick and The Harpswells
Bath Area
Wiscasset
Boothbay Harbor Region
Damariscotta/Newcastle and Pemaquid Area
Rockland/Thomaston Area
Rockport, Camden, and Lincolnville

GREIG CRANNA

Helping out on a windjammer off Rockland

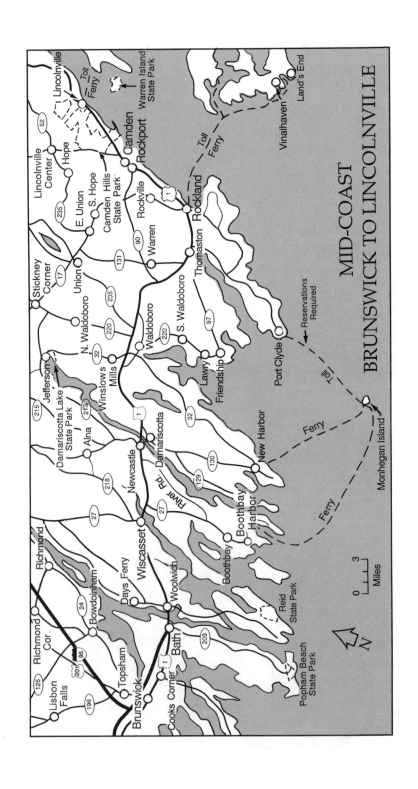

MID-COAST
BRUNSWICK TO LINCOLNVILLE

Mid-Coast Area

Beyond Casco Bay the shape of Maine's coast changes—it shreds. In contrast to the even arc of shoreline stretching from Kittery to Cape Elizabeth, the coast between Brunswick and Rockland is composed of a series of more than a dozen ragged peninsulas extending like so many fingers south from Route 1, creating a myriad of big and small harbors, coves, and bays. Scientists tell us that these peninsulas and the offshore islands are mountains drowned by the melting of the same glaciers that sculpted the many shallow lakes and tidal rivers in this area.

The 70 miles of Route 1 between Brunswick and Lincolnville are generally equated with Maine's mid-coast, but its depth is actually far greater and more difficult to define. It extends south of Route 1 to the tips of every peninsula, from Potts Point in South Harpswell and Land's End on Bailey Island to Popham Beach on the Phippsburg Peninsula and on through the Boothbays to Pemaquid Point, Friendship, Port Clyde, and Spruce Head. Along with Rockland, Camden, and the islands of Monhegan, Vinalhaven, North Haven, and Islesboro, these communities have all catered to summer visitors since steamboats began off-loading them in the late 19th century. Each peninsula differs in character from the next, but all offer their share of places to stay and eat in settings you rarely find along Route 1.

North of Route 1, this mid-coastal area also extends slightly inland. Above Bath, for instance, five rivers meld to form Merrymeeting Bay, and north of Newcastle the tidal Damariscotta River widens into 13-mile-long Damariscotta Lake. This gently rolling, river- and lake-laced backcountry harbors a number of picturesque villages and reasonably priced lodging places.

We would hope that no one who reads this book simply sticks to Route 1.

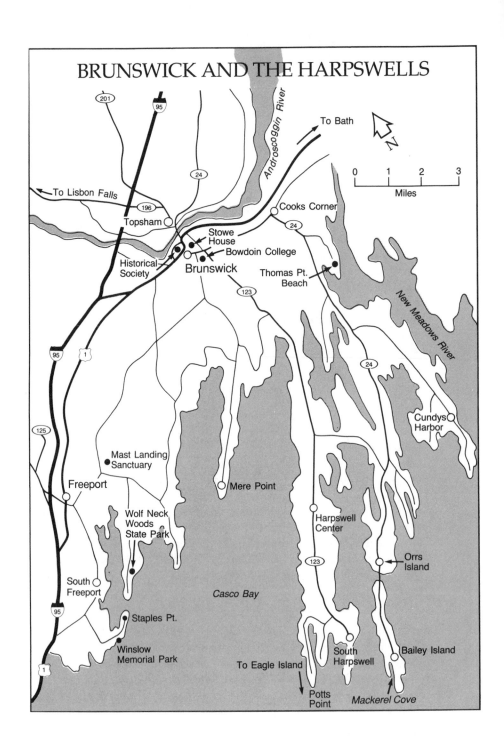

BRUNSWICK AND THE HARPSWELLS

201

95

Androscoggin River

To Bath

N

0   1   2   3
Miles

To Lisbon Falls

196

24

Cooks Corner

Topsham

24

Stowe
House

Bowdoin College

Historical
Society

Brunswick

Thomas Pt.
Beach

New Meadows River

123

95   1

24

Cundys
Harbor

125

Mast Landing
Sanctuary

Freeport

Mere Point

Wolf Neck
Woods
State Park

Harpswell
Center

Orrs
Island

South
Freeport

123

95

Casco Bay

Staples Pt.

Winslow
Memorial Park

To Eagle Island

South
Harpswell

Bailey Island

1

Potts
Point

Mackerel Cove

Brunswick and The Harpswells

Brunswick, Maine's oldest college town, is the natural centerpiece for this area. Bowdoin College was founded in 1794, and its campus is still among New England's finest. Brunswick offers summer music and theater, some interesting shops, restaurants, and galleries.

Brunswick's Maine Street is a full 12 rods wide—just as it was when the town was laid out in 1717 as an early commercial site near the junction of the Androscoggin and Kennebec Rivers, which generated power for 19th-century mills. Be sure to turn off Route 1 and drive down Maine Street with its shops and long, wide mall. Given its bandstand and frequent festivities, the town Green is often bustling with activity.

Three narrow land fingers and several bridge-linked islands stretch seaward from Brunswick, defining the eastern rim of Casco Bay. Collectively they form the town of Harpswell, better known as "The Harpswells" because it includes so many coves, points, and islands (notably Orrs and Bailey). Widely known for its seafood restaurants, Bailey Island is on the tourist path; but, otherwise, these peninsulas are surprisingly sleepy, salted with crafts, galleries, and some great places to stay. They are Maine's most convenient peninsulas, yet they seem much farther Down East.

GUIDANCE

Chamber of Commerce of the Bath-Brunswick Region (725-8797), 59 Pleasant Street, Brunswick. Open weekdays year–round, 8:30–5; also open July to September 3rd on Fridays until 8 PM, and Saturdays 3–7 PM. Staff members keep tabs on vacancies and send out lodging and dining information. The walk-in information center displays area menus and stocks a wide range of brochures. From Route 1 North follow Brunswick business district signs (these will take you down Pleasant Street).

GETTING THERE

Bus service to Brunswick and Freeport from Boston and Portland is via **Greyhound** and **Concord Trailways.**

MEDICAL EMERGENCY

Parkview Memorial Hospital (729-1641), 329 Main Street,

Brunswick. **Mid Coast Hospital** (729-0181), 58 Baribeau Street, Brunswick; and 1356 Washington Street, Bath (443-5524).

VILLAGES

Topsham, just over a bridge, feels like a natural extension of Brunswick. Historically an agricultural, mining, and mill town, it is now a suburban community with increasing commercial growth along Routes 201 and 196.

Bowdoinham, 8 miles northeast of Topsham, is a farming community with a lovely countryside. Its location on I-95, Routes 125, 138, and 24 have made it a popular home for artisans and commuters. The Cathance River is a popular fishing spot and a good place to see eagles in the winter.

TO SEE

Bowdoin College (725-3000), Brunswick. Tours of the 110-acre campus with more than 50 buildings begin at the admissions office. Phone for current hours. Because Maine was a part of Massachusetts when the college was founded in 1794, it is named after a Massachusetts governor. Nathaniel Hawthorne and Henry Wadsworth Longfellow were classmates here in 1825; other notable graduates include Franklin Pierce and Robert Edwin Peary. Founded as a men's college, the school now also welcomes women among its 1350 students. Bowdoin ranks among the nation's top colleges both in price and in status. It isn't necessary to take a tour to see the sights.

Fishway Viewing Room (725-5521), Brunswick-Topsham Hydro Station, Maine Street, Brunswick. May through June is the best time to view migrating fish; a fish ladder leads to a holding tank beside the viewing room.

MUSEUMS

Bowdoin College Museum of Art (725-3275), Walker Art Building. Open year-round, Tuesday through Saturday 10–5, Sunday 2–5; closed Mondays and holidays. One of New England's outstanding art collections housed in a building designed by McKim, Mead, and White. Colonial- and Federal-era portraits by Gilbert Charles Stuart, Robert Feke, and John Singleton Copley; also a number of paintings by Winslow Homer and other American landscape artists, plus sizable special exhibits.

Peary-MacMillan Arctic Museum (725-3416), Bowdoin College. Open same hours as the Museum of Art. A well-displayed collection of clothing, trophies, and other mementos from expeditions to the North Pole by two Bowdoin alumni. Robert Edwin Peary (class of 1877) was the first man to reach the North Pole, and Donald Baxter MacMillan (class of 1898), who was Peary's chief assistant, went on to dedicate his life to exploring Arctic waters and terrain.

Pejepscot Historical Society Museums (729-6606). Three museums are maintained by this group: The **Pejepscot Museum,** 159 Park Row,

Brunswick, is open weekdays year-round, 9–4:30; also on summer Saturdays and the first Saturday of each month, 1–4 PM. Free. Pejepscot (said to mean "crooked like a snake") is the Indian name for the local river. The museum displays changing exhibits reflecting the history of Brunswick, Topsham, and Harpswell. This building is also the site of the society's research facilities. The **Skolfield-Whittier House**, 161 Park Row, is the 17-room, mid-19th-century, Italianate double house adjacent to the Pejepscot Museum. For over 50 years the mansion was sealed, preserving its original furnishings and decor. Tours in the summer, Tuesday through Friday 10–3, Saturday 1–4. Tours are $4 adults, $2 children ages 6–12. Finally, the **Joshua L. Chamberlain Museum,** 226 Maine Street, Brunswick, is open in the summer, Tuesday through Saturday 10–4; $4 per adult, $1 per child. Call for fall hours. Here is a collection of Civil War artifacts and memorabilia of General Chamberlain, hero of Gettysburg, who also served four terms as governor of Maine and as president of Bowdoin College. The collection is housed in the partially restored home of Chamberlain, one of Brunswick's most unique structures. Combination passes to all the historical society museums are available for $6 per adult, $2 per child.

SCENIC DRIVE

A tour of The Harpswells, including Orrs and Bailey Islands. Allow a day for this rewarding peninsula prowl. From Brunswick, follow Route 24 south past Bowdoin College and watch for the right turn onto Route 123, then go 8 miles to the picturesque village of Harpswell Center. The white-clapboard Elijah Kellogg Church faces the matching Harpswell Town Meeting House built in 1757. The church is named for a former minister who was a prominent 19th-century children's book author. Continue south through West Harpswell to Pott's Point, where multicolored, 19th-century summer cottages cluster on the rocks like a flock of exotic birds that have wandered in among the gulls. Stop by the first crafts studio you see here and pick up a map/guide to other studios.

Retrace your way back up Route 123, and 2 miles north of the church turn right onto Mountain Road. This brings you to busier Route 24 on Great (also known as Sebascodegan) Island. Drive south along the narrow spine of Orrs Island to and across the only remaining cribstone bridge in the world. (Its granite blocks are laid in honeycomb fashion without cement to allow tidal flows.) This bridge brings you to Bailey Island. Continue past restaurants and lodging places, past picturesque Mackerel Cove, to the rocky Land's End (there's a small beach, gift shop, and parking lot). Return up Route 24.

TO DO

BOAT EXCURSIONS

Eagle Island (in Casco Bay)—located off Harpswell but accessible via

Eagle Tours (774-6498), Long Wharf, Portland, or from South Freeport with **Atlantic Seal Cruises** (865-6112). A classic one-man's island, just 17 acres, it takes 20 minutes to walk around. But you can easily spend that much time in Admiral Peary's shingled summer home where, on September 6, 1909, his wife received the news that her husband had become the first man to reach the North Pole. Peary positioned his house to face northeast on a rocky bluff that resembles the prow of a ship. He designed the three-sided living room hearth, which was made from island stones and Arctic quartz crystals, and stuffed many of the birds that occupy the mantel. The upstairs bedrooms appear as though someone has just stepped out for a walk, and the dining room is strewn with photos of men and dogs battling ice and snow. There is a small beach and a nature path that circles the island and takes you past the pine trees filled with sea gulls on the ocean side.

Casco Bay Lines (774-7871) offers a seasonal noon excursion from Cook's Lobster House on Bailey Island. It takes 1½ hours—circles around Eagle Island and through this northern end of Casco Bay.

GOLF
Brunswick Golf Club (725-8224), River Road, Brunswick. Incorporated in 1888, an 18-hole course known for beauty and challenging nature. Snack bar, lounge, and cart rentals.

SEA KAYAKING
H2Outfitters (833-5257), PO Box 72, Orrs Island 04066. Two-hour clinics include use of equipment; guided day trips and overnight excursions are also offered.

TENNIS
Brunswick Recreation Department (725-6656) maintains five lighted courts at Stanwood and McKeen Streets.

GREEN SPACE

BEACHES AND SWIMMING HOLES
White's Beach (729-0415), Durham Road, Brunswick. Open Memorial Day to Labor Day. A pond in a former gravel pit (water no deeper than 9 feet). Facilities include a cement pier in the middle of the pond and a small slide for children. Sandy bottom, sandy beach, lifeguards, picnic tables, grills, and snack bar.

Thomas Point Beach (725-6009), Route 24, Cook's Corner. Open Memorial Day to Labor Day, 9 to sunset. $2.50 adults, $2 children under 12. This beach is on tidal water overlooking the New Meadows River with 64 acres of lawns and groves for picnicking (more than 500 picnic tables plus snack bar, playground, and arcade). Special events are held here throughout the summer.

Coffin Pond (725-6656), River Road, Brunswick. Phone for current hours and fees. A strip of sandy beach surrounding a circular pool. Facilities include a 55-foot-long water slide, a playground, and changing rooms maintained by the town.

LODGING

INNS
Driftwood Inn and Cottages (833-5461), Bailey Island 04003. Open June through mid-October; dining room (which is open to the public) is open late June through Labor Day. Sited on a rocky point within earshot of a foghorn are three grey-shingled, traditional Maine summer houses that contain a total of 16 doubles and 9 singles (9 with half-baths); there are also 5 housekeeping cottages. Everyone dines in the pine-walled lodge dining room (so request a room away from the lodge). Almost all views are of the sea, and there is a small saltwater swimming pool set in the rocks and plenty of room, both inside and out, to lounge. The resort offers the kind of atmosphere and value possible only under longtime (over 50 years) ownership by one family. Your hosts are Mr. and Mrs. Charles L. Conrad. $65–70 per room (no minimum stay, no meals). Housekeeping cottages, available by the week, are $400–500. Breakfast is $4.85; dinner, $11.00. Weekly MAP rates: $300 per person.

Captain Daniel Stone Inn (725-9898), 10 Water Street, Brunswick 04011. Fancy new accommodations in a handsome, old Federal-style home. The 25 rooms and suites, many with whirlpool baths, all with modern amenities like color TV, telephone, VCR, alarm-clock/cassette player, almost make it seem like a luxury hotel. The atmosphere, however, with individually designed rooms, a common living room, and personal service, is that of a traditional inn. There are also two large function rooms and ample parking. Breakfast, lunch, dinner, and Sunday brunch are served in the Narcissa Stone Restaurant. Continental breakfast, included in the room rate, is set out all morning. $99–175 per room.

BED & BREAKFASTS
In Brunswick/Topsham
Brunswick Bed & Breakfast (729-4914), 165 Park Row, Brunswick 04011. Open year-round. A beautifully restored, mid-1800s Greek Revival home in the historic district on the town Green; within walking distance of shops, museums, and the Bowdoin College campus. There are six guest rooms furnished with antiques and a collection of both new and antique quilts. Four rooms have private baths. Twin parlors overlooking the mall have fires burning in the winter. A full breakfast is included. $69–89 single or double occupancy.

Middaugh Bed & Breakfast (725-2562), 36 Elm Street, Topsham 04086. Off Route 1 and I-95 in Topsham's historic district, this Greek Revival house has two very attractive, comfortable second-floor rooms, each with private bath. $60 includes a full breakfast. Children in residence.

The Samuel Newman House (729-6959), 7 South Street, Brunswick

04011. Open June through August. This 1820s home of a Bowdoin professor (Samuel Newman) is in the very shadow of the Bowdoin campus. Seven rooms share three baths. Continental breakfast with homemade breads and pastries included; $50–55 single, $60–65 double, and $75 triple.

In The Harpswells

Harpswell Inn (833-5509), 141 Lookout Point Road, RR 1, Box 141, South Harpswell 04079. Originally built as the cookhouse for Lookout Point Shipyard across the way, this three-story, white-clapboard, black-shuttered house was equipped with a bell on top for calling the workers in for lunch. Over the decades it has taken in guests under a number of names but has never been quite so gracious as now. Innkeepers Susan and Bill Menz have lived in Hawaii and Texas as well as the South, collecting antiques and furnishings along the way, and the house is filled with interesting pieces—much as though it were owned by a widely traveled sea captain. Guests enter a large living room with plenty of sitting space around a big hearth and windows overlooking Middle Bay. The 12 guest rooms vary widely and come with and without baths and water views. Children must be over 10. No smoking in the inn. $58–115 depending on room and season, breakfast included.

Bethel Point Bed and Breakfast (725-1115), 2387 Bethel Point Road, Brunswick 04011. The mailing address is Brunswick, and it's just a short drive from Bowdoin but in a very different place. The house stands facing Hen Cove near the end of a narrow point not far from Cundy's Harbor. This is a find—an 1830 house with an attractive living room and two guest rooms, sea bright and furnished appropriately. The front room has braided rugs and a writing desk, wide pumpkin-pine floorboards, a fireplace, and three windows on the water. Peter and Betsy Packard offer a warm welcome to this peaceful spot. $60–70 double per night includes a "continental plus" breakfast; $50 off-season.

Vicarage by the Sea (833-5480), Route 123, West Harpswell 04079. Open year-round. Built in the 1980s right on Curtis Cove, this cozy, Cape-style house is home for Joan Peterson-Moulton, a gracious hostess who offers two or three rooms, one with a private bath. Some rooms have ocean views, and the rocks that are uncovered at low tide are great for walking and beachcombing. This is a perfect place for dog lovers: The innkeeper's greyhound Lydia is the honorary hostess, and she's joined by other friendly canines. $55–80 includes a full breakfast.

The Johnson Bed & Breakfast (833-6053), RFD 1, Box 308, Bailey Island 04003. Closed November through May. Around the turn of the century, when guests arrived at Bailey Island by ferry, the Johnson was a four-story hotel. Later reduced to two stories, it became the Johnson family home—which it remains. George and Norma Johnson offer four comfortable guest rooms with ocean views, sharing two baths. The downstairs living room with a fireplace is a nice evening gathering spot. $60 for a double includes breakfast. The Johnsons also rent five cottages by the week, all with access to a private beach.

✐ **Senter Bed & Breakfast** (833-2874), Route 123, PO Box 149, South Harpswell 04079. Alfred Senter, owner of Brunswick's former department store and an accomplished host, also owns an exceptional contemporary home by the ocean with landscaped gardens. Spectacular views from the living room picture windows. Three bedrooms, two facing the ocean and one facing the rose garden, all with private bath. Full breakfast is included. Pets and children are welcome. $70 double, $60 single.

The Lady and the Loon (833-6871), PO Box 98, Bailey Island 04003. Gail Sprague has four antiques- and art-filled rooms with private baths. The house is situated on a bluff overlooking Ragged Island, within walking distance of a private beach. $55–70 includes breakfast. Gail is a gifted potter (the house also includes her shop) and is attuned to the local arts scene.

COTTAGES

The Bath-Brunswick Area Chamber of Commerce (see *Guidance*) lists a number of weekly cottage rentals, most on Orrs or Bailey Islands.

MOTELS

Little Island Motel (833-2392), RD 1, Box 15, Orrs Island 04066. Open early May through October. One of the most attractive motels we know of, with terrific views. Nine units, each with a small refrigerator and color TV; part of a complex that also includes a gift shop (the Gull's Nest) and a reception area where coffee and a buffet breakfast are served each morning. The complex is set on its own mini-island with a private beach, connected to other land by a narrow neck. $108–112 includes breakfast and use of boats, bicycles, and the outdoor picnic area.

Bailey Island Motel (833-2886), Route 24, Bailey Island. Located just over the cribstone bridge. A pretty, gray-shingled building ideally situated on the water's edge, offering spectacular ocean views and beautifully landscaped lawns, perfect for quiet relaxation. Rooms are clean and comfortable, with cable TV. Coffee and muffins are served each morning, included in the $65–$80 (depending on season) rates.

Note: If it happens to be a peak travel weekend and you are desperate for a bed, turn north on Route 24 into Topsham, then head up Route 196 toward Lisbon Falls. This truck route is lined with inexpensive motels that never seem to fill.

WHERE TO EAT

DINING OUT

In Brunswick

The Great Impasta (729-5858), 42 Maine Street. Open daily for lunch and dinner. A storefront at the Route 1 end of Maine Street; a find if you go for creative northern Italian fare like spinach noodle lasagna with fresh vegetables or shrimp baked with garlic, green peppers, prosciutto, and black olives. Entrées include antipasto salad and home-made bread. Entrées: $3.95–12.95.

The Stowe House (725-5543), 63 Federal Street. Open daily for breakfast, lunch, and dinner. A large but delightful wood-paneled dining room. Gourmet cuisine with specialties like sautéed shrimp and scallops in Creole sauce over linguini and sliced loin of lamb sautéed with arti-choke hearts. Harriet's Place is an inviting Victorian-style saloon. Dinner entrées: $5.95–18.75.

Narcissa Stone Restaurant (725-9898), 10 Water Street. At the Captain Daniel Stone Inn. Open every day for breakfast, lunch, and dinner. Dinner entrées include cioppino with pasta and chicken with artichoke hearts. Entrées: $8.95–21.95.

Richard's (729-9673), 115 Maine Street. This place used to be in Harpswell but has moved to the old Bowdoin Steak House building. Open for lunch and dinner Monday through Saturday. Continental fare like veal Oscar and grilled New York sirloin, but also featuring very satisfying dishes like German farmer soup, Gemischter salat, Wiener schnitzel, and Schlachtplatte. The beer list is impressive. $7.25–15.45.

In The Harpswells

J. Hathaway's Restaurant and Tavern (833-5305), Route 123, Harpswell Center. Open from 5 PM for dinner except Mondays. The Hathaways labor hard to create a casual country atmosphere and delectable dishes that include vegetable lasagna, fish and chips, and pork spareribs in the house sauce. They pride themselves on homemade dressings, soups, and desserts. $7.95–13.95.

The Original Log Cabin Restaurant (833-5546), Route 24, Bailey Island. Open mid-March to mid-October, daily for lunch and dinner. A genuine log lodge built as an enormous summer cottage; nice atmosphere with an extensive menu and children's meals. Specialties include chowders and vegetarian dishes. $3–25.

Cook's Lobster House (833-2818), Bailey Island. Open year-round for lunch and dinner. A barn of a place, right on the water, adjacent to a working fishing pier. Save your leftover french fries and muffin crumbs to feed the sea gulls on the dock out back. In July and August try to get there before the Casco Bay Liner arrives with its load of day trippers from Portland. $2.50–24.00.

Estes Lobster House (833-6340), Route 123, South Harpswell. Open mid-April through mid-October for lunch and dinner. Another large place on a causeway, with waterside picnic tables across the road. Entrées: $2.95–19.95.

EATING OUT

In Brunswick

As It Should Be (729-2826), Maine Street. This recently relocated restau-rant has expanded its Italian menu to include more Continental fare like steaks, veal, and grilled swordfish with salsa.

Miss Brunswick Diner (729-5948), 101 Pleasant Street (Route 1, north-bound). Open 6 AM–9 PM; Mexican and basic American fare.

First Wok (729-8660), 119 Maine Street. Open for lunch and dinner. Good Chinese food at reasonable prices.

In The Harpswells

Holbrook's Lobster Wharf & Snack Bar (725-0708), Cundy's Harbor (4.5 miles off Route 24). Open in-season for lunch and dinner. Lobsters and clams are steamed outdoors. Weekend clambakes; clams, crab rolls, fish-and-chips, and homemade salads and desserts like Barbara's choco-late bread pudding with ice cream. The window boxes are filled with petunias, and you sit at picnic tables overlooking buoys and lobster boats. You can get beer and wine in the store next door.

Dolphin Marina and Restaurant (833-6000), South Harpswell (marked from Route 123; also accessible by water). Open year-round, 8–8 daily. The nicest kind of small Maine restaurant—family owned and run with a combo chandlery/coffee shop partitioned from a more formal restau-rant by a model of a ketch—all overlooking a small but busy harbor. In the morning, fishermen gather on the six stools along the counter; the dining room fills for lunch and dinner (there's often a wait). Chowder, lobster stew, and homemade desserts are specialties, but there is a full dinner menu.

Mackerel Cove Restaurant (833-6656), Bailey Island. Open April through mid-October; coffee shop remains open longer. This complex includes a marina, a coffee shop (6 AM–9 PM) that caters to fishermen, and a more formal restaurant (in the pine-paneled, seafood barn tradi-tion) that serves breakfast, lunch, and dinner, specializing in seafood and homemade desserts.

Block & Tackle, Cundy's Harbor Road. Open mid-May to mid-October, 6:30 AM–8 PM. A family-run and -geared restaurant, a real find. Create your own omelet for breakfast; try shrimp stew or a real crabmeat roll for lunch, homemade clam cakes or seafood pie for dinner. The fried lobster platter is top of the menu.

SNACKS

Wild Oats Bakery (725-OATS), in the Tontine Mall, Brunswick. Open Monday through Saturday 7:30–5:30, Sunday 8–2. A delightful small bakery with light lunches, homemade breads and baked goods.

COFFEE BARS

Bohemian Coffee Roasters (725-9095), Maine Street, Brunswick. Large selection of gourmet coffees, pleasant atmosphere, outdoor seating in warm weather.

ENTERTAINMENT

Maine State Music Theater (725-8769), Packard Theater, Bowdoin Col-lege, Brunswick. Professional musical theater presentations during evenings in the summer at 8 PM, except Mondays. Also special children's shows and matinees.

Theater Project of Brunswick (729-8584), 14 School Street, Brunswick. Serious drama presented year-round.

Bowdoin Summer Music Festival (725–3322). Performances are given every Friday evening late June through August. Concerts by music school students, internationally known artists, and music school faculty. Performances are at First Parish Church and Bowdoin College Kresge Auditorium.

Bowdoin College (725-3000) performing arts groups from September to May. Concerts and theatrical performances.

SELECTIVE SHOPPING

The Lady and the Loon, Route 24, Bailey Island. Gail Sprague's shop is the kind of place where local residents go for a special gift. Birds and other wildlife are depicted in paintings and on porcelain.

Ma Culley's Old Softies (833-6455), Allen Point Road, South Harpswell. A bearded, one-legged fisherman was leaning against the small shingled shop the day we found it. He was stuffed. So were all the incredibly imaginative characters crowded into every corner of the shop. Colleen Moser introduces them one by one and says she doesn't like to sell to stores because she likes to meet the people who buy these lifelike, soft sculptures. She also makes portrait dolls but warns that the recipient must have a sense of humor.

ARTS AND CRAFTS GALLERIES

The north end of Brunswick's Maine Street has spawned some first-rate galleries in the past few years. Also, the **Harpswell Craft Guild** publishes a pamphlet that outlines a path to travel to reach hidden galleries and studios that are worth seeking out. Call first to make sure places are open; there are often midsummer and end-of-summer open houses. Weekend festivals are held in late November and early December for holiday shopping.

Icon Contemporary Art (725-8157), 19 Mason Street, Brunswick; stages changing exhibits of contemporary art.

Indrani's (729-6448), Tontine Mall, Brunswick, stocks outstanding crafts.

O'Farrell Gallery (729-8228), 58 Maine Street, Brunswick. Changing exhibits of consistently fine art.

BOOKSTORES

Gulf of Maine Books, 61 Maine Street, Brunswick. A laid-back, off-beat store that specializes in Maine and poetry: "books that fall through the holes in bigger stores."

Maine Writers & Publishers Alliance (729-6333), 12 Pleasant Street, Brunswick. An inviting bookstore stocking Maine titles and authors, maintained by the state's nonprofit organization dedicated to promoting Maine literature. Frequent workshops, catalog listing, monthly newsletters.

Potter demonstrating his craft at the Maine Arts Festival

Little Professor Bookstore, Topsham Fair Mall, has a broad inventory.
Bookland, Cook's Corner Shopping Center, Brunswick. A superstore and café in southern Maine's largest bookstore chain.

SPECIAL EVENTS

Throughout the summer: **Farmer's market** (every Tuesday and Friday, May through November), on the downtown Brunswick Mall (the town Common). **Beanhole suppers** are staged during summer months by the Harpswell Neck Fire Department.

July: **Annual Lobster Luncheon,** Orrs Island United Methodist Church. **Bailey Island Fishing Tournament** (to register phone Cooks Lobster House at 833-2818). **Great State of Maine Air Show** at the Brunswick Naval Air Station every other year (next in 1995).

August: **Topsham Fair** (early), a traditional agricultural fair complete with oxen pulls, crafts and food competitions, carnival, and livestock; held at Topsham Fairgrounds, Route 24, Topsham. **Maine Festival of the Arts,** the state's most colorful summer cultural happening, Thomas Point Beach. **A weekend in Harpswell** (late in the month), annual art show, garden club festival in historic homes, and beanhole supper. **Annual Bluegrass Festival,** Thomas Point Beach (off Route 24 near Cook's Corner). **Maine Highland Games,** Thomas Point Beach, a day-long celebration of Scottish heritage, with piping, country dancing, border collie herding demonstrations, caber tossing, and Highland fling competitions.

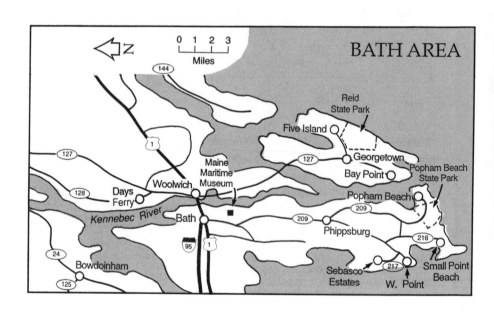

Bath Area

Over the years some 5000 vessels have been built in Bath. Think about it: In contrast to most communities—which retain what they build—here an entire city's worth of imposing structures have sailed away. Perhaps that's why, with a population of fewer than 10,000, Bath is a city rather than a town, and why the granite city hall, with its rounded, pillared facade and cupola (with a three-masted schooner for a weather vane) seems meant for a far larger city.

American shipbuilding began downriver from Bath in 1607 when the 30-ton pinnace *Virginia* was launched by Popham Colony settlers. It continues with naval vessels that regularly slide off the ways at the Bath Iron Works (BIW).

With almost 9000 workers, BIW employs about the same number of people who worked in Bath's shipyards in the 1850s. At its entrance, a sign proclaims: "Through these gates pass the world's best shipbuilders." This is no idle boast, for many current employees have inherited their skills from a long line of forebears.

Obviously, this is just the place for a museum about ships and shipbuilding, and the Maine Maritime Museum has one of the country's foremost collections of ship models, journals, logs, photographs, and other seafaring memorabilia. It even includes a 19th-century working shipyard. Both BIW and Maine Maritime Museum are sited on a 4-mile-long reach of the Kennebec River where the banks slope at precisely the right gradient for laying keels. Offshore a 35- to 150-foot-deep channel ensures safe launching. The open Atlantic is just 18 miles downriver.

In the 1850s Bath was the fourth largest port in the United States in registered tonnage, and throughout the 19th century it consistently ranked among America's eight largest seaports. Its past prosperity is reflected in the blend of Greek Revival, Italianate, and Georgian Revival styles in the brick storefronts along Front Street and in the imposing wooden churches and mansions in similar styles along Washington, High, and Middle Streets.

Today, BIW dominates the city's economy as dramatically as its red-and-white, 400-foot-high construction crane—the largest on the East Coast—does the city's waterfront. The largest civilian employer in

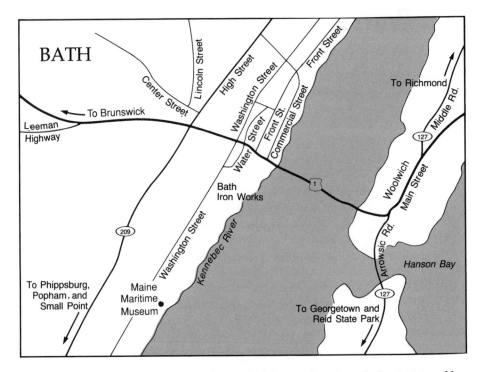

Maine, the company is descended from a firm founded in 1884 and has been filling orders for the United States Navy since 1891. During World War II, it actually produced more destroyers than did all of Japan, and it continues to do navy jobs, always keeping to its pledge to deliver ships ahead of schedule and under budget. Its story is one of many told in the Maine Maritime Museum.

Allow the better part of a day for this exceptional museum and a boat excursion from its pier, and another day to explore the Phippsburg Peninsula south of Bath. Phippsburg's perimeter is notched with coves filled with fishing boats, and Popham Beach near its southern tip is a grand expanse of sand. Reid State Park on Georgetown Island, just across the Kennebec, is the mid-coast's only other sandy strand. North of Bath, Merrymeeting Bay draws birdwatchers.

GUIDANCE

Chamber of Commerce of the Bath-Brunswick Region (443-9751 or 725-8797), 45 Front Street, Bath 04530. Open year-round, weekdays 8:30–5. From mid-June to mid-October an information center on the northbound side of Route 1, at Witch Spring Hill, is one of the state's busiest. It marks the gateway to Maine's mid-coast. There are also picnic tables and rest rooms.

For a lodging referral service (including weekends and evenings), phone 725-8797.

GETTING THERE

By car: **Route 1** passes above the city with exits from the elevated road accessing the Carlton Bridge, a bottleneck twice daily when some 9000 employees at BIW come and go to work.

By bus: **Concord Trailways** (1-800-639-3317) stops at the Coastal Plaza on Route 1, and **Mid Coast Limo** (236-2424 or 1-800-937-2424) runs to and from the Portland Jetport.

GETTING AROUND

Bath Shuttle Bus (443-6258), a 25-passenger bus, provides frequent in-town service throughout Bath, picking up at the Maine National Bank about every half hour and stopping at several points, including the Bath Shopping Center at the southern end of town. You can also flag them down.

MEDICAL EMERGENCY

Mid Coast Hospital (443-5524), 1356 Washington Street, Bath. There is also an addiction resource center here.

TO SEE

MUSEUMS

Maine Maritime Museum (443-1316), 243 Washington Street, Bath 04530. Open year-round, 9:30–5 daily; closed Thanksgiving, Christmas, and New Year's Day. Admission is $6.50 per adult and $4.00 per child ages 6–15 (maximum family admission is $20.00). Sited just south of BIW on the banks of the Kennebec River, this extensive complex includes the new brick and glass Maritime History Building and the Percy & Small Shipyard, the country's only surviving wooden shipbuilding yard (its turn-of-the-century belts for driving machinery have been restored). The size and solidity of the new building contrast with its setting and the low-slung wooden structures left from the old shipyards. Its exhibits focus, understandably, on the era beginning after the Civil War when 80 percent of this country's full-rigged ships were built in Maine, almost half of these in Bath.

The pride of Bath, you learn, were the Down Easters, a compromise between the clipper ship and old-style freighter that plied the globe during the 1870s through the 1890s, and the big, multimasted schooners designed to ferry coal and local exports like ice, granite, and lime. The museum's permanent collection of artwork, artifacts, and documents is now said to include more than a million pieces, and there is an extensive research library. Permanent exhibits range from displays on Maine's marine industries—fishing and canning as well as shipbuilding and fitting—to the story of BIW.

Did you realize that lobstering in Maine dates back to the 1820s? By the 1880s there were 23 "lobster factories" in Maine, all closed in the 1890s when a limit was imposed on the size of lobsters that could be canned. Visitors are invited to sit on the gunwale of a classic lobster boat and watch a documentary about lobstering narrated by E.B. White.

Woodworkers and wooden-boat buffs will appreciate the lofting models in the mold loft and the details of the cabinetwork in the Joiners Shop, as well as watching the apprentices building wooden boats. Children find hands-on exhibits scattered throughout this sprawling museum—from the World Trade Game in the main gallery to the mizzen in the boat near the water. Visitors of all ages should take advantage of the 50-minute, narrated boat rides aboard the *Summertime,* which departs regularly from the museum dock. Special narrated cruises to farther points are regularly offered.

Historic District. In the 18th and 19th centuries, Bath's successful shipbuilding and seafaring families built impressive mansions on and around upper Washington Street. The entire neighborhood, as well as all of Bath's downtown business section, has been entered on the National Register of Historic Places. Sagadahoc Preservation, Inc., offers walking tours; ask for a schedule at the chamber of commerce (see *Guidance*). The historical society also produces an excellent folder, "Architectural Tours—Walking and Driving in the Bath Area," available from the chamber of commerce.

1910 Farmhouse, Woolwich Historical Society Museum (443-4833), $2 per adult, $1 children aged 6–12. Route 1 and Nequasset Road, Woolwich. Open 10–4 every day July 4 to Labor Day; weekends during September. An admirable, small museum run by volunteers, this rambling farmhouse displays an intriguing collection of antique clothing and quilts, plus seafaring memorabilia, all gleaned from local attics.

SCENIC DRIVE

The Phippsburg Peninsula. From the Maine Maritime Museum, drive south on Route 209, down the narrow peninsula making up the town of Phippsburg, pausing at the first causeway you cross. This is Winnegance Creek, an ancient shortcut between Casco Bay and the Kennebec River; look closely to the left and you will see traces of the 10 tidemills that once operated here.

Continue south on Route 209 until you come to the Phippsburg Center Store on your right. Turn left on the road opposite, into the tiny hamlet of Phippsburg Center. This is one of those magical places, far larger in memory than it is in fact—perhaps because it was once larger in fact, too. Notice the huge linden tree (planted in 1774) between the stark Congregational Church (1802) and its small cemetery. Also look for the telltale stumps of piers on the shore beyond, remnants of a major shipyard. Just off Route 209 note the Phippsburg Historical Museum (open in summer Monday through Friday, 2–4).

Continue along the peninsula's east shore on the Parker Head Road, past a former millpond where ice was once harvested. At the junction with Route 209 turn left. The road threads a salt marsh and the area at Hoss Ketch Point, from which all traces of the ill-fated Popham Colony have long since disappeared. Route 209 winds around Sabino Head and ends at the parking lot for Fort Popham, a granite Civil War–era fort (with picnic benches) at the mouth of the Kennebec River. A wooded road, for walking only, leads to World War I and II fortifications that constitute Fort Baldwin Memorial Park; a six-story tower yields views up the Kennebec and out to sea.

Along the shore at Popham Beach note the telltale pilings, in this case from vanished steamboat wharfs. Around the turn of the century, two big hotels served the passengers who transferred here from Boston to Kennebec River steamers, or who simply stayed a spell to enjoy the town's spectacular beach. Now Popham Beach State Park, this immense expanse of sand remains a popular destination for fishermen, beach walkers, sunbathers, and even a few hardy swimmers. From Popham Beach return to Route 209 and follow it west to Route 217 and out to Sebasco Estates, then back up to Phippsburg Center.

TO DO

BALLOONING
Over the Rainbow Ballooning (737-8232), Dresden.
BICYCLING
Bath Cycle and Ski (442-7002), Route 1, Woolwich; rents bikes and cross-country skis.
BOAT EXCURSIONS
M/V *Ruth* based at Sebasco Estates (389-1161) offers a variety of coastal excursions on the New Meadows River and into Casco Bay.
M/V *Yankee* (389-1788) offers mid-June through Labor Day excursions from Hermit Island Campgrounds at Small Point.
Summertime (443-1316), based at the Maine Maritime Museum, offers Kennebec River cruises.
Symbian (389-2394), a 37-foot sloop, is available for 1- to 3-day cruises from the Captain Drummond House B&B in Phippsburg.
Seguin Navigation Co. (443-1677), Arrowsic. Half- and full-day sails.
Kayla D and ***Obsession*** (442-8581); ***Son Rue*** (371-2813).
CANOE AND KAYAK RENTALS
Taylor Rentals (725-7400), 271 Bath Road, Brunswick; rent a canoe to explore Merrymeeting Bay. **Dragonworks, Inc.** (666-8481), in Bowdoinham on Merrymeeting Bay, sells whitewater and sea kayaks and offers instruction.
FISHING
Surf fishing is popular at Popham Beach, and there's an annual mid-August Bluefish Tournament in Waterfront Park. **Kennebec Charters** (389-1883) and ***Kayla D* & *Obsession* Sportfishing Charters** (442-8581 or 443-3316) offer deep-sea fishing charters.

GOLF
Bath Municipal Golf Course (442-8411), Whiskeag Road, Bath. Pro shop, 18 holes. Greens fee $10. **Sebasco Lodge** (389-1161), Sebasco Estates. Nine-hole course and putting green. Primarily for hotel guests; open to the public by reservation. (Late June to early September only.)

SWIMMING
(Also see *Beaches*.)

* **Charles Pond,** Route 27, Georgetown (about 0.5 mile past the turnoff for Reid State Park; 15 miles down the peninsula from the Carlton Bridge). Often considered the best all-around swimming hole in the area, this long and narrow pond has clear water and is surrounded by tall pines.

* **Pleasant Pond** (582-2813), Peacock Beach State Park, Richmond. Open Memorial Day through Labor Day. A sand and gravel beach with lifeguards on duty. Water depth drops off gradually to about 10 feet in a 30-by-50-foot swimming area removed from boating and enclosed by colored buoys. Picnic tables and barbecue grills. Admission is $1.50 adults; $.50 ages 5–11; under 5 free.

TENNIS
Congress Avenue, Bath. Open until 9:30 PM. Four lighted outdoor courts. First come, first served. **Sebasco Lodge** (389-1161), Sebasco Estates (see *Lodging*). Courts are primarily for the use of the lodge's guests but may be reserved by others as available. (Late June to early September only.)

SPECIAL LEARNING PROGRAM
Shelter Institute (442-7938), 38 Center Street, Bath 04530. A year-round resource center for people who want to build or retrofit their own energy-efficient home. Two- and three-week daytime courses are offered May to October; Saturday morning classes are given during the winter. Tuition varies according to course taken.

GREEN SPACE

BEACHES
If you are traveling with a dog, it is important to know that they are only allowed in picnic areas, not on the beaches.

* **Popham Beach State Park** (389-1335), via Route 209 south from Bath to Phippsburg and beyond. A 3-mile-long expanse of sand at the mouth of the Kennebec River. Also a sandbar, tidal pools, and smooth rocks. Never overcrowded, but it can be windy. Day-use fees of $1.50 per adult and $.50 per child ages 5–11 (under 5 free) are charged from mid-April until mid-October.

* **Reid State Park** (371-2303), Route 127, Georgetown (14 miles south of Bath and Route 1). Open year-round, seven days per week. The bathhouse and snack bar overlook 1.5 miles of sand in three distinct beaches that seldom become overcrowded, although the limited parking area does fill by noon on summer weekends. You can choose surf or slightly warmer sheltered

backwater, especially good for children. Entrance fees of $2.00 per adult and $.50 per child ages 5–11 (under 5 free) are charged between mid-April and mid-October.

PARKS

Fort Baldwin Memorial Park, Phippsburg. An undeveloped area with a six-story tower to climb for a beautiful view up the Kennebec and, downriver, out to sea. There are also remnants of fortifications from World Wars I and II. At the bottom of the hill is the site where the Popham Colony struggled to weather the winter of 1607–1608, afterward deciding to go on to Virginia where they had originally been headed. They built the pinnace *Virginia* and sailed away.

Fort Popham Memorial Park (389-1335 in-season) is located at one tip of Popham Beach. Open Memorial Day to Labor Day. Picnic sites are scattered around the ruins of the 1861 fort, which overlooks the beach.

Josephine Newman Wildlife Sanctuary, Georgetown. Bounded on two sides by salt marsh, 119 acres with 2 miles of walking trails. Look for the sign on Route 127, 9.1 miles south of Route 1.

Bates-Morse Mountain Conservation Area comprises some 600 acres extending from the Sprague to the Morse River and out to Seawall Beach. Allow 2 hours for the walk to and from this unspoiled private beach. There's also a great view from the top of Morse Mountain. Pack a picnic and towel, but please no radios or beach paraphernalia. Seawall Beach is an important nesting area for piping plovers and least terns.

Steve Powell Wildlife Management Area (Swan Island), in Merrymeeting Bay off Richmond. See *Camping* in the "Augusta and Mid-Maine" chapter.

Hamilton Sanctuary, West Bath. Situated on a peninsula in the New Meadows River, offering a 1½-mile trail system and great birdwatching. Take the New Meadows exit off Route 1 in West Bath; left on New Meadows Road, which turns into Foster Point Road; follow it 4 miles to the sanctuary sign.

LODGING

RESORTS

Sebasco Lodge (389-1161), Sebasco Estates 04565. Open late June to early September. A traditional New England summer resort (ownership has changed only once since the 1930s), this 560-acre, self-contained complex includes a saltwater pool and a nine-hole golf course plus putting green. Other amenities include swimming at a private beach, hiking, boating, lobster cookouts, live entertainment, and special evening programs. Choose a cabin, cottage, or lodge room (98 rooms in all). Rates are MAP: $92–110 per person per night, double occupancy. B&B rates available in shoulder seasons; inquire about packages.

Rock Gardens Inn (389-1339), Sebasco Estates 04565. Open mid-June through late September. Next door to Sebasco Estates Lodge, Rock Gardens Inn accommodates just 60 guests, providing a more intimate atmosphere than the larger resort but offering access to all its facilities (see above). The inn perches on the edge of the water, banked, as you'd expect, in a handsome rock garden. Guests gather in the comfortable living room, library, and old-fashioned dining room with round tables and cornflower-blue wooden chairs. There's a welcoming Sunday cocktail party and a weekly lobster cookout. There are three rooms in the inn and ten cottages, each with living rooms, fireplaces, and sun porches. Most rooms have water views. $76–102 per person MAP; 5-night minimum in July and August. Inquire about five-day art workshops offered in June, July, and September.

INN

Grey Havens (371-2616), Seguinland Road, PO Box 308, Georgetown 04548. Open Memorial Day through Columbus Day. The same Mr. Reid who donated the land for the neighboring state park built this turreted, grey-shingled summer hotel, opened in 1904 as the Seguinland. Today, it is operated by the second generation of a Texas family who have owned it since the 1970s. A gracefully aging old lady, the hotel's atmosphere is conducive to lazy afternoons in rocking chairs on the wide porch, gazing out over Sheepscot Bay. A huge parlor window—said to have been Maine's first picture window—commands the same wonderful panorama. The parlor is hung with baskets, furnished comfortably and warmed with a huge stone fireplace. The 14 rooms upstairs range from small doubles to large, rounded turret rooms. Ten have private baths. Swimming is just up the road at Reid State Park. $90–150 double, with "hearty continental" breakfast. Two-night minimum on weekends and holidays. The comfortable, old-style dining room is open to the public.

Also see **Squire Tarbox Inn** in the "Wiscasset" chapter—it is on Westport Island, between Wiscasset and Bath.

BED & BREAKFASTS

Captain Drummond House (389-1394), Parker Head Road, PO Box 72, Phippsburg 04562. Open spring through late fall. Just off Route 209, halfway between Bath and Popham Beach, this historic, circa 1770 home was originally built as a tavern in the center of the lovely little village of Phippsburg Center. In 1977 it was restored and moved a quarter mile to its current location on a secluded, 125-foot bluff above the Kennebec River. The views of woods, coves, peninsulas, and even a lighthouse are exceptional. This is a quiet, homey, but elegant retreat where guests feel more like friends of the owners; that's why many return yearly. There are three guest rooms, one with a private, second-floor balcony and others with private entrances, plus a small suite. This suite is available only in summer. Smoking is permitted outdoors only. Leisurely breakfasts. Private baths. $75–100 double; two-room suite

$110–130 in-season. Innkeepers Donna Dillman and Ken Brigham also charter their 37-foot sloop for short day sails and overnight cruises.

Fairhaven Inn (443-4391), North Bath Road, Bath 04530. Open year-round. Hidden away on the Kennebec River as it meanders down from Merrymeeting Bay, this 1790s house has seven pleasant guest rooms, five with private baths. Everything is very neat; there are antique furnishings, and guests awaken to the aroma of unusual gourmet breakfasts. The inn's 27 acres of meadow invite walking in summer and cross-country skiing in winter (the 10-acre golf course nearby makes for even more skiing). Two-night minimum stay on holidays and on weekends in July and August. In-season rates, including a full breakfast, are $50 single; $60 double with shared bath; $70–75 double with private bath.

The Inn at Bath (443-4294), 969 Washington Street, Bath 04530. Open year-round. In the historic district, this rambling, recently restored 1830 home offers twin parlors with a marble fireplace and six carefully decorated guest rooms with a choice of twin or queen beds (all private baths), some rooms with working fireplaces. There's also a suite in a former hayloft with a sitting room. $75–95.

Popham Beach Bed & Breakfast (389-2409), Popham Beach 04562. Open early May until late October. The former Coast Guard Station, built in 1883 right on Popham Beach (decommissioned in 1971) has been restored as a posh B&B. When we visited in 1994 three guest rooms had been completed, each a tastefully decorated suite with water views; $130 includes a full breakfast.

Packard House (443-6069), 45 Pearl Street, Bath 04530. Open year-round. A gracious 1790 Georgian home in the heart of the historic district, one block from the Kennebec. Once owned by Benjamin F. Packard, partner in one of the world's most successful shipbuilding companies (the captain's quarters of the clipper *Benjamin F. Packard* are displayed at Mystic Seaport in Connecticut). Three elegant guest rooms with period furnishings. No smoking. Rates include a full New England breakfast. $65 double with shared bath; $80 for a suite with private bath and sitting room.

The Bath Bed & Breakfast (443-4477), 944 Middle Street, Bath 04530. A friendly, unpretentious B&B operated by Mike Fear, who has worked as a steeplechase jockey, sheepshearer, folksinger, and riverboater in his native England, and his wife, Betsy, a graphic designer and illustrator. Together they operate a small publishing business as well as the B&B. Rooms and suites with private baths are geared to families. In the evening, Mike sometimes plays his concertina and sings sea chanteys for guests. From $65 for a single with private bath to $150 for a three-room suite accommodating six. Rates include a full breakfast.

Elizabeth's Bed & Breakfast (443-1146), 360 Front Street, Bath 04530. Open mid-April through December. A welcoming old home overlooking the Kennebec River. Near downtown shopping. Two of the five guest rooms have river views, all are furnished with country antiques; 2½ shared baths. There is a guest living room with a TV and a resident cat. Smoking permitted downstairs only. $50–60 double, including generous continental breakfast.

The Front Porch B&B (443-5790), 324 Washington Street, Bath 04530. No view but a homey, turn-of-the-century B&B whose atmosphere is a blend of Victorian and country; practically across the street from BIW and the Maine Maritime Museum. In addition to two rooms in the house, there is an efficiency apartment with private bath in the carriage house. Rooms are $45–50; the carriage house is $55–65 for two or $75 for four; an ambitious breakfast featuring sourdough French toast and homemade blueberry syrup included.

Small Point Bed & Breakfast (389-1716), Route 216, Sebasco Estates. A comfortable, informal 1890s farmhouse handy to beaches, boats, and hiking; accepts children and pets by prior arrangement. $48 for a room with shared bath, $58–72 with private bath, full breakfast included.

Riverview (389-1124), Box 29E Church Lane, Phippsburg 04562. Open May through October. Alice Minott's riverside home is one of the oldest Capes (1830) in the area. It's in Phippsburg Center (see *Scenic Drive*) One room. Two-night minimum weekends and holidays. $30 single, $50 double with continental breakfast.

Coveside–Five Islands Bed and Breakfast (371-2807), Five Islands 04548. Open year-round. Ten miles down Route 127 from Route 1, beyond the turnoff for Reid State Park. Coveside is a 100-year-old farmhouse with a new wing and a large deck, offering three guest rooms, all with king- and queen-sized beds and water views. Coffee is served in your room or on the deck before a breakfast that might include lobster quiche or eggs Benedict. $85 in-season, $95 for one of the suites in the carriage house if they're available (Judy Ewing prefers to rent them by the week); less off-season. Inquire about winter weekends, including dinner.

1024 Washington (443-5202), 1024 Washington Street, Bath 04530. Open year-round. An imposing mansion in Bath's historic district, built in the mid-1800s by Captain Gilbert Patten, who brought all of its bricks here as ballast in his ships. Up the sweeping staircase are six high-ceilinged guest rooms filled with chintz and period furnishings plus small color televisions; some have working fireplaces. Doubles (some shared baths, some private) are $50–125.

Glad II (442-1191), 60 Pearl Street, Bath 04530. Open year-round. A 120-year-old home that's an unassuming, old-fashioned bed & breakfast within an easy walk of downtown shops and restaurants; two twin-bedded rooms, one double, air-conditioned. $50 double includes a breakfast of juice and muffins.

OTHER LODGING

Spinney's Guest House and Cottages (389-2052), RFD 3, Phippsburg

04562 (off-season: 4407 Meadowview Drive, Lakeland, FL 33809). Open May to October. This is simple, old-fashioned lodging right on Popham Beach. Four guest rooms ($55) share one bath; there are also three housekeeping cottages and two efficiency apartments ($70 per night or $450 per week). Cottages are $80 per night or $500 per week for up to four people.

⌀ **New Meadows Inn** (443-3921), Bath Road, West Bath 04530. Open year-round, with the exception of the cottages (open late May to mid-October). A good family place, with rooms for two, cottages for more, including a log cabin. Dining room with shore dinners, traditional family fare, snacks, salad bar, and buffets. Private docking and marina facilities. Rates: $30–40 for double rooms, $40–60 for cottages.

⌀ **Hermit Island** (443-2101), 42 Front Street, Bath 04530. This 255-acre, almost-island at Small Point offers 275 nicely scattered camping sites, 63 on the water. Only tents and pop-ups are permitted. Owned since 1953 by the Sewall family, Hermit Island also has a central lodge with a recreation room and snack bar where kids can meet. Campers can enjoy the island's private beaches and unspoiled woods and meadows. $22–28 per night.

Cottage listings are available from the Chamber of Commerce of the Bath-Brunswick Region (see *Guidance*) and in the Maine Publicity Bureau's "Maine Guide to Camp and Cottage Rentals." (Also see *Cottage Rentals* in "What's Where in Maine.")

WHERE TO EAT

DINING OUT

The Osprey (371-2530), at Robinhood Marina, Robinhood (just off Route 127, near Reid State Park). Open spring through fall for lunch and dinner, fewer days off-season. Reservations appreciated and a must on summer weekends. Overlooks a boatyard and, yes, there is an osprey nest on the day marker that you can see from the window. Atmosphere is minimal (the room is brightly lighted, often loud and crowded), but the cuisine is elegant. The large menu changes frequently but might include such appetizers as baked Brie in phyllo pastry with pistachio nut butter and entrées such as salmon *en papillote* with julienne of leeks, carrots, fresh herbs, and enoki mushrooms. Sauces can be rich. Entrées run $18–22 (including vegetables, breads, sorbet, and mineral water) Lunch: $5–8. In The Tavern at Riggs Cove, part of the same complex, you can dine less expensively on appetizers and soups and salads.

☞ **Kristina's** (442-8577), corner of High and Center Streets, Bath. Open daily, year-round, Tuesday through Saturday 7 AM–9 PM, Sunday 9 AM–2 PM, and Monday 7 AM–2 PM. Outdoor dining on the tree-shaded deck in summer. What began as a simple room with booths and a bakery case has grown into a sophisticated, two-level restaurant and cocktail lounge. You will still find the same great quiche, cheesecake, and other incredible breads and pastries (which you can still buy to-go at the bakery counter) for which it was first known, plus such entrées as pepper-grilled salmon fillet with Spanish gazpacho sauce ($14.95) or chicken pot pie in cheddar cheese crust ($7.95).

J.R. Maxwell's (443-4461), 122 Front Street, Bath. Open year-round, in the middle of the shopping district, in a renovated 1840s building that was originally a hotel. At lunch there are burgers, salads, crêpes, and seafood sandwiches. At dinner there are steaks, chicken, and Maine seafood. Also Sunday brunch and a children's menu. Exposed old brick walls, hanging plants. Downstairs is the Boat Builder's Pub, with live bands on weekends. Dinner for two with wine is around $40.

☞✐**Montsweag Restaurant** (443-6563), Route 1, Woolwich. A longtime favorite with good, old-fashioned cooking and old-time decor. About halfway between Bath and Wiscasset (see "Wiscasset").

EATING OUT

✐ **Front Street Deli and Club** (443-9815), 128 Front Street, Bath. Open year-round 8 AM–11 PM. A storefront with inviting booths and standard breakfast and lunch fare, soup of the day, good pies. Downstairs is "the Club," mismatched sofas and couches, same food, cocktail lounge.

✐ **Spinney's Restaurant and Guest House** (389-1122), at the end of Route 209, Popham Beach. Open weekends in April and daily May to October for lunch and dinner. Our kind of beach restaurant: counter and tables, pleasant atmosphere with basic chowder and a sandwich menu. Pete and Jean Hart specialize in fried fish and seafood but they also serve it steamed and broiled; good lobster and crabmeat rolls. Beer, wine, and cocktails. Inexpensive to moderate.

✐ **Lobster House** (389-1596), Small Point (follow Route 1 to Route 126). Open during the summer season. Mrs. Pye's is a classic lobster place specializing in seafood dinners and homemade pastry; it's down near Small Point, surrounded by salt marsh. Beer and wine are served.

✐ **The Water's Edge** (389-2756), Sebasco Estates. Open daily 11–9, Mother's Day to mid-September. The Varian family are fishermen who take pride in serving the freshest fish and seafood. Pasta and meat dishes are also served. Right on a commercial fishing wharf, the restaurant is decorated with nets, lobster pots, and photos of old vessels; there's also a take-out window and picnic tables. Reservations are advised for dinner.

✐ **New Meadows Inn** (442-8562), 393 Bath Road, West Bath (see *Other Lodging*). Shore dinners, seafood, and steaks: good family fare. Lunch buffet Monday through Friday; evening buffet on weekends. Early-bird specials.

Georgetown Fisherman's Co-op (371-2950), 13 miles south of Route 1 on Route 127 at the Five Islands wharf in Georgetown. Open seasonally, specializing in steamed lobsters and clams, lobster rolls; snack bar menu.

Truffles Cafe (442-8474), 21 Elm Street, Bath. Open Monday through Saturday 11–4. Luncheon served in a small room filled with tiny tables. Homemade specialties include spicy chicken salad, unusual soups, and delicious desserts. No smoking.

Harbor Lights Cafe (443-9883), 166 Front Street, Bath. Open year-round, 7 days a week for lunch and dinner. Mexican fare and live entertainment on weekends.

✐ **The Cabin** (443-6224), 552 Washington Street, Bath. Claims to serve "the only real pizza in Maine," plus sandwiches, pasta.

✐ **Bath House of Pizza** (443-6631), 737 Washington Street, Bath. Open daily, year-round. Freshly made pizzas, seafood, and pasta dishes.

ENTERTAINMENT

Center for the Arts at the Chocolate Church (442-8455), 804 Washington Street, Bath 04530. Year-round presentations include plays, concerts, and a wide variety of guest artists. Special children's plays and other entertainment are included on the schedule. The handsome church has been completely restored inside. There is also a very nice gallery at the Chocolate Church (so-called because of the chocolate color of this Greek Revival building).

SELECTIVE SHOPPING

ANTIQUES SHOPS
Along Front Street in Bath, note **Front Street Antiques** (190), **Pollyanna's Antiques** (182) and **Brick Store Antiques** (143).

ARTISANS
Arrowsic Pottery (443-6048), Route 127, Arrowsic (0.5 mile from the Carlton Bridge). Open daily June to August and weekdays the rest of the year. An attractive studio designed by architect Jozef Tara for his potter wife, Nan Kilbourn-Tara. Features a full line of functional pottery, including mugs, bowls, lanterns, and casseroles, all rendered in colors that reflect Maine's flowers and fields. Larger pieces made on commission: birdbaths, stoneware sinks.

Georgetown Pottery, Route 127, Georgetown (about a mile from the Carlton Bridge). Dishes and other pottery pieces, including hummingbird feeders and soap dishes, all decorated with flowers and birds.

River Front Artworks (442-7226), Customs House, 1 Front Street, Bath. Monday through Saturday 10–5. An artists' cooperative featuring 10 artists and artisans: jewelry, sculptures, painting, ceramics, quilts, and wearable art.

FLEA MARKET
Montsweag Flea Market (443-2809), Route 1, Woolwich (just south of Montsweag Farm Restaurant). A field filled with tables weighted down

by every sort of collectible and curiosity you could imagine. It is a bee-hive of activity every day during the summer and on weekends in the spring and fall. Antiques, rather than flea-market finds, are featured on Wednesdays.

SPECIAL SHOPS

Bath's Front Street, which runs parallel to the Kennebec a block from the river bank, is graced with an impressive row of mid-19th-century, red-brick commercial buildings enhanced by brick sidewalks, park benches, tasteful signs, and old-fashioned lamps. Among the gift shops, don't overlook **Reny's** (86 Front Street), one in a small chain of Maine department stores that's good for genuine bargains. **Springer's Jewelers** (76 Front Street) is a vintage emporium with mosaic floors, chandeliers, and ornate glass sales cases.

Woodbutcher Tools (442-7939), 38 Center Street, Bath. The Shelter Institute (see *Special Learning Programs*) maintains this woodworker's find, specializing in hard-to-find woodworking tools.

Dromore Bay Herb Farm (443-1574), Route 209, Phippsburg. An extremely inviting, small shop-in-the-barn selling homemade jams, jellies, pickles, and dried herbs grown here, plus a distinctive assortment of accents for the garden and home.

SPECIAL EVENTS

Three days surrounding the Fourth of July: **Bath Heritage Days,** a grand celebration with an old-time parade of antique cars, marching bands, clowns, guided tours of the historic district, craft sales, art shows, musical entertainment in two parks, a triathlon, and Firemen's Follies featuring bed races, bucket relays, and demonstrations of equipment and fire-fighting techniques. Fireworks over the Kennebec.

Second Saturday in July: **Popham Circle Fair** at the Popham Chapel features the sale of birdfeeders (shaped like the chapel) that residents make all year; profits keep the chapel going.

July and August: Wednesday evening concerts by the **Bath Municipal Band,** Library Park.

Early December: **Winter Solstice Celebration.** Bath calls itself the "Christmas City on the Kennebec" and sponsors a community sing-along at the Chocolate Church, a Christmas parade, and a Festival of Trees. Call or write the chamber of commerce for a Christmas events calendar (see *Guidance*).

Wiscasset

Wiscasset is Maine's gift to motorists toiling up Route 1. After hours of ho-hum highways, here is finally a bit of what Maine's supposed to look like. Sea captains' mansions and mid-19th-century shops line the road as it slopes toward the Sheepscot River.

Still the shire town of Lincoln County, Wiscasset is only half as populous as it was in its shipping heyday, which—as the abundance of clapboard mansions attest—came after the American Revolution but before the Civil War. Several buildings are open to the public, and many more house shops, galleries, and restaurants. The weathered remains of two early 19th-century schooners, the *Hesper* and the *Luther Little,* are picturesquely positioned just offshore and are purported to be the most photographed shipwrecks in the world.

GUIDANCE

Wiscasset does not have a chamber of commerce, but **Wiscasset Hardware** (882-6622), on Water Street (to your left just before you cross the bridge from Wiscasset to Edgecomb), stocks local brochures. Park at the Water Street entrance and walk up through the appliances; built in 1797 as a chandlery, this hospitable establishment also offers an upper deck on which to get your bearings with a cup of coffee and river view.

GETTING THERE

Concord Trailways (1-800-639-3317) stops here en route from Portland to Bangor. **Mid Coast Limo** runs to and from the Portland Jetport (1-800-834-5500 within Maine, or 1-800-937-2424 outside Maine). **Downeast Flying Service** (882-6752) offers air charters year-round. **Wiscasset Taxi** (758-1679) serves a 60-mile radius of town, including the airports in Portland, Damariscotta, and Boothbay Harbor.

PARKING

If you can't find a slot along Main Street, you can always find one in the parking lot or elsewhere along Water Street.

MEDICAL EMERGENCY

Bath Memorial Hospital (443-5524), 1356 Washington Street, Bath.

VILLAGES

Sheepscot Village. North on Route 218 from Wiscasset; look for the sign

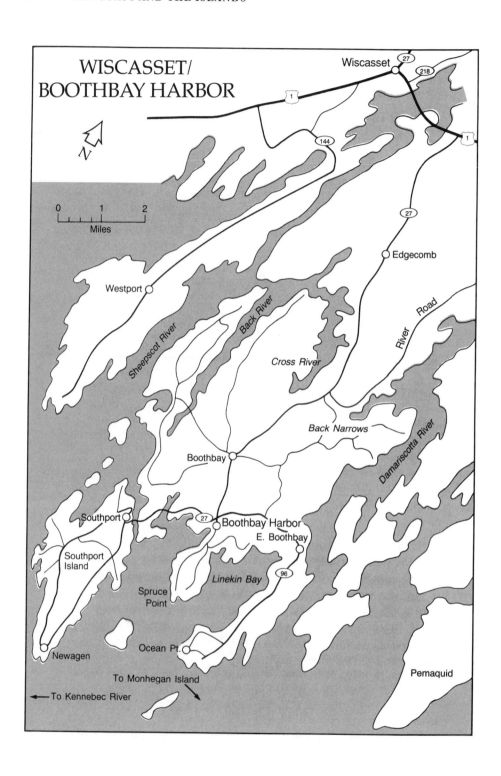

WISCASSET/
BOOTHBAY HARBOR

Wiscasset

Westport

Sheepscot River

Back River

Cross River

Back Narrows

Edgecomb

River Road

Damariscotta River

Boothbay

Southport

Boothbay Harbor

E. Boothbay

Southport Island

Linekin Bay

Spruce Point

Newagen

Ocean Pt.

To Monhegan Island

To Kennebec River

Pemaquid

0   1   2
Miles

in about 4 miles. An unusually picturesque gathering of 19th century buildings.

Head Tide Village. Eight miles up Route 218 (follow sign), an early 19th-century village that was the birthplace of poet Edward Arlington Robinson; note the Old Head Tide Church (1838), open Saturday 2–4. Watch for the swimming hole beneath the old mill dam.

TO SEE

HISTORIC HOMES

Musical Wonder House (882-7163), 18 High Street. Open daily for guided tours, mid-May to mid-October, 10–5 (fewer tours after Labor Day). An intriguing collection of music boxes, reed organs, pump organs, Victrolas, and other musical machines displayed in a fine 1852 sea captain's mansion. Visitors are taken on tours of the house during which the various machines are played and demonstrated. Tours of just the ground floor are $8 per person (or two for $15); tours of the entire house take about three hours and are $25 per person (or two for $40). The gift shop at the Musical Wonder House is open 10–6 every day that the museum is open (no admission charge). Ask about 8 PM candlelight concerts.

Nickels-Sortwell House, corner of Main and Federal Streets. Open June 1 to September 30, Wednesday through Sunday 12–5. $4 adults, $3.50 seniors, $2 children 12 and under. A classic, Federal-era mansion in the middle of town that served as a hotel for many years. Some furnishings date from the early 20th century when it was owned by a Cambridge, Massachusetts mayor. The elliptical staircase is outstanding. Today the mansion is one of the properties administered by the Society for the Preservation of New England Antiquities.

Castle Tucker (882-7364). Open during July and August, Tuesday through Saturday 11–4, and in September by appointment; you're also welcome to walk around the grounds when the house is closed. Adults $3, ages 6–12, $.50. An unusual, privately owned mansion overlooking the Sheepscot River. It was built in 1807 by Judge Silas Lee, who overextended his resources to present his wife with this romantic house. After his death it fell into the hands of his neighbors, to whom it had been heavily mortgaged, and passed through several owners until it was acquired in 1858 by Captain Richard Holbrook Tucker. Captain Tucker, whose descendants still own the house, added the elegant portico. Castle Tucker is said to be named after a grand house in Scotland. Highlights include a free-standing elliptical staircase, Victorian furnishings, and original wallpapers.

HISTORIC SITES

Lincoln County Museum (882-6817), Federal Street (Route 218). Open July and August, Tuesday through Sunday 11–4:30 (last tour at 4). $2 per adult, $1 age 12 and under. The museum is comprised of a chilling 1811 jail (in use until 1913) with damp, thick granite walls (some bearing interesting 19th-century graffiti), window bars, and heavy metal doors; plus the jailer's house (in use until 1953) with displays of tools and changing exhibits. Includes an antiques show in August.

Pownalborough Court House (882-6817), Route 128, off Route 27, Dresden (8 miles north of Wiscasset). Open during July and August, Wednesday through Saturday 10–4 and Sunday 12–4. $3 adults, $1 under 13. Worth the drive. The only surviving pre–revolutionary war courthouse in Maine, it is maintained as a museum by the Lincoln County Historical Association. The three-story building, which includes living quarters for the judge upstairs, gives a sense of this countryside along the Kennebec in 1761 when it was built to serve as an outpost tavern as well as a courtroom. This site is still isolated, standing by a revolutionary war–era cemetery and a picnic area; there are nature trails along the river. Special events include a mustering of the militia and wreath-laying ceremonies on Memorial Day and a cider pressing in October.

Lincoln County Courthouse. Open during business hours throughout the year. Built in 1824, this handsome, red-brick building overlooking the town Common is the oldest functioning courthouse in New England.

Fort Edgecomb State Memorial (882-7777), Edgecomb (off Route 1; the turnoff is just across the Sheepscot River's Davey Bridge from Wiscasset, next to Muddy Rudder restaurant). The fort is open May 30 to Labor Day, daily 9–6. Free admission. This octagonal block house (built in 1809) overlooks a narrow passage of the Sheepscot River. For the same reasons that it was an ideal site for a fort, it is today an ideal picnic site. Tables are provided on the grassy grounds.

FOR FAMILIES

Ocean Adventure (882-4033), Route 1, Edgecomb. Open May through September, Tuesday to Sunday, 10–5. $3.50 per adult, $2.50 per child 4–12. A small museum with live-animal "touch tank," underwater videos, display of commercial fishing gear, and children's playground. (Also see *To Do*.)

OTHER

World's Smallest Church, Route 218. There is barely room for two worshipers in this tiny chapel, maintained as a memorial to a former Boston Baptist minister.

TO DO

Downeast Flying Service (882-6752), Wiscasset, offers year-round sightseeing and fall foliage flights ($15 per person for a half hour); must have three passengers.

Maine Coast Railroad (882-8000 or 1-800-795-5404), at the Wiscasset Town Landing (Water Street, next to Le Garage restaurant). Memorial

Day through Columbus Day. Excursions through the coastal countryside to Newcastle and back aboard a bright red, restored 1920s train; $10 per adult, $5 per child aged 5–12, $25 per family of two adults and up to four children.

LODGING

INNS

Squire Tarbox Inn (882-7693), RD 2, Box 620 (Route 144), Wiscasset 04578 (turn off Route 1 onto Route 144 just south of Wiscasset). Open mid-May to late October. The inn is on Westport Island, 8.5 miles down a winding country road from Route 1. The handsome, Federal-style farmhouse (begun in 1763, completed in 1825) offers 11 inviting guest rooms and an atmosphere that's a mix of elegance (in the common rooms and dining room) and working goat farm. Guests are invited out to the barn to see how innkeepers Bill and Karen Mitman make their cheeses (tellicherry pepper, herb and garlic, and jalapeño as well as plain) and to take advantage of the swing hanging from the barn rafters. A path leads through the woods to a saltwater inlet where a screened area is equipped with binoculars and a birding book, and where a row-boat awaits your pleasure. Four large, formally furnished guest rooms are in the original house, while seven more country-style rooms are in the 1820s converted barn. Goat cheese is served in the gracious living room (where there's a wood stove, a scattering of sofas and chairs, and coffee-table books) at the cocktail hour. A four-course, candlelit dinner (see *Dining Out*) is served at 7 by the big, open fireplace in the attached ell, whose ceiling beams were once ship's timbers. Doubles are $125–210 in-season, including breakfast and dinner; $75–160 for bed & breakfast; add 15 percent gratuity.

The Bailey Inn (882-4214), Main Street, Wiscasset. A longtime landmark inn (formerly The Ledges) that's been renovated, renamed, and re-opened by Susan Rizzo and Joe Sullivan. Rooms are pleasant and have private baths, but inquire about what's been done to eliminate road noise. $85 including breakfast; $75 off-season.

BED & BREAKFASTS

☞ **Marston House** (882-6010), Main Street, PO Box 517, Wiscasset 04578. Open May through November. The front of the house is a shop featuring American antiques. In the carriage house behind this building—well away from the Route 1 traffic noise—are two exceptional rooms, each with private entrance, working fireplace, and private bath. They adjoin each other and can become a two-bedroom suite perfect for families. Breakfast, which is served in your room, features fresh fruit and yogurt, home-baked muffins, and fresh orange juice; it is included in the rate. $75 for a double.

The Stacked Arms (882-5436), c/o Dee Maguire, Birch Point Road, Wiscasset 04578. Open except January. A home offering two guest rooms (one with a private bath) with orthopedic beds and small refrigerators. $65–75 double; $45–50 single in-season.

OTHER LODGING

Cod Cove Inn (882-9586), junction of Routes 1 and 27, PO Box 36, Edgecomb 04556. Open year-round. A 1990s motor inn set above the Sheepscot River with 28 deluxe motel rooms, each with one or two queen-sized beds, a small refrigerator, and a terrace or balcony overlooking the river; some with gas log fireplaces. When we visited, a spa with an exercise room and hot tub was being planned. Owner operated, unusually friendly. Doubles are $88–113 in summer, $55–80 off-season, including fresh homemade muffins and coffee served each morning in the reception area.

Edgecomb Inn (882-6343 or 1-800-437-5503), Box 11, North Edgecomb 04556 (off Route 1, across the bridge from Wiscasset). Open all year. Commands a fine view of Wiscasset; 40 rooms (including efficiency suites) and 15 cottages. Next door, the Muddy Rudder serves lunch and dinner daily (see *Eating Out*). Doubles $69–89 in-season.

WHERE TO EAT

DINING OUT

Squire Tarbox Inn (882-7693), Route 144, Westport Island (also see *Inns*). Open by reservation; open mid-May through late October. A candlelit, four-course dinner is served in a former 18th-century barn with a large fireplace reflecting off ceiling beams that were once ship's timbers. Dinner is preceded by a cocktail hour featuring a complementary selection of savory goat cheeses (made here by innkeepers Karen and Bill Mitman) served variously in the living room, in the less formal game room, by the player piano, or out on the deck. Dinner begins at 7 PM. The menu changes frequently but might include scallops and fettuccine with leeks and cream sauce, or a roulade of sole and spinach. The light-as-air whey rolls are made with goat's milk. After dessert (around 9 PM) guests are invited to visit the barn to pat the friendly Nubian goats as they line up for milking. The prix fixe is $30 per person.

☞ **Le Garage** (882-5409), Water Street, Wiscasset. Open year-round, except January, for lunch and dinner. A 1920s-era garage, now an exceptional restaurant with a glassed-in porch overlooking the Sheepscot River (when you make reservations request a table on the porch). At dinner, many large, wrought-iron candelabra provide the illumination. An extensive menu features local seafood and lamb. It might include a Maine crabmeat casserole with spinach, mushrooms, and scallions ($14.95), or chicken pie ($11.50), and it always features old-fashioned finnan haddie in cream sauce ($10.95). "Light suppers" are $6.95 or $7.95 and may consist of dinner-sized pasta, cheese, and fish salads, and reasonably

A popular eatery in Wiscasset

priced vegetarian selections. The lunch menu features omelets and crêpes, soups and salads, as well as sandwiches; $5.50 for soup and a sandwich.

The Bailey Inn (882-4214), Main Street, Wiscasset (see also *Inns*). Serves breakfast, lunch, and dinner daily, year-round. Light fare is offered in the pub in the attached carriage house. Dinner is served in the more formal dining rooms (linens and candles); a recent menu ranged from fettuccine Alfredo ($8.95) and Moroccan chicken (marinated and skewered; $10.95) to seafood fettuccine with shrimp, scallops, and lobster ($15.95).

Montsweag Restaurant (443-6563), Route 1, Woolwich (south of Wiscasset). Open year-round, 11:30–8 Sunday through Thursday; Friday and Saturday until 9 (8:30 off-season). A longtime landmark in these parts, filled with old photos and nautical memorabilia, this is just as popular with the locals as it is with visitors. The menu hasn't changed much over the years; comments on it reflect the wry humor of the family management. Steak and seafood entrées priced around or under $10. Dine between 4 and 6 and entrées are $6.95–7.50.

EATING OUT

Red's Eats, Water Street, just before the bridge, Wiscasset. Open April through September until 2 AM on Friday and Saturdays, until 11 weeknights, and until 9 on Sundays. A classic hot dog stand but with tables on the sidewalk and behind, overlooking the river. A Route 1 landmark for the past 60 years, good for a quick crab roll or pita pocket as well as a hot dog ($2.50). Tell Al Gagnon we sent you.

Sarah's Pizza and Cafe (882-7504), Main Street, Wiscasset. Open daily.

This popular restaurant fills two storefronts. Offerings include exceptionally good pizza (try the Greek pizza with extra garlic) and stuffed pizza pockets, plus delicious homemade breads, soups, desserts, Mexican dishes, and lobster nine different ways. Wine and a wide choice of beers also served.

- **McLellan's Seafood** (882-6000), Route 1, North Edgecomb. Seasonal. Reasonably priced lobster, fried seafood, chowders, and sandwiches. Picnic tables for summertime dining.
- **Muddy Rudder** (882-7748), Route 1, North Edgecomb (across the bridge from Wiscasset). Open year-round 11–11 daily, Sunday jazz brunch. Your basic seafood and steak menu served in a riverside room with an outdoor deck.

The Sea Basket (882-6581), Route 1 south of Wiscasset. A cheerful diner with lobster the *New York Times* has declared to be the best in Maine.

SELECTIVE SHOPPING

ANTIQUES SHOPS

More than a dozen antiques shops (most carry a leaflet map/guide) can be found in town and just south on Route 1; many specialize in nautical pieces and country primitives.

ART GALLERIES

Maine Art Gallery (633-5055), Warren Street (in the old 1807 academy), Wiscasset. Exhibits by Maine artists; special programs are offered year-round.

Wiscasset Bay Gallery (882-7682), Water Street; changing exhibits, specializing in 19th- as well as 20th-century Maine and New England marine and landscape paintings.

ARTISANS

Sheepscot River Pottery (pastel, floral designs), Route 1 just north of Wiscasset in Edgecomb. **Sirus Graphics,** Wiscasset; mostly made-in-Maine crafts, original design T-shirts. **The Coterie,** Port Wiscasset Building, Water Street; work by Maine artisans: bird houses, tinder boxes, baskets.

Boothbay Harbor Region

The water surrounding the village of Boothbay Harbor brings with it more than just a view. You must cross it—via a footbridge—to get from one side of town to the other, and you can explore it on a wide choice of excursion boats and in sea kayaks. It is obvious from the very lay of this old fishing village that its people have always gotten around on foot or in boats. Cars—which have room to neither park nor pass each other—are an obvious intrusion. The peninsula's other coastal villages, Southport or East Boothbay, also do not lend themselves to exploration by car. Roads are walled by pines, permitting only occasional glimpses of water.

Boats are what all three of the Boothbays have traditionally been about. Boats are built, repaired, and sold here, and sailing and fishing vessels fill the harbors. Excursions range from an hour-long sail around the outer harbor to a 90-minute crossing (each way) to Monhegan Island. Fishermen can pursue giant tuna, stripers, and blues, and nature lovers can cruise out to see seals, whales, and puffins.

Good public beaches are, unfortunately, something that the Boothbays lack entirely; but the resorts and many of the more expensive motels have pools and private beaches, and there are warm-water lakes and ponds. In the middle of the summer, Boothbay Harbor resembles a perpetual carnival: crowds mill along the wharf eating ice cream cones, fudge, and taffy, shopping for souvenirs, and queuing for excursion boats. You get the feeling it's been like this every summer since the 1870s. Still, you can find plenty of timeless peace and beauty in the Boothbays. Most lodging places and summer cottages hug the ocean.

GUIDANCE

Boothbay Harbor Region Chamber of Commerce (633-2353), Box 356, Boothbay Harbor 04538 (open year-round), publishes an annual guide to the area and maintains a Route 27 office (across from the mini-mall) stocked with brochures. **The Boothbay Information Center** (633-4743) farther up Route 27 (open 9–9 daily, Memorial to Columbus Day) is an unusually friendly walk-in center that does its best to help people without reservations find places to stay. It keeps an illustrated scrapbook of options, also a cottage rental list. *Note:* You can call either of the above numbers to find out who has current vacancies.

GETTING THERE

Mid Coast Limo runs to and from the Portland Jetport (1-800-834-5500 within Maine, or 1-800-937-2424 outside Maine). **Wiscasset Taxi** (758-1679) also serves the Boothbays. Boothbay Harbor is 12 miles south on Route 27 from Route 1, 14 miles from Wiscasset, the nearest **Concord Trailways** bus stop (see "Wiscasset").

GETTING AROUND

A free **trolley-on-wheels** runs daily in-season from the parking lot at the Meadow Shopping Center on Route 27. It circulates between the Rocktide Motor Inn on the east side of the harbor and the shops on the west side. Runs daily July and August, every 30 minutes, 7–11 AM (check current schedule).

PARKING

In-town parking is limited, and if you can't squeeze into a metered space, the going fee is a flat $5. The large parking lot at the Meadow Shopping Center on Route 27, the trolley terminus, is free.

MEDICAL EMERGENCY

St. Andrew's Hospital (633-2121), Hospital Point, Mill Cove, Route 27 South, Boothbay Harbor. A well-respected shoreside hospital, St. Andrew's serves the community by land and by water (the hospital has a pier).

TO SEE

Boothbay Region Art Foundation (633-2703), 7 Townsend Avenue, Boothbay Harbor. Open daily, 11–5 weekdays and Saturday, 12–5 on Sunday. Three juried shows are held each season in the 1807 Old Brick House. Works are selected from submissions by artists of the Boothbay region and Monhegan Island.

Boothbay Region Historical Society Museum (633-3666), 70 Oak Street, Boothbay Harbor. Open July and August, Wednesday, Friday, and Saturday 10–4; off-season, Saturday 10–2 or by appointment (633-3462).

Hendricks Hill Museum, Route 27, Southport Island. Open July and August, Tuesday, Thursday, Saturday. An old boardinghouse displays pictures of Southport's old boardinghouses and hotels as well as other village memorabilia, wooden boats, and farm implements.

Boothbay Railway Village (633-4727), Route 27 (1 mile north of Boothbay Harbor). Open daily 9:30–5, mid-June through Labor Day; daily 9:30–4:30 until Columbus Day weekend. Now operated as a museum, Maine's only 2-foot, narrow-gauge railway wends its way through a re-created, miniature, turn-of-the-century village made up of 24 buildings including vintage railroad stations and a doll museum. More than 50 antique autos (1907–1949) are also on display. Admission is $6 per adult and $3 per child. Special events include a large weekend antique auto meet (more than 250 cars) in the latter part of July.

TO DO

BICYCLING

Harbour Hill House (633-4303) across from the Town Landing rents every kind of bike and **Tidal Transit Co.** (633-7140) rents mountain bikes.

BOAT EXCURSIONS

Islander Cruises (633-2500), Pier 6, Fisherman's Wharf. Operates May 20 to October 20. Trips aboard *The Islander* and *Islander III* include seal watches and music cruises.

Balmy Days Cruises (633-2284 or 1-800-298-2284). *Balmy Days II* offers supper cruises and sails every morning early June to late September and weekends in shoulder seasons to Monhegan (see "Rockland" chapter); the crossing is 90 minutes each way, and you have four hours on the island. Bring a picnic and hit the trail. *Maranbo II* offers sightseeing cruises, and *Bay Lady* (633-6990 or 633-6486), sailing out of Pier 1, is a 31-foot Friendship sloop that offers four 90-minute sails in the outer harbor, including a sunset cruise.

Cap'n Fish Boat Cruises (633-3244 or 633-2626), Pier 1 (red ticket booth). Operates mid-May to mid-October, 7 days a week. One-, two-, and three-hour excursions on the *Island Lady, Goodtime, Goodtimes Too,* and *Pink Lady*. Trips to see seals, puffins, whales, lobstering, lighthouses, etc.; also cocktail cruises, sunset cruises, and fall foliage cruises. Monday is senior citizens day. Unadvertised "noon specials" during July and August. Coffee, snacks, soft drinks, beer, wine, and cocktails are available on board. Children under 12 are half price.

BOAT RENTALS

Holladay Marine (633-4767), Route 27, West Boothbay Harbor 04575. Half- and full-day charters, with or without a captain, aboard a variety of Tartan sloops. Weekly charters also.

Midcoast Boat Rentals (882-6445), Pier 8, Boothbay Harbor; rents powerboats.

DEEP-SEA FISHING

Sport fishing boats include *Yellowbird* and *Buccaneer,* both operated by Captain Fish; *Breakaway* (633-4414 or 633-6990) by Captain Pete Ripley; and *Star II* (633-4624), available for private charter only. The catch is mackerel, tuna, shark, bluefish, and stripers.

GOLF

Boothbay Region Country Club (633-6085), Country Club Road (off Route 27), Boothbay. Open spring through late autumn. Nine holes, snack bar, carts, clubs for rent.

HORSEBACK RIDING

Ledgewood Riding Stables (882-6346), Route 27 and Old County Road, Edgecomb 04556. Horses and trails for all levels of expertise. Hourly rates.

SAILING

Several traditional sailing yachts offer to take passengers out for an hour or two, a half day, or a day. These include *Appledore* **V** (633-6598), a 60-foot windjammer that has sailed around the world; and *Heart's Desire* (633-6808), a restored, 45-foot schooner built in 1925, taking up to six people sailing from Smuggler's Cove Inn in East Boothbay. The Friendship sloop *Eastward* (633-4780) is skippered by Roger Duncan, lecturer on local history and author of the New England sailor's bible, *A Cruising Guide to the New England Coast,* plus several other sailing reference works. (Also see *Bay Lady* under Balmy Day Cruises in *Boat Excursions.*) *Tribute* (882-1020), a racing yacht, sails from Ocean Point.

SEA KAYAKING

Tidal Transit Co. (633-7140) offers guided tours.

TENNIS

Boothbay Region YMCA (633-2855), Route 27 (on your left as you come down the stretch that leads to town). An exceptional facility open to nonmembers (use-fee charged) in July and August, with special swimming and other programs for children. Well worth checking out if you will be in the area for a week or more. A wide variety of programs for all ages: tennis, racquetball, gymnastics, aerobics, soccer, swimming, and more.

Public tennis courts are located across the road from the YMCA, next to the Boothbay Region High School, Route 27, on the way into Boothbay Harbor.

GREEN SPACE

BEACHES

The beaches are all private, but visitors are permitted in a number of spots. Here are four: (1) Follow Route 27 toward Southport, across the Townsend Gut Bridge to a circle (white church on the left, monument in the center, general store on the right); turn right and follow Beach Road to the beach, which offers roadside parking and calm, shallow water. (2) Right across from the Boothbay Harbor Yacht Club (Route 27 south), just beyond the post office and at the far end of the parking lot, is a property owned by the yacht club, which puts out a float by July. There are ropes to swing from on the far side of the inlet, a grassy area in which to sun, and a small sandy area beside the water; but the water is too deep for small children. (3) **Barretts Park,** Lobster Cove (turn at the Catholic church, east side of the harbor), is a place to picnic and get wet. (4) **Grimes Cove** has a little beach with rocks to climb at the very tip of Ocean Point, East Boothbay. (Also see Knickerkane Island Park under *Parks.*)

PARKS

Damariscove Island. Over 200 rolling, treeless acres with a long gravel beach, the site of a settlement in 1605, now owned by The Nature Conservancy and open for hiking and bird-watching.

Knickerkane Island Park, Barter's Island Road, Boothbay. Paths lead from the parking lot onto a small island with picnic tables, swimming.

LODGING

The chamber of commerce lists about 50 lodging places, but families should explore the possibilities of the area's many rental cottages. Because the chamber of commerce is open year-round, it's possible to contact them in time to reserve cottages well ahead of time. See *Guidance* for the numbers you can call to check current vacancies in the area.

RESORTS

Spruce Point Inn and Lodges (633-4152; 1-800-553-0289 from outside Maine), Boothbay Harbor 04538. Open late May to late October. Sited on 15 landscaped acres, surrounded by woods and water on the tip of a peninsula, this is a small resort, just 68 rooms divided between the inn, cottages, and condominiums. Ownership changed in 1991, and since then this 95-year-old landmark has been thoroughly and tastefully renovated; the library, living room, and dining room are all unusually attractive. Just eight guest rooms upstairs in the inn itself; most are scattered in one- and two-bedroom cottages with fireplaces and kitchenettes, most with water views. The condominiums are nicely designed but without water views. Amenities include tennis, a heated spa, salt- and freshwater pools, and a free shuttle into town. MAP rates are $86–160 per person. A service charge is added. Children under four are free, and children aged 5–6 are $20–35 MAP.

☞ **Linekin Bay Resort** (633-2494), Boothbay Harbor 04538. Open late June through August. With the largest resort fleet of sailboats in New England, Linekin Bay puts the emphasis squarely on sailing, including lessons and frequent for-the-fun-of-it races. Guests also enjoy the heated saltwater pool, clay and all-weather tennis courts, canoeing, and fishing. Thirty-five rooms are divided between five waterside lodges and 37 cabins scattered through the pines, some with Franklin stoves or fireplaces. The weekly lobster and clam cookout and the Sunday buffet highlight the meals here. One-week minimum stay required except in June. $42–65 per person includes all meals and sailing.

Newagen Seaside Inn (633-5242 or 1-800-654-5242), Route 27, Southport Island, Cape Newagen 04552. Open mid-May through September. A landmark with a present style dating from the forties when it was destroyed by fire; an authentic, informal inn at the seaward tip of Southport Island, 6 miles "out to sea" from Boothbay Harbor. A fir log glowed in the large hearth and guests sat around chatting companionably on the foggy morning we last stopped by. Secluded among the pines, the inn's lawn sweeps down to a mile of bold coastline. There are 22 rooms in the main inn, all with private baths. Heated freshwater pool, large saltwater pool, two tennis courts, many lawn games, rowboats and canoes. Buffet breakfast is included; lunch and dinner are also available. Doubles $95–110 per couple, including breakfast buffet; the suites are $160 per night. Children are just $10–15 extra. Cottages begin at $650 per week; use of all facilities is included.

Ocean Point Inn (633-4200 or 1-800-552-5554), PO Box 409, East Boothbay 04544. Open mid-May to mid-October. Fifteen minutes from Boothbay Harbor, at the tip of the Ocean Point peninsula, next to the East Boothbay Town Pier on Fisherman's Passage. Long established, the complex offers 61 varied rooms in the inn, motel, and cottages, fitted with private baths, color cable TVs, and mini-refrigerators. There's also a pleasant restaurant (see *Dining Out*) and a heated pool. Doubles $85–124 in-season.

⌀ **Ocean Gate** (633-3321 or 1-800-221-5924), Route 27, Southport 04576. Open May to October. The 67 rooms are divided among several buildings, scattered through the wooded property, most with water views. The 85-acre waterfront property includes tennis courts, a dock, boats, pool, outdoor game area, and freshwater pond. There are private decks and porches, plus suites, two efficiencies, and two cottages as well. $80–130 for rooms, $80–135 for efficiencies, $90–125 for suites, and $110–210 for cottages; under age 12, free.

INNS

☞ **Albonegon Inn** (633-2521), Capitol Island 04538 (follow Route 27 to Route 238 in Southport; look for sign). Memorial Day to mid-October. "Determinedly old-fashioned," and proud of it, this inn is a true haven from the 20th century. It is an integral part of the 1880s gingerbread-style summer colony that fills Capitol Island, linked to the real world by a tiny bridge. Innkeeper Kim Peckham grew up summering on Capitol Island, and her great-grandfather stayed at the Albenagon in the 1890s (his signature is in the guest register); preserving its spirit as well as its structure is a labor of love. The summer's profits are visibly reinvested. The 11 rooms are simple but inviting. From the bed in Room 35 you can lie on your side and watch a lobsterman setting his traps. Because this place was built as, rather than converted into, an inn, you find that the shared bath system works exceptionally well: each room is fitted with a sink, and there are half and full baths for every few rooms. Best of all are the porches, hung over the water and lined with classic green rockers. Guests are welcome to grill their own steaks or burgers right here if they would rather not budge from this incredible view at sunset. Fresh-baked muffins, coffee cake, and breads are served each morning in the informal dining room that shares this view. The inn's three cottages (with private baths, also on the water's edge) tend to book up first; one (Periwinkle) has a large deck and a kitchen. $65–73 with shared bath, $73–85 double with private bath; $115 for cottage; $48 single with shared bath.

Lawnmeer Inn (633-2544 or 1-800-633-7645), Box 505, West Boothbay Harbor 04575 (on Route 27 on Southport Island, 2 miles from down-

ALBONEGON INN

A porch with a view in Boothbay Harbor

town Boothbay Harbor). Open mid-May to mid-October. The water-side location is difficult to beat, and most of the 13 nicely decorated rooms in the inn, plus a motel wing with 18 rooms (with decks) have water views; there's also a small cottage. The Lawnmeer was built as a summer hotel in the 1890s and offers attractive common rooms, also a popular restaurant (see *Dining Out*). $80–120 double or single occupancy; less off-season. Two-night minimum weekends in July and August.

BED & BREAKFASTS

Five Gables Inn (633-4551 or 1-800-451-5048 outside Maine), Murray Hill Road (off Route 96), PO Box 75, East Boothbay 04544. Open mid-May through mid-November. Built around 1865, this old summer boardinghouse has been totally renovated into an unpretentious but luxurious B&B. All 15 thoughtfully furnished rooms have ocean views and private baths; most have queen-sized beds, and 5 have working fireplaces. There are rocking chairs on the wraparound veranda and a welcoming fireplace in the common room; an extensive buffet breakfast is included in $80–130 double. Children over 8 welcome.

Welch House (633-3431), 36 McKown Street, Boothbay Harbor 04538. Open May through late October. A grand view of the harbor and islands beyond can be enjoyed from most of the 16 individually decorated rooms (some canopy beds), all with private baths. We prefer the 10 rooms in the 1850 sea captain's house to those in the adjacent Sail Loft (more modern decor). Exceptional views of harbor and islands from a third-floor observation deck, main deck, and glass-enclosed breakfast room where an electric tea kettle can always be used to make tea and coffee. Breakfast includes Martha Mason's homemade granola and a variety of homemade muffins. $50–95. Two-night minimum stay weekends between July 4 and Labor Day. Smoking only on outside decks.

Sailmaker's Inn (633-7390), Route 96 and Church Street, East Boothbay 04544. A cupola-topped Victorian home in the village of East Boothbay, built in the 1870s by sailmaker Reuben Jones. This friendly B&B offers two large guest rooms appointed with antiques (private baths). Rates include a full country breakfast (frequently featuring souffles); evening desserts served. Your Arkansas- and Iowa-born hosts, Philip and Darla Parker, are antiques dealers who delight in sharing gems like their 1920 Victrola (and records). $75–90.

Hodgdon Island Inn (633-7474), Barter's Island Road, Boothbay (mailing address: Box 492, Boothbay 04571). Open most of the year. On a quiet road overlooking an inlet, handy to swimming at Knickerkane Island Park (see *Green Space*), this B&B offers five attractive rooms (private baths) with water views in a restored sea captain's house. Syndey and Joseph Klenk are helpful hosts and justly pride themselves on their heated, chlorine-free swimming pool set in a landscaped garden. $70–85. Two-night minimum stay on holiday weekends.

Kenniston Hill Inn B&B (633-2159 or 1-800-992-2915 from outside Maine), Route 27, Boothbay 04537. Open year-round. A stately, 200-year-old pillared Colonial (one of Boothbay's oldest homes) set back from the road as it curves around to the Boothbay town Green. Ten comfortable guest rooms, all with private baths; six working fireplaces. Walk to the Boothbay Country Club for golf, or drive the couple of miles down to the harbor. The full country breakfast may include peaches-and-cream French toast, ham and Swiss in puff pastry, or three-cheese pie with tomato and sweet basil. $80–110 double or single, breakfast included. Inquire about dinner by reservation off-season.

Lion's Den (633-7367 or 1-800-887-7367), 106 Townsend Avenue, Boothbay Harbor 04538. Open year-round. Informal, family atmosphere; a short walk to downtown. Seven rooms, some with private bath and/or water views. Rates range from $47–70 for one or two people, including a full breakfast; longer and off-season stays are less. Children welcome.

Jonathan's (633-3588), 15 Eastern Avenue, Boothbay Harbor 04538. Open year-round. Named for that famous sea gull, this 100-year-old Cape offers three bedrooms (all private baths) in a quiet neighborhood, a few minutes from downtown Boothbay Harbor. $65–85, including a generous breakfast and afternoon sherry. Special rates available.

Anchor Watch (633-2284), 3 Eames Road, Boothbay Harbor 04538. Open year-round except mid-December through mid-February. Oceanfront sea captain's home overlooking islands, lobstermen hauling their catches, lighthouses. Private baths. Within walking distance of downtown. Full breakfast. $85–105.

Atlantic Ark Inn (633-5690), 64 Atlantic Avenue, Boothbay Harbor

04538. Open Memorial Day through October. Furnished with antiques and oriental rugs, this pleasant B&B is removed (but accessible by footbridge) from the bustle of the harbor. Six rooms in the inn, plus a cottage; all have private baths and most have queen-sized beds (some mahogany four-posters). Some rooms have harbor views and private balconies. The suite at the top of the house ($215) has 14 windows, cathedral ceilings, French doors opening on harbor views, a Jacuzzi, and balcony. Full breakfast includes special egg dishes (nothing as trite as bacon and eggs) and home-baked breads; sherry and/or wine is served in the afternoon. $65–215; $119 for the cottage. Two-night stays encouraged on major holiday weekends.

Seawitch Bed & Breakfast (633-7804), 5 miles south of Route 1 off Route 27, Box 27, Boothbay 04537. A new house, beautifully built along traditional lines, sequestered up a private road in 80 wooded acres near Sherman Cove. There are just two large guest rooms, each with a fireplace and sitting area; guests are welcomed with wine and appetizers in the library, and breakfast is very full. $110–120 per room.

☞✎**Emma's Guest House and Cottages** (633-5287), 110 Atlantic Avenue, Boothbay Harbor 04538. Open May to November. An old-fashioned guest house, plus efficiency cottages on Spruce Point and in East Booth Bay. Each room accommodates three or four people. Water views. Rooms are $35–50, including continental breakfast.

COTTAGES

Note: Contact the chambers of commerce for lists of rental cottages; quality is traditionally high and prices are affordable in the Boothbays. In addition the **Boothbay Cottage Connection** (663-6545) represents 80 properties.

Harborfields (633-5082), West Boothbay Harbor 04575. Open June to October. Eight housekeeping cottages, plus a suite in an 1870 house and rental of the original 1750 homestead. All accommodations have water views and private baths. Cottages are in a variety of sizes, but all have complete kitchens, fireplaces, and everything you need including flatware, cookware, wood for the fireplace, and linens. There are 10 acres of woods and fields, plus a half mile of shorefront. Cottages $520–800 per week; 1750 homestead $800 per week; suite in house $520 per week.

☞✎**Hillside Acres Motor Court** (633-3411), Route 27 (Adams Pond Road), PO Box 300, Boothbay 04537. Open mid-May through mid-October. Seven newly renovated cabins, including four efficiency units, plus an apartment and two B&B rooms, all on a quiet hillside. Electric heat, showers, color TVs. Swimming pool. Complimentary muffins, coffee cakes, and coffee are served mid-June through Labor Day. $40–68; weekly rates, too.

MOTELS

Boothbay Harbor has a number of inviting motels, but we defer to the Mobil and AAA guides.

WHERE TO EAT

DINING OUT
The Black Orchid (633-6659), 5 By Way, Boothbay Harbor. Seasonal, open for dinner except Tuesday. A family-owned trattoria serving classic Italian dishes with a twist, like fettuccine Alfredo with fresh lobster meat and mushrooms, rolled stuffed scaloppine and baked haddock with tomatoes and lemon pesto. In the less formal Bocce Club Cafe upstairs, there are seafood and raw oyster bars. No more than six people per table. No smoking. Entrées: $10.95–24.95.

Lawnmeer Inn (633-2544), Route 27, Southport Island (just across the bridge). Open for dinner and Sunday brunch. Reservations appreciated. This very pleasant dining room sports large windows overlooking the water. The menu changes frequently but might include boneless chicken breast wrapped in prosciutto with mushrooms and Marsala wine ($14.95) or roast lamb leg *au poivre* with Dijon mustard and cognac ($15.95). Entrées include salad as well as starch. Sunday brunch might feature Belgian waffles ($4.95) or *huevos rancheros* ($5.95). Some people come just for dessert.

Spruce Point Inn (633-4152), east side of outer harbor at Spruce Point. Open mid-June to mid-September; reservations advised. A gracious, old-fashioned inn with a sophisticated menu to match its decor. Entrées might include grilled marinated chicken breast ($14.75), "two texture duck" ($19.25), and lemon grass–smoked scallops ($18.75).

Newagen Seaside Inn (633-5242), Cape Newagen, Southport Island. Open seasonally, closed Tuesdays. A pleasant, old-fashioned dining room and splendid grounds to walk off entrées, which might include fresh salmon with lobster sauce, curried shrimp with fresh linguine, or grilled lamb chops. Specialties include chicken Newagen, Newagen shortcake, and house pies.

Brown Brothers Wharf (633-5440), Atlantic Avenue, Boothbay Harbor. Dining room opens in mid-June. One of Maine's better-known seafood restaurants, the largest in the area. Established in 1945. Seafood and steaks; a variety of lobster dishes. Breakfast and dinner.

Ocean Point Restaurant (633-4200), East Boothbay. Open late June to Columbus Day weekend. In a traditional dining room overlooking Linekin Bay you might dine on blackberry-glazed chicken ($10.25), vegetable lasagne ($11.25), or veal sautéed with prosciutto and snap peas ($16.95).

EATING OUT
Carriage House (633-6025), Ocean Point Road, East Boothbay. Open year-round, daily 11–10. This friendly find offers entrées ranging from a fried fisherman's platter ($12.95) and a wide choice of charbroiled beef cuts ($13.95) to a wide variety of pastas and sandwiches; luncheon

specials run $3.95–7.95, and the daily "all you can eat haddock fry" is $6.95 or $8.95.

Ebb Tide (633-5692), Commercial Street, Boothbay Harbor. Open year-round. Great breakfasts are served all day plus good things such as lobster rolls, club sandwiches, and fisherman's platters; wonderful homemade desserts like peach shortcake. An old-fashioned place with knotty pine walls, booths; look for the red-striped awning.

No Anchovies (633-2130), just off Townsend Avenue, at the entrance to the public parking lot. A pleasant, informal Italian restaurant with especially good pizza and imaginative toppings.

Thistle Inn (633-3541), 53 Oak Street, Boothbay Harbor. Open year-round, 11:30–2 and 5–9. David Welch has revived this popular local pub with its moderately priced menu (specialties include lobster pie); live music.

Fisherman's Wharf (633-5090), Boothbay Harbor (on the water). This is a big place, geared to groups and bus tours. Nicely prepared seafood, boiled lobster, and other standard fare. Three meals are served daily.

1820 House at Smuggler's Cove (632-2800), East Boothbay. A glass-walled dining room with a very pleasant atmosphere specializing in broiled fish, chicken, and steak. Moderate prices, children's menu.

Andrew's Harborside Restaurant (633-4074), Boothbay Harbor (downtown, next to the municipal parking lot and footbridge). Open 7 days a week, May to October. The chef-owner specializes in creative seafood dishes. Three meals served daily. Round Top Ice Cream is dispensed from a window at the parking lot level.

Chowder House Restaurant, Granary Way, Boothbay Harbor (beside the municipal parking lot and footbridge). Serves lunch and dinner in a restored old building that also houses several small shops. Seating is around an open kitchen and outside on a waterside deck. Chowders, obviously, plus lobster stew, salads, homemade breads, seafood, and full dinners. Serves lunch 11–5, after which the dinner menu is offered.

Maxfield's Harbour High Cafe (633-3444), Boothbay Harbor (across the street from the post office). Open daily February through December for lunch, dinner, and Sunday brunch. Indoor and deck dining. Fine family fare, including Swiss cheese pie, chowder, seven-layer salad, and a variety of seafood and meat entrées.

MacNab's (633-7222), Back River Road (first driveway on the left), Boothbay. Open daily 11–6. Billed as "the area's only Scottish tea room," serving "cock a leekie" soup and sandwiches as well tea and scones; high tea by reservation.

Tugboat Inn (633-4434), Boothbay Harbor. Open for lunch and dinner year-round. A tugboat has been incorporated into this large restaurant with water views. It includes a lounge, piano bar, and outdoor cocktail deck. Seafood and steaks. Broiled haddock, sautéed lobster, and many seafood dinners.

Everybody's (633-6113), Route 27. Open year-round for breakfast, lunch, and dinner. A casual, inexpensive place that's very popular with locals. All sorts of salad entrées plus light suppers and dinners. Sandwiches at lunchtime.

J.H. Hawk Ltd., Boothbay Harbor (right on the dock in the middle of town, upstairs). An inviting restaurant liberally decorated with nautical artifacts, offering a large menu ranging from basic burgers to pastas and steaks, pan-blackened fish, and meat in Louisiana Cajun style. Ask about live entertainment.

⌨ **Brud's Hotdogs,** in the middle of the village and on the east side of the harbor. Keep an eye out for Brud's motorized cart—he has been selling juicy dogs around town for almost 50 summers.

Crump's (633-7655), 20A McKown Street, Boothbay Harbor. A tiny English dining room serving ploughman's lunches, cappuccino and espresso, and, in the afternoon, authentic Devonshire cream teas with scones and finger sandwiches. There's also a small gift shop on the premises, with many items from Great Britain.

Dunton's Doghouse, Signal Point Marina, Boothbay Harbor. Open May through September, 11–8. Good, reasonably priced take-out food, including a decent $3.95 crabmeat roll.

LOBSTER POUNDS

⌨☞**Robinson's Wharf** (633-3830), Route 27, Southport Island (just across Townsend Gut from West Boothbay Harbor). Open mid-June through Labor Day; lunch and dinner daily, 11–8:45. Children's menu. Sit outside at picnic tables and watch the boats unload their catch. Pick out your lobster before it's cooked, or buy some live lobsters to cook at home. Seafood rolls, fried shrimp, clams, scallops, fish chowder, lobster stew, sandwiches, and homemade desserts.

Boothbay Region Lobstermen's Co-op (633-4900), Atlantic Avenue (east side of the harbor). Open mid-May to mid-October, 8 AM–8 PM. The basics: boiled lobsters and steamed clams to be eaten at picnic tables on an outside deck on the water or indoors.

Lobsterman's Wharf (633-3443), Route 96, East Boothbay (adjacent to a boatyard). Open April to October. Popular with locals. Boiled lobsters to eat at the outside tables over the water or inside. The menu also includes a wide variety of more complex entrées.

⌨ **Clambake at Cabbage Island** (633-7200). The *Argo* departs Pier 6 at Fisherman's Wharf twice daily in-season, carrying passengers to Cabbage Island for a clambake (including steamed lobsters). An old lodge, built in 1900, seats up to 100 people by a huge fireplace.

The Lobster Dock (633-7120), at the east end of the footbridge. Open seasonally noon until 8:30. When downtown Boothbay restaurants are packed, you can walk across the footbridge to this relatively peaceful little place, offering both inside and outside lunches and dinners, fried fish, and the usual sandwiches plus lobster and shore dinners, steamed clams and mussels.

SNACKS

Downeast Ice Cream Factory (633-2816), Boothbay Harbor (on the byway). Homemade ice cream and make-your-own sundae buffet; all sorts of toppings, including real hot fudge.

ENTERTAINMENT

Carousel Music Theatre (633-5297), Route 27, near Boothbay Harbor. Performances mid-May to late October. Doors open at 6:30 PM; show begins at 7. Closed Sunday. Light meals (sandwich baskets and such) and cocktails are served by the cast before they hop onto the stage to sing Broadway tunes cabaret-style and then to present a fully costumed and staged revue of a Broadway play.

Marina Deck (633-4434), Boothbay Harbor (at the Tugboat Inn). Open June through Columbus Day. A view of the harbor's lights and a good spot for a nightcap. Piano bar nightly. Specialty drinks emphasize low-alcohol choices. Light meals include salads of lobster, shrimp, or crab; steamers, burgers, and lobster rolls.

Thursday evening concerts by the Hallowell Band on the library lawn, Boothbay Harbor. July 4 through Labor Day, 8 PM.

Lincoln Arts Festival (633-4676) concerts throughout the summer in varied locations.

SELECTIVE SHOPPING

ART GALLERIES

The Butke Studio and Gallery (633-3442), Sawyer's Island, Boothbay. Housed in an old barn featuring regional paintings and crafted gifts and clothing.

Bridge House StudioGallery, in a little house smack in the middle of the footbridge linking the two sides of the harbor. Original watercolors by Captain Marion Dash. Local scenes, birds. Open intermittently.

ARTISANS

Andersen Studio, East Boothbay. Acclaimed stoneware animal sculptures of museum quality.

Nathaniel S. Wilson, East Boothbay. A sailmaker who also fashions distinctive tote bags from canvas.

Hasenfus Glass Shop, Commercial Street, Boothbay Harbor. It's called glassblowing, but it's really the heating and bending of glass tubes into all sorts of imaginative ornaments, from fully rigged sailing ships to tiny animals.

A Silver Lining, Boothbay Harbor. Working metalsmiths. Original sculpture and jewelry in brass, sterling, and gold.

Edgecomb Potter's Gallery, Route 27, Edgecomb. Lovely pottery lamps, bowls, cookware, and jewelry.

Abacus Gallery, Boothbay Harbor. An appealing shop showcasing the very best of contemporary crafts. Many pieces show the artists' wonderful sense of humor. Even if you are not buying, be sure to go browsing here.

The Gold Smith, Boothbay Harbor. In a white-clapboard house across the street from Abacus. Unusual selection of jewelry in both gold and silver.

Lupine Court, Townsend Avenue, Boothbay Harbor. Unusual crafts.

SPECIAL SHOPS

Palabra, 85 Commercial Street, Boothbay Harbor, across from Hasenfus Glass. A warren of more than a dozen rooms offering everything from kitschy souvenirs to valuable antiques. Upstairs (open by request) is a Poland Spring Museum with an impressive collection of the Moses Bottles this natural spring water used to come in, plus other memorabilia from the heyday of the resort at Poland Spring.

House of Logan, Townsend Avenue, Boothbay Harbor. Beautiful quality clothing for men and women.

Sherman's Book & Stationery Store, 7 Commercial Street, Boothbay Harbor. A two-story emporium filled with souvenirs, kitchenware, and games as well as a full stock of books, specializing in nautical titles.

Sweet Woodruff Farm (633-6977), Route 27, Boothbay 04537. Open May through December. One of the oldest homes in Boothbay, this rambling 1767 Cape houses an antiques and herb shop that features herbs that are grown and dried on the premises. Wreaths, potpourris, herb vinegars, and more. Special open houses are held in May and at the end of November.

Sherman's Book and Stationery Store (633-7262), 7 Commercial Street, Boothbay 04538. Large stock of general books and other merchandise. Maine and marine books a specialty.

SPECIAL EVENTS

April: **Fishermen's Festival**—contests for fishermen and lobstermen, cabaret ball, crowning of the Shrimp Princess, and blessing of the fleet.

Late June/early July: **Windjammer Days**—parade of windjammers into the harbor, fireworks, band concert, street dance, church suppers, parade of floats, bands, and beauty queens up Main Street. The big event of the summer.

Late July: **Friendship Sloop Days**—parade and race of traditional fishing sloops built nearby in Friendship. **Antique Auto Shows,** Boothbay Railway Village, Route 27.

Early August: **Tuna Tournament,** with prizes for the biggest catch.

Early October: **Fall Foliage Festival**—boat trips to view foliage, church suppers, and craft sales. Annual **Fall Fair** at Boothbay Railway Village.

Early December: **Harbor Lights Festival**—parade, crafts, holiday shopping.

Damariscotta/Newcastle and Pemaquid Area

The Damariscotta region encompasses the Pemaquid peninsula communities of Bristol, Pemaquid, New Harbor, and Round Pond. It also includes the inland villages around Lake Damariscotta as well as the exceptional twin villages of Damariscotta and Newcastle and their German-accented neighbor, Waldoboro. Nowhere else in Maine do you miss quite as much by simply sticking to Route 1.

Damariscotta's musical name means "meeting place of the alewives," and in spring there are indeed spawning alewives to be seen by the waterfall at Damariscotta Mills, not far from a spot where Native Americans once heaped oyster shells from their summer feasts. Native Americans also had a name for the peninsula jutting 10 miles seaward from this spot: Pemaquid, meaning "long finger."

Pemaquid loomed large on 16th- and 17th-century maps because its protected inner harbor was the nearest mainland haven for Monhegan, a busy fishing area for European fishermen. It was from these fishermen that the Pemaquid Native American, Samoset, learned the English with which he welcomed the Pilgrims at Plymouth in 1621. It was also from these fishermen that Plimoth Plantation, the following winter, secured supplies enough to see it through to spring. Pemaquid, however, lacked a Governor William Bradford in its history. Although it is occasionally referred to as this country's first permanent settlement, its historical role remains murky.

The site of Maine's "Lost City" is a delightful mini-peninsula bordered by the Pemaquid River and Johns Bay (named for Captain John Smith, who explored here in 1614). At one tip stands a round stone fort (a replica built in the early 1900s). In recent years, more than 40,000 artifacts have been unearthed in the adjacent meadow, many of them now displayed at the state-run museum that is part of the Colonial Pemaquid Restoration. An old cemetery full of crooked slate headstones completes the scene.

Since the late 19th century, when steamboats began to put into New Harbor and other ports in the area, this region has supported an abundance of summer inns and cottages. It is especially appealing to

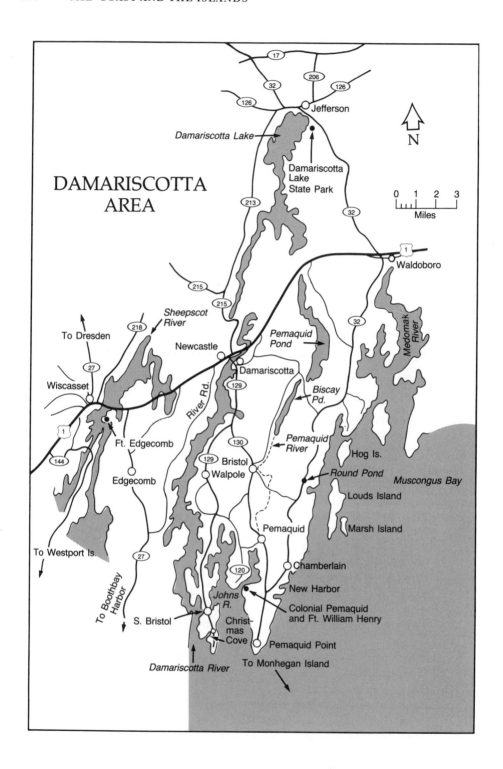

families with young children since it offers warm-water lake beaches as well as saltwater strands and smooth coastal rocks for climbing. No one should fail to clamber around the especially fascinating rocks at Pemaquid Point, one of Maine's most photogenic lighthouses.

GUIDANCE

Damariscotta Information Bureau, Damariscotta 04543, operates two seasonal offices: one on Route 1 in Newcastle just south of the Damariscotta exit (563-3176), and another on Business Route 1, in town, on Church Street (563-3175) at the top of the hill near Chapman-Hall House. Both are open mid-June through September, 10–6, closed Sunday, and can be reached year-round by mail and phone. There is also the **Damariscotta Region Chamber of Commerce** (563-8340), PO Box 13, Damariscotta 04543, with an office just off Main Street in the middle of town. Enter the side door of the building that houses the Salt Bay Cafe. The chamber is open 9–1 Monday, Wednesday, Thursday, and Friday, and 1–5 Tuesday. Both organizations will help you plan your visit.

GETTING THERE

Concord Trailways (1-800-639-8080) stops in Damariscotta and Waldoboro en route from Portland to Bangor.

Mid Coast Limo runs to and from the Portland Jetport (1-800-834-5500 within Maine or 1-800-937-2424 outside Maine). Most inns on the peninsula will pick up guests in Damariscotta, but basically this is the kind of place where you will want to have a car—or a boat—to get around. **Wiscasset Taxi** (758-1679) also serves the Damariscotta area.

MEDICAL EMERGENCY

Miles Memorial Hospital (563-1234), Bristol Road, Damariscotta.

VILLAGES

Damariscotta/Newcastle. The twin villages of Newcastle and Damariscotta (connected by a bridge) form the commercial center of the region. The main street is flanked by fine examples of 19th-century brick storefronts, many of them now restored. Shops and restaurants are tucked down alleyways. Note the towns' two exceptional churches and check the program of concerts and festivals at the Round Top Center for the Arts on Upper Main Street. Damariscotta Mills, a short drive up Route 215 from Newcastle, has some elegant houses and a great little picnic spot on Lake Damariscotta.

Waldoboro. An inscription in the cemetery of the Old German Church (see *To See*) relates the deceptive way in which landholder General Samuel Waldo lured the town's first German settlers here. The church and much of the town overlook the Medomak (pronounced with the emphasis on "Medo") River. Bypassed by Route 1, the village includes some architecturally interesting buildings, some good, small restaurants, and a theater staging films, concerts, and live performances.

Round Pond. The name was obviously inspired by the village's almost circular harbor, said to have been a pirate base (Captain Kidd's treasure may be buried here in the Devil's Oven). It was once a major shipbuilding spot, and still is a working fishing and lobstering harbor (also see *Eating Out*).

New Harbor. About as picturesque a working harbor as any in Maine. Take South Side Road to Back Cove and walk out on the wooden pedestrian bridge for a great harbor view. (Also see *Eating Out*.)

South Bristol. Be prepared to stop and find a parking space as you near this tiny village, a cluster of charming houses and shops around a busy drawbridge.

TO SEE

HISTORIC SITES

Colonial Pemaquid State Historic Site (677-2423), Pemaquid (off Route 130). Maintained by the state Bureau of Parks and Recreation and open daily Memorial Day to Labor Day, 9:30–5. $2 adults; $.50 ages 5–11; under 5 and over 65 free (ticket also admits you to Fort William Henry— see next entry). In the early 19th century, local farmers filled in the cellar holes of the 17th-century settlement that once stood here. Excavations in recent years were initiated by Rutgers University Professor Helen Camp, who noticed clay pipes and other artifacts in a newly plowed field. The state has since purchased this neck of land, and archaeologists have uncovered the foundations of early 17th-century homes, a customs house, a tavern and the jail. Inside the museum—one of very few in-the-field archaeological museums open to the public anywhere—you view dioramas of the original 1620s settlement and artifacts such as a 16th-century German wine jug and slightly less aged tools and pottery, Spanish oil jars, and wampum—all found in the cellar holes just outside. Nearby is the old burial ground dating from 1695.

Fort William Henry, off Route 130, next to the archaeological museum. Open daily Memorial Day to Labor Day, 9:30–5. $2 adults; $.50 ages 5–11; under 5 and over 65 free (ticket also admits you to the Colonial Pemaquid museum). This is a replica (built in 1907) of the third in the series of three English forts and one fortified warehouse built on this one site to fend off pirates and the French. In 1630 a stockade was built, but it was sacked and burned by pirate Dixie Bull (Captain Kidd is said to have buried treasure in a cave called Devil's Oven near New Harbor). In 1677 Governor Andros built a wooden redoubt manned by 50 men, but this was captured by Baron Castine and his Native American allies in 1689 (see the "Castine" chapter). The original of this particular fort, built in 1698, was to be "the most expensive and strongest fortification that has ever been built on American soil," but it was destroyed by the French a year later.

Fort Frederick, built in 1729, was never attacked, but during the American Revolution locals tore it down lest it fall into the hands of the British. Inside the fort are exhibits on the early explorations of Maine and a panoramic view from the ramparts. The striking 1790 captain's house adjacent to the fort is not open to the public; it serves as the lab for the ongoing research work. There are picnic tables on the grounds with great views of the surrounding water.

Pemaquid Point Lighthouse (677-2494 or 677-2726), Route 130 (at the end), Pemaquid Point. The point is owned by the town, which charges a $1 per person entrance fee during the summer (senior citizens $.50; under 12 free). The lighthouse, built in 1824 and automated in 1934, is a beauty, looking even more impressive from the rocks below than from up in the parking lot. These rocks offer a wonderfully varied example of geological upheaval, with tilted strata and igneous intrusions. The tidal pools can occupy children and adults alike for an entire day—but take care not to get too close to the water since the waves can be dangerous, catching people off balance and pulling them into the water. The rocks stretch for half a mile to Kresge Point. The **Fishermen's Museum,** housed in the former lighthouse keeper's home, is open Memorial Day to Columbus Day, Monday through Saturday 10–5 and Sunday 11–5. It contains fine photographs and ship models as well as other artifacts related to the Maine fishing industry and a description of the coast's lighthouses. Voluntary donations are requested of visitors to the lighthouse and museum. The complex also includes the **Pemaquid Art Gallery,** where works by local artists are exhibited from the end of June through mid-September. Donations requested here go toward art scholarships for local high school students. There are picnic tables and public toilets on the grounds. Next door to the lighthouse is the Sea Gull Shop and Restaurant (see *Eating Out*).

Thompson's Ice House (644-8551 in summer; 729-1956 in winter), Route 129 in South Bristol, 12 miles south of Damariscotta. Open July and August, Wednesday, Friday, and Saturday 1–4; $1 per adult, $.50 per child. One of the few surviving, commercial icehouses in New England, this 150-year-old family business uses traditional tools for cutting ice from an adjacent pond. In summer a slide and video presentation in the museum wing shows how the ice is still harvested in February; tools and ice (used all summer by local fishermen) are also on display.

Old Rock Schoolhouse, Bristol (follow signs from Route 130 to Route 132). Open during summer months, Tuesday and Friday 2–4. Dank and haunting, this 1827 rural stone schoolhouse stands at a long-overgrown crossroads in the woods.

Shell Heaps. These ancient heaps of oyster shells, left by generations of Native Americans at their summer encampments in what are now Newcastle and Damariscotta, have become incorporated into the tall hillsides along the riverbank. A close look at the soil, however, reveals the presence of the shells. The heaps—or middens, as they are called—are on private land. Inquire at the Damariscotta Information Bureau (see *Guidance*) regarding their whereabouts and permission to see them.

Samoset Memorial, New Harbor. Built of locally quarried stone, this monument is in memory of Chief Samoset, who sold land to John Brown of New Harbor, creating the first deed executed in New England. Loud's Island, off Round Pond, was Samoset's home.

Chapman-Hall House, corner of Main and Church Streets, Damariscotta (in the village, diagonally across from the First National Bank of Damariscotta). Open mid-June to mid-September daily, except Monday, 1–5. Admission $1. Built in 1754, this is the oldest homestead in the region. The house has been restored with its original kitchen. There is also an herb garden with 18th-century rosebushes.

HISTORICAL SOCIETY MUSEUM

Waldoborough Historical Society Museum, Route 220, just south of Route 1. Open late June to early September and weekends in October, 1–4:30. A complex of three buildings, including a restored school, town pound, and hall housing local memorabilia.

HISTORIC CHURCHES

This particular part of the Maine coast possesses an unusual number of fine old meetinghouses and churches, all of which are open to the public.

St. Patrick's Catholic Church, Academy Road, Newcastle (Route 215 north of Damariscotta Mills). Open year-round, daily, to sunset. This is the oldest surviving Catholic church (1808) in New England. It is an unusual building: brick construction, very narrow, and graced with a Paul Revere bell. The pews and stained glass date from 1896; and there is an old graveyard out back with forests all around.

St. Andrew's Episcopal Church (563-3533), Glidden Street, Newcastle. A charming, half-timbered building on the bank of the Damariscotta River. Set among gardens and trees, it was the first commission in this country for Henry Vaughan, the English architect who went on to design the National Cathedral in Washington, D.C.

Old Walpole Meeting House (563-5660), Route 129, South Bristol. Open during July and August, Sunday for 3 PM services, and by appointment. A 1772 meetinghouse with box pews and a pulpit with a sounding board.

Harrington Meeting House, Route 130, Pemaquid. Open during July and August, Monday, Wednesday, Friday, and Saturday 2–4:30. Donations expected. The 1772 building has been restored and serves as a museum of "Old Bristol." A nondenominational service is held here once a year, usually on the third Sunday in August.

Old German Church (832-5100), Route 32, Waldoboro. Open daily during July and August, 1–4. Built in 1772 with square-benched pews and a wineglass pulpit; note the inscription in the cemetery: "This town was settled in 1748 by Germans who immigrated to this place with the promise and expectation of finding a prosperous city, instead of which

Harrington Meeting House, 1772

they found nothing but wilderness." Bostonian Samuel Waldo—owner of a large tract of land in this area—obviously had not been straight with the 40 German families he brought to settle it. This was the first Lutheran church in Maine; it's maintained by the German Protestant Society.

SCENIC DRIVES
From Newcastle, Route 215 winds along **Damariscotta Lake** to Damariscotta Mills; continue along the lake and through farm country on Route 213 (note the scenic pullout across from the Bunker Hill Church, with a view down the lake) to Jefferson for a swim at Damariscotta Lake State Park.

Pemaquid Peninsula. Follow Route 129 south from Damariscotta, across the South Bristol Bridge to Christmas Cove. Backtrack and cross the peninsula via Harrington Meeting House Road to Colonial Pemaquid. Turn south on Route 130 to Pemaquid Point and return via Route 32 and Round Pond; take Biscay Road back to Damariscotta or continue on Route 32 into Waldoboro.

TO DO

BICYCLING
Lane's Bike Rental (677-3574) in New Harbor rents a variety of bicycles.
BOAT EXCURSIONS
Hardy Boat (Captain Vern Lewis: 677-2026 days or 882-7909 evenings),

Shaw's Wharf, New Harbor. The *Hardy III* goes to Monhegan Island daily and also offers sight-seeing trips to see puffins (with an Audubon narrator on board) and seals, plus a sunset cruise to Pemaquid Point. Inquire about the optional clambake on Monhegan.

BOAT RENTALS

Damariscotta Lake Farm (549-7953) in Jefferson rents boats and motors for use on 13-mile-long Damariscotta Lake.

FISHING

Damariscotta Lake is a source of bass, landlocked salmon, and trout.

GOLF

Wawenock Country Club (563-3938), Route 129 (7 miles south of Damariscotta). Open May to November. Nine holes; visitors are welcome.

HORSEBACK RIDING

Hill-n-Dale Riding Stables (273-2511) in Warren and **Tide's End Riding Stables** (832-4431) in Waldoboro, as well as **The Willows Ranch** (563-8543) in Damariscotta, offer trail rides.

SWIMMING

On the peninsula there is public swimming at **Biscay Pond**, off Route 32, and at **Bristol Dam** on Route 130, 5 miles south of Damariscotta (also see *Green Space*).

SPECIAL LEARNING PROGRAMS

National Audubon Ecology Camp, Hogg Island (0.25 mile offshore at the head of Muscongus Bay). Established a half-century ago, these 1- and 2-week sessions study the wildlife on the island, including ospreys, black guillemots, moose, deer, porcupines, harbor seals, eider ducks, loons, warblers, and, from a boat, the puffins that were reintroduced to nearby Eastern Egg Rock by the Audubon-related Puffin Project. There are 5 miles of spruce trails, wildflower and herb gardens, and mud flats surrounding rustic accommodations in a cluster of bungalows and a dining room in a restored 19th-century farmhouse. Famed instructors have included Roger Tory Peterson and Olin Sewall Pettingill. About 50 adult campers are accepted each session. For more information and dates, call 203-869-2017 or write National Audubon Society Ecology Camps and Workshops, 613 Riverside Road, Greenwich, CT 06831.

GREEN SPACE

BEACHES

Pemaquid Beach Park (677-2754), Route 130, Pemaquid. A town-owned area open Memorial Day to Labor Day, 9–5. Admission is $1 per adult, under 12 free. Bathhouse, rest rooms, refreshment stand, and picnic tables. Pleasant, but it can be windy, in which case try the more pebbly but more sheltered (and free) beach down the road.

Damariscotta Lake State Park, Route 32, Jefferson. A fine, sandy beach with changing facilities, picnic tables, and grills at the northern end of the lake.

NATURE PRESERVES

Rachel Carson Memorial Salt Pond, at the side of Route 32, just north of Round Pond. There's a beautiful view of the open ocean from here, and at low tide the tidal pools are filled with tiny sea creatures. Here Rachel Carson researched her book *The Edge of the Sea.*

Dodge Point Preserve on the River Road south of Newcastle offers a loop trail through pond and marsh to Sand Beach on the river. Roughly a mile south of Newcastle on the River Road, look for "FL30" (Fire Lane 30) on the river side of the road.

Witch Island, South Bristol. An 18-acre wooded island lies 0.25 mile off-shore at the east end of "The Gut," the narrow channel that serves as South Bristol's harbor. A perimeter trail around the island threads through oaks and pines, allowing views of Johns Bay. Two sheltered beaches offer swimming, picnicking, and access to a small skiff, kayak, or canoe.

PICNICKING

There are two nice picnic areas on Route 130 in Bristol, one at **Lighthouse Park** and another at **Pemaquid Beach Park.** There are also picnic tables at Damariscotta Lake State Park (see *Swimming* in *To Do*) and by the bridge in Damariscotta Mills.

LODGING

INNS

The Newcastle Inn (563-5685 or 1-800-832-8669), River Road, Newcastle 04553. Open year-round. We rarely call a place "romantic" but there's simply no other way of describing this hospitable inn. Of course, you will be happy here with your mother or sister, but chances are you will want to return with someone else. Innkeeper Ted Sprague welcomes you in one of the attractive living rooms and shows you to your room, hopefully one with a four-poster or crocheted canopy bed, a water view, or a sitting area. None of the 15 guest rooms are too frilly, just tasteful and comfortable with private baths. Guests should arrive in time to relax before dinner, a five-course event that begins at 7 PM in the candlelit dining rooms. Chris Sprague is a widely noted chef and cookbook author, and the food is superb (see *Dining Out* for details), beautifully presented and served. The three-course breakfast is also rather amazing. Guests tend to sign on for MAP one night, downshift to the B&B rate the next, and return to MAP for a third. Given the quality of food, level of comfort, and handy waterside location, this also makes a great winter getaway. $65–130 double B&B or $125–190 double MAP; a 15 percent service charge is added. Inquire about special Thanksgiving and Valentine weekends and other special packages. No smoking.

Gosnold Arms (677-3727), Route 32, New Harbor 04554. Open mid-May through mid-October (restaurant opens Memorial Day weekend). New Harbor itself is a picture-perfect clutter of lobster boats and pleasure craft. The inn, just across the road from the water, has been welcoming summer guests since 1925. Nothing fancy, it is a rambling, white-clapboard farmhouse with a long, welcoming porch, an attached barn, and scattered cottages. Eleven simple guest rooms with unstained pine walls but pleasant furnishings and firm beds (all with private bath) have been fitted into the barn, above a gathering room with a huge fireplace. There are 14 cottages, some with kitchenettes, fireplaces, and/or water views. Guests breakfast and sup on the enclosed porch overlooking the water; the dining room is also open to the public and has a reputation for fresh, local, simply prepared food (see *Dining Out*). The inn is named for Bartholomew Gosnold, who is said to have sailed into the harbor in 1602. All rates include breakfast. $75–94 double B&B in the inn, $98–124 for cottages; less off-season.

Bradley Inn (677-2105), 361 Pemaquid Point, New Harbor 04554. Open April through January 2. Chuck and Merry Robinson have recently restored this turn-of-the-century inn. The 12 guest rooms are nicely furnished (private baths), and the grounds have been handsomely landscaped. Request one of the third-floor rooms with a view of John's Bay. The entry area also serves two dining rooms (see *Dining Out*), but there is a living room with a fireplace, wing chairs, and a library of nautical books. Bicycles are available, and the inn is nicely positioned for a pleasant walk or bike ride to the lighthouse in one direction and to Kresge Point in the other. From $60 off-season to $140 in-season; also inquire about the Garden Cottage and The Barn.

Coveside Inn (644-8282), Christmas Cove, South Bristol 04568. Open early June to mid-September; motel units open through October, but restaurant closes. A holly-berry red Victorian inn with a mansard roof. There are five old-fashioned guest rooms in the inn (all have private baths, though some baths are across the hall from corresponding rooms) and a big living room that is shared with guests in the 10 modern shorefront units across the road. The motel rooms have private decks, pine paneling, and cathedral ceilings with skylights. This building and the dining room are built right out over the water. Coveside Marine, located at the inn, includes a yacht brokerage. The Coveside Waterfront Restaurant (see *Dining Out*) is popular with the yachting set, many of whom sail into Christmas Cove and row ashore for dinner. Three meals are served every day. (Christmas Cove is said to have been christened by Captain John Smith, who first arrived here one Christmas morning.) Inn rooms $85, shorefront motel rooms $95 for a double.

The Hotel Pemaquid (677-2312), Pemaquid 04554. Open mid-May to Columbus Day. A century-old classic summer hotel just 150 feet from Pemaquid Point but without water views. Everything is as neat and tidy, also as fireproof and renovated, as can be. The decor is high Victorian, the living room has a big stone fireplace and the long porch is lined with wicker chairs. Rooms in the inn itself come with and without private baths, but all rooms in the annex, the bungalows, and the motel units have private baths; there is also a housekeeping cottage. The hotel does not have a restaurant, but coffee is set out at 6:30 AM and The Sea Gull Restaurant, overlooking the ocean, is a very short walk; plenty of nearby restaurants serve dinner. No smoking. From $47 off-season with shared bath to $155 for a three-bedroom suite in August; housekeeping cottage $475–575 per week.

BED & BREAKFASTS

☞✐**Brannon-Bunker Inn** (563-5941), HCR 64, Box 045, Route 129, Damariscotta 04543. Open March to December. A rambling building that includes an 1820s Cape and a barn turned Prohibition Era dance hall turned inn. The upstairs sitting area walls are hung with memorabilia from World War I, and there are plenty of antiques and collectibles around (the adjoining antiques shop is open May through October). This is an unusually relaxed B&B. Your hosts include Mike, Beth, and Jamie Hovance, as well as their parents, Jeanne and Joe; children are welcome. Five rooms have private baths ($65), and two share ($55); there's also a three-bedroom suite with a kitchen, living room, and bath ($115). A path leads to the river, and golf is down the road at the Wawenock Country Club (see *Golf*). Breakfast features muffins and fruit, and the kitchen is available for guests' use at other times of the day.

The Flying Cloud (563-2484), River Road, Newcastle 04553. Open most of the year. A dandy of an 1840s sea captain's home, expanding on a 1790s Cape. The elegance of the furniture matches that of the floor-to-ceiling windows and fine detailing, but hosts Alan and Jeanne Davis have also taken care to provide comfortable, informal spaces like a den with a TV and sound system and a screened back porch. The five guest rooms are each named and decorated for a port-of-call of the clipper ship *Flying Cloud;* all have private baths. The master bedroom has a particularly fine water view. Breakfast may include sourdough blueberry pancakes and always features farm-fresh eggs in some form. $55–90, less off-season.

✐ **Mill Pond Inn** (563-8014), Route 215, Damariscotta Mills (mailing address: 50 Main Street, Nobleboro 04555). Open year-round. A quiet spot with a back deck overlooking a millpond. Damariscotta Lake is just a few steps away. Wildlife includes a resident bald eagle. There are two 2-person hammocks under the willow trees and a beach at the freshwater swimming hole. The 1780 gray-clapboard house with a red door offers six double rooms (all private baths), one of which has an adjoining smaller room with twin beds. Breakfast might be pancakes with fresh blueberries or omelets with crabmeat and vegetables from the inn's garden. It is served in the dining room, which has a fireplace and a picture window overlooking the lake. In winter, pack a picnic lunch and skate across the lake to a miniature island. In summer, ask for a ride in the 16-foot, restored, antique motorboat on Damariscotta Lake. You can also paddle out in a canoe or explore the rolling countryside on one of the inn's mountain bikes. Owner Bobby Whear, a registered Maine guide, also will arrange fishing trips; the catch is landlocked salmon and small-mouth bass. $60–70.

Broad Bay Inn & Gallery (832-6668), PO Box 607, Main Street, Waldoboro 04572. Open year-round. Within walking distance of village restaurants, shops, and performances at the Waldo Theatre, this is a pleasant, 1830s home with Victorian furnishings and canopy beds. The five guest rooms share three baths. Afternoon tea and sherry are served on the sun deck in summer and by the fire in winter. The art gallery in the barn exhibits works by well-known Maine artists, also sells limited-edition prints, crafts, and gifts. Host Libby Hopkins offers art work-shops. Rates include a full breakfast; on Saturday evenings, candlelight dinners may be arranged in advance (for guests and the public). Two-night minimum stay required in July and August. Ask about Thanksgiv-ing, Christmas and New Year's Eve packages. $40–70 double.

The Briar Rose B&B (529-5478), Route 32, Round Pond 04564. Open most of the year. In the center of the picturesque village of Round Pond, this lovely B&B offers large, airy accommodations, pleasing antique fur-nishings, and views of the harbor just down the road. There's a small antiques shop just inside the front door that doubles as a winter parlor. From $30 double off-season with shared bath to $70 in August for a suite with private bath.

Apple Tree B&B (677-3491), New Harbor 04554. Open year-round. A genuine old Cape a short walk from Pemaquid Beach and Fort William Henry. An attractive first-floor room has a private bath, and the two upstairs bedrooms, one with a working fireplace, share a bath. Pat Landry's kitchen usually smells of the good things served in the dining room or on the patio for breakfast. $55–70 double.

🖉☞**The Jefferson House** (549-5768), Route 126, Jefferson 04348. Jim and Barbara O'Hallaran's comfortable 1835 farmhouse feels like home the moment you walk in. The large, bright kitchen with its big old cookstove is unquestionably the center of the house, and you can also breakfast (sumptuously) on the deck overlooking the village and millpond; guests can use the canoe on the river that empties into Damariscotta Lake. Guestrooms are homey and comfortable; shared baths. $45 double, $35 single.

Glidden House (563-1859), RR 1, Box 740, Glidden Street, Newcastle 04553. Open most of the year. A Victorian house on a quiet street lined with elegant old homes. A convenient walk to the shops of both Newcastle and Damariscotta. Most guest rooms have private baths. There is also a three-room apartment. Exceptional breakfasts, included in the lodging, are served in the dining room or in the garden. $50 double with shared bath; $55 with private bath; $70 for the apartment.

Markert House (563-1309), PO Box 224, Glidden Street, Newcastle

04553. Open May to January. Another elegant Victorian, this one owned by artist Bill Markert. Nicely decorated guest rooms, within walking distance of downtown Newcastle and Damariscotta. Doubles (shared bath) $55 with full breakfast.

Captain's House (563-1482), Box 19, River Road, Newcastle 04553. Open year-round. Operated by the owners of the Bailey Inn in Wiscasset. Five guest rooms offer a pleasant view of the Damariscotta River (shared bath). A full breakfast menu is included. $50–70 double.

Barnswallow B&B (563-8568), Routes 129 and 130, HC 61, Box 135, Damariscotta 04543. Open year-round. A pristine, warmly decorated 1830s Cape with fireplaces in the dining room, living room (with TV), and reading parlor. Munchies and setups at cocktail time as well as a generous continental breakfast in the morning. Children over 12 are welcome. Two-night stay required on weekends in July and August and on some holiday weekends. All private baths; $60–75.

Snow Drift Farm Bed & Breakfast (845-2476), RR 1, Box 669, Washington 04574. Open year-round. A restored, mid-1800s farmhouse set in the country with a garden, deck, fields, nature trails, a trout stream, and pond (skating in winter). There's even a professional massage therapist available. From $35 with shared bath to $85 for a two-room suite with private bath; less off-season.

The Roaring Lion (832-4038), PO Box 756, 995 Main Street, Waldoboro 04572. Open year-round. A 1905 home with tin ceilings, fireplaces, and a big screened porch. The kitchen can cater to special, vegetarian, and macrobiotic diets. One room with private bath; three with shared bath. $55–65 double; $10 less for single occupancy. No smoking.

COTTAGES

☞✐These and other cottages and cabins in the region fill up long before summer's arrival, but you may always luck into a cancellation.

Damariscotta Lake Farm (549-7953), Jefferson 04348. Open Memorial Day to the end of September. Sited at the junction of Routes 32 and 126 at the head of Damariscotta Lake, these lined-up, one-, two-, and three-bedroom efficiency cottages have screened porches. Private sandy beach, boat rentals. There's a small pitching golf course in summer, plus a marina. One-week minimum stay required. $275 for a one-bedroom to $395 for a three-bedroom.

Thompson House and Cottages (677-2317), New Harbor 04554. Open May through October. Four apartments (one and two bedrooms) and rooms with baths in an annex to the main house. Also more than 20 cottages scattered along the harbor and back cove (less expensive) and along the ocean. Cottages accommodating up to five are $350–900 per week.

Ye Olde Forte Cabins (677-2261), Pemaquid Beach 04554 (off-season, write to Mrs. Leslie Baker, Box 2480, Litchfield 04350; 617-484-6793). Open early June through Labor Day. A parade of snug cabins up and down the grassy knoll beside Fort William Henry, all sharing a central "cook house" and a separate shower building. Four double and five single cabins with heat and half-baths. There is one housekeeping cottage with a living room, bedroom, kitchen, and full bath. $52–80 per night depending on accommodations and number of people; $550 per week for the housekeeping cottage.

✏☞**The Jamestown** (677-3677), HC62, Box 091, Pemaquid Beach 04554. Open Memorial Day through Columbus Day. On the water, next to Fort William Henry. Besides the cottage there are a variety of housekeeping units in the main house and modernized barn, all attractive and most with water views, some decks. Weekly stay required; rates range from $250–450.

MOTELS

☞✏Route 1 from Edgecomb to Waldoboro has its share of modern motels offering the usual: color TV, two double beds, private bath, often a swimming pool. There are also crescents of miniature cottages in the the more old-fashioned, motor court style. Just north of the center of Damariscotta, on Business Route 1, you will find some smaller motels and motor courts with bargain rates.

WHERE TO EAT

DINING OUT

The Newcastle Inn (563-5685), River Road, Newcastle 04553. Open nightly June through end of October; Friday and Saturday off-season. Chris Sprague has received well-deserved raves from *Food & Wine* magazine, *Yankee* magazine, and the *Maine Sunday Telegram*. Her dazzling, five-course dinners are offered to the public by reservation and cost $75 for two. The cocktail hour, with complimentary hors d'oeuvres, begins at 6 PM, followed by dinner at 7. Chris's husband, Ted, serves as host, bartender, and sommelier. You might begin with a lobster risotto or smoked bacon and wild mushrooms in puff pastry, then savor a purée of fennel soup or wild mushroom consommé followed by a salad, and finally dine on rack of lamb with Shiitake mushrooms or roasted salmon with black pepper and almonds and celery root purée. The meal might be topped off with bittersweet-chocolate soufflé or a chocolate hazelnut terrine with caramel sauce. The inn has a full bar and a small but carefully selected, moderately priced wine list.

Coveside Waterfront Restaurant (644-8282), Christmas Cove. Open June through mid-September. A little out of the way but a nice excuse to drive down to the tip of Route 129, where you will actually be on an island connected to South Bristol by one of the world's smallest drawbridges. The restaurant, part of an inn complex (see *Inns*), is built out over the water with views of the picturesque harbor and the mouth of the Damariscotta River beyond (Christmas Cove was supposedly named by explorer Captain John Smith when he arrived on December

25, 1614). This place is a beloved standby—especially with yachtsmen. Three meals are served daily. Dinner specialties include pan-fried crabcakes served with Remoulade, grilled marinated shrimp, and steamed seafood in parchment. There are also burgers and seafood salad plates. About $30–70 for two.

Gosnold Arms (677-3727), New Harbor. Open Memorial Day weekend through mid-October. An old-fashioned summer hostelry (see *Inns*) with a public dining room that seats 80. The kitchen specializes in the freshest local seafood in straightforward preparations, such as broiled salmon steak with dill, seafood casserole, and sea scallops broiled or deep fried. Dinner is served on the enclosed porch with a view of the harbor. From $8.95 for a fried boneless chicken breast to whatever the salmon or lobster is priced at. The blackboard specials always include roast lamb on Sundays. Full liquor and beer list.

Bradley Inn (677-2105), Pemaquid Point Road. There are two restaurants in this spacious old inn, one sea green and decorated with nautical seafaring memorabilia and the second, less formal (checked tablecloths), overlooking the garden. The same menu serves both, and there's live jazz or folk music on Friday and Saturday nights, piano music other nights. The à la carte menu might include entrées like grilled pesto-mustard-crumb salmon with white-bean–tomato-basil relish ($16.75), or Eastland mussels with tomato-basil Romano sauce on linguine ($16.00); a white chocolate–raspberry sambuca crème caramel might be dessert.

Snow Turtle Inn (832-4423), Route 32 and Old Route 1, Waldoboro. Serving dinner Tuesday through Saturday 5–9; Sunday brunch and dinner 11:30–8; year-round. The painting of Windsor Castle has hung above the mantel in the dining room ever since this house was built by a successful sea merchant in 1803. Its deep greens have determined the color the wood trim is painted; the pink tablecloths and candles provide an eye-pleasing complement. Serving up to 45 in the two dining rooms and an additional 25 on the sun porch in summer, the Snow Turtle offers such entrées as steak, veal Marsala, baked haddock, sautéed Cajun scallops, roast duckling, and raspberry chicken. Aileen Allen, who with her husband, Larry, runs the inn, is the chef; her daily specials feature such fresh fish as salmon, blackened red snapper, and lemon-pepper catfish. Entrées run $8.95–16.95.

☞ **Bill's Cafe and Book Store** (832-4613), Jefferson Street, Waldoboro. Open year-round for breakfast, lunch, and dinner, except Thursday. Dedicated to the "presumption that well prepared and graciously served meals need not be expensive." No smoking. The walls are lined with used books (browsing encouraged), and there are just seven tables. Omelets are featured at breakfast; homemade soup, sandwiches, and salads at lunch; and the dinner menu is varied, ranging from Angus steak in béarnaise sauce ($13.00) through crabcakes ($10.00) or pasta with scallops and bacon ($10.50) to fettuccine Alfredo ($8.00). Desserts include café-made ice cream and chocolate fondue. Beer and wine are served.

EATING OUT

On or just off Route 1

Moody's Diner (832-7468), Route 1, Waldoboro. Open 24 hours (except midnight–5 AM on Friday and Saturday nights). A longtime landmark well known for its cream pies and family-style food. Unbeatable breakfasts such as corned beef hash and eggs; suppers of meatloaf, stews, burgers, and such. Very digestible prices—two slices of their famous pie and coffee will run you about $3—in a clean and warm, old classic diner. Run by several generations of the Moody family along with other employees who have been there so long they have become part of the family, too. To re-create Moody's menu at home, take home a copy of their cookbook.

Backstreet Landing (563-5666), Elm Street Plaza, Damariscotta. Open daily, year-round. Just behind Main Street, overlooking the upper Damariscotta River, this very pleasant, low-key restaurant and gathering place has good, dependable food. Three meals are served each day, plus Sunday brunch. Seafood entrées, homemade soups and chowders, quiches, lunch specials, and light late-evening snacks. This is a popular place with locals.

Salt Bay Cafe (563-1666), Main Street, Damariscotta. Open year-round for lunch and dinner. A pleasant, greenhouselike entrance; conventional booths and tables. Serves simple favorites such as fried clams, french-fried vegetables, burgers, sandwiches, and soups; also pastas, steaks, local seafood.

Pine Grove Family Restaurant (563-3765), Route 1, just north of Damariscotta. Open year-round. Open early for breakfast but closes somewhat early, too. A comfortable dining room with moderate prices and the motto, "Where friendliness adds flavor to your food." Fried seafoods and old-fashioned good food. Service can be a bit slow, but there is a take-out window for those in a hurry.

Morse's Kraut House (832-5569), some 8 miles north of Route 1 on Route 220 in North Waldoboro. Open daily except Sunday year-round 7–4. Set in fields of cabbage, this is probably New England's single most famous source of sauerkraut (harvested and prepared on the premises since 1910). The kraut is hand cut and processed according to an old German recipe. Try it on a Reuben or bratwurst (there are picnic tables), and bring some home. Other Maine food products are also sold.

Laura Cabot's Bakery and Cafe (832-6337), 13 Friendship Street, Waldoboro. The booths have stained-glass insets, and the brick walls are hung with Eric Hopkins prints. Peasant breads, prepared salads, soups and sandwiches available for takeout or for eating in the shop or up on the back deck overlooking the Medomak River.

On the Pemaquid Peninsula

Anchor Inn (529-5584), Round Pond. Open daily for lunch and dinner,

Memorial Day through Columbus Day. A real find, a tiered dining room overlooking the harbor in the small fishing village of Round Pond. Try the native crabcakes for either lunch or dinner. Dinner options include Italian seafood stew (loaded with fish, shrimp, scallops, and mussels), charbroiled steaks, and linguine with black olives, feta, and roasted vegetables in a sherried tomato sauce.

The Sea Gull Shop (677-2374) next to the Pemaquid Lighthouse at Pemaquid Point. Open daily in-season, 8–8. The unbeatable ocean view is what this place is all about. Standard menu. BYOB.

Samoset Restaurant (677-2142), New Harbor. Open year-round for breakfast, lunch, and dinner daily. No view but good food; the local hangout. Cocktails are served. Homemade split-pea soup and a half sandwich hit the spot on a drizzly day.

LOBSTER POUNDS

Shaw's (677-2200), New Harbor (next to the New Harbor Co-op). Open late May to mid-October, daily for lunch and supper. You can't get nearer to a working harbor than this very popular dockside spot. You stand in line at the counter to order your lobster and then wait for your name to be called when it's ready. In addition to lobster and steamed clams, the menu includes a variety of basic foods like meatloaf, fish cakes, stews, shrimp, roast turkey, scallops, and sandwiches. Liquor is also served. Choose to sit at a picnic table either out on the dock over the water or in the inside dining room.

Pemaquid Fisherman's Co-op (677-2801), Pemaquid Harbor. Boiled lobster, steamed clams and mussels, and shrimp to be enjoyed at outdoor tables over the harbor.

Farrin's Lobster Pound and Chowder House (644-8500), Route 129 at "the Gut" in South Bristol. Open summer months, 8–8, weekends into October. Another classic spot from which to savor a lobstering atmosphere. This complex includes a general store and fish market, and the dining deck is upstairs overlooking the water; a place for lobster stewed as well as steamed, also clams, shrimp, and fried seafood. Beer is on the menu.

Captain's Catch Seafood (677-2396), Pemaquid Beach Road, New Harbor. Open throughout the summer season, 11–8 daily. Indoor and outdoor picnic-style dining. Lobsters, clams (steamed or fried), seafood baskets, and dinners; fish fry every Friday; homemade desserts.

Dana's Chart House (677-3315), at the Pemaquid Restoration. Open Memorial Day through October, lunch through dinner. There's a take-out section adjacent to the pier (you can come by boat) and a large dining room. From a $1.50 hot dog to lobster pie ($10.95).

SNACKS

Round Top Ice Cream (563-5307), Business Route 1, Damariscotta. Open Memorial Day to Columbus Day. You'll find delicious Round Top ice cream offered at restaurants throughout the region, but this is the original

Round Top, on the grounds of the farm where it all began in 1924 (an expanded creamery is now just over the hill). The ice cream comes in 36 flavors, including raspberry, Almond Joy, and fresh blueberry. This is the granddaddy of all ice-cream stands in the area, and we don't think the interior has changed since 1924. There are stools inside and umbrella-topped tables outside. Also on the grounds is the Round Top Center for the Arts, offering concerts, classes, exhibitions, and festivals (see *Entertainment*).

Zecchino's Submarines, Damariscotta, near the town landing (in back of Gilliam's fish market). A variety of submarine sandwiches, plus chili, soups, and salads.

ENTERTAINMENT

Round Top Center for the Arts (563-1507), Upper Main Street, Damariscotta. On the grounds of the old Round Top Farm, this energetic, nonprofit organization offers an ambitious schedule of concerts, classes, exhibitions, and festivals. Check locally for evening outdoor concerts in summer—it could be anything from the Portland Symphony Orchestra to rousing ethnic music by Mama Tongue. Bring a blanket and a picnic and enjoy both the music and the lovely setting.

Waldo Theatre (832-6060), Main Street, Waldoboro. March through December, a schedule of films, concerts, and live performances. Inquire about outlets for advance sales of concert tickets in Damariscotta, Rockland, and Thomaston.

SELECTIVE SHOPPING

ANTIQUES SHOPS
Partridge Antiques, Route 1, Newcastle. The fine 18th-century European furniture and paintings displayed in this huge, peak-roofed barn draw connoisseurs from across the country. Turn into the lane by the chain-link fence.

Robert L. Foster, Route 1, Newcastle. A conglomeration of individual dealers' stalls, flea market tables outside, and an auction hall with auctions scheduled on Saturday and Sunday mornings and Thursday evenings; good entertainment as well as bargains.

Kaja Veilleux Antiques (563-1002), Newcastle Square, Newcastle. In the handsome, old, red-brick shipping agent's offices near the center of the village. Fine antiques and free verbal appraisals on Thursdays.

Cooper's Red Barn, Business Route 1, Damariscotta. Old pine and oak furniture, rough or refinished. Gifts, crafts, old books, china, and glass.

ART GALLERIES
Schooner Galleries (563-8031), Route 1, Edgecomb, and Main Street, Damariscotta. Specializing in 18th- and 19th-century marine paintings

by artists such as Thomas Bush Hardy, Frank Mason, and W.H. Drake, plus works by local artists.

Le Va-tout Gallery (832-4552), RR 1, Box 375, Waldoboro 04572. Open in-season Wednesday through Sunday 12–5, and by appointment. A small gallery featuring the work of Maine artists and craftspeople. Owner Don Slagel has created an exceptionally pleasant spot, including lovely gardens dedicated to Maine composer Walter Piston. B&B accommodations are also offered here.

ARTISANS

David Margonelli, furniture maker (633-3326), River Road, Edgecomb. About 4 miles down a lovely, tree-shaded road from the villages of Newcastle and Damariscotta. Showroom is open in-season Monday through Saturday 10–5, and by appointment. Exquisite, completely handmade furniture with a classic influence. David and Susan make it all themselves.

Ax Wood Products (563-5884), Route 129, Walpole (10 minutes from Damariscotta). Open year-round. Barnaby Porter makes rustic wooden objects, both functional and decorative. Specialties include imaginative wind vanes in such shapes as a Friendship sloop, a mackerel, and a Wind Maiden; and miniature houses built inside hollow tree stumps (the latter have been featured in the Fifth Avenue windows of Tiffany's). Special orders are welcomed.

Gil Whitman Gallery (882-7705), Route 1, Edgecomb. Open weekdays 9–5, and by appointment. Metal sculptures with "the Maine ingredient," which is usually just a touch of humor. Commissions are welcomed.

Damariscotta Pottery, off Main Street (downstairs at Weatherbird), Damariscotta. A treasure trove of watercolored pottery. Reminiscent of Mallorcan ware, it is decorated in primitive floral and animal designs. You can watch this charming pottery being made and painted right in the shop.

Pemaquid Floorcloths (529-5633), Route 32, Round Pond. Hand-stenciled, canvas floor coverings in the traditional country style. Open by chance and by appointment.

Laberge Stained Glass Design (529-5264), Round Pond. Art glass—windows, cabinet doors, hangings, mirrors, lamp shades, etc. There is also a small gallery of paintings and photographs by local artists (open June to September).

Village Weavers (529-5523), Round Pond. Open Monday through Saturday 12–5, and by appointment. Textiles woven by two artists in this studio include table linens, rugs, window hangings, and clothing. Handwrought ironwork by **The Scottish Lion Blacksmith** is also on display.

Blueledge Studio Pottery (529-5501), Round Pond. Decorative and functional porcelain pottery.

Wingset (529-5906), Round Pond. Working decoys and waterfowl art. Also British outdoor wear by Barbour.

SPECIAL SHOPS

☞ **Reny's** (563-3177), Main Street, Damariscotta. First opened in Camden in 1949, Reny's has since become a small-town, Maine institution from Biddeford to Fort Kent. Operated by Robert H. Reny and his two sons Robert D. and John E., the stores sell quality items—ranging from TVs to sheets and towels and whatever "the boys" happen to have found to stock this week. "We don't know what to call ourselves," Robert H. tells us, "but we have a lot of fun doing it." We enjoy shopping at Reny's too; it's not just the unexpected quality and prices, it's a certain something that's still distinctly Maine. The headquarters for the 15-store chain are in Damariscotta's former grade school; on Main Street look for Reny's and Reny's Underground.

✐ **Maine Coast Book Shop** (563-3207), Main Street, Damariscotta. A truly exceptional bookstore with engaging, knowledgeable staff members who delight in making suggestions and helping customers shop for others. This is certainly one of the state's best bookstores.

Victorian Stable, Water Street, Damariscotta. Seasonal. An old stable whose box stalls are now filled with the outstanding work of more than 100 Maine craftspeople.

2 Fish, Elm Street (across from Sun Cafe), Damariscotta. An eclectic assortment of clothing, jewelry, and treasures from the world over.

Mostly Needlepoint and Yarns, Main Street, Damariscotta. In the handsome Nathaniel Austin House. Yarns, kits, and help on needle projects.

✐ **Granite Hall Store,** Route 32, Round Pond. Open Tuesday through Sunday 10–5. A general store filled with Scottish-, Irish-, and Maine-made woolens, Eskimo sculptures, a few antiques and baskets, toys, books, a good selection of greeting cards, penny candy, hot roasted peanuts, homemade fudge, and, at an outdoor window, ice cream.

SPECIAL EVENTS

Second weekend in July: **Damariscotta River Oyster Festival,** Damariscotta—a celebration of the oyster aquaculture conducted in the river. Oysters fixed every way (especially *au naturel*), music, crafts, and a canoe race through the rapids of the Damariscotta River.

Early August: **Olde Bristol Days,** Old Fort Grounds, Pemaquid Beach. **Parade**—fish fry, chicken barbecue, bands, bagpipers, concerts, pancake breakfast, road race, boat race, firemen's muster, crafts, and the annual **Bristol Footlighters Show** (which has been going on for more than 40 years).

Rockland/Thomaston Area

Rockland's brick downtown is the commercial center for a wide scattering of towns and islands. It's also the site of the William A. Farnsworth Library and Art Museum, housing an exceptional collection of Maine-based paintings, including works by three generations of Wyeths.

Blessed with a wide, deep harbor, Rockland is home port for a number of the passenger-carrying schooners known as "windjammers" as well as a sizable fleet of lobster and fishing boats. It celebrates its status as "Lobster Capital of the World" (it's Maine's leading lobster distribution center) the first weekend in August with the mammoth and colorful Maine Lobster Festival. Rockland is also the departure point for ferries to the islands of Vinalhaven, North Haven, and Matinicus (see the *Islands* section of this chapter).

Southwest of Rockland, two peninsulas separate Muscongus Bay from Penobscot Bay. One is the fat arm of land on which the villages of Friendship and Cushing doze. The other is the skinnier St. George Peninsula with Port Clyde at its tip, the departure point for the year-round mail boat to Monhegan Island (again, see *Islands*).

The peninsulas are divided by the 10-mile-long St. George River, at the head of which sits Thomaston, a beautiful old town that has produced more than its share of wooden ships. Although its handsome Main Street mansions stand today in white-clapboard testimony to the shipbuilders' success a century ago, Thomaston is best known as the site of the state prison—and its popular prison shop.

GUIDANCE

Rockland-Thomaston Chamber of Commerce (596-0376), Public Landing, Rockland (write PO Box 508, Rockland 04841). Open weekdays, 9–5 in summer and 8–4 in winter. The chamber serves as an information source for the entire Rockland area, which includes Thomaston, the peninsula villages, and the islands. They have cottage listings for North Haven, Vinalhaven, and the area from Owls Head to Cushing.

GETTING THERE

By air: **Knox County Airport** (594-4131), at Owls Head, just south of Rockland, schedules daily service to Boston and New York. Keep in mind, however, that the airport is on a peninsula that is particularly susceptible to fog—so flights may be diverted to Bangor or Augusta if

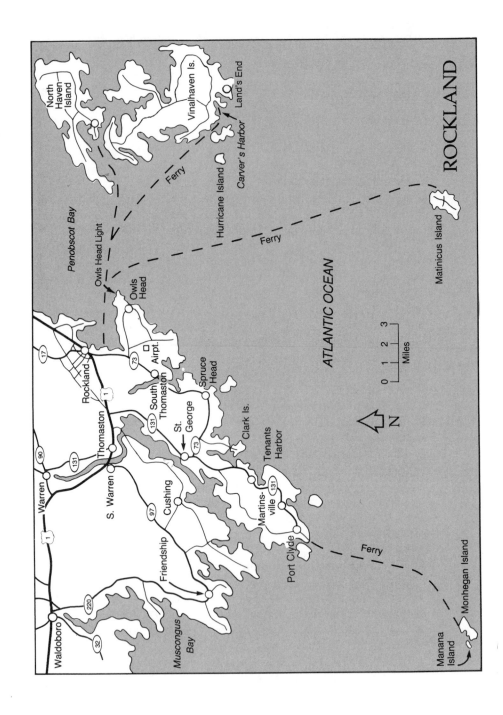

conditions are poor. For charter flights to and from Portland and the islands, check with **Penobscot Air Service, Ltd.** (596-6211). **Colgan Air** (596-7604 or 1-800-272-5488) also links Rockland with Boston, Bar Harbor, and Augusta, and **Land's End** (594-5311) is a charter service geared to longer flights. **Mid Coast Limo** runs to and from the Portland Jetport (1-800-834-5500 within Maine, or 1-800-937-2424 outside Maine). **Schooner Taxi** (594-5000) is the local reliable.

By bus: **Concord Trailways** (1-800-639-3317) offers service to Rockland with a stop right at the Maine State Ferry Service pier.

MEDICAL EMERGENCY

Penobscot Bay Medical Center (596-8000), Route 1, Glen Cove, Rockland.

VILLAGES AND ISLANDS

Friendship. Best known as the birthplace of the classic Friendship sloop, first built by local lobstermen to haul their traps (originals and reproductions of this sturdy vessel hold races here every summer). Friendship remains a quiet fishing village.

Tenants Harbor has a good little library and, beyond, rock cliffs, tidal pools, old cemeteries, and the kind of countryside described by Sarah Orne Jewett in *Country of the Pointed Firs.* Jewett lived just a few bends down Route 131 in Martinville while she wrote the book.

Union is a short ride from the coast but surrounded by gentle hills and farm country (the Union Fair and Blueberry Festival is a big event). This place is also a good spot to swim, to eat, and to explore an unusually interesting historical museum.

Islands. An overnight or longer stay on an island is far preferable to a day trip. From Rockland you can take a Maine State (car) Ferry to **Vinalhaven** and **North Haven.** Together these form the Fox Islands, with just a narrow passage between them. Yet the islands are very different. On Vinalhaven, summer homes are hidden away along the shore, and what visitors see is the fabulously funky old fishing village of Carver's Harbor. On North Haven, most of the clapboard homes (mainly owned by wealthy summer people) are set in open fields. **Matinicus,** also accessible from Rockland, is the most remote Maine island and quietly beautiful. Tiny **Monhegan,** accessible from Port Clyde, offers the most dramatic cliff scenery and the most hospitable welcome to visitors. For details, see the descriptions of each island at the end of this chapter.

TO SEE

William A. Farnsworth Library and Art Museum (596-6457), 19 Elm Street, Rockland. Open year-round, daily June through September (10–5, except Sunday 1–5), otherwise closed on Monday. Admission to the museum and the homestead (see next entry) is $5 adults, $4 senior citizens, $3 students aged 8–18, under 8 free. This exceptional art museum was established by Lucy Farnsworth, an eccentric spinster who lived frugally in just three rooms of her family mansion. When she died in 1935 at age 96, neighbors were amazed to find that she had left $1.3 million to preserve her house and build the handsome museum next door. In 1994 the museum's exhibit space virtually doubled, permitting installation of the permanent exhibit "Maine in America," tracing the evolution of Maine landscape paintings. The museum features Hudson River School artists like Thomas Cole, and 19th-century marine artist Fitz Hugh Lane; American impressionists Frank Benson, Willard Metcalf, Childe Hassam, and Maurice Prendergrast; early 20th-century greats like George Bellows, Rockwell Kent, and Charles Woodbury; and such "modernists" as John Marin and Marsden Hartley. It is also well known for its collection of works by three generations of Wyeths: Look for *Eight Bells at Port Clyde* by N.C., *Her Room* by Andrew, and *Portrait of Orca Bates* by Jamie Wyeth. Louise Nevelson, who lived in Rockland as a child, is also well represented with both painting and sculpture. Note the new changing exhibit gallery and Main Street museum store. The original Georgian Revival library houses an extensive collection of reference materials and serves as the site for regularly scheduled lectures and concerts.

Farnsworth Homestead (596-6457), Elm Street, Rockland. Open June through September only; Monday through Saturday 10–5 and Sunday 1–5. Joint admission to the homestead and museum is $5 adults, $4 senior citizens, $3 students 8–18, under 8 free. The Farnsworth Homestead was built in 1850 by Miss Lucy's father, a tycoon who was very successful in the lime industry and also owned a fleet of ships. Brimming with lavish, colorful Victorian furnishings (all original), it remains—according to a stipulation in Miss Lucy's will—just as it was when she died at the age of 96. Curious details of the decor include draperies so long that they drag on the floor to indicate that the family could afford to buy more fabric than was required. Nevertheless the walls are hung with inexpensive copies of oil paintings known as chromolithographs, a fireplace mantel is glass painted to resemble marble, and doors are not made of fine wood grains but, rather, have been painted to imitate them. How strange that a woman whose home shows so little appreciation for the fine arts should leave all her money for the establishment of an art museum.

The Olson House (354-0102), Hathron Point Road, Cushing. Open June through September, Wednesday through Sunday 11–4. $3 adult, $1 ages 8–18. Administered by the Farnsworth Museum, this house served as a backdrop for many works by Andrew Wyeth, including *Christina's World.*

Montpelier (354-8062), Thomaston. Open May 30 to Labor Day, Wednesday through Sunday from 9–5:30. Free. This is not the original but rather a reproduction of the grand mansion built on this spot in 1794 by General

WILLIAM A. FARNSWORTH LIBRARY AND ART MUSEUM

N.C. Wyeth, Portrait of a Young Artist

Henry Knox, the portly (5-foot 6-inch, 300-pound) Boston bookseller who became a revolutionary war hero, then our first secretary of war. He married a granddaughter of Samuel Waldo, the Boston developer who owned all of this area (and for whom the county is named), and built himself as elaborate a mansion here as any to be found in the new republic. It has an oval dining room facing the St. George River, high ceilings, and long windows, not to mention a semi-flying staircase. Montpelier and its collection of Colonial- and Federal-period furnishings provide a unique glimpse of General Knox and his family by showing their impact on national, state, and local history. By 1871, however, it had fallen into disrepair and was torn down, then rebuilt as a Great Depression project at a cost of $300,000 (financed by Philadelphia magazine publisher and Camden summer resident Cyrus Curtis). Today the replica is once again in need of an angel to underwrite the extensive repairs required.

Owls Head Transportation Museum (594-4418), adjacent to the Knox County Airport off Route 73, Box 277H, Owls Head (just south of Rockland). Open year-round. April through October daily, 10–5; November through March 10–4 weekdays and 10–3 weekends. Regular admission is $4.00 adults, $2.50 under 12, under 5 free. Inquire about the frequent spring-through-fall special weekends (when admission is $5 adults and $3 under 12). Founded in 1974, this has become one of the country's outstanding collections of antique planes and automobiles, unique because everything works. On weekends there are special demonstrations of such magnificent machines as a 1901 Oldsmobile and a 1918 "Jenny" airplane; and sometimes rides are offered in a spiffy Model-T. In the exhibition hall, you can take a 100-year journey through the evolution of transportation, from horse-drawn carriages to World War I fighter planes; from a 16-cylinder Cadillac to a Rolls Royce; from the Red Baron's Fokker Triplane to a Ford Trimotor. There are also wagons, motorcycles, and bikes. All vehicles have been donated or lent to the museum, which is largely a volunteer effort.

Marshall Point Lighthouse Museum (372-6450), open June through September daily, except Monday, 1–4; May and October, Saturday and Sunday 1–5. A road leads to this vintage 1885 light from the village of Port Clyde; it was deactivated in 1971 and now houses a small museum dedicated to the long and fascinating history of the town of St. George (of which Port Clyde and Tenants Harbor are a part).

Shore Village Museum (594-0311), 104 Limerock Street, Rockland. Open June 1 to October 15, 10–4 daily; by appointment the rest of the year. Free admission. A large and fascinating collection of historic artifacts of the United States Coast Guard, including one of the most extensive collections of lighthouse materials (working foghorns, flashing lights, search-and-rescue gear, buoys, bells, and boats), plus Civil War memorabilia and a collection of 34 dolls dressed in period costumes up to the Gay Nineties. There is also a small museum shop.

Matthews Museum of Maine Heritage, Union Fairgrounds (just off Route 17 west of Rockland). Open July 1 to Labor Day, daily except Monday, 12–5. Adult $2, senior citizen $1, child $.50. A collection of more than 5000 artifacts showing the ingenuity and craftsmanship of the area's settlers in the 1800s.

Friendship Museum, Friendship. Junction of Route 220 and Martin's Point Road. Open July to Labor Day, Monday through Saturday 12–4, Sunday 2–4. Free. This former schoolhouse contains local memorabilia, including an exhibit on Friendship sloops.

LIGHTHOUSES

Maine has more lighthouses than any other coastal state, and Penobscot Bay boasts the largest number of lighthouses of all. Two in the Rockland area are accessible by land. One is the **Rockland Light,** perched at the end of the almost mile-long granite breakwater (turn off Route 1 onto Waldo Avenue just north of Rockland, then follow Samoset Road to the end). Parking is free, and you can walk all of the way out on the breakwater to the light. Locals bring their lunches here on pretty days. The other lighthouse is the **Owls Head Light,** built in 1825 atop sheer cliffs, but with safe trails down one side to the rocks below—good for scrambling and picnicking. From Rockland or the Owls Head Transportation Museum, take Route 73 to North Shore Drive Road. After about 2 miles you come to a small post office at an intersection. Go down Main Street for 0.25 mile and make a left onto Lighthouse Drive (the road turns to dirt). Park and walk a short way to the lighthouse. Lighthouse buffs should also be sure to visit the **Shore Village Museum** and **Marshall Point Lighthouse Museum** (see above).

TO DO

BOAT EXCURSIONS
Annie McGee (594-9049, RFD 279, Rockland 04841), a pinky schooner, offers day sails for up to six passengers from Rockland Harbor.

Wendameen (236-3472), the classic 67-foot schooner, has been beautifully restored by owner/captain Neal Parker, who takes passengers on overnight cruises from Rockland.

Atlantic Expeditions (372-8621). The 50-foot *Finback* sails from the Rockland Landings Marina at 8 AM, returning at 3 PM, on puffin watching tours to Matinicus Rock and Seal Island National Wildlife Refuge.

M/V *Monhegan* (596-5660), a former ferry-turned-excursion boat, offers lunch and dinner cruises and harbor tours from Rockland.

The Three Cheers (594-0900), a lobster boat built with guests in mind, offers "lobster fishing and lighthouse cruises."

Also see the Maine State Ferry Service described under *Islands* in this chapter. Ferry passage to North Haven and Vinalhaven is cheap and takes you the distance.

COASTAL CRUISE
(See also *Windjammer Cruises.*)
The *Pauline* (236-3529 or 1-800-999-7352) at Windjammer Wharf, Box 1050, Rockland, is a graceful, 83-foot motor vessel belonging to the owners of the windjammer *Stephen Taber* that also offers weekly cruises off the Maine coast. A former sardine carrier, she has been converted into a handsome passenger motorboat, accommodating 12 guests. Able to cruise at up to 9 knots, the *Pauline* offers a wider range of travel than the sailing windjammers. One day she may motor to Monhegan to attend an arts festival; the next, you could be off to Roque Island way Down East. Amenities and services on board are also a bit more luxurious than on a windjammer. The weekly per person fare is under $1000, including all meals.

DEEP-SEA FISHING
Charter boat *Henrietta* (Captain John Earl: 594-5411) departs daily in-season at 7:30 AM and returns by 4:30 PM.

ROLLER SKATING
Rockland Skate Center (594-1023), 299 Park Street, Rockland.

SPECIAL LEARNING PROGRAMS
Hurricane Island Outward Bound School (594-5548), Mechanic Street, Rockland. Courses lasting 5 to 26 days are offered on Hurricane Island

in Penobscot Bay, May to October. There are courses tailored to every age and to both sexes; they focus on sailing, rock-climbing, and outdoor problem solving. An international program begun in Wales, Outward Bound challenges participants to do things they never thought they could and then push themselves just a little further. For details, write Box 429, Rockland 04841.

The Island Institute (594-9209), 60 Ocean Street, Rockland. An organization dedicated to the preservation of Maine's beautiful islands; its activities include the development of an "island trail" for kayakers. Call or write for membership information.

(See also Bay Island Sailing School in the "Camden" chapter.)

WINDJAMMER CRUISES

More Maine windjammers are now based in Rockland than anywhere else. Three- and six-day cruises range from $300 to $700 (slightly less early and late in the season). You can spend a week between May and October gunkholing around Penobscot Bay on one of these tall-masted schooners—choose a new reproduction or an authentic old coasting schooner. Go where the winds and the captain decide, help haul the sails or not as you wish, and get elbow deep in lobsters and clams at a bake on a deserted island. These are not luxury cruises; you will have a small cabin with sink, shared heads (toilet and sink), and a shower that may be no more than an on-deck, hand-held sprayer under which you can wash your hair while wearing your bathing suit. But the experience is incomparable, and many passengers return year after year. All of the following vessels are inspected and certified each year by the Coast Guard.

American Eagle (1-800-648-4544), North End Shipyard, Rockland, is 92 feet long and accommodates 28 guests in 14 double cabins; there is a hot freshwater shower. She was originally built as a fishing vessel in 1930 and fished out of Gloucester until 1983, when Captain John Foss brought her to Rockland's North End Shipyard. There he spent the next two years restoring and refitting her. The *Eagle* was built with an engine (so she still has one) as well as sails, and she offers some comfortable below-deck spaces. The *Eagle* frequently sails farther Down East than most of the other windjammers.

Isaac H. Evans (594-8007 or 1-800-648-4544), North End Shipyard, Rockland, is 65 feet long with 11 double cabins for 22 passengers. She is just over a hundred years old, having been built in New Jersey in 1886 as an oyster-fishing schooner. She has been completely rebuilt in recent years. Hot freshwater shower on board. Captain Ed Glaser is a veteran seaman who plays the guitar and concertina.

Heritage (1-800-648-4544 or 1-800-542-5030 outside Maine), North End Shipyard, Rockland, is one of the newest schooners, designed along the lines of a 19th-century coaster and built by her captain in the early 1980s. Captain Doug Lee is a marine historian who, with his wife and co-captain, Linda, designed and built the *Heritage* in Rockland's North

Shore Shipyard. Their two daughters, Clara and Rachel, were raised aboard ship and sail as crew all summer long. She is 95 feet long and accommodates 33 passengers. There are showers in the deckhouse.

J&E Riggin (594-2923 or 1-800-869-0604) was built in 1927 for the oyster-dredging trade. A speedy 89-footer, she was extensively rebuilt in the 1970s before joining the windjammer trade. Facilities include hot showers. Captain Dave Allen is a second-generation windjammer captain, and his family has been sailing vessels out of nearby Brooklin (where the *Riggin* frequently drops anchor) since the War of 1812—so he comes by his Maine humor rightfully. His wife, Sue, is also a Maine native and an excellent cook. The couple rebuilt the vessel themselves.

Stephen Taber (236-3520 or 1-800-999-7352), Windjammer Wharf (at the State Ferry Landing), Box 1050, Rockland, was launched in 1871 and is the oldest documented United States sailing vessel in continuous use. She is 68 feet long and accommodates 22 passengers. She has a hand-held, hot-water shower on deck. Ken and Ellen Barnes, both licensed captains, bought, restored, and continue to sail the *Taber* after careers as (among other things) drama professors. Their enthusiastic following proves that they approach each cruise as a new production, throwing their (considerable) all into each sail.

Victory Chimes (594-0755 or 1-800-745-5651), PO Box 1401, Rockland, is the only original three-masted schooner in the windjammer trade and, at 170 feet, the largest. In 1991 the vessel celebrated its return to the Maine windjammer fleet in which she had served for 35 years before an interlude on the Great Lakes under ownership by Domino's Pizza. She carries 44 passengers on 3- and 6-day cruises. Her present co-owner and captain, Kip Files, has sailed on the *Victory Chimes* for many years.

Nathaniel Bowditch (273-4062 or 1-800-288-4098) comes by her speed honestly: She was built in East Boothbay as a racing yacht in 1922. Eighty-two feet long, she took special honors in the 1923 Bermuda Race and served in the Coast Guard during World War II. She was rebuilt in the early 1970s. A Maine guide from Rangeley, Captain Gib Philbrick came to the coast to sail aboard a windjammer in 1966 and has been at it ever since. He and his wife, Terry, met aboard the *Bowditch* (she was a passenger). They remain a great team.

Summertime (1-800-562-8290 outside Maine; 1-800-924-1747 in-state), 115 South Street, Rockland, is a 53-foot pinky schooner offering 3- and 6-day cruises for up to six passengers throughout the summer. In the spring and autumn, she offers day sails out of Stonington, Castine, and Bucks Harbor.

Most of these vessels are members of the Maine Windjammer Association, which distributes information on all members: 1-800-807-WIND, PO Box 1144, Blue Hill 04614. (Also see *Windjammers* under "What's Where in Maine" at the front of the book.)

GREEN SPACE

BEACHES
Johnson Memorial Park, Chickawaukee Lake, Route 17 (toward Augusta); **Birch Point Park,** Owls Head; and **Ayer Park,** Union.
PICNICKING
Route 1 picnic area overlooking Glen Cove, between the towns of Rockland and Camden; **Johnson Memorial Park,** Chickawaukee Lake, Route 17; **Sandy Beach Park,** Atlantic Street, Rockland.

LODGING

INNS
East Wind Inn (372-6366 or 372-6367), PO Box 149, Tenants Harbor 04860. Open year-round. Originally a sea captain's house and sail loft, set on the edge of picturesque Tenants Harbor. The parlor has a piano that guests are welcome to play. The inn is very clean and conveys a sense of being well run; it boasts 16 pleasant rooms, furnished with antiques, some with harbor views, most sharing baths. There are 10 additional guest rooms (private baths) in the adjacent (modern) Meeting House. Rates vary according to season, ocean view, and baths; doubles during the May to October season run $74–96 with continental breakfast; a suite is $96, and an apartment, $130. The dining room, open to the public, serves three meals each day in-season (see *Dining Out*).

Craignair Inn (594-7644), Clark Island, Spruce Head 04859. Open mid-May to October. Sited on a granite ledge by the shore, this unusual building was originally erected for workers at a nearby granite quarry. The 22 guest rooms are divided between the main house (all shared baths) and units in back (private baths); bedrooms are small but pleasing, furnished with antiques. In the downstairs common rooms you'll find more antiques. The water-view dining room, open to the public for dinner, showcases innkeeper Terry Smith's extensive collection of plates and other souvenirs from her travels in the Far East (see *Dining Out*). Walking is the thing to do here, down the miles of paths meandering from the inn and on Clark Island. There's also good bird-watching and swimming in the old quarry hole. Lodging includes a full breakfast. Doubles priced from $62–90; less off-season. Two-night minimum stay on holiday weekends. Weekly rates are available.

Ocean House (372-6691), PO Box 66, Port Clyde 04855. Open May 15 to November 1. The logical place to spend the night before boarding the morning ferry to Monhegan. Seven of the nine upstairs guest rooms in this building have private baths (two share). Note the water view from the upstairs porch. In the nearby **Seaside** annex (open year-round), rooms vary more in quality, but the overall feel is pleasant. Inquire about artists' workshops conducted by well-established artists, staged regularly spring through fall. A former garage has been converted into a large, professionally equipped studio. In the attractive dining room in the main inn, breakfast is served to both guests and the public, 7–noon; a 6:30 dinner ($15) is also available by reservation (BYOB). Rooms are $47–66.

(In the "Rockport, Camden, and Lincolnville" chapter also see the Samoset Resort, which overlooks Rockland Harbor.)

BED & BREAKFASTS

☞ **The Outsiders' Inn** (832-5197), corner of Routes 97 and 220, Box 521A, Friendship 04547. Open year-round, except for a few weeks in midwinter. Comfortable atmosphere in an 1830 house that was formerly the village doctor's home. Guests can take advantage of Bill and Debbie Michaud's kayaking expertise; eight kayaks are available for rent and guided expeditions in nearby Muscungous Bay. Pleasant doubles with private bath are $65, $50 with shared. A small cottage in the garden is $350 per week. Inquire about sailing seminars and packages on the Friendship sloop *Gladiator.*

☞ **Old Granite Inn** (594-9036), 546 Main Street, Rockland 04841. A mansion built in the 1840s of local granite, attached to a 1790s wooden Cape, a bit like a duck out of water given its commercial surroundings. This is the perfect place to stay before boarding a windjammer or taking the ferry to Vinalhaven, or North Haven, or Mattinicus. It's right across from the Main State Ferry Landing (see *Islands*) and the Concord Trailways stop. John (an artist) and Stephanie (a chef) Clapp have deftly restored the rich woodwork in this wonderful old building, creating 12 inviting guest rooms (three with private bath) furnished with cottage furniture and other antiques. Though front rooms have views, you might want to be in back, away from traffic. The living room and dining room are both delightful, and the Clapps are helpful about exploring the area. $45–100 (for the back suite) per night.

The Captain Lindsey House (596-7950), 5 Lindsey Street, Rockland 04841. Open in July of 1995, this fine old captain's house is furnished with a mix of antiques (for sale) and contemporary furnishings; there are seven rooms and two suites, all with private baths. Innkeeper Susan Barnes is a seasoned windjammer chef: She's a member of the family that also owns Maine's oldest surviving windjammer (the *Stephen Taber*) and its only sardine-carrier-turned-commercial-motor-yacht (the *Pauline*). She includes breakfast in the $96–135 rates. There are discounts for *Taber* and *Pauline* passengers, as well as dining discounts at The Waterworks, the neighboring brew pub/restaurant Susan also runs.

☞ **Weskeag Inn** (596-6676), Route 73, PO Box 213, South Thomaston 04858. Open year-round (weekends-only in winter). Convenient to Owls Head Transportation Museum and the Knox County Airport (where they'll gladly pick you up). An 1830s home overlooking the Weskeag estuary with its reversing falls. From the dining room and deck, you can watch lobstermen hauling their traps. Nine rooms range from singles with shared bath to doubles with private baths; some rooms have two double beds. Request a water view. Rates are $60–80 including full breakfast.

LimeRock Inn (594-2257 or 1-800-LIME-ROCK), 96 Limerock Street, Rockland 04641. The thin edge of the wedge: This is the first Camden-style B&B to open in Rockland. An 1890s Queen Anne–style mansion has been thoroughly restored, its eight guest rooms (all private, baths) furnished with splendid reproduction antiques (the innkeepers own a furniture store in Intervale, New Hampshire). Rates range from $85 for a small room decorated in floral prints to $160 for a large room with a mahogany four-poster and whirlpool bath or for a turret room with a "wedding canopy" bed. The inn's 36-foot sailing yacht is available for day sails at $50 per person, lunch included. Room rates include a full breakfast and afternoon tea.

Mill Pond House (372-6209), Tenants Harbor 04860. Open year-round. No children or pets are permitted. This 200-year-old house with a water view across the road offers three rooms with private or shared bath and a sitting room with TV. Rates include continental breakfast. Double with shared bath $45; with private bath $55.

Cap'n Frost B&B (354-8217), 241 W. Main Street, Thomaston 04861. Closed January and February. On Route 1 just southwest of Thomaston village, this is a pleasant old Cape filled with antiques appropriate to its early American decor. Bicycles, croquet, grill, and picnic tables are provided for guests. Rates are $45 and up, including a full breakfast.

Friendship By The Sea (832-4386), PO Box 24, Friendship 04547. A vintage 1805 Cape, set in a meadow, surrounded by woods. Open most of the year. Three attractive rooms with shared baths; common rooms include a pleasant living room and dining room with fireplace and deck. Walk to a working harbor or quiet cove. $55 per couple.

Harbor Hill (832-6646), Town Landing Road, PO Box 35, Friendship 04547. Open July and August. An 1800s farmhouse, this comfortable B&B sits above the fishing village of Friendship, offering views of the islands in Muscongus Bay. Full breakfast, plus dinners with prior arrangements. Three doubles with private baths are $85–90; there is also an efficiency apartment for up to four people at $90 a night or $450 per week.

COTTAGES AND EFFICIENCIES

A list of cottages, primarily in the Owls Head and Spruce Head areas, is available from the Rockland-Thomaston Chamber of Commerce (see *Guidance*).

Island View Oceanfront Cottages (594-7527), PO Box 128, Spruce Head 04859 (off-season: CJF Villa 142, Fripp Island, SC 29920; 803-838-5170). Open June to November. Two- and three-bedroom cottages with fireplaces and oceanfront decks set among spruce trees at the edge of the water. Furnished and equipped with everything (except linens and blankets), including washer/dryers and dishwashers; 14-foot, 6-horse-power motorboats for rent. Weekly rates are $535 for two-bedroom cottages and $565 for three-bedroom cottages.

The Mermaid (594-0616), 256 Main Street, Rockland 04841. Open year-round. This is one of Rockland's oldest center-chimney Colonial homes, across from the public landing. No breakfast. Guest apartment and efficiency with all linens and supplies provided. $250 a week; inquire about overnight rates.

MOTELS

Trade Winds (596-6661) in Rockland has a large restaurant and a full health club; **The Navigator** (594-2131), across from the state ferry terminal, has a restaurant.

WHERE TO EAT

DINING OUT

Jessica's, A European Bistro (596-0770), 2 South Main Street (Route 73), Rockland. Open year-round, every day except Tuesday; serves dinner and Sunday brunch. Reservations are recommended. In a restored Victorian home, this is an exceptional restaurant with an enthusiastic local following. Nicely prepared Continental cuisine includes a wide variety of meat entrées and pastas as well as seafoods, served in an inviting atmosphere. Paella is $14.40, veal Zürich, $14.

Cafe Miranda (594-2034), 15 Oak Street, Rockland. Open for lunch Tuesday through Saturday, dinner except Monday. Be sure to reserve, because this small, bright dining room—a ray of southwestern colors and flavors—is usually filled with savvy locals. The open kitchen features a brick oven and seafood grill, and the menu, fresh pastas and herbs. Our pink-pottery platter of curried mussels and shrimp (both in the shells) served on polenta with sweet peppers and onions, mopped up with flatbread (olive oil provided), was a bargain at $12.50. Wine and beer, espresso and cappuccino are served.

The East Wind Inn (372-6366), Tenants Harbor. Open for dinner and Sunday brunch. A dining room overlooking the working harbor with a porch on which cocktails are served in summer. The menu features local seafood and produce. Dinners might include poached salmon and spinach ($15.95), East Wind seafood stew ($18.95), and grilled clam with garden vegetables ($14.95).

Craignair Inn (594-7644), Clark Island, Spruce Head. Open for dinner Monday through Saturday. A pleasant dining room with limited water views. The à la carte menu is varied. Appetizers may include crab puffs, bouillabaisse ($15.95), "Tikka Kabab" (lamb cubes marinated in yogurt, lemon, and spices, $13.95), and black bean enchiladas ($11.95).

(Also see Marcel's at the Samoset Resort in the "Rockport, Camden, and Lincolnville" chapter.)

EATING OUT

In Rockland

The Landings Restaurant & Pub (596-6563), 1 Commercial Street. Right on the harbor with outside as well as inside seating, serves from 11–9:30 from a menu that ranges from a hot dog to steak, lobster, or a full-scale clambake. Fried clams, fish-and-chips, and a good selection of sandwiches.

The Brown Bag (596-6372), 606 Main Street (north of downtown). Open Monday through Saturday 6:30 AM–4 PM. This recently expanded store-front restaurant offers an extensive menu. Make your selection at the counter and carry it to your table when it's ready.

Second Read Bookstore (594-4123) 369 Main Street. Open 9–5:30, much later on music nights, 12–4 on Sunday. Vegetarian fare includes the "best hummus in the state," baked Brie, and maybe a roasted eggplant, pepper, and fresh mozzarella sandwich; there are usually soup and salad specials, also light meat dishes like teriyaki chicken. Cappuccino and espresso complement the bookish atmosphere (this is a second-hand bookstore); there's frequently folksinging or jazz on Saturday nights.

El Taco Tico (594-7568), 294 Main Street, is a good little Mexican restaurant; beer and wine served.

Wasses Wagon (found either at 2 North Main Street or the corner of Park and Union Streets); a local institution for hot dogs.

In Thomaston

Harbor View Tavern (354-8173). Open year-round. Tucked right down on the harbor on Snow's Pier, this is a real find. All sorts of photographs and memorabilia ornament the walls, and some very contented-looking goldfish swim about in the water tank of a huge, old coffeemaker. Try the broiled scallops, the peel-your-own Maine shrimp, or mussels and cream.

Thomaston Cafe and Bakery (354-8589), Main Street. Open 7 AM–2 PM, also for dinner Friday and Saturday and for Sunday brunch. Home-made soups, great sandwiches, specials like fishcakes with homefries, salads.

Dave's Restaurant (594-5424), Route 1, north of Thomaston. Seafood dinners and the area's only smorgasbord with old-fashioned classics, such as macaroni and cheese, beans and franks, etc. Breakfast and lunch buffets, plus a large salad bar. Breakfast is served all day.

Elsewhere

The Harpoon (372-6304), corner of Drift Inn and Marshall Point Road, Port Clyde. Open May through mid-October. In July and August, open for lunch and dinner every day. Spring and fall, dinner only, Wednesday through Sunday. This engaging little seafood restaurant in the seaside village of Port Clyde (just off Route 131, around the corner from the harbor) serves the local catch. Try the Cajun seafood, lazy lobster, fried combo plate, or prime rib.

Dip Net Coffee Shop, Port Clyde. Seasonal 8–4. Counter and table seating, but the preferred spot on any decent day is the deck overlooking this picturesque harbor. The idea is to park your car and buy your ticket for the 10 AM boat to Monhegan—then unwind over a breakfast of homemade coffee cake, muffins, or, better yet, fresh strawberry pie! The lunch menu runs to chowder, quiche, lobster stew, and tantalizing desserts.

Farmer's Restaurant (372-0525), Route 131, Tenants Harbor. Excellent value, no water view but good food; favored by local residents.

Hannibals (785-3663), on The Common, Union. Open daily 7 AM–8 PM, Sunday 7 AM–2 PM, closed Tuesday. Vegetarian specialities include tofu cutlet ranchero, but you can also get a "macho burger," barbecue baby back ribs and, best of all, Maine shrimp baked with sun-dried tomatoes, feta cheese, garlic, and spices. Children's menu.

LOBSTER POUNDS

Miller's Lobster Company (594-7406), Wheeler's Bay, Route 73, Spruce Head. Open 10–7, Memorial to Labor Day. Right on a working harbor, this is an old-fashioned, family-owned and -operated business with a loyal following. The lobsters and clams are cooked in seawater.

Cod End (372-6782), on the Wharf, Tenants Harbor. Open mid-June to mid-September every day 8–7:30; spring and fall 8–6. Lobster and clam picnics on their deck plus lobster rolls, chowders, and ice cream. Seafood packed for travel, live or cooked.

Waterman's Beach Lobsters (594-2489), off Route 73, South Thomaston. Open daily 11–7 in the summertime. Oceanfront feasting on the deck: lobster and clam dinners, seafood rolls, homemade pies.

ENTERTAINMENT

The Farnsworth Museum (596-6457) stages a year-round series of Sunday concerts, free with museum admission; reservations advised.

The Strand Cinema (594-7266), Main Street, Rockland, stages first-run films.

The Second Read Bookstore (594-4123), 369 Main Street, Rockland, has live music, usually jazz or folksinging, Friday and Saturday evenings.

SELECTIVE SHOPPING

Rockland's Main Street is a relatively well-preserved example of 19th-century commercial architecture, with local department, hardware and furniture stores. Note especially: **The Store,** featuring a wide selection of cooking supplies; **Coffin's,** a family clothing store; **Goldsmith's Sporting Goods,** a source of foul-weather gear; and **Senter Crane's,** an old-fashioned department store with a vintage elevator. **The Reading Corner** is a full-service bookstore with an interesting interior. The **Farnsworth Museum Store** occupies a space that was a florist shop until 1994 (corner of Main and Elm Streets).

ANTIQUES

More than a dozen antiques stores, scattered between Rockland and Thomaston, publish their own guides, which are available locally.

ART GALLERIES

Gallery One (596-0059), 365 Main Street, Rockland, and **Caldbeck Gallery** (594-5935), 12 Elm Street across from the Farnsworth Museum, Rockland, are both prestigious Maine exhibit spaces.

Open Air Gallery (372-8037), Route 73 in St. George, exhibits the work of Robert "Dan" Daniels, a retired construction welder and radiator repairman whose whimsical metal sculptures of birds, animals, and people have caught the imagination of passers-by and turned them into collectors of these original works.

BOOKSTORES

The Reading Corner (596-6651), Main Street, Rockland. A full-service bookstore filling two unusual storefronts.

New Leaf Books, Main Street, Rockland, is a feminist bookshop.

Thomaston Books & Prints (354-0001), 105 Main Street, Thomaston. Open daily. An attractive, new, full-service bookstore.

Lobster Lane Bookstore (594-7520), Spruce Head. Marked from the Off-Island Store. Open June to September, Thursday through Sunday and weekends through October. Vivian York's stock of 50,000 books is well known in bookish circles. Specialties include fiction and Maine.

SPECIAL STORES

Prison Shop at the Maine State Prison in Thomaston, Main Street (Route 1), at the southern end of town. A variety of wooden furniture—coffee tables, stools, lamps, and trays—and a choice of small souvenirs, all carved by inmates. Prices are reasonable and profits go to the craftsmen.

Newavom (354-6995), Route 1 just south of Thomaston. Open Monday through Saturday 1–4; closed in winter. An unusual workshop and showroom featuring custom-knitted textiles, hand-loomed rugs and throws, needlework packets, Portuguese and South American rugs and wall hangings, jewelry, sculpture, and hand-painted furniture.

Schoolhouse Farm vegetable stand, Route 1 south of Thomaston. Baskets of produce just harvested from the surrounding fields, jams and jellies, wheels of cheese, and fresh-baked muffins and breads.

Sheepskin Shop (273-3061), Route 90, Warren, selling everything from car seats to coats and vests made out of sheepskin.

Nobel Clay (372-6468 or 1-800-851-4857), Route 131, Tenants Harbor. Open year–round, 10–6. Trish Inman and Steve Barnes produce and sell functional white-and-blue glazed pottery decorated with whimsical designs.

Kohn's Smokehouse (372-8412), Route 131, south of Route 1 in St. George. Smoked fish, mussels, chicken, pheasant, bacon, salamies, using an old German recipe.

SPECIAL EVENTS

June: **Warren Day**—a pancake breakfast, parade, art and quilt shows, chicken barbecue, and auction.

July: **Fourth of July** celebrations in most towns, with parades. Thomaston's festivities include a big parade, foot races, live entertainment, a craft fair, barbecue, and fireworks. **Schooner Days** (Friday, Saturday, and Sunday closest to July 4)—see the wonderful windjammers vie for first place in a spectacular race that recalls bygone days. The best vantage point is the Rockland breakwater next to the Samoset Resort.

August: **Maine Lobster Festival** (first weekend in the month plus the preceding Wednesday and Thursday)—this is probably the world's biggest lobster feed, prepared in the world's largest lobster boiler. Patrons queue up on the public landing to heap their plates with lobsters, clams, corn, and all the fixings. King Neptune and the Maine Sea Goddess reign over the event, which includes a parade down Main Street, concerts, an art exhibit, contests such as clam shucking and sardine packing, and a race across a string of lobster crates floating in the harbor. **Union Fair and Blueberry Festival** (late August)—a real agricultural fair with tractor- and oxen-pulling contests, livestock and food shows, a midway, the crowning of the Blueberry Queen, and, on one day during the week, free mini-blueberry pies for all comers.

THE ISLANDS

Monhegan

Though barely a mile square—among Penobscot Bay's smallest—this storied island 10 miles offshore boasts 600 species of wildflowers, more than 400 years of intriguing history, and unequaled beauty. Two-thirds of Monhegan is, moreover, laced with 17 miles of footpaths that run along dramatic cliffs pounded by surf and through tall stands of pine.

"Beached like a whale" is the way one mariner in 1590 described the shape of the island: 150-foot headlands sloping down to coves, a low and quiet tail. Miraculously, the beauty survives today. Prospect Hill, the only attempted development, foundered around 1900. It was Theodore Edison, son of the inventor, who amassed property enough to erase the first traces of Prospect Hill and keep the island's 125 cottages bunched along the sheltered Eastern Harbor. In 1954 Edison helped to organize Monhegan Associates, a nonprofit corporation dedicated to preserving the "natural, wild beauty" of the island. Ironically, considering Edison's descent, this is one of the country's few communities to shun electricity until relatively recently. A number of homes and one inn still use kerosene lamps. Vehicles are limited to a few trucks to haul lobstering gear and visitors' luggage to and from the dock. Deer saunter through the middle of the village.

Monhegan is a genuine art colony. Jamie Wyeth summers in a house built by Rockwell Kent. The museum displays an etching by George Bellows of a prayer meeting in the village church. Some 20 artists open their studios to visitors (hours are posted on "the barn") during the course of a summer week. Cathedral Woods is studded with "fairy houses" (a local art form).

The island has three inns and a sprinkling of bed & breakfasts and summer cottages; off-season lodging is limited but possible. The less than 100 residents, who for generations have made their living from the sea (the lobstering season here begins in January), are joined in summer by some 400 visitors (day-trippers aside) seeking time and space to appreciate nature and quiet, to walk, to paint, and to reflect. An unusual number of people come alone.

GETTING THERE

Day-trippers and those who do not need to leave parked cars come on the **Balmy Days II** (see "Boothbay Harbor Region," *Boat Excursions;* note that you can take the bus to Wiscasset and a taxi to Boothbay Harbor) or the **Hardy III** (see "Damariscotta Area," *Boat Excursions*). Longer-term visitors tend to prefer the **Laura B** **mail boat** from Port Clyde (reservations are necessary: Monhegan Boat Line, PO Box 238, Port Clyde 04855; or call 372-8848) because they can park their car at Port Clyde (about $3 per day); the ticket for the 1-hour mail-boat trip is $24 round-trip. The *Laura B* runs year-round: twice daily in-season, once daily in spring and fall, and on Monday, Wednesday, and Friday in winter. When you make a reservation, request a copy of the booklet *An Introduction to Monhegan Island* by the late Dr. Alta Ashley. Visitors are advised to arrive properly shod for the precipitous paths, also equipped with sweaters and windbreakers. Wading or swimming from any of the tempting coves on the back side of the island tends to be lethal. Flashlights, heavy rubber boots, and rain gear are also good ideas. There is no bank on the island. Camping is prohibited. Do not bring bicycles, and dogs are better off at home (they must be leashed at all times). Smoking is not allowed outside the village center, and please don't pick the flowers.

TO SEE

The **Lighthouse,** built in 1824 and automated in 1959, offers a good view from its perch on the crest of a hill. The former keeper's cottage is now the **Monhegan Museum** (open daily July 4 through September 30, 11:30–3:30), a spellbinding display of island art, artifacts, flora, fauna,

The Laura B

some geology, lobstering, and an artistic history of the island, including documents dating back to the 16th century.

Manana Island (across the harbor from Monhegan) is the site of a famous rune stone with inscriptions purported to be Norse or Phoenician. At Middle Beach on Monhegan you may be able to find someone willing to take you over in a skiff.

TO DO

HIKING

Pick up a trail map before setting out. Day-trippers should take the **Burnt Head Trail** out and loop back by the village via **Lobster Cove** rather than trying a longer circuit; allow at least 5 hours (bring a picnic) to circuit the island. Our favorite hike is **Burnt Head** to **White Head** along high bluffs, with a pause to explore the unusual rocks in **Gull Cove**, and back through **Cathedral Woods**. On another day head for **Blackhead** and **Pulpit Rock**, then back along the shore to **Green Point** and **Pebble Beach** to watch the action on **Seal Ledges**.

LODGING

INNS

Island Inn (596-0371, or January to May 1-800-722-1269), Monhegan Island 04852. Open June to mid-September. With 45 rooms, the largest inn on the island. All the rooms have views, either of the ocean (and sunset) or of the meadows (and sunrise). Six doubles have private baths; the rest, both singles and doubles, share baths; four rooms and a suite are in the adjacent Pierce House. Rooms are small, clean, and plain. Downstairs are two small living rooms, part of the original pre-1850 house that is the nucleus of this 1900 inn; note the hand-painted murals and other local art. The large, old-fashioned dining room serves three meals a day to the public as well as to overnight guests. Doubles are $113–153, including breakfast and dinner.

Monhegan House (594-7983). Open Memorial Day through Columbus Day. An 1870s summer inn with 32 rooms. No closets, shared baths, but clean, comfortable, and bright. The downstairs lobby is often warmed by a glowing fireplace, and has ample seating for foggy mornings. The Bluebird Cafe here is a popular spot for breakfast (see *Eating Out*) with locals as well as guests of the inn. Singles are $42; doubles, $70; $80 for three people (breakfast is extra). (For advance reservations off-season, contact Jean Lord, Box 345, Monhegan 04852; the telephone number is the same.)

☞ **The Trailing Yew** (596-0440), Monhegan Island 04852. Open mid-May through early October. Operated since 1926 by Josephine Day and managed by Faryl Henderson, "The Yew" is an institution in its own right: 40 very basic rooms divided between the main house, adjacent buildings, and cottages on the grounds and even a bit up the road. Expect shared baths, a combination of electricity (in the bathrooms) and kerosene lamps, and simple food (usually there's some form of "cod"). Before meals, guests gather around the flagpole outside the main building to pitch horseshoes and compare notes; family-style dining at shared tables features lots of conversation. Birders tend to have their own table. The dining room is also open to the public. About $50 per person per day, including breakfast and dinner and all taxes and tips; ages 5–10, $15–30.

BED & BREAKFAST

Shining Sails Guesthouse (596-0041), Box 346, Monhegan Island 04852. Open year-round. Bill Baker and Amy Melenbacker have renovated a waterside home on the edge of the village. There are three rooms here, two with views of the meadow and of the ocean; also four efficiencies, two with ocean views. All rooms are tastefully decorated, as is the common room, which has a water view and Franklin stove. An ample continental breakfast is served May through Columbus Day. Rooms are $70–75, $425–490 per week; apartments are $75–95 per night, $490–630 weekly.

COTTAGES AND EFFICIENCIES

Note: Cooking facilities come in handy here: You can buy lobster and good fresh and smoked fish (bring meat and staples) and a limited line of vegetables.

Tribler Cottage (594-2445), Monhegan Island 04852-0307, has been in the same family for over three generations. Open May through October. Proprietors Martha Yandle and Richard Farrell (a photographer whose pictures decorate the walls) offer 4 one-bedroom apartments with fully equipped kitchens, sheets, towels, and all utilities; also one housekeeping room. The Hillside Apartment has a sun deck and living room with fireplace. Summer rates are $70–95 per day for two; $400–550 per week for two (minimum one-week rental period in-season; 5 percent discount on stays of two weeks or longer). $60 per night and $385 per week in winter.

Hitchcock House (594-8137), Horn's Hill, Monhegan Island 04852. Open year-round. Hidden away on top of Horn's Hill with a pleasant garden. Barbara Hitchcock offers several rooms and efficiencies with views of the meadows. The studio, a separate cabin, has a kitchen and bedroom. Rooms are $50 per night, $320 per week; efficiencies are $70 per night, $450 per week.

Shining Sails Real Estate (596-0041) manages two dozen or so rental cottages, available by the weekend as well as by the week.

WHERE TO EAT

The Bluebird Cafe at the Monhegan House is the place for breakfast.

The Island Inn (mid-June to mid-September). Open to the public for all three meals. Dinner is a set $18 per person ($20 on Sunday, buffet night). You might begin with vegetable beef and barley soup or a juice and dine on a choice of five entrées, maybe chicken parmigiana or cold sliced smoked trout with horseradish. A salad, vegetable, bread, and dessert (perhaps fresh peach pie or raspberry sherbert with a cookie) and coffee are included. BYOB.

The Trailing Yew (mid-May to mid-October). Open to the public by reservation. $13.50 for fruit cup, main entrée, salad, and dessert, whatever is being served that night. Ask when you reserve. The big attraction here is the conversation around communal tables.

The Careless Navigator serves breakfast, lunch and dinner. A two-floor restaurant with water views, varied menu, beer and wine.

North End Pizza, open seasonally for lunch, and dinner, is good for daily specials as well as a wide variety of pizzas. Run by a young fisherman and his wife.

At the **Fish "R" Us Fish Market,** you'll find smoked products and picnic fixings as well as lobsters.

SELECTIVE SHOPPING

ART GALLERIES

The **Lupine Gallery** offers original works and reproductions by Monhegan artists.

Open Studios: Many of the resident artists welcome visitors to their studios for browsing and buying; pick up a schedule, check "The Barn," or look for shingles hung outside listing the hours they're open.

SPECIAL SHOP

Carina. The spiritual successor of the old Island Spa, offering booths for sipping coffee, and a discerning selection of books, quality crafted items, and fresh-baked goods and vegetables.

Vinalhaven

Vinalhaven is a large (8-mile-long) island 13 miles off Rockland with a year-round fishing fleet of over 200 boats. Summer visitors may out-number residents five to one, but it still feels like the locals are in charge here. Vinalhaven gets relatively few day-trippers, accommodations are limited, and summer people seem to disappear once off the ferry; most are from families who have been coming here for generations. Unless you are renting a cottage, do not bring a car. Lodging places cluster in **Carver's Harbor,** the pure 1880s village at which the ferry docks. Bi-cycles are all you need to reach the quarries (great swimming holes) and nature preserves where you can walk, pick berries, bird-watch, and generally unwind.

In 1880, when granite was being cut on Vinalhaven to build Boston's Museum of Fine Arts and New York's Court House, there were 3380 people living on Vinalhaven, a number now reduced to about 1000—a mix of descendants of 18th-century settlers and the stonecutters who came here from Sweden, Norway, Finland, and Scotland. In recent years the island has also attracted a number of artists, including Robert Indiana, who works year-round in the middle of the village.

GETTING THERE

In the past couple years, the nightmare quality of taking a car to Vinalhaven has eased thanks to the addition of a second ferry, but it can still be enough of a hassle in July or August to cancel out the relaxing effect of the island itself. **The Maine State Ferry Service** (in Rock-land: 596-2203; in Carver's Harbor: 863-4421) has its own system: Each ferry takes no more than 17 vehicles (usually less since there is always a truck or two), and only a few of these spaces can be reserved (reserva-tions are $5 but must be made no less than 30 days in advance). Cars are taken in order of their position in line. For the morning boats you must be in line the night before. During the summer season getting off the island can entail lining up a day in advance and then moving your car for every ferry (five times a day). It's $24 for car and driver; $8 per adult and $6 per child, $4 per bicycle. Winter fares are lower. Call 867-4621 to find out about shuttle service between Vinalhaven and North Haven.

Coastal Transit (596-6605), the island's van service, meets every boat and will take you to the northern end of the island to the water taxi to North Haven.

TO SEE

Vinalhaven Historical Society Museum, open July through Labor Day, Monday through Friday, 11–3, Sundays noon–4. Housed in the old town hall, the museum displays photos and mementos from the island's granite and fishing industries. Check out the nearby Carver Cemetery.

TO DO

BICYCLING
Vinalhaven has more than 30 miles of paved roads, but most places you will want to find are a short ride out of Carver's Harbor. **Tidewater Inn** (see *Lodging*) rents bikes.
HIKING
See *Green Space.*

GREEN SPACE

Lane's Island Preserve lies off the road on the southern side of Carver's Harbor (cross the Indian Creek Bridge and look for the sign on the left). It includes 45 acres of fields, marsh, moor, and beach.

Grimes Park, just west of the ferry terminal, is a 2-acre point of rocky land with two small beaches. Note the rough granite watering trough once used by horses and oxen.

Armrust Hill is on the way to Lane's Island, hidden behind the medical center. The first place in which granite was commercially quarried, it remained one of the most active sites on the island for many decades. Note the many small pits ("motions") as well as four major quarries. The main path winds up the hill for a splendid view.

Booth Quarry. Continue east on Main Street 1.5 miles past the Union Church to the Booth Brothers Granite quarry (also known as the "swamp quarry"). This is a town park and popular swimming hole.

Note: This list is just a sampling of possibilities.

LODGING

Fox Island Inn (863-2122), PO Box 451, Carver Street, Vinalhaven 04863. Open Memorial Day through October. A restored, century-old town house near the library, just a 10-minute walk from the ferry landing, through the village and up the hill. Gail Reinertsen, a competitive long-distance runner, is a warm and helpful host, knowledgeable about the island and happy to dispense directions to her favorite beauty spots.

Several bikes are available to guests. Rooms are nicely decorated, and the living room is well stocked with books. Breakfast is buffet style, and guests are welcome to use the kitchen to prepare picnics, light meals, and snacks. Most rooms share (immaculate) baths. Doubles are $40–60; there's also a three-room suite; rates include breakfast. To reserve off-season, call Gail at 904-878-2643.

Tidewater Inn (863-4618), Carver's Harbor, Vinalhaven 04863. Open year-round. An outstanding little motel featuring waterfront units with private sun decks and kitchen units, located on the water in the heart of the village. All accommodations have private baths. Rates depend on whether your room is on the water and whether you want a kitchen unit. $68 doubles, $85 for waterfront units with kitchens; lower rates in the winter. The Tidewater also rents bicycles.

Libby House (863-4696; winter: 516-765-3756), Water Street, Vinalhaven 04853. Open July and August. Built in 1869, this handsome, rambling home is wonderfully furnished with Victorian pieces, including great, heavily carved beds. The comfortable common rooms are often filled with the sound of music, for when he's not playing host, the innkeeper is a music teacher. It's a short walk from here to Lane's Island Preserve. Breakfast is included. $55–75 for doubles with shared bath; a three-room apartment is $90; a suite $135.

WHERE TO EAT

The Haven (863-4969), Main Street, Vinalhaven. Open year-round. In summer for breakfast (5–10) and dinner (until 9) Tuesday through Saturday. Off-season just Wednesday, Friday, and Saturday (call). This is a very special place. Two dining rooms—an open-beamed room overlooking the water and a smaller streetside café—flank a kitchen in the middle. At breakfast the waterside room is the local gathering place: coffee served in heavy mugs, plenty of talk in the deep green booths. Dinner is elegant, with reservations a must in-season in the waterside room. Imaginatively prepared fish and pasta dishes with a stress on fresh ingredients; lighter meals served on the street side. Liquor served.

The Nighthawk, Main Street. Open until 8; closed Sundays. A vintage storefront bakery with tables scattered around, great sandwiches, soups, baked goods, a distinctly island place. Buy a sandwich on homemade bread and head out for a picnic.

Sand Dollar, Main Street. Open for breakfast, lunch, and dinner. A good dinner bet: lots of good food, local ambience, BYOB (Boongies is across the street).

Steamin' Kettle, Harbor Wharf. Open for lunch and dinner. Closed Tuesday. Indoor and outside seating, mostly seafood.

SELECTIVE SHOPPING

The Fog Gallery, featuring the work of such well-known Vinalhaven artists as Robert Indiana and Eric Hopkins.

North Haven

A low-key, private sort of resort with pebble beaches, very walkable country roads beside rolling, wildflower-filled meadows, vistas of Penobscot Bay, and a pleasant town park on the north side of the island. The **North Island Museum,** operated by the local historical society, will help you understand the island's history.

GETTING THERE

See *Getting There* for Vinalhaven. Same story except you line up in Rockland in the lanes marked NH rather than VH. The Maine State Ferry Service office in North Haven is: 867-4441. For shuttle service from North Haven to Vinalhaven, call 867-4621. Again, you don't need a car. The only place to stay has bicycles.

LODGING

Pulpit Harbor Inn (867-2219), North Haven Island 04853. Open year-round. A small, very special country inn with six guest rooms. Breakfast is included with overnight lodging. $70–90. Bicycles are available for use by guests and can be rented by nonguests. Dinner is no longer served, but Copper's Landing and the Coal Wharf both serve dinner. When these seasonal restaurants close, guests can use the kitchen facilities.

SELECTIVE SHOPPING

There are grocery, clothing, and antiques shops, and two art galleries. The **North Island Yarn Shop,** in the village of North Haven, sells yarn, sweaters, and special sweater kits made from wool sheared from local sheep and spun on the island.

Matinicus

Home to about 35 hardy souls in winter, most of whom make their living lobstering, Matinicus's population grows to about 200 in summer. A very quiet, unspoiled spot in Penobscot Bay, the island has a small village composed of the post office and powerhouse. There are also two beautiful sand beaches, one at each end of the island. On nearby

Matinicus Rock there is a protected nesting site for puffins.

GETTING THERE

Dick Moody, who runs the post office, also operates the 40-foot *Mary and Donna* between Matinicus and Rockland on Monday, Friday, Saturday, and Sunday in summer (and specially chartered trips at other times). The regular round-trip is $30, and reservations are a must (366-3700). The *Mary and Donna* also makes day trips to Matinicus Rock to see the puffins on weekends ($10 extra if you aren't taking the boat to or from Rockland that day). The Maine State Ferry serves the island about once a month (596-2202) in winter, three times in summer; fare is $25 round-trip; $35 if you bring your car. And you can charter a plane from **Penobscot Air Service Ltd.,** Owls Head (596-6211).

LODGING

Tuckanuck Lodge (366-3830), with five rooms and shared bath, is the only place to stay on the island. Rates are moderate. The lodge also rents bikes to guests.

For **cottage rentals:** call Donna Rogers (366-3011). For more information, write to the Matinicus Chamber of Commerce, Box 212, Matinicus 04851.

Rockport, Camden, and Lincolnville

All I could see from where I stood
Was three long mountains and a wood;
I turned and looked another way,
And saw three islands in a bay.

—Edna St. Vincent Millay

These opening lines from "Renascence" suggest the view from the top of Mount Battie. Millay's home town—Camden—lies below the mountain on a narrow, curving shelf between the hills and bay.

Smack on Route 1, Camden is the most popular way station between Kennebunkport or Boothbay Harbor and Bar Harbor. Seemingly half its 19th-century captains' homes are now B&Bs. Shops and restaurants line a photogenic harbor filled with private sailing and motor yachts. It's also a poor man's yacht haven.

Here, in 1935, artist Frank Swift refitted a few former fishing and cargo schooners to carry passengers around the islands in Penobscot Bay. He called the boats "windjammers." A half dozen members of Maine's current windjammer fleet are still based here (the rest are in neighboring ports) and several schooners offer day sails. You can also get out on the water in an excursion boat or a sea kayak.

From the water you can see two aspects of Camden that you can't see from land. The first is the size and extent of the Camden Hills. The second is the size and number of the palatial old waterside "cottages" along Beauchamp Point, the rocky promontory separating Camden from Rockport. Here, as in Bar Harbor, summer residents were wise and powerful enough to preserve the local mountains, seeding the creation of the present 6500-acre Camden Hills State Park, one of Maine's more spectacular places to hike.

Camden's first resort era coincided with those colorful decades during which steam and sail overlapped. As a stop on the Boston-Bangor steamboat line, Camden acquired a couple of big (now vanished) hotels. In 1900 when Bean's boatyard launched the world's first six-masted

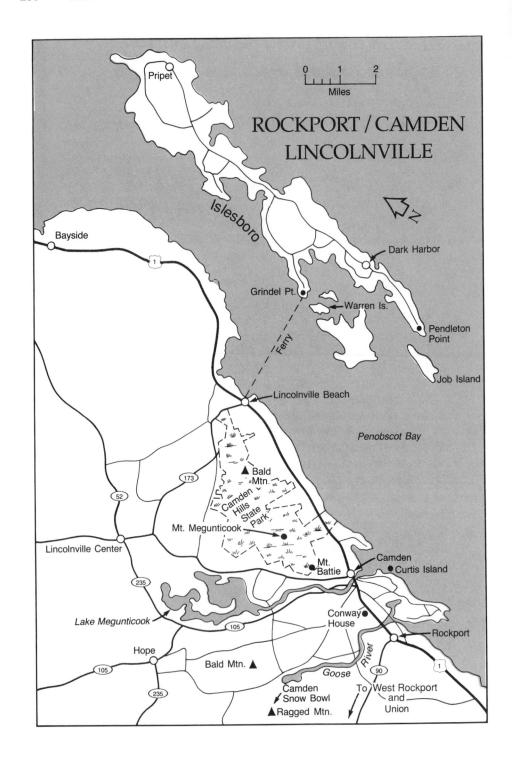

ROCKPORT / CAMDEN
LINCOLNVILLE

Pripet

0   1   2
Miles

Islesboro

N

Bayside

Dark Harbor

1

Grindel Pt.

Warren Is.

Ferry

Pendleton
Point

Job Island

Lincolnville Beach

Penobscot Bay

173

▲ Bald
Mtn.

Camden
Hills
State
Park

52

Mt. Megunticook

Lincolnville Center

Camden
● Curtis Island

235

Mt.
Battie

Lake Megunticook

105

Conway ●
House

River

Rockport

Hope

Bald Mtn. ▲

Goose

90

1

105

Camden
Snow Bowl

To West Rockport
and
Union

235

▲ Ragged Mtn.

schooner, onlookers crowded the neighboring ornate steamboat wharf to watch.

In contrast to Boothbay and Bar Harbor, Camden has always been a year-round town that's never been overdependent on tourism. Camden's early business was, of course, building and sailing ships. By the mid-1800s, a half dozen mills lined the series of falls on the Megunticook River, just a block or two from the waterfront. The vast wooden Knox Woolen Co.—the "Harrington Mill" portrayed in the movie *Peyton Place*—made the felts used by Maine's paper mills to absorb water from paper stock. It operated until 1988, and the complex is now the New England headquarters for a major credit card company, the most recent among dozens of companies to locate in Camden.

Culturally enriched by its sophisticated populace—work-a-day residents, retirees, and "summer people" alike—Camden (along with Rockport) offers a bonanza of music, art, and theatrical productions surprising in quality. There are also programs in computer sciences and photography, as well as the long-acclaimed summertime Salzedo Harp Colony.

Ironically, only a small fraction of the thousands of tourists who stream through Camden every summer take the time to discover the extent of its beauty. The tourist tide eddies around the harborside restaurants, shops, and galleries and continues to flow on up Route 1 towards Bar Harbor. Even in August you are likely to find yourself alone atop Mount Battie (accessible by car as well as on foot) or Mount Megunticook (highest point in the Camden Hills), or in the open-sided Vesper Chapel, with its flowers and sea view. Few visitors see, let alone swim in, Megunticook Lake or set foot on the nearby island of Islesboro.

A dozen years ago you could count the number of places to stay here on your fingers, but Camden has since become synonymous with bed & breakfasts, which, at last count, totaled more than 20. Still the number of rooms in town are less than 200, and on most summer weekends that's not enough. Be sure to reserve as far ahead as possible.

GUIDANCE

Rockport-Camden-Lincolnville Chamber of Commerce (236-4404), PO Box 919, Public Landing, Camden 04843. Open year-round, Monday through Friday 9–5 and Saturday 10–5; also open Sunday 12–4, mid-May through mid-October. You will find all sorts of helpful brochures here, plus maps of Camden, Rockport, Lincolnville, and Islesboro, as well as knowledgeable people to send you in the right direction. The chamber keeps tabs on available vacancies during the high season, also on what is open off-season and what cottages are for rent (a list is ready for requests each year by January). Be sure to secure their booklet, as well as the Camden-Rockport Historical Society's "A Visitor's Tour," which outlines tours of historic districts in Camden and Rockport.

GETTING THERE

By air: **Knox County Airport,** at Owls Head, about 10 miles from Camden (see the "Rockland" chapter), offers daily flights to and from Boston. **Bangor International Airport** (see the "Bangor" chapter) offers connections to all parts of the country.

By bus: **Concord Trailways** stops on Route 1 south of Camden en route from Bangor to Portland and Boston.

By limo: **Mid Coast Limo** (1-800-834-5500 within Maine, or 1-800-937-2424 outside Maine) offers connections to the Portland Jetport.

PARKING

Parking is a problem. In-town parking has a stringently enforced 2-hour limit (just 15 minutes in a few spots, so be sure to read the signs). There are a few lots outside the center of town (try the Camden Marketplace and a lot on Mechanic Street); there's an advantage here to finding lodging within walking distance of the village.

MEDICAL EMERGENCY

Penobscot Bay Medical Center (594-9511), Route 1, Rockport.

VILLAGES AND ISLAND

Rockport's harbor is as picturesque as Camden's, and the tiny village is set high above it. Steps lead down to Marine Park, departure point in 1816 for 300 casks of lime shipped to Washington, DC, to help construct the Capitol building. A granite sculpture of Andre the Seal recalls the legendary performer who drew crowds every summer in the early and mid-1980s. The village (part of Camden until 1891) includes the restored Rockport Opera House, site of the summer Bay Chamber Concerts, the noted Maine Coast Artists gallery, the Maine Photographic Workshop program, and a salting of restaurants and shops.

Lincolnville is larger than it looks as you drive through. The village's landmarks—the Lobster Pound Restaurant and Maine State Ferry to Islesboro—serve as centerpieces for proliferating shops, restaurants, and B&Bs.

Islesboro. A 10-mile-long, stringbean-shaped island just 3 miles off Lincolnville Beach, Islesboro is a private kind of place. Its two communities are Dark Harbor (described by Sidney Sheldon in his best-seller *Master of the Game* as the "jealously guarded colony of the super-rich") and Pripet, a thriving, year-round neighborhood of boat builders and fishermen. The car-carrying **Maine State Ferry** (call 789-5611 or 734-6935; $4 per passenger, $12 per car, $4 per bicycle) from Linconville Beach lands mid-island, at Grindle Point, next to the old lighthouse and keeper's cottage that's now the seasonal **Sailors' Memorial Museum.** You at least need a bike to get any sense of this place. The **Islesboro Town Office** (734-2253) in Dark Harbor is a friendly source of information and can refer you to local realtors who handle cottage rentals.

The only place to stay is **Dark Harbor House** (see *Inns*), which also offers dinner by reservation to passing yachtsmen. **Oliver's,** open May through October (734-6543) in Dark Harbor, also offers fine dining and lighter fare in a second-floor pub. There are summer musical and theatrical performances at the **Free Will Baptist Church** and Earl and Bonnie MacKenzie offer day sails and dinner cruises on their *Flying Fish* (734-6984 or 734-6714), a 45-foot, gaff-rigged schooner built in 1936. Check out the **Up Island Church,** a fine old structure with some beautiful wall stencils and fascinating old headstones in the adjacent graveyard. The luncheonette in **The Dark Harbor Shop** is the local gathering place.

TO SEE

MUSEUMS
Old Conway House Complex (236-2257), Conway Road (off Route 1 just south of Camden). Open during July and August, Tuesday through Friday 10–4; admission $2; students $1, children over 6, $.50. Administered by the Camden-Rockport Historical Society, this restored, early 18th-century farmhouse has been furnished to represent several periods. The barn holds collections of carriages, sleighs, and early farm tools, and there is a Victorian privy and a blacksmith shop.

Knox Mill Museum, MBNA offices, Mechanic Street, Camden. Open weekdays, 9–5. A sophisticated little museum dramatizes the 125 years of operation of the Knox Woolen Mill. Exhibits include a film, many photographs, and some machinery. The prime supplier of felts for the endless belts used in paper maunfacturing, this was the "Harrington Mill" in the 1957 film *Peyton Place,* filmed in Camden.

SCENIC DRIVE
Around Beauchamp Point: Drive or, better yet, bicycle (see *Bicycling* under *To Do*) around Beauchamp Point. Begin on Chestnut Street and follow this peaceful road by the lily pond and on by the herd of Belted Galloway cows (black on both ends and white in the middle). Take Calderwood Lane through the woods and by the **Vesper Hill Children's Chapel,** built on the site of a former hotel and banked with flowers, a great spot to get married or simply to sit. Continue along Beauchamp Avenue to Rockport Village to lunch or picnic by the harbor, and return via Union Street to Camden.

TO DO

BICYCLING
Fred's Bikes (236-6664), Chestnut Street, across from the YMCA, rents a variety of mountain and road bikes, kiddie kart trailers, and accessories, and delivers them to inns and B&Bs. Inquire about evening group rides.

Mainely Mt. Bike Tours (785-2703), Union, offers 2- and 3-hour guided mountain bike tours.

BOAT EXCURSIONS

(See also Windjammer Cruises.)

Figaro Cruises (1-800-473-6169), PO Box 1336, Camden 04843. A 51-foot centerboard yawl built for ocean racing accommodates six passengers—a size that one guest assures is perfect for getting in some sailing and sharing heads (there are two)—on 3- and 6-day cruises; vegetarian fare is a specialty. Inquire about a Yoga Cruise.

Yacht charters are offered spring to autumn along the Maine coast. Most charters run for a week, although sometimes it is possible to charter a boat just for a long weekend, with or without crew. For more information, contact **Windward Mark Yacht Charters** (236-4300; 1-800-633-7900 outside Maine). **Bay Island Yacht Charters** (236-2776) has yachts available for bare-boat charter out of Rockland as well as other ports the length of Maine's coast. **Blue Seas Adventure Co.** (236-6904) rents a variety of power and sail boats by the day or more.

Appledore (236-8353), an 86-foot schooner (the largest of the day-sailing fleet), has sailed around the world and now offers several trips daily, including sunset cruises.

Surprise (236-4687), a traditional, historic, 57-foot schooner, gets rave reviews from those who take its 2-hour sails. Captain Jack and wife, Barbara Moore, spent 7 years cruising between Maine and the Caribbean, educating their four children in the process.

Olad (236-2323), a 47-foot schooner, offers 2-hour sails.

Shantih II (236-8605 or 1-800-599-8605) offers day sails, sunset sails, and a sail/inn package out of Rockport.

Betselma (236-2101), a motor launch, provides hourly sight-seeing trips (owner Les Bex was a longtime windjammer captain) of the harbor and nearby coast.

Lively Lady, a traditional lobster boat, takes passengers on 1- and 2-hour cruises that include watching lobster traps being hauled.

Maine State Ferry from Lincolnville Beach to Isleboro (789-5611). At $4 round-trip per passenger and $2 per bicycle, this is the bargain of the local boating scene; see Islesboro under *Villages and Island.*

GOLF

Goose River Golf Club (236-8488), Simonton Road, Camden. Nine holes, but you can play through twice using different tees. Cart rentals. Clubhouse.

Samoset Golf Course (594-2511 or 1-800-341-1650), Rockport, has 18 holes on a course that *Golf Digest* selected as one of the five most beautiful in the country. Many of the fairways skirt the water, and the views are lovely. Carts are available.

HIKING

The Camden Hills are far less recognized than Acadia National Park as a hiking haven, but for the average once-or-twice-a-year hiker, they offer ample challenge and some spectacular views. Mount Battie, accessible by a steep half-mile trail from Route 52, is the only peak also accessible by car. The 1-mile Maiden Cliff Trail (park off Route 52, 2.9 miles from Route 1) is favored by locals for its views from the top of 800-foot sheer cliffs overlooking Lake Megunticook; it connects with the 2.5-mile Ridge Trail to the summit of Mount Megunticook (1300 feet). A complete trail map is available from most B&Bs and from the gatekeeper at Camden Hills State Park (see *Green Space*).

SEA KAYAKING

Maine Sport Outfitters (236-8797 or 1-800-722-0826) on Route 1 just south of town is a phenomenon rather than merely an outfitter. Be sure to stop. They offer courses in kayaking and canoeing, guided excursions around Camden Harbor and out into Penobscot Bay, and island-based workshops. They also rent kayaks and canoes. Contact them for their catalog of activities.

Ducktrap Sea Kayak Tours (789-5950) in Lincolnville Beach also offers guided tours.

Mt. Pleasant Canoe and Kayak (785-4309), West Rockport, offers a 2-hour sunset trip on Megunticook Lake as well as guided coastal tours.

SWIMMING

Saltwater swimming from Camden's **Laite Memorial Park and Beach,** upper Bayview Street; at **Lincolnville Beach,** Route 1 north of Camden; and in Rockport at **Walker Park.** Freshwater swimming at Megunticook Lake (**Barret Cove Memorial Park and Beach;** turn left off Route 52 northwest of Camden), where you will also find picnic grounds and a parking area; **Shirttail Beach** on Route 105; and at the **Willis Hodson Park** on the Megunticook River (Molyneaux Road). At the **Camden YMCA** (236-3375), Chestnut Street, visitors can pay a day-use fee that entitles them to swim in the Olympic-sized pool (check hours for family swimming, lap swimming, etc.), use the weight rooms, and play basketball in the gym.

TENNIS

There are two public tennis courts at the **Camden Snow Bowl** on Hosmer's Pond Road. In addition, **Samoset Resort** (594-2511), Rockport, has indoor and outdoor courts.

WINDJAMMER CRUISES

Windjammer cruises are offered mid-June to mid-October. A half dozen schooners and a ketch sail from Camden and Rockport on 3- to 6-day cruises through Penobscot Bay. For brochures and sailing schedules, contact the **Maine Windjammers Association** (374-5400 or 1-800-807-WIND). (See also *Windjammer Cruises* under *To Do* in the "Rockland" chapter and under "What's Where.")

Angelique (236-8873), PO Box 736, Camden, is a 95-foot ketch that was built expressly for the windjammer trade in 1980. Patterned after

19th-century English fishing vessels, she offers a pleasant deck-level saloon and below-decks showers.

Timberwind (236-6095 or 1-800-759-9250), PO Box 247, Rockport 04856, was built in Portland in 1931 as a pilot schooner. This pretty, 70-foot vessel was converted to a passenger vessel in 1969. She has an enclosed, hand-held shower on deck. The *Timberwind* is the only windjammer sailing out of Rockport Harbor, next door to Camden.

Roseway (236-4449 or 1-800-255-4449), Yankee Schooner Cruises, PO Box 696, Camden, was built in 1925 as a fishing schooner and later spent 32 years as a pilot vessel, escorting ships in and out of Boston Harbor. She has been sailing out of Camden since 1975. There are enclosed, hot, freshwater showers on deck.

Lewis R. French (1-800-469-4635) was launched on the Damariscotta River in 1871. Before becoming a passenger vessel, she carried cargo along the coast. She was completely rebuilt between 1973 and 1976. Sixty-four feet long, she accommodates 23 passengers. Hot, freshwater shower on board. Native Maine Captain Dan Pease met his wife, Kathy, when she came aboard for a vacation. Now their son, Joe, comes along every chance he gets. No smoking.

Mary Day (1-800-992-2218 in the US and Canada; 1-800-540-2750 in Maine), Box 798, Camden 04843, was the first schooner built specifically for carrying passengers. She's among the swiftest; her co-captains are Steve and Chris Cobb. Features include a fireplace and parlor organ and hot, freshwater showers on deck.

Grace Bailey (236-2938 or 1-800-736-7981), Maine Windjammer Cruises, PO Box 617, Camden; for years known as the *Mattie,* she has taken back her original name following a thorough restoration. Built in 1882 in New York, she once carried cargo along the Atlantic coast and to the West Indies. She has below-decks showers.

Mercantile (see *Grace Bailey*), was built in Maine in 1916 as a shallow-draft coasting schooner. Seventy-eight feet long, she has been in the windjammer trade since its beginning in 1942. Each cabin has its own private head, and there are below-decks showers nearby.

Mistress (see *Grace Bailey*), the smallest of the fleet, carries just six passengers. A topsail schooner built along the lines of the old coasting schooners, she is also available for private charter. All three cabins have private heads, but there is no shower on board.

SKIING

Camden Snow Bowl (236-3438), Hosmer's Pond Road, Camden. With a 950-foot vertical drop, nine runs for beginner through expert, and night skiing, this is a comfortably sized area where everyone seems to know everyone. Facilities include a base lodge, a rental and repair shop, and a cafeteria.

Camden Hills State Park also marks and maintains some trails for cross-country skiing, and there's a ski hut on Mount Battie.

SPECIAL LEARNING PROGRAMS

Camden Yacht Club Sailing Program (236-3014), Bayview Street, provides sailing classes for children and adults, boat owners and nonboat owners, during July and August; among them is an excellent week-long course just for women. There is also a lecture series open to the public.

Bay Island Sailing School (236-2776 or 1-800-421-2492), headquartered in Camden but based at Journey's End Marina in Rockland, an ASA-certified sailing school offering beginner, coastal cruising, and bare-boat certification programs ranging from intensive weekend workshops to 5-day hands-on cruises. $395–995.

Maine Photographic Workshops (236-8581), Rockport 04856. A nationally respected, year-round school offers a choice of 200 programs that vary in length from 1 week to 3 months for every level of skill in photography, cinematography, television production, and related fields. Teachers are established, recognized professionals who come from across the country, as do the students. There is also a gallery with changing exhibitions open to the public. The school provides housing for most of its students and helps to arrange accommodations for others.

The Artisans School (236-6071), Box 539, Rockport 04856. Open to visitors year-round, 10–5 Monday through Saturday (and sometimes on Sunday if you call ahead). Perpetuating the art of wooden boatbuilding, this school offers 2-year apprenticeships, 6-week internships, and 6-week volunteer stints. A wide variety of boats have been built here, reflecting the maritime heritage of the Atlantic from Newfoundland to the Bahamas. The Visitors' Gallery overlooks the boatbuilding in progress on the main floor below. There are also exhibits of models, boats, photographs, and marine art.

Maine Sport Outfitters (236-8797), PO Box 956, Rockport 04856. This Route 1 complex is worth a stop whether you are up for adventure sports or not. This place is more than simply a store or kayaking, canoeing, mountain biking center; it has evolved over the years from a fly-fishing and canvas shop into a multitiered store that's a home base for adventure tours. Inquire about a wide variety of local kayaking tours and multiday kayaking workshops geared to all levels of ability, based at its facilities on Gay Island.

Center for Furniture Craftsmanship (236-3032), Camden. June to October. Two-week, hands-on workshops for beginning and intermediate woodworkers.

GREEN SPACE

Camden Hills State Park (236-3109 or 236-0849), Route 1, Camden 04843. In addition to Mount Battie, this 6500-acre park includes Mount Megunticook, one of the highest points on the Atlantic seaboard, and a shoreside picnic site. You can drive up the road that starts at the park entrance, just north of town. Admission through the gate is $2 adults; $.50 ages 6–12; 5 and under free. At the entrance, pick up a "Hiking at Camden Hills State Park" map. For highlights of this 25-mile network see *Hiking*. In winter many of the trails are suitable for cross-country skiing, given snow. There are 112 campsites here.

Warren Island State Park, also administered by Camden Hills State Park, is just a stone's throw off the island of Islesboro. There are picnic tables, trails, and tent sites here. Accessibility is the problem: You can arrange to have a private boat carry you over from the mainland, rent your own boat in Camden, or paddle out in a sea kayak (see *Sea Kayaking*).

Marine Park, Rockport. A nicely landscaped waterside area with sheltered picnic tables. Restored lime kilns and a train caboose are reminders of the era when the town's chief industry was processing and exporting lime.

Merryspring (236-4885), Camden. A 66-acre preserve with walking trails, an herb garden, a lily garden, a rose garden, raised beds, a demonstration garden, and an arboretum. The preserve is bisected by the Goose River and is accessible by way of Conway Road from Route 1 in Camden. Weekly talks in the summertime. The organization is dedicated to planting and preserving flowers, shrubs, and trees in this natural setting and to interpreting them through workshops and special events. Donations are encouraged.

Fernald's Neck Nature Conservancy Preserve. Near the junction of Route 52 and the Youngtown Road, a heavily wooded peninsula juts into Lake Megunticook. One walking trail leads to 60-foot cliffs. Trails can be boggy: wear boots or old shoes.

Camden Amphitheatre, Atlantic Avenue, Camden. A magical setting for summertime plays and concerts and a good place to sit, think, and read anytime. Tucked behind the library and across the street from the harbor park—a gentle, manicured slope down to the water.

Curtis Island, in the outer harbor. A small island with a lighthouse that marks the entrance to Camden. It is a public picnic spot, and a popular sea kayaking destination.

LODGING

All listings are Camden 04843 unless otherwise indicated. Rates are for high summer; most have off-season rates as well. *Note:* If you choose one of the many B&Bs in historic houses on Elm, Main, or High Streets (all are Route 1), you might want to ask what pains have been taken to muffle passing traffic.

Camden Accommodations (1-800-236-1920), a reservations service representing most places to stay in the Camden area. It also coordinates rentals for some six dozen cottages and condos.

RESORT

Samoset Resort (594-2511 or 1-800-341-1650), 220 Warrenton Street,

Rockport 04856. Open year-round, a full-service resort set in 230 waterside acres, with 132 rooms and 18 suites, some handicapped accessible, many with ocean views, all with balconies or patios, private baths, color TVs, and climate-controlled air-conditioning and heat. Seventy-two time-share units with full kitchens and washer/dryers are also available for nightly rentals. The two-bedroom Flume Cottage, perched on a rocky outcropping above the water, is available by the week in-season and nightly off-season. Amenities include an outstanding 18-hole golf course, indoor golf center, indoor and outdoor tennis courts, a Nautilus-equipped fitness club, racquet ball courts, a glass-enclosed swimming pool, and an outdoor pool. A children's program is offered during school holiday periods. This is a popular meeting and convention site. The dining room, Marcel's (see *Dining Out*), is generally rated among the best on the mid-coast. The adjacent lounge has a large fireplace and floor-to-ceiling windows overlooking the water. $120–270 in summer; $100–145 in winter. Time-share units are $255–300 (one bedroom), $295–340 (two bedroom) in summer, less by the week and off-season. Ask about packages.

INNS

The Belmont (236-8053 or 1-800-238-8053), 6 Belmont Avenue. Open mid-May through New Year's Eve. An 1890s Edwardian house with a wraparound veranda; offers six guest rooms and suites, each furnished with nice touches such as matching bedspreads and wallpaper. All have private baths. Our favorite is the third-floor room. In the living room, accented by Oriental rugs on shining wood floors, guests are invited to relax in comfortable wing chairs and chat about the day's adventures or enjoy a cocktail from the bar. Chef Gerald Clare (one of the owners) offers imaginative "New American" fare (see *Dining Out*) in an inviting dining room that's recognized as one of the best on the Maine coast. A full country breakfast—egg dishes or perhaps blueberry pancakes—is included in lodging. $95–145 in summer, $75–105 in winter, single or double occupancy. Two-night minimum stay on weekends July through October.

Dark Harbor House (734-6669), Box 185, Main Road, Dark Harbor, Islesboro 04848. Open mid-May to mid-October. The only place to stay on Islesboro and one of the most pleasant inns along the Maine coast. Built on a hilltop at the turn of the century as a summer cottage for the president of the First National Bank of Philadelphia, this imposing, yellow-clapboard inn offers elegance from a past era. Inside you'll find a summery living room with glass doors opening onto a porch and a cozier library with a fireplace just right for crisp autumn afternoons. Fine antiques are found throughout the Dark Harbor House and its seven bedrooms. All have private baths, and some feature balconies. There's also a two-room suite with a wet bar and a fold-out sofa bed in its living room, as well as a two-room master suite complete with an enclosed sun-porch sitting room, fireplace, and canopied queen-sized mahogany bed. An à la carte dining and full wine service is served to guests and to the public with reservations. Entrées might be *paupiettes* of sole with native crabmeat, chicken roulades with leek, Gruyère, and prosciutto, or locally caught steamed lobster. Dessert might be lemon mousse, raspberry-blueberry crisp, or chocolate caramel walnut torte. Picnic baskets can be prepared for day trips. Doubles are $95–245 including a full, four-course breakfast; 2-night minimum on holiday weekends. Dinner entrées run $16.95–21.50.

Whitehall Inn (236-3391), 52 High Street (Route 1). Open Memorial Day to Columbus Day weekend. There's an air of easy elegance and comfort to this rambling, family-owned inn on Route 1, east of the village. The large, low-beamed lobby and adjoining parlors are fitted with Oriental rugs and sofas, games, and puzzles. The Millay Room, with its vintage 1904 Steinway, looks much the way it did on the summer evening in 1909 when a local girl, Edna St. Vincent Millay, read a poem, "Renascence," to assembled guests, one of whom was so impressed that she undertook to educate the young woman at Vassar. The inn offers 40 guest rooms in the main inn, 10 more divided between the Maine and Wicker Houses across Route 1. These rooms are simpler than most to be found in neighboring B&Bs, but each has its appeal. Most have private baths. All have the kind of heavy, old phones your children have never seen. A tennis court is across the street, and it's just a short walk to the Salzedo Harp Colony (summer concerts) and a "sneaker" beach (which means you have to wear shoes because of the rocks) on Camden's outer harbor. Families are welcome but asked to dine early. Doubles are $130–165 MAP July through mid-October; a single room with shared bath is $60 B&B during this period; doubles are $100–135 B&B. Cheaper Memorial Day through June. Add 15 percent service.

Camden Harbour Inn (236-4200), 83 Bayview Street. Open year-round. A landmark 1874 inn on a knoll overlooking the harbor and mountains. Thoroughly renovated (and fireproofed) in the late 1980s, the inn nevertheless retains the feel of an old summer hotel in its parlor. All 22 rooms have private baths (no TVs or phones), and many have balconies, patios, or fireplaces. Each room is different, and all are furnished in genuine and reproduction antiques, including many four-poster and canopy beds. Request a water view. On summer evenings, dinner is served on a large outdoor porch as well as in the dining room. Doubles $175–225 in high season; lower in "mid-season" and off-season. Between April 29 and December 1, rates include a full breakfast; from December 2 to April 28, a complimentary continental breakfast is offered. Inquire about packages.

The Blue Harbor House (236-3196 or 1-800-248-3196), 67 Elm Street (Route 1). Open year-round. The feel here is that of a friendly B&B but dinner as well as breakfast is served at separate tables on the spacious sun porch. We haven't sampled dinner (multicourse, candlelit, $25) but can vouch for breakfast, which can be a lobster quiche, cheese soufflé, or blueberry pancakes with blueberry butter. The 10 guest rooms vary, but all are pleasantly decorated with country antiques, stenciling, and hand-made quilts; all have private baths. There are also two carriage house suites with whirlpool tubs. Bicycles are available to guests. Doubles $85–125; 2-day Thanksgiving and winter packages with dinner, $195. Inquire about "Sail Inn," a 6-day package with 2 nights on the schooner *Timberwind*, 2 nights here, and 1 at the Castine Inn (offered May, June, July, and September); $625 per person double occupancy, including all lodging, sailing, and food.

Youngtown Inn (763-4290), Route 52 and Youngtown Road, Lincolnville 04849. This 1810 farmhouse is 4 miles from Camden Harbor at the end of Megunticook Lake, near Lincolnville Center. The decor is country, and all six rooms have private baths. Rooms 5 and 6 convert to a suite for four. The dining room (see *Dining Out*) and pub downstairs have a genuinely hospitable atmosphere, complete with pumpkin-pine floors, beamed ceilings, and fireplaces. $80–95 single or double occupancy in summer, $60–80 in winter includes a full country breakfast: maybe fresh fruit, muffins or croissants, French toast stuffed with apple slices, or an egg dish. Ask about packages.

Hartstone Inn (236-4259), 41 Elm Street (Route 1). Open year-round. This 1835 house offers a comfortable parlor with soapstone fireplace and a library with many books on sailing and Maine, plus cable TV. All ground-floor rooms are shared space for guests. The seven guest rooms are bright and airy, most with queen-sized beds, two with fireplaces; all have private baths. In addition, the restored carriage house harbors efficiency apartments. Rates include a full breakfast in the dining room or a continental breakfast in bed. Dinner, served only to inn guests, is moderately priced and features a four-course meal (guests may also request lobster in advance). $75–120 double (less off-season). Ask about special workshop weekends.

BED & BREAKFASTS

The Maine Stay (236-9636), 22 High Street (Route 1). Open year-round. This is one of the oldest homes in Camden's High Street Historic District. A Greek Revival house with an attached barn, it offers eight guest rooms, four with private bath, all carefully furnished in antiques. The lower-level guest room in the attached carriage house is especially appealing, with well stocked, built-in bookshelves, a wood stove, and glass doors opening onto a private patio with lawn and woods beyond (the 2-acre property includes a wildflower garden and benches). We also find the third-floor rooms (shared bath) particularly appealing. The two parlors (with fireplaces), the TV den, and dining room are all salted with interesting furnishings and curiosities collected during innkeeper (former captain) Peter Smith's wide-ranging naval career. Peter, his wife, Donny, and her twin sister, Diana Robson, are all unusually helpful hosts. Guests gather for a very hot breakfast at the formal dining room table; afternoon tea is also included in the $75–115 double room rate. Pets can be accommodated in the barn.

Hawthorn Inn (236-8842), 9 High Street (Route 1). Open year-round. An 1890s turreted Victorian on the water side of High Street with a path leading down to the harbor, the Hawthorn offers elegant accommodations ranging from four rooms upstairs off the three-story staircase to two garden rooms downstairs; also three suites in the adjacent carriage house with harbor views and whirlpool tubs. Afternoon tea and lemonade are available in the tasteful parlor where a fire frequently glows in the unusual, soapstone-faced hearth. A full breakfast, served at the dining room table, is included. Breakfast trays are provided to units with their own kitchens. Doubles $95–170. Two-night minimum July through Labor Day.

Norumbega (236-4646), 61 High Street (Route 1). Open year-round. With one of the most imposing facades of any B&B anywhere, this turreted stone "castle" has long been a landmark just north of Camden. Inside, the ornate staircase with fireplace and love seat on the landing, formal parlor with fireplace, and dining room capture all the opulence of the Victorian era. Its 12 guest rooms, some with fireplaces and all with king-sized beds and private baths, are located both upstairs and downstairs, the latter with private terrace entrances. Doubles $205–270, including full breakfast and afternoon wine and cheese; penthouse $425. Two-night minimum on weekends.

Edgecombe-Coles House (236-2336), 64 High Street (Route 1), HCR 60, Box 3010. Open year-round. This gracious 1890s summer home above Route 1, overlooking Penobscot Bay, is a mile north of the center of Camden and a mile from Camden Hills State Park. Bicycles are available to reach both. The country decor is enhanced by special collections of whimsical animals and other antiques that innkeepers Terry and Louise Price display throughout. The rooms offer a choice of garden/forest view or ocean view, and double, queen-, or king-sized bed. All have private baths, and one bedroom has a working fireplace. There are also fireplaces in the living room, dining room, and den. A full breakfast is served in the dining room; continental breakfast is delivered to guests' rooms if they prefer. $100–170 for two. Two-night minimum stay in July and August and on holiday weekends.

Windward House (236-9656), 6 High Street (Route 1). Open May through October. This handsome, clapboard Greek Revival home, surrounded by a lawn and gardens, offers seven welcoming guest rooms, all with private baths and furnished throughout with antiques. Full "gourmet" breakfast included, served in the sunny dining room. Doubles $85–130.

The Blackberry Inn (236-6060), 82 Elm Street. Open year-round. The decor in this 1860 Italianate Victorian includes marble mantels, Oriental rugs, and Bar Harbor wicker, and there's a courtyard where guests can relax, perhaps in the company of the friendly resident black Labrador. All 10 rooms have private baths; some rooms are air-conditioned and feature king-sized beds, whirlpool baths, TV, wood-burning fireplaces, and ceiling fans. $85–150 in summer. A full "gourmet" breakfast in the dining room is included, plus an "afternoon hospitality hour."

Nathaniel Hosmer House (236-4012), 4 Pleasant Street. Open year-round. A block away from the Route 1 traffic, this location is quiet yet convenient. In the Hosmer family from the time it was built in the early 1800s until 1985, this historic house stands in an attractive neighborhood near the center of town and all the shops and restaurants. The pleasant rooms are simply furnished and have private baths. A full breakfast is included. $85–115 double.

Twin Gables (236-4717), Spear and Beauchamp Streets, PO Box 189, Rockport 04856. Open June through October. In a quiet neighborhood near the harbor and a meadow where black-and-white Belted Galloway cows graze, this 1855, 17-room house offers two accommodation choices: a double or twin bedroom with private bath, and a suite with sitting room and private bath. Full breakfast included. $85–120; 2-night minimum.

The Inn at Sunrise Point (236-7716 or 1-800-435-6278), PO Box 1344, Lincolnville. Open May through October. Set on a 4-acre waterfront estate just over the town line in Lincolnville, this small, luxurious B&B is owned by Jerry Levitin, author of the *Country Inns and Back Roads* guidebook series. Levitin himself tends to be on the road in summer, but an affable innkeeper is on hand to welcome guests either to one of the three rooms with water views in the main house (all with fireplaces) or to one of the four deluxe oceanside cottages, all skillfully furnished and fitted with fireplaces and Jacuzzis. All accommodations have queen- or king-sized beds, phones, and color TVs with VCRs; plush robes are also provided in each bath. Common rooms include a glass conservatory that lets the sun shine in, plus a snug, wood-paneled library with fireplace that's just right for cooler days. Rooms are $125–200; cottages are $195–300; full breakfast and afternoon appetizers included.

☞ **The Spouter Inn** (789-5171), Route 1, PO Box 176, Lincolnville 04849. Open year-round. Just across the road from Lincolnville Beach and the ferry to Islesboro, this early 1800s home invites guests to enjoy the view from a rocker on the front porch or to relax by the fire in the attractive library and parlor. The four rooms have water views and are tastefully decorated (some with fireplaces). They are named for naval ranks (First Mate, Captain, Admiral, and Commodore) and increase in luxury accordingly. Doubles $75–85; $125 for the Commodore's suite, which includes a living room, bedroom, kitchen, bath, and private sun deck and accommodates up to four. Full breakfast included. Two-night minimum on weekends and holidays during high season. Innkeeper Paul Lippman also runs Ducktrap Sea Kayak tours, and guests find themselves in a great spot from which to paddle off to Bayside or Islesboro or Camden and Rockport.

☞ **Sign of the Owl** (338-4669), Route 1, RR 2, Box 85, Lincolnville Beach 04849. Open year-round. Nine miles north of Camden. Three double rooms with shared bath. Well-behaved pets welcome. Also on the premises is a gift and antiques shop specializing in Victorian pieces and oriental paintings, scrolls, porcelains, and note papers. Doubles $45–65.

Victorian B&B (236-3785 or 1-800-382-9817), Lincolnville Beach 04849. Open year-round. Sequestered down by the water is this spacious 1880s house with seven guest rooms, all with private baths, two with ocean views and fireplaces. $85–125.

A Little Dream (236-8742), 66 High Street. Open year-round. If you like ruffles and furbelows, you will love this Victorian confection: all ribbons and collectibles, with a touch of English country. A full breakfast, served in the dining room, may include a smoked-salmon or an apple-Brie omelet, banana-pecan waffles, or lemon-ricotta soufflé pancakes. Doubles $95–139, for a large room with VCR and private sun deck. Two-night minimum on holiday weekends.

OTHER LODGING
All listings are in Camden 04843 unless otherwise indicated.

🖝**High Tide Inn** (236-3724), Route 1. Open May to October. Set far enough back from Route 1 to preclude traffic noise, this friendly complex appeals to singles and couples (who tend to choose one of the five rooms in the inn) and families, who opt for one of the 6 cottages or 19 motel units (some with connecting, separate sleeping rooms). Most accommodations have views. The complex is set on 7 quiet acres—formerly a private estate—of landscaped grounds and meadow that slope to the water, where there's over 250 feet of private beach. Home-baked continental breakfast, included in lodging in-season, is served on the glass-enclosed porch; the living room also has ample windows with views of the bay. The porch, living room and bar all have working fireplaces. Rates: $60–175 in-season, less May through late June; 2-night minimum weekends in July and August and over holidays.

☞ **The Owl and Turtle Harbor View Guest Rooms** (236-9014 or 236-8759), PO Box 1265, 8 Bayview Street. Open year-round. In the middle of all the harbor hubbub but high above it, with the best harbor view in town. There are only three rooms, and repeat business is heavy, so book early for the summer months. Each room has air-conditioning, TV, telephone, and private bath; two face directly over the water. Private parking is provided. Downstairs is one of the state's best bookshops. No smoking; no pets. Rates include continental breakfast brought to the room. $70–85; less off-season.

✐ **The Lodge at Camden Hills** (236-8478 or 1-800-832-7058 outside Maine), PO Box 794, Route 1. Open year-round. This complex of modern, shingled cottages—21 units, including 11 efficiencies—are scattered among pines on a hill overlooking Penobscot Bay. Some one-bedroom cottages are equipped with Jacuzzis and fireplaces as well as token kitchens; suites have fireplaces. $99–160 in-season; children are $15 over age 12, otherwise free.

Lord Camden Inn (236-4325), 24 Main Street. Open year-round. In a restored, 1893 brick Masonic hall, the "inn" occupies several floors above a row of Main Street shops. Restored antique furnishings, including some canopy beds, blend with modern amenities: color TVs, private baths, in-room telephones, and elevator service. Most rooms have two double beds and balconies overlooking the town and harbor or the river and hills beyond; there are also three luxury suites on the first floor. Rates include continental breakfast and the paper. $118–175, depending on the view, in summer.

Highland Mill Inn (236-1057), PO Box 961, corner of Mechanic and Washington Streets. Open year-round. A former shirt factory on the Megunticook River now offers 24 rooms, each with a balcony overlooking the river and the old mill wheel. Park in a reserved space and walk to shops, restaurants, and the harbor. Handicapped accessible. Doubles $79–139.

Reunion Inn & Grill (236-1090), 49 Mechanic Street. Geared to business guests but possibly just what you're looking for: handsome suites in a renovated 1800s mill house overlooking the river on a quiet side street above a restaurant (see *Dining Out*). $90–120.

WHERE TO EAT

DINING OUT

The Belmont (236-8053), 6 Belmont Avenue, Camden. Open for dinner early May through New Year's Eve. There is a lot of creativity in the kitchen here, reflected in rave reviews from the *New York Times* and others. Gerald Clare is the chef who, along with his co-owner, John Mancarella, oversees the 55-seat dining room of this fine inn (see *Lodging*). Pad Thai, a popular appetizer here, reflects Mr. Clare's skill with Asian ingredients like lemon grass, ginger, and Kaffir lime leaves. The dish combines rice noodles and bean sprouts with chicken, shrimp, or lobster ($8.50). Entrées might include salmon, crisply seared and served in lime-scented broth ($17); desserts are an art form (around $6).

Marcel's (594-2511), Rockport (at the Samoset Resort). Open every day year-round for breakfast, lunch, and dinner. The dining fare merits the formality it receives (if gentlemen haven't brought a coat they are given one). Specialties include grilled loin of lamb, sliced and served with a dressing of dried pears, garlic, and mushrooms ($16), and tournedos topped with béarnaise, bordelaise, horseradish, and peppercorn cream ($19.50). There's piano music at dinner and entertainment in the adjacent Breakwater Lounge.

Reunion Inn & Grill (236-1090), 49 Mechanic Street, Camden. Dinner except Monday. David Grant earned rave reviews as chef/owner of Aubergine (now The Belmont) before disappearing and resurfacing as chef/owner of this renovated 1800s mill house overlooking the Megunticook River. The menu changes constantly but, on the day we stopped by, you could dine from an extensive à la carte menu on salmon with oysters pan-fired with homemade tartar sauce ($15) or on duck confit with ginger and strawberries ($13). A wide choice of wines is available by the glass as well as by the bottle.

☞**O'Neil's** (236-3272), 21 Bayview Street, Camden. Open for lunch and dinner daily, almost year-round. Recently expanded to offer multilevel seating but retaining its distinctive atmosphere and menu featuring entrées prepared on a wood-fired brick oven, grill, and rotisseries. You can even have wood-grilled Maine lobster with crab and shrimp stuffing (market price), but the spit-roasted marinated chicken ($12.95) and grilled salmon with braised fennel, cherry tomato salad, and fried leeks ($14.95) can hit the spot, as can any of the one-person pizzas. Vegetarians can also dine well here.

Cassoulet (236-6304), 27 Elm Street, Camden. Open for lunch and dinner. A seasonally changing menu that's shifted its accent from French peasant to Italian, with mixed reviews as a result. This is a storefront dining room seating only 24, so reservations are recommended. Good wine list. $15 on an à la carte menu.

Peter Ott's (236-4032), Bayview Street, Camden. Open spring, summer, and fall for dinner only; closed Monday. Known as a steak house, this pleasant restaurant also serves fresh local seafood and a very good chicken teriyaki. Try the linguini with sea scallops, artichoke hearts, and fresh tomatoes in a lemon and herb pepper sauce ($15.95). Good desserts, too, and potent liqueur-laced coffees.

The Sail Loft (236-2330), Rockport. Open year-round for lunch and dinner daily and Sunday brunch. A longtime favorite of residents and visitors alike, the Sail Loft overlooks Rockport Harbor and the activities of the boatyard below (owned by the same family). The lunch menu might include avocado stuffed with crabmeat, creative omelets, and mussels steamed in garlic and wine. At dinner, entrées feature native seafood and prime beef. Small, melt-in-your-mouth blueberry muffins come with every meal. Dinner entrées run $19.50–37 (the shore dinner).

Youngtown Inn (763-4290), corner of Route 52 and Youngtown Road, Lincolnville. Dinner and Sunday brunch. Four miles from Camden, this inn (see *Inns*) serves dinner in dining rooms that are warmed by fireplaces on cool evenings. Chef-owner Manuel Mercieris French offers a varied menu ranging from sautéed mushrooms and bacon in cream and Parmesan over fusili ($10.95) to roast rack of lamb ($16.95).

☞ **Chez Michel** (789-5600), Lincolnville Beach (across the road from the beach). Serving lunch and dinner. This pleasant restaurant serves exceptional food with a French flair. Moderately priced entrées include bouillabaisse, scallops Provençal, fresh Atlantic poached salmon, crabcakes, and vegetarian pastas and couscous. A well-kept secret among Camdenites who have become loyal regulars.

Camden Harbour Inn (236-4200), 83 Bayview Street, Camden. Open year-round. A 19th-century inn (see *Inns*) with dining overlooking Camden Harbor. The extensive menu ranges from a choice of pastas to the "fisherman's dinner"—a mix of haddock, shrimp, and scallops topped with blended olive oil and lemon and oven broiled ($15.95). Weekly specials might include stuffed summer squash ($11.95) and shrimp and scallops pesto ($14.95). Entrées include salad.

EATING OUT

Cappy's Chowder House (236-2254), Main Street, Camden. Open year-round (hours vary depending on the season). An extremely popular pub—they claim that "sooner or later, everyone shows up at Cappy's," and it's true. Good food with reasonable price tags: eggs, granola, treats from the on-premises bakery for breakfast; croissant sandwiches, burgers, full meals for lunch; seafood entrees, special pasta dishes, meat dishes for dinner. The chowder has been written up in *Gourmet*. Upstairs in the Crow's Nest (open in the summertime only), you will find a quieter setting, a harbor view, and the same menu as downstairs. Kids get their own menu with selections served in a souvenir carrying box; a place mat with puzzles, crayons for coloring, and sometimes even balloons are provided. This is also a good bet if you're in a hurry and just want a chowder and beer at the bar.

The Waterfront (236-3747), Bayview Street, Camden. Open daily year-round (closes for a short while in the dead of winter). Located right on the harbor, with lots of windows and an outside deck with an awning; a worthy tourist place that's better for lunch than dinner.

Sea Dog Brewing Co. (236-6863), 43 Mechanic Street, Camden. Housed in the former Knox mill with views of the waterfall; a large, cheerful, family-run brew pub decorated with windjammer and other nautical paraphernalia, featuring a large, moderately priced menu and generous portions. Everything from burgers and crab rolls, through soups and salads, to grilled shrimp and Italian sausage en brochette. The specialty brews are lagers and ales with a half dozen staples and several monthly specials.

Village Restaurant (236-3232), Main Street, Camden. Open year-round. Long a favorite with locals, this traditional restaurant serves lots of fried local seafood and fish chowder. The dining room overlooks Camden Harbor.

Gilbert's Public House (236-4320), Bayview Street, Camden. Tucked underneath the shops along Bayview Street (you enter through a side door just off the street), this is a good place for a beer and a sandwich, snacks or light meals for the kids, or a simple supper before the evening's activities. There's an international flavor to the "pub food" offered:

Mediterranean shrimp salad, wurst platter, egg rolls, veggie stir fry, and nachos are among the favorites. There's also a frozen drink machine here, plus frothy and colorful daiquiris, margaritas, and the like. Live music for dancing in the evening.

The Helm (236-4337), Route 1, Rockport (1.5 miles south of Camden). Open for lunch and dinner April to late October; closed Monday. There's a French accent to the menu, with such dishes as coquilles Saint-Jacques and bouillabaisse, plus Maine shore dinners. The menu includes about 50 entrées. One dining room overlooks the Goose River. Children's menu, too. At the take-out window you can order real onion soup, fresh rabbit pâté, among other treats, plus delicious crabmeat rolls and sandwiches on French bread.

Spinnaker (596-6804), Route 1, Rockport. Open year-round for lunch and dinner. Salad bar, daily soup-and-sandwich specials, steaks, fresh seafood, and a variety of lobster dishes.

Mama and Leenie's (236-6300), Elm Street, Camden. Open year-round for breakfast pastries, lunch, tea, and dinner. A warm, mothering atmosphere with fresh meat pies and a fragrant bakery. Hearty home cooking includes soups, sandwiches, salads, cheesecake, and pineapple upside-down cake. No liquor. This is a small place with only a handful of tables, plus a few more on an adjacent, shaded, outdoor patio. Service can be slow when they're busy.

Fitzpatrick's Deli Cafe (236-2041), Sharp's Wharf, Bayview Street, Camden. Open March through early January for breakfast, lunch, and dinner. Fitzi's is easy to miss as you walk from Bayview to the public landing. But it's a find: a wide variety of sandwiches and salads plus quiche of the day and special soup-salad-sandwich plates. You order at the counter, and they call you by name when it is time to pick up your food. Popular with regulars. Outside patio for summertime dining.

Camden Deli (236-8343), Main Street, Camden. Choose among about 35 sandwiches, combining all of the regular deli meats and cheeses; the Possible Dream is whatever you can come up with, and the New Deli Special changes daily. The back room overlooks the harbor.

Rockport Corner Shop (236-8361), Rockport (right in the middle of the village, across from the Rockport Photo Workshop, so there are a lot of students). Open year-round for breakfast and lunch. Regulars greet each other warmly, but newcomers are made to feel welcome, too. Help yourself to coffee. An exceptional find with almost no decor but plenty of atmosphere. Fresh coffee cakes are baked each morning; all salads are made with garden-grown vegetables. Omelets, chowders, and lentil burgers are specialties. There is a vegetarian bent, but choices do include fish and meat dishes. No liquor. Very reasonable prices.

Miss Plum's, Route 1, Rockport. Open most of the year, except in the dead of winter. Painted deep plum, this is a real, old-fashioned ice-cream parlor with all of the flavors made on the premises. There are homemade cones and edible dishes and nostalgic treats such as egg creams and extra-thick frappes. Miss Plum's also serves breakfast in summer and lunch year-round. The menu lists hot dogs, nachos, soups (including cold summer soups), and a variety of sandwiches.

LOBSTER POUNDS

☞✐**Lobster Pound Restaurant** (789-5550), Route 1, Lincolnville Beach. Open every day for lunch and dinner, the first Sunday in May through Columbus Day. Also serves breakfast between July 4th and Labor Day. This is a mecca for lobster lovers—some people plan their trips around a meal here. Features lobster, steamed or baked, also clams, other fresh seafoods, roast turkey, ham, steaks, and chicken. This is a family-style restaurant that seats 260 inside and has picnic tables near a sandy beach and take-out window. Always popular (always crowded).

Captain Andy's (236-2312), Upper Washington Street, Route 105, Camden. Call and order your lobsters with all the fixings, and they'll be delivered right to you at the harbor park or town landing for a delicious picnic. Note **Capt'n Andy's North** (236-6155), open daily 11–8:30 on the water side of Route 1 north of the village, just south of Camden Hills State Park. The take-out menu includes boiled lobsters, steamers, and clam baskets to be consumed at the picnic tables.

TAKEOUT

The Market Basket (236-4371), Routes 1 and 90, Rockport. The daily menu includes a selection of two or more unusual soups plus generously portioned Greek and garden salads. This is a specialty food store, so you can buy French bread (the best we've had anywhere), cheeses, pâtés, slices of cheesecake, and a good bottle of wine or imported beer to top things off. Head for Marine Park.

☞ **Scott's Place** (236-8751), Elm Street, Camden. This tiny building in the parking lot of a small shopping center serves hundreds of toasted crabmeat and lobster rolls, marinated chicken sandwiches, burgers, hot dogs, and chips. Prices are among the best around: under $1 for a hot dog, under $6 for a lobster roll. This is one of several small take-out buildings around town, but it is the only one open year-round.

☞ **Ayer's Fish Market** (236-3509), Main Street, Camden. A great little fish store with live lobsters, too. But the pièce de résistance is what has to be the best lunch bargain in town: a large serving of steamy fish chowder for just $1.50. What goes into it varies from day to day, and it is sometimes chunkier than at other times; but it is always delicious.

(Also see The Helm under *Eating Out* and Captain Andy's under *Lobster Pounds*.)

ENTERTAINMENT

Bay Chamber Concerts (236-2823), Rockport Opera House, Rockport 04856. Thursday and Friday evening concerts are given during July and

August (also monthly winter concerts from October through May) in this beautifully restored opera house with its gilded interior. Outstanding chamber music presented every year for more than 30 years. Summer concerts are preceded by free lectures.

Camden Civic Theatre (John Ferraiolo, 594-5161), Camden Opera House, PO Box 362, Main Street, Camden 04843. A variety of theatrical performances is presented in this newly restored, second-floor theater with plum seats and cream-and-gold walls. Tickets are reasonably priced.

Camerata Singers (Sandra Jerome, director: 236-8704). This award-winning, 15-member, *a capella* singing group presents a summer series in July and a Twelfth Night concert in January. Performances are given in Camden, Belfast, and Waldoboro.

Maine Coast Artists (see *Art Galleries*) sponsors a series of lectures and live performances June through September.

Bay View Street Cinema (236-8722), Bayview Street, Camden. Showings daily. A mixed bag of old favorites, foreign and art films, and some current movies.

SELECTIVE SHOPPING

ANTIQUES
At the chamber of commerce (see *Guidance*), pick up the leaflet guide to 33 antiques shops scattered between Camden, Rockport, and Lincolnville.

ART GALLERIES
Maine Coast Artists Gallery (236-2875), Russell Avenue, Rockport. Major exhibitions May through October; open 7 days a week 10–5. Ongoing special exhibitions off-season; call for details. Free admission, but contributions encouraged. A late 19th-century livery stable, then a firehouse, then the town hall, and, since 1968, one of Maine's outstanding art centers. Showcasing contemporary Maine art, the gallery sponsors several shows each season, an art auction, a craft show, gallery talks, and an evening lecture series.

Harbor Square Gallery, 58 Bayview Street, Camden. Art and sculpture, finely crafted furniture, and jewelry are displayed in this two-floor gallery; it includes Good Hands, a studio creating one-of-a-kind designs in gold and silver.

Maine's Massachusetts House Galleries (789-5705), Route 1, Lincolnville (2 miles north of Lincolnville Beach). Open year-round Monday through Saturday 9-5; Sunday in summer and fall, 12–5. A large barn gallery that's been a landmark since 1949, exhibiting works by Maine artists: oils, watercolors, and sculpture.

Pine Tree Shop and Bay View Gallery, Bayview Street, Camden. One of the largest galleries in the mid-coast area. Original paintings and sculptures by contemporary Maine artists plus several thousand posters and prints. Expert custom framing, too.

A Small Wonder Gallery (236-6005), Commercial Street (across from the Camden Chamber of Commerce). A small gallery with well chosen, limited-edition graphics, watercolors, art glass.

ARTISANS

Anne Kilham Designs (236-0962), 165 Russell Avenue, Rockport. Anne Kilham's distinctive designs on postcards, note cards, and prints are now distributed throughout the country. She is frequently here in her studio and in the shop that sells her watercolors and oils as well as paper products, placemats, and more.

Windsor Chairmakers (789-5188), Route 1, Lincolnville Beach. Filling two floors of an old farmhouse, the inviting display encompasses not only Windsor chairs but also tables, highboys, and four-poster beds, all offered in a selection of finishes including "distressed" (instant antique). The owner welcomes commissions—he's always ready to make a few sketches as you describe your ideas—and enjoys chatting with visitors and showing them around the workshop.

Brass Foundry (236-3200), Park Street, West Rockport (diagonally across from Mystic Woodworks). Custom metal castings in bronze and aluminum. Also hand-blown glass vases, bowls, and goblets.

James Lea (236-3632), 9 West Street, Rockport. Showroom is open by appointment Monday through Friday. Jim Lea is a third-generation craftsman fashioning museum-quality furniture reproductions using antique tools as well as more modern devices; all work is done on commission.

BOOKSTORES

ABCDEF of Books (236-3903), 23 Bay View Street, Camden. Open daily except Sunday from July 4 through Labor Day, otherwise closed Monday April through December; closed completely Jaunary through March. A Camden literary landmark: An unusually extensive and (recently) organized collection of rare and used books featuring maritime, art, New England, and history titles.

Down East (594-9544), Route 1, Rockport. The headquarters for Down East Enterprises (publishers of *Down East Magazine, Fly Rod & Reel, Fly Tackle Dealer,* and *Shooting Sportsman,* as well as a line of New England books) is a fine old mansion that includes a book and gift shop.

The Owl and Turtle Bookshop, Bayview Street, Camden. Six rooms full of books, including special ones devoted to arts and crafts, boats, sports, and young adults and children. Special orders and searches for out-of-print books. Great for browsing.

SPECIAL SHOPS

All shops in Camden and are open year-round unless otherwise indicated.

- **Camden 5 & 10.** "Yes you can buy underwear in downtown Camden!" is the slogan of this huge, old five-and-dime on Mechanic Street, just off Main.
- **The Grasshopper Shop,** Bayview Street. A favorite with all ages: clothing, home furnishings, crockery, linens, baskets, cards and gifts.

Unique 1, Bayview Street. Woolen items made from Maine wool, designed and hand loomed locally. Also some pottery.

The Smiling Cow, Main Street. Seasonal. Three generations ago, a mother and five children converted this stable into a classic gift shop, one with unusual warmth and scope. Customers help themselves to coffee on the back porch overlooking a waterfall and the harbor.

Ducktrap Bay Trading Company, Bayview Street. Decoys and wildlife art. Many of these really special pieces have earned awards for their creators. There are also some less expensive carvings plus jewelry.

Etienne Fine Jewelry, Main Street. Gallery of designer jewelry in 14- and 18-carat gold; very contemporary and unusual pieces made on the premises.

Stitchery Square, Bayview Street. Everything for needlework, including unusual, hand-colored needlepoint kits of Maine scenes, also finished pieces.

L.E. Leonard, 67 Pascal Avenue, Rockport. An old general store with a fine selection of antique and contemporary furnishings from Indonesia and India; pieces ranging from jewelry to carved beds.

Danica Design Candles (236-3060), Route 90, West Rockport. In a striking building of Scandinavian design, a candle factory and shop.

SPECIAL EVENTS

July: **Fourth of July**—a full weekend of special events culminating in fireworks over the harbor. **Great Schooner Race** (see "Rockland/Thomaston Area").

Late July: **Annual Open House and Garden Day,** sponsored by the Camden Garden Club. Very popular tour of homes and gardens in Camden and Rockport held every year for four decades. Third Saturday and Sunday in July—**Arts and Crafts Show,** Camden Amphitheater.

Early August: **Maine Coast Artists Annual Art Auction,** Maine's largest exhibit and auction of quality, contemporary Maine art.

Mid-August: **Downeast Jazz Festival,** Camden Opera House.

Late August: **Union Fair and Blueberry Festival,** Union Fairgrounds (see "Rockland/Thomaston Area").

Mid-September: **Rockport Folk Festival,** Rockport Opera House.

Early October: **Camden Fall Festival**—crafts and harvest market, chicken barbecue, street dancing, lobster-eating contest.

Early December: **Christmas by the Sea**—tree lighting, Santa's arrival, caroling, holiday house tour, refreshments in shops, Christmas Tree Jubilee at the Samoset Resort.

IV. EAST PENOBSCOT BAY REGION

Belfast, Searsport, Stockton Springs, and Bucksport
Castine
The Blue Hill Area
Deer Isle, Stonington, and Isle au Haut

Windjammer anchored off Butter Island

TED DILLARD

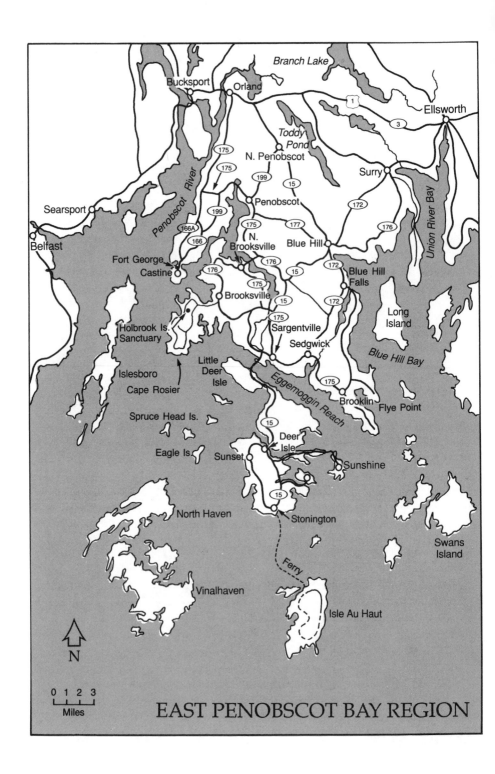

Branch Lake

Bucksport
Orland
Ellsworth
1
3

Toddy
Pond
N. Penobscot
175
175
199
15
Surry
172

Searsport
199
Penobscot
176

Belfast
166A
166
175
177
N.
Brooksville
Blue Hill
172
Penobscot River
Fort George
Castine
176
176
15
Blue Hill
Falls

Brooksville
175
172

175
15
Sargentville
172
Long
Island

Holbrook Is.
Sanctuary
Sedgwick
Blue Hill Bay

Islesboro
Little
Deer
Isle
Eggemoggin Reach
175

Cape Rosier
Brooklin
Flye Point

Spruce Head Is.

15

Eagle Is.
Sunset
Deer
Isle
Sunshine

North Haven
15
Stonington

Union River Bay

Swans
Island

Vinalhaven
Ferry

Isle Au Haut

N

0 1 2 3
Miles

EAST PENOBSCOT BAY REGION

Belfast, Searsport, Stockton Springs, and Bucksport

Penobscot Bay narrows at its head so that, following Route 1 east from Belfast, you have the sense of following a mighty river. With its sheltered harbors, this area was once prime shipbuilding country.

In 1845 Searsport alone managed to launch eight brigs and six schooners. In Searsport's Penobscot Marine Museum you learn that more than 3000 different vessels have been built in and around Penobscot Bay since 1770. Searsport also once boasted more sea captains than any town its size, explaining the dozens of 19th-century mansions, many now B&Bs, still lining the Searsport stretch of Route 1.

Neighboring Belfast has had a history of unusual commercial diversification, including a highly successful sarsaparilla company, a rum distillery, and a city-owned railroad, not to mention poultry and shoe enterprises. Belfast can also boast 11 shipyards and over 360 ships raised in its shipbuilding past. Many sea captains made their homes here, and the streets are lined with a number of their fine old houses, many of which have become bed & breakfasts in recent years. The Victorian brick downtown has become a genuinely interesting place to shop.

Bucksport, north of Searsport at the mouth of the Penobscot River, began as an important shipping port in 1764. After the British burned it, settlers rebuilt, and it is still a strong shipping force today. Bucksport overlooks New England's biggest fort, a memorial to its smallest war.

Just north of Searsport lies Stockton Springs, a small town with neither large shopping area nor business district. What it does have is some good restaurants, inns, and Sandy Point, offering great views and a nice little beach.

Pleasant lodging places are scattered along the bay between Belfast and Bucksport, making this a logical hub from which to explore the entire region, from Camden to Bar Harbor.

GUIDANCE

Belfast Area Chamber of Commerce (338-5900) maintains a year-round office and seasonal information booth on the waterfront. Information can be obtained year-round by writing PO Box 58, Belfast 04915.
Searsport & Stockton Springs Chamber of Commerce (548-2213),

PO Box 139, Searsport 04974, maintains a seasonal information booth (548-6510) on Route 1 and publishes a guide to the area, as well as provides information about antiques shops.

GETTING THERE

By air: **Ace Aviation** (338-2970) in Belfast offers charter service to all points.

By car: The most direct route to this region from points south and west is via I-95, exiting in Augusta and taking Route 3 to Belfast.

MEDICAL EMERGENCY

Waldo County General Hospital (338-2500 or 1-800-649-2536), Northport Avenue, Belfast.

VILLAGES

Frankfort. Granite quarrying was a major industry here in the mid-1800s, and granite from Mt. Waldo was used in the Washington Memorial as well as in the area's own Fort Knox. Today, quarrying is no longer an industry, and Frankfort is a quiet town with turn-of-the-century homes and many empty quarry pits.

Liberty is home to Lake St. George State Park, as well as a number of unique businesses. Liberty Tool Company on Main Street draws large crowds with its bizarre mix of antiques and items found in an old-fashioned hardware store. The octagonal post office houses the historical society and is itself a museum with all of its original equipment. It is open on weekends in the summer.

Northport. Where some of Belfast's earliest settlers first landed, this deceptively sleepy looking little town has a yacht club, golf club, pretty gingerbread cottages lining the bay, a popular Saturday night dance club, and a well-known Mexican restaurant.

Prospect. The site of Maine's largest fort and host to hundreds of tourists who come to explore it, this town is otherwise quite rural.

Orland. The epitome of a New England town, with the Narramissic River ambling through its center and a church that is widely popular with photographers. The best time to wander through is during River Days, usually the last week in June, when an "anything goes" raft contest, live music, barbecue, crafts festival, and more celebrate the town and its river.

TO SEE AND DO

MUSEUMS

Penobscot Marine Museum (548-2529), Route 1, Searsport. Open Memorial Day to mid-October, Monday through Saturday 9:30–5 (Sunday 1–5). Adults $5.00; ages 7–15, $1.50. (The library is open weekdays, year-round). Housed in a cluster of public and private buildings that formed the town's original core. Displays in the 1845 town hall trace the evolution of sailing vessels from 17th-century mast ships to the Down Easters of the 1870s and 1880s—graceful, square-rigged vessels that were both fast and sturdy cargo carriers. In other buildings there are fine marine paintings, scrimshaw, a variety of lacquerware, Chinese imports, and more. You learn that Searsport didn't just build ships; townspeople owned the ships they built and sailed off in them to the far reaches of the compass, taking their families along. In 1889 Searsport boasted 77 deep-sea captains, 33 of whom manned full-rigged Cape Horners. There are pictures of Searsport families meeting in far-off ports, and, of course, there is the exotica they brought home—much of which is still being sold in local antiques shops. The Fowler-True-Ross house tells the story of two prominent captains' families. Not everyone led the life of a sea captain, however, and the museum's exhibit "Working the Bay: The Ports and People of Penobscot Bay" places some attention on the working-class people who made their living here in the granite, lime, ice, fishing, and lobstering industries. The museum sponsors lecture, film, and concert series and operates a gift store.

Perry's Tropical Nut House (338-1630), Route 1, east of Belfast. Open spring through fall until 9:30 PM in high season. A nutty store in every way, this landmark began in the 1920s when the South produced more pecans than it could sell, a situation that inspired a Belfast man who had investments in southern groves to sell pecans to the new tourist traffic coming up Route 1 in Maine. Irving Perry was soon doing so well that he moved his shop to the old cigar factory that it still occupies, along with the original shop building tacked on. He traveled throughout South America and other parts of the world collecting nuts (the display includes every nut species known to man) as well as alligators, monkeys, ostriches, peacocks, gorillas, and other dusty stuffed animals now on display. It is all a bit fusty now, and Perry himself is long gone, but everyone still has to stop and pose next to the various exotica and outsized carved elephants.

HISTORIC SITES

Fort Knox State Park (469-7719), Route 174 (off Route 1), Prospect (just across the Penobscot from Bucksport). Open daily May 1 to November 1, 9 AM–sunset. $1 per adult. Built in 1844 of granite cut from nearby Mount Waldo, it includes barracks, storehouses, a labyrinth of passageways, and even a granite spiral staircase. There are also picnic facilities. The fort was to be a defense against Canada during the boundary dispute with New Brunswick called the Aroostook War. The dispute was ignored in Washington, and so in 1839 the new, lumber-rich state took matters into its own hands by arming its northern forts. Daniel Webster represented Maine in the 1842 treaty that formally ended the war, but Maine built this fort two years later, just in case. It was never entirely completed and never saw battle.

Bucksport Historical Society Museum (469-3623), Main Street, Bucksport. Open July and August, Wednesday through Friday 1–4, and by appointment. Admission $.50. Housed in the former Maine Central Railroad Station; local memorabilia.

Northeast Historic Film (496-0924), 377 Main Street, Bucksport 04416. Housed in the vintage, 1916 Alamo Theater on Main Street, Bucksport, is the region's only "moving image" archives—source of silent, Maine-made films. The museum is devoted to staging and chronicling them.

Searsport Historical Society (548-6663), Route 1, Searsport. Open July through September, Wednesday through Sunday 1–5. A collection of local artifacts, photos, maps, clothing, and town records.

Belfast Museum (338-2078 or 338-1875), 6 Market Street, Belfast. Open Thursday and Sunday in the summer, 1–4, and by appointment year-round. Local area artifacts, paintings, scrapbooks, and other displays.

HATCHERY

Craig Brook National Fish Hatchery (469-2803), East Orland (turn off Route 1 in Orland, just east of Bucksport). Open daily 8–4:30. Opened in 1871, this is the country's oldest salmon hatchery. Situated on the shore of a lake, it offers a visitors center with aquariums, also a nature trail, picnic tables, and a 19th-century icehouse.

CEMETERIES

The **Bowditch Cemetery** on Route 1 in Searsport has an unusual number of memorials to mariners lost at sea or buried on foreign shores. It is named for the famous Nathaniel Bowditch of Salem, MA, author of the navigational guide by which most seamen of his era sailed. His idea was that if he helped them navigate in this world's water, he could do so in the next as well.

In the **Bucksport Cemetery,** near the Verona Bridge, a granite obelisk marks the grave of Colonel Jonathan Buck, founder of Bucksport. The outline of a leg on the stone has spurred many legends, the most popular being that a woman Judge Buck sentenced to death for witchcraft is carrying through a promise to dance on his grave. Attempts to remove the imprint have failed, and it is still there.

AIRPLANE RIDE

Ace Aviation Inc. (338-2970) offers scenic flights from Belfast Municipal Airport; two-person minimum.

BOAT EXCURSION

Check with the Belfast Chamber of Commerce for information about current cruises of the bay.

GOLF

Country View Golf Course (722-3161) in Brooks is the most scenic in the area: nine holes, par 36, cart rental, club rentals, lessons, clubhouse.

SWIMMING

Lake St. George State Park (589-4255), Route 3, Liberty. Open May 15 to October 15. A great way station for travelers going to or from Down East. A deep, clear lake with a small beach, lifeguard, bathhouse, parking facilities, 31 campsites, and boat launch.

Swan Lake State Park, Route 141, Swanville (north of town; follow signs). This beach has picnicking facilities on Swan Lake.

Belfast City Park, Route 1, Belfast (south of town). Swimming pool, tennis courts, picnicking facilities, and a gravel beach.

Sandy Point Beach, off Route 1 north of Stockton Springs (it's posted "Hersey Retreat"; turn toward the water directly across from the Rocky Ridge Motel). No facilities, but a great spot to cool off if you're headed up or down Route 1; particularly popular with windsurfers.

Mosman Beach Park, Searsport. Town dock, boat ramp, swimming, fishing.

TRAIN EXCURSION

Belfast and Moosehead Lake R.R. Co. (338-2330), May through October, operates 2½-hour excursions from the Belfast waterfront along the Passagassawakeag River to the rural village of Brooks and back, with an attempt at a holdup by the infamous "Waldo Station Gang." They also offer rides on Maine's only coal-fired standard-gauge steam locomotive from Unity station. Rail & Sail combos available in conjunction with *Voyageur,* a former Mississippi steamboat on the Penobscot River.

GREEN SPACE

(Also see *Swimming.*)

Moose Point State Park, Route 1, south of Searsport. Open May 30 to October 15. A good spot for picnicking; cookout facilities are in an evergreen grove and open field overlooking Penobscot Bay.

Fort Pownall and **Fort Point State Park,** Stockton Springs (marked from Route 1; accessible via a 3.5-mile access road). This is the site of a 1759 fort built to defend the British claim to Maine (the Kennebec River was the actual boundary between the English and French territories). It was burned twice to prevent its being taken; only earthworks remain. The adjacent park, on the tip of a peninsula jutting into Penobscot Bay, is a fine fishing and picnic spot. A pier accommodates visitors who arrive by boat. The lighthouse is another great spot. Views from the point are back down to the Camden Hills.

LODGING

INNS AND BED & BREAKFASTS

In Belfast 04915

Hiram Alden Inn (338-2151), 19 Church Street. A handsome 1840s home in downtown Belfast offers eight guest rooms (five are available year-round), most with marble-top sinks, shared baths. Nicely furnished with iron bedsteads and antique quilts. There is an upstairs sitting room as well as a gracious downstairs living room. The price includes a full breakfast such as blueberry-nut pancakes or ham on French toast. $45–50.

Horatio Johnson House (338-5153), 36 Church Street. A handsome 1840s Belfast home with three guest rooms, all private baths. Rates include a

BRIAN SWARTZ/BANGOR DAILY NEWS

Fort Point Lighthouse in Stockton Springs

full breakfast such as Belgian waffles and bacon, depending on the chef's mood. $45 single, $55 double.

The Jeweled Turret Inn (338-2304), 16 Pearl Street. Open year-round. A handsome gabled and turreted house built ornately inside and out in the 1890s. The fireplace in the den is said to be made of stones from every state in the Union at that time, from the collection of the original owner. Each of the seven guest rooms is decorated in shades reminiscent of the gem it is named for and furnished with antiques and plenty of knick-knacks. We like the Amethyst Turret room, a romantic setting with four-poster queen bed in an octagonal turret, lace curtains, and hardwood floors. Private baths; full breakfast and tea included in the rate. $65–85 double.

In Searsport 04974

Homeport Inn (548-2259 or 1-800-742-5814), Route 1. Open year-round. An 1861 captain's mansion complete with widow's walk that overlooks the bay. Dr. and Mrs. George Johnson were the first Searsport B&B hosts, and they now offer 10 elegantly decorated guest rooms; also a two-bedroom cottage on the water. Rooms in the front of the house are old-fashioned with shared baths, but those in the back have private baths and bay views. The landscaped grounds include flower gardens and slope to the water. A full breakfast is included in the rates, which range from $30 (single with shared bath) to $75 (double with private bath), lower rates November through April. The cottage is $500 per week.

Captain Green Pendleton B & B (548-6523), Route 1. Open year-round. Another fine old captain's home with 80 acres set well back from Route 1. The three bedrooms, one downstairs (with private bath) and two upstairs, are comfortably furnished with a welcoming feel. All have working fireplaces, and there's a Franklin fireplace in the guest parlor. A path circles the meadow, a cross-country ski trail goes through the woods, and there's a large, spring-fed pond. The Greiners are warm and helpful hosts. $65 per night downstairs, $55 upstairs, includes tax as well as a full breakfast.

Thurston House B&B Inn (548-2213), 8 Elm Street. Open year-round. Carl and Beverly Eppig offer four guest rooms in an attractive 1830s village house, originally built as a parsonage. Two rooms are upstairs and have private baths. The two on the first floor of the carriage house share a bath and have a private entrance (good for a family of five). A full breakfast and state tax is included in $40–60.

The Captain Butman Homestead (548-2506), Route 1. A classic 1830s farmhouse on 5½ acres. It's open summers only because hosts Lee and Wilson Flight teach school in Massachusetts. This was home for two generations of Searsport deep-water captains, and there's a view of the water from one upstairs window and a right-of-way down to Penobscot Bay. The three guest rooms share 1½ baths. A full breakfast is included in $45 double. If you have high school–aged children, you might want to ask about the Downeast Outdoor Education School, an exciting 2-week program (Wilson took a group to Calgary to explore the rocks and dinosaur parks in 1994 and hopes to go to Newfoundland in 1995).

Summerwood Inn (548-2202), Route 1. Open year-round. A 1790s farmhouse with four guest rooms and a sitting room. $40–65 includes a continental breakfast.

Carriage House Inn (548-2289), Route 1. Open year-round, a Victorian sea captain's home with matching carriage house (now an antiques and art gallery). When Gary and Linda Farmer stayed at the inn, it was for sale. One thing led to another, and they now offer four pretty rooms in this historic house, which was once a summer home and studio for Maine painter Waldo Pierce. Full breakfast is included. $65–75 double.

In Stockton Springs 04981

The Hichborn Inn (567-4183), Church Street, PO Box 115. Open year-round except Christmas. This stately, Victorian Italianate mansion complete with widow's walk is up a side street in an old shipbuilding village that's now bypassed by Route 1. Built by a prolific shipbuilder (N.G. Hichborn launched 42 vessels) and prominent politician, it remained in the family, preserved by his daughters (there's a story!), until 1939. For Nancy and Bruce Suppes, restoring this house has meant deep involvement in its story—and its friendly ghosts. Bruce, an engineer on supertankers, has done much of the exceptional restoration work himself. There's a comfortable "gent's parlor," where evening fires burn; also a music room and an elegant library. Elaborate breakfasts are served either in the carefully restored dining room or on the sun porch. We recommend the "Harriet Room" with its deftly created bath and glimpse of water. Books, magazines, and water views are by all the beds, and Nancy brings hot coffee with your wake-up call. Your hosts will pick you up at the dock in Searsport or Belfast, and provide transport to dinner or for picking up boat supplies. $40–80 per night, less off-season.

In Bucksport 04416

Jed Prouty Tavern (469-1271), 5254 Main Street. Open year-round. The 1798 building, billed as "the fifth oldest continuously run hostelry in America," has 14 upstairs rooms with private baths and phones, canopy beds, reproduction antiques, and matching curtains, wallpaper, and coverlets ($75–125 depending on room and time of year). Forty additional rooms in a four-story, motel-style building are built into the bluff across the street, overlooking the Penobscot River and Fort Knox ($65–85).

WHERE TO EAT

DINING OUT

Nickerson Tavern (548-2220), Route 1, Searsport. Open Tuesday through Sunday 5:30–9. Patrons drive from Bar Harbor and Bangor to this handsome 1860s sea captain's house on Route 1. Under new ownership, the tavern's elegance and quality has been upheld, and meals continue to be delightful. Entrées include veal sautéed with wild mushrooms, scallions, and sage in a Marsala cream sauce, chicken with a light coating of crushed hazelnuts in raspberry sauce, and shrimp sautéed with Cajun spices, garlic, and ale, finished with sweet butter. All entrées come with a delectable bread basket and fresh vegetables with dip, but the appetizers are also outstanding, and desserts are irresistible. Reservations are a must. Entrées are $12.50–18.50.

Macleods (469-3963), Main Street, Bucksport. Open weekdays 11–9, weekends 5–9. A pubby bar with booths, informal atmosphere, dependable dining. Good lunch specials (try a croissant sandwich). Entrées include scampi and linguini ($12.95), MacLeod's mixed grill ($12.95), and Jambalaya ($9.95).

Jed Prouty Restaurant and Tavern (469-3113), 52 Main Street, Bucksport. Open for dinner. The dining room is decorated with pink flowery wallpaper and lacy curtains, and the menu is large and traditional: seafood (fried, pan-fried, or broiled) and the usual choice of steaks. Dinner entrées: $11.95–17.95.

L'Ermitage (469-3361), 219 Main Street, Bucksport. Open Tuesday through Sunday for dinner. Dine on traditional French fare in the dining rooms of a Victorian house. It may be the only place in Maine you will find blueberry trifle. Entrées begin at $12.95.

EATING OUT

Darby's Restaurant and Pub (338-2339), 105 High Street, Belfast. Open for lunch and dinner. A friendly, storefront café with salads, burgers, and upscale lunch sandwiches. A reasonably priced dinner find: entrées range from pad Thai ($10.95) and fish-and-chips ($8.95) to Moroccan lamb ($11.95). Wine and beer.

90 Main (338-1106), Belfast. A delightful, family-operated café with deli and bakery. Open for lunch, dinner, and Sunday brunch. Specializes in seafood, pastas, and organic produce at reasonable prices.

Sail Inn, Route 1, Stockton Springs, just south of Fort Knox and the Verona Island bridge. Open 7 AM–8 PM (11–7 in winter). A classic diner perched high on the bluff above the head of Penobscot Bay, with a six-stool counter, booths, and deck. Blackboard specials (crab roll $4.75), deep-fried chicken, sandwiches, pizza, clam or scallop stew, chowder.

Young's Lobster Pound (338-1160), Mitchell Avenue (posted from Route 1 just across the bridge from Belfast), East Belfast. Open in-season 7–6:30. A pound with as many as 30,000 lobsters. Order and enjoy the view of Belfast across the Passagassawakeag River while you wait.

Weathervane (338-1774), City Landing, Belfast. One in a northern New England chain. Same menu for lunch and dinner, daily. "Appetizers & Satisfiers" can include calamari, smelts, or crabmeat stew. Fried seafood dinners are a specialty. You can also have lobster or steak, a burger or crabmeat roll, a sloe gin fizz, or wine by the glass.

Light's Diner (548-2405), Route 1, Searsport. Open daily for all meals. Orange vinyl booths, full salad bar, reasonably priced lobster dinners. The daily special is usually the best bet. Try the custard pie.

Seafarer's Tavern (548-2465), Route 1, Searsport. Open for lunch and dinner except Sunday. Right in the middle of the village, good for sandwiches and pizza; also homemade desserts, chicken Parmesan, or ribs.

Jordan's Restaurant (548-2555), Route 1, Searsport. Open for breakfast, lunch, and dinner. Large menu, eat-in or takeout; specials ranging from seafood to beef; also a children's menu.

ENTERTAINMENT

Penobscot Theater Company (942-3333), Main and Union Streets, Bangor. October through February series; inquire about summer performance sites.

MythWeaver Theater (338-3848). Performances at various locations, including Belfast Opera House.

Chamber Theatre of Maine (354-8807). Based in Thomaston, but contemporary and classic plays staged throughout Waldo County.

The Belfast Maskers (338-9668). A year-round community theater that's making waves with performances in its Waterfront Theater. Check local listings.

SELECTIVE SHOPPING

ANTIQUES SHOPS

Searsport claims to be the "Antiques Capital of Maine." After counting 29 shops on Route 1, we may be inclined to agree. A directory is available at the chamber of commerce (see *Guidance*). With so many options, allow plenty of time for browsing.

The **Searsport Antique Mall,** open daily year-round, is a cooperative of 74 dealers. Everything from 18th-century furniture to 1960s collectibles is spread over two floors. Next door, **Hickson's Flea Market** has both indoor shops (most have specialties) rented for the season, and outdoor tables where anyone can set up. **The Pumpkin Patch,** we're told by an experienced dealer, is one of the best shops in the state. They've been in business close to 20 years and have 26 dealers represented. Mary Harriman ran a truck stop until 1989. When it closed, she opened the **Hobby Horse,** which has since grown to house 20 shops, 30 tables, and a lunch wagon. **The Searsport Flea Market,** held weekends in-season, is also big.

(Also see the Big Chicken Barn under *Special Shops* in "Bar Harbor and Acadia Area.")

ART GALLERIES

Artfellows (338-5776), 16 Main Street, Belfast. Open Monday through Saturday 9–5. A cooperative gallery that represents the work of 40 artists working in a variety of media. Changing exhibits; annual **Invitational Painters Show.**

J.S. Ames Gallery (338-1558), 68 Main Street, Belfast. Open Monday through Saturday, 10–5. Features prints by well-known artists and printmakers.

Frick Gallery (338-3671), 139 High Street, Belfast. Contemporary art.

MH Jacobs Art Gallery (338-3324), 44 Main Street, Belfast. Original paintings.

BOOKSTORES

Victorian House/Book Barn (567-3351), Stockton Springs. Open April through December, 8–8; otherwise by chance or appointment. A large collection of old, out-of-print, and rare books.

Fertile Mind Bookshop (338-2498), 13 Main Street, Belfast. An outstanding browsing and buying place featuring Maine and regional books and guides, maps, records, and cards.

Canterbury Tales (338-1171), 52 Main Street, Belfast. A full-service bookstore.

Mr. Paperback (338-2735), Belmont Avenue, Belfast. A full-service bookstore.

SPECIAL SHOPS

Coyote Moon (338-5659), 54 Main Street, Belfast. A nifty, reasonably priced women's clothing and gift store.

Waldo County Co-op, Route 1, Searsport Harbor. Open June to October daily, 9–5. A showcase for the local extension service. Dolls, needlework, wooden crafts, quilts, pillows, jams, and ceramics—and lots of them.

Northport Landing (338-5555), Route 1 between Lincolnville and Belfast. Open mid-May to mid-October, 10–6. A barn filled with crafted gifts, antiques, and art.

Silkweeds (548-6501), Route 1, Searsport. Specializes in "country gifts": tinware, cotton afghans, rugs, wreaths.

Ducktrap River Fish Farms, Inc. (338-6280), 57 Little River Drive, Belfast. This company produces more than 25 varieties of smoked seafood, which they sell nationwide to restaurants, gourmet food stores, and individuals. Among their products are smoked trout, shrimp, mussels, and a selection of smoked pâtés. Visitors may view (through windows) the processes involved, and purchase the products in the store. It's best to call first.

SPECIAL EVENTS

July: **Belfast Bay Festival**—midmonth week of events; giant chicken barbecue, midway, races, and parade.

December: **Searsport Victorian Christmas**—second weekend in December; open houses at museum, homes, and B&Bs.

Castine

Castine is one of Maine's most photogenic coastal villages, the kind writers describe as "perfectly preserved." Even the trees that arch high above Main Street's clapboard homes and shops have managed to escape the blight that has felled elms elsewhere.

Situated on a peninsula at the confluence of the Penobscot and Bagaduce Rivers, the town still looms larger on nautical charts than on road maps. Yacht clubs from Portland to New York visit annually.

Castine has always had a sense of its own importance. According to the historical markers that pepper its tranquil streets, Castine has been claimed by four different countries since its early 17th-century founding as Fort Pentagoet. It was an early trading post for the Pilgrims but soon fell into the hands of Baron de Saint Castine, a young French nobleman who married a Penobscot Indian princess and reigned as a combination feudal lord and Indian chief over Maine's eastern coast for many decades.

Since no two accounts agree, we won't attempt to describe the outpost's constantly shifting fortunes—even the Dutch owned it briefly. Nobody denies that in 1779 residents (mostly Tories who fled here from Boston and Portland) welcomed the invading British. The Commonwealth of Massachusetts retaliated by mounting a fleet of 18 armed vessels and 24 transports with 1000 troops and 400 marines aboard. This small navy disgraced itself absurdly when it sailed into town on July 5, 1779. The British Fort George was barely in the making, manned by 750 soldiers with the backup of two sloops, but the American privateers refused to attack and hung around in the bay long enough for several British men-of-war to come along and destroy them. The surviving patriots had to walk back to Boston, and many of their officers, Paul Revere included, were court-martialed for their part in the disgrace.

Perhaps it was to spur young men on to avenge this affair that Castine was picked (150 years later) as the home of the Maine Maritime Academy, which occupies the actual site of the British barracks and keeps a training ship anchored at the town dock, incongruously huge beside the graceful, white-clapboard buildings of a very different maritime era.

In the mid-19th century, thanks to shipbuilding, Castine claimed to be the second wealthiest town per capita in the United States. Its genteel qualities were recognized by summer visitors who later came by steamboat to stay in the eight hotels. Many built their own seasonal mansions.

Only two of the hotels survive. But the town dock is an unusually welcoming one, complete with picnic tables, parking, and rest rooms. It remains the heart of this walking town, where you can amble uphill past shops or down along Perkins Street to the Wilson Museum. Like many of New England's most beautiful villages, Castine's danger seems to lie in the perfect preservation of its beauty, a shell unconnected to the lives that built it. Few visitors complain, however. Castine is exquisite.

GUIDANCE

Town Office (326-4502). The town clerk is helpful. Inquire about the map/guide to Castine's inns, shops, and restaurants, usually available.

GETTING THERE

By air: See the "Bar Harbor" and "Portland" chapters for air service.

By car: The quickest route is the Maine Turnpike to Augusta and Route 3 to Belfast, then Route 1 to Orland and Route 175; follow signs.

MEDICAL EMERGENCY

Blue Hill Memorial Hospital (374-2836), the largest facility in the area, has a 24-hour emergency room. **Castine Community Health Services** (326-4348) has a doctor on call.

TO SEE

State of Maine (326-4311). Open daily July and August, weekdays, 1–4. Free. Visitors are welcome to come aboard and tour the ship, a former troop ship that dates from 1952 and still takes Maine Maritime Academy cadets on an annual cruise. Midshipmen serve as guides.

MUSEUM

Wilson Museum (326-8545), Perkins Street. Open May 27 to September 30, Tuesday through Sunday 2–5. Housed in a fine waterside building donated by anthropologist J. Howard Wilson, a summer resident who amassed many of the displayed Native American artifacts as well as ancient ones from around the world. There are also changing art exhibits, collections of minerals, old tools, and farm equipment, an 1805 kitchen, and a Victorian parlor. **Hearse House** and a blacksmith shop are open Wednesday and Sunday afternoons in July and August, 2–5. The complex also includes the **John Perkins House,** open only during July and August, Wednesday and Sunday 2–5 ($4 admission); a pre–revolutionary war home, restored and furnished in period style. Guided tours and crafts and fireside cooking demonstrations.

HISTORIC SITE

Fort George. Open May 30 through Labor Day, daylight hours. The sorry tale of its capture by the British during the American Revolution (see above) and again during the War of 1812, when redcoats occupied the town for 8 months, is told on panels at the fort—an earthworks complex of grassy walls (great to roll down) and a flat interior where you frequently find Maine Maritime Academy cadets being put through their paces.

TO DO

BOAT EXCURSION
Balmy Days (338-4652 or 596-9041), a vintage, 1932 coastal Maine workboat, offers tours of Castine Harbor Sunday through Wednesday at 11 AM; charters also available.
FISHING
We are told that you can catch flounder off the town dock and mackerel at Dyce's Head, below the lighthouse.
GOLF AND TENNIS
Castine Golf Club (326-4311), Battle Avenue. Offers nine holes and four clay courts.
SWIMMING
British Canal, Backshore Road. During the War of 1812, the British dug a canal across the narrow neck of land above town, thus turning Castine into an island. Much of the canal is still visible.
Maine Maritime Academy (326-4311) offers, for a nominal fee, gymnasium facilities to local inn guests. This includes the pool, weight room, and squash and racquetball courts.

GREEN SPACE

Witherle Woods is an extensive wooded area webbed with paths at the western end of town.
The ledges below **Dyce's Head Light,** also at the western end of town, are great for clambering. **Castine Conservation Commission** sponsors nature walks occasionally in July and August. Check local bulletin boards.

LODGING

All lodging listings are for Castine 04421.
Castine Inn (326-4365), PO Box 41, Main Street. Open May through October. A rare bird among Maine's current plethora of B&Bs and inns: a genuine, 1890s summer hotel that's been lovingly and deftly restored, right down to the frieze beneath its roof. It offers 20 light and airy, but unfrilly (the furniture is Maine made—solid but not fancy), guest rooms, all with private baths and many with harbor views. Guests enter a wide, welcoming hallway and find a pleasant sitting room and a pub, both with frequently lit fireplaces and interesting, original art. Innkeeper Margaret Hodesh, an artist herself, has painted a mural of Cas-

tine on all four walls of the dining room (see *Dining Out*)—a delightful room with French doors leading out to a broad veranda overlooking the inn's terraced, formal gardens (a popular place for weddings) and the town sloping to the harbor beyond. Children over five welcome. Margaret and co-host Mark Hodesh take some trouble to orient guests to the region, annually updating their own guide to sights and shops. $75–11ひ includes a full breakfast.

Pentagoet Inn (326-8616 or 1-800-845-1701), PO Box 4, Main Street. Open May to October. The main inn is a very Victorian summer hotel with a turret and gables. Rooms in the inn itself are rather small but unusually shaped and cozy, and the room in neighboring **Ten Perkins Street** (a 200-year-old home) has a working fireplace. In all there are 16 guest rooms, each with private bath. There are two sitting rooms and a pink-walled dining room that opens onto the garden. $154–174 per couple MAP; children over age 12 are welcome.

The Manor (326-4861), Box 276, Battle Avenue. A summer mansion built in 1895 by the commodore of the New York Yacht Club. Guest rooms are spacious, some with fireplaces; and public rooms are opulent but informal. The long marble oyster bar off the library is open to the public. Children and "well-behaved pets" are welcome both here and at **The Holiday House** (326-4335) on Perkins Street, another nicely restored mansion, this one on the water; also owned by Paul and Sarah Brouillard. Inquire about family suites with two rooms on a bath. Together the two houses offer a total of 30 rooms. $65–135 in-season plus 15 percent gratuity, includes continental breakfast.

The Village Inn (326-9510), Water Street. Open year-round. Four unpretentious but livable rooms upstairs above Bag's Bake House; $75 with private bath, $55 with shared bath in summer, less off-season.

WHERE TO EAT

DINING OUT

☞ **Castine Inn** (326-4365), Main Street. Open daily for breakfast and dinner. The ambience, quality, and value of this dining room is well known locally, filling it most nights. Crabmeat cakes in mustard sauce are a specialty, available either as an appetizer ($4.50) or main course ($14.00). Broiled salmon, with lemon and egg sauce ($15.50), is a real treat, but it's no hardship to settle for the chicken and leek pot pie ($13.00). The menu changes frequently but always features local seafood and produce. A mural of Castine by innkeeper/artist Margaret Parker Hodesh wraps around all four walls of the room, punctuated by windows and French doors overlooking the inn's spectacular garden.

Pentagoet Inn (326-8616), Main Street. Open May to October, dinner by reservation. Lindsey and Virginia Miller have expanded and brightened the dining room. Chowder and lobsters are staples of the frequently changing dinner menu. There is an extensive wine list. Dinner at 7. $35 prix fixe.

The Manor (326-4861), Battle Avenue. Seasonal. Dinner is served to the public in this opulent summer mansion. The menu might include grilled sweet chili chicken ($16), Portuguese mussels ($16) or lobster cakes ($19).

EATING OUT

Bah's Bake House (326-9510), Water Street. Open 7 AM–9 PM daily, until 8 PM on Sunday. A few tables and a great deli counter featuring sandwiches on baguette bread, daily-made soups, salads, and baked goods.

Dennett's Wharf (326-9045), Sea Street (off the town dock). Open daily spring through fall for lunch and dinner. An open-framed, waterside structure said to have been built as a bowling alley after the Civil War. Seafood, smoked fish, and seafood pasta salads, and waterside dining.

The Breeze (326-9034), town dock. Seasonal. When the summer sun shines, this is the best place in town to eat: fried clams, hot dogs, onion rings, and soft ice cream. The public facilities are next door and, with luck, you can dine at the picnic tables on the dock.

ENTERTAINMENT

Cold Comfort Productions (366-3510), PO Box 259. A resident company performs a series of popular productions from early July through late August. Performances are either in Emerson Hall on Court Street, at the Maine Maritime Academy, or occasionally outside.

SELECTIVE SHOPPING

ARTISAN

Chris Murray, Waterfowl Carver (326-9033), Main Street. Accomplished decoy artist Chris Murray maintains a shop behind his house. He sells the highly detailed birds for which he is known (and the books and tools necessary for making them) and conducts classes in carving.

BOOKSTORE

Compass Rose (326-9366), Main Street. A fully stocked bookstore with a large selection of children's titles; specializes in summer reading, regional titles, and Penguin classics.

SPECIAL SHOP

Water Witch (326-4884), Main Street. Jean de Raat sells original designs made from Dutch Java batiks, English paisley prints, and Maine-made woolens.

SPECIAL EVENTS

July: **Sea Kayaking Symposium** sponsored by L.L. Bean.
June–October, Tuesdays: Windjammers usually in port.

The Blue Hill Area

In Maine, "Blue Hill" refers to a specific hill, a village, a town, a peninsula—and also to an unusual gathering of artists, musicians, and craftspeople.

The high, rounded hill overlooks Blue Hill Bay. The white wooden village is graced with no fewer than 75 buildings on the National Historic Register: old mansions, an 1840s academy, a fine town hall, a busy music hall, two gourmet restaurants, some lively cafés, a half dozen galleries, and two potteries.

Blue Hill is a shade off the beaten path, one peninsula west of Mount Desert, and nowhere near a beach; but it always has had its own following—especially among craftspeople, artists, musicians, and writers. Most tourists whiz on by up Route 1 to Mount Desert, and relatively few stray as far as the village of Blue Hill—let alone as far as Deer Isle, attached to the southern tip of the Blue Hill peninsula by Maine's most amazing bridge. Deer Isle itself wanders off in all directions, and a number of its villages, although technically linked to the mainland by causeways, retain the atmosphere of islands.

Follow narrow roads through the countless land fingers around Blue Hill and search out the studios of local craftspeople and artists. What you remember afterward is the beauty of clouds over fields of wildflowers, quiet coves, the loveliness of things woven, painted, and blown, and conversations with the people who made them.

GUIDANCE

A map/guide is available from PO Box 520, Blue Hill 04614, or by calling the Liros Gallery at 374-5370.

GETTING THERE

Follow directions to Castine (see *Getting There* in "Castine"), but turn off Route 1 onto Route 15 south instead of Route 175 (it's between Orland and East Orland).

MEDICAL EMERGENCY

Blue Hill Memorial Hospital (374-2836), the largest facility in the area, has a 24-hour emergency room.

TO SEE

Parson Fisher House (374-2161), 0.5 mile south of Blue Hill Village on Route 15/176. Open July through mid-September, Monday through Saturday 2–5. A house built in 1814 by Blue Hill's first pastor, a Harvard graduate who augmented his meager salary with a varied line of crafts and by teaching (he founded Blue Hill Academy), farming, and writing. His furniture, paintings (his *Morning View of Blue Hill Village* is in the Farnsworth Museum in Rockland), books, journals, and woodcuts are exhibited. $2 admission.

Holt House, Water Street, Blue Hill. Open during July and August, Tuesday and Friday 1–4. The Blue Hill Historical Society collection is housed in this restored, Federal, 1815 mansion near the harbor, noted for its stenciled walls. The annual quilt show is held here.

Blue Hill Library (374-5515), Main Street. Open daily except Sunday. A handsome WPA project building with periodicals and ample reading space; changing art shows in summer.

Merrill House, Route 172, Sedgwick (1 mile north of the village, opposite Sedgwick Town House). Open Sunday July and August, 2–4. A 1795 house displaying one-man shows, prints, paintings, books, and artifacts.

Bagaduce Lending Library (374-5454), Blue Hill. Open Tuesday and Wednesday 10–3. This is another Blue Hill phenomenon: some 500,000 volumes of sheet music, some of it more than a century old, most of it special for one reason or another, all of it available for borrowing. The collection includes 1400 pieces either written about Maine, by Maine composers, or published in Maine. Stop by just to see the fascinating picture over the entrance depicting Blue Hill at the center of concentric, creative circles.

(Also see *Art Galleries* under *Selective Shopping*.)

TO DO

SAILING

Buck's Harbor Marine (326-8839), South Brooksville, is the place from which day-sail charters leave. Captain Gil Perkins (326-4167) offers half- and full-day cruises on his 30-foot sailboat *2nd Fiddle* and his power cruiser *Queen Mary*.

The *Summertime* (1-800-562-8290 outside Maine, and 1-800-924-2747 inside), a 53-foot pinky schooner, offers day sails and longer cruises from several ports around Penobscot Bay.

SEA KAYAKING

The Phoenix Center (374-2113), Route 175, Blue Hill Falls. With a salt pond on its acreage, the center is well positioned to teach and guide half-day and full-day sea kayaking on both sides of the Blue Hill peninsula.

WOODEN BOAT SCHOOL IN BROOKLIN

Boat building at the Wooden Boat School in Brooklin

Wilderness canoe camping, backpacking and rock-climbing trips are also offered. Inquire about 2–5-day, inn-to-inn sea kayaking expeditions.

Reversing Falls at South Blue Hill and the area between Snow Cove and the Bagaduce Estuary in Brooksville are popular with canoeists and kayakers. A 15-mile flatwater run is possible between Walker Pond in Brooksville and Castine.

SPECIAL LEARNING PROGRAM

Wooden Boat School (359-4651), off Naskeag Point Road, south of the village of Brooklin. A spinoff from *Wooden Boat Magazine* more than 14 years ago, this seafaring institute of national fame offers more than 90 summer courses between June and October, ranging from building your own sailboat, canoe, or kayak to navigation and drawing and painting. Facilities are a former estate on Eggemoggin Reach, and visitors are encouraged to come to the library and to shop in the "Big House." The former brick barn now houses three separate boatbuilding spaces, and you can wander down to the Boathouse, now a classroom and evening gathering spot. For a course catalog write: Wooden Boat School, PO Box 78, Brooklin 04616. Accommodations available.

GREEN SPACE

CONSERVATION AREA

Holbrook Island Sanctuary is a state wildlife sanctuary of more than 1230 acres, accessible by car only from North or South Brooksville. No camping is permitted, but there is a lovely picnic area adjacent to a pebble beach. A network of old roads, paths, and animal trails lead along the shore and through marshes and forest.

Blue Hill. Our friends at the Blue Hill Bookstore tell us that this was not the setting for the children's classic, *Blueberries for Sal*, by Robert McClosky—a longtime summer resident of the area. But we choose to disbelieve him. It looks just like the hill in the book and has its share of in-season blueberries. The big attraction, however, is the view of the Mount Desert mountains. To find the mile-long trail to the top, drive north from Blue Hill Village on Route 172 and take a left across from the Blue Hill Fairgrounds; after 0.8 mile, a sign on the right marks the start of the path.

LODGING

RUSTIC RESORTS

☞✿**Hiram Blake Camp** (326-4951), Cape Rosier, Harborside 04642. Open mid-May to mid-October. Well off the beaten track, with more than 75 seasons in the same family, this is the kind of place you come to stay put. All cottages are situated within 200 feet of the shore, with views of Penobscot Bay. There are 6 one-bedroom cottages, five with two bedrooms, and three with three bedrooms; each has a living room with a wood-burning stove; some have a fireplace as well. Each has a kitchen, a shower, and a porch. Guests with housekeeping cottages cook for themselves in the four shoulder months, but in July and August everyone dines in the dining room, which doubles as a library because thousands of books are ingeniously filed away by category in the ceiling. There are rowboats at the dock, a playground, and a recreation room with table tennis and board games; also ample hiking trails. The camp is run by the children, grandchildren, and great-grandchildren of Captain Hiram Blake, who founded it in 1916. $550 per week for a two-bedroom cottage sleeping a family of four, plus $135 per week per adult for meals, $85 for children age 12 and under. Rates drop during "housekeeping months" to $300–450 per week.

✐ **Oakland House** (359-8521 or 1-800-359-RELAX), Herricks, Sargentville 04673. Open May to late October. A picturesque old place with a mansard roof, run by Jim Littlefield as it was by Jim's forebears back to 1889. His family has been living on this choice piece of property by Eggemoggin Reach since 1776. Meals are served in the delightful old dining room, but there are no longer any guest rooms upstairs. Instead there are 16 cottages (each different, all with water views, and many with living rooms and fireplaces) scattered over the property, each accommodating four to six people. There is also a 10-room guest house. The resort caters to families with children. There is swimming at a private lake beach, also sailing, deep-sea fishing, badminton, croquet, and a choice of hiking trails. Dinner is served between 6 and 7 (liquor is not allowed in the dining room), and the fixed entrée varies with the night: roast beef on Saturday, turkey on Sunday, and always a lobster picnic on Thursday. All three meals are large. Three-fourths of the guests here are repeaters. $252–840 per adult per week depending on the accommodation and season; children's prices vary from free to two-thirds the adult rate, depending on age. Housekeeping cottages in the four shoulder months (when the dining room is closed) are $250–375 weekly; the 10-room house is $1050 a week.

INNS AND BED & BREAKFASTS
In Blue Hill 04614

John Peters Inn (374-2116), Peters Point. Open May through October. An imposing mansion, a fantasy place with columns and airy, superbly furnished rooms (nine with fireplaces), is set on 25 shorefront acres, a mile from the center of town. Guest rooms offer great views, private baths; some have outside decks, and four have kitchens. There's a glassed-in breakfast room, a pool, and lawns sloping down to the water. A canoe, rowboat, and small sailboat are available to guests. $95–150 includes an ambitious breakfast and gratuity. No children under age 12.

☞✐**Blue Hill Farm** (374-5126), Box 437. Open year-round. An attractive old farmhouse on 48 acres laced with walking/cross-country ski trails. Few inns offer as pleasant a gathering area—the former barn has been reworked as an open-beamed combination breakfast room and living room with plenty of light and space to read quietly alone or mingle with other guests. Innkeepers Jim and Marcia Schatz are usually around, either manning the desk or the adjoining kitchen. Upstairs are seven small guest rooms, each with a private bath. The attached farmhouse offers seven more old-fashioned guest rooms with shared baths (including one appealing single) and more comfortable common rooms, one with a wood stove. Jim and Marcia enjoy tuning guests into this unusual community. $58–85 double includes a very full breakfast.

Blue Hill Inn (374-2844), near the junction of Main Street and Route 177. Open year-round. A classic 1830s inn within walking distance of downtown shops but on a quiet, elm-lined street. There are 11 guest rooms, some with sitting rooms and/or working fireplaces, all with antiques and

CHRISTINA TREE

View of Eggemoggin Reach

private baths. Public rooms are also furnished with antiques and Oriental rugs. In good weather guests gather for cocktails in the garden. A number of Kneisel Hall concerts (see *Entertainment*) are performed here during the course of the summer. A full breakfast, six-course candlelight dinner, and hors d'oeuvres are included in $110–160 double, plus 15 percent service charge. Rental bikes are available.

Mountain Road House (374-2794), RR1, Box 98, Mountain Road. One mile from the village on the way up Blue Hill Mountain, this gracious house offers three rooms with private baths, two with bay views. $55–75 includes a full breakfast.

Elsewhere on the Blue Hill peninsula

☞ **Buck's Harbor Inn** (326-8660), Box 268, South Brooksville 04617. Open year-round. Technically in the town of South Brooksville but really smack in the middle of the delightful yachting center of Buck's Harbor. A mansard-roofed building with six bedrooms, 2½ baths, and pleasant common rooms. The dining room is open to the public November to April 1 on Saturday nights, and in summer the neighboring Landing Restaurant (see *Dining Out*) offers fine food and views. We like the feel of this place, from the sea-bright rooms to the glass-faced breakfast room; a full breakfast features fresh fruit. Pets are accepted off-season. From $50 single, $50–60 double; $70 for the suite with an attached room, ideal for a family with one child.

Eggemoggin Reach Bed & Breakfast (359-5074), RR1, Box 33A, Herrick Road, Brooksville 04673. Susie and Mike Canon built this many-windowed, waterside house as a retirement retreat but have transformed it nicely into an unusually luxurious getaway spot. When we stopped by in '94, there were six rooms (two rooms to a bath) and two more unusually spacious rooms with private baths (one, "The Wheelhouse," also has its own living room and cathedral ceilings). Plans were to convert another two rooms into one more sumptuous suite. Two "studios" with efficiency stoves, cathedral ceilings, sitting areas, and private, screened-in porches face Deadpans Cove. The view from the porch in the main house is across Penobscot Bay to the Camden Hills. Breakfast is very full. $130–142.

WHERE TO EAT

DINING OUT
Firepond (374-2135), Main Street, Blue Hill. Open May through December, lunch and dinner daily. This village restaurant is exceedingly popular, and even with its recent expansion, dinner reservations are a good idea. Request a table on the porch, within earshot of an old mill stream (and don't forget a sweater). The specialties are delicately flavored veal and lamb, maybe with crab or sun-dried tomatoes, and seafood dishes like scallops with leeks; also roast duckling or tournedos of beef with the chef's sauce of the day. Dinner entrées run $14.95–19.95. You can also dine from the "Light Fare" menu on salads, soups, and entrées ranging from grilled chicken Caesar salad ($8.95) to baked lobster and artichoke hearts ($14.95).
Jonathan's (374-5226), Main Street, Blue Hill. Open daily year-round for lunch and dinner. Two pleasant dining rooms. The menu is large and features seafood, local produce, and products made in imaginative ways. The specialty of the house is shrimp flavored with ouzo and feta cheese on linguine. The wine list is extensive. Dinner entrées come with soup, vegetable, and French bread. With his wife, Leah, chef-owner Jonathan Chase has authored *Saltwater Seasonings*, a glossy, coastal Maine cookbook. $11.95–17.95.
Surry Inn (667-5091), Route 172, Contention Cove, Surry. Open nightly for dinner. This pleasant dining room overlooking a cove is well known locally for reasonably priced, fine dining. The menu changes often but always includes a choice of interesting soups—maybe Hungarian mushroom or lentil vegetable. The selection is wide and might include veal tarragon, medallions of pork sautéed with herbs and red wine vinegar, spicy garlic frog legs, and scallops with pesto and cream. Entrées run $14–17.
The Blue Hill Inn (374-2844), Union Street, Blue Hill. Dinner to nonguests is by reservation only, but the candlelit dining room is large enough and the fare ambitious enough to encourage dinner patrons. The $30 prix fixe menu changes nightly. You might begin with a salad of lobster, potatoes, and peas, then dine on salmon with pernod or beef

fillet with blue-cheese sauce, and finish with parfait glacé. Open year-round but serving weekends only in deep winter.

The Landing Restaurant (326-9445), Buck's Harbor, South Brooksville. Open May to October, Tuesday through Saturday from 3 PM. Chef-owner Fred Channell has established a reputation for pleasant dining. The restaurant overlooks the area's most scenic yachting harbor (you can sail in) and features local fish and produce, breads and desserts made daily, vegetarian and children's menu. Moderately priced.

The Lookout (359-2188), Flye Point (2 miles off Route 175), North Brooklin. Seasonal. Open for dinner 6–9; Sunday brunch. This classic old summer hotel has a spectacular view of Herrick Bay on one side and the Acadia Range on Mount Desert beyond Blue Hill Bay on the other. It has been in the same family for 200 years and an inn since 1891 (when the farmhouse was enlarged). The menu might include grilled salmon with cucumber dill sauce ($16.25) or grilled quail with maple syrup ($15.95).

EATING OUT

The Left Bank Bakery and Cafe (374-2201), Route 172, Blue Hill. Open daily 7 AM–10 PM. A sensational success as a place both to eat and to hear nationally known musicians (see *Entertainment*). It is known for its baked goods, soups, freshly picked salads, spinach pie, fruit pies, and reasonably priced dinners like mushroom bean Stroganoff or apricot chicken. In summer, frequent nightly programs pack the place.

Jean Paul's Bistro (374-5852), Main Street, Blue Hill Village. Open for lunch and tea. The menu is light: summer soups and salads, maybe some grilled chicken. The preferred seats are outside under umbrellas or better yet, in one of the Adirondack chairs that can be grouped together around tables on the lawn overlooking the water.

Sarah's Shoppe (374-5181), Main Street, Blue Hill. Open 7 AM–9 PM daily. A snug little restaurant that features blueberry pancakes for breakfast, homemade soup *du jour* and quiche for lunch, and broiled garlic shrimp and steamed crabmeat for dinner.

The Pantry Restaurant (374-2229), Water Street, Blue Hill. Open weekdays for breakfast and lunch (7:30–2:30) in the handsome brick building by the bay. Soups and chowders a specialty.

Pie in the Sky Pizza (374-5570), Mill Street, Blue Hill. Open daily for lunch and dinner: pizzas, calzones, and subs. This is such a popular spot, you may want to plan on coming early to be sure to get a booth or a table on the porch by the brook. The soups are especially good, and we recommend the pesto pizza with a Greek salad.

Bagaduce Lunch, Route 176, North Brooksville (at the Reversing Falls). A great spot with picnic tables by the river.

Benjamin's Pantry, Sedgwick, next to the post office. Open 6:30–1:30. Breakfast specials include biscuits, blueberry pancakes or muffins, cinnamon rolls, and pie. Homemade soup, sandwiches, and specials such as meatloaf or sweet-and-sour pork for lunch; omelets and root beer floats all day.

Morning Moon Cafe (359-2373), Brooklin. A tiny oasis in the middle of Brooklin Village. Fresh-dough pizza, full menu: traditional American fare. Open daily 7 AM–2 PM, except Monday, also for dinner Thursday through Sunday 5–8.

ENTERTAINMENT

MUSIC

Kneisel Hall Chamber Music Festival (374-2811), PO Box 648, Blue Hill 04614. Faculty and students at this prominent old summer school for string and ensemble music present a series of Sunday afternoon and Friday evening concerts, early July through mid-August.

The Left Bank Bakery and Cafe (374-2201), Route 172, northern fringe of the village of Blue Hill. A 55-seat café that's become a stop on the national folk music, jazz, and poetry circuit.

WERU (374-2313), a nonprofit community radio station based in Blue Hill Falls (89.9 FM), is known for folk music, jazz, and reggae. It's based in the former hen house on Route 175, which is owned by Paul Stookey (of Peter, Paul, and Mary fame). Here is also the studio of composer and pianist Paul Sullivan, known for his distinctly Maine compositions.

Bagaduce Chorale (326-8532), Blue Hill. A community chorus staging several concerts yearly ranging from Bach to show tunes.

Surry Opera Company (667-2629), Morgan Bay Road, Surry. Zen master Walter Nowick founded this company in 1984 and mounts fairly spectacular productions most summers, often incorporating performers from Russia and other countries. Performances are held throughout the area, but home base is Walter Nowick's Concert Barn.

SELECTIVE SHOPPING

ART GALLERIES

Leighton Gallery (374-5001), Parker Point Road. Open June to mid-October. Exhibits in the three-floor gallery change every few weeks, but there are some striking staples: Judith Leighton's own oils, the wonderful variety of sculpted shapes in the garden out back, and the unforgettable wooden animal carvings by local sculptor Eliot Sweet.

Liros Gallery (374-5370), Main Street, Blue Hill. An established gallery specializing in fine paintings, old prints, maps, and Russian icons.

Jud Hartman Gallery and Sculpture Studio (374-9917), Main Street, Blue Hill. Changing exhibits complementing Jud Hartman's own realistic bronze sculptures of northeastern Native Americans.

S.L. Kinnery Studio and Gallery (374-5894), the Levy House, Main Street, Blue Hill. Tuesday through Sunday 11–6 in summer, otherwise by appointment. Contemporary American, Native American, shamanistic images: paintings, photographs, carvings, jewelry.

Quinn Gallery (667-8490), Route 172, Surry. A truly eclectic and quality collection of paintings, photography, jewelry, pottery, blown glass.

Baker Gallery (359-2714), Route 175, Brooklin. Open Theoretically open Monday through Saturday 11–5, but closed when we stopped by. Housed in an old Odd Fellows Hall that itself demands a photo; realist landscape paintings in oil and watercolor, functional stoneware.

ARTISANS

Rowantrees Pottery (374-5535), Union Street, Blue Hill. Open year-round, daily in summer (weekdays 7–5, Saturday from 8:30, and Sunday from 12) and on weekdays in winter (7–3:30). Find your way back behind the friendly white house into the large studio. It was a conversation with Mahatma Gandhi in India that got Adelaide Pearson going on the idea of pottery in Blue Hill by using glazes gathered from the town's abandoned copper mines, quarries, and bogs. Fifty years later, Sheila Varnum continues to make the deeply colored glazes from local granite and feldspar. She invites visitors to watch tableware being hand thrown and to browse through the upstairs showroom filled with plates, cups, vases, and jam pots.

Rackliffe Pottery (374-2297), Route 172, Blue Hill. Open Monday through Saturday 9–5; also Sunday afternoons. Phyllis and Phil Rackliffe worked at Rowantrees for 22 years before establishing their own business. They also use local glazes, and their emphasis is on individual small pieces rather than on sets. Visitors are welcome to watch.

Handworks Gallery (374-5613), Main Street, Blue Hill. Open Memorial Day to late December, Monday through Saturday 10–5. An upstairs, middle-of-town space filled with unusual handwoven clothing, jewelry, furniture, rugs, and blown glass.

North Country Textiles, Route 175, South Penobscot (326-4131), and Main Street, Blue Hill (374-2715). Open May through December in Blue Hill, summer months on Route 175. A partnership of three designer/weavers: Sheila Denny-Brown, Carole Ann Larson, and Ron King. The shop displays jackets and tops, mohair throws, guest towels, and coasters, all in bright colors and irresistible textures.

Scott Goldberg Pottery, Route 176, Brooksville. Open daily May to October. Scott Goldberg and Jeff Oestreich display their own stoneware pottery as well as work by others.

Gail Disney (326-4649), Route 176 between South Brooksville and Brooksville Corners. Visitors are welcome year-round. Handwoven cotton and wool rag rugs, custom made.

Janet Redfield (326-4778), Harborside. One more reason to find the Cape Rosier Road (it's off Route 176 just north of South Brooksville). Exceptional stained glass: lamp shades, planters, windows. Call to make sure someone's home.

BOOKSTORES

Blue Hill Books (374-5632), 2 Pleasant Street (two doors up from the post office). A long-established, full-service, family-run bookstore that's one of the best Down East.

North Light Books (374-5422), Main Street, Blue Hill. A full-service, family-run bookstore specializing in art, architecture, and photography books.

Wayward Books (359-2397), Route 15, Sargentville. Open mid-May through December 10–5, Saturday 12–5. A good used bookstore.

SPECIAL SHOPS

Blue Hill Tea & Tobacco Shop (374-2161), Main Street. Open Monday through Saturday 10–5:30. An appealing shop dedicated to the perfect cup of tea or coffee, a well-chosen wine, and the right blend of tobacco.

Blue Hill Yarn Shop (374-5631), Route 172 north of Blue Hill Village. Open Monday through Saturday 10–4. A mecca for knitters in search of a wide variety of wools and needles. Lessons and original hand knits are sold.

Sow's Ear Winery, Brooksville. Tom Hoey turns the juice of organically grown apples into a strong, dry, English cider. Many of the apples are from his own small orchard, where 60 varieties grow. Tastings and tours during July and August. Follow directions for weaver Gail Disney's shop (see *Artisans,* above); she's Hoey's wife.

H.O.M.E. Co-op (469-7961), Route 1, Orland. Open daily in-season, 9–5. A remarkable complex that includes a Crafts Village (visitors may watch pottery making, weaving, leatherwork, woodworking); a museum of old handicrafts and farm implements; a large crafts shop featuring hand-made coverlets, toys, and clothing; a market stand with fresh vegetables, herbs, and other garden produce; and a chapel with services open to the public on Wednesday afternoons. There is a story behind this non-profit enterprise, which has filled an amazing variety of local needs. Be sure to stop.

SPECIAL EVENTS

Mid-July: **Full Circle Summer Fair,** sponsored by WERU-FM—the stress is on everything natural and on crafts.

Last weekend in July: **Blue Hill Days**—arts and crafts fair, parade, farmers' market, antique car rally, shore dinner, boat races.

August: **St. Francis Annual Summer Fair.**

Labor Day weekend: **Blue Hill Fair,** at the fairgrounds. Harness racing, a midway, livestock competitions; one of the most colorful old-style fairs in New England.

December: a weekend of Christmas celebrations.

Deer Isle, Stonington, and Isle au Haut

The narrow, soaring suspension bridge across Eggemoggin Reach connects the Blue Hill peninsula with a series of wandering land fingers linked by causeways and bridges. These are known collectively as "The Island" or "Deer Isle" and include the towns of Deer Isle and Stonington, the villages of Sunset and Sunshine, and the campus of the nationally respected Haystack Mountain School of Crafts. Many prominent artisans have come here to teach or study—and stayed. Galleries in the village of Deer Isle display outstanding work by dozens of artists and craftspeople who live, or at least summer, in town. Stonington, by contrast, remains a working fishing harbor, little changed since John Marin painted it in the twenties. Most of its buildings were built between 1880 and World War I, boom years during which Deer Isle's pink granite was shipped off to face buildings from Rockefeller Center to Boston's Museum of Fine Arts.

In Stonington you can still glimpse the way of life that formed—but has long since faded from—most coastal Maine villages. Stonington's buildings are scattered on smooth rocks around a harbor still filled with lobster boats, not pleasure craft. Visitors are welcome to tour the Stonington Canning Co., one of Maine's last sardine-packing plants (the label is Port Clyde and you can buy a case). Daily life still eddies around Atlantic Avenue Hardware and Bartlet's Supermarket, around Billings Diesel and Marine and the new Commercial Pier, home base for one of Maine's largest fishing/lobstering fleets.

Of course, windjammers put in regularly, and sea kayaks are increasing. On Main Street, you can now buy a painting for $6000, lunch on a goat cheese and smoked salmon sandwich, and buy striking locally crafted jewelry, pottery and clothing.

Creeping resortification? Only in July and August—the months when visitors stream over the Eggemoggin Reach bridge to visit crafts studios salted through Deer Isle and to explore the kind of coves and lupine-fringed inlets usually equated with "the real Maine." Isle au Haut, a mountainous island 8 miles off Stonington, is accessible by mail boat. It's a glorious place to walk trails maintained by the National Park Service.

GUIDANCE

Deer Isle–Stonington Chamber of Commerce (348-6124) maintains a seasonal information booth on Route 15 at Little Deer Isle, just this side of the bridge. Hours are theoretically 10–4, but, since this booth is a volunteer effort, it may or may not be open.

The *Annual Bay Community Register,* listing some useful touring information, is available from **Penobscot Bay Press** (367-2200), Box 36, Stonington 04681. The press also publishes *Island Advantages* and the *Weekly Packet,* published weekly for 111 years.

GETTING THERE

Follow directions to Castine, but continue on Route 1 to Orland and take Route 15 on down through Blue Hill to Deer Isle.

MEDICAL EMERGENCY

Island Medical Center (367-2311), Airport Road, Stonington. (Also see "The Blue Hill Area.")

TO SEE

Haystack Mountain School of Crafts (348-2306), Deer Isle (south of Deer Isle Village, turn left off Route 15 at the Gulf gas station; follow signs 7 miles). Mid-June through Labor Day, 3-week sessions are offered, attracting some of the country's top artisans in a variety of crafts. Visitors are welcome to join the campus tours offered daily at 1 PM, June through August, and to shop at "Goods in the Woods," the campus source of art supplies and craft books. Phone to check when visitors are also welcome to view student shows and to attend lectures and concerts. The school itself is a work of art: a series of small, spare buildings clinging to a steep, wooded hillside above Jericho Bay.

Salome Sellers House, Route 15A, Sunset. Open July to Labor Day, Wednesday and Friday 2–5. This is the home of the Deer Isle–Stonington Historical Society, an 1830 house displaying ship models, Native American artifacts, and old photos; interesting and friendly.

TO DO

BOAT EXCURSIONS

Mail Boat to Isle au Haut (367-5193) departs Stonington at least twice daily except Sunday, year-round. See *Green Space* for a description of the island; note that the island's famous hiking trails cluster around Duck Harbor, a mail boat stop only during summer months; a ranger usually meets the morning boat to orient passengers to the seven hiking trails, the picnic area, and drinking water sources (otherwise a pamphlet guide serves this purpose). Be sure to check the schedule, and in July and August come as early as possible for the first ferry. The boat tends to fill up, and it's first come, first served; if you miss the first boat, you can at least make a later one. Fares are $9.00 one-way per adult weekdays, $11.00 on Sundays; $4.50 per child under 12 ($5.00 on Sunday, less off-season). The boat takes kayaks and canoes for a fee, but not to Duck Harbor.

The Miss Lizzie (367-5193). Operates June to mid-September and departs from the Atlantic Avenue Hardware dock at 2 PM; 1½-hour cruise among the islands of Penobscot Bay. $9.00 per adult, $4.50 per child under age 11.

Palmer Day IV (367-2207). Seasonal 2 PM sailings. Captain Reginald Greenlaw offers narrated cruises of Penobscot Bay. $10 per adult, $5 per child under age 10. Longer excursions to Vinalhaven and North Haven are also offered on Thursday.

The Eagle Island Mailboat (348-2817) leaves Sylvester's Cove at Sunset; daily in-season.

GOLF AND TENNIS

Island Country Club (348-2379), in Deer Isle, welcomes guests mid-June to Labor Day; nine holes.

GREEN SPACE

Ames Pond, east of town on Indian Point Road, is full of pink-and-white water lilies in bloom June to early September.

Holt Mill Pond Preserve. A walk through unspoiled woodland and marsh. The entrance is on Stonington Cross Road (Airport Road)—look for a sign several hundred feet beyond the medical center. Park on the shoulder and walk the dirt road to the beginning of the trail, then follow the yellow signs.

Isle au Haut. Isle au Haut (pronounced *aisleaho*) is 6 miles long and 3 miles wide; all of it is private except for the 2800 acres of national park that are wooded and webbed with hiking trails. More than half the island is preserved as part of Acadia National Park (see "Bar Harbor/ Acadia Area"). Camping is forbidden anywhere except in the five Adirondack-style shelters at Duck Harbor (each accommodating six people) that are available by reservation only. To secure a reservation form, phone 288-3338 or write to Acadia National Park, PO Box 177, Bar Harbor 04609; the cost is $25 to secure a site, and the form must be sent on or as soon after April 1 as possible. Camping is permitted mid-May through mid-October, but in the shoulder season you have to walk 5 miles from the town landing to Duck Harbor. In summer months the mail boat arrives at Duck Harbor at 11 AM, allowing plenty of time to hike the island's dramatic Western Head and Cliff trails before returning on the 5:30 boat. Longer trips, like that to the summit of Mount Champlain near the northern end of the island, are also possible. Trails are pine-carpeted and shaded, with water views. For more about day trips to the island, see *Boat Excursions.*

Crockett Cove Woods Preserve (a Maine Nature Conservancy property) comprises 100 acres along the water, with a nature trail. Take Route 15 to Deer Isle, then the Sunset Road; 2.5 miles beyond the post office, bear right onto Whitman Road; a right turn at the end of the road brings you to the entrance, marked by a small sign and registration box. From Stonington, take the Sunset Road through the village of Burnt Cove and turn left on Whitman Road.

Barred Island Preserve is a 2-acre island just off Stinson Point, accessible by a wide sandbar; request permission for access from Goose Cove Lodge (see *Rustic Resort*).

LODGING

RUSTIC RESORT

Goose Cove Lodge (348-2508), Sunset 04683. Open mid-May to mid-October. One-week minimum stay during July and August. Situated on a secluded cove, this lodge is popular with families, hikers, and bird-watchers. Guests sleep in cabins and in two annexes to the main lodge, all different but simply furnished, most with refrigerators. The dining room has a fine water view and a great central fireplace. There is a vegetarian choice to the four-course dinner. Children dine early while adults gather for hors d'oeuvres in the living room, and after dinner, guests regroup for a movie, music, a lecture, or a slide show, often staged by other guests. There is swimming at the private beach and hiking on Barred Island. Rates, which include breakfast and dinner, are $97–107 per person; off-season B&B rates are $93–146 per couple. Children four and under are $35, otherwise half the adult rate.

INNS

In Stonington 04681

Pres du Port (367-5007), Box 319, West Main and Highland Avenue. Open July and August and sometimes spring and fall—a find. An unusually cheery, comfortable B&B with three imaginatively furnished guest rooms with double beds and screened and glassed-in porches with harbor views. Charlotte Casgrain is a warm, locally knowledgeable hostess who enjoys speaking French. $40–60 double with a buffet breakfast, less for a single.

Ocean View House (367-5114), Main Street, Box 261. Open July and August only. A white-clapboard, Victorian inn set on a knoll near the dock, built to board quarry workers employed on Crotch Island. Midwesterners Christine and Jack Custer have created bright, cheerful rooms; the three guest rooms share baths, but all have bay views. $60 per room; breakfast of homemade pastries.

Captain's Quarters Inn and Motel (367-2420). Open year-round. A lineup of several waterfront buildings creatively renovated into 15 suites and housekeeping units, a coffee shop, a gift shop, and a gallery. You can buy lobsters at the cooperative, boil them in your room, and eat them on the deck overlooking the harbor. The brochure includes floor plans and rates for each room. Both #10 and #11 have working fireplaces. Rates are $36–90 per unit in-season; $20–55 in winter. The complex is accessible by water; both pets and children are welcome. Guests receive a 50 percent discount on meals at the Bayview Restaurant, under the same ownership (see *Eating Out*). Coffee, espresso, and cappuccino sold in the lobby can be enjoyed on the deck.

On Deer Isle 04627

The Inn at Ferry Landing (348-7760), Old Ferry Road, RR 1, Box 163. Overlooking Eggemoggin Reach is this 1850s seaside farmhouse with magnificent water views, spacious rooms, patchwork quilts, and a great common room with huge bay windows. There are seven guest rooms, all with private baths, including a master suite with a wood stove, skylights and sunken tub. $80–110, full breakfast included.

Holden Homestead (348-6832), Route 15. Open seasonally. Formerly a church parsonage. Host Cynthia Bancroft Melnikas is a fifth-generation Holden. The breakfast buffet features blueberry muffins along with gourmet coffees. $38–43 single, $43–48 double, $63 for the suite.

King's Row Inn (348-7781), Box 426. A very Victorian sea captain's house set high on a hill overlooking the water. Kate Olson offers six guest rooms, all with water views and furnished with Victorian antiques; some private baths. From $75 double to $100 for the suite; continental breakfast is served in the conservatory. No smoking and no children.

Pilgrim's Inn (348-6615). Open mid-May through mid-October. Squire Ignatius Haskell built this house in 1793 for his wife, who came from Newburyport, Massachusetts, and demanded an elegant home. The story goes that he built the house in Newburyport and had it shipped up to Deer Isle, where it stands in the middle of the village overlooking Northwest Harbor and his millpond. Of the 13 guest rooms, 8 have private baths and 5 on the top floor share two baths (one with a shower). All rooms have water views, and many have fireplaces. Downstairs there are four common rooms, and a dining room is in the old barn, known for its gourmet fare (see *Dining Out*). Eighteenth-century colors predominate, and the inn is furnished throughout with carefully chosen curtains and rugs, antiques, and local art (much of it for sale). $70 single MAP plus 13 percent gratuity; the one-bedroom cottage up the street is $120 EP, $140–185 double MAP. Weekly rates are also available.

Deer Isle Village Inn (348-2564), PO Box 456. Open all year. Paul and Bobbie Zierk offer pleasant rooms in the middle of Deer Isle Village with swimming in a pond behind. $60 double occupancy (shared bath) includes a full breakfast.

On Isle au Haut 04645

The Keeper's House (367-2261), PO Box 26. This turn-of-the-century lighthouse keeper's house sits back in firs behind its small lighthouse on a point surrounded on three sides by water. Most guests arrive on the mail boat from Stonington just in time for a dip and a glass of sparkling cider before dinner (guests who want something stronger should be advised to bring it). Dinner is by candlelight, and guests tend to sit together, four to a table, and after dinner to wander down to the smooth rocks to gaze at the pinpoints of light from other lighthouses and communities in Penobscot Bay. There are four guest rooms in the main house, a self-contained room in the tiny "Oil House," and another in the "woodshed." It's a hike to the island's most scenic trails in Duck Harbor on the southeastern end of the island. $250–300 per couple includes all meals and use of bikes; add $18 per person round-trip for the ferry plus $3–5 per night for parking.

MOTEL

Bridge Inn (348-6115), Little Deer Isle 04650. Open May through mid-October. A nicely sited motel just beyond the Deer Isle suspension bridge, overlooking Eggemoggin Reach. The 20 rooms are clean, and new owner James Biggoine has expanded the restaurant, serving breakfast, lunch, and dinner. Rooms: $50–60.

WHERE TO EAT

DINING OUT

Pilgrim's Inn (348-6615), Main Street, Deer Isle Village. Open mid-May to late October. Reservations only for dinner at 7, Friday through Wednesday. Fixed price of $28.50 for a five-course dinner, including hors d'oeuvres served after 6 PM in the living room or on the deck. Meals begin with soup, then salad, followed by an entrée that varies with the night: maybe halibut with artichokes and cream, poached salmon with *beurre blanc*, or paella. Lettuce is from the backyard, chickens from Deer Isle, breads and desserts are baked daily. The dining room is a converted barn; tables are covered with checked tablecloths and lighted by candles.

Eaton's Lobster Pool Restaurant (348-2383), Deer Isle. Seasonal. Monday through Saturday 5–9; Sunday 12–9. For the best value, be sure to order lobster à la carte and by the pound instead of the higher priced "lobster dinner." The restaurant is still in the family that settled the spot, and it is the area's premier lobster pound, one of the best in Maine. It offers a full menu and a fine view. BYOB. We've received both rave reviews and complaints from readers.

Goose Cove Lodge (348-2508), Route 15A, Sunset. Open May to mid-October. Outside guests are welcome by reservation for the four-course dinner (there's always a vegetarian option) in this rustic dining room that's set in the pines with water views. Under the owners Joanne and Dom Parisi, the dining room is gaining a reputation for its "New American cuisine."

EATING OUT

Fisherman's Friend Restaurant (367-2442), School Street, Stonington (just up the hill from the harbor). Open March or April to November, 11–9. Simple decor but outstanding food. You can lunch on a superb clam or haddock chowder or crabmeat roll, or dine handsomely on a mini-fisherman's platter. Appetizers include baked stuffed clams and Maine shrimp cocktail. Everything is fresh caught and homemade. Don't pass up the pies.

Penobscot Bay Provisions (367-2920), West Main Street, Stonington. Open year-round, June through August, Tuesday to Saturday 8–5; Sunday 10–2; shorter hours off-season. This is the best picnic source for many miles around. Rich and May Howe have thrown in the corporate rag and gone year-round with this amazing store. A blackboard menu lists sandwiches (the hard salami and goat cheese was memorable), and shelves and a cooler are stocked with made-in-Maine cheeses and bottled, canned, and otherwise preserved products. Breads are baked daily.

Bayview Restaurant (367-2274), Sea Breeze Avenue, Stonington (near the dock). Open mid-May to mid-October, daily 8 AM–8 PM or later. A pleasant dining space with reasonably priced candlelight dinners featuring local seafood, broiled and baked as well as fried. BYOB.

The Finest Kind (348-7714), marked from Route 15 between Stonington and Deer Isle Village. Open April through November, lunch and dinner; Sunday breakfast from 8 AM. Neat as a pin, a log cabin with a counter and booths. Dinner from $6.25 for chopped steak to $12.95 for prime rib. Pizzas, fried seafood, salad bar, calzones, draft and imported beers.

Austin Wood's Ice Cream, Main Street, Stonington. Open May to December, 8 AM–9 PM. The ice cream is from Hancock County Creamery, and the view is of the harbor. Sandwiches are also available on a deck overlooking the harbor.

The Bridge Inn Restaurant (348-6115), Little Deer Isle. Open for breakfast, lunch, and dinner, specializing in seafood, pasta and lobster dinners.

SELECTIVE SHOPPING

Pick up a current (free) copy of the *Maine Cultural Guide* published by the Maine Crafts Association (348-9943). It covers all of Maine but is produced locally (visitors are welcome in the office, marked from Route 15 just north of Deer Isle Village). It is helpful in tracking down the art galleries and crafts studios, which are more plentiful here than anywhere else in the state. It's available at most local galleries.

ART GALLERIES AND ARTISANS

Deer Isle Artists Association, Route 15, Deer Isle Village. Open mid-

June to September. A series of four-person shows; members' exhibition every summer.

Turtle Gallery (348-2538), Deer Isle Village. Open June through September, Monday through Saturday and Sunday 2–4. One of Maine's top small galleries. A series of one-person shows: prints, paintings, sculpture, and photographs.

Hoy Gallery (367-6339 or 367-5628), East Main Street, Stonington (at the foot of Furlow Hill as you enter the village). Open daily July through September, 10–5. A big, white barn set back from the street and filled with Jill Hoy's bold, bright Maine landscapes. (Note the sample on our cover.)

Eastern Bay Gallery (367-5006), Main Street, Stonington. Open mid-May through October, daily in summer and Monday through Saturday in slow season. This long-established and outstanding gallery sells works by more than 40 artists and craftspeople within a 50-mile radius. The space, filled with fine clothing, jewelry, pottery, and such, is itself worth the trip to Stonington.

The Blue Heron (348-6051), Route 15, Deer Isle (near the center of the village). An old barn is stocked with crafted gifts and clothing from around the world; also kitchen utensils, cookbooks, baskets, and boxes. A gallery, adjacent to the shop, features changing exhibits of crafted items.

Pearson's Jewelry (348-2535), Old Ferry Road (off Route 15), Deer Isle. Ron Pearson has an international reputation for creative designs in gold and silver jewelry as well as delicately wrought, tabletop sculpture in other metals. From $22 for small silver earrings to $8000 for a gold necklace. The shop also displays work by local blacksmith/sculptor Douglas Wilson.

Kathy Woell (348-6141), 156 Old Ferry Road, Deer Isle. Open Monday through Saturday 10–5. This home/studio is tucked away deep in the pines, filled with soft, vivid scarves and hats, vests, jackets, and coats— each one of a kind. "I put colors together. That's the gift I have," says Woell, a former painter who discovered weaving as her media at Haystack.

William Mor (348-2822), Reach Road, Deer Isle. Open mid-June through October. Hand-thrown pottery in interesting shapes, functional and handsome. Designs are based on oriental folk pottery; the studio, kiln, and shop are in a garden setting. Oriental rugs are also sold.

SPECIAL SHOPS

Island Supply Co. (367-5558), Main Street, Stonington. Open daily late May to mid-October. Silk kimonos from Japan and Indian skirts and tops, which owner Kathyrn Butler personally spends her winters prowling sources for; natural fibers are the common denominator.

Gallery of the Purple Fish, Main Street, Stonington. Open when the windjammers are in port and otherwise by chance. Evelyn and Jan Kok maintain this weathered old waterside building (said to be a former fishermen's church) as a gallery, filled with paintings and wonderful clutter. Evelyn also hand-inks bookmarks and cards and strums on her guitar; visitors may find themselves dancing and singing.

Dockside Books and Gifts, West Main Street, Stonington. Seasonal. Al Webber's waterside bookstore has an exceptional selection of Maine and marine books, also gifts and a great view with a harbor balcony where you can sit and read.

The Periwinkle, Deer Isle. A tiny shop crammed with books and carefully selected gifts.

Dry Dock (367-5528), Main Street, Stonington. Open Monday through Saturday in-season. Indian clothing, salt-glazed pottery, gourmet cooking utensils, children's books, and handmade toys.

Harbor Farm (348-7737), Route 15 at the causeway in Little Deer Isle. Open year-round. A rehabbed schoolhouse that's stocked with a large and imaginative range of gifts and home furnishings.

SPECIAL EVENTS

July: **Independence Day** parade and fireworks. **Lobster boat races** (mid-month).

August: **Stonington Fisherman's Festival.**

V. DOWN EAST

Bar Harbor and Acadia Area
Washington County, Campobello, and St. Andrews

Trenton Lobster Pound

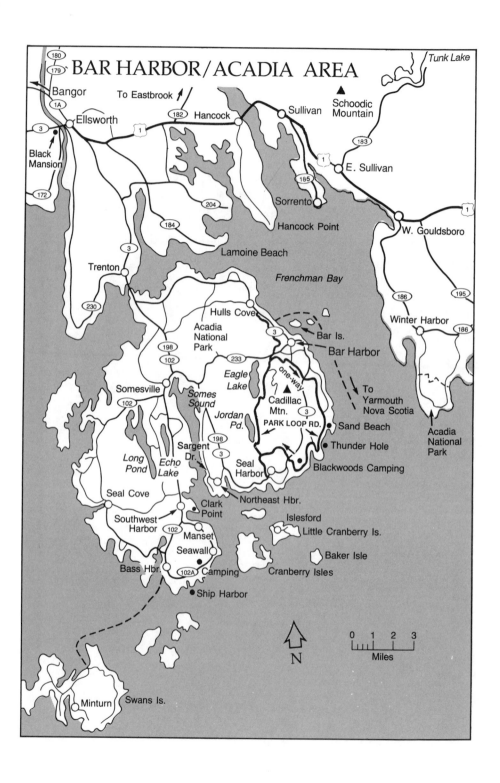

BAR HARBOR/ACADIA AREA

Tunk Lake

180
179

Bangor
1A
To Eastbrook
Schoodic Mountain

182 Hancock
Sullivan

Ellsworth
1
3

Black Mansion
172

E. Sullivan
1
183

185
Sorrento
204

Hancock Point
184

W. Gouldsboro
1

Lamoine Beach

Trenton
3

Frenchman Bay

230
186
195

Hulls Cove
Winter Harbor
186

Acadia National Park
3
Bar Is.

198
102
Bar Harbor

233
Eagle Lake
one-way

Somesville
Somes Sound
Cadillac Mtn.
To Yarmouth Nova Scotia

102
Jordan Pd.
3
PARK LOOP RD.
Sand Beach
Acadia National Park

198
Sargent Dr.
3
Thunder Hole

Long Pond
Echo Lake
Seal Harbor
Blackwoods Camping

Seal Cove
Clark Point
Northeast Hbr.

Southwest Harbor
102
Islesford
Little Cranberry Is.

Manset
Seawall
Baker Isle

Bass Hbr.
102A
Camping
Cranberry Isles

Ship Harbor

0 1 2 3
Miles
N

Minturn
Swans Is.

Bar Harbor and Acadia Area

Mount Desert is New England's second-largest island, one conveniently linked to the mainland and laced with roads ideally suited for touring by car, bike, or skis. It also sports more than 120 miles of hiking paths.

The island's beauty cannot be overstated. Seventeen mountains rise abruptly from the sea and from the shores of five large lakes. There are also countless ponds and streams, an unusual variety of flora and fauna, and more than 300 species of birds.

Native Americans first populated the area, using it as hunting and fishing grounds. Samuel de Champlain named it L'Isle de Monts Deserts in 1604. Although it was settled in the 18th century, this remained a peaceful, out-of-the-way island even after a bridge was built in 1836 connecting it to the mainland. In the 1840s, however, landscape painters Thomas Cole and Frederick Church began summering in Bar Harbor, and their images of the rugged shore were widely circulated. Summer visitors began arriving by steamboat, and their number was soon augmented by travelers taking express trains from Philadelphia and New York, bringing guests enough to fill more than a dozen big hotels. By the 1880s, many of these hotel patrons had already built their own mansion-size "cottages" in and around Bar Harbor. These grandiose summer mansions numbered more than 200 by the time the stock market crashed. Many are now inns.

The legacy of Bar Harbor's wealthy "rusticators" is Acadia National Park. A cadre of influential citizens, which included Harvard University President Charles W. Eliot, began to assemble parcels of land for public use in 1901, thus protecting the forests from the portable saw mill. Boston textile heir George Dorr devoted his fortune and energy to amassing a total of 11,000 acres and convincing the federal government to accept it. In 1916 Acadia became the first national park east of the Mississippi. It is now a 40,000-acre preserve, encompassing almost half the island.

Four-fifths of the park's 5 million annual visitors limit their tour to the introductory film in the visitors center and to the 27-mile Park Loop Road, which includes the summit of Cadillac Mountain, the highest point on the eastern seaboard north of Brazil. Plenty of uncrowded beauty is left for the enterprising minority: hikers, bicyclists, and participants in the Park Service's program of nature walks and cruises.

Mount Desert Island is 16 miles wide and 13 miles long, but it seems far larger because it is almost bisected by Somes Sound, the only natural fjord on the East Coast. Bar Harbor is the big town, and the village holds one of New England's largest clusters of hotels, motels, inns, B&Bs, restaurants, and shops. These are within easy reach of the park visitors center, on the one hand, and the *Bluenose* ferry to Nova Scotia, on the other. The shops and restaurants line Cottage, Mount Desert, West, and Main Streets, which slope to the Town Pier and to the Shore Path, a mile walk between mansions and the bay.

Bar Harbor lost its old hotels and many of its mansions in the devastating fire of 1947, which also destroyed 17,000 acres of woodland. The island's summer social scene has since shifted to Northeast Harbor, where a deceptively sleepy lineup of shops and galleries cater to visiting and resident yachtsmen.

Southwest Harbor lacks the pretensions of Northeast Harbor and the crowds of Bar Harbor and offers easy access to both mountain and shore paths. One of the best views of Cadillac Mountain and its neighbors is from the porch and boathouse of the island's oldest hotel, The Claremont, in Southwest Harbor.

During July and August, Mount Desert is expensive, crowded, and exquisite to behold. Between Labor Day and Columbus Day it is cheaper, less crowded, and still beautiful. The rest of the year is off-season. If you take advantage of the solitude and bargains available in June (which tends to be rainy) or February (which can be spectacular if snow conditions permit cross-country skiing), be sure you have access to a fireplace.

East of Ellsworth, the shopping center for the eastern coast, Route 1 continues along Frenchman Bay. Superb views of Mount Desert's pink-shouldered mountains can be enjoyed from the shore in Sullivan and from the Hancock and Schoodic peninsulas. Schoodic Point, with its own mountain to hike, is a part of Acadia National Park. The B&Bs and rental cottages scattered along the eastern rim of the bay are generally less expensive than those on Mount Desert.

GUIDANCE

(Also see Acadia National Park under *Green Space.*)

Bar Harbor Chamber of Commerce (year-round: 1-800-288-5103 or 288-5103), PO Box 158, 93 Cottage Street, Bar Harbor 04609; maintains seasonal information booths. Write for the free vacation guide to sights and lodging.

Thompson Island Information Center (288-3411) is open daily May to mid-October (8–8 during high season) on Route 3, just after you cross the causeway. It is a walk-in center that offers rest rooms, national park information, and help with lodging reservations on all parts of the island.

Mount Desert Chamber of Commerce (276-5040), Northeast

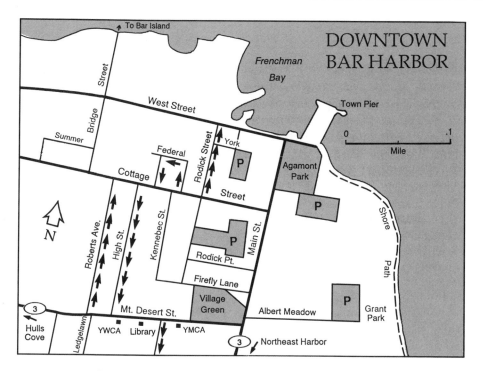

DOWNTOWN BAR HARBOR

Harbor, maintains a seasonal walk-in cottage at the town dock.

Southwest Harbor Chamber of Commerce (1-800-423-9264 or 244-9264) maintains a seasonal information booth on Route 102.

Ellsworth Chamber of Commerce (667-5584 or 667-2617), 163 High Street, Ellsworth (in the Ellsworth Shopping Center; look for Burger King), also maintains a well-stocked, friendly information center.

GETTING THERE

By air: **Colgan Air** (1-800-272-5488) services Hancock County/Bar Harbor Airport in Trenton (between Ellsworth and Bar Harbor) from Boston and Rockland. Avis, Hertz, and Budget rental cars are available at the airport. (Also see Bangor International Airport in the *Bangor* section of this chapter for connections with most American cities.)

By boat: **Marine Atlantic *Bluenose* Ferry** (1-800-432-7344 in Maine; 1-800-341-7981 elsewhere in the continental United States); carries passengers and cars between Bar Harbor and Yarmouth, Nova Scotia. The trip takes just 6 hours. Service is daily late June to late September, three times per week in the shoulder seasons, and twice per week in winter. See "Portland Area" for details about the *Scotia Prince* ferry from Yarmouth to Portland.

By private boat: A number of visitors arrive under their own sail; contact the Mount Desert or Bar Harbor Chambers of Commerce (see *Guidance*) for details about moorings, or contact the Bar Harbor harbor master at 288-5571.

By bus: **Vermont Transit** serves Bar Harbor May through October.
Concord Trailways also serves Bangor from Portland and Boston, and
has movies and music en route.

By car: From Boston and New York there are three routes. The longest
is Route 1 from Kittery. The shortest is I-95 to Bangor to 395, then to
Route 1A to Ellsworth. The third is a compromise: I-95 to Augusta,
then Route 3 east to Bar Harbor.

GETTING AROUND

Local ferries: **Beal and Bunker, Inc.** (244-3575), Northeast Harbor,
operates daily ferry service to the Cranberry Islands. **Swan's Island
Ferry** (244-3254), Bass Harbor, has daily ferry service to Swan's Island;
service twice weekly to Frenchboro.

Both **National Park Tours** (288-3327) and **Oli's Trolley** (288-9899)
offer narrated, 2½-hour bus tours through Bar Harbor and along the
Park Loop Road, and 1-hour trolley tours, daily in-season.

MEDICAL EMERGENCY

Maine Coast Memorial Hospital, Ellsworth (667-4520). **Mount
Desert Island Hospital** (288-5081), Bar Harbor, provides 24-hour
emergency care. **Southwest Harbor** (244-5513). **Northeast Harbor**
(276-3331).

VILLAGES

Corea. You won't find any boutiques or shopping areas in this peaceful
little area, only a serene fishing village at the end of a peninsula. It's
perfect for true solitude.

Hancock and Hancock Point are home to a famous conducting school
and some widely popular inns and restaurants, yet are set away from
the hustle and bustle of the island. Quiet, remote, and truly Down East.

Bass Harbor. A village in Southwest Harbor, on the "quiet side" of the
island, this is a working fishing harbor with ferry service to Swan's Island; good for bicycling.

TO SEE

On the way to Bar Harbor

Bar Harbor Oceanarium, Route 3 (at the entrance to the island), West
Street. Open 9–5, except Sunday, mid-May to late October. Everything
you ever wanted to know about a lobster, plus the Thomas Bay Marsh Walk.
$4.75 per adult, $3.50 per child. Rewarding, but the price is too high.

Natural History Museum, College of the Atlantic (288-5015), Route 3,
Bar Harbor. Open mid-June to Labor Day, 9–5 daily; evening speaker
series, 7:30 on Wednesday. This is a nice little museum with mounted
birds and animals, skeletons of local species, a "discovery corner," and
sea tanks; $2.50 per adult, $.50 per child.

In Bar Harbor

Oceanarium Lobster Hatchery (288-2334), One Harbor Place, West Street. Open Monday through Saturday 9–5, mid-May to late October. A working lobster hatchery with thousands of lobsters being raised for future release. $3 per adult, $2 per child. Fun but the admission price is too high.

Bar Harbor Whale Museum (288-2339), 52 West Street. A gift shop and museum with all you ever wanted to know about whales. Free admission (donations accepted).

Bar Harbor Historical Society (288-3838), Jesup Memorial Library, 34 Mount Desert Street. Open mid-June to October, Monday through Saturday 1–4, also by appointment. A fascinating collection of early photographs of local hotels, steamers, cottages, the cog railroad, and the big fire of 1947.

Robert Abbe Museum at Sieur de Monts Spring (288-3519), posted from both Route 3 (south of the Jackson Laboratory) and the Park Loop Road. Open May to October, 9–5 daily during July and August, otherwise 10–4. Don't miss this exceptional collection of New England Native American artifacts: sweet-grass baskets, jewelry, moccasins, a birch bark canoe, dioramas of Native American life during all seasons, an authentic tepee. Changing exhibits teach about early life on Mt. Desert Island, recent archaeological excavations, culture and traditions, and more. $2 per adult, $.50 per child. The museum overlooks the Nature Center and the **Wild Gardens of Acadia,** a pleasant walk where more than 300 species of native plants are displayed and labeled.

In Otter Creek

Jackson Laboratory (288-3371), Route 3. Open to the public mid-June through August; phone ahead to check times for the audiovisual presentation about one of the world's largest mammalian-genetics research facilities. Cancer, diabetes, and birth defects are among the problems researched.

In Northeast Harbor

Asticou Terraces, including Thuya Garden and Thuya Lodge (276-5130). Open July to Labor Day, 7–7; the lodge is open daily 10–5. $2 donation. An exquisite, 215-acre municipal park complex begun by landscape artist Joseph Henry Curtis around 1900. Curtis created a system of paths and shelters on Asticou Hill, now open to the public along with his home, Thuya Lodge, which houses an important collection of botanical books and floral paintings. Thuya Garden behind the lodge was designed by landscapist and artist Charles Savage; it's semi-formal, with perennial beds and a reflecting pool. The gardens descend in terraces, then through wooded paths to the harbor's edge.

Asticou Azalea Gardens, Route 3 (near the junction of Route 198). Open April through October. Also designed by Charles Savage. A delightful place to stroll down windy paths and over ornamental bridges. Azaleas (usually in bloom the last weeks in June), rhododendrons, laurel, and Japanese-style plantings.

Great Harbor Collection at the Old Firehouse Museum (276-5262), Main Street. Open June to September, daily 10–5. A collection of historical artifacts representing life past on Mount Desert. Exhibits include an early fire engine, parlor room, kitchen, photographs, clothing, sleighs, and a player piano; demonstrations.

From Northeast Harbor

Cranberry Isles. Accessible by boat (see *Boat Excursions*) from Northeast Harbor in-season. Note the park ranger–led trips to **Baker Island** and the guided tours to the **Islesford Historical Museum** on **Little Cranberry Island** (244-9224). The museum is open daily late June through September, varied hours depending on the ferry schedule. It traces the area's history from 1604; there are some juicy smuggling stories told here about the War of 1812.

In Somesville

Mount Desert Historical Society (244-7872), Route 102. Open July and August, Wednesday and Sunday 2–5. Two tidy little buildings, one dating back to 1793, connected by a moon bridge. Collections include mill town and marine-related items, furniture, books.

In Southwest Harbor

Mount Desert Oceanarium, Clark Point Road. Open mid-May to mid-October, 9–5 daily except Sunday. A large, old, waterside building filled with exhibits, including 20 tanks displaying sea life, whale songs, a "lobster room," and a touch tank. $4.75 per adult, $3.50 per child.

Wendell Gilley Museum (244-7555), Route 102. Open May through December, 10–4 (10–5 July and August), daily except Monday; Friday through Sunday only in May, November, and December. A collection of more than 200 bird carvings by the late woodcarver and painter Wendell Gilley. $3 per adult, $1 per child under age 12.

(Also see the Ship Harbor trail under *Green Space—Acadia National Park.*)

From Bass Harbor

Frenchboro Historical Society (334-2929), open seasonally. Old tools, furniture, local memorabilia. A good excuse to explore this very private island 8 miles offshore. Bring a bike. Check with the state ferry service: 334-2929.

Swan's Island Educational Society (526-4350), open seasonally. Six miles offshore, Swan's is a pleasant island that's good biking. The museum, housed in the Seaside Hall, Atlantic Street, includes a store, school, old tools, and photographs. It's a 0.75-mile walk from the ferry (244-3254) to the hall.

Seal Cove Auto Museum, Pretty Marsh Road off Route 102, between Bass Harbor and Somesville. Open daily June to September, 10–5. A collection of over 100 antique cars and 30 motorcycles, the life's work of a private collector; $5.00 per adult, $1.50 per child.

Painting on Swans Island

At Indian Point

Blagden Preserve, a 110-acre Nature Conservancy preserve in the north-
western corner of the island includes 1000 feet of shorefront and paths
that wander through the woods. It offers a view of Blue Hill Bay and is
a tried and true seal-watching spot. From Route 198 north of
Somesville, turn right on Indian Point Road, bear right at the fork, and
look for the entrance; sign in and pick up a map at the caretaker's house.

In Ellsworth

Colonel Black Mansion (Woodlawn), West Main Street. Open June to
mid-October, weekdays 10–5 (last tour starts at 4:30). Off the island,
but be sure to stop en route. An outstanding Georgian mansion built as
a wedding present in 1862 by John Black, who had just married the
daughter of the local agent for a Philadelphia land developer, owner of
this region. Supposedly, the bricks were brought by sea from Philadelphia, and it took Boston workmen three years to complete it. It is now
open to the public, furnished just as it was when the Black family used
it (three generations lived there). Besides the fine period furniture and
spiral staircase, there is a lovely garden and a carriage house full of old
carriages and sleighs. $4 per adult, $2 per child.

Stanwood Homestead Sanctuary and Museum (667-8460), Route 3.
Open daily mid-June to mid-October, 10–4; sanctuary open year-round.
Don't miss this exceptional place: a 100-acre nature preserve that is a
memorial to Cordelia Stanwood (1865–1958), a pioneer ornithologist,

nature photographer, and writer. The old homestead (1850) contains family furnishings and a collection of stuffed birds, eggs, and old photos. There are gardens, a picnic area, and a gift shop. $2.50 per adult, $1.50 for seniors, and $.50 per child for the museum; no admission charge for the sanctuary.

East of Ellsworth

Schoodic Peninsula. The tip of the peninsula that forms the town of Gouldsboro is known as the Schoodic Peninsula and is part of Acadia National Park; the one-way loop road begins beyond Winter Harbor. Look sharp (an unmarked left after the Frazier Point Picnic Area) for the side road up to Schoodic Head. Park here and follow the short trail to the summit. The loop road leads to **Schoodic Point,** where flocks of people feed bread to flocks of sea gulls. There are also flat, smooth rocks ideal for clambering, and Little Moose Island with its Arctic flora is accessible at low tide. (Also see Isle au Haut, another part of Acadia National Park, in the "Deer Isle, Stonington, and Isle au Haut" chapter.)

WINERY

Bartlett Maine Estate Winery (546-2408), Route 1, Gouldsboro. Open June to mid-October, Tuesday through Saturday 10–5, Sunday 12–5. Also mid-November to December 23, Tuesday through Saturday 10–4, Sunday 12–4. Founded in 1983, Maine's first (and only) winery, specializing in blueberry, apple, and pear wines; also limited raspberry, strawberry, and honey dessert wines. Guided tours hourly; tasting room and gift packs.

FOR FAMILIES

In addition to the whale and lobster oceanariums and auto museums listed above, there are several attractions along Route 3: the **Acadia Zoological Park** ($4.50 per adult, $3.50 per child), as well as elaborate mini-golf and go-cart options.

TO DO

AIRPLANE RIDES

Acadia Air (667-5534), Route 3 at Trenton Airport. Flight instruction, aircraft rentals, and a number of well-worth-it sight-seeing and whale-sighting flights. **Island Soaring Glider Rides** (667-SOAR), also at the airport, offers a motorless soaring flight daily.

BICYCLING

The 57-mile network of gravel carriage roads (see *Green Space*) constructed by John D. Rockefeller in 1915 lends itself particularly well to mountain biking.

Acadia Bike & Canoe Company (288-9605), 48 Cottage Street, Bar Harbor, rents child trailers and every kind of bike; also provides detailed maps. **Acadia Outfitters** (288-8118), 106 Cottage Street, Bar Harbor, rents mountain bikes also. **Bar Harbor Bicycle Shop** (288-3886), 141

Acadia Mountains from across Frenchman Bay

Cottage Street, Bar Harbor, rents a wide variety of bikes and offers handy access to the park. **Northeast Harbor Bike Shop** (276-5480), Main Street, Northeast Harbor, also has rentals. **Southwest Cycle** (244-5856), Main Street, Southwest Harbor, rents mountain and 10-speed bicycles. **Cadillac Mountain Bike Adventures** (288-3278), 110 Main Street, Bar Harbor, provides guided sunrise breakfast rides from the top of Cadillac Mountain. "Lakeside lunch" and "sunset dinner" tours are also offered.

BIRDING

For special programs led by park naturalists, consult "Acadia's Beaver Log," available at the park visitors center (see *Green Space*).

BOAT EXCURSIONS

All excursions are seasonal.

Acadian Whale Watcher (288-9794), Golden Anchor Pier, West Street, Bar Harbor. Sunset cruises June to October.

Beal and Bunker Co. (244-3575). Operates daily from Northeast Harbor to the Cranberry Islands.

Islesford Ferry Co. (276-3717), Northeast Harbor dock. Nature and sunset cruises; also naturalist-guided cruise to Baker Island.

BOAT RENTALS

Harbor Boat Rentals (288-3757), at the Pier, Bar Harbor. Powerboats and sailboats available. (Also see *Sailing*.)

CANOEING AND KAYAKING

Most ponds on Mount Desert offer easy access. Long Pond, the largest lake on the island, has three access points. Boats can be launched at Echo Lake from Ike's Point, just off Route 102. Seal Cove Pond is less used, accessible from fire roads north of Seal Cove. Bass Harbor Marsh is another possibility. Canoe rental sources offer suggestions and directions. Kayaking is a recent but booming sport, easier to master than saltwater canoeing.

Acadia Bike & Canoe Company (288-5483), 48 Cottage Street, Bar Harbor. Both canoe and kayak rentals; offers half-day and sunrise kayaking tours on Frenchman Bay and Blue Hill Bay.

National Park Canoe Rentals (244-5854), Route 102, 2 miles west of Somesville (at the north end of Long Pond). Open daily May through October. Half- and full-day rentals; rooftop carriers available.

Life Sports (667-7819), 34 High Street, Ellsworth. Rents canoes, kayaks, and windsurfers; runs clinics in kayaking and windsurfing.

Canoe Works (422-9095), Route 1, Sullivan. Guy Cyr is known nationally as a canoe maker and mender; he also rents canoes by the day and half day.

Coastal Kayaking Tours (288-9605 or 1-800-526-8615), Cottage Street, Bar Harbor. Offers half- and full-day tours in the area; also offers 3- and 5-day island camping tours (no previous paddling experience required). Two-person kayaks only.

Schoodic Kayak Tours (963-7958) in Corea offers guided tours along the eastern shore of Frenchman's Bay, featuring the most spectacular views of Acadia.

GOLF

Kebo Valley Club (288-3000 or 288-5000), Route 233, Bar Harbor. Open daily May through October. Eighteen holes; "oldest golf grounds in America," since 1892.

Bar Harbor Golf Course (667-7505), Routes 3 and 204, Trenton. Eighteen holes.

Causeway Golf Club (244-3780), Southwest Harbor. Nine-hole course, club and pull-carts, pro shop.

HIKING

Acadia National Park is a recognized mecca for rock climbers as well as hikers. Several detailed maps are sold at the visitors center, which is also the source of an information sheet that profiles two dozen trails within the park. These range in difficulty from the Jordan Pond Loop Trail (a 3⅓-mile path around the pond) to the Precipice Trail (1½ miles, very steep, with iron rungs as ladders). There are seven trails to mountain summits on Mount Desert.

Schoodic Mountain, off Route 183 north of Sullivan, provides one of east-

MAINE OFFICE OF TOURISM

Kebo Valley Club, Bar Harbor

ern Maine's most spectacular and least-known hikes, with 360-degree views, including the peaks on Mount Desert across Frenchman Bay. The Bureau of Public Lands has recently improved the parking area and trail system here. Take your first left after crossing the railroad tracks on Route 183; bear left at the "Y" and in 0.8 mile bear right to the parking lot. The hike to the top of Schoodic Mountain (1069 feet) should take less than 45 minutes; a marked trail from the summit leads down to sandy Schoodic Beach at the southern end of Donnell Pond (good swimming and a half dozen primitive campsites); return to the parking lot on the old road that's now a footpath (½ mile). From the same parking lot you can also hike to the bluffs on Black Mountain; from here the trail continues to other peaks, and another trail descends to Schoodic Beach.

HORSE-DRAWN TOURS

Wildwood Stables (276-3622), follow the Park Loop Road from the visitors center; turn left at the sign a half mile beyond Jordan Pond House. Two-hour horse-drawn tours in multiple-seat carriages offered six times a day.

SAILING

The *Natalie Todd* (288-4585) sails from the Bar Harbor pier, late June through early October. Maine's only three-masted commercial schooner, it was built in 1941 in Brooklyn as a two-masted schooner dragger. Captain Steven Pagels found the vessel in Gloucester in 1986 and rebuilt her in Thomaston as a three-masted, gaff-rigged schooner. The 2-hour cruises through Frenchman Bay are offered several times a day in high season, less frequently in slower summer weeks. Check current handouts for other day sails.

Mansell Boat Company (244-5625), Route 102A, Manset (near Southwest Harbor); offers sailing lessons.

For sailboat charters and rentals, contact **Classic Charters** (244-7312), Northeast Harbor; **Hinckley Yacht Charters** (244-5008), Bass Harbor; **Mansell Boat Rental** (244-5625); or **Morris Yachts** (244-5509), Southwest Harbor.

SWIMMING

Within Acadia there is supervised swimming at **Sand Beach,** 4 miles south of Bar Harbor, and at **Echo Lake,** 11 miles west. At **Seal Harbor** there is a small, free, town beach with parking in a small lot across Route 3.

At **Lake Wood** near Hull's Cove there is a pleasant freshwater beach that is ideal for children. The trick is finding it: Turn off Route 3 at the Cove Motel and take your second left up a dirt road (there is a small official sign), which leads to a parking area; there is a short walk down to the beach. No facilities or lifeguard, but warm water.

The clearest water and softest sand we have found in the area is at **Molasses Pond** in Franklin.

TENNIS

Atlantic Oakes by the Sea (288-5218), Route 3, Bar Harbor, offers use of its courts. Also check with chambers in Northeast Harbor and Southwest Harbor.

CROSS-COUNTRY SKIING

More than 43 miles of carriage roads at Acadia National Park are maintained as ski-touring trails. Request a "Winter Activities" leaflet from the park headquarters (write to Superintendent, PO Box 177, Bar Harbor 04609).

SNOWMOBILING

The motor and unpaved (see above) roads are open for snowmobiles.

GREEN SPACE

ACADIA NATIONAL PARK

The park maintains its own visitors center (288-5262 or 288-4932) at Hulls Cove, open early May through October. From mid-June to August 31, hours are 8–6 daily; during shoulder seasons, hours are 8–4:30. The park headquarters at Eagle Lake on Route 233 (288-3338) is open daily throughout the winter 8–4:30. For more information about the park, write to Superintendent, PO Box 177, Bar Harbor 04609. The glass-and-stone visitors center, set atop 50 steps, shows its 15-minute **introductory film** every half hour. Books, guides, and postcards may be purchased here. This is also the place to pick up a free map and a copy of the current "Acadia's Beaver Log" (a listing of all naturalist activities), to rent a cassette tape tour, and to sign up for the various programs offered. **Special evening programs** are scheduled by the national park staff nightly, June through September, at the amphitheaters in Blackwoods and Seawall campgrounds. Visitors ages 7–12 are eligible to join the park's **Junior Ranger Program;** inquire at the visitors center.

Within the park are more than 50 miles of carriage roads donated by John D. Rockefeller. These incredible gravel roads take bikers, hikers, joggers, and cross-country skiers through woods, up mountains, past lakes and streams. The paths also lead over and under 17 spectacular stone bridges. On this network of roads, you are truly immersed in nature, experiencing the peace and tranquility of days gone by. In recent years, volunteers have rallied to refurbish and improve these truly spectacular carriage roads.

There is a weekly charge of $5 per car or $2 per hiker or biker along the 27-mile Park Loop Road, the prime tourist route within the park. It is possible, however, to get to mountain trails and some popular spots, such as the drive up Cadillac, without charge.

Sights along the Loop Road include the following:

Sand Beach, actually made up of ground shells, not sand; a great beach to walk down and from which to take a dip, if you don't mind 50-degree water; there are changing rooms and lifeguards.

Thunder Hole. The water rushes in and out of a small cave, which you can view from behind a railing. The adjacent rocks can keep small children scrambling for hours.

Cadillac Mountain. From the smooth summit, you look out across Frenchman Bay, dotted with porcupine islands that look like giant stepping-stones. This is a great spot for a picnic, so come prepared.

WALKS

Ship Harbor, Route 102A (near Bass Harbor), offers a fine nature trail that winds along the shore and into the woods; it is also a great birding spot.

The Shore Path. This mile-long path runs from Agamont Park near the Bar Harbor Town Pier and along the bay. It's also accessible from Grant Park, off Albert Meadow at the corner of Main and Mount Desert Streets.

LODGING

GRAND OLD RESORTS

The Claremont (244-5036), Claremont Road, Southwest Harbor 04679. Open May to mid-October. Mount Desert's oldest hotel (110 years in 1994), substantially renovated. Sited with spectacular views of Cadillac Mountain across Somes Sound and the waterfront estates in Northeast Harbor. This is a classic, grand resort hotel with rockers on the veranda, spacious common rooms that include a game room lined with books, and a large dining room designed so that every table has a water view.

Food is excellent, with an emphasis on fresh fish (see *Dining Out*). In the old resort tradition, jacket and tie are required for dinner, but the atmosphere is relaxed and friendly. Lunch is served at the Boat House, right on the water with splendid views of the mountains and Northeast Harbor. The hotel has 24 old-fashioned double rooms, simply furnished but comfortable, and there are more rooms in Phillips and Clark Houses, including a large suite in each; there are also 12 cottages, each with living room and fireplace. Recreation options include tennis on clay courts, croquet, badminton, and water sports; rowboats are available. The Croquet Classic in August is the social high of the season. A room in the hotel is $165–185 double, MAP, in-season; $145–175, EP, in the cottages; $80–125 double, B&B, off-season in the hotel. A gratuity is added: 15 percent in the rooms, 10 percent in the cottages.

Asticou Inn (276-3344), Route 3, Northeast Harbor 04662. Cranberry Lodge is open May to late December, and the main house, mid-June to mid-September. The epitome of elegance, the Asticou Inn caters to a distinguished clientele, with superb food, simply furnished rooms with water views, luxurious public rooms with Oriental rugs and wing chairs by the hearth, and a vast porch overlooking formal gardens. In all, there are 50 rooms and suites, all with private baths, divided between the main house and smaller lodges, which include the Cranberry Lodge across the road (6 rooms here have fireplaces). Facilities include a cocktail lounge, tennis courts, and a heated swimming pool. Dinner dances on Thursday evenings in July and August; music many summer nights. $150–286 double, MAP. $65–135 in Cranberry Lodge, off-season. Add 15 percent gratuity.

INNS AND BED & BREAKFASTS

In Bar Harbor

According to the Bar Harbor Chamber of Commerce, there are some 3000 beds in town of every type from motel units to suites in elegant inns. In recent years the number of inns and B&Bs, almost all in former "cottages," has increased. One word of caution: Never come to Bar Harbor in July or August without a reservation. You will find a room, but it may well cost more than $300. We cannot claim to have inspected every room in town, but we offer this partial listing of places that we have actually checked out. All the following are in Bar Harbor 04609.

Inn at Canoe Point (288-9511), Box 216. Open year-round. Two miles north of Bar Harbor near the entrance to the Acadia National Park Visitors Center. Separated from Route 3 by its own small pine forest, overlooking the bay. The five guest rooms have water views and private baths. The master suite, with its fireplace and French doors onto a deck, is ideal for a romantic getaway. The garret suite, occupying the whole third floor, is ideal for families, and the garden room exudes the charm of a traditional Bar Harbor cottage guest room. All rooms have been imaginatively, elegantly furnished. Guests gather in the Ocean Room for breakfast to enjoy the fireplace, grand piano, and 180-degree view. In-season: $125–225; off-season: $80–150.

The Inn at Bay Ledge (288-4204 or 1-800-848-6885), 1385 Sand Point Road. Open April through November. Perched on a cliff overlooking the ocean, surrounded by towering pines. The inn offers 10 guest rooms, all with bay views and private baths. Spa amenities include a sauna, hot tub, steam bath, heated pool, and weight room; but the best feature is a private, grottolike pebble beach, accessible via 79 steps designed with a series of landings on which to pause and appreciate the view. Rates are $95–250.

Nannau Seaside B&B (288-5575), Box 710, Lower Main Street. Open May through October. This vintage 1904, shingled, 20-room "cottage" was originally built as a "mother-in-law" cottage for the people who lived next door. Vikki and Ron Evers rescued it from a dilapidated state and restored it to its former elegance (it was recently featured in *Old House Interiors*). In its peaceful location on Compass Harbor just a mile from downtown Bar Harbor and abutting the national park, Nannau offers rooms ranging from a third-floor aerie ($75 double) with a shared bath to a bedroom with private bath, fireplace, and a large bay window on the ocean ($115). A large breakfast, maybe eggs Florentine or frittata, is served, and the Evers invite guests to make themselves at home in the parlor and living room where there are plenty of books; frequently a dog is napping on the hearth. A path leads down to the water, and there is an easy walk to the point. No smoking. $65–105 in shoulder seasons.

Bayview (288-5861 or 1-800-356-3585), 111 Eden Street (Route 3). Open from early May to late October. This former estate, which overlooks Frenchman Bay, is now a complex of Hotel Château with 26 motel units (each with bath, water view, phone, and TV), the original mansion (now an inn with six rooms), and a cluster of town homes (each with two fireplaces, two baths, and two or three bedrooms). There is a restaurant and bar. It is very elegant, as it should be at $95–260 for a room in the inn, $165–225 in the hotel, and $195–425 for a town home; less in shoulder seasons.

Breakwater 1904 (288-2313 or 1-800-238-6309), 45 Hancock Street. The newest of the town's former colossal "cottages" to become an inn, this place is elegant and awe-inspiring. A 1904 English Tudor estate with six guest rooms furnished with antiques (or reproductions) and Laura Ashley prints, private baths with Victorian cast-iron tubs, water views, vast common rooms (including a billiards room lined with books), and wicker rockers on the porch overlooking the lawn that sweeps to the Shore Path and bay beyond; $175–295 includes a "gourmet" breakfast and afternoon wine and cheese.

The Tides (288-4968), 119 West Street. Open May through October. A Greek Revival mansion, vintage 1887, overlooking the "bar" as well as "the harbor" and a short walk from the middle of town. At low tide you can walk down the line and out to "Bar Island," part of Acadia. The three guest rooms have recently been made into two-room suites with sitting rooms, four-poster beds, fireplaces, and window seats with water views. The veranda, with its wicker chairs and fireplace, is a popular gathering spot for afternoon hors d'oeuvres. $195–235. No smoking, pets, or children.

Balance Rock Inn By the Sea (288-9900 or 1-800-274-5334), 21 Albert Meadow. A secluded bayside "cottage" with 14 guest rooms that pull out all the stops: features may include water views, whirlpool baths, steam baths, saunas, canopied beds, fireplaces, TVs, VCRs. Facilities include a heated pool and fitness center. Full breakfast and afternoon tea included in rates. $150–350 in-season.

Manor House Inn (288-3759), 106 West Street. Open May through mid-November. This 1887 "cottage" is on the National Register of Historic Places. All 14 rooms have private baths, and most are furnished with Victorian pieces. Four have working fireplaces. Rare woodwork and nicely preserved details add comfort and beauty. The gardens are quite lovely. $50–150 per room includes a full buffet breakfast.

Ledgelawn Inn (288-4596 or 1-800-274-5334), 66 Mount Desert Street. Open May through November. A turn-of-the-century "cottage" and carriage house gilded to the hilt. Built in 1904, this was the last large summer residence built on Mount Desert. Each room is different, but many are furnished with antiques, some with whirlpool tubs, saunas, and steam baths, working fireplaces, verandas, private entrances, and sitting areas. There are 21 rooms in the main building, 8 in the carriage house, and many of the furnishings are original. Facilities include a bar, pool, and Jacuzzi. $55–245.

Thornhedge Inn (288-5398), 47 Mount Desert Street. Open May to mid-October. This cheerful yellow mansion, its porch garnished with geraniums, offers 13 guest rooms, all with baths and 5 with fireplaces. The house was built for the Boston publisher who persuaded Louisa May Alcott to write *Little Women* and was one of the first bed & breakfast inns in Bar Harbor. Continental breakfast served in the dining room; wine and cheese at 5 PM. $80–140.

Mira Monte Inn and Suites (288-4263 or 1-800-553-5109 outside Maine), 69 Mount Desert Street. Open May to mid-October. A gracious 1865 mansion with a welcoming porch and some rooms with private balconies overlooking the deep, peaceful lawn in back or the formal gardens on the side. Marian Burns, a native of Bar Harbor, offers 12 rooms with private baths; 8 with fireplaces; and all with antiques, private phones, clock radios, and TVs. Also two suites in a separate building, each with fireplace, kitchenette, lace canopy bed, two-person whirlpool, and private deck. Guests may take advantage of the inviting library and sitting room with fireplaces. The per night rate includes a full breakfast and afternoon refreshments. $90–150 per room, $125–180 for suites. 10–20 percent discount in shoulder season and for longer stays.

☞ **Bass Cottage in the Field** (288-3705), The Field. Open late May to mid-October. Anna Jean Turner is the gracious hostess of this grand old home, just off Main Street but in a quiet world of its own, set above the town pier and park. It's been in her family since 1928. The large, enclosed porch is stacked with magazines and local menus, furnished with wicker, and brimming with flowers. The stamped tin ceilings are high, and there is stained glass. The 10 rooms are traditionally furnished and airy; some with private baths. Smoking on porches only. $50–85 double, $35 single in-season.

Holbrook House Inn (288-4970), 74 Mount Desert Street. Open mid-May through mid-October. A restored 1876 "cottage." Thirteen rooms, all with private baths, furnished with antiques. Room one is especially nice, with a private entrance and deck, and view of Cadillac Mountain. The library is nice for relaxing. A full breakfast and afternoon refreshments are served on the sun porch. $75–125 double.

McKay Lodging (288-3531 or 1-800-TO-MCKAY), 243 Main Street. Open year-round. Two Victorian houses, the Main House and the Summer House (open May through October, no smoking), offer a total of 23 rooms, each different but all with brass beds, TVs, direct-dial phones; most with private baths and refrigerators. $60–120 includes continental breakfast.

Canterbury Cottage (288-2112), 12 Roberts Avenue. Open May to mid-October. A small, centrally located B&B whose owners share a lifetime familiarity with the island. The Victorian house is architecturally interesting (its original owner was the B&M stationmaster, and its architect specialized in railroad stations), and rooms are comfortably and tastefully decorated. No children, pets, or smokers. $75–85 double includes breakfast in the country kitchen.

In Northeast Harbor 04662

Harbourside Inn (276-3272). Open June through September. An 1880s, shingle-style inn set in 4 wooded acres, with 14 guest rooms on three floors, all with private baths, some kitchens. There are also working fireplaces in all the first- and second-floor rooms. All are large and bright with interesting antiques and fine rugs. Guests mingle over breakfast muffins served on one of the wicker-furnished sun porches. There is also a comfortable living room, but most guests spend their days in adjacent Acadia National Park (its wooded paths are within walking distance) or on boat excursions out of Northeast Harbor, also just down the road. Your hosts, the Sweet family, are longtime island residents. $90–150 (for a suite).

The Maison Suisse Inn (276-5223) PO Box 1090. Open May through October. This is a gem—just steps from Northeast Harbor's shops and galleries but set back from Main Street by a rustic garden with plenty of room for relaxing. This elaborate turn-of-the-century "cottage" has spacious common rooms with fireplaces and 10 guest rooms (4 are suites), all with private baths; a full breakfast at a restaurant across the street is included. $105–155 double; suites $175–215; $10 per child, $15 per extra person over 18; less in May and June.

In Southwest Harbor 04679

☞ **Penury Hall** (244-7102), Box 68, Main Street. Open year-round. An attractive village house with three guest rooms sharing two baths, all nicely decorated with interesting art and tempting reading material salted about. This was the first bed & breakfast on the island, and Toby Strong takes his job as host seriously (wife Gretchen is a retired town manager). Toby does the cooking and housekeeping and makes guests feel part of the family. Breakfast includes juice, fresh fruit, a choice of eggs Benedict, blueberry pancakes, or a "penurious omelet." A canoe, a 21-foot sloop, and a windsurfer are available, and you can relax in the sauna after hiking or cross-country skiing. $45–60.

The Inn at Southwest (244-3835), PO Box 593, Main Street. Open March to November. A high Victorian "cottage" in the village with a wraparound porch and harbor views, nicely restored in Waverly and Laura Ashley fashions and antiques. Pleasant sitting room with fireplace, games, and magazines, where afternoon refreshments are served. All nine rooms have private baths; $45–98 double includes a full breakfast.

Kingsleigh Inn (244-5302), Box 1426, Main Street. Open all year. A spacious, Colonial Revival home in the village. The eight guest rooms all have private baths, and some have water views; the entire third floor is a comfortable suite with fireplace and a telescope. Coffee and tea are available anytime, and a full breakfast is included; $75–165 (for the turret suite) in summer; $55–95 off-season. Tom and Nancy Cervelli, guests tell us, are warm and helpful hosts.

Harbour Cottage Inn (244-5738), PO Box 258. Open year-round except November. A mansard-roofed house originally built in 1870 as an annex to Mount Desert's first (and long gone) summer hotel. The eight guest rooms all have private baths, ranging from a claw-foot tub to steam showers and whirlpools. Recommended as a great place to honeymoon off-season (by friends who did). $60–135 double (depending on room and season), including breakfast and 5:30 nibbles; $5 less for single occupancy.

Lindenwood Inn (244-5335), Box 1328. Open all year. A turn-of-the-century sea captain's home set among stately linden trees. Recently renovated by Jim King (original owner of the Kingsleigh), it's been decorated with art and furnishings gathered in his travels. The nine guest rooms all have private baths, and many have private balconies. The annex offers cottages and housekeeping apartments. A full breakfast is served in the paneled dining room (where the fire is lit most mornings). Swing on the porch or relax in the parlor. $45–135 double; $20 per extra person.

View of Northeast Harbor from Thuya Garden Path

The Island House (244-5180), Box 1006. Open all year. Right across from the harbor is this large 1850s house, part of an early summer hotel (ask to see the scrapbook of historical memoirs). Ann Bradford offers four double rooms with two shared baths, also an cozy efficiency apartment with a loft in the Carriage House. $40–95 includes a full breakfast; no minimum stay required.

The Heron House (244-0221), HC-33, Box 101. Open year-round. After 16 years of vacationing in the area, Sue and Bob Bonkowski redecorated this comfortable house into a B&B of their own (1994 was their first season). Three pleasant guest rooms share two baths. Guests are greeted by two Irish wolfhounds and two cats, and are welcome to use the living room and den to relax in. $50–60 depending on season, includes full breakfast served family style.

In Bass Harbor 04653

Pointy Head Inn and Antiques (244-7261), HC 33, Box 2A. Open mid-May to late fall. This rambling old sea captain's home on Route 102A overlooks the ocean. Doris and Warren Townsend offer six guest rooms, some with water/mountain views, two with private baths, the rest sharing two. "Mature" children only. An antiques shop with wood carvings by Warren is on the premises. A favorite with artists and photographers; $45–85 per room; $15 per extra person, includes full breakfast.

Bass Harbor Inn (244-5157), Shore Road, PO Box 326. Open May through October. A vintage 1832 house, Barbara and Alan Graff offer nine rooms, ranging from doubles with shared baths to a top-floor suite with kitchenette. One room with a half-bath has a fireplace. $60–100 includes great breakfast breads and pastries.

In Seal Cove

🖉 **Seal Cove Farm** (244-7781), HCR 62, Box 140, Mount Desert 04660. Open year-round. Overlooking a lake, the century-old farmhouse on Route 102 offers three spacious rooms, one with private bath. This is a great place for children; there are sheep, ducks, geese, chickens, turkeys, and goats from which the Brooks family makes several varieties of cheese. A full country breakfast is included. $54–65; $11 per extra person.

In Lamoine 04605

☞ **Lamoine House** (667-7711), Route 184, Box 180. Open all year. Just a few miles off Route 3, Lamoine is a quiet byway with its own beach and water views. This B&B is a simple, friendly old farmhouse across the road from the water. Two guest rooms, one upstairs and one down, share the family bath and living room. Molly Gilley is a serious gardener and baker, and the reasonable rates—$18–26 single and $26–34 double—include a full country breakfast.

East of Mount Desert

☞🖉**Crocker House Country Inn** (422-6806), Hancock Point 04640. Open daily mid-April to Columbus Day, weekends (Thursday through Sunday) late October to New Year's Eve. Just 30 minutes north of Bar Harbor, Hancock Point has a different feel entirely: quiet, with easy access to water, hiking trails, crafts shops, and concerts. The three-story, 1880s inn has 11 guest rooms, 9 in the inn itself and 2 on the second floor of the carriage house. All rooms have private baths (new and nicely done with natural woods) and country antiques, quilts, and stenciling. There is a pleasant, unpretentious feel to this inn, and families feel welcome; the common rooms are spacious, and there's more lounging space on the ground floor of the carriage barn near the hot tub. The second smallest post office in the United States sits across the road next to the tennis courts, and the nearby dock is maintained by the Hancock Improvement Association. Breakfast and dinner are served in the dining room, which is open to the public (see *Dining Out*). $65–95 double includes breakfast.

Le Domaine (422-3395 or 422-3916), Route 1, Hancock 04640. Best known for the French fare of its dining room (see *Dining Out*), this cozy European-style inn also has seven rooms, each with private bath. The rooms are each named for a different herb, and each has a unique style. We especially like Rosemary, with a private deck overlooking the gardens and pretty floral decor. Chives, with a built-in wooden corner seat perfect for reading, is nice also. Although the house is right on Route 1, this is a relatively quiet section of the road, and a large garden in back offers a peaceful haven. A path through the woods leads to a tranquil trout pond. $180 per couple, MAP, plus 15 percent gratuity.

Island View Inn (422-3031), HCR 32, Box 24, Sullivan Harbor 04664. This is a spacious, gracious, turn-of-the-century summer "cottage" set well back from Route 1 with splendid views of Frenchman Bay and the dome-shaped mountains on Mount Desert. The seven guest rooms, five with private baths and three with water views, are nicely decorated, and there is ample and comfortable common space; a full breakfast is included. $40–70; no charge for children five years and younger, otherwise $10 per extra person in room. An 18-foot sailboat is available for guests to rent, and there is a mooring for guests who sail in.

Sullivan Harbor Farm (422-3735), Route 1, Sullivan Harbor 04664. Built in 1820 by Captain James Urann, who launched his vessels from the shingle beach across the road. The house overlooking Frenchman Bay is cheerfully, tastefully decorated and includes a library and an enclosed porch on which breakfast is served. The three guest rooms with double beds share a bath ($55–65). "Cupcake," a seasonal cottage, also has water views; six people can sleep there for $600 per week. Another cottage, "Milo," sleeps four. A canoe is available and hosts Joel Franztman and Leslie Harlow, who delight in tuning guests in to local hiking and paddling possibilities, operate a salmon smokehouse on the premises.

The Black Duck (963-2689), PO Box 39, Corea 04624. A quiet place in a serene fishing village—in other words, no boutiques and gift shops—this is the perfect place for those looking to truly get away from it all. Barry Canner and Robert Travers offer four guest rooms, comfortably furnished with antiques, contemporary art, and Oriental rugs. Common areas display collections of antique toys and lamps, and the living room has a cozy fireplace. Twelve acres of land and waterfront property invite hiking, photography, artistic pursuits, and quiet relaxation. A dog, three cats, and Dolly the pot-bellied pig will welcome you, so please leave your pets at home. Two waterfront cottages also available. $55–80.

COTTAGES

"Maine Guide to Camp & Cottage Rentals," available free from the Maine Publicity Bureau (623-0363), lists some great rental cottages within easy striking distance of Mount Desert.

Emery's Cottages on the Shore (288-3432), Sand Point Road, Bar Harbor 04609. Open May to mid-October. Twenty-two cottages (fourteen with kitchens), electric heat, showers, cable TVs, and private pebble beach. No pets. $400–610 per week; $62–88 per day; less off-season.

Hinckley's Dreamwood Motor Court (288-3510), Route 3, Box 15, Bar Harbor 04609. Open May to mid-October. Sited under tall pines. Twenty-five cottages (nineteen with kitchens), three 2-bedroom units (some with fireplaces); also a four-bed house and four-bedroom cottage that sleeps as many as eight. Three-night minimum stay. Facilities include a heated pool. Moderately priced.

Salisbury Cove Cottages (288-4571), PO Box 723, Bar Harbor 04609. Open late May to October. Classic Maine motor court cottages; paneled in pine with tidy screened porches, kitchenettes; accommodates two to six people. $50–85 double.

Edgewater Motel and Cottages (288-3491), Box 566, Bar Harbor 04609. Open April through October. Just eight units right on Frenchman Bay in Salisbury Cove; four units have Franklin stoves and complete kitchens, and all have balconies and TVs. $65–85 per night, $430–595 per week.

Eden Village Motel and Cottages (288-4670 or 1-800-356-4670), Box 1930 (10 minutes north of Bar Harbor on Route 3), Bar Harbor 04609. The housekeeping cottages are set on 25 acres. They accommodate two to seven people, and are equipped with fireplaces and screened porches. $390–410 per week; nightly and lower off-season rates. Motel rooms are $49–69.

Edgewater Cabins (422-6414), Sullivan. Open late April to November. Emery and Lydia Dunbar have passed on management of their Route 1 store but still accommodate summer guests in seven old-style Maine cottages, all with splendid views across Frenchman Bay. Inexpensive.

HOTELS AND MOTELS

Bar Harbor Inn (288-3351 or 1-800-248-3351), Newport Drive. Overlooking the water but centrally located in Bar Harbor, next to the municipal pier. In previous editions, categorial placement of this complex has puzzled us, and it was sometimes listed under "inns." Owner David Witham, however, describes it as a hotel, with 24-hour guest service, bellman service, a restaurant open for all three meals, and room service. The lobby with its formal check-in desk is grandiose, and the "Reading Room" dining room began as an elite men's social club in 1887. The 51 guest rooms were the first new hotel rooms available in town after the 1947 fire. In 1988 a deluxe 64-unit Oceanfront Lodge replaced a standard 15-unit motel, and it offers large, tastefully furnished rooms, each with a private balcony overlooking the bay. Spring of 1994 brought the addition of yet another building: 38 large modern rooms that do not have water views, but are less expensive. All rooms have private baths, phones, color TVs, and access to the pool, Jacuzzi, and 7 acres of manicured lawns on the water. The lodge is open year-round and in winter is half its high-season price ($59–89). Summer rates range from $115–230, with deluxe continental breakfast included. Children 15 and under are free; ask about two- to four-night packages, which bring the rack rates down. With 153 units, the inn does get its share of tour groups, but its location is unbeatable and it's a good value at Bar Harbor prices, especially for families.

Atlantic Oakes By-the-Sea (288-5801 or 1-800-33MAINE), Box 3, Eden Street (Route 3, next to the *Bluenose* ferry terminal), Bar Harbor 04609. Open year-round. This is a modern facility on the site of Sir Harry Oakes's 10-acre estate: The eight different buildings house 152 units, many with balconies, 12 with kitchens. There's also an eight-room bed & breakfast in the original Oakes summer mansion. Facilities include a pebble beach, heated outdoor pool, indoor pool, five tennis courts, and pier and float handy to the *Bluenose* ferry. $118–151 in-season; $48–113 off-season.

Wonder View Inn (288-3358 or 1-800-341-1553), PO Box 25, 50 Eden Street, Bar Harbor 04609. Open mid-May to mid-October. Both pets and children are welcome in the 79-unit motel built on 14 acres, the site of an estate once owned by Mary Roberts Rinehart, author of popular mystery stories. Handy both to the *Bluenose* ferry and to downtown Bar Harbor, the motel overlooks Frenchman Bay, and its extensive grounds are nicely landscaped. Includes a swimming pool and the Rinehart Dining Pavilion, which serves breakfast and dinner. $55–115.

CAMPGROUNDS

There are two campgrounds within Acadia National Park: **Blackwoods** (288-3274), open all year and handy to Bar Harbor; and **Seawall** (244-3600) near Southwest Harbor, open late May to late September. Sites at Seawall are meted out on a first-come, first-served basis, but Blackwoods reservations can be made at least eight weeks in advance from June 15 to September 15 by calling 1-800-365-2267.

Note: Although Blackwoods and Seawall frequently fill during July and August, waterside sites in nearby **Lamoine State Park** (667-4778), open mid-May to mid-October, are often empty. This attractive, 55-acre park is just minutes from Route 3 on Route 184 in Lamoine. Facilities include picnicking and a boat launch but no hot showers. The park is just up the road from **Lamoine Beach** (great for walking and skipping stones). There are also more than a dozen commercial campgrounds in this area.

OTHER LODGING

Mount Desert Island YWCA (288-5008), 36 Mount Desert Street, Bar Harbor 04609. Open all year. Offers 26 rooms (singles and doubles) and a dorm room for eight women. Gym and tennis courts.

Mount Desert Island AYH Youth Hostel (288-5587), 41 Mount Desert Street (behind St. Savior's Episcopal Church), PO Box 32, Bar Harbor 04609. Open mid-June through August to AYH members. Twenty beds, kitchen facilities. $8 per person, reservations advised. For membership information contact AYH, Greater Boston Council, 1020 Commonwealth Avenue, Boston, MA 02215 (617-731-5430 or 617-731-6692).

Appalachian Mountain Club's Echo Lake Camp (244-3747), AMC/Echo Lake Camp, Mount Desert 04660. Open late June through August. Accommodations are platform tents; family-style meals are served in a central hall. There is a rustic library reading room and an indoor game room. The focus, however, is outdoors: There are boats for use on the lake, daily hikes, and evening activities. Reservations should be made on April 1. Rates for the minimum 1-week stay (Saturday to Saturday) are inexpensive per person but add up for a family. All meals included. For a brochure, write to Echo Lake Camp, AMC, 5 Joy Street, Boston, MA 02108.

Swan's Island Vacations (526-4350), Box 27, Minturn 04659. Year-round. Maili Bailey coordinates rentals for cottages, houses, and apartments on Swan's Island, a picturesque lobstering island accessible from Bass Harbor. Accommodations range from $280–900 per week. There is also a guest house at Burnt Coat Harbor.

WHERE TO EAT

DINING OUT
In Bar Harbor

George's Restaurant (288-4505), 7 Stephen's Lane (just off Main Street behind the First National Bank). Open mid-June through October. Dinner from 5:30–10 PM. Creative, fresh, vaguely Greek cuisine in a summery house with organdy curtains. Extensive choice of appetizers, grazers, and entrées. You might dine on Cajun baked oysters, a green salad, and lobster strudel; all entrées $19.50. Two levels of prix fixe available (one with appetizer, one with grazer). Desserts include Chocolate Seduction, or try Sweet Degustation—a platter of tastes.

The Porcupine Grill (288-3884), 123 Cottage Street. Open most of the year for dinner, daily from 6 PM. Reservations recommended. Well-chosen antiques, photos of the Porcupine Islands, and fresh flowers complement imaginative dishes like lobster and sun-dried tomato tart and grilled leg of lamb with mint peppercorn sauce. $12.50–18.00, extensive wine list, cocktails a specialty.

124 Cottage Street (288-4383). Early-bird specials 5–6; pleasant, flowery atmosphere, Szechuan shrimp, Bombay chicken, mussels sautéed in a spicy marinara. Entrées $12.95–20.95 (bouillabaisse); all dinners include breads and the extensive salad bar.

Maggie's Classic Scales (288-9007), 6 Summer Street. Dinner 5–10:30. Chef-owned restaurant featuring New England cuisine well prepared, fresh seafood specialties; entrées $10–19.

Cafe Bluefish (288-3696), 122 Cottage Street. Dark wood, books, cloth napkins patterned with different designs, and mismatched antique china create a pleasant atmosphere. Chef-owner Bobbie Lynn Hutchins, a fourth-generation Bar Harbor native, specializes in chicken, vegetarian, and seafood entrées like Cajun crusted salmon ($15.95), mushroom bean Stroganoff ($10.95), and seafood strudel ($13.95).

The Reading Room (288-3351), Bar Harbor Motor Inn, Newport Drive. Opened in 1887 as an elite men's club, the horseshoe-shaped, formal dining room has a view of the harbor; frequent piano music at dinner. Open for all three meals, specializing in daily lobster bakes on the outdoor terrace. Dinner entrées range from grilled breast of chicken with sauce of wild blueberries and cranberries ($15.95) to steak and lobster tail ($27.95). Sunday champagne-brunch buffet from 11:30–2:30.

Testa's at Bayside Landing (288-3327), 53 Main Street. Open 7 AM–midnight, June 15 through September, when the family moves to Palm Beach where they run a second restaurant. Three daily meals are served in the comfortable dining rooms. Italian and seafood specialties include spaghetti Testa au gratin, with diced chicken, peppers, and mushrooms. Blueberry and strawberry pies. In Bar Harbor since 1934.

✐ **Freddie's Route 66** (288-3708), 21 Cottage Street. Open May to mid-October, 5–10 PM only. Fun 1950s nostalgia dining room decorated with antique grocery store over the bar, Starlite Drive-in theater with 1950s movies and speakers in your booth, Seeburg jukebox. Specializes in seafood and road house specialties (hot roast turkey dinner with all the fixings is one choice). Children's plates. Entrées $8.95–14.95.

The Fin Back (288-4193), 78 West Street. No smoking. Lunch and dinner daily, reservations suggested. A small, chef-owned restaurant featuring deliciously healthy entrées like chicken served with ancho chili and mango sauce, and pork tenderloin with wild rice cakes. The crabcakes are famous. Entrées run $15–19.

Mark Andrews (288-3292), 101 Cottage Street. Open year-round for breakfast, lunch, dinner. Known for very fresh fish, also Mexican dishes. Dinner entrées $7.25–15.95; prices come down off-season.

The Unusual Cabaret (288-3306), 14½ Mount Desert Street. Staff members perform musical numbers throughout dinner, and there is an original production following the meal. Menu includes lobster sautée and spinach lasagne. $9.75–16.75.

Elsewhere on Mount Desert

Jordan Pond House (276-3316), Seal Harbor, Park Loop Road. Open for lunch 11:30–2:30, for tea on the lawn 2:30–5:30, and also for dinner 5:30–8. Seasonal. Best known for its popovers at tea, this landmark is also pleasant, and less crowded, for dinner (jackets suggested). Specialties include crabmeat au gratin, prime rib, and crabmeat and Havarti quiche. Children's dinner includes beverage. The dining room overlooks the pond and mountains. The restaurant dates from the 1870s but was rebuilt after a fire destroyed it in 1979. From $2.75 for grilled cheese to $14.50 for lobster.

Asticou Inn (276-3344), Northeast Harbor. Open mid-June to mid-September for breakfast, lunch, and dinner. Thursday night buffet and dance. Grand old hotel atmosphere with waterside formal dining room (window seats, however, are reserved for longtime guests). Specialties include filet mignon and lobster *au poivre* (in light *beurre blanc* with angelhair pasta). Jacket, tie, and reservation required. $15–23.

Bistro at Seal Harbor (276-3299), Seal Harbor. Mid-June to mid-October, dinner nightly from 6 PM. Many innkeepers describe this as the best place around. Sadly, we were unable to try it, but the choices sound delicious, with such appetizers as crabcakes with creole mustard sauce, and a bistro salad with feta, apples, and spiced pecans. Entrées sound just as appealing, including grilled loin lambchops with garlic rosemary butter, and seafood gumbo. Owners Donna Fulton and Teresa Clements spend time in New Orleans (and love Cajun cooking) and

California and have worked to develop the best domestic wine list possible. Seasonal desserts might include plum crisp, and a standard is the Seal Harbor chocolate torte. $5–21.

Redfield's (276-5283), Main Street, Northeast Harbor. This trendy storefront café, open for espresso and gourmet takeout during the day and for dinner until 9 PM, has become a local legend in just 2 years. Chefowner Scott Redfield was formerly chef at Cranberry Lodge. The rear dining room doubles as a daytime art gallery. Sample menu includes nightly vegetarian offerings and grilled marinated quail. $16.95–18.95.

The Claremont (244-5036), Clark Point Road, Southwest Harbor. Open late June through Labor Day; lunch at the Boathouse, mid-July through August. The formal dining room has been designed so that most tables have at least some water view. Both the food and the service enjoy a long-standing tradition (responsible for jacket and tie requirement) and a fine local reputation. Dinner choices change frequently, perhaps including tournedos of beef in béarnaise sauce, or grilled lamb tenderloin with mint pesto. Entrées average $16. The Boathouse, down on the water below the hotel, is a great place for predinner cocktails or for lunch; the view may just be the most spectacular on the island.

The Burning Tree (288-9331), Route 3, Otter Creek. Open 5–10:30. Admired for its fresh fish, imaginatively prepared. Dine inside or on a lattice-enclosed porch on entrées like Cajun lobster, saffron scallops, and four-cheese pasta; moderately priced.

Clark Point Cafe (244-0255), Clark Point Road, in the village of Southwest Harbor. Pleasant, informal atmosphere with a varied menu, ranging from pasta and seafood stew to veal and lobster dishes. Good service. $11–16.

Seafood Ketch (244-7463), on Bass Harbor. Open May to November, 7 AM–9 PM daily. Lisa, Stuart, and Ed Branch work hard to make this place special. Known for homemade breads and desserts, also for fresh, fresh seafood. Dinner specialties include baked lobster-seafood casserole ($13.95) and baked halibut with lobster sauce ($13.95); luncheon fare includes burgers, BLTs, and crabmeat rolls.

Deck House Restaurant (244-5044), end of Swan's Island Ferry Road, Bass Harbor. A very special place featuring, in addition to an excellent menu, nightly cabaret theater by the serving staff, beginning at 8:30 PM. Entertainment cover. Full bar. Reservations are a must.

East of Mount Desert

Le Domaine (422-3395), Route 1, Hancock. Nicole Purslow, *propriétaire et chef,* prepares very French entrées, generally rated the best cuisine Down East. The atmosphere is that of a French country inn, complete with a small, European-style bistro. Nicole's mother, Marianne Purslow-Dumas, established the restaurant in the 1940s. She had fled France during World War II and come to live with a relative, Pierre Monteaux, who had established a conducting school—which still thrives and holds summer concerts—in Hancock. Every summer resident in and around Bar Harbor knows this story, along with the shortcut to Le Domaine from Mount Desert (turn off Route 3 onto 204 in Lamoine and follow our map). Dinner is an elegant experience, with a fire burning in the dining room, soft music, and candlelight. After the hot rolls, you might start with a tomato salad (tomatoes topped with a wonderful blend of herbs and cheeses), and move on to *escalope de veau sauté aux champignons* (veal medallions sautéed with mushrooms). Daily specials vary. Dessert choices might include crème brulée or traditional flan. Thursday is bistro night, $30 per person prix fixe.

Crocker House Country Inn (422-6806), Hancock Point. Open nightly for dinner, 5:30–9. A pleasant country inn atmosphere and varied menu; the specialty is Crocker House scallops, sautéed with mushrooms, scallions, garlic, and tomatoes with lemon and wine sauce. In summer request the sun porch. Sunday brunch is big here, as are desserts. Entrées: $16.95–21.95.

EATING OUT

In Bar Harbor

✐ **Fisherman's Landing** (288-4632), 47 West Street. Open in-season 11:30–8. Right on the dock. Boiled lobster dinner, steamed clams, hamburgers, hot dogs, and fried foods; liquor license.

✐ **Epi Sub & Pizza** (288-5853), 8 Cottage Street. Open 7 AM–11 PM. Tops for food and value but zero atmosphere. Cafeteria-style salads, freshly baked calzone, pizza, quiche, pasta, and crabmeat rolls. Clean and friendly; game machines in back.

Bubba's (288-5871), 30 Cottage Street. Open 11:30 AM–1 AM but serving food to 8:30 PM only. Steam-bent oak and mahogany in art deco style creates comfortable atmosphere. Soup and sandwiches, full bar.

Island Chowder House (288-4905), 38 Cottage Street. Open 11–11. Bentwood chairs and bright decor; homemade soups, thick chowder, seafood pasta, and chicken. Lunch and dinner specials.

Miguel's Mexican Restaurant (288-5117), 51 Rodick Street. Open 5–10 nightly. Best Mexican food Down East: fajitas, blue corn crabcakes with roasted red pepper sauce.

Lompoc Cafe & Brew Pub (288-9392), 34 Rodick Street. Open daily for lunch, dinner, and late night dining, specializing in house-made beer, espresso, international and vegetarian entrées; live entertainment.

West Street Cafe (288-5242). Open for lunch and dinner. Features homemade soups and pies, fried and broiled seafood, and four different lobster dishes. Children's menu and early-bird specials are available.

Nakorn Thai Restaurant (288-4060), 30 Rodick Street. Open daily for lunch and dinner, closing Saturday and Sunday at 4 PM. Locally liked, reasonably priced.

Elsewhere on Mount Desert

Chart Room (288-9740), Route 3, Hulls Cove. Open for breakfast, lunch, and dinner. A dependable, family-geared, waterside restaurant with seafood specialties. Moderate.

Docksider (276-3965), Sea Street, Northeast Harbor. Open 11:30–9. The lunch menu is available all day: chowder, salads, burgers, sandwiches, clam rolls, seafoods, and shore dinner. Wine and beer.

Outback Cafe & Deli (276-3335), Main Street, Northeast Harbor. Sequestered in the back of the Pine Tree Market; a few tables inside and more in the garden. Breakfast through dinner, closed Monday.

Cafe Drydock (244-3886), 108 Main Street, Southwest Harbor. Open May to October, 7 AM–10 PM. An informal dining find specializing in seafood and pasta dishes; specialty drinks like "Maine Mudslide" and "Creamsicle." Entrées: $9–17.

The Deacon Seat (244-9229), Clark Point Road, Southwest Harbor. Open 5 AM–4:30 PM except Sunday. A great place for breakfast and the local gathering spot, near the middle of the village. A choice of 22 sandwiches to take out for picnics.

Ellsworth

The Mex (667-4494), 185 Main Street, Ellsworth. Open daily for lunch and dinner. Front tiled booths, inner dining room with white stucco walls, beaded curtains, heavy wooden chairs and tables. The Mex serves great Mexican food—we always order too much. (The bean soup is a meal in itself.) Sangria, Margaritas, and Mexican beer. Service can be slow.

Maidee's (667-6554), Main Street, Ellsworth. A former diner with oriental and standard American fare.

In Winter Harbor

Fisherman's Inn (963-5585), Route 186, Winter Harbor. Open April to October, then weekends until Christmas, dinner only; 4:30–9 on weekdays and Saturday; 12–9 on Sunday. A cozy restaurant near the entrance to the park. Specialties include Tony's famous baked stuffed shrimp and steamed local crabmeat in butter.

Donut Hole (963-7074), down by the water. A local hangout with a blackboard menu featuring fried seafood and homemade doughnuts.

Chase's Restaurant (963-7171). Open all day in-season. A convenient, nononsense eatery at the entrance to the park. Booths, salad bar, fried lobsters and clams, good chowder; will pack a picnic.

LOBSTER POUNDS

Why the lobster prices are so cheap at the clutch of restaurants around the Trenton Bridge we've never been able to figure. The **Trenton Bridge Lobster Pound** (667-2977), open in-season 8:30–8, has been in George Gascon's family a long time, and the view is great; but the preferred spot (it has a spectacular view) is the **Oak Point Lobster Pound** (667-8548), 4 miles down Route 230 from Route 3. Open in-season for lunch and dinner. Picnic tables and weatherproofed dining on Western Bay: lobster rolls, stews, and seafood dinners; excellent blueberry pie.

Beal's Lobster Pier (244-7178 or 244-3202), Clark Point Road, Southwest Harbor. Dock dining on picnic tables at the oldest lobster pound in the area. Crabmeat rolls, chowder, fresh fish specialties, and lobster (packed and shipped air freight, too).

Tidal Falls Lobster Pound (422-6818), Hancock (a half mile off Route 1). Open 11–8 in-season. It is getting so that local summer people cannot find a table overlooking the reversing falls. This is the kind of place where you bring your own wine, salad, and dessert; drink in the view; and feast on steamed lobster, mussels, and crabs. A weatherproofed pavilion has a lobster weather vane.

SNACKS

Jordan Pond House (276-3316), Park Loop Road. Tea on the lawn at the Jordan Pond House (served 2:30–5:30) has been *de rigueur* for island visitors since 1895. The tea comes with freshly baked popovers and homemade ice cream. Reservations suggested.

J.H. Butterfield Co. (288-3386), 152 Main Street, Bar Harbor. "Fancy foods since 1887," the sign says, and John Butterfield preserves the quality and atmosphere of the grocery that once delivered to every one of Bar Harbor's summer mansions. The reasonably priced sandwiches are the best takeout we've found in town, and the chocolate and lemon cakes are legendary. Carry your order to a bench across the way on the town Green or around the corner to Grant Park, overlooking the Shore Path and the bay.

Rooster Brother (667-8675), Route 1, Ellsworth. Just south of the bridge. Gourmet groceries, cheese, fresh-roasted coffee blends, takeout.

COFFEE BAR

Parkers Coffee and Tea House (288-2882), right next door to Criterion Theater, a perfect place for a cup of coffee or tea and pie after the show. Open early morning to late night.

ENTERTAINMENT

MUSIC

Bar Harbor Music Festival (288-5744), The Rodick Building, 59 Cottage Street, Bar Harbor. Mid-July to mid-August. For more than 25 years this annual series has brought top performers to the island. The 8:30 PM concerts are staged at a variety of sites around town.

Mount Desert Festival of Chamber Music (276-5039), Neighborhood House, Main Street, Northeast Harbor. A series of six concerts presented for more than 25 seasons during mid-July through mid-August.

Arcady Music Festival (288-3151 or 288-2141). Late July through August. A relative newcomer (this is its 14th season) on the Mount Desert music scene. A series of concerts held at the College of the Atlantic (each concert performed in Bangor and Dover-Foxcroft as well).

Pierre Monteux Memorial Concert Hall (442-6251), Hancock, is the setting for a series of summer concerts presented by faculty and students at the respected Pierre Monteux School for Conductors.

(Also see *Entertainment* in "The Blue Hill Area.")

FILM

Criterion Theater (288-3441), Cottage Street, Bar Harbor. A vintage 1932, art deco, 891-seat theater, worth the ticket in itself; first-run and art films at 8 PM nightly. Rainy day matinees.

The Grand Theater (667-9500), Main Street, Ellsworth. A classic old theater. When not in use for live performances, first-run and art films are shown.

Ellsworth Cinemas (667-3251), Maine Coast Mall, Route 1A, Ellsworth. Two evening shows; matinees on weekends, holidays, and rainy days. First-run films.

THEATER

Acadia Repertory Theatre (244-7260), Route 102, Somesville. Performances during July and August, Tuesday through Sunday at 8:15 PM, Sunday matinees at 2. A resident theater group based in the Somesville Masonic Hall (8 miles from Bar Harbor) performs a half dozen popular plays in the course of the season.

The Grand Theater (667-9500 or 1-800-462-7616), Main Street, Ellsworth. Live performances by singers, comedians, and theatrical groups. Check current listings.

Deck House Cabaret Theatre (244-5044), Swan's Island Ferry Road, Bass Harbor. July and August, dinner at 6:30. Waiters and waitresses stage a cabaret show at 8:15 (see *Dining Out*).

The Unusual Cabaret (288-3306), 14½ Mount Desert Street, Bar Harbor. Cabaret throughout dinner, original production after the meal (see *Dining Out*).

SELECTIVE SHOPPING

ART AND FINE CRAFTS GALLERIES

Worth the trip: The **Barter Family Gallery and Shop** (422-3190), North Sullivan. Open mid-May through December, Monday through Saturday 9–5 or by appointment. We put this one first, although it's way off the beaten track, because it's our favorite in the region. You will find Philip Barter's paintings in the best Northeast Harbor and Blue Hill galleries (we first saw them in a Massachusetts museum). Mostly landscapes, they are primitive, bold, and evocative of northern Maine. Barter's furniture creations and pen-and-ink landscapes are also displayed. This is the Barter home, and the gallery and shop (featuring Maine and Scottish woolen products, local crafts, and Irish tweeds) is staffed by the family. Phone for directions. It's less than 15 miles from Ellsworth.

Along Main Street in Northeast Harbor. The quality as well as quantity of artwork showcased in this small yachting haven is amazing. **Smart Studio & Art Gallery** (276-5152) offers changing exhibits of watercolors, oils, and serigraphs. **The Wingspread Gallery** (276-3910) has an outstanding assemblage of unusual art; changing exhibits in the main gallery and a selection by well-established artists in the back room. **Redfield Artisans Gallery** (276-3609); the furniture (all made right here) is exquisite, and there are small, affordable pieces. Also imaginative stone sculptures and impressionist paintings. **Shaw Contemporary Jewelry** (276-5000); Samuel Shaw's designs are bold and fun, executed in everything from baked enamel over bronze to pure silver and gold. A new glass gallery showcases hand-blown glass; a shop that keeps deservedly expanding.

Eclipse Gallery (288-4054), 12 Mount Desert Street, Bar Harbor. Oils, watercolors, graphics, and sculpture by nearly 200 contemporary American artists.

Island Artisans, 99 Main Street, Bar Harbor. A cooperative run by 24 area craftspeople. The quality and variety of work is outstanding.

Lone Moose (288-4229), West Street, Bar Harbor. For almost 20 years, a waterfront collection of "made in Maine" pottery, textiles, baskets, furniture, jewelry, watercolors, and glass.

Beyond Bar Harbor

Jones Gallery, Main Street, Southwest Harbor. Contemporary works by New England artists. Jewelry, boxes, and more.

West Side Gallery (244-4329), Main Street, Southwest Harbor. Old prints, etchings, lithos, and paintings.

Susanne Grosjean (565-2282), Sullivan Road, 3.5 miles north of Route 1. Distinctive, award-winning rugs; showroom and made-to-order crafts.

Spring Woods Gallery (442-3007), Route 200, off Route 1 in Sullivan. Open daily except Sundays, 10–5. This is a family gallery representing five members of the Breeden family. It features fine arts, jewelry, and sculpture.

Gull Rock Pottery (422-3990), Eastside Road, 1.5 miles off Route 1. Open year-round. Torj and Kurt Wray wheel-throw blue and white stoneware with hand-brushed designs.

Pine Tree Kiln, Route 1, West Sullivan. Ruth and Denis Vibert and Dorothea and Frank Stoke have made this shop standing behind an easy-to-miss clapboard home into an insider's landmark. Their own ovenproof stoneware is outstanding, as is the selection of prints, jewelry, weaving, glass, and leather by other Maine craftspeople. Books and cards are also sold here.

Maine Kiln Works, Route 186, West Gouldsboro. Open year-round, Monday through Saturday 10–5. An amazing number of unusual items: dinnerware, ceramic sinks, soap dishes, and lamps are made on the spot; there are also unusual quilts and work by other local craftspeople.

U.S. Bells (963-7184), Route 186 in Prospect Harbor. Open daily 8–5 except Sunday. Richard Fisher creates (designs and casts) superb and distinctive wind-bells.

BOOKSTORES

Sherman's Bookstore and Stationery (288-3161), Main Street, Bar Harbor. A great browsing emporium; really a combination five-and-dime, stationery store, gift shop, and well-stocked bookshop.

Port in a Storm Bookstore (244-4114), Route 302, Somesville. Open year-round, Monday through Saturday 9:30–5:30 and Sunday 1–5. A 19th-century general-store building with water views, two floors of books, discs and cassettes, soft music, reading nooks, coffee. Linda Lewis and Marilyn Mays have created a real oasis for book lovers.

Mr. Paperback, Maine Mall, Route 1A, Ellsworth; and 227 Main Street, Bar Harbor. Fully stocked bookstores with popular titles and magazines.

Oz Books (244-9077 or 1-800-281-9077), Main Street, Southwest Harbor. A first-rate children's bookstore.

SPECIAL SHOPS

Darthia Farm (963-771), West Bay Road (marked from Route 1), Gouldsboro. Open May through October, 8–6. A 133-acre organic farm with resident sheep, Scotch Highland cattle, turkeys, collies, and cows. Visitors are welcome to inspect the farm as well as the farm stand, justly famed for its vinegars, jams, and cheeses (there's even crême fraiche); Hattie's Shed, a weaving shop also at the farm, features coats, jackets, scarves, and shawls.

Sullivan Harbor Salmon (422-3735), Route 1, Sullivan Harbor. The salmon is local and visitors are welcome to tour the smoke house; shipping is a specialty.

Willey's, Route 1A, Ellsworth. A large, Maine-based clothing store specializing in name-brand sporting clothes plus a large selection of guns. Sidewalk sales and some discounted clothing.

Life Sports, 34 High Street (Route 1), Ellsworth. A large, trendy store that features camping and hiking, running, tennis, racquetball, fishing, and swim clothes. Life Sports also rents and sells canoes, kayaks, and windsurfers, and even offers windsurfing and kayaking clinics.

Acadia Shops, 85 Main Street, Bar Harbor, with branches in the park at Jordan Pond House, Cadillac summit, and Thunder Hole. Maine-made clothing and gifts, souvenirs.

By Way of Maine (244-7027 or 1-800-423-0403), Main Street, Southwest Harbor. An outstanding selection of things made in Maine; also a mail-order catalog.

L.L. Bean Outlet, High Street, Ellsworth. Clothing, sporting equipment, and a wide variety of discounted items from Maine's most famous store.

Big Chicken Barn (667-7308), Route 1 south of Ellsworth. Maine's largest used bookstore fills the vast innards of a former chicken house on Route 1. Annegret and Mike Cukierski have 80,000 books in stock: hardbacks, paperbacks, magazines, and comics; also used furniture and collectibles. Browsers are welcome.

SPECIAL EVENTS

Throughout the summer: **Band concerts**—Bar Harbor Village Green (check current evenings).

June: **Antique Auto Rally, Lobster Races.**

July: **Independence Day**—midnight square dance with breakfast for dancers, followed by sunrise dance on top of Cadillac Mountain, street parade, and seafood festival. **Art Show**—Bar Harbor's Agamont Park (later in the month). **Dulcimer and Harp Festival,** Bar Harbor. **Southwest Harbor Days**—craft show, parade, sidewalk sales. **Ellsworth Craft Show** (end of month).

August: **Crafts Show** and **Art Show,** Bar Harbor. **Winter Harbor Lobster Festival,** Winter Harbor—includes road race, lobster feed, and lobster boat races.

September: **Marathon road race, bicycle race.**

Bangor Area

It is no coincidence that the year 1820—when big-city merchants began buying timberland along the upper reaches of the Penobscot River—was also the year in which the Massachusetts District of Maine became a state and planted a white pine in the center of its official seal.

By the 1830s the Penobscot River was filled with pine logs, all of which were processed in the sawmills just above Bangor, where they were loaded aboard ships. By 1834–1836 land brokers offices were springing up as land speculation reached its peak. Townships and lots were sold sight unseen several times over. In 1835 it was reported that two paupers who had escaped from Bangor's almshouse had each cleared $1800 by speculating in timberland (the land offices worked around the clock) by the time they were caught the next morning.

By the 1850s, Bangor was the world's leading lumber port, handing over $3 million worth of lumber in its peak year. During this boom, a section of the city came to be known as the "Devil's half acre," where loggers flooded in after a long winter's work (and with a long winter's pay) to frequent the numerous taverns and brothels.

The Bangor of today is substantially different. The only Paul Bunyan around now is the 31-foot-high statue next to the chamber of commerce office. A 1911 fire wiped out the business district, and the end of the logging boom combined with urban renewal left the "Devil's half acre" a distant memory. Still, Bangor is Maine's second largest city, and Bangor International Airport is the departure point for craft (admittedly air instead of sailing) bound for faraway points of the globe.

Two neighborhoods actually hint at the city's past grandeur. One is the West Market Square Historic District, a mid-19th-century block of shops. The other is the Broadway area, studded with the Federal-style homes of early prominent citizens and lumber barons' mansions. Across town, West Broadway holds a number of even more ornate homes, including the turreted Victorian home of author Stephen King (look for the bat and cobweb fence).

GUIDANCE

Greater Bangor Chamber of Commerce (947-0307), 519 Main Street (just off I-95 Exit 45 to 495 East/Exit 3B; across from the Holiday Inn),

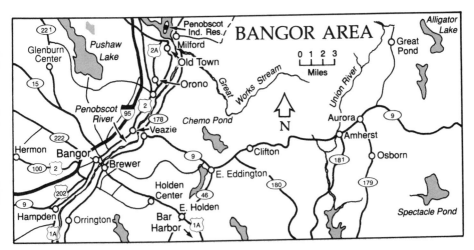

maintains a seasonal Bangor Visitors Information Office (947-0307) in Paul Bunyan Park on lower Main Street (Route 1A).

The **Maine Publicity Bureau** maintains two rest area/information centers on I-95 in Hamden between Exits 43 and 44: northbound (862-6628) and southbound (862-6638).

GETTING THERE

By air: **Bangor International Airport** (947-0384) is served by Delta Airlines, Continental Express, Northwest Airlink, and United Airlines. **Rental cars** are available at the airport.

By bus: **Greyhound** offers daily service to the downtown terminal. **Concord Trailways** offers express trips, complete with movies and music, daily from Portland and Boston.

By car: I-95 from Augusta.

MEDICAL EMERGENCY

Eastern Maine Medical Center (945-7000), Bangor. **St. Joseph Hospital** (947-8311), Bangor.

VILLAGES

Hampden. Adjacent to Bangor, but offering a more rural setting. The academically excellent Hampden Academy and a well-known truck stop are found here.

Orono. Home of the University of Maine, but still a small town. Downtown there are some nice shops and local dining landmarks, and on campus a multitude of cultural activities are available.

Old Town. Definitely a mill town, also the home of the famous Old Town Canoe factory. There's a great little museum worth visiting.

Indian Island. In 1786 the Penobscot tribe deeded most of Maine to Massachusetts in exchange for 140 small islands in the Penobscot River;

they continue to live on Indian Island, which is connected by a bridge to Old Town. The 1970s discovery of an 18th-century agreement that details the land belonging to the tribe (much of it now valuable) brought the island a new school and a large community center, which attracts crowds to play high-stakes bingo (phone 1-800-255-1293 for the schedule). A general store in the center sells locally made crafts, as does the Moccasin Shop at Ernest Goslin's house on Bridge Street. A **Penobscot Nation Museum** (827-6545), 6 River Road, is theoretically open weekdays 1–4 ($1 per adult, $.50 per child), but it was not open when we stopped by. The island is accessible from Route 2, marked from I-95, Exit 51.

Winterport. An old river town, once home of many sea captains, now a quiet little area with a historic district. Walking tour brochure available from area businesses.

TO SEE AND DO

MUSEUMS

Cole Land Transportation Museum (990-3600), 405 Perry Road (junction I-95 and 395), Bangor. Open May 1 to early November, daily 9–5. $2 per adult; senior citizens, $1; age 18 and under free. A collection of 19th- and 20th-century Maine vehicles: snowplows, wagons, trucks, sleds, rail equipment, and more.

University of Maine museums (581-1901), Route 2A, Orono. **Hudson Museum** (open Tuesday through Friday 9–4, Saturday 9–3, Sunday 11–3) has an exceptional anthropological collection including a special section on Maine Native Americans and Maine history. **University of Maine Museum of Art** (581-3255), 109 Carnegie Hall (open weekdays 9–5, Saturday 1–4), shows a fraction of its 4500-work collection; changing exhibits.

Old Town Museum (866-4393), North Fourth Street Extension, Old Town. Open early June through mid-August, Wednesday to Sunday 1–5. A former waterworks building houses exhibits on the Penobscot tribe and on local logging; early photos; an original birchbark canoe.

Maine Forest and Logging Museum (581-2871), Leonard's Mills, off Route 178 in Bradley (take Route 9 north from Brewer; turn left on 178 and watch for signs). Open weekends mid-May through mid-October and the site of "Living History Days" on two weekends, one in mid-July and another in October. A covered bridge, waterpowered sawmill, millpond, pit saw, stone dam, barn, and trapper's line camp mark the site of a late 19th-century logging community.

HISTORIC HOMES AND SITES

Bangor Historical Society Thomas A. Hill House (942-5766), 159 Union Street (at High Street), Bangor. Open March to mid-December, Tuesday through Friday 12–4 (also Sunday, July through September). Admission is $2 per adult, $.50 per student. Downstairs has been restored to its 19th-century grandeur with Victorian furnishings and an elegant double parlor, while changing exhibits of city memorabilia are housed upstairs in this Greek Revival house. Architecture buffs might also want to check out the neighboring **Isaac Farrar Mansion** (941-2808), 166 Union Street, open weekdays 9–4 ($1 admission). A restored Greek Revival lumber baron's mansion with marble fireplaces, mahogany paneling, and stained-glass windows.

Mount Hope Cemetery in Bangor is one of the nation's oldest garden cemeteries, designed by noted Maine architect Charles G. Bryant.

BUS TOURS AND BOAT EXCURSIONS

Best of Bangor Bus Tours, sponsored by the Bangor Historical Society, are offered on Thursday in July, August, and September, departing from the Bangor Visitors Information Office at 519 Main Street (see *Guidance*) at 10:30 AM; $3 per adult, $1 per child.

Voyageur (948-5500), Bangor's new 193-passenger vessel sails daily except Tuesday in the summer, offering 1- and 2-hour cruises on the Penobscot River. Combined rail and sail excursions are also offered, featuring a ride on the Belfast & Moosehead Railroad along with the river cruise.

FISHING

Bangor Salmon Pool. A gathering spot for salmon traveling upstream to spawn; located 2 miles south of Bangor, Route 9 off North Main Street, Brewer.

GOLF

Bangor Municipal Golf Course (945-9226), Webster Avenue; 18 holes. **Penobscot Valley Country Club** (866-2423), Bangor Road, Orono; 18 holes. **Hermon Meadow Golf Club** (848-3741), Hermon; nine holes.

SWIMMING

Jenkin's Beach. Popular beach on Green Lake for families with children. Store and snack bar.

Violette's Public Beach and Boat Landing (843-6876), East Holden (between Ellsworth and Bangor). $2 admission. Popular spot for college students and young adults. Swim float with slide, boat launch, and picnic tables.

DOWNHILL AND CROSS-COUNTRY SKIING

Hermon Mountain (848-5192), Newburg Road, Hermon. (3 miles off I-95 on Exit 43 Carmel, or off Route 2 from Bangor). Popular local ski area, with 17 runs (the longest is 3500 feet); rentals available; base lodge, night skiing, snowboarding.

Hermon Meadow Ski Touring Center (848-3471) Approximately 6 miles of groomed trails on a golf course.

LODGING

Highlawn Bed and Breakfast (866-2272) 193 Main Street, Orono 04773. This majestic white house with front columns has been a bed & breakfast for nine years this season. Six of the seventeen rooms in this 1803 house are pretty guest rooms, but only three are rented at a time, giving each a private bath. Full breakfast (maybe pancakes or omelets) is included in the $40–60 rate.

The Lucerne Inn (843-5123), RFD 2, Box 540, Lucerne-in-Maine 04429. A 19th-century mansion on Route 1A, overlooking Phillips Lake in East Holden. Best known as a restaurant (see *Dining Out*), it also has 25 rooms with private baths, working fireplaces, heated towel bars, whirlpool baths, phones, and TVs. $78–128 depending on the season for standard rooms, $98–143 for suites, including a full breakfast.

☞✐**Hamstead Farm** (848-3749), RFD 3, Box 703, Bangor 04401. Open year-round. Barns and outbuildings trail picturesquely behind a snug 1840s farmhouse. There are three pleasant guest rooms (one with private bath) with a cozy, country-style decor. Resident animals include 70 turkeys, 40 cows, 15 breed sows, 100 feeder pigs, and any number of kittens. The farm is set on 150 acres; a path leads into the village of Hermon. $45–50 double, $35–40 single includes a farm breakfast.

Colonial Winterport Inn (223-5307), Route 1A, Main Street, PO Box 525, Winterport 04496. Ten miles west of Bangor on Route 1A, a chapter in local history has been reclaimed by Ontario couple Duncan and Judie Macnab. The vintage 1834 inn originally served travelers and freight vessels sailing upriver; in winter months they had to off-load here because the river usually became icebound at this point (hence "Winterport"). This is a full-service inn with seven guest rooms furnished in Victorian antiques and floral prints; $50–65 per couple including breakfast ($10 per additional person), $125 per person off-season includes 2 nights and one dinner.

WHERE TO EAT

DINING OUT

Lucerne Inn (843-5123), Route 1A, East Holden (11 miles out of Bangor, headed for Ellsworth). Open for lunch and dinner daily, Sunday brunch. A grand old mansion with a view of Phillips Lake. Specialties include shrimp Nicoise and veal Normandy. $11.95–19.95.

Seguino's Italian Restaurant (942-1240), 735 Main Street, Bangor. A series of small dining rooms and terraces creates an intimate atmosphere in this big old house. The menu is vast: a dozen varieties of antipasti, pasta dishes, veal dishes, and seafood and chicken choices. Try the veal Saltimbuca ("jump in the mouth," sautéed in wine, garlic, and butter, with mozzarella, prosciutto, ham, and sage). $10–16.

Pilot's Grill (942-6325), 1528 Hammond Street (Route 2, 1.5 miles west of Exit 45B off I-95), Bangor. Open daily 11:30–9:30. Most people will tell you this is the best place to eat in town: a large, long-established place with 1950s decor and a huge, all-American menu. $7–15.

The Greenhouse (945-4040), 193 Broad Street, Bangor. Lunch Tuesday through Friday, dinner Tuesday through Saturday. Tropical plants and an exotic menu are not what you'd expect to find in Bangor. We suggest coming for lunch on a warm summer day: there's a large riverside deck. $10–18.

☞ **Jasmine's** (866-4200), 28 Mill Street, Orono. Open weekdays for lunch and dinner, weekend brunch menu 9–1:30. An intimate restaurant featuring northern Italian cuisine made with fresh, regional products. The first Wednesday and Thursday of every month are "Calamari Club" nights, serving a variety of unique calamari dishes. Tuesdays are "pasta 'til busta" nights (all you can eat pasta with choice of sauce). Regular menus include a large variety of seafood, veal, chicken, and vegetarian dishes. $7.95–11.95.

EATING OUT

Bagel Shop (947-1654), 1 Main Street, Bangor. Open Monday to Thursday 6–6; Friday 6–5; Sunday 6–2. A big, genuine, reasonably priced kosher restaurant, delicatessen, and bakery that features egg dishes, bagels, and chocolate cheesecake.

✎ **Governor's Take Out and Eat In** (947-7704), 643 Broadway in Bangor; and Stillwater Avenue in Stillwater (827-4277). Open from early breakfast to late dinner: big breakfast menu, hamburgers to steaks, specials like German potato soup, fresh strawberry pie, ice cream.

Dysart's (942-4878), Coldbrook Road, Hermon (I-95, Exit 44). Open 24 hours. Billed as "the biggest truck stop in Maine"—one room for the general public and another for drivers. Known for great road food and reasonable prices. Homemade bread and seafood are specialties.

Pat's Pizza (866-2111), Mill Street, Orono. A local landmark, especially popular with high school and university students and families. Now franchised throughout the state, but this is the real thing with booths and a jukebox, back dining room and downstairs tap room, plus Pat and his family still in charge. Pizza, sandwiches, full dinners.

ENTERTAINMENT

Maine Center for the Arts, at the University of Maine campus in Orono, has become *the* cultural center for the area. It's now home to the **Bangor Symphony Orchestra** (942-5555), the oldest continuously running community symphony orchestra in the US.

Penobscot Theater (942-3333), 183 Main Street, Bangor.

Maine Masque Theater (581-2000). Classic and contemporary plays presented October through May at the University of Maine, Orono.

Bass Park (942-9000), 100 Dutton Street, Bangor. Complex includes **Bangor Auditorium, Civic Center, State Fair,** and **Raceway** (featuring harness racing, Thursday through Sunday, May to July).

SELECTIVE SHOPPING

BOOKSTORES
Betts' Bookstore (947-7052), 26 Main Street, Bangor, a full-service bookstore specializing in Stephen King titles.
Mr. Paperback. Bangor is home base for this eastern Maine chain, with stores here at Main Square (942-6494) and Airport Mall (942-9191). All are fully stocked stores with Maine sections.
BookMarc's (942-3206), 10 Harlow Street, Bangor. A great little full-service bookstore.
The Booksource, Crossroads Plaza, Bangor. A superstore with special emphasis on multimedia and children's books.

CANOES
Old Town Canoe Factory Outlet Store (827-5513), 130 North Main Street, Old Town. Varieties sold include fiberglass, wood, Kevlar, Crosslink, and Royalex. Factory tour video shows how canoes are made.

SPECIAL SHOPS
Winterport Boot Shop, Twin City Plaza, Brewer. Largest selection of Redwing workboots in the Northeast. Proper fit for sizes 4–16, all widths.
The Briar Patch (941-0255), on West Market Square, Bangor. A large and exceptional children's book and toy store.
The Grasshopper Shop (945-3132), West Market Square, Bangor. So many items, they now have two stores across the street from each other. Trendy women's clothing, toys, jewelry, gifts, housewares.
The Bangor Mall, Hogan Road (just west of the I-95 Exit 49 interchange). Boasts more than 80 stores and has spawned a number of satellite minimalls. Since this is precisely the kind of strip most visitors come to Maine to escape, we won't elaborate; but it certainly has its uses.

SPECIAL EVENTS

May: **Bangor Antiquesfest,** Bass Park.
July: **Bangor State Fair,** Bass Park—agricultural fair with harness racing.
December: **Festival of Trees,** Bangor Mall.

Washington County, Campobello, and St. Andrews

As Down East as you can get in this country, Washington County is a ruggedly beautiful and lonely land unto itself. Its 921-mile coast harbors some of the most dramatic cliffs and deepest coves—certainly the highest tides on the eastern seaboard—but relatively few tourists. Lobster boats and trawlers still outnumber pleasure craft.

Created in 1789 by order of the General Court of Massachusetts, Washington County is as large as the states of Delaware or Rhode Island. Yet it is home to just 32,000 people widely scattered among fishing villages, canning towns, logging outposts, Native American reservations, and saltwater farms. Many people (not just some) survive here by raking blueberries in August, making balsam wreaths in winter, and lobstering, clamming, and digging sea worms the remainder of the year.

Less than 10 percent of the visitors who get as far as Bar Harbor come this much farther. The only "groups" you see are scouting for American bald eagles or osprey in the Moosehorn National Wildlife Refuge, for puffins, auks, and arctic terns on Machias Seal Island, or for whales in the Bay of Fundy. You may also see fishermen angling for Atlantic salmon in the tidal rivers or for landlocked salmon and smallmouth bass in the lakes.

Recently word has begun to spread that you don't drop off the end of the world beyond Eastport or Campobello despite the fact that since 1842—when a boundary was drawn across the face of Passamaquoddy Bay—New England maps have included only the Maine shore and Campobello Island (linked to Lubec, Maine, by a bridge), and Canadian maps have detailed only New Brunswick. In summer when the ferries are running, the day trip from either Eastport or Campobello to St. Andrews (the Bar Harbor of New Brunswick) is, in fact, one of the most scenic in the East; you drive one way and take the ferries the other. The drive is up along the St. Croix River to Calais and via Deer Island—which entails two delightful car ferry rides (one of them free) across Passamaquoddy Bay.

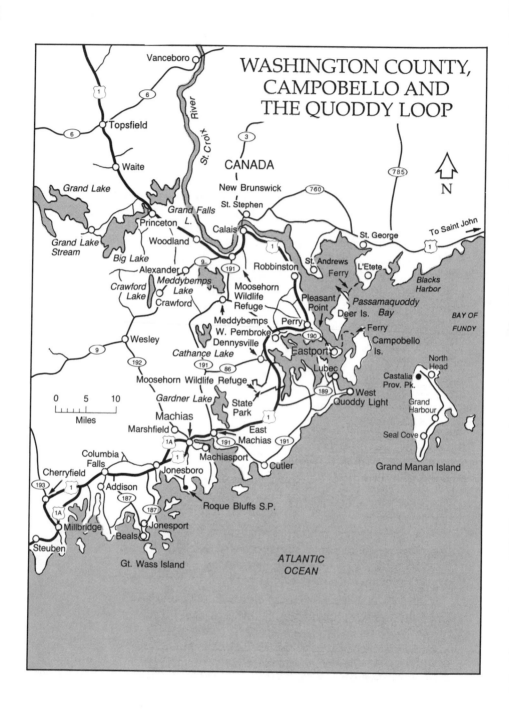

WASHINGTON COUNTY, CAMPOBELLO AND THE QUODDY LOOP

For exploring purposes, Washington County is divided into four distinct regions: (1) the 60-mile stretch of Route 1 between Steuben and Lubec (this actually includes some 600 miles of rugged coast), an area for which Machias is the shopping, dining, and information center; (2) Eastport and Cobscook Bay, the area of the highest tides and an end-of-the-world ambience; (3) Calais and the St. Croix Valley, including the lake-splotched backwoods and the fishermen's havens at Grand Lake Stream; and (4) St. Andrews, New Brunswick.

Wherever you explore in Washington County—from the old sardine-canning towns of Eastport and Lubec to the coastal fishing villages of Jonesport and Cutler and the even smaller villages on the immense inland lakes—you find a Maine that you thought had disappeared decades ago. You are surprised by the beauty of old buildings such as the 18th-century Burnham Tavern in Machias and Ruggles Mansion in Columbia Falls. You learn that the first naval battle of the Revolution was won by Machias men; that some local 18th-century women were buried in rum casks (because they were shipped home that way from the Caribbean); and that Pirate Captain Richard Bellamy's loot is believed to be buried around Machias.

And if any proof were needed that this has always been one isolated piece of coast, there is Bailey's Mistake. Captain Bailey, it seems, wrecked his four-masted schooner one foggy night in a fine little bay 7 miles south of Lubec (which is where he should have put in). Considering the beauty of the spot and how far he was from the Boston shipowner, Bailey and his crew unpacked their cargo of lumber and settled right down on the shore. That was in 1830, and many of their descendants have had the sense to stay put.

Local historians will also tell you why the "Fundy Isles" now belong to Canada rather than to the United States. Daniel Webster, the story goes, drank a few too many toasts the night Lord Ashburton sailed him out to check the boundaries. Campobello and Deer Island, let alone Grand Manan, were barely visible to Webster when he conceded them.

GUIDANCE

Washington County (1-800-377-7948); call to request printed information.

The Machias Bay Area Chamber of Commerce (255-4402), PO Box 606, Machias 04654. Request a copy of "Maine's Washington County" as well as the Machias Bay area directory—a B&B and inn pamphlet. The chamber maintains a year-round information center in the Emporium, a small shopping complex on Route 1, Machias.

The **Calais Information Center** (454-2211), 7 Union Street, Calais. Open year-round and staffed by the Maine Publicity Bureau, it provides material on the entire county and state.

New Brunswick information of all kinds is available by phoning (within North America) 1-800-561-0123. Request a copy of the "New Brunswick Travel Guide."

(Also see *Guidance* for each region.)

GETTING THERE

By air: See the "Bar Harbor and Acadia" chapter, including the *Bangor* section, for scheduled airline service. Charter service is available to the following airports: **Eastport Municipal** (853-2951); **Machias Valley** (255-8709); **Lubec Municipal** (733-5532); and **Princeton Municipal** (796-2744).

By bus: **Vermont Transit** and **Concord Trailways** both serve Bangor year-round; some summers Trailways comes as close as Ellsworth (check: 1-800-639-3317).

By car: There are three equally slow ways to come: (1) I-95 to Augusta, then Route 3 to Belfast (stop at Lake St. George for a swim), then Route 1; (2) I-95 to Bangor, then Route 1A to Ellsworth, then Route 1; (3) for eastern Washington County, take I-95 to Bangor, then the Airline Highway (Route 9) for 100 miles straight through the blueberry barrens and woods to Calais. The state maintains camping and picnic sites at intervals along this stretch, and food and lodging can be found in Beddington, Wesley, Alexander, and Baring.

GETTING AROUND

East Coast Ferries (506-747-2159), based on Deer Island, serve both Campobello (45 minutes) and Eastport (30 minutes). Generally these run every hour from around 9 AM to around 7 PM, mid-June to mid-September, but call Stan Lord to check. The Campobello ferry takes 15 cars, and the Eastport ferry (a fishing boat lashed to a barge) takes 12. **Deer Island** itself is more than a mere stepping-stone in the bay. Roughly 9 miles long and more than 3 miles wide, it's popular with bicyclists and bird-watchers. It boasts the world's largest lobster pound, the original salmon aquaculture site, and a staffed lighthouse. The free, 18-car **Deer Island–L'Etete (New Brunswick mainland) Ferry** (506-453-2600) crossing takes 20 minutes, departing April through September every hour, 7–7, but call to confirm.

MEDICAL EMERGENCY

Calais Regional Hospital (454-7531). **Down East Community Hospital** (255-3356), Machias.

THE ATLANTIC COAST: MILBRIDGE TO CAMPOBELLO

GUIDANCE

The **Machias Bay Area Chamber of Commerce** (255-4402), see *Guidance* in the introduction to this chapter. **The Campobello Tourist Bureau** (506-752-7043), at the entrance to the island, is open daily May to Columbus Day.

TO SEE

Entries are listed geographically, traveling east.

Steuben, the first town in Washington County, is known as the site of the 3135-acre **Petit Manan National Wildlife Refuge** (see *Hiking*).

Milbridge, a Route 1 town with a wandering coastline, is the administrative home of one of the oldest wild-blueberry processors (Jasper Wyman and Sons). The town also supports one of the county's surviving sardine canneries, a Christmas wreath factory, a commercial center with a fine crafts cooperative, and a movie theater. **McClellan Park,** overlooking Narraguagus (pronounced *nair-a-gway-gus*) Bay, offers picnic tables, fireplaces, campsites, rest rooms, and drinking water.

Cherryfield. A few miles up the Narraguagus River, Cherryfield boasts stately houses and a fine Atlantic salmon pool. The **Cherryfield-Narraguagus Historical Society** (546-7979), Main Street (just off Route 1), is open July and August, Wednesday and Friday 1–4, otherwise by appointment May through October. Picnic tables in **Stewart Park** on Main Street and in **Forest Mill Dam Park** on River Road are on the banks of the river. Cherryfield (why isn't it called *Berryfield?*) bills itself "Blueberry Capital of Maine"; there are two processing plants in town.

Columbia Falls is an unusually picturesque village with one of Maine's most notable houses at its center. **The Ruggles House** (1 mile from Route 1; open June to mid-October, Monday through Saturday 9:30–4:30, Sunday 11–4:30) is a Federal-style mansion built by wealthy lumber dealer Thomas Ruggles in 1818. It is a beauty, with a graceful flying staircase, a fine Palladian window, and superb woodwork. Legend has it that a woodcarver was imprisoned in the house for three years with a penknife. There is an unmistakably tragic feel to the place. Mr. Ruggles died soon after its completion, and his heirs petered out in the 1920s.

Jonesport and Beals Island. Jonesport and Beals are both lobstering and fishing villages. Beals is the home of the **Beals Island Regional Shellfish Hatchery** (497-5769), open to the public May through November, daily 9–4. Beals is connected by a bridge to Jonesport, and by a shorter bridge to **Great Wass Island,** probably the county's most popular place to walk (see *Hiking*). Jonesport is the kind of village that seems small the first time you drive through but grows in dimensions as you slow down. Look closely and you will find a colorful marina, several restaurants, grocery stores, antiques shops, bed & breakfasts, chandleries, a hardware/clothing store, a realtor, and much more. Together the towns are home for eastern Maine's largest lobstering fleet, but the big buy at the cooperative in Jonesport is crabmeat.

Jonesboro is represented on Route 1 by a brief lineup of general stores, a church, and a post office. The beauty of this town, however, is in its shoreline, which wanders in and out of points and coves along the tidal Chandler River and Chandler Bay on the way to **Roque Bluffs State Park** (see *Swimming*), 6 miles south of Route 1. A public boat launch with picnic tables is 5 minutes south of Route 1; take the Roque Bluffs Road but turn right onto Evergreen Point Road.

Machias is the county seat, an interesting old commercial center with the Machias River running through town and over the Bad Little Falls. **The Burnham Tavern** (255-4432), tucked up behind the old-fashioned five-and-dime, is open early June to Columbus Day, Monday through Friday 9–5; otherwise by appointment. A 1770s, gambrel-roofed tavern, it's filled with period furnishings and tells the story of British man-of-war *Margaretta*, captured on June 12, 1775, by townspeople in the small sloop *Unity*. This was the first naval battle of the American Revolution. Unfortunately, the British retaliated by burning Portland.

Machias was a hotbed of patriot zeal at the outbreak of the Revolution, an era that can also be savored at **Micmac Farm** in Machiasport. Micmac Farm contains one of Maine's best restaurants (see *Dining Out*), filling two rooms of a low-beamed house built in 1772 by a patriot who fled here from Nova Scotia.

Thanks in part to the presence of the University of Maine at Machias, the town calendar includes frequent concerts and plays (see *Entertainment*). There are also concerts on the Tracker organ in the graceful 1836 **Congregational Church** (centerpiece of the annual Blueberry Festival). Also note the picnic tables and suspension bridge at the falls and the many headstones worth pondering in neighboring **O'Brien Cemetery.**

Early in the 19th century, Machias was second only to Bangor among Maine lumber ports. In 1912 the town boasted an opera house, two newspapers, three hotels, and a trotting park. Today it retains its share of fine houses and is home to the **Maine Wild Blueberry Company,** which processes 250,000 pounds of berries a day and ships them as far as Japan. Billed as the world's largest processor of wild blueberries, Maine Wild is the brainchild of Dr. Amr Ismail, a courtly and portly Egyptian who is generally recognized as Maine's most colorful and effective blueberry promoter.

Machiasport. This picturesque village includes the **Gates House** (open late May through mid-September, Monday through Friday 12:30–4:30), a Federal-style home with maritime exhibits and period rooms. **Fort O'Brien** is an earthwork mound used as an ammunitions magazine during the American Revolution and the War of 1812. We recommend that you continue on down this road to the fishing village of Bucks Harbor and take one of the roads to **Jasper Beach,** so named for the wave-tumbled and polished pebbles of jasper and rhyolite that give it a distinctive color. The road ends with great views and a beach to walk in **Starboard.**

Cutler. From East Machias follow Route 191 south to this small fishing village that's happily shielded from a view of the Cutler navy communications station—said to be the world's most powerful radio station. Its 26 antenna towers (ranging from 800 to 980 feet tall) light up red at night and can be seen from much of the county's coast. Cutler is the departure point for Captain Andy Patterson's excursions to see the puffins on Machias Seal Island (see *Boat Excursions*). Beyond Cutler, Route 191 follows the shoreline through moorlike blueberry and cranberry country but with disappointingly few views. Much of this land is now publicly owned and although paths lead down to the bluff, as yet they are not well marked for public access. In South Trescott bear right onto the unmarked road instead of continuing north on Route 191 and follow the coast through Bailey's Mistake (see chapter introduction) to West Quoddy Light.

West Quoddy Light State Park, South Lubec Road, Lubec. Open mid-April through October, sunrise to sunset. Marking the easternmost tip of the United States, the red-and-white-striped lighthouse dates back to 1858. The park, adjacent to the lighthouse, offers benches from which you are invited to be the first person in the United States to see the sunrise. There is also a fine view of Grand Manan Island, a pleasant picnic area, and a 2-mile hiking trail along the cliffs to Carrying Place Cove. Between the cove and the bay, roughly a mile back down the road from the light, is an unusual coastal, raised-plateau bog with dense sphagnum moss and heath.

West Quoddy Marine Research Station (733-8895), PO Box 9, Lubec 04652 (down the road from the light). Open 10–6 in-season. A visitors center has exhibits about local whales, which include finbacks, humpbacks, and minkes; there are whale tapes, seminars, and nature walks.

Lubec. Most visitors now pass through this "easternmost town" quickly—on their way over the FDR Memorial Bridge to Campobello Island. Take a minute to find the old town landing where there's a public boat launch and a breakwater and a view of "The Sparkplug," as the distinctive little Lubec Channel Light is known. It is just offshore amid very fast-moving currents. Once there were 20 sardine-canning plants in Lubec; the wonder is that there are still two, one now processing salmon (farmed in pens in the bay). Barney Rier has preserved much of the flavor of Lubec's heyday in **The Old Sardine Village Museum** (733-2822), Route 189, on your way into Lubec. Open June through September, Wednesday through Friday 2–5, Saturday 2–3:45. $3 per adult, $2 per teen. A large warehouse-like structure is filled with displays depicting the growth of the food-canning industry from the first hand-formed can of the 1830s; a variety of old machines, photos, and blueberry cannery equipment is also on view.

Roosevelt Campobello International Park (506-752-2922), Welshpool, Campobello Island, New Brunswick, Canada (for a brochure write Box 97,

Lubec 04652). Open daily Memorial Day weekend to mid-October 9–4:45 eastern daylight time (10–5:45 Canadian Atlantic daylight time). Although technically in New Brunswick, this manicured, 2800-acre park with a visitors center and shingled "cottages" is the number-one sight to see east of Bar Harbor. You turn down a side street in Lubec, and there is the bridge (built in 1962) and Canadian customs. The house in which Franklin Delano Roosevelt summered as a boy has disappeared, but the airy "Roosevelt Cottage," a wedding gift to Franklin and Eleanor, is maintained just as the family left it, charged with the spirit of the dynamic man who contracted polio here on August 25, 1921. During his subsequent stints as governor of New York and then as president of the United States, F.D.R. returned only three times. Neighboring Hubbard Cottage, with its oval picture window, gives another slant on this turn-of-the-century resort. There's a visitors center here with an uninspired 15-minute introductory film, and the grounds are backed with flower beds. Beyond stretch more than 8 miles of trails to the shore and then inland through woods to lakes and ponds. There are also 15.4 miles of park drives, modified from the network of carriage drives that the wealthy "cottagers" maintained on the island. Beyond the park is **East Quoddy Head Lighthouse,** accessible at low tide, a popular whale-watching station but a real adventure to get to (attempt only if you are physically fit). Note the small car ferry to Deer Island that runs during July and August (see *Getting Around*) and the description of The Owen House under *Inns and Bed & Breakfasts.* Campobello Park was granted to Captain William Owen in the 1760s and remained in the family until 1881, when it was sold to Boston developers who built large (long-gone) hotels.

TO DO

AIRPLANE RIDES
Sunrise Air-Lubec (733-2124), Lubec. Scenic rides, photos, and fish spotting. **David Rier** (255-8458), scenic rides from the Machias airport.
PUFFIN-WATCHING AND BOAT EXCURSIONS
Machias Seal Island is a prime nesting spot for puffins in June and July, also a place to see razor bill auks and arctic terns in August and September. Although just 9 miles off Cutler, the island is maintained by Canada as a lighthouse station and wildlife refuge. But **Captain Barna Norton** (497-5933) of Jonesport, who has been offering bird-watching cruises to Machias Seal since the 1940s, refuses to concede the island. Since it was never mentioned in the 1842 Webster-Ashburton Treaty, he insists that it was claimed by his grandfather in 1865. Thus he continues to offer puffin-watching and other birding trips to the island, ably assisted by his son John, emphasizing his views on the island by shading himself with an umbrella displaying an American flag on top.

Captain Andrew Patterson's **Bold Coast Charter Company** (259-4484) is based in Cutler, just 9 miles from Machias Seal Island to which he also offers frequent bird-watching trips from May to August. Captain Patterson also uses his 40-foot passenger vessel *Barbara Frost* to cruise the coast, to visit the Cross Island Wildlife Refuge at the mouth of Machias Bay, and, on special request, to go to Grand Manan Island.

CANOEING

The **Machias River,** fed by the five Machias lakes, drops through the backwoods with technically demanding rapids and takes three to six days to run. The Narraguagus and East Machias Rivers are also good for trips of two to four days. For rentals, lessons, advice, and guided tours, see **Sunrise County Canoe Expeditions** (454-7708) in the *Calais and the St. Croix Valley* part of this chapter.

FISHING

Salmon fishing is the reason many people come to this area (see Cherryfield under *To See*); the Narraguagus and Machias Rivers are popular places to fish mid-May through early June. Six Mile Lake in Marshfield (6 miles north of Machias on Route 192), with picnic facilities, shelters, and a boat ramp, is known for trout. For information about licenses, guides, and fish, write to the regional headquarters of the **Inland Fisheries and Wildlife Department,** Machias 04654.

GOLF

Great Cove Golf Course (434-2981), Jonesboro Road, Roque Bluffs, offers nine holes, water views, clubhouse, rental clubs, and carts.

Herring Cove Golf Course (506-752-2449), in the Herring Cove Provincial Park (open mid-May to mid-November), has nine holes, a clubhouse restaurant, and rentals.

HIKING

(Also see West Quoddy Light State Park under *To See* and Schoodic Mountain in the "Bar Harbor and Acadia Area" chapter.)

Great Wass Island. A 1540-acre tract at the southern tip of the Jonesport-Addison peninsula. The interior of the island supports one of Maine's largest jack-pine stands and has coastal peatlands maintained by the Maine chapter of The Nature Conservancy. There is a choice of trails; we prefer the 2-mile trek along the shore to Little Cape Point, where children can clamber on the smooth rocks for hours. Bring a picnic.

Petit Manan National Wildlife Refuge, Petit Manan Point, Steuben (6 miles off Route 1 on Pigeon Hill Road). A varied area with pine stands, cedar swamps, blueberry barrens, marshes, and great birding; a 5-mile shore path hugs the woods and coastline.

Roosevelt Campobello International Park. At the tourist information center pick up a trail map. We recommend the trail from Southern Head to the Duck Ponds. Seals frequently sun on the ledges off Lower Duck Pond and loons are frequently seen off Liberty Point. Along this dramatic shoreline at the southern end of the island, also look for whales

July through September. At Eagle Hill Bog a boardwalk spans a peat bog with interpretive panels.

The Bold Coast. Trails are presently being developed from Route 191 to the cliffs east of Cutler, overlooking Grand Manan Channel. Maine's Bureau of Public Lands owns 100 acres of uneven moor and rugged shoreline here; a loop path from the road to the cliffs and along the shore is due to be completed sometime in 1995. For details contact the bureau regional office in Old Town at 827-5936.

PICNICKING

McClellan Park in Milbridge, 5 miles south of town at Baldwin's Head, overlooking the Atlantic and Narraguagus Bay (from Route 1, follow Wyman Road to the park gates). A town park on 10½ acres donated in 1926 by George McClellan, a one-time mayor of New York City and subsequently a professor of economic history at Princeton. There's no charge for walking or picnicking. (Also see *Campgrounds.*)

SWIMMING

Roque Bluffs State Park, Roque Bluffs (6 miles off Route 1). There is a pebble beach on the ocean, frequently too windy to use even in August. A sheltered sand beach on a freshwater pond is the ideal place for children. Facilities include tables, grills, changing areas with vault toilets, and a children's playground.

Gardner Lake, Chases Mills Road, East Machias, offers freshwater swimming, a picnic area, and a boat launch. **Six Mile Lake,** Route 192, North Machias, is also good for a dip. On Beals Island, the **Backfield Area,** Alley's Bay, offers saltwater swimming.

WHALE-WATCHING

The unusually high tides in the Bay of Fundy seem to foster ideal feeding grounds for right, minke, and humpback whales and for porpoises and dolphins. East Quoddy Head on Campobello and West Quoddy Head in Lubec are favored viewing spots. Two father-and-son teams, the Nortons (see *Puffin-Watching and Boat Excursions*) and the Harrises (see *Boat Excursions* under *Eastport*), offer whale-watching cruises. **Cline Marine** (506-529-4188) also offers 2-hour whale-watching cruises from Head Harbour on Campobello Island.

LODGING

INNS AND BED & BREAKFASTS

Entries are listed geographically, heading east.

☞✐**Ricker House** (546-2780), Cherryfield 04622. Open year-round. A classic Federal house built in 1803 with a double parlor, furnished comfortably with plenty of books and an inviting country kitchen. There are three guest rooms (two with river views), nicely furnished with antiques and old quilts, sharing one bath. A path leads to a picnic table by the river, and the tennis courts across the road are free; there are also lawn games: horseshoes

Living room in the Roosevelt Cottage on Campobello Island

BRIAN SWARTZ

and croquet. The Conways keep a two-volume photo album, "Adventures from Ricker House" on their coffee table and are delighted to help guests explore the area, especially on foot or by canoe. $45–50 per room ($10 per extra person) includes a full breakfast.

Pleasant Bay Bed & Breakfast (483-4490), PO Box 222, West Side Road, Addison 04606. Open year-round. After raising six children and a number of llamas in New Hampshire, Leon and Joan Yeaton cleared this land and built themselves a large, gracious house with many windows and a deck and porch overlooking the Pleasant River. Opening onto the deck is a large, sunny room with couches, a piano, and a fireplace, and an adjoining open kitchen and dining room, all with water views. A more formal living room is well stocked with puzzles and books for foggy days. This is a 110-acre working llama farm, and guests are invited to meander the wooded trails down to the bay, either accompanied or unaccompanied by llamas. There are three guest rooms, one particularly attractive one with private bath, all with water views, also an apartment above the barn. $45–65 per couple ($10 per additional child) includes a splendid breakfast of fresh fruit and, if you're lucky, Joan's popover/pancake.

Tootsie's Bed and Breakfast (497-5414), RFD 1, RRO, Box 252, Jonesport 04649. This was the first bed & breakfast in Washington County, and it is still one of the nicest. Charlotte Beal ("Tootsie" as her grandchildren call her) offers two rooms—nothing fancy, but homey and spanking clean—and routinely makes a 6 AM breakfast for guests who need to leave at 6:45 to catch Barna Norton's boat (see *Puffin-Watching*). The shipshape house sits in a cluster of lobstermen's homes on the fringe of this fishing village, handy to Great Wass Island. $25–40 includes a full breakfast. Pets are occasionally accommodated if they are small and well behaved.

Jonesport "By The Sea" (497-2590), PO Box 541, Main Street, Jonesport 04649. Open year-round. Sited in the center of the village with five rooms and an antiques shop; $40–50 includes continental breakfast.

Chandler River Bed & Breakfast (434-2651; off-season: 908-679-2778), Jonesboro 04648. Open July and August only. Operated by the Kerr family for 30 years; the feel is that of someone's summer home that just happens to have six extra bedrooms, one that's actually a five-person suite; all share one full and one half-bath; $45 per room includes breakfast.

Riverside Bed & Breakfast (255-4134), East Machias 04630. Open year-round. This Victorian house fronts on Route 1, but the back rooms and deck overlook the East Machias River. Tom and Carol Paul owned an antiques shop in Newport before creating this attractive way station, which is pure 1890s—right down to the antique linens. Note the old train-baggage rack over the claw-foot tub. In 1994 there were two rooms in the main house (private baths) and a guest house suite with a balcony and kitchen facilities; another downstairs suite was planned for '95; $45–75 includes a full breakfast; the specialty is blueberry stuffed French toast. Carol is well known in the area for the quality of her dinners (see *Dining Out*).

Little River Lodge (259-4437), Box 237, Cutler 04626. Open May through October. Built in 1845 as a logging camp, converted to a hotel in 1870 when the Eastern Steamship ferries stopped here; nicely decorated. Carl and Nancy Sundberg offer seven bedrooms, some with fireplaces, sharing three baths. We slept well and woke up renewed here. A dining room overlooks Cutler Harbor. Dinner is served by reservation and has a great local reputation (see *Dining Out*). Double $40–60, $75 with private bath, includes breakfast.

Home Port Inn (733-2077 or 1-800-457-2077), 45 Main Street, Lubec 04652. Open April through October. Tim and Miyoko Carman offer seven antiques-furnished rooms (two on the ground floor, all with private baths) in a gracious old hilltop Lubec home, built in 1880. Breakfast and dinner are served (see *Dining Out*). $60–75 double.

Peacock House (733-2403), 27 Summer Street, Lubec 04652. Open late May 15 to October 15. An 1880s house on a quiet side street, home to four generations of the Peacock family (owners of the major local cannery). There are five guest rooms that, like the formal common rooms, are immaculate; one is handicapped accessible. $55–75 with a full breakfast.

☞⌀**Christie's of South Bay** (733-2529), Box 6490, Lubec 04652. Gloria Christie is well known around Lubec as a superb gardener, baker, and cook, and the kitchen of her roadside farmhouse is frequently filled with the aroma of baking herb breads, lasagna, pizza, or whatever she happens to be preparing. Breakfast may well be quiche or freshly made croissants with fresh fruit. The three guest rooms (shared baths) are simply but nicely furnished. Picnics and dinner by advance notice. Pets and children welcome. $48–58 includes breakfast and the 7 percent Maine tax.

The Owen House (506-752-2977), Welshpool, Campobello, New Brunswick, Canada EOG 3HO. Open May through September. This amazing inn is reason enough to visit Campobello. Probably the most historic house on the island, it was built in 1829 by Admiral William Fitzwilliam Owen, son of the British captain to whom the island was granted in 1769. Joyce Morrell, an artist who maintains one room as her gallery, has furnished the nine guest rooms (five with private baths) with friendly antiques, handmade quilts, and good art. Guests gather around an immense breakfast table in the formal dining room, also around one of the many fireplaces in the evening. There are 10 acres of land, and you can walk to the Welshpool dock and take the ferry to Deer Island and back to get out on the bay. $60–73 Canadian plus 11 percent tax (no GST).

COTTAGES

The choice of rental cottages in Washington County has increased substantially in recent years. The Machias Bay Chamber publishes the "Vacation Rental Guide"; and a number of additional listings can be found in the booklet "Maine Guide to Camp & Cottage Rentals," available from the **Maine Publicity Bureau** (see *Information* in "What's Where in Maine"). Summer rentals in this area still begin at around $300 per week. Our own family has spent many rewarding weeks over the years at **Windrise Farm** (434-2701) in Jonesboro.

Micmac Farm Guest Cabins (255-3008), Machiasport 04655. Open May to November. Best known for their restaurant (see *Dining Out*), Barbara and Daniel Dunn also offer several housekeeping cabins. Each has two double beds and a view of the Machias River through sliding glass doors. A real find at $50–60 daily per unit, $300–375 per week.

MOTELS

Machias Motor Inn (255-4861), Route 1 next to Helen's. Bob and Joan Carter maintain a two-story, 35-unit motel; most rooms are standard units, each with two double, extra-long beds, cable TV, and a phone. Rooms feature decks overlooking the Machias River. There are six efficiency units, and Helen's Restaurant, serving three meals, is part of the complex. $60 double, $70–80 for efficiencies, $85 for a two-bedroom apartment. Pets accepted.

Blueberry Patch Inn (434-5411), Jonesboro 04648. Jerry and Daisy Herger's spick-and-span motel on Route 1 is in the village of Jonesboro next door to the Whitehouse Restaurant. Each unit has a refrigerator, air-conditioning, phone, TV, and coffee; two efficiencies, a pool, and sun deck surrounded by berries. $30–45 in-season.

CAMPGROUNDS

McClellan Park, Milbridge. Open Memorial to Columbus Day. See *Picnicking* under *To Do* for more on this dramatically sited town-owned park that's free for day use but charges $3 for tenting, $5 for full campsites; 18 campsites and water are available, but no showers. For details phone Town Hall at 546-2422.

Henry Point Campground, Kelly Point Road, Jonesport. Open April through November. Surrounded on three sides by water, this is another great town-owned campground that's usually got space (its crunch weekend is July 4). Neither showers nor water are available, but you can shower and use the laundromat at the Jonesport Shipyard across the cove. Good water is also available from an outside faucet at the town hall. This is a put-in place for sea kayaks. Turn off Route 187 at the Purple House.

Herring Cove Provincial Park (506-752-2396), Campobello Island. Adjoining the Roosevelt Campobello International Park is this provincial-park campground offering 87 campsites; there's a beach, a golf course, and extensive hiking trails.

(Also see Cobscook Bay State Park in "Eastport and Cobscook Bay.")

WHERE TO EAT

DINING OUT

Micmac Farm Restaurant (255-3008), Machiasport. Open year-round (except for 2 weeks at Christmas), Tuesday through Saturday 6 PM–9 PM, by reservation. Located down a bumpy dirt road off Route 92. You wouldn't think anyone could find it, but it tends to be full most summer evenings. Last season the Dunns had to turn away customers, but they don't want to enlarge and risk losing "some of the present ambience and charm." The restaurant is in an exquisite riverside house built in 1776 by Ebenezer Gardner, a patriot refugee from Nova Scotia. Just 25 diners can be seated in the low-beamed dining room, and meals are served by candlelight. From her minute kitchen, Elizabeth Dunn produces a choice of five entrées, which might include tenderloin Stroganoff, lobster graziella, and filet mignon bordelaise. Full dinners run $15–18. BYOB, since the town is dry.

Riverside Inn (255-4134), East Machias. Dinner nightly except Friday by reservation. Tables line the sun porch overlooking the East Machias River and fill a lacy, flowery dining room. Innkeeper Carol Paul's reputation as a chef is golden. A choice of chicken, beef, and seafood entrées is offered, part of a soup-to-dessert menu that might include fillet of sole with wild rice or beef bourguignon. Full dinners run $14.95–15.95. BYOB.

Seafarer's Wife (497-2365), Jonesport. Open except January Tuesday through Saturday, 5:30–8:30 PM by reservation only. Two very Victorian rooms in a Main Street house, with long-skirted waitresses serving a choice of a half dozen entrées ranging from chicken to "Fisherman's Bounty" (a baked medley of shrimp, lobster, halibut, scallops, and more). Faye Carver is the owner-chef and her local reputation is sterling. Complete dinners, from hors d'ouevres through soup and salad to dessert, are $13.95–19.95. BYOB.

The Home Port Inn (733-2077), 45 Main Street, Lubec. Open nightly Memorial Day weekend through September. The attractive dining room in the back of this inn contains just eight well-spaced tables. Innkeeper Tim Carman has brought extensive restaurant experience to this effort and provides a full menu featuring seafood dishes like coquilles Saint-Jacques. Entrées run $8.99–13.99.

Little River Lodge (259-4437), Cutler. Seasonal. Dinner is served by reservation in the small dining room of this attractive, locally favored inn overlooking the harbor. $15–20 prix fixe.

EATING OUT

Entries are listed geographically, heading east.

Milbridge House (546-2020), Main Street, Milbridge. Open early and late, a great family-owned restaurant that's bigger and more attractive than it looks from the road. Don't pass up the pies.

The Red Barn (546-7721), Main Street (junction of Routes 1 and 1A), Milbridge. Open daily year-round, 6 AM. There is a counter in the back, an abundance of deep booths in the main, pine-paneled dining room, and more seating in the overflow "banquet" room. The menu is large: pastas, burgers, steak, seafood, and fried chicken. Children's menu, great cream pies. Inexpensive to moderate.

Cherryfield Inn Restaurant, Cherryfield. Open year-round 6–1:30 for breakfast and lunch, Wednesday through Saturday for dinner; Friday night fish-fry, Saturday night smorgasbord.

The Blue Beary (546-2052), Route 1, Cherryfield. Open 11–9, a friendly dining room; also a picnic area featuring fresh-dough pizza (try the garlic and cheese), homemade soups and pies.

Perry's Seafood, Route 1, Columbia. Open daily, 6 AM–9 PM. Easy to pass by without noticing, favored by locals for dinner as well as other meals; try the homemade onion rings and the special of the day.

Tall Barney, Main Street, Jonesport. Open 7–7. Don't be put off by the exterior of this local gathering spot, set back behind its parking lot across from the access to the big bridge. It is particularly welcoming for breakfast on a foggy morning. The papers are stacked on the counter, and the booths are filled with local people. Just don't sit at the long table down the middle of the front room the way we did. No one says anything, but it's obvious, after a while, that it's reserved for the local lobstermen, who come drifting in one by one.

JP Lobster (497-5971), Main Street, Jonesport. Open daily 11:30–10:30 in-season, check in shoulder seasons. This relatively new but old-style lobster pound (the lobsters are kept healthy in tanks of circulating seawater) is run by one of the area's long-standing fishing families. The crabmeat stew ($5.75) is alone worth the 11-mile drive down Route 187 from Route 1. The pies are also outstanding.

The Whitehouse (434-2792), Route 1, Jonesboro. Open 5 AM–9 PM. Look for the red-striped awnings. Inside are cheery blue booths, a counter, and friendly service. Memorable breakfasts, outstanding fish chowder (much better than the lobster); specialties include fried seafood platters and delectable pies.

The Artist's Cafe at the Ferris Wheel Emporium, Route 1, Machias. A small upstairs café featuring unusual homemade soups and sandwich breads adjoining a small but noteworthy art gallery.

Helen's Restaurant (255-6506), 32 Main Street, Machias (north of town on the water). Open 5:30 AM–9:30 PM. Geared to bus groups en route from Campobello to Bar Harbor, but there's plenty of room for everybody. Generous servings: a wide choice of seafood, meat entrées, salads, fish stews, and sandwiches. "Whipped" pies are a specialty: strawberry, blueberry, and a dozen more. Try blueberry pancakes in-season.

Graham's Restaurant (255-3351), Lower Main Street, Machias. Open year-round for all three meals. A diner atmosphere for breakfast and lunch, but the dining room (with banquet room) features live boiled lobster, seafood, salad bar, homemade pies, and cocktails at dinner.

Hillside Restaurant (733-4223), Route 189, Lubec. Open every day except Tuesday in-season, 11 AM–9 PM. "We're not fancy, and we don't have a view, but we serve the kind of food that brings folks back," boast the ads for this main-drag eatery. Get some fish chowder and a lobster salad sandwich from the take-out window and bring it down to the breakwater.

Lupine Lodge (752-2487), Campobello. Open 12–9. A former log "cottage" that has been hoakied up by a developer, but the restaurant retains its old hearth and some charm; a predictable menu, moderately priced.

Players (752-2467), Campobello. A café at the golf club, good for breakfast, lunch, and informal dinner, specializing in fish-and-chips; vague views of the water.

Friar's Bay Restaurant, Campobello. This is the third obvious place to eat on Campobello and gets both rave reviews and complaints from patrons; we're told the quality depends on who's on the job. Good water views.

SNACKS

Sugar Scoop Bakery (546-7048), Main Street, Milbridge. Open Tuesday through Saturday 5 AM–6 PM. Good for a cup of coffee and a freshly baked doughnut or turnover, even a chicken pie or baked beans and brown bread.

The Islander (497-2000), Alleys Bay Road, Great Wass Island. Open in-season 3–9 PM. The back of the house is toward the water and in summer becomes a great take-out place, with a deck for consuming fried clams and soft ice cream. The place to stop after a 4-mile hike (see *Hiking*).

ENTERTAINMENT

Milbridge Theater (546-2038), Main Street, Milbridge. Open nightly May through November, 7:30 show time; Saturday and Sunday matinees for children's films; all seats $3.50. A very special theater: a refurbished movie house featuring first-run and art movies with truly affordable prices. Fresh popcorn, ice-cream parlor.

University of Maine, Machias (255-3313, ext. 284), offers both a winter and summer series of plays, musicals, and concerts.

DownRiver Theater Productions (255-4997) stages plays June through August at Gay's Wreath Building, Marshfield Ridge Road, Machias. Productions are a mix of safe musicals like *The Sound of Music* and *Cabaret* and original plays. Tickets are $8 per adult, $7 for seniors and students.

Machias Bay Chamber Concerts (255-3889), Center Street Congregational Church, Machias. A series of eight chamber music concerts, July through early August, Tuesday at 8 PM. Top groups such as the Kneisel Hall Chamber Players and the Vermeer Quartet are featured.

SELECTIVE SHOPPING

Entries are listed geographically, heading east.

Hands On! A Gallery of Fine Maine Crafts (546-7926), Route 1, Milbridge. Open daily June through September, 9:30–5:30. An outlet for work by 35 outstanding local craftspeople, including weavers, potters, quilters, a jeweler, a metal sculptor, and a woodworker. So special that they demand mention are contemporary quilts by Carol Schutt, Old World Pottery Mocha Ware by Roscoe Mann (the two are married), and metal sculptures by Peter Weil.

Sea-Witch (546-7495), Milbridge. Describing itself as "the biggest little gift shop in Washington County," this is a trove of trinkets and treasures: collector dolls, spatterware, stuffed animals, local seafood, and berry products.

Columbia Falls Pottery (483-4075), Main Street, Columbia Falls. Open year-round. Striking, bright, sophisticated terra-cotta creations by April Adams and Alan Burnham: mugs, platters, kitchenware, lamps, wind chimes, and more.

Crossroads Vegetables (497-2641), posted from Route 187 (off Route 1), Jonesport. Open daily, 9–5:30 in-season. Bonnie and Arnold Pearlman have built their house, windmill, sauna, and barn and have reclaimed acres of productive vegetable garden from the surrounding woods. In addition to their outstanding vegetables (salad lovers get their greens picked to order; Bonnie adds the edible parts of flowers like nasturtium), they also sell the hand-hollowed wooden bowls that Arnold carves all winter and the dried flower wreaths that Bonnie makes.

The Ferris Wheel Emporium (255-4649), Machias. Open May to December. This is a showcase for more than 5 dozen Washington County craftspeople and entrepreneurs who can't afford their own stores. The array of antiques, clothing, wooden toys, and pottery makes for good browsing.

The Sow's Ear (255-4066), 7 Water Street, Machias. A gift store featuring jewelry, clothing, books, toys, and cards.

Country Duckling (255-8063), 1 Water Street, Machias. Locally made handcrafted gifts.

Downeast 5 & 10 Cents (255-8850), Water Street, Machias. Open Monday through Saturday 9–5 and until 8 on Friday. A superb, old-fashioned Ben Franklin store: two stories of crammed aisles.

Connie's Clay of Fundy (255-4574), Route 1, East Machias. Open year-round. Connie Harter-Bagley's combination studio/shop is filled with her distinctive, glazed earthenware in deep colors with minimal design. Bowls, pie plates, platters, lamps, and a variety of small essentials like garlic jars and ring boxes.

CHRISTMAS WREATHS

Wreath-making is a major industry in this area. You can order in the fall and take delivery of a freshly made wreath right before Christmas. Prices quoted include delivery. Sources are: **Cape Split Wreaths** (483-2983), Box 447, Route 1, Addison 04606; **Simplicity Wreath** (483-2780), Sunset Point, Harrington 04643; **The Wreath Shoppe** (483-4598), Box 358, Oak Point Road, Harrington 04643 (wreaths decorated with cones, berries, and reindeer moss); and **Maine Coast Balsam** (255-3301), Box 458, Machias 04654 (decorations include cones, red berries, and bow).

SPECIAL EVENTS

July: **Independence Day** celebrations in Jonesport/Beals (lobster boat races, easily viewed from the bridge); Cherryfield (parade and fireworks); and Steuben (fireman's lobster picnic and parade). **Homecoming Celebration,** in Machiasport, sponsored by the historical society, features clam/lobster feed, tour of the Gates House, church services, and Milbridge annual homecoming.

August: **Blueberry Festival and Machias Craft Festival** (third weekend) in downtown Machias—sponsored by Penobscot Valley Crafts and Center Street Congregational Church: concerts, food, major crafts fair, and live entertainment.

EASTPORT AND COBSCOOK BAY

There is a haunting, end-of-the-world feel to Eastport with its 19th-century storefronts along Water Street and its sole-surviving sardine factory. Eastport prides itself on being the birthplace of the sardine industry (the canning process was invented by Julius Wolfe in 1875, and, at one time, 18 canneries were all operating full tilt). Today the town is making a comeback as a base for salmon farming operations. You can see the pens in both Cobscook and Passamaquoddy Bays from the overlook in the new park at Shackford Head.

Eastport was occupied by the British for four years during the War of 1812, a tale told in the Barracks Museum. One of the old cannons used to fend off the enemy still stands in front of the Peavey Library. A "city" of 2500 people (less than half its turn-of-the-century population), Eastport has many gaps in its old waterfront, which has been walled with a pink granite seawall to form Overlook Park.

This is a good spot from which to get out on Passamaquoddy Bay, either in a sailboat or an excursion boat, to watch the area's summer gathering of whales, and to view "Old Sow," a whirlpool off Deer Island that's billed as the world's second largest. If nothing else, take the ferry to Deer Island and back.

Eastport is on an island connected to the mainland by a series of causeways linking other islands. In the center of the Pleasant Point Indian Reservation, situated on one of these islands, the Waponahki Museum tells the story of the Passamaquoddy tribe, past and present.

GUIDANCE

Eastport Chamber of Commerce (853-4644), 78 Water Street, Eastport 04631. Open late May to mid-September, Monday through Friday 11–3.

TO SEE

Barracks Museum, 23A Washington Street, Eastport. Open Memorial Day to Labor Day, Tuesday through Saturday 11–4. Originally part of Fort Sullivan, occupied by the British during the War of 1812, this house has been restored to its 1820s appearance as an officers' quarters and displays old photos and memorabilia about Eastport in its golden era.

Quoddy Tides Foundation Marine Library, 123 Water Street, Eastport. Open Monday through Friday 10–4; Saturday 10–12. A small, waterfront aquarium, library, and gift shop maintained by the county's largest newspaper.

Waponahki Museum & Resource Center (853-4001), Route 190, Pleasant Point. Open weekdays 9–11 and 1–3. Easy to miss, a small red building near the big IGA. Photos, tools, baskets, and crafts tell the story of the Passamaquoddy tribe.

Reversing Salt Water Falls. From Route 1 in West Pembroke, take the local road out along Leighton Neck, which brings you to a 140-acre park with hiking trails and picnic sites that view the incoming tidal current as it passes between Mahar's Point and Falls Island. As the saltwater flows along at upwards of 25 knots, it strikes a series of rocks, resulting in rapids.

TO DO

AIRPLANE RIDES

Quoddy Air (853-0997) offers scenic rides, whale-watching, and charters.

BOAT EXCURSIONS

Whale-watching (853-4303). Captain George Harris and his son Butch sail from Eastport public pier, 1:30 daily in summer. $15 per adult, $7.50 per child 12 and under.

Sailing (726-5151). Bay of Fundy sloop ***Anna,*** a 39-foot recreational version of a once-common workboat in these waters, was built by Tom and Barbara Barnett, who offer day sails out of Eastport, 10 AM and 2 PM. The shallow keel allows them to sail far up tidal creeks as well as across the bay. $15 per adult, children 10 and under $10, minimum charge $45.

Ferry to Deer Island and Campobello. For details about **East Coast**

QUODDY TIDES

Deer Island Ferry and Landing at Eastport

Ferries Ltd. (506-747-2159), based on Deer Island, see *Getting Around* in the chapter introduction.

CANOEING

(See *Calais and the St. Croix Valley.*)

GREEN SPACE

WALKS

Shackford Head (posted from Route 190 south of Eastport) is a new 95-acre park with a mile-long trail from the parking lot to a "viewpoint" overlooking Campobello and Lubec in one direction and Cobscook Bay in the other.

Moosehorn National Wildlife Refuge, Edmunds: 6700 acres bounded by Cobscook Bay and the mouth of the Dennys and Whiting Rivers, with several miles of rocky shoreline.

Gleason's Point, Perry. Take the next right north of The Wigwam on Route 1 and follow it to the beach and boat landing.

LODGING

INNS AND BED & BREAKFASTS

☞ **Weston House** (853-2907), 26 Boynton Street, Eastport 04631. Open year-round. A very elegant, Federal-style house built in 1810 by a Harvard graduate who became a local politician. There are five large guest rooms, one with a working fireplace, views of the bay and gardens, antiques. You can have the Audubon Room (John James Audubon slept here on his way to Labrador in 1833). Rates are $53.50–74.90 for a double, including state tax and a sumptuous breakfast in the formal dining room. Another room with private bath is available with notice ($80.25 including tax). In the off-season, rates also include afternoon tea (complete with scones) and sherry. Dinner and a picnic lunch are also available. The common rooms are furnished with Oriental rugs and wing chairs; but if you want to put your feet up, there is a very comfortable back room with books and a TV, and the gardens are also good places for relaxing. Jett and John Peterson decorate the house for holidays and enjoy guests on all occasions.

☞✐**Todd House** (853-2328), Todd's Head, Eastport 04631. Open year-round. A restored 1775 Cape with great water views. Breakfast is served in the common room in front of the huge old fireplace. In 1801, men met here to charter a Masonic Order, and in 1861 the house became a temporary barracks when Todd's Head was fortified. The house has changed little in a century. The four large double rooms vary in decor, view, and access to baths and range from $45–55. There are also two efficiency suites ($70–80), both with water views. Guests are welcome to use the deck and barbecue. Innkeeper Ruth McInnis welcomes well-behaved children and pets.

The Inn at Eastport (853-4307), 13 Washington Street, Eastport 04631. An early 19th-century house built by the owner of a schooner fleet, now a comfortable, welcoming B&B with four rooms, one with a canopy bed, all with antiques and private baths. Guests can gather in two front parlors (one with a TV) or in the outdoor hot tub. $55–65 includes innkeeper Brenda Booker's very full breakfast, maybe Belgian waffles or scrambled eggs with salmon.

Lincoln House (726-3953), Dennysville 04628. A yellow, four-square mansion built in 1787 by Judge Theodore Lincoln, reportedly an ancestor of President Lincoln. (Audubon stayed here while studying the region's birds.) There are six nicely furnished guest rooms sharing four baths; the two front rooms are the classics, with working fireplaces. The public rooms have wide-pine floorboards, hooked rugs, and an abundance of antiques. Innkeepers Carol and Jerry Haggerty have also restored the 1820 MacLauchlan House just across the Dennys River where they offer four more guest rooms, some handicapped accessible, all with private baths. The dining room is open to the public (see *Dining Out*). $58–72 per person MAP from June through September; add 15 percent service.

MOTEL

The Motel East (853-4747), 23A Water Street, Eastport 04631. This two-story motel has 14 units, some handicapped accessible, all with water views, some with balconies overlooking Campobello Island. Amenities include direct-dial phones, cable TV, some kitchenettes. Handicapped accessible. $70 per night; $85 for a suite.

CAMPGROUND

Cobscook Bay State Park (726-4412), Route 1, Dennysville. Open mid-May to mid-October. Offers 150 camping sites, most of them for tents and many with water views. There are even showers (unusual in Maine state campgrounds). The 864-acre park also offers a boat launch area, picnicking benches, and a hiking and cross-country ski trail. (*Cobscook* means "boiling tides.")

WHERE TO EAT

DINING OUT

Lincoln House (726-3953), Dennysville. Dinner is by reservation at 7 PM, with just one set entrée that changes nightly. It's a prix fixe, multicourse meal, $17.50 plus tax and 15 percent gratuity. Specialties include shrimp Provençal, veal Amelio, and roast tip loin of beef with béarnaise. There are two small dining rooms in this 18th-century house.

EATING OUT

Cap'n T's (853-2307), 75 Water Street, Eastport. Open daily 11–9. Homemade chowders are the specialty, along with baked haddock with lobster sauce and baked scallops; good water views.

La Sardina Loca (853-2739), 28 Water Street, Eastport. Open irregularly for lunch and dinner until midnight. A cheerful bit of Mexico; omelets a specialty.

Kinney's on the Deck (853-4466), Water Street, Eastport. Open daily 9–8 in-season. Built onto the back of a flower shop, this is a great spot on a sunny day when you take advantage of the deck ovelooking the bay. Try the lobster and crabmeat rolls, and don't pass up the pies.

New Waco Diner, Water Street, Eastport. Open year-round, Monday through Saturday 6 AM–9 PM. A friendly haven with booths and a long shiny counter, with menu choices posted on the wall behind. You can get a full roast turkey dinner; there is also beer, pizza, and great squash pie.

Crossroads Restaurant (726-5053), Route 1, "at the Waterfall," Pembroke. Open 11–9 daily. Bigger than it looks from outside, a great road food stop, serving the best lobster roll in the area; deep-fried seafood pies are specialties; liquor served.

ENTERTAINMENT

The **Eastport Arts Center** (853-4166), which occupies the second and third floors of the 1887 Masonic Hall at the corner of Water and Dana Streets, showcases area artists; also includes a 100-seat theater, the site of a performing arts series—drama, music, and more.

SELECTIVE SHOPPING

Raye's Mustard Mill (853-4451 or 1-800-853-1903), Route 190 (Washington Street), on the way into Eastport. Open daily, 9–5 in summer; winter hours vary. In business since 1903, this company is billed as the country's last remaining, stone-ground mustard mill. This is the mustard in which Washington County's sardines were once packed, and it's sensational. When the yellow flag is flying out front, they're grinding, and visitors are welcome to watch. Otherwise don't fail to stop by the Pantry.

Studio 44 (44 Water Street), Eastport, displays paintings featuring works by Philip Harvey as well as bright, original pottery.

Smoked Salmon (853-4831), 37 Washington Street, Eastport. Jim Blankman uses an old method to process the town's newest product; also rainbow steelhead trout. Will ship anywhere.

Mainely Quilts (853-2933), Route 1 just north of the Eastport turnoff. Housed in a former schoolhouse, an outlet for fabrics and blankets from the local Guilford Industries mill, also a source of quality handmade quilts.

The Wigwam and **The Trading Post,** both Route 1 in Perry, are outlets for local Passamaquoddy craftswork.

Fountain Books, Main Street, Eastport. A funky former pharmacy filled with books, retaining the old soda fountain, adding cappuccino.

SPECIAL EVENTS

July: **Independence Day** is celebrated for a week in Eastport with parades, an air show, and fireworks. **Cannery Wharf Boat Race** (last weekend).

August: **Annual Indian Ceremonial Days,** Pleasant Point Reservation.

September: **Eastport Salmon Festival,** the weekend after Labor Day—a celebration of Eastport's new industry; salmon, trout, and Maine baked potatoes are grilled dockside, and free tours of fish farms in the bay are offered, along with live entertainment, games, and an art show.

CALAIS AND THE ST. CROIX VALLEY

GUIDANCE

Calais Information Center (454-2211), 7 Union Street, Calais. Open year-round, daily 8–6 July through October 15, otherwise 9–5 (rest rooms). Operated by the Maine Publicity Bureau, a source of brochures for all of Maine as well as the local area. Though it's not set up as a walk-in information center, the **Calais Area Chamber of Commerce** (454-2308) is also helpful.

Grand Lake Stream Chamber of Commerce, PO Box 124, Grand Lake Stream 04637. Request the brochure listing local accommodations and outfitters and get a map showing hiking/mountain biking trails.

GETTING THERE

By car: The direct route to Calais from points west of Washington County is Route 9, "The Airline Highway." From the Machias area take Route 191.

TO SEE

Calais. The largest city in Washington County, Calais (pronounced *cal-us*) is a busy border, crossing point and shopping center for eastern Washington County. Its present population is 4000, roughly 2000 less than it was in the 1870s, the decade in which its fleet of sailing vessels numbered 176.

Moosehorn National Wildlife Refuge (454-3521), PO Box 1077, Calais 04619. Established in 1937, this area is the northeast end of a chain of wildlife and migratory bird refuges extending from Florida to Maine, managed by the United States Fish and Wildlife Service. The refuge comprises two units, some 20 miles apart. The larger, 16,000-acre area is in Baring, 5 miles north of Calais on Route 1. Look for eagles, which seem to be nesting each spring at the intersection of Charlotte Road and Route 1.

"Indian Days," Pleasant Point Reservation

Grand Lake Stream. A remote but famous resort community on West Grand Lake, with access to the Grand Lake chain. Grand Lake Stream claims to have been the world's biggest tannery town for some decades before 1874. Fishing is the big lure now: landlocked salmon, lake trout, smallmouth bass, also pickerel and white perch. Some of the state's outstanding fishing lodges and camps are clustered here.

St. Croix Island Overlook, Red Beach. Eight miles south of Calais on Route 1 the view is of the island on which Samuel de Champlain and Sieur de Monts established the first white settlement in North America north of Florida. That was in 1604. Using the island as a base, Champlain explored and mapped the coast of New England as far south as Cape Cod.

TO DO

CANOEING
Sunrise Canoe Expeditions (454-7708), Cathance Lake, Grove Post Office 04638. March to October. Offers advice, canoe rentals, and guided trips down the Grand Lake chain of lakes and the St. Croix River, which runs along the Maine–New Brunswick border; good for a 3- to 6-day run spring through fall. We did this trip with Sunrise (putting in at Vanceboro) and highly recommend it. In business more than 20 years, Sunrise is headed by photographer and naturalist Martin Brown; expeditions to the Arctic and Rio Grande are offered as well as to the Machias,

St. John, and St. Croix Rivers. Canoes for local use are $25 per day.

FISHING

Salmon is the big lure. Ranging from 8 to 20 pounds, Atlantic salmon are taken by fly fishermen in the Dennys and St. Croix Rivers, mid-May through early July. **Grand Lake Stream** is the focal point for dozens of lakes, ponds, and streams known for smallmouth bass and landlocked salmon (May through mid-June). There are also chain pickerel, lake trout, and brook trout. Fishing licenses, available for 3 days to a season, are also necessary for ice fishing. For information on fishing guides, lodges, and rules, write to the **Regional Headquarters of the Inland Fisheries and Wildlife Department,** Machias 04653.

GOLF

St. Croix Golf Club, Calais. A tricky, nine-hole course on the banks of the St. Croix River.

SWIMMING

Reynolds Beach on Meddybemps Lake by the town pier in Meddybemps (Route 191) is open daily 9 AM–sunset. Meddybemps is a very small, white, wooden village with a church, general store, and pier; a good spot for a picnic and a swim. **Red Beach** at Calais on the St. Croix River is named for the sand on these strands, which is deep red. There is also swimming in dozens of crystal clear lakes. Inquire about access at local lodges and general stores.

LODGING

BED & BREAKFAST

Brewer House (454-2385), Route 1, PO Box 94, Robbinston 04671. On Route 1, 12 miles south of Calais, is this striking 1828 mansion with graceful Ionic pillars. The interior, filled with treasures amassed by antiques dealers David and Estelle Holloway, is very Victorian. The living room and five bedrooms are filled with fanciful pieces, and there are views of Passamaquoddy Bay across the road. $50–75 includes a very full breakfast, not the kind you probably eat at home, elegantly served in the sunny breakfast room. Estelle sells antiques next door at The Landing.

SPORTS LODGES

Weatherby's (796-5558), Grand Lake Stream 04637. Open early May through October 15. A rambling, white, 1870s lodge with flowers along the porch, set in roses and birches by Grand Lake Stream, the small river that connects West Grand Lake with Big Lake. Ken and Charlene Sassi make you feel welcome. There is a big sitting room—with piano, TV, and hearth—in the lodge; also a homey, newly redecorated dining room with a tin ceiling and better than down-home cooking (served by the owner-chef). Each of the 15 cottages is unique, but most are log-style with screened porches, bath, and a Franklin stove or fireplace. *Fishing* is what this place is about, and it's a great place for children. $80 per person double occupancy, MAP, $100 single; $50 per child. Motor-boats are $34 per day, and a guide, $120; family rates available; 15 per-cent gratuity added. Inquire about the canoe/camping option.

Leen's Lodge (796-5575), Box 40, Grand Lake Stream 04637. November 1 through April 30 write: Newport 04953 or phone 368-5699. We're glad to report that this landmark sporting lodge is back in business un-der new ownership after several years' hiatus. Cabins, each with a fire-place or Franklin stove, a refrigerator, and gas heat, are scattered along the shore of West Grand Lake. They range in size from one bedroom to eight. The Tannery Room in the main lodge, a pine-paneled gathering space equipped with games, books, a TV, and BYOB bar, overlooks the lake, as does the many-windowed dining room. $85–125 per day MAP; half price for children and discounts for groups, but add 15 percent gratuity; lunch, boat rentals and guide service are extra.

Indian Rocks Camps (796-2822 or 1-800-498-2821), Grand Lake Stream 04637. Open year-round. Five, century-old log cabins and a central lodge compose this friendly compound that caters to families in sum-mer as well as to fishermen, cross-country skiers, snowmobilers, and ice fishermen in winter. Amenities include miniature golf. $62 per person includes all meals; $25 per person (no meals) in the housekeeping cabins.

Lakeside Inn and Cabins (796-2324), Princeton 04668. Open May through November. A handsome old inn with twin chimneys and seven guest rooms; also five basic housekeeping cabins on Lewy Lake (the outlet to Big Lake, also a source for the St. Croix River). Rooms in the inn are simple and nicely furnished, with in-room sinks, and, although baths are shared, there are plenty. Betty Field is a warm, grandmoth-erly host. $50 per person includes all meals; $38 double B&B in the inn; cabins from $40 per couple per day, no meals.

CAMPGROUND

Georgia Pacific's woodland office in Millinocket (723-5232) dispenses a sportsman's map and information about camping on its extensive wood-land holdings ($3).

Also see Cobscook Bay State Park in the *Eastport and Cobscook Bay* section.

WHERE TO EAT

DINING OUT

The Chandler House (454-7922), 20 Chandler Street, Calais. Open 4–11 daily except Sunday. Chef-owned, specializing in seafood like black-ened whitefish. Entrées: $9.00–18.95.

Bernardini's, 89 Main Street, Calais. Open year-round for lunch and din-ner except Sunday. An attractive storefront trattoria, entrées $11–20.

The Townhouse Restaurant (454-8021), 84 Main Street, Calais. Open mid-April to mid-October, 11–9 except Sunday. Seafood specialties include haddock with lobster sauce ($12.95).

Patrick's Restaurant (454-8810), 114 North Street, Calais. Open 6–9. A

welcome addition to the strip on North Street. An attractive dining room
featuring entrées like salmon steak ($13.95) and seafood scampi ($13.95).

Redclyffe Dining Room (454-3279), Route 1, Robbinston. Open 5–10 for
dinner. The view of the bay is superb, and the food, we're told, is good too.

Heslin's (454-3762), Route 1, Calais (south of the village). Open May
through October, 5–9. A popular local dining room specializing in steak
and seafood entrées and "French cooking." Moderate.

EATING OUT

Wickachee (454-3400), 282 Main Street, Calais. Open year-round, 6 AM–
10 PM. Steak and seafood with a big salad bar are the dinner specialties,
but even dinner entrées start at $4.

Angelhom (454-3066), 63 Main Street, Calais. Open early; good road food,
within walking distance of the border.

SELECTIVE SHOPPING

Pine Tree Store, Grand Lake Stream. Open daily, year-round. A general
store that also carries many sportsmen's essentials.

The Something Special Shop, Grand Lake Stream. Open Memorial Day
to Labor Day. Joan Barton turned her garage into a gift shop more than
20 years ago, and it seems to get better every year. A nice selection of
crafts and gifts.

SPECIAL EVENTS

July: **Indian Festival and Indian Township,** Princeton.

August: **North Country Festival,** Danforth. **International Festival,**
Calais—a week of events including a parade, suppers, canoe and raft
races.

NEW BRUNSWICK: ST. ANDREWS

As we have already mentioned, St. Andrews is much like Bar Harbor,
but a Bar Harbor with the genteel charm and big hotels that it lost in
the 1947 fire. The big hotel in St. Andrews is the Algonquin, a 200-
room, many-gabled, neo-Tudor resort dating from 1915 and still managed by the Canadian Pacific Railroad. The Algonquin is enthroned
like a queen mother above this tidy town with Loyalist street names like
Queen, King, and Princess Royal. St. Andrews was founded in 1783 by
British Empire Loyalists, American colonists who so strongly opposed
breaking away from the mother country that they had to leave the new
United States after independence was won. Most came from what is
now Castine, many of them unpegging their houses and bringing them
along in the 1780s. Impressed by this display of loyalty, the British

government made the founding of St. Andrews as painless as possible, granting them a superb site; British army engineers dug wells, built a dock, constructed a fort, and laid out the town on its present grid. Each Loyalist family was also given a house lot twice the usual size. The result is an unusually gracious, largely 19th-century town, hauntingly reminiscent of Castine. The focal point remains Market Wharf, where the first settlers stepped ashore, and Water Street, lined with shops specializing in British woolens and china.

GUIDANCE

St. Andrews Chamber of Commerce (506-529-2555), Reed Avenue, St. Andrews, New Brunswick, Canada EOG 2XO; office open year-round, information center, May through October.

Complete lodging listings for both St. Andrews and Grand Manan are detailed in the *New Brunswick Travel Guide,* available toll-free in Canada and the United States (1-800-561-0123), or by writing Economic Development & Tourism, PO Box 12345, Fredericton, New Brunswick, Canada E3B 5C3.

GETTING THERE

By car: Route 1 via Calais. From the border crossing at Calais, it's just 19 miles to St. Andrews.

By car ferries: See *Getting Around* at the beginning of this chapter.

TIME

Note that New Brunswick's Atlantic time is one hour ahead of Maine.

TAXES

The Canadian Goods and Services Tax (GST) is a 7 percent tax imposed on food, lodging, and just about everything else in Canada—known locally as the "Go South Tax," hence the traffic backup at the border. Visitors who spend more than $100 on goods and short-term accommodations will get most of it back by mailing in a Revenue Canada application and appending all receipts. New Brunswick also tacks on an 11 percent food and lodging tax; the latter does not apply to smaller B&Bs.

TO SEE

Ross Memorial Museum (506-529-3906), corner of King and Montague Streets, open daily late May to early October; a vintage 1824 mansion displaying the fine decorative art collection of Reverend and Mrs. Henry Phipps Ross of Ohio. The **Charlotte County Archives** (506-529-4248; open weekdays), 123 Frederick Street, is housed in the 1830s "Gaol."

Ministers Island Historic Site (506-529-5081), Chamcook, New Brunswick. Open June to mid-October. One of the grandest estates on the continent has recently been opened to the public as a Provincial Historic Site. Built around 1890 on an island connected by a "tidal road" (accessible only at low tide) to St. Andrews, Covenhoven is a 50-room mansion with 17 bedrooms, a vast drawing room, a bath house, and a gigantic and ornate livestock barn. The builder was Sir William Van Horne, the driving force in constructing the Canadian Pacific Railway from sea to sea. Because of the tides and nature of the island, only set, 2-hour guided tours are offered. Phone before coming.

Huntsman Marine Science Centre (606-529-1202), off Route 127, Brandy Cove Road, St. Andrews. A nonprofit aquaculture research center sponsoring educational programs and cruises; the aquarium-museum features hundreds of living plants and animals found in the Quoddy region, including resident harbor seals.

Atlantic Salmon Information Centre (506-529-8889), in Chamcook, 5 miles east of St. Andrews on Route 127. Open spring to fall, 10–6. A staffed interpretation area dramatizes the history of Atlantic salmon and current conservation efforts. A nature trail threads the salmon nursery area and adjoining woods.

TO DO

GOLF
The **Algonquin golf course** (see *Resort*) is New Brunswick's oldest (it dates from 1894) and is considered its best. The 18-hole Donald Ross seaside course was designed by Donald Ross. There is also a nine-hole "Woodland" course. Both are open to the public.

WHALE-WATCHING
Cline Maine (506-526-4188) offers seasonal bird- and whale-watching tours from St. Andrews and Campobello.

LODGING

RESORT
The Algonquin (506-529-8823, or in the United States: 1-800-828-7447), St. Andrews, New Brunswick, Canada EOG 2X0. Open May to October. The last of the truly grand coastal resorts in northeastern America; a 200-room, Tudor-style hotel with formal common rooms and dining rooms, also banquet space geared to the many groups that keep it in business. Although the golf course is the big draw, amenities also include tennis courts, a pool, and spa. The rack rate averages $120 per couple, but special packages, including "mini vacations" that capitalize on weekends, bring it down to $136 (Canadian) for 2 days, breakfast included, children free. Inquire about golf and "romance" packages.

INN
The Rossmount Inn (506-529-3351), St. Andrews, New Brunswick, Canada EOG 2XO. Open year-round. A boxy, three-story mansion set atop a hill with commanding views, this is a real period piece. The period is high Victorian, with ornate chandeliers, woodwork, and

Algonquin Hotel, St. Andrews, New Brunswick

appropriate furniture. The house was built in 1891 by the same Reverend and Mrs. Ross who endowed the Ross Museum in town. Come for high tea or dinner, if you can't spend the night, or for one of the off-season murder mystery weekends for which this place seems to have been created. There are 18 guest rooms, each different, all with private baths. The 84-acre estate includes walking trails leading to the summit of Chamcook Mountain, the highest point in the Passamaquoddy Bay area. $68–99 (Canadian) per couple EP in-season, less mid-October through mid-June.

BED & BREAKFASTS

A number of small B&Bs in St. Andrews provide a reasonable alternative to the big hotels. Their zip code is New Brunswick EOG 2XO (Canada).

Pansy Patch (506-529-3834), 59 Carleton Street. Open mid-May to mid-September. Built fancifully in 1912 to resemble a Norman cottage, right across from the Algonquin. Marilyn O'Connor offers four guest rooms with water views and antiques. We particularly like room number 3. Breakfast, served in the country kitchen, is included in $75–95 per couple (Canadian).

Pippincott (506-529-3445), 208 Prince of Wales Street. Open year-round. On the high end of town, look for Bob and Eleanor Parke's gracious house with a big garden. The suite is $80 (Canadian), and the smaller guest room is $60, including a big breakfast and tea, both with homemade pastries and jams.

The Walker Estate (506-529-4210), 109 Reed Avenue. Built in 1912 as a summer mansion, it now offers four guest rooms plus a master suite with a working fireplace and Jacuzzi. $90–125 Canadian and $160 for a family of up to six; includes continental breakfast and afternoon tea.

MOTEL

St. Andrews Motor Inn (506-529-4571), 111 Water Street, St. Andrews, NB EOG 2X0. A three-story motel with 33 units and a heated swimming pool. All rooms have two queen-sized beds and color TVs, some with kitchenettes, and all with private balconies overlooking Passamaquoddy Bay; $79.95–89.95 includes coffee and doughnuts.

WHERE TO EAT

DINING OUT

The Algonquin (506-529-8823), 184 Adolphus Street, St. Andrews. Dining rooms are the Passamaquoddy Veranda with windows overlooking formal gardens. Full dinner with tax is $42 Canadian. The Sunday buffet is $7.50 Canadian.

L'Europe Dining Room and Lounge (506-529-3818), 63 King Street, St. Andrews. Chef-owner Alexander Ludwig's specialities are a pleasing mix of French and German classics ranging from Wiener schnitzel ($15.60) to duck a l'orange ($24.00) to rack of lamb ($26.90); seafood entrées range from broiled sea bass ($17.50) to lobster with morel mushrooms in a lobster sauce ($33.00); prices are Canadian and include homemade pâté and salad as well as breads and vegetable. Candlelight and fine linen but no view.

Rossmount Dining Room (506-529-3351), Route 127, east of St. Andrews. Open for breakfast, lunch, high tea, and dinner. The menu changes frequently, but entrées might include charbroiled New York steak ($18.95) and poached Atlantic salmon ($19.95).

The Gables (506-529-3440), 143 Water Street, St. Andrews. Open 11–10. Reasonably priced, good food, and a water view; what more can you ask, especially with wine by the glass and a wide selection of beers? Specialties include fresh fish ranging from fried haddock and chips ($9.50 Canadian) to a seafood platter ($21.95). Salmon steak is $14.95, and you can always get a veggie burger ($7.50) or a sausage dinner ($8.95).

EATING OUT

Passamaquoddy Fish & Chip, on the wharf, St. Andrews. Out on the wharf, featuring great fried fish—not your usual pre-frozen blocks, either. Even the fish sandwich is real.

SELECTIVE SHOPPING

Cottage Craft Ltd., Town Square, St. Andrews. Dating back to 1915, Cottage Craft showcases yarns, tweeds, and finished jackets, sweaters, and skirts; also distinctive handwoven throws made in homes throughout Charlotte County. Skirt and sweater kits as well as the finished products are the specialties.

VI. WESTERN MOUNTAINS AND LAKES REGION

Sebago and Long Lakes Region
Bethel Area
Rangeley Lakes Region
Sugarloaf and the Carrabassett Valley

Lake Country

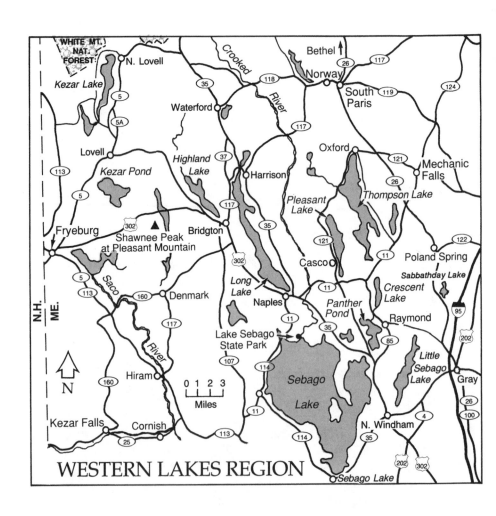

WESTERN LAKES REGION

Sebago and Long Lakes Region

Fifty lakes lie scattered in the area that the eye can see from the summit of Pleasant Mountain. Ten are in the town of Bridgton. With such a multitude of options for those who love water recreation, it is easy to see why this region became a popular summer destination over 100 years ago.

Before the Civil War, Bridgton's pioneer tourists could actually come by boat all the way from Boston. From Portland, they would ride 20 miles through 28 locks on the Cumberland and Oxford Canal, thence across Sebago Lake, up the Songo River, Brandy Pond, and Long Lake to Bridgton.

Later, summer travelers made the journey on Bridgton's "2-footer" railroad line, and they now arrive by car, but many waste little time getting onto or into water. At the Naples Causeway, aqua bicycles, sailboards, and every form of boat are for rent, and here is also where you can board an excursion boat for the ride across Brandy Pond and through the only surviving lock from the 1830 canal. The fishing is good; Sebago, Maine's second largest lake, is known for its salmon. This is also Maine's most popular waterskiing area; both rentals and lessons are available.

And for those who don't love the water, the region has plenty of land recreational opportunities, too—golf, tennis, mineral collecting, horseback riding, biking, and camping; the list is endless.

Fryeburg, just west of the lakes, was the first village settled, both in Oxford County and in the Mt. Washington region. This community has long been dependent on agriculture, and their agricultural fair in early autumn is the largest in the state. Fryeburg is also headquarters for canoeing the Saco River. Sandy-bottomed and clear, the Saco meanders for more than 40 miles through woods and fields, rarely passing a house. Too shallow for powerboats, it is perfect for canoes. There is usually just enough current to nudge along the limpest paddler, and the ubiquitous sandbars serve as gentle bumpers. Tenting is permitted most places along the river, and there are six public campgrounds. Outfitters rent canoes and provide shuttle service.

Most summer visitors stay in lakeside cottages—of which there are hundreds. The few motels and long-established inns, as well as the mushrooming crop of bed & breakfasts, tend to fill up on many summer weekends with parents visiting their children at camps, of which there also seem to be hundreds.

This southwestern corner of the state has enough to keep camp parents busy all week. From the country's last living Shaker community at Sabbathday Lake, quarries for rockhounds, and the State of Maine Building at Poland Springs, to the reconstructed, late 19th-century village of Willowbrook at Newfield, the region is brimming with history and sights to see.

But most lakes region visitors don't come to look at anything. They swim and fish, and fish and swim. They take powerboats for a cruise around a lake or paddle canoes on a lazy river. On rainy days, they browse through the area's abundance of antiques and crafts stores. In winter, come sun or snow, they ski downhill at Shawnee Peak (alias Pleasant Mountain) or ski cross-country almost anywhere.

GUIDANCE

Bridgton-Lakes Region Chamber of Commerce (647-3472), Box 236, Bridgton 04009. The chamber maintains a seasonal (daily from mid-June to Labor Day, weekends from Memorial Day through October) walk-in information bureau on Route 302. Request a copy of the chamber's "Bridgton-Lakes Region Map and Guide." Year-round information is also available from the town office (647-8786).

Naples Business Association (693-3285; winter: 693-6365), PO Box 412, Naples 04055, publishes a map/guide to the Sebago–Long Lakes Region just south of Bridgton; it also maintains a seasonal information bureau next to the town's historical society museum on Route 302.

Windham Chamber of Commerce (892-8265), PO Box 1015, Windham 04062, maintains a seasonal information booth on Route 302 and publishes a booklet guide.

Oxford Hills Chamber of Commerce (743-2281), PO Box 167, Norway 04628, publishes a directory to the area.

The Harrison Business and Professional Association (583-2978), 36 Tolman Road, Harrison 04040, publishes a brochure describing local lodging and dining.

Fryeburg Information Center (935-3639), Route 302, Fryeburg. The Maine Publicity Bureau staffs this state-owned log cabin on the New Hampshire line. A source of pamphlets on the state in general, western Maine in particular.

GETTING THERE

By air: **Portland Jetport,** served by five minor carriers, is a half-hour to an hour drive from most points in this area. **Rental cars** are available at the airport.

By car: From New York and Boston, take I-95 to the Westbrook exit (Exit 8), then Route 302, the high road of the lakes region.

For the Sabbathday Lake/Poland Spring/Oxford area, take I-95 to Gray (Exit 11) and Route 26 north.

For Newfield and south of Sebago area, take Route 25 from I-95 at Westbrook (Exit 8).

MEDICAL EMERGENCY

Northern Cumberland Memorial Hospital (647-8841), South High Street, Bridgton. **Stephens Memorial Hospital** (743-5933), Norway.

VILLAGES

Norway and **South Paris** form the commercial center for Oxford County. Downtown streets sport intriguing shops, Route 26 offers shopping centers, and the area abounds with historic sites, including the home of Hannibal Hamlin, Lincoln's vice president. Sleds, toboggans, and children's furniture are manufactured in South Paris. Pennesseewassee Lake (better known as Norway Lake) offers fishing, swimming, and boating.

Naples is at the heart of the region, and its pretty causeway and numerous recreation options make this a logical place to stop. Many fine inns and restaurants are right nearby.

TO SEE

State Fish Hatchery and Game Farm, Route 26/100 north, Gray. Open daily 10–4; $.50. A 1300-acre farm, set up to breed ring-necked pheasants, has become a refuge for injured or threatened animals: moose, deer, raccoons, bears, bobcats, porcupines, minks, skunks, fishers, coyotes, and a variety of birds and fish.

Oxford Plains Speedway/Dragway (539-4401), Route 26, Oxford. Open April to September, Saturday at 7:30 PM, Sunday at 2 PM, and for special events. The Oxford 250 draws competitors from throughout the world during July.

MUSEUMS

Sabbathday Lake Shaker Community and Museum (926-4597), Route 26, New Gloucester (8 miles north of Gray). Open Memorial Day to Columbus Day, except Sunday, 10–4:30. Guided tours: $4 adults, $2 children. Extended tours: $5.50 adults, $2.75 children. Under 6 free. Welcoming the "world's people" has been a part of summer at Sabbathday Lake since the community's inception in 1794.

Founded by Englishwoman Ann Lee in 1775, Shakers numbered 6000 Americans in 18 communities by the Civil War. Today, with fewer than 10 Shaker Sisters and Brothers, this village is the only one that still functions as a religious community rather than as a museum. These men and women still follow the injunction of founder Mother Ann Lee to "put your hands to work and your heart to God." Guided tours are offered of the 17 white-clapboard buildings; rooms are either furnished or filled with exhibits to illustrate periods or products of Shaker life. Among other things, the shop sells herbs and herbal teas, yarn from the community's sheep, and *Shaker Your Plate: Of Shaker Cooks and Cook-*

Shaker Village at Sabbathday Lake

ing, a delightful book about the community's cooks and cooking by Sister Frances Carr, the community's present leader. During warm-weather months, services are held at 10 AM on Sundays in the 18th-century meetinghouse on Route 26. Sit in the World's People's benches and listen as the Shakers speak in response to the psalms and gospel readings. Each observation is affirmed with a Shaker song—of which there are said to be 10,000. This complex includes an extensive research library housing Shaker books, writings, and records open to scholars by appointment.

Willowbrook at Newfield (793-2784), Newfield (off Route 11). Open May 15 to September 30, daily 10–5. $6.50 per adult, $3.25 per student, under 6 free. This is a quiet, peaceful place that shouldn't be missed. Although it's off the beaten track, the drive through the quiet country-side is easy and relaxing, and once you get there, well worth it. Devastated by fire in 1947, the village was almost a ghost town when Donald King began buying buildings in the 1960s. The complex now includes 37 buildings displaying more than 11,000 items: horse-drawn vehicles, tools, toys, a vintage 1894 carousel, and many other artifacts of late 19th-century life. Linger in the ballroom, ring the schoolhouse bell, picnic in the area provided. This is a perfect place to get away from it all. A restaurant and ice-cream parlor for light lunches, an old-time country store, and a Christmas gift shop open most of the year are located on the premises.

The Jones Museum of Glass and Ceramics (787-3370), Douglas Hill (off Route 107), Sebago. Open mid-May to mid-November, Monday through Saturday 10–5 and Sunday 1–5. $5 per adult, $3 per student. More than 7000 works in glass and china. Displays include ancient Egyptian glass, Chinese porcelains, Wedgwood teapots, and French paperweights. There are also gallery tours, frequent lecture-luncheon seminars, and identification days (visitors bring their own pieces to be identified).

Orlin Arts Center at Bates College (786-6255), Campus Avenue, Lewiston. Lovers of artist Marsden Hartley may want to seek out this small but excellent collection of bold, bright canvases by Hartley, a Lewiston native (call ahead to find out what's on display).

HISTORIC HOMES

Daniel Marrett House, Route 25, Standish. Tours mid-June to September 1, Tuesday, Thursday, Saturday, and Sunday noon–5. $3.00 adults, $2.50 seniors, $1.50 children. Money from Portland banks was stored here for safekeeping during the War of 1812. This Georgian mansion, built in 1789, was bought by Standish's third parson, Daniel Marrett, in 1793. It remained in his family until 1944; architecture and furnishings reflect the changing styles over 150 years, and the formal gardens are in full bloom throughout the summer.

Parson Smith House (892-5315), 89 River Road, South Windham. Open mid-June to Labor Day, Tuesday, Thursday, Saturday, and Sunday 12–5; $2. A Georgian farmhouse with an exceptional stairway and hall; some original furnishings.

Peabody–Fitch House Museum, Ingalls Road (off Route 107), South Bridgton. Open June 5 through Labor Day, Tuesday through Sunday 10–4. $2 for adults, $1 for seniors and children. A Federal- period home in an unspoiled rural setting; includes a blacksmith shop. House still under restoration.

HISTORIC SITES

State of Maine Building from the 1893 Columbia Exposition in Chicago, Route 26, Poland Spring. Open July and August, daily 9–1; June and September, weekends 9–1. $1 admission. A very Victorian building that was brought back from the 1893 Columbian Exposition in Chicago to serve as a library and art gallery for the now-vanished Poland Spring Resort (the water is now commercially bottled in an efficient, unromantic plant down the road). Houses the Poland Spring Preservation Society with museum displays from the resort era on the second floor and art on the third. While you are there, peek into the All Souls Chapel next door for a look at its nine stained-glass windows and the 1921 Skinner Pipe Organ.

Hamlin Memorial Hall, Paris Hill, off Route 26. Open year-round, Tuesday through Friday 11:30–5:30, and Saturday 10–2; also Wednesday 7–9. The old, stone Oxford County Jail now houses the public library and museum. Worth a stop for the American primitive art; also local minerals and displays about Hannibal Hamlin (who lived next door), vice president during Abraham Lincoln's first term. This stop may not sound very exciting, but the setting is superb: a ridgetop of spectacular, early 19th-century houses with views west to the White Mountains.

Songo Locks, Naples (2.5 miles off Route 302). Dating from 1830, the last of the 27 hand-operated locks that once enabled people to come by boat from Portland to Harrison. It still enables you to travel some 40 watery miles. The boat traffic is constant in summer.

Naples Historical Society Museum (693-6790), Village Green, Route 302, Naples. Open July and August, Tuesday through Friday 10–3. The old brick complex includes the old jail, some great memorabilia, and slide presentations on the Cumberland and Oxford Canal, the Sebago–Long Lake steamboats, and vanished hotels like the Chute Homestead.

Bridgton Historical Society Museum (647-2765), Gibbs Avenue, Bridgton. Open June to August, except Monday, 1–4. Housed in a 1902 former fire station, the collection includes slides on the old narrow-gauge railroad.

Hopalong Cassidy in the Fryeburg Public Library, 98 Main Street, Fryeburg. Open year-round; Tuesday, Thursday, and Saturday 10–5, Friday 5–8, Wednesday 10–8. The library is housed in an 1832 stone schoolhouse. It is decorated with many paintings by local artists and also contains a collection of books, guns, and other memorabilia belonging to Clarence Mulford, creator of Hopalong Cassidy.

TO DO

AIR RIDES

Naples Flying Service (693-6591), Naples Causeway. Operates daily in-season, 9–7. Offers 25-mile scenic flights over the Sebago–Long Lakes area.

Parasailing (693-3888), Naples Causeway.

Destinations Unlimited (743-9781 or 1-800-526-TOUR), South Paris. Hot-air balloon rides, located at the Norway-Paris town line.

BOAT EXCURSIONS

Songo River Queen II (693-6861), Naples Causeway. Operates daily July through Labor Day; weekends during June and September. Offers a 2½-hour Songo River ride and a 1-hour Long Lake cruise. The 90-foot-long stern-wheeler was built in 1982; snack bar and rest rooms. The ride is across Brandy Pond and through the only surviving lock from the 1830 canal. It is a pleasant ride to the mouth of Sebago Lake down the Songo River, which is about as winding as a river can be. The distance is just 1.5 miles as the crow flies, but 6 miles as the Songo twists and turns.

Mail Boat Rides (693-6861), Naples Causeway. Operates daily in-season (see above) except Sunday. This pontoon offers varied rides on Songo and Long Lakes. No toilets on board.

BOAT RENTALS

Available throughout the region. Inquire at local chambers. (See also *Canoeing.*)

CANOEING

The only hitch to canoeing the **Saco River** is its popularity. On Friday afternoons in August, would-be canoeists are backed up bumper to bumper along the access roads at Swan's Falls and Canal Bridge in Fryeburg.

Saco River Canoe and Kayak (935-2369), PO Box 111, Route 5, Fryeburg (across from the access at Swan's Falls). "For canoeing, the Saco is the number one river east of the Mississippi," enthuses Fred Westerberg. "Nowhere else can you canoe so far without having to portage. Nowhere else can you find this kind of wilderness camping experience without the danger of remoteness. Nowhere on the river are you far from help if you need it." Westerberg, a registered Maine guide, runs Saco River Canoe and Kayak with the help of his wife, Prudy, and daughters, Beth and Chris. They also offer shuttle service and canoe rentals, which come with a map and careful instructions geared to the day's river conditions.

Saco Bound (603-447-2177 or 603-447-3801), Route 302, Center Conway, New Hampshire (just over the state line, south of Fryeburg). The largest canoe outfitter around. Offers rentals, guided day trips during the summer (Tuesdays and Thursdays in July and August), whitewater canoeing on the Androscoggin River, a campground at Canal Bridge in Fryeburg, and a shuttle service. Its base is a big, glass-faced store stocked with kayaks and canoes, trail food, and lip balm. Staff members are young and enthusiastic.

Canal Bridge Canoes (935-2605), Route 302, Fryeburg Village. Pat and Carl Anderson offer rentals and a shuttle service.

Woodland Acres (935-2529), Route 160, Brownfield. Full-facility camping, canoe rentals, and a shuttle service.

River Run Canoe (452-2500), Brownfield. Free primitive camping on River Run's 130 wooded acres, with canoe rentals, shuttle service.

FISHING

Fishing licenses are available at town offices and other local outlets; check marinas for information. Salmon, lake trout, pickerel, and bass are plentiful.

GOLF AND TENNIS

Bridgton Highlands Country Club (647-3491), Bridgton, has a nine-hole course, snack bar, carts, and tennis courts. Other nine-hole courses include **Lake Kezar Country Club** (925-2462), Route 5, Lovell; **Naples Country Club** (693-6424), Route 114, Naples; and **Summit Golf Course** (998-4515), Poland Spring.

Tennis at Brandy Pond Camps (693-6333), old Route 114, Naples.

HIKING

Douglas Mountain, Sebago. A Nature Conservancy preserve with great views of Sebago and the White Mountains. The trail to the top is a 20-minute walk, and there's a ¾-mile nature trail at the summit; also a stone tower with an observation platform. Take Route 107 south from the town of Sebago and turn right on Douglas Mountain Road; go to the end of the road to find limited parking.

Pleasant Mountain, Bridgton. Several summits and interconnecting trails, the most popular of which is the Firewarden's Trail to the main summit. A relatively easy, 2½-mile climb from base to summit through rocky woods.

HORSEBACK RIDING

Sunny Brook Stables (787-2905), Sebago, offers trail rides pitched to beginners and intermediate riders. $15–18 per hour.

Secret Acres Stables (693-3441), Lambs Mill Road, Naples (1 mile off Route 302), offers trail rides and lessons.

MINI-GOLF

Steamboat Landing (693-6429), Route 114, Naples. Open weekends Memorial Day to late June, then daily until Labor Day 10–10 (1–10 on Sunday). A delightful 19-hole course with a Maine theme in a wooded setting.

Maplewood Miniature Golf and Arcade (655-7586), Route 302 across from State Park Road, Casco. Eighteen holes and a full arcade with video games, pinball, snacks.

ROCKHOUNDING

This area is particularly rich in minerals. Rockhounds should stop at

Perham's of West Paris (674-2341 or 1-800-371-GEMS), Route 26, West Paris. Open 9–5 daily. Looking deceptively small in its yellow-clapboard, green-trim building (right side, heading north), this business has been selling local gemstones since 1919. Aside from displaying an array of locally mined amethyst, tourmaline, topaz, and many other minerals, as well as selling gem jewelry, Perham's offers maps to four local quarries in which treasure-seekers are welcome to try their luck. Whether you are a rockhound or not, you will want to stop by this mini-museum, said to attract 90,000 visitors per year.

Snow Falls Gorge, off Route 26, West Paris. Whether you are hunting for gems or not, be sure to stop by this beautiful spot (you can ask directions at Perham's). A waterfall cascades into the gorge, and there's a bridge for great viewing; also hiking trails.

SWIMMING

Sebago Lake State Park (693-6613, June 20 to Labor Day; 693-6231, otherwise), off Route 302 (between Naples and South Casco). The day-use area includes beaches, tables, grills, a boat ramp, lifeguards, and bathhouses. There is a separate camping area (see *Campgrounds*) with its own beach; also a summer program of conducted hikes on nature trails and presentations in the amphitheater. Songo Lock is nearby.

The town of Bridgton maintains a tidy little beach on **Long Lake** just off

Main Street, another on **Woods Lake** (Route 117), and another on **Highland Lake.** The town of Fryeburg maintains a beach, with float, on the **Saco River,** and **Casco** maintains a small, inviting beach in its picturesque village.

Range Pond State Park (998-4104) in Poland offers swimming and fishing.

In addition, most camps, cottages, and lodges have their own waterfront beaches and docks, and there are numerous local swimming holes.

CROSS-COUNTRY SKIING

Carter's Farm Market (539-4848), Route 26, Oxford. Extensive acreage used to grow summer vegetables is transformed into a ski center during the winter. Equipment rentals, lessons, 10 km of groomed trails, some lighted trails for night skiing, and food.

DOWNHILL SKIING

Shawnee Peak at Pleasant Mountain (647-8444), Route 302, Bridgton. An isolated, 1900-foot hump, 1 mile west of the center of town. Maine's oldest ski area, it has a vertical drop of 1300 feet, 30 trails, 98 percent snowmaking, and night skiing. Lifts include one triple chair and three double chairs. Other amenities include ski school, rentals, and child care.

LODGING

RUSTIC RESORTS

The western lakes area offers some unusual old resort complexes, each with cabin accommodations, dining, and relaxing space in a central, distinctively Maine lodge. In contrast to similar complexes found farther north, these are all geared to families or to those who vacation here for reasons other than hunting and fishing.

Migis Lodge (655-4524), PO Box 40, South Casco 04077 (off Route 302). Open early June through Columbus Day weekend. There are seven rooms in the two-story main lodge, and 30 cottages scattered in the pines on 97 acres. All cottages have fireplaces, and guests enjoy use of the private beach, tennis, lawn games, waterskiing, sailboats, canoes, and boat excursions. Children under 4 are not permitted in the dining room during the high season (July to Labor Day), so the resort provides a supervised dining and play time 6:30–8:30; older children are also welcome to join in. $100–155, includes three meals; children's rates.

Aimhi Lodge (892-6538), North Windham 04062. Open spring through fall. More than 70 years in the same family, this classic complex accommodates 75 guests. The lodge and 25 cabins are sited on Little Sebago Lake. The cabins have one to three rooms, Franklin stoves, and screened porches. Down-home cooking; turkey every summer Sunday since the 1930s, at least; the Holdtman/Hodgson family has been running the lodge since the 1920s. Facilities include game rooms, lawn games, a beach, sailboats, canoes, and rental boats. Rates include three meals.

Farrington's (925-2500), Lake Kezar, Center Lovell 04016. Open late June to Labor Day, serving all meals; open again for foliage season on a B&B basis. A great old summer resort on Lake Kezar. There are 16 guest rooms and 30 cottages with one to three bedrooms each. Meals are served in the pine-paneled dining room with white tablecloths and white bentwood chairs. Facilities include a sand beach, waterskiing, boats, movies, a recreation hall, and tennis. Moderate rates considering they include three meals.

Quisisana (925-3500; off-season: 914-833-0293), Lake Kezar, Center Lovell 04016. Late June through Labor Day. One-week minimum stay in high season. Founded in 1917 as a place for music students and music lovers to relax in the pines by one of Maine's clearest lakes. Each evening climaxes with performances in the lakeside music hall: musical theater, opera, and concerts performed by staff recruited from top music schools. There are 16 guest rooms in two lodges; also 38 one- to three-room cottages (some with fireplaces) scattered through the woods and around the soft beach, which curves to a grassy point. Waterskiing, boats, and fishing guides are all available. The white-frame central lodge includes a big, homey sitting room and the kind of dining room you don't mind sitting in three times a day. Lodge rooms $80–102, cottages $90–138, all three meals included.

Northern Pines (655-7624), PO Box 279, Route 85, Raymond 04071. Open early June through Labor Day; September and October weekends; Christmas, New Year's week, and February 5–21. A holistic health resort housed in a 1920s women's camp on the shores of Crescent Lake. A few rooms are available in the main lodge, but others are sprinkled through the woods in a wide variety of cottages that range from rustic log cabins with fireplaces to a yurt. There are usually fewer than 30 guests. Some take part in supervised fasting, but most simply take advantage of the daily regimen, which begins at 6:30 AM with exercises, including aerobics and yoga; evening program and optional lectures. Meals are vegetarian and delicious. Summer facilities include sailboats, canoes, paddleboats, and a lakeside hot tub; cross-country skiing and ice skating January through March. The central lodge (closed in winter) has a massive, two-sided fireplace, and there is a large library. $125–229 daily; $744–1352 weekly, meals included.

INNS

Oxford House Inn (935-3442), Fryeburg 04037. Open year-round, this spacious 1913 house in the middle of Fryeburg has a view across the Saco River to the White Mountains. The public restaurant is popular for dinner (see *Dining Out*), but there is ample space for inn guests to relax. The five upstairs guest rooms are all large and nicely decorated, with private baths. Request one with a view. $75–95, includes a full breakfast.

Lake House (583-4182 or 1-800-223-4182), Routes 35 and 37, Waterford 04088. Open year-round. Our favorite in this area. A graceful old stagecoach inn with vestiges of the old ballroom under the eaves. Suzanne and Michael Uhl-Myers have totally overhauled this landmark in the middle of picturesque Waterford Village. They now offer five spacious guest rooms, including a two-room suite and a one-room cottage, all with private baths. Downstairs there is a comfortable sitting room, away from the two small, public dining rooms. Lake Keoka is just across the street. $79–125.

Kedarburn Inn (583-6182), Route 35, Waterford 04088. London natives Margaret and Derek Gibson bring an English accent to this pleasant 1850s house. The inn offers seven guest rooms, including two with private baths and one 2-room suite with private bath. Margaret has also recently opened a crafts shop on the ground floor, filled with items made by local artists as well as her own crafts, including her specialty quilts. $69–75 double, breakfast and an English afternoon tea included.

Center Lovell Inn (925-1575), Route 5, Center Lovell 04016. Closed November and April. A striking old inn with a cupola and a busy public dining room (see *Dining Out*). Janice and Richard Cox saw their dream come true when they won the inn through an essay contest in May of 1993. They run the inn with the help of Janice's mother, Harriet, and her husband, Earle (known to guests as "Mom" and "Pop"). There are four guest rooms on the second floor (the two with shared bath can become a suite), nicely furnished with antiques and art. In the 1835 Harmon House there are five smaller rooms, some with private bath. $87–144 MAP (more for suite).

Westways (928-2663), Center Lovell 04016. Open May through October. Built as a summer retreat for the self-made Maine millionaire who founded the Diamond Match company, this lakeside home offers seven guest rooms (three with private bath) and nine cottages. The low-beamed living room has a massive fireplace and furnishings that range from plush to baronial. The game room, with a two-lane bowling alley, is in a neighboring library. The view is of Lake Kezar with its backdrop of mountains, and there is a dock for sunning and swimming. Guests can also play tennis, fish, or canoe. Vacation homes, some old, some new, with three to seven bedrooms are scattered on the resort's 100 acres. $95–165 double in high season. $800–1700 weekly for vacation homes.

The Cornish Inn (625-8501), Route 25, PO Box 266, Cornish 04020. Open all year. A classic, old village inn with 15 rooms (some shared baths); antique decor and hand-stenciled wall borders. Candlelit dinners served every night but Wednesday in summer; a Spirits Room open every night with a bar menu. $53–79, includes breakfast.

Tarry-a-While (647-2522), Ridge Road, Bridgton 04009. Open mid-June to Labor Day. This resort has a delightful Swiss ambience. Ten guest rooms upstairs in the Gasthaus (an old summer hotel), 16 in the four chalets; all private baths, some handicapped units. Owners Hans (who is Swiss) and Barbara (she's from the States) Jenni are known for their hospitality. There are 30 acres of lakeside grounds on one of the most peaceful lakes in the area (there are no marinas or children's camps). Guests have free access to three fine beaches, canoes, rowboats, aqua bikes, pedal boats, tennis, and bicycles. Motorboats, sailboats, windsurfers, and waterskiing are extra. $100–120 double, includes a Swiss buffet breakfast. Three housekeeping cottages also available. $500–950 per week.

BED & BREAKFASTS

Noble House (647-3733), Box 180, Bridgton 04009. Open year-round, but October 15 to June 15 by prior reservation only. There is a formal feel to the public rooms with their grand piano, crystal, and Oriental rugs. This was a senator's manor, and it shows—set among stately oaks and pines with a view of mountains. The 10 guest rooms vary from a single to large family suites; all are decorated with antiques. There are niceties such as Australian fleece mattress covers; also new rooms in a rear annex, three with whirlpool bath. In winter, both downhill and cross-country skiing are nearby. There is a private beach (with a hammock, canoe, and dock) on Highland Lake across the road. $70–110 double, includes full breakfast and use of a canoe and pedal boats.

* **Sebago Lake Lodge** (892-2698), PO Box 110, White's Bridge Road, North Windham 04062. Open year-round. A rambling, old white inn on a narrows between Jordan Bay and the Basin, seemingly surrounded by water. Debra and Chip Lougee, both Maine natives, have refurbished the rooms to create eight units with their own kitchens (one is a suite with an enclosed porch) and four standard rooms with kitchen privileges. A light buffet breakfast is set out in the gathering room, a pleasant space to read, play games, or watch TV. There are also nine moderately priced cottages. Facilities include an inviting beach, picnic tables and grills; there is also a fishing boat, rowboat, canoe, and motorboat rentals. Fishing licenses are available. $48 for a room, $98–120 per housekeeping unit; cheaper off-season. Cottages $395–695 per week.

Maine-lly Llamas Farm (929-3057), Route 35, Hollis. May to November. A small working farm in a historic area. John and Gale Yohe offer comfortable guest rooms and a chance to learn about the farm or take a nature trek with their gentle llamas. Other animals include turkeys and Angora rabbits. Organically grown vegetable and flower gardens. Rooms are in the carriage house, with a separate staircase. $55 single, $65 double includes a full country breakfast. Guided llama treks are $20/hour for two llamas, $10 each additional llama.

Bear Mountain Inn (583-4404), Routes 35 and 37, South Waterford 04081. Open year-round. One of the area's first farmhouses to take in guests, still with an informal farmhouse feel. There are seven guest rooms, four full baths, and a two-room suite with bath. Read and Sheila Grover offer "healthy" vacations. The place is geared to groups (it accommodates 16 to 20 people), but everyone is welcome. The 40 acres include frontage on

Bear Pond. Amenities include an exercise machine, table tennis, and hiking trails. $45 single, $55 double; includes a full breakfast.

The Inn at Long Lake (693-6226), PO Box 806, Naples 04055. Built in 1906 as an annex to the (vanished) Lake House Resort, this four-story, clapboard building has been renovated and is again an inn. Irene and Maynard Hincks offer 16 guest rooms, ranging from cozy deluxe rooms to two-room suites. The inn is furnished to reflect the period that was popular when the annex was built, but with modern amenities like private bath, TV, and air conditioner. The Great Room on the ground floor has a magnificent fieldstone fireplace and, with the adjacent porch, makes a perfect setting for special events like the murder-mystery weekends offered. Views are across pastures to Long Lake. $75–115 per room, $45–80 in winter.

Augustus Bove House (693-6365), Routes 302 and 114, Naples 04055. Open year-round. This welcoming, 150-year-old brick mansion was originally the Hotel Naples, one of the first summer hotels in the area. The 11 guest rooms (4 share baths) are all different sizes and colors, and furnished with comfortable antiques. A first-floor suite with refrigerator, microwave, and pull-out couch is good for handicapped individuals and families. Set back from the road yet handy to all of the water sports at nearby Naples Causeway and to Sebago Lake State Park. No smoking or alcohol. A hearty breakfast is included in $75–85 in summer, less off-season.

Admiral Peary House (935-3365 or 1-800-237-8080), 9 Elm Street, Fryeburg 04037. Once the residence of Maine's famed Arctic explorer. Four large guest rooms, each with antiques, private bath, and air-conditioning. The top-floor "North Pole" room, with its king brass bed and views of the mountains, is delightful. Guests can play billiards or relax in the living room, outdoor spa, or perennial gardens. Amenities include a clay tennis court and bicycles. $89–98 includes a full breakfast. No smoking.

Tolman House Inn (583-4445), PO Box 551, Tolman Road, Harrison 04040. Open year-round. A former carriage barn, artfully transformed into an unusually inviting inn. Nine guest rooms with private baths and antiques; a dining and lounging area overlooking lovely gardens. The inn is situated on 100 hillside acres sloping to the tip of Long Lake. There is a game room in a former icehouse. The moderate rate includes a full breakfast; weekly rates are available. Children under 2 stay free, but there are no cribs. $60–75 for a double.

Snowbird Lodge (583-2544), Route 2, Harrison 04040. There's a large common room, paneled in knotty pine and with a big stone fireplace, piano, TV, VCR, stereo, and some games. Some baths are private but rooms are very basic. The 100-acre property includes birch and pine woods, plus a pond complete with sandy beach. Moderately priced, includes a full breakfast.

✍ **Moose Crossing Farm** (743-7656), 203 Christian Ridge Road, South Paris 04281. This is a nicely renovated, 18th-century farmhouse set high on Christian Ridge with long views west to the White Mountains. Anne and Allen Gass raise black and brown sheep; they offer woodland trails (good for cross-country skiing), two comfortable guest rooms, a hearty breakfast. $55 per room, shared bath.

COTTAGES

The "Lakes Region Cottage Directory," listing some 2 dozen cottages and cottage clusters, is available from the **Bridgton–Lakes Region Chamber of Commerce** (see *Guidance*). Many area cottages are also listed in the "Maine Guide to Camp & Cottage Rentals," free from the **Maine Publicity Bureau** (623-0363), PO Box 2300, Hallowell 04347-2300. Specific cottages that we recommend include the following:

Crescent Lake Cottages (655-3393), 178 Plains Road, Raymond 04071. Cozy, clean, and nicely sited; one- and two-bedroom cottages with a private sand beach on Crescent Lake. Lawn games, tennis, shuffleboard, recreation lodge; set on 8 acres. Inexpensive.

Hewnoaks (925-6051), Center Lovell 04016. Six unusually attractive, distinctive cottages overlooking Lake Kezar. Rates are moderate.

CAMPGROUNDS

See *Canoeing* for information about camping along the Saco River. In addition to those mentioned, the **Appalachian Mountain Club** maintains a campground at Swan's Falls. The "Maine Camping Guide," available from the **Maine Campground Owners Association** (782-5874), 655 Main Street, Lewiston 04240, lists dozens of private campgrounds in the area.

Sebago Lake State Park (693-6613; 693-6611 before June 20 and after Labor Day), off Route 302 (between Naples and South Casco). Open through mid-October. On the northern shore of the lake are 1300 thickly wooded acres with 250 campsites, many on the water; the camping area has its own beach, hot showers, a program of evening presentations, and nature hikes. For information about reservations, phone 1-800-332-1501 or 207-287-3824 from outside the state.

✍ **Point Sebago** (655-3821), RR 1, Box 712, Casco 04015. More than just a campground: 500 campsites, most with trailer hookups, on a 300-acre lakeside site, plus 160 rental trailers ranging from small trailers to large models of near mobile home size. Campers have access to the beach, marina, dance pavilion, child day care, teen center, excursion boats, soccer and softball fields, horseshoe pitches, 10 tennis courts, video-game arcade, general store, and combination restaurant/nightclub/gambling casino; full daily program beginning with 8 AM exercises and ending at 1 AM when the club closes. A golf course will open in June of 1995.

✍ **Papoose Pond Resort and Campground** (583-4470), RR 1, Box 2480, Route 118, 10 miles west of Norway in North Waterford 04267-9600. Family geared for 40 years, this facility is on 1000 wooded acres with a half mile of sandy beach on mile-long Papoose Pond; facilities include 25 cabins with baths, 18 cabins without baths, 10 housekeeping cottages, 8 bunkhouse trailers, 13 tent sites, 59 tent sites with electricity and water, 28 more with sewage as well, a dining shelter, and a kitchen and bathhouse. Amenities include a recreation hall, store, café, movie tent, sports area, 50 boats (canoes, rowboats, sailboats, paddleboats, kayaks), fishing equipment, and a vintage 1916 merry-go-round. From $19 for a tent site to $166 for a four-bedroom cottage.

OTHER LODGING

Wadsworth Blanchard Farm Hostel (625-7509), Hiram 04041. Open May through October. An attractive Hosteling International (HI) facility that's an 18th-century farmstead, and handy to canoeing on both the Saco and Ossippee Rivers. $10 per person in the dorm rooms, $30 for a private family room; access to the kitchen is included in all rates.

WHERE TO EAT

DINING OUT

Epicurian Inn (693-3839), Routes 302 and 35, Naples. Open for dinner except Monday, year-round. A mansard-roofed, French-style house specializing in "classical French and New American Cuisine served in an atmosphere of cozy elegance." Featured entreés weekly in addition to the regular menu. On a typical evening, these may include sole with bananas, marinated bluefish, and veal with chanterelles. Reservations sometimes needed days ahead of time. $15.95–19.95, includes sorbet after entrées; also a selection of cheese and fruit.

Lake House (583-4182 or 1-800-223-4182), Routes 35 and 37, Waterford. Open from 5:30 PM daily. A picturesque old inn with two intimate dining rooms. The wine list is impressive, with over 100 selections from around the world. Dinner specialties include Atlantic salmon, with a light sauce of tequila, lime, and butter, and veal Waterford (sautéed and topped with ham, Gruyère cheese, pimento, and mushrooms). Homemade desserts include parfait pie and flaming desserts for two. $16–21.

Center Lovell Inn (925-1575), Center Lovell. Open nightly (reservations requested); breakfast by reservation only. The northern Italian specialties include swordfish florentine, shrimp *fra diavolo* (in spicy tomato sauce with red and green bell peppers on rice), and veal Picatta. There are two pleasant dining rooms and a wraparound porch in summer. $14.95–20.95.

Westways on Kezar Lake (928-2663), Route 5, Center Lovell. Open nightly during summer; call to check off-season. Ask for a table on the dining porch with views over Kezar Lake and the mountains beyond. The dining room itself is formal, almost baronial. The core menu is supplemented by nightly specials, perhaps prime rib. There's a full wine list. No smoking in the dining room. Reservations requested. $11.95–18.95.

The Olde House (655-7841), just off Route 302 on Route 85, Raymond. Open for dinner daily. Elegant candlelight dining in a 1790 home that was once a well-known guest house. Specialties include Weiner schnitzel (sautéed veal with lemon sauce) and coquilles Saint Jacques mornay (scallops in light cream sauce with duchess potatoes topped with dilled Havarti). $11.95–19.95.

Oxford House Inn (935-3442), 105 Main Street, Fryeburg. Open nightly in summer and fall, winter and spring hours modified. Entrées include veal oxford, champagne poached salmon, and scallops l'orange. The setting is the former living room and dining room of a handsome 1913 house. $17–22.

Maurice Restaurant Francaise (743-2532), 113 Main Street, South Paris. Open daily for lunch and dinner and for Sunday brunch (no lunch on Saturday). A reasonably priced, classic French restaurant with four dining rooms. The specialty is scampi à la Provençal. Reservations recommended. $9.75–15.50.

Olde Rowley Inn (583-4711), Route 35, North Waterford. Open for lunch and dinner. Low-beamed dining rooms in a 200-year-old stage stop; specialties include game, seafood, and roast pork. $8.95–18.95 at dinner.

Bridgton Lobster Pound (647-8610), Route 302, Bridgton. Open year-round for lunch and dinner. A classic, 25-year-old seafood restaurant with fish tanks, fishnet decor, worn wooden tables, and a sink in the dining room to wash off the lobster and butter. You can get a hot dog or a cheeseburger, but the specialties are lobster and fried seafood dinners. Beer and wine. Moderate.

EATING OUT

Cracked Platter (583-4708), Maine Street, Harrison. Open 6 AM–1 AM daily, except 7 AM–1 PM on Sunday. This is a terrific place, worth waiting for if you are driving up from the south. The menu is large, and the cooking is down home; friendly family atmosphere.

Shaner's Family Dining (743-6367), 193 Main Street, South Paris. Open for breakfast, lunch, and dinner, a large, cheerful, family restaurant with booths, specials like fried chicken, liver and onions, and chicken pie; creamy homemade ice cream in an unusual choice of flavors.

Cole Farms (657-4714), Route 100/202, Gray. Open 5 AM–10:30 PM daily except Monday. Specialties include the fried fish plate and seafood Newburg. This is Maine cooking from family recipes. Everything from soups and chowders to ice cream and pastries made on the premises. No liquor.

ENTERTAINMENT

FILM
Magic Lantern, Main Street, Bridgton, presents film classics and first-run cartoons.

Windham Hill Mall on Route 302 has a cinema that shows first-run movies.

MUSIC

Sebago–Long Lakes Region Chamber Music Festival (627-4939), DeerTrees Theater, Harrison. A series of concerts held mid-July through mid-August.

THEATER

DeerTrees Theater (583-6747), Harrison. Once a popular 1930s summer theater, abandoned until the 1980s, when the town of Harrison and individual volunteers turned it into a nonprofit organization. It is once again becoming a cultural center for the area, with the chamber music festival, comedians, and shows by the resident theater company "The Dear Deer Players."

Celebration Barn Theater (743-8452), South Paris. Summer workshops in acrobatics, mime, and juggling by resident New Vaudeville artists who stage concerts Friday and Saturday nights in summer.

SELECTIVE SHOPPING

ANTIQUES SHOPS

Those with a fondness for browsing can find many flea markets and antiques shops along Route 302, with Bridgton being the regional center for antiques.

Wales & Hamblen Antiques Center (647-8344), 134 Main Street, Bridgton. A showcase for the wares of 30 dealers; the 1882 building itself has been restored with original woodwork and shelving.

BOOKSTORES

Annie's Book Stop (892-9366), Cumberland Farms Plaza, Route 302, North Windham. Current best-sellers at major discounts, children's corner, out-of-print and used books.

Books 'n' Things (743-7197), Oxford Plaza, Route 26, Oxford. Billing itself as "Western Maine's Complete Bookstore," a fully stocked store with a full children's section and a branch store in Bethel.

Downtown Bookshop (743-7245), 200 Main Street, Norway. Closed Sunday. A source of general titles, stationery, cards, and magazines.

CRAFTS SHOPS

Glassworks, Route 114 (2.8 miles off Route 302), Naples. Open Memorial Day to Labor Day, 10–4. The showroom and studio of glassblower Glenn Ziemke and jeweler Kathe Ziemke. Glenn designs and hand blows perfume bottles, paperweights, goblets, and vases in striking color combinations. Kathe makes porcelain earrings and porcelain bead necklaces.

Bridgton Arts and Crafts Society, Depot Street, Bridgton. Open during July and August, Tuesday through Saturday. Displays a variety of handicrafts by members.

Emphasis on Maine, 36 Main Street, Bridgton. Open daily. Displays work by more than 700 New England artists and craftspeople—superior stuff.

SPECIAL SHOPS

Sportshaus, 61 Main Street, Bridgton. Open daily. Known for its original Maine T-shirts; also a selection of casual clothes, canvas bags, tennis rackets, downhill and cross-country skis, athletic footwear, swimwear, and golf accessories. All housed in a pillared, 18th-century house.

Sheep Shop at Chardia Farm (583-2996), 1533 Maple Ridge Road, Harrison. A working farm selling wool and sheepskin products, hand-spun yarn, and shearling coats, vests, hats, and gloves.

United Society of Shakers (926-4597), Route 26, New Gloucester. Open Memorial Day to Columbus Day; sells Shaker herbs, teas, handcrafted items.

SPECIAL EVENTS

July: **Independence Day** is big both in Bridgton and Naples. Bridgton events include a lobster/clambake at the town hall, a road race, a concert, arts and crafts fair, and fireworks. In Naples, the fireworks over the lake are spectacular. Also in early July, the **Oxford 250 NASCAR Race** draws entrants from throughout the world to the Oxford Plains Speedway. In late July, a major **crafts fair** at the town hall is sponsored by the Bridgton Arts and Crafts Society; the 3-day **Lakes Region Antique Show** is held at the high school; and the **Bean Hole Bean Festival** in Oxford draws thousands.

August: **Gray and Windham Old Home Days,** both in the beginning of the month, include a parade, contests, and public feeds. In Lovell, the **Annual Arts and Artisans Fair** (mid-month) is held on the library grounds: chicken barbecue, book and crafts sale.

September: **Oxford County Agricultural Fair** in West Paris is usually held during the second week.

October: **Fryeburg Fair,** Maine's largest agricultural fair, is held for a week in early October, climaxing with the Columbus Day weekend. This is an old-fashioned agricultural happening—one of the most colorful in the country.

December: **Christmas open house and festivals** in Harrison, Paris Hill, and Naples.

Bethel Area

Bethel is a natural farming and trading site on the Androscoggin River. Its town Common is the junction for routes west to the White Mountains, north to the Mahoosucs, east to the Oxford Hills, and south to the lakes.

When the train from Portland to Montreal began stopping here in 1851, Bethel also became an obvious summer retreat for city people. But unlike many summer resorts of that era, it was nothing fancy. Families stayed the season in the big, white farmhouses, of which there are still plenty. They feasted on home-grown and home-cooked food, then walked it off on nearby mountain trails.

Hiking remains a big lure for many visitors. The White Mountain National Forest comes within a few miles of town, and trails radiate from nearby Evans Notch, many of them used for the llama treks now becoming popular in Maine. Just 12 miles northwest of Bethel, Grafton Notch State Park also offers some short hikes to spectacles such as Screw Auger Falls and to a wealth of well-equipped picnic sites. Blueberrying and rockhounding are local pastimes, and the hills are also good pickings for history buffs.

The hills were once far more peopled than they are today—entire villages have vanished. Hastings, for example, now just the name of a National Forest campground, was once a thriving community complete with post office, stores, and a wood alcohol mill that shipped its product by rail to Portland, thence to England.

The Bethel Inn, born of the railroad era, is still going strong. Opened in 1913 by millionaire William Bingham II and dedicated to a prominent neurologist (who came to Bethel to recuperate from a break- down), it originally featured a program of strenuous exercise—one ad- mired by the locals (wealthy clients actually paid the doctor to chop down his trees) as well as by the medical profession. This strenuous exercise is still recognized as a pioneer concept in physical therapy, and the inn still has an extensive exercise program (golf, tennis, swimming, boating, and cross-country skiing) as well as a sports center.

Bethel is best known these days as a ski town. Sunday River, 6 miles to the north, claims to "offer the most dependable snow in North America" and, despite its relatively low altitude, has managed to produce

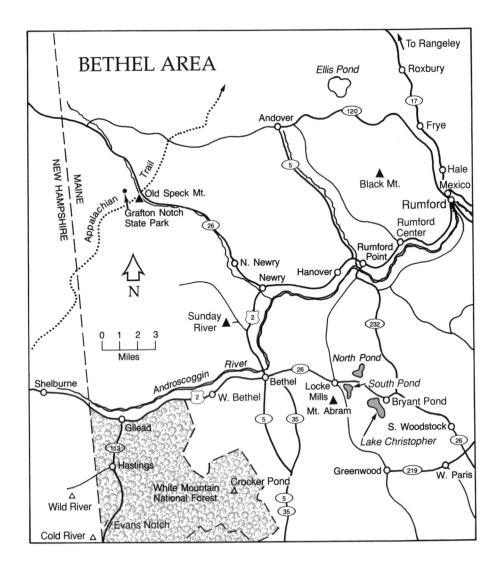

BETHEL AREA

dependable snow conditions even when snow is scarce. Powered by its snow guns (powered in turn by water from the Androscoggin), it has doubled and redoubled its trails, lifts, and lodging. Its facilities and prices are geared to families—and attract them in droves, up to 10,000 skiers per day. Mount Abram, a few miles east of the village, has undergone major changes in the last couple of years but remains one of Maine's friendliest low-key family areas. A wide choice of inns, bed & breakfasts, shops, and restaurants complete the inviting scene.

For Bethel, however, tourism has remained the icing rather than the cake. Its lumber mills manufacture pine clapboards, furniture parts, and most of this country's broom handles. Three dairy farms ship 7000 gallons of milk per week. Bethel also hosts Gould Academy, a co-ed prep school with a handsome campus. Brooks Brothers is the name of the hardware store, not a men's clothier; and, even though Main Street has its share of quality crafts shops, it also has Preb's—carrying envelopes, diapers, liquor, ice cream, Timex watches, toys, and stationery.

Skiers tend to see Bethel as "a quick hit" that you simply get to— and out of—without stopping on the way to the snow-covered trails 75 miles north of Portland. In summer, it's a very different story. As it has been since settlement, Bethel is a natural way station—between the White Mountains and the coast, and between the lake resorts and children's camps to the south and Rangeley to the north. From Bethel, Route 2 follows the Androscoggin north, and Route 232 north from Bryant Pond threads a deep valley. Either way, you can't avoid Mexico, the classic old paper mill town in which you pick up Route 17 (see "Rangeley Lakes Region"—*Getting There*).

GUIDANCE

Bethel Area Chamber of Commerce (824-2282), PO Box 439, Bethel 04217, publishes an excellent area guide and maintains a reservation service (824-3585 or 1-800-442-5826). Look for the "?" sign outside the chamber's office/information center on Lower Main Street (Route 26).

Sunday River maintains its own toll-free reservation number (1-800-543-2SKI), good nationwide and in Canada; the service is geared toward winter and condo information, but also serves local inns and B&Bs.

Bethel Outdoor Adventures (836-3607 or 1-800-533-3607), Route 2, West Bethel. Geared to travelers entering Maine from New Hampshire; a combination gift store, adventure center, and State of Maine Information Center, well stocked with statewide pamphlets and information.

GETTING THERE

By air: **Portland Jetport,** served by Continental Express, United, Delta, USAir, and TW Express, is 75 miles from Bethel. All major car rentals are available at the airport. **Bethel Air Service** (824-4321) offers air taxi/charter service.

By car: Bethel is a convenient way stop between New Hampshire's White Mountains (via Route 2) and the Maine coast. From Boston, take the Maine Turnpike to Gray, Exit 11; Bethel is 55 miles north on Route 26. There are restaurants en route in South Paris (see "Sebago and Long Lakes Region").

MEDICAL EMERGENCY
Bethel Area Health Center (824-2193), or Sheriff's Department (1-800-482-7433).

TO SEE

MUSEUM
Bryant Pond Telephone Museum (336-9911), Rumford Avenue, Bryant Pond. This was the last town in the country to use an old-style crank phone (until 1983), and visitors are welcome to see an exhibit of the magneto telephone system. Open the last Saturday in September or by appointment.

HISTORIC SITES
Moses Mason House (824-2908), 15 Mason Street, Bethel. Open July and August, 1–4 daily except Monday, and by appointment the rest of the year; $2 per adult, $1 per child. This exquisite Federal-style mansion, home of the Bethel Historical Society, is proof of the town's early prosperity. Restored to its original grandeur when it was owned by Dr. Moses Mason, one of Bethel's most prominent citizens in the 1800s, it has Rufus Porter murals in the front hall and fine furnishings, woodwork, and special exhibits.

Woodstock Historical Society Museum (665-2450), Route 26, Bryant Pond. Open Memorial Day to Labor Day, Saturday 1–4 or by appointment. An old barn housing a collection of old furniture, glass, uniforms, books, wooden toys, pictures, and, of course, a crank phone.

COVERED BRIDGE
Artist's Covered Bridge, Newry (across the Sunday River, 5 miles northwest of Bethel). A weathered town bridge built in 1872 and painted by numerous 19th-century landscape artists, notably John Enneking. A great spot to sun and swim. Other swimming holes can be found at intervals along the road above the bridge.

SCENIC DRIVES
Evans Notch. Follow Route 2 west to Gilead and turn south on Route 113, following the Wild and then the Cold Rivers south through one of the most spectacular mountain passes in northern New England. (Also see *Hiking* and *Campgrounds*.)

Grafton Notch State Park. A beautiful drive even if you don't hike (see *Hiking*).

Patte Brook Multiple Use Management Demonstration Area. A 4-mile, self-guided tour with stops at 11 areas has been set up along Patte Brook near the National Forest's Crocker Pond campground in West Bethel.

The tour begins on Forest Road No. 7 (Patte Brook Road), 5 miles south of Bethel on Route 5. A glacial bog, former orchards and home-sites, an old dam and pond are among the clearly marked sites.

TO DO

AIRPLANE RIDES
Bethel Air Service (824-4321). Steve Whitney and Dan Bilodeau offer daily scenic flights of the area with views of the Bethel and Appalacian Mountain areas year-round. Also offer flight instruction, air taxi/charter, and public lounge.

BICYCLING
Sunday River's Mountain Bike Park (824-3000 or 1-800-543-2SKI), Sunday River Ski Area, Newry. A chair lift accesses 38 miles of bike trails. Lift and trail passes are $17, sold at the White Cap Base Lodge. Lodging, lift, and meal packages available. Rental bikes are $27 per day with lift and trail pass.

Bethel Outdoor Adventures (836-3607) offers scheduled, guided mountain bike tours as well as custom tours. Rental bikes are also available in Bethel from **Mahoosuc Mt. Sports** (824-3786), Main Street, Bethel; **Tom O'Rourke's Bike Shop** (665-2267), Route 26, Bryant Pond; and **Great American Bike Renting Company** (824-3092; they also do bike tours), Sunday River Road, Bethel.

CANOEING
Popular local routes include the **Ellis River** in Andover (13 easy miles from a covered bridge in East Andover to Rumford Point); the **Androscoggin River** (the reach from Gilead to West Bethel has many islands, splendid mountain views); and the **Sunday River** (Newry to Bethel beginning at the covered bridge, great white water in spring). A chain of water connects **North, South,** and **Round Ponds** and offers a day of rewarding paddling, with swimming holes and picnic stops en route.

Bethel Outdoor Adventures (836-3607), Route 2 in West Bethel, offers shuttle service and a map of the Androscoggin as well as canoe rentals and guided trips. Guided trips are also available from **Mahoosuc Mountain Adventures,** Newry. Rentals can be found at **Tom O'Rourke's Bike Shop** (665-2267), Route 26, Bryant Pond, and from **Bob's Corner Store** (see *Fishing*).

CHAIR LIFT RIDES
Sunday River Ski Resort (824-3000) offers scenic chair lift rides up the mountain (you must walk down, since the chair is not equipped to carry passengers down). Weekends and holidays mid-June to Columbus Day weekend. The views of the Mahoosuc Mountains are particularly nice in autumn.

DOGSLEDDING
Mahoosuc Mountain Adventures (824-2073), Bear River Road, Newry 04261. Polly Mahoney and Kevin Slater offer combination backcountry

skiing and mushing trips. You can be as involved with the dogs as desired: an hour, a day, or a 3-day, 2-night trip.

Bethel Outdoor Adventures (see *Canoeing*) also offers dogsledding trips.

FISHING

Temporary nonresident licenses are available at the **Bethel Town Office,** Main Street, or at **Bob's Corner Store & Texaco Station** (875-2419), Route 26 South, Locke Mills. Full- and half-day fishing trips on Kezar and Sebago Lakes are available through **White Birch Guide Service.**

GOLF

Bethel Inn and Country Club (824-2175), Bethel. An 18-hole, championship-length course and driving range. Club and golf cart rentals are available.

HIKING

White Mountain National Forest, although primarily in New Hampshire, includes 41,943 acres in Maine. A number of the trails in the Evans Notch area are spectacular. Trail maps for the Baldface Circle Trail, Basin Trail, Bickford Brook Trail, and Caribou Trail are available from the Evans Notch Ranger District (824-2134), Bridge Street, Bethel— open Monday through Friday 8–4. Detailed maps are also available from the chamber (see *Guidance*).

Grafton Notch State Park, Route 26, between Newry and Upton. From Bethel, take Route 2 east to Route 26 north for 7.8 miles. Turn left at the Getty station (Newry Corner) and go toward New Hampshire for 8.7 miles. **Screw Auger Falls** is 1 mile farther—a spectacular area at the end of the Mahoosuc Range. Other sights include **Mother Walker Falls** and **Moose Cave,** a ¼-mile nature walk. The big hike is up **Old Speck,** the third highest mountain in the state; up Old Speck Trail and back down the Firewarden's Trail is 5½-miles.

Step Falls can be found just before the entrance to Grafton Notch State Park. From the Getty station at Newry Corner, go 7.9 miles. On the right will be a white farmhouse, followed by a field just before a bridge. There is a road leading to the rear left of the field where you may park. The well-marked trail is just behind the trees at the back. Please respect the private property adjoining the trail and falls. This scenic area on Wight's Brook, maintained by the Nature Conservancy, has been enjoyed by local families for generations.

In Shelburne there are hiking trails on **Mount Crag, Mount Cabot,** and **Ingalls Mountain,** and there are more trails in **Evans Notch.** For details, check the AMC *White Mountain Guide* and *Fifty Hikes in Southern Maine* by John Gibson, published by Backcountry Publications, Woodstock, VT 05091.

✐ LLAMA TREKKING

Telemark Inn & Llama Farm (836-2703), RFD 2, Box 800, Bethel 04217. Treks offered April through October. "Llamas are a natural for these mountains," enthuses owner Steve Crone. You lead a llama, and it carries

SHARON MCNEIL

Skiing at Sunday River

your gear plus the tent and food supplied by Steve and his fellow guides, who prepare a feast on top of the mountain and set up camp. You can also learn about the flora and fauna around you and how to photograph it. Treks range from 1 to 6 days, and packages can include camping or lodging at Steve's Telemark Inn (see *Inns*).

ROCKHOUNDING
This corner of Oxford County is recognized as one of the world's richest sources of some minerals and gems. More than a third of the world's mineral varieties are said to occur here. Gems include amethyst, aquamarine, tourmaline, and topaz. Mining has gone on around here since tourmaline was discovered at Mount Mica in 1821. Although **Perham's** of West Paris (see "Sebago and Long Lakes Region" and *Rockhounding* under "What's Where in Maine") is the famous starting point for most rockhounders, Jim Mann's **Mt. Mann** shop on Main Street, Bethel, is a trove of information as well as the source for fine gemstone jewelry that he has mined himself, then cut and set (he also designs settings to order). By summer of 1995, Jim plans to offer educational tours of a large mine in the area. Jim admits that he spends too much of his day talking with fellow rockhounders about the rock specimens on display.

SWIMMING
There are numerous lakes and river swimming holes in the area. It is best to ask the chamber (see *Guidance*) about where access is currently possible. "Never fail" spots include the following:
Artist's Covered Bridge. Follow Sunday River signs north from Bethel, but continue on Sunday River Road instead of turning onto the ski-area

access road. Look for the covered bridge on your left. Space for parking, bushes for changing.

Wild River in Evans Notch, Gilead, offers some obvious access spots off Route 113, as does the **Bear River,** which follows Route 26 through Grafton Notch.

CROSS-COUNTRY SKIING

Sunday River Ski Touring Center (824-2410), Bethel (based at Sunday River Inn, near the ski area). A total of 40 km of double-tracked trails loop through the woods, including a section to Artist's Covered Bridge. Thanks to the high elevation, careful trail prepping, and heavy-duty grooming equipment, snow tends to stick here when it's scarce in much of Maine. The center offers guided night skiing, rentals, instruction, and snacks.

Bethel Inn and Country Club (824-2175), Bethel. Forty km of trails meander out over the golf course and through the woods, offering beautiful mountain views, solitude, and challenges suitable for all levels. Skating and classic trails, rental equipment, and lessons available.

Carter's X-Country Center (539-4848), Middle Intervale Road (off Route 26 south of the village), Bethel. Dave Carter, a member of one of Bethel's oldest families and a longtime cross-country pro (he helped launch the Jackson Ski Touring Foundation in the 1970s), maintains some 65 km of wooded trails on 1000 acres, meandering from 600 up to 1800 feet in elevation; an easy loop connects two lodges and runs along the Androscoggin River. Reasonably priced equipment rentals and lessons.

Telemark Inn & Llama Farm (836-2703), West Bethel. Though it's not a formal touring center, the inn maintains 20 km of trails and unlimited backcountry skiing terrain for its guests; the public is invited to use them, too (number of skiers limited; please call first). Because of their elevation (1500 feet) and wooded nature, the trails hold snow when there's relatively little around.

Also see Mahoosuc Mountain Adventures under *Dogsledding* and contact the Bethel Ranger Station for details about cross-country trails in the White Mountain National Forest (see *Hiking*).

DOWNHILL SKIING

Ski Mount Abram (875-2601), Locke Mills. A year ago, Rick and Micki Hoddinott got together with four other partners and spared this longtime skiing tradition from a sad fate. The mountain belonged to the bank when the Hoddinotts bought it, with the goal of promoting family skiing at "good Maine rates."

The area was recently expanded to 35 trails and slopes, which hold some pleasant surprises, including two new black diamond trails and a "cruiser" trail. The vertical drop is 1030 feet.

Facilities include 65–70 percent snowmaking; two double chair lifts and three T-bars; an expanded "barn red" lodge with lounge, snack shop, Keenan Co. ski shop, nursery, and ski rentals; and 60 condominiums. PSIA ski school is offered, and there is a variety of special programs, including two-for-one skiing on Tuesdays.

Lift tickets are divided into three categories: adult, teen, and junior. Adults ski on weekends for $28 full day, $20 half day, and $49 for a 2-day pass. Teen prices are $21, $16, and $37; juniors (ages 6–12) ski for $15, $12, and $25. Midweek prices are $18 for adults and teens, $12 for juniors. Children under age 5 ski free. Learn-to-ski packages include lessons, rentals, and lift tickets. The best deal is the 3-day, $45 learn-to-ski option.

Sunday River Ski Area (824-3000; resort reservations: 1-800-543-2SKI), Bethel 04217. Sunday River has become synonymous with snow. Powered by the incessant output of its snow guns and grooming fleet, it has shown substantial growth every year for the past 14 years. Owner Les Otten seems determined to outstrip Killington in Vermont and make Sunday River New England's largest ski resort. It was as part of Killington's management team that 23-year-old Otten first came to 12-trail Sunday River. That was in 1972, an era when environmentalists were calling the shots in Vermont, curtailing Killington's growth—so it happened that a big Vermont resort bought a little Maine ski area. Killington's Sherburne Corporation installed a chair lift and some snowmaking equipment, then got the green light to expand again on its own turf. In 1980 it sold Sunday River to Otten. It was from Killington that Otten imbibed an obsession with snowmaking and a sense of how trails can multiply along a range of mountains. What it lacks in altitude (the highest peak is just 2793 feet), the resort makes up for in easy access to water, the essential ingredient in snowmaking.

At Sunday River, 101 trails now lace seven interconnected mountain peaks, including the Jordan Bowl, new in 1994. Challenges include a 3-mile run from a summit and White Heat—"the steepest, longest, widest lift-served expert trail in the East." The trails are served by seven quad chair lifts (three high-speed detachable), five triple chair lifts, and two doubles. The vertical "descent" is 2300 feet. Snowmaking is on 90 percent of the skiing terrain.

Facilities include three base lodges and a Mountaintop Peak Lodge, ski shops, and several restaurants; a total of 5000 beds are in condominium hotels with pools and Jacuzzis, town houses, a new slope-side Summit Hotel, a Snow Cap Inn (really a lodge), and the Snow Cap Ski Dorm (geared to groups).

The 1993 season saw the debut of the Silver Bullet Ski Express, a train that runs from Portland to Sunday River on the historic Grand Trunk Railroad route. A success, the train has been the trigger for a proposed real estate development called Bethel Station, which in addition to serving as a home base for the ski train would offer hotels, shops, restaurants, and a first-run movie theater.

The ski school offers Guaranteed Learn-to-Ski in One Day and

Perfect Turn clinics, SKIwee for ages 4–6, Mogul Meisters for ages 7–12, a Junior Racing Program, and a Maine Handicapped Skiing Program.

Lift tickets are $79 per adult and $48 per junior for two days on weekends; less midweek. Many lodging packages available.

ICE SKATING
In winter, a portion of Bethel's Common is flooded, and ice skates can be rented from the cross-country center in the Bethel Inn.

SNOWMOBILING
Local enthusiasts have developed a trail system in the area. Contact the chamber (see *Guidance*) for information on where to get maps. Maine and New Hampshire also maintain 60 miles of trails in the Evans Notch District.

SLEIGH RIDES
Steve Crone offers sleigh rides in winter (see *Llama Trekking*); so does Sunday River Ski Resort (see *Downhill Skiing*), and the Bethel Inn and Country Club (see *Inns*).

LODGING

Also see Lake House, Bear Mountain Inn, Kedarburn Inn, Westways, Farrington's, and Quisisana in "Sebago and Long Lakes Region."

INNS
Bethel Inn and Country Club (824-2175), Bethel 04217. This rambling, yellow structure with mansionlike cottages dominates the town Common. There are 65 guest rooms, all with phones and private baths. The common rooms downstairs are large and formal, but there is nothing starchy about the downstairs Mill Brook Tavern. The formal dining room is one of the loveliest around, with a fireplace and windows overlooking the mountains (see *Dining Out*). There are also 40 condominiums and a recreation center with a pool and hot tub, two saunas, exercise room, game room, and lounge. The pool is outdoors but heated to 91 degrees for winter use. Other amenities include an 18-hole golf course, tennis court, a boathouse with canoes and sailfish, and a sandy beach on Songo Pond; winter facilities include an extensive cross-country ski network (see *Golf, Cross-Country Skiing, and Sleigh Rides*). $70–150 per person double occupancy in rooms; $140–360 per condo unit (no meals). Many packages are available, including bargain-priced weekends in late fall and spring.

✐ **Philbrook Farm Inn** (603-466-3831), Shelburne, NH 03581. Open May through October and December 26 through March. Although it is 2 miles into New Hampshire, this grand old inn is very much a part of the Bethel area, the last survivor among the dozens of local farms that began taking guests in the 1860s. A framed child's drawing in a hallway reads, "Only generations can come here. We are the fifth generation." Actually, the fourth and fifth generations of Philbrooks run the place, but newcomers

are welcome. The 19 guest rooms are furnished with the kind of hand-me-downs for which most innkeepers scour antiques stores and auctions. The five cottages (summer only) are very Victorian. There is a pine-paneled dining room, and the maze of public rooms includes spacious summer parlors. The rambling white building is secure on its own 1000 acres, sited on a knoll above the floodplain of the Androscoggin River. In winter, it caters to cross-country skiers; in summer, to hikers. It is accessible from Route 2 in Shelburne and from Bethel by a dirt road. $105–135 double, MAP (breakfast and dinner) plus 15 percent gratuity; $500 per week for a housekeeping cottage.

Telemark Inn (836-2703), RFD 2, Box 800, Bethel 04217. It is a challenge to describe this unusual retreat, set 2.5 miles up a private road among birch trees, surrounded by national forest. Owner Steve Crone says, "We don't fit anywhere," but the truth is, the place fits in too many categories, offering a little bit of everything. It's the perfect place for Crone's herd of llamas, and he was the first in New England to offer treks. In summer there are family vacation packages, guided hiking trips, canoeing, and mountain biking. Winter brings cross-country skiing (ranked as a top ski touring center by *Cross Country Magazine*), skating parties, elegant dining, and a beautiful sense of isolation. The inn itself is beautifully built, with paneling and a mineral-rich fireplace. It accommodates 12–17 guests, who dine at a huge, round dining table supported by slim tree trunks. Rooms share baths. $70–90 per room with breakfast; many packages available (see *Llama Trekking* and *Cross-Country Skiing*). Truly a spectacular spot for nature lovers.

Sunday River Inn (824-2410), RFD 2, Bethel 04217. Primarily a winter inn; open only to groups in summer and fall. A large fireplace, a selection of books, and quiet games are in the living room, and an adjacent room can be used for small conferences. A game room and sauna are also available to guests. Sleeping arrangements range from dorms to private rooms in the inn or adjacent chalet. The inn maintains its own extensive cross-country trail system and is handy to Sunday River Ski Area (see *Cross-Country Skiing* and *Downhill Skiing*). $40–75 per person includes two meals; children's rates.

L'Auberge (824-2774 or 1-800-760-2774), Mill Hill Road, Bethel 04217. A former barn (belonging to a long-vanished mansion), renovated many times for many uses, has for 18 years been a gracious inn. Completely renovated in spring of 1994, the seven guest rooms are decorated in individual styles from Colonial to Early American. The Theater Suite is unique and fun, with a large dressing room (where cots for kids can be put) and a staircase and balcony on the back wall—left over from the days when the building was a theater (this room was the stage). A baby grand piano stands in the large living room, which also has a hearth, plenty of books, and comfortable seating. Dinner is served to the public (see *Dining Out*). You can walk to village shops and restaurants just around the corner. $75–125 double with breakfast.

Sudbury Inn (824-2174), Lower Main Street, Bethel 04217. A nicely restored village inn built in 1873 to serve train travelers (the depot was just down the street). The 15 guest rooms are all different shapes and decors, but all have private baths. The downstairs public rooms are attractive, and the dining rooms are among the best around (see *Dining Out*); basement-level Suds Pub is a year-round evening gathering spot (see *Après-Ski*). $70–90 double, includes a full, "made-to-order" breakfast. (Also see Summit Hotel under *Ski Lodges and Condominiums*—"Sunday River.")

BED & BREAKFASTS

Chapman Inn (824-2657), Bethel 04217. A family find. A rambling white Federal house on the Common in the National Historic District. A variety of options under one roof. It offers six spacious, carefully furnished rooms (two private, four sharing two baths) and three apartments with full kitchens. Breakfast is served in the elegant dining room. Facilities include an inviting TV room, a game room with pool table and two saunas, and a dormitory that sleeps 24. Handy to cross-country trails at the Bethel Inn, also to village shops and restaurants. $45–75 per room or apartment, $25 for the dorm; all rates include a full breakfast; midweek and ski-week specials.

Douglass Place (824-2229), Bethel 04217. A handsome, 20-room home that once took in summer boarders. Dana and Barbara Douglass have raised four daughters here and now graciously welcome guests. There are four guest rooms, one queen-sized bed and three with twin beds, a game room (with piano and pool table), a big homey kitchen where breakfast is served, attractive living and dining rooms, grounds, a gazebo, and a large barn. $45–55, includes continental breakfast with homemade muffins and fresh fruit.

Hammons House (824-3170), Broad Street, Bethel 04217. Sally Taylor has turned this exquisite 1859 home on the Common into a bed & breakfast. There are four spacious double rooms, two to a bath (two rooms can be joined to make a suite). A rear sun porch has been converted into an unusual, two-story conservatory overlooking the gardens (the upstairs is a nice reading spot). There are a number of pleasant, relaxing spaces and formal gardens in back. Also an antiques shop in the building once used as an amateur theater. $55–80 double or $90–150 for the suite. No smoking.

Holidae House (824-3400 or 1-800-882-3306), PO Box 851, Bethel 04217. A gracious Main Street house (the first in Bethel to be electrified), built in the 1890s by a local lumber baron. Five guest rooms and two efficiency apartments are furnished in comfortable antiques (the master bedroom in the rear of the house has a four-poster); each has cable TV, phone, and private bath. The common rooms include a lacy, formal living room and a family room with a wood stove. $40–85 double, includes a very full breakfast. Efficiencies $65 and up off-season to $150 in-season for four in the apartment that sleeps 8–10 (each extra person is $25). Dinner on request.

The Norseman (824-2002), Route 2, Bethel 04217. A fine old (parts date to 1799) farmstead with 10 light, pleasant guest rooms and 22 more units in the old barn. Guests in the house have access to the big, comfortable living room, with its fireplace made from local stones, and the dining room, with a similar hearth where breakfast is served. The motel units are spacious and handicapped accessible; amenities include laundry room and game room. $48–98 (breakfast is included in inn rooms but not with motel units).

☞ **Abbotts Mill Farm** (364-2697), RFD 2, Box 3702, Bryant Pond 04219 (7 miles north of Bryant Pond, off Route 232 and 3 miles south of Route 2). Grace McKivergan is a handweaver and spinner who sells her brightly braided rugs and woven mats in the barn attached to this rambling farmhouse, itself filled with samples of her ingenious work. The swimming pool, screened porch with rockers, and big country kitchen all seem to promise comfort and peace. The three upstairs guest rooms share a bath. The surrounding 16 acres include cross-country ski trails, foothills, and a brook for fishing (license required); and there's sugaring here in March. A blackboard menu notes the $10 dinner available on request. No children under 10; no smoking, please. $37 single, $48 double.

Field View B&B (665-2333), Rumford Road, Bryant Pond 04219. Irene and Sterling Mills raised four children in this tidy farmhouse, and now they extend a down-home Maine welcome to guests who find their way here. Nothing fancy, but one of the two guest rooms has a canopy bed and private balcony. $45–50 includes a full breakfast.

SKI LODGES AND CONDOMINIUMS

Sunday River (824-3000; resort reservations: 1-800-543-2SKI), PO Box 450, Bethel 04217. Now offers more than 5000 "slope-side beds." There are nine condominium hotels, ranging from studios to three-bedroom units. Each complex has access to a pool, Jacuzzi, sauna, laundry, recreation room, and game room; **Cascades** and **Sunrise** offer large common rooms with fireplaces, and **Fall Line** has a restaurant. **Merrill Brook Village Condominiums** have fireplaces, and many have whirlpool tubs. **South Ridge** also offers fireplaces in each unit—from $120 for a studio to $480 for a three-bedroom unit; rates are lower off-season. Rooms in the 68-room **Snow Cap Inn,** which has an atrium with fieldstone fireplaces, exercise room, and outdoor Jacuzzi, are $110–150. The 147-room **Summit Hotel and Conference Center,** with both standard and kitchen-equipped units and a health club with tennis courts, pool, and conference facilities, offer rooms from $150–540 (for two bedroom) per night (less for multiday stays) in winter, much less in summer.

Pine-Sider Lodge (665-2226), 481 Gore Road, Bryant Pond 04219-6113.

Bill and Ernestine Riley designed and built Pine-Sider for families and groups. Closed April and May. The lodge is divided into four efficiency units (the Rileys live in one), sleeping four to eight people, just 5 minutes from Mount Abram, 20 minutes from Sunday River. $250–325 per week in summer; $160–275 per weekend (lower midweek, 2-night minimum), or $500–675 per week in winter.

☞ **The River View Motel** (824-2808), Route 2, 357 Mayville Road, Bethel 04217. An attractive motel offering 32 two-bedroom suites, each with a fully equipped kitchen, living room, dining area, and large modern bath; each unit sleeps four comfortably (one queen, two twin beds) and has cable TV, phone, air-conditioning, and daily maid service. The complex also offers a riverside nature path, playground, Jacuzzi, sauna, game room, and tennis court. $50 double in summer ($65 for four people), $69–90 double in winter ($89–140 for four), plus $2 gratuity per night.

MOTELS

Bethel Spa Motel (824-2989), Main Street, Bethel 04217. The 10 units are upstairs in the middle of the village, over shops. Nothing fancy, but comfortable with phone and color cable TV. $28 single, $40 double.

Mollyockett Motel (674-2345), West Paris 04289 (20 minutes south on Route 26 from Bethel). A 20-unit motel with highly rated rooms, three efficiencies, and an attractive stone addition that houses the heated indoor pool, sauna, and whirlpool. $55–85.

CAMPGROUNDS

In the **Evans Notch area** of the White Mountain National Forest there are five campgrounds: Basin (21 sites), Cold River (12 sites), Crocker Pond (7 sites), Hastings (24 sites), and Wild River (11 sites). All accept reservations during the May 13 to October 11 season. Phone: 1-800-280-2267, Monday through Friday (Pacific time, so from the East Coast, phone between 12–9 or Saturday and Sunday 1–6). For information, phone the Evans Notch Ranger Station (824-2134), Bridge Street, Bethel.

Littlefield Beaches (875-3290), RFD 1, Box 4300, Bryant Pond 04219. Open Memorial Day to October. A clean, quiet family campground surrounded by three connecting lakes. Full hookups, laundry room, miniature golf, game rooms, swimming. Daily and seasonal rates are available, reduced rates in June and September.

OTHER LODGING

The Maine House (1-800-646-8737), Lake Road, Bryant Pond. A unique option in lodging, this self-service guest house does not have a live-in manager or owner. The facility is either rented to a large group, or there is a volunteer host. The 1791 house on Lake Christopher was once the winter home of President Rutherford B. Hayes's daughter, Frances. The current owners purchased the house in 1992 (they also own similar facilities in Vermont and on the Cape). The eight simply furnished bedrooms (shared baths) offer a variety of accommodations from bunk beds to queen beds. Facilities also include a rec room and steam bath.

WHERE TO EAT

DINING OUT

Bethel Inn and Country Club (824-2175), Bethel Common. An elegant, formal dining room with a hearth and large windows overlooking the golf course and hills, with a year-round veranda. All three meals are open to the public. Traditional New England fare; 16 entrées, starting at $14 for Yankee pot roast, including salad, potato or rice, and vegetable. Specialties include salmon and prime rib; don't pass up the desserts.

☞✐ **Mother's** (824-2589), Main Street, Bethel. Open daily for lunch and dinner. A green-and-white gingerbread house with three dining rooms, eclectically furnished with books, old pictures and oddments, and stoves. Lunch specialties are homemade soups and sandwiches. At dinner you can go with The Stew Pot ($6.95), a vegetarian stir fry ($8.95), or lamb chops with mint sauce ($14.95). Pastas are a specialty.

Sudbury Inn (824-2174), Main Street, Bethel. Open for breakfast, lunch, and dinner. A pleasant dining room and summer porch in a 19th-century village inn. Both lunch and dinner menus include pizza and salads, but chef Irv Skaff has put this place on Maine's culinary map, and it would be a shame to miss the chicken Chambord ($14) or flamed tenderloin *au poivre* ($18).

Legends at the Summit (824-3500), Sunday River. A fairly formal atmosphere to complement dinner entrées like roast quail ($18.95). Breakfast, lunch, and an evening pub menu also available.

L'Auberge (824-2774 or 1-800-760-2774), Mill Hill Road, Bethel. A country inn with three cozy dining rooms and a first-class chef. The menu might include an appetizer of escargot *en croute* ($6) and entrées like roast duck with Chambord-soaked cherries ($16), fettuccine *fruits de mer* ($19), and lemon caper chicken ($13).

(Also see The Olde Rowley Inn and The Lake House in Waterford, and Westways on Kezar Lake in "Sebago and Long Lakes Region.")

EATING OUT

Moose's Tale Food & Ale, The Sunday River Brewing Co. (824-4ALE), junction of Sunday River Road and Route 2. Dining areas surround brewing kettles and tanks. Patrons can choose from a variety of house brews to wash down soups and salads, burgers, and pizza. Often has live entertainment evenings.

Cisco & Poncho's (824-2902), Snows Falls. Closed Monday. Relocated from Bethel, this place still serves outstanding Mexican cuisine, but beware: hot means *hot*.

✐ **The Only Place** (836-3663), Route 2, West Bethel (3.5 miles west of Bethel). An oasis with a strong local reputation for its pizza, subs, and hot sandwiches; specialties such as *fritalini* platter (little fried dough morsels with cold cuts and cheese). Draft beer; wine and soda by the carafe.

Skidder's Deli (824-3696), lower Main Street, Bethel. Great deli meats plus baby back ribs, homemade pastries, box lunches.

Breau's (824-3192), just west of Bethel on Route 2; will deliver, and the pizza is good. Homemade clam "chowdah," chili, burgers, subs, and salads are on the menu, too. Open from 7 AM for full breakfast.

Mexico Chicken Coop Restaurant (364-2710), Route 2 in Mexico. Don't let the outside put you off. This is a great way stop if you are heading north up Route 17 from Bethel to Rangeley. The specialties are Italian, chicken, a huge salad bar, and fresh-baked pastries.

COFFEE BARS

Java House, Lower Main Street, Bethel. Indoor and outdoor seating, homemade muffins, pastries and breads, Green Mountain Coffee Roasters coffee. Open daily from 7 AM.

ENTERTAINMENT

APRÈS-SKI

The Backstage Restaurant and Lounge, Summer Street, Bethel. A great après-ski place, good for anytime snacks (buffalo chicken wings, mozzarella sticks, chili); also pasta, burgers, ribs, and steak. Open year-round.

Suds Pub, downstairs at the Sudbury Inn. Entertainment Thursday through Saturday, otherwise a friendly pub with 5 draft and 25 bottled beers; a reasonably priced pub menu. Open year-round.

SELECTIVE SHOPPING

ANTIQUES SHOPS

Hammons House and **Holidae House** in Bethel and the **Rumford Center Inn** in Rumford Center (Route 2) all maintain seasonal antiques shops. There is also **Bethel Depot Antiques** in Bryant Pond.

ART GALLERY

Baker's Art Gallery (824-2088), Sunday River Road. Open in summer only. A framing and matting shop that sponsors summer workshops in watercolor, drawing, oils, and color theory.

ARTISANS

Bonnema Potters (824-2821), Lower Main Street, Bethel. Open daily 8:30–5:30. Distinctive stoneware, noteworthy for both design and color: lamps, garden furniture, dinnerware, and the like produced and sold in Bonnema's big barn. Seconds are available.

The Wood & Glass Gallery, top of Main Street, Bethel. A gallery featuring handmade wood and glass gifts.

BOOKSTORE

Books 'n' Things (1-800-834-READ), Main Street, Bethel. A branch store of Oxford's bookshop. A large selection with specialties in regional titles, nature books, and gifts. A great children's section with playroom.

CRAFTS SHOPS

Groan and McGurn's Tourist Trap and Craft Outlet (836-3645), Route 2, West Bethel. Begun as a greenhouse—to which the owners' specially silk-screened T-shirts were added. Now there is so much that an ever-changing catalog is available.

Mountainside Country Crafts (824-2518), Sunday River Road, Bethel. "Thousands" of crafted creations, many of them made locally.

Meg 'n Gram Shop (824-2948), Route 26, Bethel. Daily 9–5 or when the flag is flying. A little shop specializing in wood crafts made in the adjoining workshop. Special orders welcomed.

SPECIAL SHOPS

Maine Line Products (824-2522), Main Street, Bethel. Made-in-Maine products and souvenirs, among which the standout is the Maine Woodsman's Weatherstick. We have one tacked to our back porch, and it's consistently one step ahead of the weatherman—pointing up to predict fair weather and down for foul.

Mt. Mann (824-3030), Main Street, Bethel. Jim Mann mines, cuts, and sets his own minerals and gems (see *Rockhounding*).

Keenan Co. Apparel Ski Outlet (824-2717), Main Street, Bethel. A branch of the Kingfield and Skowhegan stores; great clothing and sportswear, frequent sales.

Prebs Marketplace (824-2820), Main Street, Bethel. Open Monday through Saturday from 8:30 AM–10 PM. A full-service pharmacy; also the Western Union agent, Agency Liquor Store, and local source of Ben & Jerry's ice cream.

Mainely Fibers, Main Street, Bethel. Knitting, spinning, and basket-weaving supplies. Specializes in handspun yarns.

SPECIAL EVENTS

February: **Winter Carnival** at Carter's X-Country Ski Center.

March: **Pole, Paddle and Paw Race**—a combination ski and canoe event at the end of ski season.

July: **Strawberry Festival,** Locke Mills Union Church (date depends on when strawberries are ready; announced in local papers). **Mollyockett Day** (midmonth weekend)—road race, parade, bicycle obstacle course, fiddler contest, fireworks. Festivities honor an 18th-century medicine woman who helped the first settlers.

August: **World's Fair,** North Waterford (first weekend). **Sudbury Canada Days,** Bethel—children's parade, historical exhibits, old-time crafts demonstrations, bean supper, and variety show. **Blueberry Festival** at Locke Mills Church.

Autumn: **Blue Mountain Crafts Fair** at Sunday River Ski Resort.

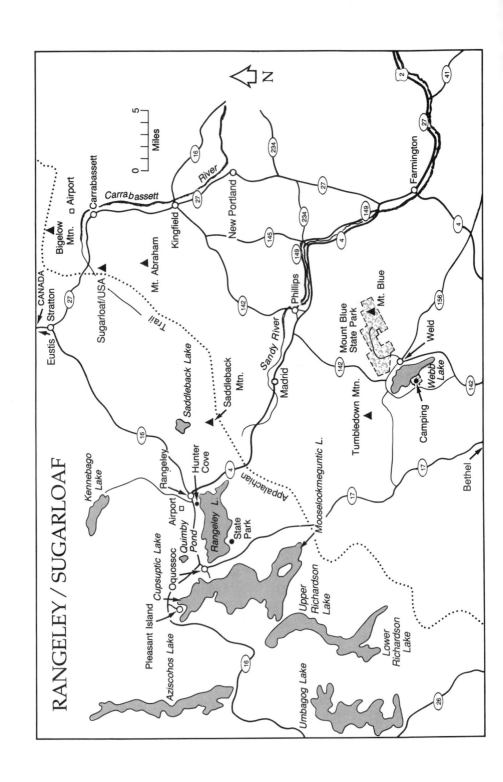

RANGELEY / SUGARLOAF

Rangeley Lakes Region

Seven lakes—Aziscoos, Richardson, Cupsuptic, Mooselookmeguntic, Kennebago, Umbagog, and Rangeley—plus dozens of ponds are scattered among magnificently high, fir-covered mountains, all within a 20-mile radius of the village of Rangeley. The big summer lures are fishing (landlocked salmon and brook trout) and hiking, and in winter there's snowmobiling and both alpine and cross-country skiing.

The Rangeley lakes region offers a sense of splendid isolation, thanks to 450 square miles of commercially forested land and genuine beauty, plus the mountains that hump up in every direction, inviting you to climb.

This has been a resort area since steamboat days, as evidenced by the dozens of vintage, rustic log lodges and cottages. Resort hotels are a thing of the past in this area, but photographs and postcards of days gone by can be found by browsers poking through area antiques shops.

In summer the town's population quadruples, but in winter, loggers outnumber skiers in the IGA. The skiers are here for Saddleback Mountain—a 4116-foot-high, 40-trail mountain with a high-altitude touring network that may just be New England's best-kept ski secret. On snowy weekends, it generally attracts only about 800 skiers. About the same number of snowmobilers take advantage of one of Maine's most extensive and best-groomed trail networks, found in the Rangeley area.

Doc Grant's Restaurant proclaims that Rangeley is 3107 miles from the North Pole and the same distance from the equator. It feels like a million miles from everywhere, especially if you spend some days in one of the traditional sporting camps scattered widely throughout the surrounding forest. The Maine classic, *We Took to the Woods*, written by Louise Dickinson Rich around 1940 near Lower Richardson Lake (which flows into Upper Richardson, which flows into Mooselookmeguntic), conveys a sense of the splendid isolation still possible.

GUIDANCE

Rangeley Lakes Region Chamber of Commerce (864-5364 or 1-800-MT-LAKES), PO Box 317, Rangeley 04970. Open year-round, Monday through Saturday 9–5. The chamber maintains a walk-in information center in the village, publishes a handy "Accommodations and

Services" guide and an indispensable map, keeps track of vacancies, and makes reservations.

GETTING THERE

By air: **Mountain Air Service** (864-5307) will pick you up at the **Portland Jetport** as well as other New England airports; also serves remote ponds and camps.

By car: From points south, take the Maine Turnpike to Exit 12 (Auburn), then Route 4. From New Hampshire's White Mountains, take Route 16 east. From the Bethel area, take Route 17 north (see *Scenic Drive*).

MEDICAL EMERGENCY

Franklin Memorial Hospital (778-6031) in Farmington is at least a 20-minute drive. **Rangeley Ambulance** (911).

VILLAGES

Byron. On Route 17 between Rangeley and Mexico, this rural area boasts a natural beauty as well as the **Coos Canyon** rest stop and picnic area. Sometimes high water rushes over the rocks in the river, and sometimes the water lazily makes its way along the canyon; nevertheless, it's always a sight worth seeing. Across the street is the Coos Canyon schoolhouse, now a community building, and a bulletin board with some interesting historic articles posted. Gold was first found in Maine in the Swift River in Byron.

Phillips, once the center of the Sandy River–Rangeley Lakes "2-footer" line, is now a quiet residential area. The town comes to life with Old Home days in late August.

Weld is another quiet residential area, centrally located between several good hiking options, including Mount Blue. You can also enjoy Mount Blue State Park beach area in summer, and good cross-country skiing and snowmobiling trails in the winter. There are a couple of good inns here, and Kawanhee Inn (see *Rustic Resorts and Sporting Camps*) overlooks Lake Webb.

TO SEE

MUSEUM

Wilhelm Reich Museum (864-3443), off Route 4/16, Rangeley. Open July and August, Tuesday through Sunday 1–5, Sundays in September 1–5; $3 per adult; children under 12 free. The 200-acre property, "Orgonon," is worth a visit for the view alone. Wilhelm Reich was a controversial pioneer psychiatrist and scientific thinker concerned with "objectifying the presence of a ubiquitous life force." He is buried on a promontory overlooking a sweep of lake and mountains next to one of his many inventions, a "cloudbuster." There are nature trails, children's activities, and a bookstore. The museum occupies a stone observatory that Reich helped design; it contains biographical exhibits, scientific equipment, paintings, and a library and study that remain as Reich left them.

HISTORIC SITES

Rangeley Lakes Region Historical Society (864-3317), Main and Richardson Streets, Rangeley. Open June 5 through September 17, Monday through Saturday 10–noon. This is a great little museum occupying the only brick building in the middle of town, featuring photographs and local memorabilia from Rangeley's days of grand old hotels, trains, and lake steamers. Note the jail cell in the basement.

Sandy River–Rangeley Lakes Railroad (353-8382). Runs May through October on the first and third Sundays of each month, and continuously through Phillips Old Home Days in late August. $3 per adult, $1.50 per child 6–12. From 1873 until 1935, this narrow-gauge line spawned resort and lumbering communities along its 115-mile length. Begun as seven distinct lines, it was eventually acquired by the Maine Central, which built shops and a large roundhouse in Phillips. Over the past decade, volunteers have produced a replica of the old steam locomotive, and others have helped lay a mile of track so that you can rattle along in an 1884 car just far enough to get a sense of getting around Franklin County "back when." A depot houses railroad memorabilia.

Phillips Historical Society (639-4001). Open August, Friday and Saturday 2–4, and by appointment June through October (phone 872-8745). The library and historical society are both in an 1820 house in the middle of the village. The collection includes many pictures of the railroad (see above) and an attic full of clothes for children to try on.

Weld Historical Society (585-2586), Weld Village. Open July and August, Wednesday and Saturday 1–3, and by appointment. The 1842 Museum House is filled with period furniture and clothing; also photographs. The original Town House (1845) houses farming, logging, and ice-cutting tools. A Heritage Day Fair is held here the last Saturday in July.

SCENIC DRIVE

Route 17, a posted scenic highway, is well worth taking to or from the area, even if it takes you a little out of your way. The road winds through a wide, mountain-walled valley by Coos Canyon, an interesting rock formation, waterfall, and picnic site in Byron (where gold was first found in America). The road also passes between the Height O'Land, a point where six lakes spread out below you (surrounded by mountains), and Rangeley Lake Overlook, which provides breathtaking views in the other direction. All along Route 17 are scenic turnout spots and many sights to remember.

TO DO

AIRPLANE RIDES

Mountain Air Service (864-5307) offers 15-minute scenic flights, longer fire patrol flights, and flight instruction.

BOAT EXCURSIONS

In addition to the following scheduled tours, there are half a dozen places that offer tours by appointment only. Check in the chamber of commerce "Visitor's Guide" pamphlet.

Expeditions North (864-3622), Route 17, Oquossoc, offers party-boat tours of Rangeley Lake.

The Queen (864-5608) offers weekend tours of Rangeley Lake from the Town Dock at 1:30 and 3:30 PM on a 20-passenger Chris Craft Cruiser.

BOAT RENTALS

Check with the chamber of commerce about the more than a dozen places in town that rent motorboats, canoes, sailboats, and waverunners, and be sure to rent one, because you are not really in Rangeley unless you are out on a lake one way or another.

CANOEING

Rangeley is the departure point for an 8-mile paddle to Oquossoc. On **Lake Mooselookmeguntic** there is a 12-mile paddle to Upper Dam, then a portage around the dam and another 8 miles to Upper Richardson Lake through the Narrows to South Arm. Check with the chamber of commerce about campsites (see *Guidance*). For canoe rentals, see *Boat Rentals,* above.

FISHING

Brook trout are plentiful in local streams. In the lakes, the big catch is land-locked salmon, for which the season is early spring through September. A number of fishing camps supply boats, equipment, and guides (see *Rustic Resorts and Sporting Camps*). The **Rangeley Region Sport Shop** (864-5615), Maine Street in Rangeley, specializes in fly-fishing and tying equipment; also a source of advice on where to fish and with whom (a list of local guides is posted).

GOLF

Mingo Springs Golf Course (864-5021), Proctor Road (off Route 4), Rangeley, offers 18 scenic holes; instruction, carts, and club rentals.

HIKING

The regional map published by the chamber of commerce (see *Guidance*) outlines more than a dozen well-used hiking paths, including a portion of the Appalachian Trail that passes over **Saddleback Mountain.** The longest hike is up **Spotted Mountain** (4½ miles to the top), and the most popular is the mile trail to the summit of **Bald Mountain;** both yield sweeping views of lakes, woods, and more mountains. Other favorites are Bemis Stream Trail up **Elephant Mountain** (6 hours round-trip) and the mile walk into **Angels Falls**—which is roughly 4 miles off Route 17; be sure to use a current trail guide.

In Weld, the tried-and-true trails are **Bald Mountain** (3 miles round-trip), **Mount Blue** (3¼ miles), and **Tumbledown Mountain** (a particularly varied climb with a high altitude).

MOOSE-WATCHING

Registered Maine guide **Rich Gacki** (864-5136) in Oquossoc offers guided canoe trips departing the Rangeley Inn most mornings at 5 AM. This is a 3-hour expedition; reservations are required by 6 PM the previous evening.

SWIMMING

Rangeley Lake State Park offers a pleasant swimming area and scattered picnic sites (see *Green Space*). Day-use fee; free under age 12. There is also a town beach with lifeguards and a playground at **Lakeside Park** in the village of Rangeley, and almost all lodging places offer water access. **Mount Blue State Park** also has a nice swimming area (see *Green Space*).

TENNIS

Public courts are maintained in Lakeside Park, Rangeley, and in the village of Oquossoc.

SKIING

Saddleback Mountain (864-5671; snow phone: 864-3380), Box 490, Rangeley 04970. This is a very big downhill ski area with a very small, fiercely loyal following. Saddleback itself, 4116 feet high and webbed with 40 trails, forms the centerpiece in a semicircle of mountains rising above a small lake. Twelve thousand acres—comprising most of this natural bowl—are now under Saddleback ownership, and a major four-season resort is planned. Trails and slopes include glade skiing, a 2.5-mile beginner trail, and an above-treeline snowfield in spring. The vertical drop is 1830 feet. Most trails are a shade narrower and twistier than today's average, but most intermediate runs such as Haymaker and White Stallion are memorable cruising lanes. Experts will find plenty of challenge on Bronco Buster, Powderkeg, and the Nightmare Glades terrain. Facilities include cafeteria, lounge, ski school, shop, rentals, nursery, and mountain warming hut. Lift tickets are $30 weekends ($18 juniors), $15 midweek.

Nordic Touring Center at Saddleback (864-5671) claims to be the highest altitude (2500 feet) cross-country touring center in New England. It offers 40 km of groomed trails, guided tours, rentals, instruction, norpining, and special events. We have seldom skied anything as beautiful as the isolated Rock and Midway Pond Trails—high, sheltered, and tracked by coyotes, bobcats, and snowshoe rabbits as well as by machine.

Mount Blue State Park (585-2347) also offers extensive cross-country skiing trails.

SNOWMOBILING

Rangeley Lake State Park offers 3 miles of marked trails with access to the lake; also a connecting trail with 20 more miles of groomed trails in **Mount Blue State Park.** Rangeley's snowmobile club maintains more than 140 miles of trails.

GREEN SPACE

(Also see *Campgrounds*.)

Rangeley Lake State Park (864-3858) covers 691 acres, including more than a mile of shoreline on the southern rim of Rangeley Lake between Routes 17 and 4. Open May 15 to early October. There are 40 scattered picnic sites, a pleasant swimming area, a boat launch, and children's play area; $2 per person.

Mount Blue State Park (585-2347), Weld (off Route 156). Open May 30 to October 15. The 6000-acre park includes Mount Blue itself, towering 3187 feet above the valley floor, and a beachside tenting area (136 sites) on Lake Webb. The lake is 3 miles wide and 6 miles long, good for catching black bass, white perch, pickerel, trout, and salmon. Boats may be rented from the ranger, and there is a recreation hall complete with fireplace. The view from the Center Hill area looks like the opening of a Paramount picture. Despite its beauty and the outstanding hiking, this is one of the few state camping facilities that rarely fills up. $1.50 per person admission.

Small's Falls, Route 4 (12 miles south of Rangeley). The Sandy River drops abruptly through a small gorge, which you can climb behind railings. A popular picnic spot and a swimming hole for daring youths. You can follow the trail to the **Chandlers Mill Stream Falls,** equally spectacular.

Hunter Cove Wildlife Sanctuary, off Route 4/16 west of Rangeley Village. Offers color-coded trails, winding in and out of the trees along a cove.

Dogs and sled in the Rangeley Lakes region

MAINE OFFICE OF TOURISM

LODGING

INNS
Rangeley Inn and Motor Lodge (864-3341), Rangeley 04970. Open year-round. A blue-shingled, three-story landmark, partly an annex to a vanished grand hotel that stood across the road, overlooking the lake; the classic old hotel lobby dates from 1907. There are 50 guest rooms, 12 with claw-foot tubs, some with water views; also 15 nicely decorated motel units, some with kitchenettes, whirlpool baths, and wood stoves, overlooking Haley's Pond, a bird sanctuary. Over the past 20 years, Fay and Ed Carpenter have remodeled all of the rooms, brightening them with flowery papers and comfortable antiques, installing private baths including some whirlpool baths, and decorating the halls with photos of 19th-century Rangeley. The dining room is large and excellent (see *Dining Out*), and there is plenty of lounging space for guests in the columned lobby, with its grand piano, and in the TV room. Popular with bus groups, but also a good spot for couples. Rates that include breakfast and dinner are available. $69–107 double.

Country Club Inn (864-3831), PO Box 680, Rangeley 04970. Open except April and November. Surrounded by an 18-hole golf course and overlooking the lake, this is a golfer's dream. Built by a millionaire sportsman in the late 1920s, this place has the feel of a private club. Massive stone fireplaces face each other across a gracious living room walled in knotty pine and stocked with books and puzzles. You are drawn to the view of lakes and mountains from the deck and from tables in the dining room. The 20 rooms are bright motel units, with picture windows and private baths. In winter you can cross-country ski from the door, and in summer there's an outdoor pool. $144–160 MAP double occupancy, less in winter.

BED & BREAKFASTS
✎ **Mallory's B&B Inn** (864-2121, 864-5316, or 1-800-722-0397), Box 9, Hyatt Road, Rangeley 04970. Open June 15 through October 15. A turn-of-the-century estate on the north shore of Rangeley Lake, with five bright guest rooms, four with water views, sharing three full baths. Our favorite is "Anna Maria," with an antique double bed and windows on two sides. There are two delightful common rooms; downstairs offers large comfortable couches, a fireplace, a piano, and a decorative "rocking moose." Upstairs, a TV, board games, and plenty of books are on hand for rainy days. The landscaped lawns slope to the lake out front, and there's a floating dock for swimming; a canoe, paddleboats, and mountain bikes are available, and the heated, indoor basketball court can be a blessing on rainy days. Scenic seaplane tours are available when Jay, a full-time pilot, is home, and Mingo Springs (see *Golf*) is next door. The Mallorys are delightful hosts. Children wel-

come, pets possible; $55–$65 double includes breakfast, $15 per extra child 12 and up, $10 for ages 2–11.

Lake Webb House (585-2479), PO Box 127, Route 142, Weld 04285. Open year-round. A pleasant, welcoming old farmhouse near the lake and village. Cheryl England makes the quilts that grace the beds in her four guest rooms (which share two baths). We would request one of the front rooms (choice of queen and twin beds). There's a pleasant family room with a wood stove. $45 double, includes a full breakfast featuring Maine blueberries and maple syrup.

Northwoods (864-2440), Main Street, Rangeley 04970. Open June through October and January through March. An expansive, vintage 1912 house in the village with lake views. Four guest rooms (the front ones have lake views and big bathrooms); $60–75 double with breakfast.

COTTAGES

Rangeley still has an unusual number of these traditional, family-geared "camps."

Sundown Lodge and Cottages (864-3650; 516-485-3059 in winter), Box 40, Oquossoc 04964. Open June to September. Just three delightful one- and two-bedroom cottages right on Mooselookmeguntic Lake, and another 4 miles away. Fireplaces, lawn games, and rental bikes, boats, canoes. $350–465 weekly.

Hunter Cove (864-3383), Mingo Loop Road, Rangeley 04970. Open year-round. Nine cottages on Rangeley Lake set on 6 wooded acres, each accommodating two to six people. Recently renovated, walled in knotty pine; handy to golf, Saddleback, and the village. Daily $80–120, weekly $500–750.

Mooselookmeguntic House (864-2962), Haines Landing, Oquossoc 04964. The grand old hotel by this name is gone, but the 10 log cabins are well maintained and occupy a great site with a beach and marina. Many of the one- and two-bedroom cabins are on the water and have fireplaces or wood stoves. $350–575 per week.

Sunset Point Cottages (864-3712; 802-863-4721 in winter, evenings). Five old-fashioned housekeeping cottages. Two or three bedrooms, gas lights, refrigerators and stoves, screened porches, and sandy beach on Mooselookmeguntic Lake.

Mountain View Cottages (864-3416), off Route 17, Box 284, Oquossoc 04964. Five well-spaced, two- to four-room cottages on the west shore of Rangeley Lake. $500–600 per week.

North Camps (864-2247), PO Box 341, Oquossoc 04964 (write E.B. Gibson). Open spring through hunting season. Fourteen cottages on Rangeley Lake among birches on a spacious lawn. Cottages have fireplaces or wood stoves, screened porches, and access to the beach, tennis, sailboats, fishing boats, and canoes. During July and August, rentals are available by the week only. Nightly rates and rates that include all three meals are available in spring and fall. $265–510 weekly.

Clearwater Sporting Camps (864-5424), Oquossoc 04964. Five cottages, all different, are scattered on private waterfront ledges along Mooselookmeguntic Lake. Michael and Tina Warren also offer boat rentals, a boat launch, swimming, and guide service. Camps $70 per day double; $475 per week.

Note: Some of the area's most famous old cottage clusters have been subdivided but are still available through local realtors. The former Flybuck, Quimby Pond, and Saddleback Lodge properties are all now handled by local realtors. **Rangeley Lakes Region Chamber of Commerce** (see *Guidance*) also keeps listings of available cottages.

CONDOMINIUMS

Saddleback Ski and Summer Lake Preserve (864-5671), Box 490, Rangeley 04970. There are two condo complexes at the ski resort— most units are exceptionally luxurious with views over the lake. Some two dozen are usually available for rent. From three to five bedrooms, many with hot tubs, cable TV; all have access to the clubhouse with its game room. $125–245 per night in summer, $140–365 in winter; weekly rentals also available.

RUSTIC RESORTS AND SPORTING CAMPS

The complexes easily accessible by public roads tend to cater to families, while the more remote "camps" (accessible only by water and private woodland roads) are geared to serious fishermen. All offer more than basic comfort and pride themselves on their meals.

Kawanhee Inn (585-2000), Weld 04285. (In winter contact Sturgis Butler and Marti Strunk, 778-3809 evenings; 7 Broadway, Farmington 04938.) Dining room open mid-June to Labor Day; cottages available from mid-May to mid-October. A traditional Maine lodge set atop a slope overlooking Lake Webb. There are 14 rooms in the inn itself; also 11 cabins that accommodate two to seven people each. Meals are served in the large pine dining room and on the screened veranda overlooking the water (see *Dining Out*). The open-beamed lobby has a massive central fireplace, a pool table, and numerous corners in which to read and talk. Guest rooms in the main lodge are simple and homey, and the cabins are delightful, each with its own fireplace and screened porch with rockers. There is a private beach and dock; canoes are available, and the local hiking is outstanding. Pets are welcome in a some of the cottages. Rooms start at $65 double; cabins from $500 per week (one bedroom), also by the day if available. Room rates include continental breakfast.

Bald Mountain Camps (864-3671), PO Box 332, Oquossoc 04964. Open Memorial Day to Labor Day. This is the surviving part of a complex that dates from 1897. Nicely old-fashioned, with fireplaces in 15 cabins and a log-style dining room, a safe sand beach, tennis courts, and lawn games. Right on Mooselookmeguntic Lake and exuding the kind of hospitality found only under long-term ownership. Stephen Philbrook is your host. $95 per person, all meals included; less for children and during May and June.

☞ **Bosebuck Mountain Camps** (243-2945; 486-3238 in winter), Wilsons Mills 04293. Open May through November. Accessible by boat or by a 14-mile private gravel road (phone to check gate times before you decide to drop by), the camps are sited at the remote end of Aziscoos Lake. The lodge houses a dining room overlooking the water and a sitting room filled with books; all heat is from wood stoves, and the 11 cabins have electric lights powered by a generator that runs 8 hours a day. Tom and Susan Rideout cater to serious fishermen, giving access to the Parmachenee area and to the Big and Little Magalloway Rivers (fly-fishing only). Three full meals are included in the rate: $75 per person per night ($70 for stays of longer than 3 days). If the moosehorn (radio phone) doesn't answer, keep trying. Dogs welcome. Family rates in July and August ($53 per person) when fishing eases off. Fishing package rate available in July.

Grant's Kennebago Camps (864-3608; 282-5264 in winter; 1-800-633-4815), PO Box 786, Oquossoc 04964. Open after ice breaks up and through September. A serious fly-fisherman's haven located 9 miles up a private dirt road on Kennebago Lake. Large, excellent meals are served in the comfortable dining room with terrific lake views. Cabins are rustic, knotty pine with wood stoves and a screened-in front porch overlooking the water. Each has a dock and boat exclusively for your use during your stay. $92 per adult, $30 per child including all meals; less for a 7-day stay.

Lakewood Camps (summer: 243-2959; 392-1581 in winter), Middledam 04216. Open after ice breaks up through September. The specialty is landlocked salmon and trout; fly-fishing in 5 miles of the Rapid River. Twelve truly remote cabins; meals feature fresh-baked breads, cakes, and pies. Access is from Andover. This is very much the same place described in *We Took to the Woods*. $85 per person (2-day minimum), double occupancy includes three full meals; $40 per child under 12, $15 under age 5, pets $5. Tax and gratuity not included.

CAMPGROUNDS

For information and reservations in both the state parks described below, phone 287-3821.

Rangeley Lake State Park (864-3858), between Routes 17 and 4, at the southern rim of Rangeley Lake. Some 50 campsites are well spaced among fir and spruce trees; facilities include a beach and boat launch, picnic sites, and a children's play area. $16 for nonresidents. There are also a number of private campgrounds and wilderness sites accessible only by boat; inquire at the chamber of commerce (see *Guidance*).

Mount Blue State Park (585-2347), Weld. Campsites cost $12 for out-of-staters, $10 for residents, and tend to get filled up after those in better-known parks (see *Green Space*).

WHERE TO EAT

DINING OUT

Also see restaurants described in "Sugarloaf and the Carrabassett Valley."
Porter House in Eustis and **The White Wolf** in Stratton are popular
dining destinations for Rangeley visitors.

Rangeley Inn (864-3341), Main Street, Rangeley. Closed mid-April to late
May; otherwise open for breakfast and dinner daily. A large hotel dining room with a high, pink, tin ceiling and a reputation for the best food
around, thanks to Sue Carpenter. Entrées range from the pasta of the
evening (under $10) to tournedos *au poivre* ($16.25). Some people
come just for desserts like and praline tulip cups. $9.95–18.95.

Kawanhee Inn (585-2243), Weld. Open for dining nightly, mid-June to
September. One of Maine's most picturesque, traditional-style lodges is
the setting for candlelight dining in the open-beamed dining room or
screened porch overlooking Lake Webb. Fresh flowers garnish the
tables, and meals are thoughtfully prepared. Fresh fish and Maine lobsters, crisp salads and warm breads, great desserts.

Country Club Inn (864-3831), Rangeley. Open every evening summer
and fall, weekends in winter by reservation only. The inn sits on a rise
above Rangeley Lake, and the dining room windows maximize the view.
Entrées run from $12.25 for a chicken dish to $15.95 for filet mignon.

Fineally's (864-2955), Saddleback Mountain Road, Rangeley. Open
Wednesday through Sunday year-round for dinner. Cozy, informal, with
Mexican specialties and standard fare like veal Marsala ($10.95) and
linguini with meatballs ($6.95).

EATING OUT

White Birch Cafe (864-5844), Main Street and Richardson Avenue,
Rangeley Village. Open for breakfast and lunch; Sunday for breakfast
only. Knotty pine walls, the favorite place in town for breakfast: pancakes,
bagels, Belgian waffles. Fresh Maine seafood and homemade desserts.

Red Onion (864-5022), Main Street, Rangeley. Open daily for lunch and
dinner. A friendly Italian American dining place with a sun room and
bier garten; fresh-dough pizzas and daily specials.

The Four Seasons Cafe (864-5291), Oquossoc. There's a bar, wood stove,
and standard menu but good, reasonably priced specials.

Doc Grant's Restaurant and Cocktail Lounge, Main Street, Rangeley.
Meals served 7 AM–8 PM seasonally. A lively lounge with light lunches
available until 1 AM; a game room with pool tables and video games,
draft beer, cocktails. Seafood rolls, chicken in the basket, omelets.

Gingerbread House (864-3602), Oquossoc. Open year-round, summer 6
AM–9 PM, otherwise 7–2; closed Tuesday. The marble soda fountain is
the big attraction, but there is also a variety of sandwiches and daily
breakfast and lunch specials; breakfast is always available.

Trading Post Restaurant and Tackle Shop, Route 16, Magalloway Plantations (30 miles west of Rangeley). Home-cooked food; for fly-fishermen, a large assortment of custom-tied flies.

Mike's Sports Pub & Grub (864-5616), Rangeley Village. Open daily for lunch and dinner. A pubby place with a big-screen TV featuring sports events; good for chili, sandwiches, or Yankee pot roast.

People's Choice (864-5220), Rangeley. Open year-round for breakfast, lunch, dinner. Standard fare. Weekend entertainment in the lounge includes live bands and the largest dance floor around (everyone comes).

ENTERTAINMENT

Rangeley Friends of the Performing Arts sponsors a July and August series of performances by top entertainers and musicians at local churches, lodges, and the high school. For the current schedule check with the chamber of commerce.

(Also see People's Choice under *Eating Out*.)

SELECTIVE SHOPPING

Accents of Rangeley (864-5347), Kennebago Road, Rangeley. Maine books, maps, cookbooks, children's books, stationery, and calendars.

Rodney Richard's Woodcarving (864-5072), Main Street, Rangeley. "The Mad Whittler," known for his chain-saw sculptures, welcomes visitors.

First Farm (864-5539), Gull Pond Road, Rangeley. Open seasonally, Monday, Tuesday, Friday, Saturday 10–5. Roughly a mile north of the town, marked from Route 16. Kit and Linda Casper's farm and farm shop have become a Maine legend.

Alpine Shop (864-3741), Main Street, Rangeley. A long-established village landmark: clothing, gifts.

(Also see Rangeley Region Sport Shop under *Fishing*.)

SPECIAL EVENTS

January: **Rangeley Lakes New England Sled Dog Races. Rangeley Snodeo.**

March: **Annual Sled Dog Race. Bronco Buster Ski Challenge** at Saddleback.

July: **Independence Day** parade and fireworks; **Old-Time Fiddler's Contest;** and **Logging Museum Festival Days.**

August: **Sidewalk Art Festival; Annual Blueberry Festival;** and **Phillips Old Home Days** (third week).

November: **Hunter's Ball.**

December: **Christmas Fair** at the Episcopal Church; and **Walk to Bethlehem Pageant,** Main Street, Rangeley. **Giving Tree Celebration.**

Sugarloaf and the Carrabassett Valley

Sugarloaf/USA is Maine's biggest ski mountain. The second highest mountain in the state, it faces another 4000-footer across the Carrabassett Valley—a narrow defile that accommodates a 17-mile-long town.

Carrabassett Valley is a most unusual town. In 1972, when it was created from Crockertown and Jerusalem townships, voters numbered 32. The school and post office are still down in Kingfield, south of the valley; the nearest drugstore, supermarket, and hospital are still in Farmington, 36 miles away. There are relatively few full-time residents, but there are now more than 5000 "beds." Instead of uptown and downtown, people say "on mountain" and "off mountain."

On mountain, at the top of Sugarloaf's access road, stands one of New England's largest self-contained ski villages: a dozen shops and a dozen restaurants, a seven-story brick hotel, and a church. A chair lift hoists skiers up to the base lodge from lower parking lots and from hundreds of condominiums clustered around the Sugarloaf Inn and its Sugartree Health Club. More condominiums are scattered farther down the slope, all served by a chair lift. From all places you can also ski down to the Carrabassett Valley Ski Touring Center, Maine's largest cross-country trail network.

More than 800 condominiums are scattered among firs and birches. To fill them in summer, Sugarloaf has built an 18-hole golf course, fostered a lively special events program, promoted rafting and hiking, and even seriously attempted to eliminate black flies.

Off mountain, down on Route 27, bargains are still to be found in the friendly, sometimes funky, ski lodges that predate the on-mountain bed boom. Most of the valley is still owned by paper companies and by the Penobscot Indian Nation. The old railway bed, along which narrow-gauge trains once puffed up the valley, is now a combination cross-country skiing and jogging trail.

In summer the focus shifts from the mountain to the golf course and the surrounding backwoods. The Appalachian Trail passes over Bigelow Mountain, while lodging places in the village of Stratton, north of Sugarloaf, cater to hikers. Just north of the village, Route 27 crosses a corner of Flagstaff Lake and continues through Cathedral Pines, an impressive sight and a good place to picnic. The 30,000-acre Bigelow Preserve, which embraces the lake and great swatches of this area, offers swimming, fishing, and camping. Eustis, a small outpost on the lake, caters to sportsmen and serves as a PO box for sporting camps squirreled away in the surrounding woodland.

Kingfield, at the southern entrance to the Carrabassett Valley, was founded in 1816. This stately town was the one-time home of the Stanley twins, inventors of the steamer automobile and of the dry-plate coating machine for modern photography. The town offers some first-rate dining, shopping, and lodging.

The Carrabassett River doesn't stop at Kingfield. Follow it south as it wanders west off Route 27 at New Portland, then a short way along Route 146 to see the striking, vintage 1841 Floodproof Wire Bridge. Continue on Route 146 and then west on Route 16 if you are heading for The Forks and the North Woods; to reach the coast, take Route 27 south through Farmington, a gracious old college town with some decent dining.

GUIDANCE

Sugarloaf Area Chamber of Commerce (235-2100), RR #1, Box 2151, Carrabassett Valley 04947. The chamber is well stocked with brochures on the area as well as statewide information. It also offers an area-wide, year-round reservation service (235-2500 or 1-800-THE-AREA) for lodging places on and off the mountain. Sugarloaf's toll-free reservations and information number for the eastern seaboard is 1-800-THE-LOAF; you can also call 237-2000.

GETTING THERE

By air: **Portland International Jetport** (779-7301), 2½ hours away, offers connections to all points. **Riverbend Express** (628-2877) offers ground transport year-round. **Rental cars** are available at the Portland International Jetport.

By car: From Boston it theoretically takes 4 hours. Take the Maine Turnpike to Exit 12 (Auburn), then Route 4, to Route 2, to Route 27; or take I-95 to Augusta, then Route 27 the rest of the way. (We swear by the latter route, but others swear by the former.)

GETTING AROUND

In ski season, the **Valley Ski Shuttle Bus** runs from the base lodge to the Carrabassett Valley Ski Touring Center and Route 27 lodges. It operates five times a day on weekends and holidays, three times on weekdays.

MEDICAL EMERGENCY

Franklin Memorial Hospital (778-6031), Farmington.

Sugarloaf/USA has its own emergency clinic, and the **Kingfield Area Health Center** (265-4555) has a full-time nurse and physician's assistant.

TO SEE

MUSEUMS

Stanley Museum (265-2729), School Street, Kingfield. Open year-round except April and November, Tuesday through Sunday 1–4. Suggested donation: $2 per adult, $1 per child. Housed in a stately wooden school donated by the Stanley family in 1903, this is a fascinatingly varied collection of inventions by the Stanley twins F.O. and F.E. (it was their invention of the airbrush in the 1870s that made their fortune). Exhibits range from violins to the steam car for which the Stanleys are best known. Three Stanley Steamers (made between 1905 and 1916) are on exhibit; also fascinating photos of rural Maine in the 1890s and elsewhere through the 1920s by Chanosonetta Stanley Emmons, sister of the two inventors.

The Western Maine Children's Museum (235-2211), RR 1, Box 2153, Carrabassett Valley 04947. Open in winter: weekends 1–5, Monday 3–7, additional hours during school vacations; otherwise hours vary. Hands-on exhibits include math and science tables, a dress-up corner, computers, and a real plane where kids hear the control tower as they take off. $2.50 per child; adults free.

Nordica Homestead Museum (778-2042), Holley Road, off Route 4 in Farmington. Open June to Labor Day, Tuesday through Sunday 10–noon and 1–5; also September and October by appointment. $2 per adult, $1 per child 6–12. This 19th-century farmhouse is the unlikely repository for the costumes, personal mementos, and exotic gifts given the opera star Lillian Norton, who was born here (she later changed her name to "Nordica").

Nowetah's American Indian Museum, Route 27, New Portland. Don't dismiss the sign as just another tourist trap. This collection of Native American artifacts from the US, Canada, and South America is fascinating. Nowetah Timmerman, a native of the Susquehanna and Cherokee tribes, has had her collection open to the public since 1969. The museum is clean and bright, and all items are well-researched and clearly labeled. A special room holds over 300 Maine baskets and bark containers. Free admission. There is also a gift shop selling Native American crafts made by Nowetah and her family.

HISTORIC SITES

Kingfield Historical Society (265-4871), Church Street, Kingfield. Open August, Sunday 1–4; also by appointment in July, September, and October. Local memorabilia of the narrow-gauge railroad, the Stanley family, and Maine's first governor, William King; also 19th-century clothes, dolls, and a general store.

Dead River Historical Society (246-6901), Stratton. Open weekends in summer, 11–3. Displays memorabilia from the "lost" towns of Flagstaff and Dead River, photos of early 1900s logging operations, logging tools.

BRIDGES

Fireproof Wire Bridge, on Wire Bridge Road, off Route 146 (not far) off Route 27 in New Portland. Nowhere near anywhere, this amazing-looking suspension bridge across the Carrabassett River has two massive, shingled stanchions. The bridge is one of Maine's 19th-century engineering feats (it was built in 1841). There's a good swimming hole just downstream and a place to picnic across the bridge; take a right through the ball field and go 0.5 mile on the dirt road. Note the parking area and path to the river.

TO DO

BICYCLING

Mountain bikers are discovering that the winter ski trails on Sugarloaf make for some great rides. Bring your own or rent a bike at the **Sugarloaf Mountain Bike Shop** (237-6998), where maps and information are also available.

FISHING

Thayer Pond at the Carrabassett Valley Recreation Center, Route 27, is a catch-and-release pond open to the public, with fly-fishing lessons, boat rentals, and fish for a fee.

The village of Eustis, north of Stratton, is serious fishing country, with the **Arnold Trail Sport Shop** serving as a source of equipment, information, and canoe rentals. In Eustis, both **Tim Pond** and **Tea Pond,** described under *Sporting Camps,* are traditional fishing camps. The **Arnold Trail Service Station** (Irving), **Pines Market,** and **Northland Cash Supply** in Stratton also carry fishing gear. Inquire about fly-fishing schools at Sugarloaf.

GOLF

Sugarloaf Golf Club (237-2000), Sugarloaf/USA. A spectacular, highly rated, 18-hole course designed by Robert Trent Jones II, teaching pro. Weekend and midweek golf schools and packages are offered in-season.

HIKING

There are a number of 4000-footers in the vicinity and rewarding trails up **Mount Abraham** and **Bigelow Mountain.** The Appalachian Trail signs are easy to spot on Route 27 just south of Stratton; popular treks include the 2 hours to Cranberry Pond or 4 hours plus (one way) to Cranberry Peak. Pick up detailed hiking maps locally or check the AMC *Mountain Guide* or *Fifty Hikes in Southern Maine* (Backcountry Publications) by John Gibson, which detail several spectacular hikes in the 17-mile Bigelow Range (35,027 acres now lie within the Bigelow Preserve).

SWIMMING

Cathedral Pines, Route 27, Stratton. Just north of town, turn right into the campground and follow signs for the public beach on Flagstaff Lake. No charge.

(Also see Fireproof Wire Bridge in *To See*.)

WHITEWATER RAFTING

Day trips on the Kennebec are offered; $150 midweek to $200 weekends includes 2 nights' lodging, the ride, cookout, meals.

(Also see "The Upper Kennebec Valley and Jackman"—*Whitewater Rafting*.)

CROSS-COUNTRY SKIING

Carrabassett Valley Ski Touring Center (237-2205). Open in-season, 9 AM–dusk. This is Maine's largest touring network, with 85 km of trail loops, including race loops for timed runs. Rentals and instruction are available. The center itself includes the Klister Kitchen, which serves soups and sandwiches; space to relax in front of the fire with a view of Sugarloaf; and a rental area.

Holly Farm Resort (778-4869), Farmington (marked from Route 27). Trails meander across fields and into the woods; 11 km of groomed trails. This rustic family lodge has a dining room, an indoor pool, and a sauna.

Titcomb Mountain Ski Touring Center (778-9031), Morrison Hill Road (off Route 2/4), Farmington. A varied network of 20 km of groomed trails and unlimited ungroomed trails; used by the University of Maine at Farmington.

Troll Valley Cross-Country Ski and Fitness Center (778-3656), Red Schoolhouse Road, Farmington. Gently rolling terrain and scenic views; 25 km of groomed trails designed for the tourer rather than the racer. Ski school, rentals, and guided tours.

Fly-fishing near Sugarloaf

SUGARLOAF NEWS BUREAU

DOWNHILL SKIING

Sugarloaf/USA (general information: 237-2000; snow report is ext. 6808; on-mountain reservation number is 1-800-THE-LOAF). Sugarloaf Mountain Corporation was formed in 1955 by local skiers, and growth was steady but slow into the 1970s. Then a boom decade produced one of New England's largest self-contained resorts, including a base village complete with a seven-story brick hotel and a forest of condominiums. Sugarloaf has been expanding and improving snowmaking and services ever since. Snowmaking now even covers its snowy cap.

Trails number 101 and add up to 39 miles. The vertical drop is a whopping 2820 feet. The 15 lifts include a new SuperQuad, a four-passenger gondola, two quad chairs, a triple chair, eight double chairs, and two T-bars. Facilities include ski school, cub ski school, ski shop, rentals, base lodge, cafeteria, nursery (day and night), game room, and a total of 18 bars and restaurants. Services include a first-rate nursery and children's ski school programs for 3-year-olds to teens; also mini-mountain tickets for beginners.

Call for current 1-day lift rates (also multiday, early and late season, and packaged rates). Under age 6 lifts are free.

DOGSLED RIDES

T.A.D. Dog Sled Services (246-4461 or 237-2000), PO Box 147, Stratton 04982. Tim Diehl offers rides by his team of Samoyeds, "The White Howling Express." The 1½-mile rides leave approximately every half hour throughout the day during ski season from his base on Route 27 just north of the Sugarloaf access road. Drop by just to see his friendly, frisky dogs, all of whom were "unwanted pets" until Diehl adopted and trained them. He owns 19 and usually uses a team of 10 to pull the light, two-person (a child can also be snuggled in under the blanket) tobog-gan sled. You glide along low to the ground (lower than the feathery tails of the white Samoyeds), through the woods on trails Diehl main-tains. In summer, cart rides are offered.

ICE SKATING

Sugarloaf Ski Touring Center (237-2205) maintains a lighted rink and rents skates.

SNOWMOBILING

Snowmobile trails are outlined on many maps available locally; a favorite destination is Flagstaff Lodge (maintained as a warming hut) in the Bigelow Preserve.

HEALTH SPAS

Sugarloaf Sports and Fitness Center (237-2000), Sugarloaf Inn Resort, Carrabassett Valley. Amenities include a pool, racquetball courts, sau-nas, outdoor hot tubs, steam rooms, Jacuzzis in the dressing rooms, and a beauty salon. Available to all guests at the Sugarloaf Inn and Sugarloaf Mountain condominiums and to the public on the basis of available space.

Herbert Hotel (265-2000), Kingfield. An attractive sauna and a Jacuzzi room—with a moose head pictured in tiles above the hot tub—can be rented by the hour.

LODGING

Sugarloaf/USA Inn and Condominiums (1-800-THE-LOAF or 237-2000), Carrabassett Valley 04947. Some 330 ski-in, ski-out condominiums are in the rental pool. Built gradually over the last 20 years (they include the first condos in Maine), they represent a range of styles and sites; when making a reservation, you might want to ask about convenience to the base complex, the Sugarloaf Sports and Fitness Center (to which all condo guests have access), or the golf club. From $110 for a studio to $460 for a five-bedroom condo during ski season; less in summer and through special packages. The 42-room **Sugarloaf Inn** offers attractive standard rooms and fourth-floor family spaces with lofts. Amenities include a comfortable living room with fireplace, a solarium restaurant (see *Dining Out*), a 24-hour, manned front desk, access to the Sugartree Health Club and to the mountain via the Snubber Chair. $72–156 per night, less in summer.

Sugarloaf Mountain Hotel (1-800-527-9879), RR 1, Box 2299, Carrabassett Valley 04947. So close to the base complex that it dwarfs the base lodge, this is a massive, seven-story, 119-room brick hotel with a gabled roof and a striking central tower. Built at a cost of $9 million, it has been turned into condominiums, and many of the units are "quarter shared." All rooms are large and tastefully furnished, and most have small refrigerators and microwaves. There are also four 2-bedroom suites, each with a living room and kitchen, and two palatial tower penthouses, each with three bedrooms, three baths, and a hot tub. Amenities include a library and a health club with a large hot tub and plunge pool, sauna, and steam room. $90–160 per night, multiday discounts, less in summer.

INNS AND BED & BREAKFASTS

Some Sugarloafers prefer to stay a full 17 miles south of the mountain in Kingfield because it is such a classic Maine village.

The Herbert (265-2000 or 1-800-THE-HERB), PO Box 67, Kingfield 04947. Open year-round. "We're away from 'condomania,'" says Bud Dick, a long-time Sugarloaf skier who has lovingly restored this hotel, billed as a "palace in the wilderness" when it opened in 1918 in the center of Kingfield. In 1982, when Dick purchased it, the hotel was downright derelict, with 230 broken water pipes and no electricity. The "fumed oak" walls of the lobby now gleam, and there's a fire in the hearth beneath the moose head. Soak up the warmth from richly upholstered chairs and enjoy music from the grand piano by the big windows. The peach-colored dining room is now frequently filled for all three meals, and the fare is exceptional (see *Dining Out*). The 33 rooms are simple but tasteful, and bathroom units have Jacuzzis. $52–58 in summer and fall, $56–80 during ski season; includes continental breakfast.

Three Stanley Avenue (265-5541), Kingfield 04947. Designed by a younger brother of the Stanley twins, now an attractive bed & breakfast next to the more ornate One Stanley Avenue, also owned by Dan Davis (see *Dining Out*). There's a nice feel to this place, and each room is different. Number 2 has twin beds and a bath with claw-foot tub, and number 1, an ornate sleigh bed with claw-foot tub. We also like number 6 (no bath), and number 4 is good for a family (one double, one twin bed). Although there is no common room, guests are welcome to use the elegant sitting room with its flak wallpaper and grandfather clock next door at One Stanley Avenue. In summer, the lawns and woods are good for walking. Breakfast is included. $50–60, less midweek and in summer.

Inn on Winter's Hill (1-800-233-WNTR), RR 1, Box 1272, Winter Hill Road, Kingfield 04947. A Georgian Revival mansion (rare in Maine) designed by the Stanley brothers for Amos G. Winter (his son, Amos Jr., founded the Sugarloaf Mountain Ski Area). The historic house enjoys many distinctions, including being the first in Maine with central heat. In the historic section, there are four luxury rooms that share a private upstairs sitting area. Another 16 units are in the new section, a replica of the original (burned) barn. Amenities include a pool, hot tub, tennis, lounge, and elegant dining room (see *Dining Out*). $75–125 summer, $68–138 winter. Inquire about special packages.

River Port Inn (265-2552), Route 27, Kingfield 04947. An 1840 roadside farmhouse on the edge of town with comfortable, nicely decorated guest rooms, a living room, and big, friendly dining area in which guests tend to linger over home-baked breakfasts and bottomless cups of coffee. $40–80 per room depending on day and season.

Widow's Walk (246-6901 or 1-800-943-6995), PO Box 150, Stratton 04982. A Victorian home in Stratton Village (closed Columbus Day through December 1 and some weeks in summer). The six guest rooms (five have twin beds, the sixth, a double and a twin) are very basic with shared baths, but Mary and Jerry Hopson are friendly hosts and the living room is inviting, with games for children. This is a popular stop for Appalachian Trail hikers. $46 double during ski season includes a full breakfast; $30 double in summer with breakfast. No smoking.

SKI LODGES AND MOTELS

Lumberjack Lodge (237-2141), Carrabassett Valley; off-season: RR 1, Box 2230, Kingfield 04947. Open ski season and (more or less) the rest of the year. A three-story, chalet-style complex of eight efficiency units (each sleeps up to eight people) with a sauna and a game room. As near as you can get to the slopes on Route 27; also the nearest lodging to the touring center. Owner Paul Schipper skis every day and may just know more about the mountain than anybody. $18–32 per person depending on the number of guests.

Spillover Motel (246-6571), PO Box 427, Stratton 04982. An attractive, two-story, 20-unit (12 nonsmoking) motel just south of Stratton Village. Spanking clean, with two double beds to a unit, color cable TV, phone. $40–65 plus $5 for each additional person, includes continental breakfast.

SPORTING CAMPS

Tim Pond Wilderness Camps (243-2947), Eustis 04936. Open after the ice breaks up through November. Accessible only by a private road in the remote wilderness northeast of Rangeley; in business since the 1860s and billed as "the oldest continuously operating sporting camp in America." The lure is fly-fishing for native square-tailed trout, far more prized than its hatchery-spawned kin. There are 10 log cabins, each with a fieldstone fireplace or wood stove; three meals are served in the lodge. Canoes and motorboats are available for use on this clear, remote lake, surrounded by 4450 acres of woodland, also good for hiking. $98 single per night, includes three meals; half price for children under age 12; no charge under age 5. Family rates during August.

The Sugarloaf Area Chamber of Commerce (see *Guidance*) keeps a list of second homes, ranging from classic, old A-frames to classy condos; the average price is $100 a day in ski season for a fully equipped house sleeping at least six; less in summer.

WHERE TO EAT

DINING OUT

One Stanley Avenue (265-5541), Kingfield. Closed May to December; otherwise open after 5 PM except Monday. Reservations are a must. Small, but the number one restaurant in western Maine. Guests tend to gather for a drink in the very Victorian parlor, then proceed to one of the two intimate dining rooms. Specialties include veal and fiddlehead pie, sweetbreads with applejack and chives, maple cider chicken, and saged rabbit with raspberry sauce. We have seldom savored more tender meat or moister fish, and the herbs and combinations work well. Owner-chef Dan Davis describes his methods as classic, the results as distinctly regional. $13–23 includes fresh bread, salad, vegetables, starch, coffee and teas, but it's difficult to pass on the wines and desserts.

The Herbert (265-2000), Main Street, Kingfield. Dinner is served after 5 PM, Wednesday to Monday. Sunday brunch 12–2:30. This elegant, old hotel dining room is decorated in lacy colors; tables are nicely set; service is friendly; dress is casual; and the wine list is extensive. A recent summer menu (read the history on the front while you wait) included chicken Dijon (breast meat sautéed with mushrooms, scallions, sun-dried tomatoes, and capers in a Dijon cream sauce, $13.95) and shrimp Athens (sautéed with tomatoes, garlic, dill, and black olives, topped with feta cheese, $15.95).

Hug's Italian Cuisine (237-2392), Route 27, Carrabassett Valley. A small eatery featuring northern Italian delicacies such as pesto Alfredo, carbonado, veal scampi, and prepared Huguette. A place not to miss, if you can get in.

Porter House (246-7932), Route 27, Eustis. Serving dinner "364 days a year." A country farmhouse located 12 miles north of Sugarloaf; also a pilgrimage point for Rangeley Lake visitors. There are four small dining rooms, a fire, and candlelight. Sip a specialty cocktail while you study the menu, which (of course) includes Porter House steak. Entrées run from $7.95 for fresh vegetable sautée to $16.95 for top sirloin with roast duckling; children's menu available. All breads, soups, and desserts are homemade. Full bar and wine list. Your chef/hosts are Beth and Jeff Hinman.

The Seasons (237-6834), Sugarloaf Inn, Carrabassett Valley. Breakfast daily, and dinner by reservation after 5 PM nightly in winter, Thursday through Sunday in summer and fall. Request a table in the glass-walled section of the dining room, particularly pleasant in winter because it overlooks the slope below Sugarloaf's base lodge. Spacious and softly lit; weekend entertainment in the adjacent Cirque Bar. Specialties include mustard chicken and baked haddock served with red bell peppers and topped with a saffron-orange cream sauce. $9.95–16.95.

The Truffle Hound (237-2355), Village West at Sugarloaf/USA, Carrabassett Valley. Open weekends in summer, for lunch and dinner in winter. Reservations are suggested for this cozy, candlelit place. Specialties include country pâté with the French delicacy, truffles.

Tufulio's (235-2010), Valley Crossing, Carrabassett Valley. Open nightly after 4:30. The menu is Italian, and the atmosphere congenial, with Maine's only nine-piece-band player piano. Specialties include veal Marsala, steak, and amaretto cheesecake; children's menu. Moderate.

Julia's (265-5426), The Inn on Winter's Hill. Offers both a prix fixe menu and à la carte dining in a formal, mansion setting. With the prix fixe, try one of Julia's wine tastings (a different wine with each course of the meal). Entreés might include beef Wellington ($21.95), Rock Cornish game hen ($16.95), and blueberry-apple duck breast ($20.95); prix fixe for $35.

F.L. Butler Restaurant & Lounge (778-5223), Front Street, Farmington. Open for lunch weekdays, dinner Monday through Saturday. Steaks, broiled fish, and Italian dishes served in a restored, Colonial-style tavern. $6.95–12.95.

Fiddleheads Restaurant (778-9259), 23 Pleasant Street, Farmington. Open for lunch and dinner except Monday. An upbeat, relaxed dining room furnished in hickory and oak; brick hearth. Specialties include fettuccine with prosciutto and mushrooms. $6.95–13.95.

EATING OUT

✐ **Longfellow Restaurant & Riverside Lounge** (265-4394), Kingfield. Open year-round for lunch and dinner (from 5 PM). An attractive, informal dining place in a 19th-century building decorated with photos of

19th-century Kingfield. There's a pubby area around the bar, an open-beamed dining room, and an upstairs dining space with an outdoor deck overlooking the river. Great for lunch (homemade soups, quiche, crêpes, and a wide selection of sandwiches); a find for budget-conscious families at dinner. Specialties include steak teriyaki, chicken Longfellow, seafood, and Italian dishes. Children's plates are available. $5.50–12.50.

The Bag (237-2451), Sugarloaf Mountain. Open for lunch and dinner. Unbeatable Bag Burgers, great pizza, homemade soups, curly french fries, entertainment, booths, and a friendly bar.

The White Wolf (246-2922), Stratton. Open daily for breakfast, lunch, and dinner. A find featuring homemade soups, reasonably priced entrées with local ingredients (dinner includes full salad bar), and some of the best desserts (try the peanut butter pie) in western Maine. The sure touch belongs to Sandy Isgrow, a former chef's assistant at One Stanley Avenue (see *Dining Out*). There's a nice feel to the front dining room with its flowery curtains by the bar (breakfast and lunch) and to the larger space in back where dinner is served. Breakfast from 8 AM, $.99 and up; lunch specials from $2.25; and dinner (the board changes daily according to what is fresh and in-season) runs from $3.95 for a Big Beef Burger to $16.95 for a venison game combo.

The Woodsman, Route 27, Kingfield, north end of town. Pine paneled, decorated with logging tools and pictures, a friendly, smoky barn of a place, good for stacks of pancakes, great omelets, endless refills on coffee, homemade soups and subs, local gossip.

Nostalgia Tavern, a warm place with an old-fashioned feel. Nightly specials might include a 16-ounce prime rib ($9.95) and veal and eggplant Parmesan ($10.95). Kids are sure to love the five peanut butter sandwich choices (one is peanut butter and pickles).

D'Ellies (237-2490), Village West at Sugarloaf. An on-mountain treasure: great make-your-own sandwiches on freshly made bread with your choice of condiments (like Pesto Mayo). The turkey, chicken, soups, and stews are made on the spot, all to-go, along with morning coffee and muffins.

Carrabassett Yacht Club (235-2730), Route 27 at the Valley Motel. Dinner nightly, nice atmosphere. Menu includes gourmet pizza and fresh seafood; children's menu available.

Trail's End (246-7511), Eustis. Open for lunch and dinner most days. Full bar, hefty sandwiches, hearty entrées like rare prime rib and charbroiled ham steak, and homemade pies. Caters to skiers, snowmobilers, hunters, fishermen, and woodsmen.

ENTERTAINMENT

APRÈS-SKI

Sugarloaf Brewing Company (237-2211). A brand new microbrewery on the shuttle route. A great place to relax with a Carrabassett Ale, Misery

Bitter, or Dead River Porter after a vigorous day on the slopes.

SELECTIVE SHOPPING

Patricia Buck, "Emporium of the Western Mountains" (265-2101), Main Street, Kingfield, and two shops in the Alpine Village at Sugarloaf/ USA. Open daily. Features Patricia Buck's own patterned sweaters, hats, and leg warmers; also carries arts and crafts supplies, books, cards, gourmet coffees, spices, clothing, antiques, and myriad stocking stuffers. Don't miss the second-floor art gallery in the Kingfield store. Yet another branch can be found in Farmington.

Devaney, Doak & Garret (778-3454), 29 Broadway, Farmington. The outstanding general bookstore in the area.

Keenan Auction Company (265-2011), Kingfield. Open daily. A great family clothing store featuring brand names at discounts: Woolrich, Oshkosh, Maine Guide, and Nike are all here, plus bargain baskets full of ski mittens, goggles, and the like.

Mountain Video Inc. (265-2585), Route 27 just north of Kingfield and in Village South at Sugarloaf. Large selection of videos; also carries books.

SPECIAL EVENTS

January: **White White World Winter Carnival**—broom hockey, chili cookoff, bartenders' race, and discounts at Sugarloaf/USA.

March: **Sugarloaf Corporate Challenge Weekend;** and **St. Patrick's Day Leprechaun Loppet**—a 15-km, citizens' cross-country race.

April: **Easter Festival**—costume parade, Easter egg hunt on slopes, and sunrise service on the summit; **Reggae Festival** weekend.

May: **Sugarloaf Marathon.**

August: **Kingfield Days Celebration**—4 days with parade, art exhibits, potluck supper; **Old Home Days,** Stratton-Eustis-Flagstaff; **weekend jazz series.**

September: **Kingfield 10K Foot Race and Sugarloaf Uphill Climb; Franklin County Fair,** Farmington.

October: **Skiers' Homecoming Weekend,** Sugarloaf Mountain.

December: **Yellow-Nosed Vole Day,** Sugarloaf Mountain; and **Chester Greenwood Day,** Farmington, which honors the local inventor of the earmuff with a parade and variety show in Farmington.

VII. THE KENNEBEC VALLEY

Augusta and Mid-Maine
The Upper Kennebec Valley and Jackman

Participants in the Great Kennebec River Whatever Week

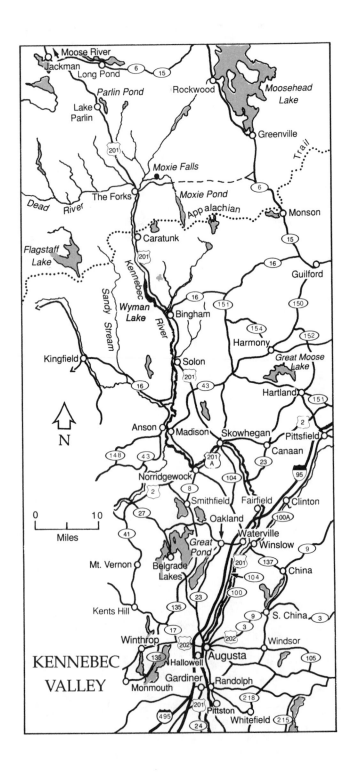

Augusta and Mid-Maine

Augusta, the capital of Maine, rises in tiers above the Kennebec River at its head of shipping navigation. This position provided a good hunting and fishing ground for the area's earliest inhabitants, the Norridgewock and Kennebec tribes of the Algonquins. In 1625 the Pilgrims sailed to this spot and traded "seven hundred pounds of good beaver and some other furs" with the Native Americans for a "shallop's load of corn." They procured a grant to the Kennebec, from Gardiner to a waterfall halfway between Augusta and Waterville, with a strip of land 15 miles wide on either side of the bank. At the Native American village of Cushnoc (present-day Augusta), they built a storehouse and, with the proceeds of their beaver trade, were soon able to pay off their London creditors.

With the decline of the fur trade and rising hostilities with the Native Americans, these settlers sold the tract of land to four Boston merchants for just 400 pounds. The merchants had plans—farming, timber, and shipyards. War halted these plans, and the settlers fled, but they returned in 1754 when the British built Fort Western. The area was selected as the capital in 1827, and a state house, designed by Charles Bulfinch and built of granite from neighboring Hallowell, was completed in 1832. During the mid-19th century, this area boomed: Some 500 boats were built along the river between Winslow and Gardiner, and river traffic between Augusta and Boston thrived. The era is still reflected by the quaint commercial buildings lining the river downstream in Hallowell (known for shopping and dining) and in Gardiner (recently restored; also a place to dine and browse).

Today Augusta remains worth a visit, if only to see one of the most interesting state museums in the country; exhibits vividly depict many aspects of landscape, industry, and history. Not far downriver from the museum door are some enticing restaurants, and shops line Water Street in Hallowell and Maine Street in Gardiner.

This lower Kennebec Valley is rolling, open farmland, spotted with lakes. Just north of the city the seven lakes in the Belgrade Lakes Region form an old resort area, blessed with cottage colonies that need not advertise and plenty of recreation from mail boat excursions to canoe rides, to relaxation plain and simple. East of the city the China Lakes form another low-profile haven. Good summer theater can be found in Waterville (upriver), Monmouth (another old resort area west of town), and Skowhegan (also known for its art school). In the past few years, attractive old homes throughout this region have opened their doors to guests—who are discovering not only the beauty of the immediate area but also that "mid-Maine" is the only true hub in this sprawling state, handy to many parts of the coast, the western lakes and mountains, and the North Woods.

GUIDANCE

Kennebec Valley Chamber of Commerce (623-4559), PO Box E, University Drive, Augusta 04332. The office is off I-95 (the exit for Route 27) in the civic center complex. This is a year-round source of information, primarily on the area from Augusta to Gardiner.

Belgrade Lakes Region, Inc., PO Box 426, Belgrade 04917, maintains a seasonal (late June to September) information booth on Route 27 and also publishes a pamphlet guide to the area.

China Area Chamber of Commerce (445-2890), Box 317, South China 04358. Year-round.

Mid-Maine Chamber of Commerce (873-3315), PO Box 142, Waterville 04901. Open year-round.

GETTING THERE

By air: **Colgan Air** connects Augusta with Boston and Presque Isle.

By bus: **Vermont Transit** serves Augusta and Waterville.

By car: You don't have to take the Maine Turnpike to reach the Augusta area; from points south, I-95 is both quicker and cheaper (I-95 and the turnpike merge just south of Augusta). If you are not in a hurry, the most scenic route to Augusta from points south is to follow the Kennebec River up Route 24 through Bowdoinham and Richmond.

MEDICAL EMERGENCY

Kennebec Valley Medical Center (626-1000), 6 East Chestnut Street, Augusta. **Mid-Maine Medical Center** (873-0621), North Street, Waterville. **Waterville Osteopathic Hospital** (873-0731), Waterville, also offers emergency service. **Redington-Fairview General Hospital** (474-5085), Fairview Avenue, Skowhegan.

VILLAGES

Richmond. If you follow the Kennebec River from Brunswick to Gardiner, you will be rewarded first with views of Merrymeeting Bay and then of rolling farmland sloping to the river. Richmond, at first glance, seems to be just another small mill town, but its onion-domed churches recall its Russian population, which numbered as many as 500 in the 1950s and 1960s. Cross the bridge in the middle of the village to find the Pownalborough Court House, which we have described in "Wiscasset."

Hallowell. This village is much the same as it was over 100 years ago. The store names may be different, but the Water Street commercial blocks, with two- and three-story, vintage mid-19th-century buildings, are definitely worth a stroll; known throughout New England for its number of antiques shops. Also note the restaurants we've described under *Where to Eat.*

Gardiner. Located where the Kennebec and Cobbossee Rivers meet, this old industrial (shoe, textiles, and paper) town has been nicely restored. Nineteenth-century Maine Street remains a great place in which to stroll and eat; also see *Entertainment.*

TO SEE

State House (287-2301), State Street, Augusta. Open year-round, Monday through Friday 8:30–4:30. Much modified since the original design by Charles Bulfinch; its size has actually doubled. A 180-foot dome has replaced the original cupola. There are markers that will lead you on a self-guided tour, or guided tours are available.

Blaine House (287-2301), State Street, Augusta. Open year-round, Monday through Friday 2–4, and by appointment. A 28-room mansion built in the 1830s by a Captain James Hall of Bath, later purchased by James Blaine, a Speaker of the United States House of Representatives, a United States senator, and twice secretary of state. Blaine was known as the "plumed knight" when he ran for the presidency in 1884, battling "Rum, Romanism and Rebellion." His daughter gave the mansion to the state in 1919, and it has since served as home for Maine governors.

Colby College (872-3000), Waterville 04901 (2 miles from Exit 33 off I-95; marked). Founded in 1813, Colby College enrolls close to 1700 students from 45 states and 22 foreign countries. Its 900-acre campus includes a performing arts center and an art museum featuring Maine works by Winslow Homer, Andrew Wyeth, and John Marin (open daily). Student-led tours are offered weekdays throughout the year.

MUSEUMS

Maine State Museum (287-2301), State Capitol Complex, State Street (Route 201/27), Augusta. Open weekdays 9–5, Saturday 10–4, and Sunday 1–4. Admission: $2 per adult, $1 per child or senior, maximum of $6 per family. Turn into the parking lot just south of the capitol building. This outstanding museum isn't even marked from the street! You have to know that it is in the State Library in order to find it.

Without question, it is the best state museum in New England. Allow at least an hour. The newest exhibit, "12,000 Years in Maine," traces the story of Maine's Native Americans with reproductions of petroglyphs and genuine ancient artifacts. This fascinating exhibit also dramatizes early European explorations and 19th-century attempts to explore the state's antiquities. Elsewhere, the museum re-creates a variety of Maine's landscapes and traditional industries: fishing, agriculture,

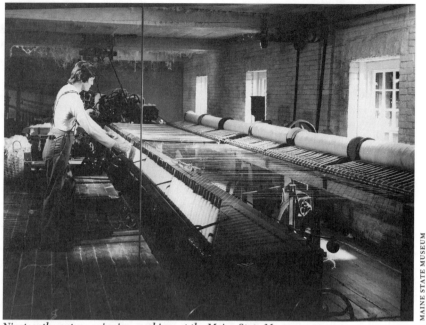

MAINE STATE MUSEUM

Nineteenth-century spinning machines at the Maine State Museum

granite-quarrying, ice harvesting, shipbuilding, and lumbering. "Made in Maine" depicts more than a dozen 19th-century industrial scenes: textile mills and shops producing shoes, guns, fishing rods, and more. What makes these scenes most fascinating is the incredible, lifelike quality and attention to detail. The 1846 narrow-gauge locomotive "Lion" stands like a mascot in the lobby.

Children's Discovery Museum (622-2209), Water Street, Augusta. A new, interactive, hands-on learning museum for children through the fifth grade. Hours and days vary.

HISTORIC SITES

Fort Western Museum on the Kennebec (626-2385), City Center Plaza, 16 Cony Street, Augusta. Open Memorial Day to July 4, 1–4 daily; July 4 to Labor Day, 10–4 weekdays, 1–4 weekends; Labor Day to Columbus Day, 1–4 weekends only. Groups and school programs year-round. $4.50 adults/$2.50 children. The original 16-room garrison house has been restored to reflect its use as a fort, trading fort, and lodge from 1754 to 1810. The blockhouse and stockade are reproductions.

Redington Museum and Apothecary (872-9439), 64 Silver Street, Waterville. Open mid-May through September, Tuesday through Saturday 2–6, and by appointment. $2 admission; $1 age 18 and under. The local historical collection: furniture, Civil War and Native American relics, a children's room, period rooms, and a 19th-century apothecary.

Monmouth Museum (933-4444), Monmouth (at the intersection of Routes 132 and 135). Open Memorial Day to October 1, Tuesday through Sunday 1–4; year-round by appointment (933-2287 is the answering machine, or call Annie Smith: 933-2752). $3 per adult, $1 per child. A collection of buildings: 1787 Blossom House, stencil shop (1849), blacksmith shop, freight shed, and carriage house.

Waterville-Winslow Two Cent Bridge, Front Street, Waterville. Until recently the only known remaining toll footbridge in the country. Toll-taker's house on Waterville side. Free.

Fort Halifax, Route 201, Winslow (1 mile south of the Waterville-Winslow bridge at the junction of the Kennebec and Sebasticook Rivers). Just a blockhouse remains, but it is original, built in 1754; the oldest block-house in the United States.

Cumston Hall, Main Street, Monmouth. Open year-round, weekdays during business hours. Vintage 1900, this ornate wooden building would look more at home in India than mid-Maine. Monmouth native Harry H. Cochrane not only designed but decorated the building with murals, detailing, and stained glass. He also composed the music and conducted the orchestra at the building's dedication. It houses the town offices, library, and the Theater at Monmouth, a repertory theater specializing in Shakespeare (see *Entertainment*).

Arnold Historical Society Museum (582-7080), off Route 17, Pittston. Open July and August, Saturday, Sunday, and holidays 10–4 and by appointment. $1.50 per adult, $.50 per child over age 6. An 18th-century house in which Benedict Arnold and Aaron Burr stayed for a couple of nights in the fall of 1775 on their way to attempt to capture Quebec. The army camped on Swan Island in Richmond (see *Green Space*), and about 600 men and supplies continued upriver in *bateaux*—the flat-bottomed boats that are exhibited here in the barn. The house is furnished to period, and picture panels depict the Arnold expedition.

Norlands Living History Center (897-4366), RD 2, Box 1740, Livermore 04254. Take Norlands Road off Route 108 between Livermore and Livermore Falls. Open July and August, daily 10–4 for general tours of all buildings. $4.50 per adult, $2 per student. Also open by reservation for live-in weekends and week-long programs, year-round. An incredible 450-acre, living history complex re-creates life in the late 19th century. The working farm with barn and farmer's cottage, church, stone library, and Victorian mansions of the Washburn family are open to visitors. This is the genuine 1870–1890 rural experience; visitors become scholars in the one-room schoolhouse and hear the story of the famous Washburn sons. Those living-in assume the identity of a 19th-century character, carrying out chores (cooking, mending, working the farm) just as they would have if they had been living here then. Chris's husband and oldest son went for a weekend and have never been the same. Try it. Come for a special weekend like Heritage Days in June, the Autumn Celebration in late September, or Christmas early in December. Three-day live-in weekends are also offered in February, April, May, and November and cost $195.

TO DO

BALLOONING
Balloon Drifters (622-1211), Augusta State Airport. Offers free flights and tethered rides.

BOAT EXCURSIONS
Great Pond Marina (495-2213), Belgrade Lakes Village. Operates the mail boat on Great Pond (the inspiration for the book and movie *On Golden Pond*); the mail boat ride costs $7 per adult, $5 per senior, $4 per child. Also moorings, boat rentals (canoes, sailboards, sailboats, fishing boats).

FISHING
Belgrade Lakes are known as a source of smallmouth bass; **Day's Store** in Belgrade Lakes Village devotes an entire floor to fishing gear. Boat rentals are available (see *Boat Excursions*).

GOLF AND TENNIS
Natanis Golf Club (622-3561), Webber Pond, Vassalboro. Eighteen holes; tennis courts. **Waterville Country Club** (465-7773), Waterville (off I-95). Eighteen holes, clubhouse, carts, and caddies.

SWIMMING
Peacock Beach State Park, Richmond (just off Route 201, 10 miles south of Augusta). A small, beautiful sand beach on Pleasant Pond; lifeguards and picnic facilities. $1 per adult, free under age 12.

Public beaches include **Sunset Camps Beach** on North Pond, Smithfield; and **Willow Beach** (968-2421), China. Although public access is limited at the Belgrade and China lakes, every cottage cluster and most rental "camps" there are on the water.

Lake St. George State Park (589-4255), Route 3 in Liberty. A pleasant, clean, clear lake with a sandy beach and changing facilities, a perfect break if you are en route from Augusta and points south to the coast.

GREEN SPACE

Pine Tree State Arboretum (621-0031), Hospital Street, Augusta. (At Cony Circle—the big rotary across the bridge from downtown Augusta—turn south along the river; it's a short way down on the left, across from the Augusta Mental Health Institute.) Trails through woods and fields, past 300 specimens of Maine plants.

Swan Island. A state-owned wildlife management area. Day use and overnight camping; prior reservations (287-1150) necessary for both, since only 60 visitors are allowed on the island at any one time. $3 day visit/ $5 overnight camping. The landing is in Richmond Village, where Department of Inland Fisheries and Wildlife employees transport visitors to the island. Tours are available in an open, slat-sided truck; plenty of area for walking. The southern area is restricted, but staff will accompany you on a tour (also see *Campgrounds*).

(Also see *Swimming*.)

LODGING

BED & BREAKFASTS

Maple Hill Farm (622-2708), RFD 1, Box 1145, Hallowell 04347. Little more than 4 miles from the turnpike and downtown Augusta, this pleasant old house with a new addition sits on 62 acres. Scott Cowger bought the property at auction and turned it into the comfortable, welcoming place it is today. The seven guest rooms (some with shared bath) are furnished in a pretty country style, with bedspreads that were made in Hallowell. A suite with a whirlpool tub is available. There is a trail leading through the woods to a spring-fed swimming hole by a quarry, and the carriage house has been transformed into a roomy function space. Full breakfast is included in the $53–70 rates.

Home-Nest Farm (897-4125), Baldwin Hill Road, Box 2350, Kents Hill 04349. Closed March and April. This is a wonderful old family estate, with three historic homes on the extensive property. The main house, built in 1784, offers a panoramic view of the White Mountains. Lilac Cottage (1800) and the Red Schoolhouse (1830) are available for rent as separate units. The property has been in host Arn Sturtevant's family for six generations; his grandchildren are the eighth generation to sleep there. Arn can relate some interesting family tales while showing you Civil War memorabilia. The sheep are a lot of fun to watch. $50 per room, $80–95 for houses with one to three bedrooms; breakfast included.

Independence Farm (622-0284), Box 857, Augusta 04330. Although the mailing address says Augusta, this 1820s farmhouse actually overlooks Webber Pond in Vasselboro. Now that their eight children are grown, Pat (a craftsperson with her own store in Hallowell) and Bob Riedman raise llamas on their 55-acre spread, as well as geese and coon cats. Two large guest rooms have private baths, and a third is frequently used for children. There's a canoe for summer use, and in winter cross-country ski rentals (and trails) are available at the nearby golf club. $55 double includes a full farm breakfast.

Richmond Sauna and Bed and Breakfast (737-4752), off Route 197, Richmond 04357. Open year-round. A handsome Federal home with five guest rooms, kitchen privileges, sauna, hot tub, and pool. There are actually six saunas, available by the hour. Use of all facilities for guests who pay $60 per couple, $45 single.

The Senator (622-5804), Western Avenue (just off I-95), Augusta 04330. A popular spot for politicians and business travelers. Rooms are large and plush; some have TV, phone, and refrigerator in the bathroom. Outdoor heated pool, Jacuzzi, fitness room with a sauna. Unlike many motels, pets are allowed here. $74–98 depending on season.

CAMPS AND COTTAGES

Bear Spring Camps (397-2341), RFD 2, Box 1900, Oakland 04941. Open mid-May to October. A gem of a family resort with 75 percent repeat business. Serious fishermen come in early May for trout and salmon, and in July there is still bass. Each of the 32 cottages (niceties include open fireplaces) is right on the water with its own dock and motorboat (sailboat rentals are available). Also available are a tennis court and a variety of lawn games, and the swimming is great (the bottom is sandy). Meals are served in the main house. Weekly rates are $445 per couple in shoulder months to $1400 for eight in high season, including all meals.

Castle Island Camps (495-3312), Belgrade Lakes 04918. Open May through mid-September. In winter, contact Horatio Castle, 1800 Carambola Road, West Palm Beach, FL 33406 (407-641-8339). A dozen comfortable-looking cottages clustered on a small island (connected by bridges) in 12-mile Long Pond. This is the second generation of Castles to maintain the camps, geared to fishing (the pond is stocked; rental boats are available). Meals are served in the small central lodge; weekly and children's rates are available. $48 per person per night; $322–329 per week, including all three meals.

CAMPGROUNDS

Steve Powell Wildlife Management Area (Swan Island), in Merrymeeting Bay off Richmond. State-owned Swan Island is managed as a wildlife preservation area in Merrymeeting Bay, a vast tidal bay that's well known among bird-watchers. Limited camping is available, along with a motorboat shuttle from Richmond, only through the Department of Inland Fisheries and Wildlife: 287-1150.

Lake St. George State Park (589-4255), Route 3, Liberty, offers 38 campsites and a boat launch ($13 for nonresidents).

WHERE TO EAT

DINING OUT

Slate's (622-9575), 167 Water Street, Hallowell. Breakfast, lunch, and dinner Tuesday through Friday, brunch and dinner Saturday, brunch only on Sunday. Coffeehouse atmosphere in three adjoining storefronts with brick walls, tin ceilings, changing art, a great bar, and a patio in back. The brunch menu is huge and hugely popular. The dinner menu changes daily but might include scrod baked with Brie and fresh blueberries, or cashew chicken on rice. Live music Friday night, Saturday night, and during Sunday brunch. $8.95–14.95.

La Casa Ristorante (623-2938), 37 Water Street, Hallowell. Closed Sunday; otherwise open for lunch and dinner. A homey decor in an old building. Specialties include ravioli filled with three Italian cheeses, homemade sauce. Moderate.

Village Inn (495-3553), Route 27, Belgrade Lakes. Open year-round for dinner nightly and lunch on Sunday. Lunch served in July and August. A rambling old place with a lake view and early-bird specials. The specialty is duckling, roasted for up to 12 hours and served with a choice of sauces ($11.50–15.95). Entrées $9.95–16.95.

Bachelders Tavern (268-4965), Route 126 and Hallowell Road, Litchfield. Open daily for lunch and dinner. Dutch chef-owners Clare and Dirk Keijer create memorable meals in an elegant old stage stop, center of the village. A screened summer deck overlooks a pond and garden. Specialties include Mediterranean dishes, Maine seafood, and certified Black Angus beef. Entrées $10.95–21.00. Reservations recommended.

Johann Sebastian B. (465-3223), 40 Fairfield Street, Oakland. Open Wednesday to Saturday for dinner in summer; Friday and Saturday the rest of the year. A Victorian house in the Belgrade Lakes area. Specialties include chicken cordon bleu and sauerbraten; homemade European pastries and dessert drinks. $11.00–21.50.

Feather Bed Inn (293-2020), Mount Vernon. Sunday 8–3, otherwise 5–9 by reservation. Continental fare served in pleasant dining rooms in a restored 1800s house overlooking Lake Minnehonk. The specialty is roast duck in orange and allspice sauce. Entrées from $16.95.

Ashlie's (582-3005), 103 Water Street, Hallowell. Open for lunch and dinner. Housed in the old Cobbossee National Bank building; the vault is still behind the bar. An all-American menu specializing in steaks and seafood. Lunch buffet for $4.95, also good sandwiches. Entrées: $8.95–16.95.

River Cafe (622-2190), 119 Water Street, Hallowell. Open for lunch and dinner except Sunday. Mediterranean/American specialties include shish kebob and shish Tawook (marinated chicken tips cooked over an open flame and rolled in Lebanese bread). Reservations required for dinner. $7.95–14.95.

Senator Restaurant (622-5804), 284 Western Avenue, Augusta. Open daily from 6:30 AM through dinner. A big, all-American dining room (buses are welcome). Seafood specialties include seafood medley (a little bit of everything) and native Maine crabcakes; full (generous) salad bar. Entrées: $12.95–16.95.

Silver Street Tavern (873-2277), 2 Silver Street, Waterville. Open for lunch Tuesday through Friday, dinner Tuesday through Sunday, and Sunday brunch. Turn-of-the-century pub atmosphere (tin ceiling). Specialties include teriyaki sirloin and coquilles Saint-Jacques. $7.50–16.95.

EATING OUT

The A-1 Diner (582-4804), 3 Bridge Street, Gardiner, is a current hot spot for dinner as well as breakfast and lunch. Open Monday through Saturday for all three meals, but just from 7 AM to noon on Sunday (opening at 5 AM weekdays, at 6 AM Saturday). A vintage 1946 Worcester diner with plenty of formica, blue vinyl booths, blue and black tile, a 14-stool, marble-topped counter, and a neon blue and pink clock with the slogan "Time to Eat." The waitress seems to know everyone in the place at breakfast, and everyone seems to know each other. But with Mike Giberson and Neil Andersen running it, things are done with a unique flair.

The breakfast menu includes banana-almond French toast, and a wide variety of omelets, as well as eggs and hash; the meatloaf has a Cajun accent, the split-pea soup, an Italian, and the chili, a Latin. Greek lemon soup is a specialty. Beverages range from herbal tea to imported beers and wines. But you can always get tapioca pudding, and the route to the rest room is still outside and in through the kitchen door.

Burnsie's Homestyle Sandwiches (622-6425), State Street, Augusta, between the capitol and the rotary. Open 8–4 weekdays only. This is the perfect place if you are visiting the Maine State Museum. Keep your car parked where it is and walk up past the Capitol to this out-of-place house, a source of famous lobster rolls, Reubens, and a variety of sandwiches, many named for local legislators. Although there is no real place to eat in the shop, if it's a nice day the picnic tables in the park just across the river, adjoining Fort Western, offer the best view in town.

Pedro's (582-5058), 161 Water Street, Gardiner. Open for lunch and dinner Tuesday through Saturday. A comfortable, casual place with a Mexican and southwestern menu.

My Cousin's Place (634-3016), Route 2 between Skowhegan and Norridgewock. Open for breakfast and lunch. Convenient and friendly with tables overlooking the river.

ENTERTAINMENT

Theater at Monmouth (933-2952), PO Box 385, Monmouth 04259. Performances Wednesday through Sunday in July, Tuesday through Sunday in August; matinees and children's shows vary. Housed in Cumston Hall, a striking turn-of-the-century building designed as a combination theater, library, and town hall. A resident company presents classics (last season included two Shakespeare productions: *The Taming of the Shrew* and *The Tempest*).

Waterville Summer Music Theater (872-2707), in the Waterville Opera House. Performances during July and August, Tuesday through Saturday at 8 PM; Wednesday and Sunday matinees.

Johnson Hall (582-3730), Water Street, Gardiner. The second-floor, 450-seat theater, dating from 1864, is presently under restoration, but a 100-seat studio performance space designed for workshops and small performances has already been restored. This is home for the Institute for the Performing Arts (classes in magic, juggling, etc.) offered by Benny and Denise Reehl, the powers behind the semi-annual New England Vaudeville Festival. Check local calendars for periodic performances.

SELECTIVE SHOPPING

The mid-19th-century commercial buildings along Water Street in Gardiner have hatched some interesting shops.

The heart of the Belgrade Lakes Village is **Day's Store** (495-2205). Open year-round, recently expanded to serve as general store; state liquor store; fishing license, gear, boot, and gift source; and rainy-day mecca. **Maine Made Shop,** open late May to Labor Day, stocks pottery, books, and Maine souvenirs.

ANTIQUES SHOPS

The picturesque riverside lineup of shops in Hallowell harbors fewer antiques dealers than it did a few years ago, but it is still a worthwhile browsing street. **Dealer's Choice,** 108 Water Street, is a 70-plus dealer mall with a wide range. **Hatties Antiques,** 148 Water Street, specializes in fine antique jewelry, antique lamps, clocks, and art glass. **The Kennebec Valley Art Association,** 160 Water Street, is open Tuesday through Saturday 1–4.

BOOKSTORES

The Iron Horse Bookstore (872-0939), 10 Railroad Square, Waterville. The big store, adjoining the Railroad Square Cinema and Café (see *Entertainment* and *Eating Out*), is a serious, full-service store with special readings, soft music, and coffee. A branch store on Route 27 in Belgrade Lakes Village adjoins the Village Inn and overlooks Great Pond.

Children's Book Cellar (872-4543), 5 East Concourse, Waterville.

Leon H. Tebbets Bookstore, 164 Water Street, is a book lover's delight; 36,000 closely packed titles (closed Sunday in winter).

FACTORY OUTLETS

Carleton Woolen Mills Factory Outlet (582-6003), Griffin Street, Gardiner. Fabrics, woolens, and notions.

Cascade Fabrics, Oakland. Open Monday through Saturday 8:30–4:30. A genuine mill store.

Dexter Shoe Factory Outlet (873-6739), Kennedy Memorial Drive, Waterville.

SPECIAL EVENTS

July: **The Great Kennebec River Whatever Week**—10 days of activities ending with the Kennebec River Whatever Race, running downriver from Augusta to Gardiner (beginning of the month). **China Connection**—public supper, pageant, road race, greased pig and pie-eating contests in China. **Old Hallowell Days** (third week). **Annual Scottish Games & Gathering of the Scottish Clans,** sponsored by the St. Andrew's Society of Maine, Thomas College, Waterville.

September: **Common Ground Fair,** Windsor—Maine's celebration of rural living, a gathering of organic farmers and Maine craftspeople.

The Upper Kennebec Valley and Jackman

Commercial rafting on the Kennebec began in 1976 when fishing guide Wayne Hockmeyer discovered the rafting potential of up to 8000 cubic feet of water per second (released every morning from late spring through mid-October from the Harris Hydroelectric Station) churning through dramatic, 12-mile-long Kennebec Gorge.

On his first ride through the gorge, Hockmeyer had to contend with logs hurtling all around him, but, as luck would have it, 1976 also marked the year in which environmentalists managed to outlaw log runs on the Kennebec. More than 15 rafting companies now compete for space on the Kennebec, but no more than 800 rafters are allowed on the river at a time. In order to compete, outfitters based in and around the Forks have added their own lodging, and the more elaborate "base camps" now remain open year-round.

Empty as it seemed when rafting began, this stretch of the Upper Kennebec had been a 19th-century resort of sorts. The 100-room, three-story Forks Hotel was built at the confluence of the Kennebec and Dead Rivers in the middle of The Forks in 1860 and was well known for its steady flow of liquor (Maine was legally dry at the time). Nineteenth-century guests were well aware of the area's many miles of wilderness hiking trails and sights (such as spectacular Moxie Falls). A half dozen remote sportsmen's camps on fishing ponds date from this period.

Route 201, as it follows the Kennebec River north through Skowhegan and Solon to Bingham, The Forks, and Jackman, traverses lonely but beautiful wilderness. Wildlife abounds: more than 100 species of birds have been seen in the region, and this section of the Kennebec is the only US river in which five types of game fish are found. The route is known as the Arnold Trail because Benedict Arnold came this way in 1775 to Quebec City, which—it's worth noting—is just 86 miles north of Jackman.

GUIDANCE

Upper Kennebec Valley Chamber of Commerce (672-4100), PO Box 491, Bingham 04920, maintains a seasonal storefront, walk-in information booth on Route 201 in the middle of Bingham. Open daily.

Skowhegan Chamber of Commerce (474-3621), PO Box 326, Skowhegan 04976, maintains a seasonal information center in town on Route 201 north. This is actually the gateway to the Upper Kennebec Valley and serves as a source of advice on lodging throughout the valley.

Jackman–Moose River Chamber of Commerce (668-4094) also maintains a seasonal information center on Route 201 in Jackman.

MEDICAL EMERGENCY

Bingham Area Health Center (672-4808); Ambulance Service (672-4410).

TO SEE

Skowhegan History House (474-3140 or 474-6632), Norridgewock Avenue. Open June to Labor Day, Tuesday through Sunday 1–5. A Greek Revival brick house exhibiting 19th-century furnishings, artifacts, and local maps.

Margaret Chase Smith Library Center (474-7133), Skowhegan. Open Monday through Friday 10–4. Set above the Kennebec, an expanded version of Senator Smith's home is a research and conference center housing records, scrapbooks, news releases, tape recordings, and memorabilia from 40 years in public life.

Skowhegan Indian and Norridgewock Monument. Billed as "the world's largest sculptured wooden Indian," this 62-foot-high statue is dedicated to the memory of the Maine Abenakis. It's just off Route 201 near the Kennebec. Abenaki heritage is particularly strong in this area. In the early 18th century, French Jesuit Sabastian Rasle established a mission in nearby Norridgewock, insisting that Native American lands "were given them of God, to them and their children forever." Rasle and his mission were wiped out by the English in 1724. The site of the village is marked by a pleasant riverside picnic area in a pine grove. (Take Route 201A from Norridgewock toward Madison across the bridge and up a steep hill. Turn left 3 miles from the top of the hill on Father Rasle Monument Road; it's 3 more miles to the cemetery and picnic site.) Note that Route 201A rather than 201 follows the Kennebec here. In the middle of Norridgewock, you might also want to stop by Oosoola Park to see the totem pole topped by a frog (this is also a good picnic spot and boat launch site). Ancient Native American petroglyphs have been found in Emden.

TO DO

AIRBOAT TRIP

Maine Whitewater (672-4814), Gadabout Gaddis Airport, Bingham 04920. Daily, 14-mile scenic rides on the Kennebec between Solon and Bingham.

CANOEING

The Moose River Bow Trip is a Maine classic: A series of pristine ponds form a 42-mile meandering route that winds back to the point of origin, eliminating the need for a shuttle. The fishing is fine; remote campsites are scattered along the way, and the put-in place is accessible. One major portage is required. Canoe rentals are available from a variety of local sources (check with the two local chambers of commerce), and guided canoe trips can be arranged through some of the larger rafting companies.

FISHING

Fishing is what the sporting camps are all about. The catch is landlocked salmon, trout, and togue. Rental boats and canoes are available (see *Rustic Resorts*).

GOLF

Moose River Golf Course (668-5331), Moose River. Mid-May through mid-October; club rental, putting green, nine holes.

HIKING

Hiking possibilities abound in this area. *Take a Hike* by Susan Varney (available locally and from Voyager Whitewater) describes 20 hikes in the Upper Kennebec Valley Region. The standout is Moxie Falls, an 89-foot waterfall that is considered the highest in New England, set in a dramatic gorge. It's an easy ⅔-mile walk from the trailhead. Turn off Route 201 onto Moxie Road on the south side of the bridge across the Kennebec in The Forks. Park off the road at the trailhead sign on the left.

MOOSE-WATCHING

The best time to see a moose is dawn or dusk. Favorite local moose crossings include Moxie Road from The Forks to Moxie Pond; the Central Maine Power Company road from Moxie Pond to Indian Pond; the 25 miles north from The Forks to Jackman on Route 201; and the 30 miles from Jackman to Rockwood on Route 16. Drive these stretches carefully; residents all know someone who has died in a car/moose collision.

MOUNTAIN BIKING

Local terrain varies from old logging roads to tote paths. Rentals are available from **Sky Lodge Resort** (1-800-416-6181) and **Northern Outdoors** (1-800-765-RAFT).

WHITEWATER RAFTING

See the introduction to this chapter. Selecting an outfitter can be the most difficult exercise of the rafting trip. The safety records for all are excellent, or they wouldn't be in this rigorously monitored business. April through October all offer the basics: a river ride with a hearty steak cookout at its end and a chance to view (and buy) slides of the day's adventures. The standard charge is $75 weekdays, $95 weekends. If you don't like getting your feet wet (especially early and late in the season when the water is frigid), you might ask about self-bailing rafts, but the big variant among outfitters is the nature of the lodging. It ranges from tent sites to inns and cabins to condo-style units—which they package into rates. To save calling around for availability you might call **Raft Maine** (1-800-723-8633; Monday through Friday, 9–5, Saturday 9–noon), representing 12 outfitters.

Note: Although whitewater rafting began as a big singles sport, it is becoming more and more popular with families, who combine it with a visit to Quebec City, just 86 miles north of Jackman.

Northern Outdoors Inc. (663-4466 or 1-800-765-RAFT), PO Box 100, The Forks 04985. Wayne and Suzie Hockmeyer were the first rafters on the Kennebec, and Northern Outdoors is still the biggest outfitter. Its "Outdoor Resort Center" at The Forks includes an attractive open-timbered building with high ceilings, a huge hearth, comfortable seating, a cheerful dining room (see *Dining Out*), a bar, a pool, a private lake, platform tennis, and a hot tub. Fishing and mountain biking are also available. Accommodations vary from camping to cabins, from lodge double rooms to "logdominiums" (condo-style units with lofts and a kitchen/dining area). Kennebec River day and overnight trips, Dead River runs, and canoe and kayak clinics are offered, and in winter the lodge caters to snowmobilers and cross-country skiers.

New England Whitewater Center (663-4455 or 1-800-766-7238), Box 15, West Forks 04985. The second largest outfitter offers some of the fanciest and funkiest lodging in the area; the Sterling Inn in Caratunk, a 19th-century stage stop, dates from 1816 and offers country inn–style

Rafting the Kennebec River

NORTHERN OUTDOORS

guest rooms, and the Marshall Hotel features linoleum-covered floors and a lively dining/bar/pool room.

Wilderness Expeditions (534-2242 or 1-800-825-WILD), PO Box 41, Rockwood 04478. Wilderness maintains a base camp in The Forks with a pleasant central lodge and more than 20 riverside cabin tents. This is an offshoot of The Birches Resort in Rockwood, a beautifully sited, full-service resort on Moosehead Lake; packages combine Kennebec and Dead River rafting with stays at The Birches.

Crab Apple White Water (663-4491 or 1-800-553-RAFT), The Forks 04985. The Crab Apple Acres is an 1830s edifice with a fan light over the door and flowery wallpaper in the seven guest rooms. Neighboring motel units serve as the base camp.

Maine Whitewater (672-4814 or 1-800-345-MAIN), Gadabout Gaddis Airport, Bingham 04920. Jim Ernst operates the second oldest rafting company on the river. His Bingham base complex includes a restaurant, hot tub, a private airport, and a campground.

Downeast Whitewater (663-2277 or 1-800-677-7238), maintains the attractive, seasonal, Dew Drop Inn bed & breakfast on Pleasant Pond in Caratunk, as well as the Kelley Brook Resort with a restaurant and riverside campground and cabins on Route 201.

Unicorn Rafting Expeditions (725-2255 or 1-800-UNICORN), PO Box T, Brunswick 04011, caters to families with its packages and classic log cabins strung along Lake Parlin, alongside a sleek new lodge.

Voyagers Whitewater (663-4423 or 1-800-289-6307), The Forks 04985, caters to small groups of six people per raft and serves a country gourmet feast at its quaint B&B on Route 201 in The Forks.

Eastern River Expeditions (1-800-634-7238) offers a variety of rafting trips from Rivers Inn, its Greenville base. In addition to trips in Kennebec Gorge and on the Dead River, Eastern River offers a family-geared run on the Upper Kennebec from East Outlet.

Magic Falls Rafting (1-800-207-7238 or 207-663-2220) has a base camp with campground on the banks of the Dead River in The Forks and offers "funyaks" (an inflatable cross between a canoe and a kayak) as well as rafts.

Moxie Outdoor Adventures (663-2231 or 1-800-866-6943), operates out of Lake Moxie Camps, one of the oldest and best-known sporting camps around.

SNOWMOBILING

Snowmobile rentals are available in Jackman, which prides itself on the quality of its groomed trail system with many long views.

GREEN SPACE

Moxie Falls (90 feet high) is said to be the highest falls in New England (see *Hiking*). **Caratunk Falls** is a 36-foot falls located near Solon.

Wyman Dam (155 feet high) walls the Kennebec River between Moscow and Bingham. It was built in the 1930s by Central Maine Power. It raises the river 123 feet, creating the most popular rafting route in the Northeast. **Wyman Lake** stretches out for many miles behind it, and there is a public boat access from Route 201.

Attean View. Heading north toward Jackman from The Forks, only one rest area is clearly marked. Stop. The view is splendid: Attean Lake and the whole string of other ponds linked by the Moose River, with the western mountains as a backdrop. There are picnic tables.

LODGING

RUSTIC RESORTS

These are classic sporting camps geared to fishermen and hunters.

Harrison's Pierce Pond Sporting Camps (672-3625; this is a radio phone, so let it ring and try again if it doesn't work; Columbus Day to May 15, or when unable to get through, call 603-279-8424), Box 315, Bingham 04920. Open May through October. Sited on the Appalachian Trail, 15 miles down a dirt road from Bingham. Fran and Tim Harrison have brought new life to this classic, old log camp set on a hillside and overlooking a stream with a waterfall in the distance. Nine-mile-long Pierce Pond is a short walk across the stream and through the woods. Each of the nine log cabins has a bedroom and token bath; rates include three abundant meals per day. Word has gotten out about Fran's cooking, and some people actually drive the bumpy road for Sunday turkey or Friday lobster. $59–63 per person per day or $345–370 per week, includes all meals (based on double occupancy); half price for children, special family rates July 15 through August 16.

Cobb's Pierce Pond Camps (628-2819 in summer; 628-3612 in winter), North New Portland 04961. There are 11 guest cabins, accommodating from two to eight persons; each has a screened porch, wood stove, bathroom, and electricity. Home-cooked meals and between-meal snacks are served in the main lodge. The camp dates from 1902, and the Cobb family has been running it for almost 35 years; 90 percent of their guests are repeats. It is the kind of place that doesn't advertise. It has a loyal following among serious fishermen; sand beaches nearby. $65 per person per day includes three meals.

Attean Lake Resort (668-3792; 668-7726 in winter), Jackman 04945. Sited on an island in Attean Lake, surrounded by mountains; 20 seasonal cabins, luxurious by sports lodge standards, with open fireplaces and even a small Oriental carpet, nightlights, and an attentive cabin boy. The resort also maintains three cabins along the Moose River trip (see *Canoeing*). Fishing boats and canoes are available. The resort is easily accessible from Jackman; you phone from the shore, and a boat fetches you. $150–200 includes meals.

OTHER LODGING

☞ **Mrs. G's Bed & Breakfast** (672-4034 or 1-800-672-4034), Box 389, Meadow Street, Bingham 04920. A tidy house on a side street in the middle of town. Frances Gibson (Mrs. G) delights in orienting guests to the full range of local hiking, biking, rafting, and cross-country skiing possibilities. There are four cheerful guest rooms; also a delightful loft dorm room; shared baths. $30 single and $50 double includes a fabulous full breakfast and state tax.

Sky Lodge Resort (668-2171 or 1-800-416-6181), PO Box 428, Jackman 04945. Open year-round. A splendidly built lodge on Route 201 with two-story fieldstone hearth in the living room. Seven guest rooms in the lodge have fireplaces ($75 per person MAP) and there are five fully equipped, three-bedroom log cabins ($100 for four people) and a motel ($59 double). The lodge will outfit you for mountain biking, canoeing, whitewater rafting and cross-country skiing; facilities include a seasonal pool and hot tub, a billiards/game room, and a gym with table tennis, basketball, and exercise equipment.

Briarwood Mountain Lodge (668-7756), Route 201, Jackman 04945. This is a spiffy, 20-room, three-story motel with a heated pool (seasonal) set in an attractive deck with a great view, hot tub, cable TV, and restaurant and bar with weekend entertainment. $54 double, $46 single, lodging packages.

(Also see the lodging described for each *Whitewater Rafting* outfitter.)

WHERE TO EAT

DINING OUT

The Village Candle Light (474-9724/2978), 1 Madison Avenue, Skowhegan. Open for dinner except Monday. The specialties are seafood, native vegetables, home baking. Entrées $6.95–13.95.

Harrison's Pierce Pond Camps (672-3625), Bingham. We don't want to understate the taxing trip into Harrison's (see *Rustic Resorts*), but if you happen to be spending a few days in this area and want a very special meal, it's worth the ride for the turkey dinner on Sunday, baked stuffed pork on Monday, steak teriyaki "Juline" on Tuesday, and so on; reservations at least one day in advance required.

Northern Outdoors (663-4466), Route 201, The Forks. The pine-sided dining room in the lodge is informal, hung with great photos of The Forks in its big-time logging and old resort days, and the food is very good; nightly specials. Moderately priced.

Loon's Look-Out Restaurant at Tuckaway Shores Cabins (668-3351) on Big Wood Lake, Jackman. Take Spruce Street off Route 201, bear right onto Forest Street, and it's at the end on the right-hand side. Open Friday through Sunday 5–9. A great little Italian place with specialties like chicken parmigiana and *bistecca a la pazzarella* (steak chunks sautéed with bell peppers, onions, mushrooms, and spices). Call ahead. $8.95–10.00.

EATING OUT

Old Mill Pub (474-6627), 41-R Water Street, Skowhegan. Open Monday through Saturday for lunch and dinner. A picturesque old mill building set back from the main drag with a seasonal deck overlooking the Kennebec. A friendly bar and scattered tables; sandwiches (a good Reuben), quiche, and specials for lunch; spinach lasagna or stir-fry shrimp for dinner.

Bloomfield's Cafe & Bar (474-8844), 40 Water Street, Skowhegan. Open daily 11 AM–11:30 PM. Stained glass, ferns, tile floors, and an exquisite copper moose head create a pleasant atmosphere in this corner store eatery. Pete's Wicked Ale and Moosehead are available, and the selection of sandwiches is wide; try "Bloomies Bomber."

☞ **Thompson's Restaurant** (672-3245), Main Street, Bingham. Open daily from 6 AM–8:30 PM year-round. An inviting eatery in business since 1939. Terry and Daniel Hilton have preserved the old-fashioned look, complete with red awning and deep booths, and the menu includes homemade doughnuts, fresh fish, pea soup on Thursday, baked beans on Saturday, and (always) custard pie; pizza, wine, and beer also served.

Briarwood Mountain Lodge (669-7756), Jackman. The big dining room is in the rear of the motor lodge, with plate-glass windows overlooking the Moose River Valley—a spread of trees with mountains rising in the distance. All three meals served.

ENTERTAINMENT

Lakewood Theater at Skowhegan, the Cornville Players (474-7176), RFD 1, Box 1780, Skowhegan 04976. Mid-June through August. A community group performs in one of Maine's oldest summer theaters. Broadway plays and children's performances. **Park Street Players** at Constitution Hall, Skowhegan State Fair Grounds, Route 201, Skowhegan. A regional theater staging summer plays and musicals. Curtain time is 8 PM.

SPECIAL EVENTS

August: **Skowhegan State Fair,** one of the oldest and biggest fairs in New England—harness racing, a midway, agricultural exhibits, big-name entertainment, tractor and oxen pulls.

September: **Oosoola Fun Day,** Norridgewock, includes the state's oldest frog jumping contest (up to 300 contestants) around a frog-topped totem pole; also canoe races, crafts fair, flower and pet contests, live music, barbecue. **Fly-in,** Gadabout Gaddus Airport, Bingham.

VIII. NORTHERN MAINE

Moosehead Lake Area
Katahdin Region
Aroostook County

MAINE OFFICE OF TOURISM

View of Mount Katahdin from Abol Stream

MOOSEHEAD AND KATAHDIN REGIONS

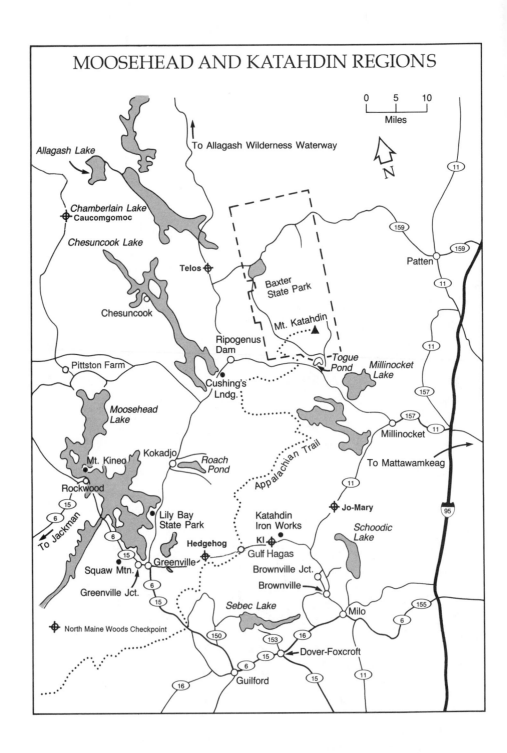

0   5   10
Miles

N

To Allagash Wilderness Waterway

Allagash Lake

11

Chamberlain Lake
Caucomgomoc

159

Chesuncook Lake

159

Patten

Telos

Baxter State Park

11

Chesuncook

Mt. Katahdin

11

Ripogenus Dam

Togue Pond

Millinocket Lake

Pittston Farm

Cushing's Lndg.

157

Moosehead Lake

157

11

Millinocket

Mt. Kineo   Kokadjo

Roach Pond

To Mattawamkeag

Rockwood

Appalachian Trail

15

Jo-Mary

6

To Jackman

Lily Bay State Park

6

Katahdin Iron Works

Schoodic Lake

95

15

Hedgehog

KI

Gulf Hagas

Squaw Mtn.

Greenville

Brownville Jct.

6

Brownville

Greenville Jct.

15

Sebec Lake

Milo

155

North Maine Woods Checkpoint

150

153   16

6

Dover-Foxcroft

15

6

15

Guilford

16

11

The North Woods

Like "Down East," Maine's "North Woods" may seem a bit of a mirage, always over the next hill. In fact, 17.6 of Maine's 22 million acres are forested, and much of that woodland lies in what we've described in this book as the "Western Mountains and Lakes Region."

Still, one particular tract of forest tends to be equated—mostly by out-of-staters—with the North Woods. That section is the 6.5 million acres bordered to the north and west by Canada, which on highway maps shows no roads. This is the largest stretch of unpeopled woodland in the East, but wilderness it's not.

Private ownership of this sector, technically part of Maine's 10.5 million acres known as the "Unorganized Townships," dates from the 1820s when Maine was securing independence from Massachusetts. The mother state, her coffers at their usual low, stipulated that an even division of all previously undeeded wilderness be part of the separation agreement. The woodlands were quickly sold by the legislature for 12½ to 38 cents per acre, bought cooperatively by groups to cut individual losses.

The vast inland tracts, mostly softwood, increased in value in the 1840s when the process of making paper from wood fibers was redis-covered. It seems that the method first used in A.D. 105 had been for-gotten, and New England paper mills were using rags at the time.

By the turn of the century pulp and paper mills had moved to their softwood source and assumed management responsibility and taxes for most of the unorganized townships. Mergers have since increased the size (decreased the number) of these companies, and ownership of some of the largest (namely Great Northern and Scott) is now based in Britain and South Africa. North Maine Woods, Inc., a consortium of 20 major landowners, now pays the lion's share of the area's land tax and the cost of maintaining thousands of miles of private gravel roads, the ones not shown on the state highway maps but open to visitors who pay a fee and promise to abide by the rules (rule number one: Drive slowly and pull over to permit logging trucks to pass).

The private roads have multiplied since the termination of log drives in the 1970s and have changed the look and nature of the North Woods. Many remote sporting camps, for a century accessible only by wa-ter and more recently by air, are now a bumpy ride from the nearest town.

457

Many of the sporting camps themselves haven't changed since the turn of the century. Some have hardly altered since the 1860s, the era when wealthy "sports" first began arriving in Greenville by train from New York and Boston, to be met by Native American guides. The genuine old camps are Maine's inland windjammers: unique holdovers from another era. Many simply cater to descendants of their original patrons.

For the general public, two North Woods preserves have been set aside to provide a wilderness experience. These are 200,000-acre Baxter State Park and the 92-mile ribbon of lakes, ponds, rivers, and streams designated as the Allagash Wilderness Waterway.

There are three major approaches to this "North Woods." The longest, most scenic route is up the Kennebec River, stopping to raft in The Forks (see "The Upper Kennebec Valley and Jackman"), and along the Moose River to the village of Rockwood at the dramatic narrows of Moosehead Lake, then down along the lake to Greenville, New England's largest seaplane base. (You can, of course, also drive directly to Greenville, exiting from I-95 at Newport.)

From Greenville you can hop a float-plane to a sporting camp or set off up the eastern shore of Moosehead to the woodland outpost of Kokadjo and on to the Golden Road, a 98-mile, private logging road running east from Quebec through uninterrupted forest to Millinocket. As Thoreau did in the 1850s, you can canoe up magnificent Chesuncook Lake, camping or staying in the tiny old outpost of Chesuncook Village. With increased interest in rafting down the west branch of the Penobscot River through Ripogenus Gorge and the Crib Works, this stretch of the Golden Road has become known as the West Branch Region.

For those who come this distance simply to climb Mount Katahdin and to camp in Baxter State Park, the quickest route is up I-95 to Medway and in through Millinocket; it's 18 miles to the Togue Pond Gatehouse and Baxter State Park.

Northern reaches of Baxter State Park and the lakes beyond its northern bounds are best accessed from the park's northern entrance via Patten. Both Ashland and Portage are also points of entry, and Shin Pond serves as the seaplane base for this northernmost reach of the North Woods.

GUIDANCE

North Maine Woods (435-6213), Box 421, Ashland 04732, is a consortium of the 20 major landowners that manages the recreational use of 2.8 million acres of commercial forest in northwestern Maine. It publishes a map/guide that shows logging roads and campsites and a list of outfitters and camps.

Maine Sporting Camp Association, PO Box 89, Jay 04239, publishes a booklet guide to its 44 members. See *Sporting Camps* under "What's Where."

Moosehead Lake Area
Including Lower Piscataquis

Moosehead Lake is 40 miles long with some 320 miles of mountainous shoreline, most of it owned by lumber companies. Greenville is the sole "organized" town.

Around the turn of the century, you could board a Pullman car in New York City and ride straight through to Greenville, there to board a steamer for Mount Kineo, a palatial summer hotel perched on an island in the lake. Greenville began as a farm town, but it soon discovered its most profitable crops to be winter lumbering and summer tourists—a group that, since train service and grand hotels have vanished, now consists largely of fishermen, canoeists, whitewater rafters, and hunters, augmented in winter by skiers, snowmobilers, and ice fishermen.

But you don't have to be a sportsman to enjoy Moosehead Lake. Immense and backed by mountains, it possesses unusual beauty and offers a family a wide choice of rustic, old-fashioned "camps" at reasonable prices. The town remains a lumberman's depot and jump-off point for excursions into the wooded wilderness to the north. Greenville is New England's largest seaplane base, with three competing flying services ready to ferry visitors to remote camps and campsites.

The community of Rockwood, a half-hour drive north of Greenville on the west shore of the lake, is even more of an outpost: a cluster of sporting camps and stores between the lake and the Moose River. The river connects with a chain of rivers and ponds that trail off to the west all the way to Jackman. Rockwood sits at the lake's "Narrows," across from its most dramatic landmark: the sheer cliff face of Mount Kineo, a place revered by Native Americans. According to local legend, the mountain is the petrified remains of a monster moose sent to Earth by the Great Spirit as a punishment for sins. It was also the Native Americans' source of flint. The Mount Kineo House, which once stood at the foot of this outcropping, accommodated 800 guests. The resort flourished for many years under the ownership of the Maine Central Railroad (which offered service to Rockwood) and included a golf course, a yacht club, and stables.

The big hotel has long since vanished, but a defunct, three-story annex, a row of shingled Victorian "cottages"—one now a small inn serving meals to the public—and the nine-hole golf course survive. Accessible only by shuttle boat from Rockwood, much of Kineo is now a state-owned nature preserve with exceptional hiking trails.

Most Greenville visitors explore Moosehead's eastern shore at least as far as Lily Bay State Park, and many continue to the outpost village of Kokadjo (population 5), prime moose-watching country. It's another 40 miles northeast over paper company roads to Chesuncook Lake and to Ripogenus Dam, from which logging roads lead north into the Allagash and east to Baxter State Park and Millinocket.

GUIDANCE

Moosehead Lake Region Chamber of Commerce (695-2702), Box 581, Greenville 04441. A four-season source of information. The walk-in information center up on Indian Hill (Route 15 south of town) is open daily in summer; Tuesday to Saturday in winter.

Moosehead Vacation and Sportsmen's Association (534-7300), PO Box 366, Rockwood 04478, a source of year-round information about the Rockwood area.

GETTING THERE

By air: **Folsom's Air Service** (see *Getting Around*) offers charter service to Bangor, Augusta, and Portland.

By car: From points south, the obvious route is to take the Maine Turnpike to Exit 39 (Newport). Proceed up Route 7 to Dexter, then continue north on Route 23 to Sangerville (Guilford), then up Route 15 to Greenville. Note the longer, more scenic route up through The Forks and Jackman suggested in our introduction to this part.

GETTING AROUND

By air: **Folsom's Air Service** (695-2821), Greenville. Billed as "Maine's largest seaplane operator," founded by Dick Folsom in 1946, now headed by his son Max. Until recently, Folsom's radio phone was the only link with the outside world for many camps; his fliers are adept at landing their seaplanes at most North Woods camps. Folsom's will also book you into a camp and transport you and your canoe into the Allagash, or just give you a scenic flight.

Currier's Flying Service (695-2778), Greenville Junction. An enterprising, serious outfit offering scenic flights, service to camps; will book camps and guides or set up guided backcountry, cross-country ski trips.

Jack's Flying Service (695-3020) caters to Allagash canoe trips and also offers fly-in to housekeeping cottages.

By boat: Service to Mount Kineo from Rockwood is offered regularly in summer via the **Kineo Shuttle** (every hour May through October, 1–5; call 534-8812). **The Wilderness Boat** (534-7305) based at The Birches and **Moosehead Water Taxi** (534-8847) also serve the peninsula.

By car: If you plan to venture out on the network of private roads maintained by the lumber companies, be forewarned that it may be expensive, both in terms of gate fees and damage to your car's suspension. You need a high car, and, preferably, four-wheel drive.

MEDICAL EMERGENCY

Charles A. Dean Memorial Hospital and ambulance service (695-2223), Greenville. Emergency aid is also available from **Maine State Police Headquarters** (1-800-452-4664).

TO SEE

Moosehead Marine Museum (695-2716 in-season; for year-round information write: PO Box 1151, Greenville 04441). Home for the *S/S Katahdin*, a restored, vintage 1914 steamboat that cruises daily late June through September, weekends after Memorial Day (9–5). One of 50 steamboats on the lake at its height as a resort destination, the Katahdin was the last to survive, converted to diesel in 1922 and, in the 1930s, modified to haul booms of logs, something we can remember her doing in 1975, the year of the nation's last log drive. This graceful, 115-foot, 150-passenger boat was restored through volunteer effort and re-launched in 1985. The museum's displays depict the lake's steamboat history from 1836. The 3-hour cruise is $12 per adult, $10 per senior, $6 per child over 5. Six-hour Thursday trips to Mount Kineo, with time to walk around the run, are $18 per adult, $16 per senior, and $10 per child.

Evelth-Crafts-Sheridan House (695-2992), Main Street, Greenville. Open July 4 to Labor Day, Wednesday through Friday 1–4; $1 admission. Home of the Moosehead Historical Society, a genuinely interesting 19th-century home.

SCENIC DRIVES

Along the Western Shore

Follow Route 6/15 north through Greenville Junction. If **Squaw Mountain**'s chair lifts are running (see *To Do*), the ride is well worth taking for the views. Continue to **Rockwood** and take the shuttle (see *Getting Around*) to **Mount Kineo;** allow the better part of a day for exploring this dramatic spot (see *Hiking* and *Eating Out*). From Rockwood you can continue north for 20 miles to the Northern/Bowater checkpoint ($8 gate fee for out-of-staters, $4 for Maine resident vehicles). **Pittston Farm,** a short distance beyond, was once the hub of Great Northern operations for this entire western swath of North Woods. It's now a lodge known for lumber camp–style cooking (see *Eating Out*). Note that from Rockwood you can also continue on to Quebec City (via Jackman).

Along the Eastern Shore

Lily Bay State Park (695-2700), 8 miles north of Greenville, offers a sandy beach, a grassy picnicking area, and camping.

Kokadjo, 18 miles north of Greenville, is a 100-acre island of independently owned land on First Roach Pond, in the center of lumber company-owned forest. Most of the buildings here were once part of a lumbering station and are now camps attached to the Kokadjo Trading Post (see *Eating Out*); Northern Pride Lodge (see *Inns*) rents canoes and boats. If you continue north a few miles, you will hit the Bowater/Great Northern Paper checkpoint at **Sias Hill** ($8 per out-of-state vehicle and $4 per Maine license plate). The road surface improves here and is fairly smooth (but you must now pull over to let lumber trucks pass); it improves even more in a dozen miles when you hit the **Golden Road** (see part introduction). Turn right (east).

Cushing's Landing, at the foot of Chesuncook Lake, is worth a stop. The woodsman's memorial here was created from a post in the doorway of a Bangor tavern; it is decorated with tools of the trade and an iron bean pot. This is also the logical boat launch for visiting **Chesuncook Village,** one of the few surviving examples of a 19th-century North Woods lumbermen's village, now on the National Register of Historic Places. In summer, access is by charter aircraft from Greenville or by boat from Chesuncook Dam. In winter, you can come by snowmobile. Writing about the village in 1853, Henry David Thoreau noted, "Here immigration is a tide which may ebb when it has swept away the pines." Today a church, a graveyard (relocated from the shore to a hollow in the woods when Great Northern raised the level of the lake a few years ago), an inn, and a huddle of houses are all that remain of the village. (See Chesuncook Lake House under *Inns* and Katahdin View Lodge and Camps under *Camps* for lodging and boat shuttle.)

Ripogenus Dam, just east of Chesuncook Lake, is the departure point for a number of whitewater rafting expeditions (see *Whitewater Rafting/Kayaking*). This is one of the two major centers for whitewater rafting in Maine—the other is The Forks (see *Whitewater Rafting* in "The Upper Kennebec Valley and Jackman"). Beginning at the dam, the West Branch of the Penobscot drops more than 70 feet per mile—seething and boiling through Ripogenus Gorge—and continues another 12 miles with stretches of relatively calm water punctuated by steep drops. You can get a view of the gorge by driving across the dam. **Pray's Store** (723-8880) sells most things you might need and rents cottages (open year-round).

The Telos Road leads to the **Allagash Wilderness Waterway,** a 92-mile-long chain of lakes, ponds, rivers, and streams that snake through the heart of the North Woods. The traditional canoe trip through the Allagash takes 10 days, but 2- and 3-day trips can be worked out. Brook trout, togue, and lake whitefish are plentiful. For details see *Canoeing the Allagash* in "What's Where." Also see *Canoe Rentals and Trips*.

TO DO

AIRPLANE RIDES
All the flying services listed under *Getting Around* also offer scenic flights.
BOAT EXCURSIONS
See *S/S Katahdin* at the Moosehead Marine Museum under *To See*.
Jolly Rodgers Moosehead Cruises (534-8827/8817). Roger Lane's *Socatean* sails from Moose River in Rockwood late May through Columbus Day, offering narrated cruises around the lake; ask about lunch and dinner Mount Kineo cruises.
CANOE RENTALS AND TRIPS
Allagash Canoe Trips (695-3668), Greenville. A family business since 1953, offering professional guides and top equipment. Week-long expeditions into the Allagash Wilderness Waterway (there are also special teen trips); also a 4-day trip on the Penobscot River and on Chesuncook Lake.
Allagash Wilderness Outfitters (695-2821), PO Box 629, Star Route 76, Greenville 04441. Supplies gear for a canoe camping trip.
Wilderness Expeditions (534-2242 or 534-7305), PO Box 81, Rockwood 04478. A source of rental equipment and advice. Guided trips on the West Branch of the Penobscot or into the Allagash Wilderness Waterway; towing service and ground transportation. Canoe and kayak clinics are also offered.
Note: All the flying services will ferry canoes into remote backcountry (see *Getting Around*).
CHAIR LIFT RIDES
Chair Lift Ride at Squaw Mountain (695-2272), Route 6/15 between Greenville and Rockwood; generally weekends in summer and fall, but call ahead. The view of lake and mountains is spectacular.
FISHING
Troll for salmon and trout in Moosehead Lake and fly-fish in the many rivers and ponds—rental boats and boat launches are so plentiful that they defy listing.
There are two prime sources of fishing information: the **Inland Fisheries and Wildlife** office (695-3757) in Greenville, and the **Maine Guide Fly Shop and Guide Service** (695-2266), Main Street, Greenville. At the Fly Shop, Dan Legere sells 314 different flies and a wide assortment of gear; he also works with local guides to outfit you with a cabin cruiser and guide or to set up a river float trip or a fly-in expedition. For a list of local boat rentals, check with the **Moosehead Lake Area Chamber of Commerce** (see *Guidance*). Also see listings in *Rustic Resorts*, all of which are on water and cater to fishermen.
GOLF
Squaw Mountain Village Resort on Moosehead Lake (695-3609). A

nine-hole course with lounge and restaurant.

Mount Kineo Golf Course (695-2229), a spectacularly sited, newly revived course at Kineo, accessible by frequent boat service from Rockwood; carts and club rentals.

HIKING

Easy hikes featuring great views can be found on:

Mount Kineo, an islandlike peninsula that offers steep but rewarding paths to the lookout tower at the top of the 750-foot-high cliff; a shore path also circles the peninsula. It's accessible from Rockwood by shuttle (see *Getting Around*).

Gulf Hagas, billed as the "Grand Canyon of Maine," is just 8 miles east of the Wilson checkpoint near the Greenville airport (see the "Katahdin Region" for details).

Borestone Mountain Sanctuary, 10 miles out the Eliotsville Road from Route 6/15 at Monson, offers an information center (June 1 through October 1, 8 AM–dusk) maintained by the National Audubon Society; it's at Sunrise Pond, halfway up the 3-mile trail leading to a summit with a 360-degree view.

The Moosehead Lake Region Chamber of Commerce (695-2702) also furnishes information on climbing **Big Spencer, Elephant Mountain,** and walking into **Little Wilson Falls,** a majestic, 57-foot cascade in a forested setting.

HORSEBACK RIDING AND WAGON RIDES

Northern Maine Riding Adventures (564-3451 or 564-2965), PO Box 16, Dover-Foxcroft 04426. Judy Cross, a registered Maine guide and skilled equestrian, offers 1-hour trail rides, centered riding clinics, and day trips from her four-season facility; also overnight treks based at her camp in the backwoods around Katahdin Ironworks. Special needs riders are welcome.

Rockies Golden Acres (695-3229), Greenville. Trail rides: 1½ to 2-hour rides through the woods to Sawyer Pond; mountain views. Call after 7 PM.

Moosehead Wilderness Trail Rides (534-7305). Laura Munster, based at The Birches in Rockwood, offers trail rides, also overnights with camping and cookouts.

MOOSE-WATCHING

"Moosemainea," sponsored by the Moosehead Lake Chamber of Commerce mid-May through mid-June (see *Moose-Watching* in "What's Where") makes up the largest, most colorful moose-watching event in New England; but chances are you can spot the lake's mascot any dawn or dusk, especially if you avail yourself of boat trips offered by **Wildlife Cruise** (534-7577) or the **Wilderness Boat** (534-7305), both departing from Rockwood. **Moose Safaris** (695-2375), based at Moose Station in Greenville, specializes in van trips into off-road bogs, swamps, and trout ponds.

MOUNTAIN BIKING

The Birches (534-7305 or 1-800-825-WILD) in Rockwood offers mountain bike rentals for use on its extensive cross-country ski network.

SWIMMING

See Lily Bay State Park under *To See.*

WHITEWATER RAFTING/KAYAKING

Moosehead Lake is equidistant from Maine's two most popular rafting routes—Kennebec Gorge and Ripogenus Gorge. **Wilderness Expeditions** (534-2242 or 1-800-825-WILD), PO Box 41, Rockwood 04478, based at the Birches in Rockwood (see *Rustic Resorts*), is a family-run business specializing in half-day white-water rafting trips on the Kennebec at East Outlet (minimum age is 7); longer expeditions on the Kennebec from a base camp in The Forks and on the Penobscot from another base near Baxter State Park. **Eastern River Expeditions** (695-2411/2248 or 1-800-634-7238), Box 1174, Greenville 04441. May through mid-October. From their Greenville base, Sandy Neily and John Connelly offer day trips on the Kennebec and Dead Rivers; also through Ripogenus Gorge and Big Eddy on the Penobscot as well as a family-geared trip from the East Outlet.

CROSS-COUNTRY SKIING

Formal touring centers aside, this region's vast network of snowmobile trails and frozen lakes constitutes splendid opportunities for backcountry skiing. We've skied from the cabins at Chesuncook Lake House, Pray's Cottages at Ripogenus Dam, and Northern Pride Lodge in Kokadjo, all open in winter for cross-country skiers as well as snowmobilers.

Birches Ski Touring Center (534-7305), Rockwood. The resort maintains a 35-mile network of trails, currently expanding to take advantage of a recently acquired 11,000-acre forested spread across the wooded neck between Brassua Lake and Moosehead. You can also ski to Tomhegan, 10 miles up the lake, or out past the ice-fishing shanties to Kineo. Rentals and instruction; snowshoes, too.

Little Lyford Pond Camps (see *Rustic Resorts*) offers groomed trails. In Chesuncook Village, both **Chesuncook Lake House** and **Katahdin View Lodge** cater to cross-country skiers.

DOWNHILL SKIING

Moosehead Resort and Ski Area (695-2272 in Maine; 1-800-348-6743 out-of-state), Greenville 04441. A ski area resort since 1963, with one of New England's first base-area hotels, owned by Scott Paper (1970–1974) and then sold to the state under whose ownership it languished for 11 years. It continues to struggle. The vertical drop is 1750 feet; there are 18 trails, 20 percent snowmaking. Lifts include one double chair, one triple chair, one T-bar, and one Poma lift. Other facilities include a base lodge, cafeteria, restaurant, motel-style lodge, ski school, and ski shop.

SNOWMOBILING

The Moosehead Lake Vacation and Sportsmen's Association maintains some 500 miles of trails in the area. Snowmobile rentals are available from **Kokadjo Sporting Camps** (695-3890) in Kokadjo and from **Rockwood Sales & Service** (534-7387), Rockwood. Ask the chamber about guided tours sponsored by the Moosehead Riders Snowmobile Club. Moosehead Resort and Ski Area also caters to snowmobilers.

LODGING

INNS

Greenville Inn (695-2206), Norris Street, Box 1194, Greenville 04441. Open April through November; inquire whether open in winter. A true lumber baron's mansion set atop a hill just off Main Street, with a sweeping view of Moosehead Lake. Rich cherry, mahogany, and oak paneling, embossed walls, working fireplaces, and an immense, leaded-glass window depicting a single spruce tree—all contribute to the sense of elegance. There are six second-floor rooms (two with wonderfully working fireplaces), also a more rustic suite in the Carriage House (ideal for families) and two pine-paneled cottages with views. Four new cottages are due for completion in 1995. The dining room, open to the public, is considered the best in northwestern Maine (see *Dining Out*). Your hosts are Elfi, Susie, and Michael Schnetzer. Rates (including continental breakfast) run from $85 for a small but charming room with private bath to $95 for the original master bedroom with a working fireplace and large bath; the carriage house is $90 ($15 extra for each added person), less in spring.

The Lodge at Moosehead (695-4400), Box 1175, Lily Bay Road, Greenville 04441. Jennifer and Roger Cauchi have transformed a vintage 1916 hunting lodge into a phenomenon. Each of the five guest rooms (four with lake views) has been designed with immense care around a theme. In the "trout" room, for instance, brightly painted leaping trout have been sculpted into the bed's four posters and matching mirrors; the fabric-covered walls are pattered with hooks and flies. For each room, local sculptor Joe Bolf has created equally spectacular beds depicting themes like moose, bear, and loon. All rooms have cable TVs, gas fireplaces, and baths with Jacuzzi tubs. Breakfast and dinner in the glass-walled dining room is for guests only, and even the gift shop is off-limits to passersby. Roger, a former travel agent, delights in playing concierge, arranging fishing, hiking, rafting, or whatever else guests may desire. Rates, including a full breakfast and evening hors d'oeuvres, are $135–185 June 16 through October 31; $125–160 off-season, including dinner as well as breakfast.

Chesuncook Lake House (745-5330 or c/o Folsom's: 695-2821), Box 656, Route 76, Greenville 04441. Open year-round. An unpretentious, 1864 farmhouse built on the site of an older log cabin that served as the center for the lumbering camp (see Chesuncook Village under *To See*). There are 12 guest rooms and three housekeeping cabins. Maggie McBurnie, a native Parisian, serves three meals a day in summer; her husband, Bert, born and schooled in Chesuncook, meets guests at Cushing's Landing at the south end of the lake and ferries them in. Otherwise you can fly in from Greenville. Registered Maine guides and boats are available. In winter, cross-country ski tours are offered. $85 per person includes three meals in the inn, which closes in winter; the year-round rate in the cabins is $25 per person per day with a 3-day minimum; $35–38 per person, per day in the summer.

Northern Pride Lodge (695-2890), HCR 76, Box 588, Kokadjo 04441. Open year-round. Built as a lumber baron's hunting lodge in this wilderness outpost (year-round population: 5), the lodge offers six guest rooms, each with enough beds for a family or group of friends; shared baths. The living room has a hearth, stained-glass windows, and a sense of opulence; the dining room, on a glassed-in porch overlooking First Roach Pond, is open to guests daily, and to the public Thursday through Sunday. There are also 24 campsites, rental canoes, and motorboats. In winter the lodge caters to snowmobilers and cross-country skiers. $80 per couple includes breakfast; rates with all three meals are also offered.

BED & BREAKFASTS

Sawyer House (695-2369), PO Box 521, Lakeview Street, Greenville 04441. Open year-round. Handy to the flying services, and an ideal stop if you fly in from Portland en route to a remote sporting camp or inn; good for anyone who likes being in Greenville with a view of the lake. There's a first-floor suite that can accommodate up to four ($70 double) and two second-floor rooms with private bath ($60 double); rates include a full breakfast. Pat Zieten is a warm, helpful host.

Devlin House (695-2229), PO Box 1102, Greenville 04441. A modern home high on the hill west of town with splendid views over meadows to the lake; a ground-level suite with a sitting room, and two rooms with king-sized beds, private baths, air-conditioning, and TV. Ruth Devlin is a longtime local resident who enjoys sharing her knowledge of the area. $40–80.

Manitou Cottage (695-3082), PO Box 1208, Greenville 04441. Open year-round. Mimi and Russ Whitten (a Maine guide), after operating popular wilderness sporting camps for many years, have created a comfortable retreat in the middle of Greenville. Set back from the street, the cottage offers harbor views, a two-room downstairs suite with private bath, and two bright, cheery upstairs rooms with shared bath. The only TV is in the pleasant common room; continental breakfast is served in the old-fashioned kitchen. $40–65; special rates for the whole house.

Kineo House (534-8812), PO Box 397, Rockwood 04478. Open December through April and May through October. The only place to stay on Kineo, a nature preserve at the narrows of Moosehead Lake accessible only by boat or snowmobile from Rockwood. The eight guest rooms (private baths) are in Oak Lodge, one of the cottages once clustered around a mammoth—now all but vanished—grand hotel. The classic, old, nine-hole golf course survives, and hiking trails now lead up the sides of the sheer-faced Mount Kineo for which the old hotel was named. Lynn and Marshall Peterson serve lunch to the public, also dinner by reservation, and operate the Kineo shuttle (see *Getting Around*). Shuttle and breakfast are included in $65 double, $15 per extra person.

Lyman Blair House (695-2375 or 695-3386), PO Box 1326, Greenville 04441. Set high on Blair Hill with views across Moosehead Lake to Big Squaw, this is an expansive 1890s house set in 14 sloping acres. When we stopped by, 10 guest rooms ($85–125) were being readied for the '95 season.

RUSTIC RESORTS

The Birches Resort (534-7305/2241 or 1-800-825-WILD), PO Box 41, Rockwood 04478. Open year-round. The Willard family has turned this thirties sporting camp into one of the most comfortable family-geared resorts in the North Woods. It's sited in a birch grove overlooking Mount Kineo. Fifteen hand-hewn log cabins are strung along the lake, each with a porch, a Franklin stove or fireplace in a sitting room, and one to three bedrooms. Some cabins have kitchens, but three meals are available in summer. The main lodge includes a cheerful, open-timbered dining room, an inviting lobby with a trout pool, and a living room with hearth room. Upstairs are four guest rooms with decks overlooking the lake (shared bath), and there are also 12 "cabin tents" near the lodge and several yurts scattered through the resort's 11,000 acres. Facilities include an outside hot tub and sauna; windsurfers, sailboats, kayaks, canoes, fishing boats and mountain bikes are available. Cross-country skiing rentals and expeditions are also offered. From $76 double with breakfast in the lodge. Housekeeping cottages are $650–950 per week in summer (less off-season) without meals. Cabin tents begin at $17 single per day. A variety of rafting, canoeing, and other packages are also available. The dining room is open to the public (see *Dining Out*).

Little Lyford Pond Camps (Folsom's radio phone: 695-2821), Box 1269, Greenville 04441. Open sporadically. Sited in a sheltered, alpine-looking valley, these camps were built in the 1870s as a logging company station on a tote road. The 10 shake-roofed log cabins (without plumbing or electricity) sleep from two to seven. Three meals are served in the main lodge; facilities also include a conference center, sauna, and solar shower. Gulf Hagas is a short hike and cross-country ski trails are maintained. In winter you can ski or fly in, but in summer the pontoon planes don't like to land. The camps are 3.5 miles off the Appalachian Trail, 12 miles via a gated logging road from Greenville. $75 per person includes all meals, plus use of canoes.

Nugent's Chamberlain Lake Camps (695-2821), HCR 76, Box 632, Greenville 04441. Open year-round. Dates just from the 1930s, but built entirely by Al and Patty Nugent. This is one of the most remote camps, nicely sited and still so old-fashioned that it should be on the National Register of Historic Places. In 1987 the state awarded the lease of these camps to John Richardson and Regina Webster. Sited within the Allagash Wilderness Waterway, 50 miles north of Millinocket between Baxter State Park and Allagash Mountain, they are best reached via Folsom's Air Service (see *Getting Around*); otherwise it's a 5-mile boat or snowmobile ride up Chamberlain Lake. The eight housekeeping cabins have the traditional front overhang and outhouses; they sleep 2 to 10. Boats are available. AP, MAP, or housekeeping plans available. $22–60 per person. Pets and children welcome.

West Branch Ponds Camps (695-2561), Box 35, Greenville 04441. A 10-mile drive from the main road at Kokadjo. Open after the ice breaks up and through September; inquire about winter season. First opened as a moose-hunting lodge in the 1880s; the newest log cottage was built in 1938. Directly across the pond is the majestic bulk of Whitecap Mountain. There are wonderfully weathered old cabins (each with log beds, heat, electricity, bath; three with Franklin stoves) and a square central lodge with a bell on top. Andy and Carol Stirling are third-generation owners, and Carol is well known for her cooking. Motorboats and canoes are available. The lodge has plenty of books and comfortable corners, and the camps have wood stoves. $50 per person per day includes three meals and use of a canoe; children are half price.

☞ **Maynards in Maine** (534-7703), Rockwood 04478. Open May through hunting season. "The only thing we change around here is the linen," says Gail Maynard, who helps run the sportsmen's camp founded by her husband's grandfather in 1919. Overlooking the Moose River, a short walk from Moosehead Lake, Maynards includes a dozen tidy, moss-green frame buildings furnished with dark Edwardian furniture, much of it from the grand old Mount Kineo hotel. The lodge is filled with stuffed fish, moose heads, and Maynard family memorabilia, and furnished with stiff-backed leather chairs. A sign cautions, "Do Not Wear Hip Boots or Waders into the Dining Room." Two meals a day are served and one "packed." $48 per person with three meals, $288 per week for cabins.

CAMPS

Tomhegan Wilderness Resort (534-7712), PO Box 308, Rockwood 04478. Open year-round. A 10-mile ride up a dirt road from Rockwood Village; 1.5 miles of frontage on Moosehead Lake. Nine hand-hewn cottages with kitchens and living rooms, rocking chairs on the porches, full baths, and wood stoves; also efficiency units in the lodge. Boats and canoes are available; cross-country skiing and snowmobiling in winter. Moderate.

✎ **Rockwood Cottages** (534-7725), Box 176, Rockwood 04478. Open year-round. Ron and Bonnie Searles maintain clean, comfortable housekeeping cottages with screened-in porches overlooking the lake and Mount Kineo just across the narrows. They are happy to advise about exploring Kineo and this less-developed end of the lake. Boats, motors, and fishing licenses are available, and guests have free docking. There's also a sauna, a barbecue, and an impressive moose head. $60 per couple, $10 per additional person; $360 per couple per week, $60 per additional person. Pets welcome.

Beaver Cove Camps (695-3717 or 1-800-577-3717), Greenville 04441. Open year-round. Eight miles north of Greenville on the eastern shore of Moosehead Lake are six fully equipped housekeeping cabins, each with full kitchen and bath. Owner Jim Glavine is a registered Maine guide specializing in fly-fishing. Guided hunting and snowmobile or ski touring also offered. $65 per night or $390 double per week.

☞ **Spencer Pond Camps** (radio service: 695-2821), Star Route 76, Box 580, Greenville 04441. Open May to November. Bob Croce and Jill Martell are the new owners of this long-established cluster of six housekeeping camps (sleeping 2 to 10) in an unusually beautiful spot, accessible by logging road from Lily Bay Road. Gas and kerosene lights and hand-pumped water; a base for birding, hiking, and mountain climbing. Canoes and boats available. $15–18 per person; 2-night minimum stay for two people.

Medawisla (radio phone year-round: 695-2690), HCR 76, Box 592, Greenville 04441. Open May through November. In this remote corner of the woods, not far from Kokadjo, the LeRoys offer six fully equipped cabins with wood stoves, flush toilets, and hot showers. Each can sleep from 2 to 10 people. Popular for fishing in spring, hunting in fall, and as a getaway in summer. Meals available during deer season only. Boats and canoes are available. The loons of the sound track from the movie *On Golden Pond* were taped here. From $60–90 double, housekeeping; weekly rates.

Frost Pond Camps (Folsom's radio phone: 695-2821), HCR 76, Box 620, Greenville 04441 (in winter: 723-6622; 36 Minuteman Drive, Millinocket 04462). Open May to November; located 3 miles beyond Ripogenus Dam. These eight rustic housekeeping cabins are on Frost Pond (good for trout) and handy to Chesuncook Lake (landlocked salmon). Rick and Judy Givens also outfit Allagash Wilderness canoe trips and offer 10 wooded campsites. $19.50–24.50 per night.

CAMPGROUNDS

Lily Bay State Park (695-2700), 8 miles north of Greenville. Ninety-three sites, many spaced along the shore; boat launch and beach.

The State of Maine Bureau of Forestry (695-3721) maintains free (first come, first served) "authorized sites" (no fire permit required) and "permit sites" (permit required), scattered on both public and private land along Moosehead Lake and on several of its islands.

Bowater/Great Northern Paper woodlands office in Millinocket (723-

5131) is also the source of a map detailing roads and primitive camp-sites in that company's vast domain. After paying the gate fee ($8 for out-of-state vehicles, $4 for Maine plates), sites are $6 per out-of-state vehicle, $3 for Maine plates.

WHERE TO EAT

DINING OUT
Greenville Inn (695-2206), Norris Street, Greenville. Dinner served nightly by reservation from 6 PM. Thanks to Austrian-born chef Elfi Schnetzer, this former lumber baron's dining room is the toast of north-western Maine. Appetizers might include smoked venison with cumberland sauce ($8) or fresh Maine chevre with olives, tomatoes, and rosemary olive oil ($6). There are usually just seven entrées—al-ways a trio of lamb chops with herbed butter ($17) and a choice of well-dressed fish dishes like Atlantic salmon fillet with sauce verte ($16); frequently orange apricot grilled roast duckling ($15). Leave room for Susie Schnetzer's pastry creations.

The Birches (534-2242), Rockwood. Open year-round; daily in summer and fall, vacation weeks and weekends in winter. This popular resort (see *Rustic Resorts*) has one of the area's most attractive dining rooms—log-sided with a massive stone hearth, a war canoe turned upside down in the open rafters, and hurricane lamps on the highly polished tables. Specialties include chicken cordon bleu and pork roast with glazed apple stuffing, $12.95–14.95. Reservations suggested.

Northern Pride Lodge (695-2890), Kokadjo. The dining room in this clas-sic lumber baron's hunting lodge (see *Inns*) is a modified sun porch overlooking First Roach Pond. Dinner is served to the public Thursday through Sunday and ranges from spaghetti to filet mignon ($9.95–14.95). Reservations suggested.

EATING OUT
Pittston Farm (call Folsom's Air Service: 695-2821). Open except for the last 2 weeks in April. "Authentic" only begins to describe this classic outpost, a wilderness farm built around 1910 as a major hub of Great Northern's logging operations. Sited at the confluence of the North and South Branches of the Penobscot River a little more than 20 miles north of Rockwood, the white-clapboard lodge and its outlying barns and fields are now owned by Ken Twitchel (a veteran lumber camp cook) and his wife, Sonja. Visitors are welcome for "all you can eat" meals, which include thick, tasty soups and at least two kinds of meat, several vegetables (some grown outside), a salad bar, and freshly baked rolls, bread and pastries. Buffet suppers ($7.95) are served at 5 PM and 6 PM and might be a good idea to reserve for (Folsom's will fly you in and back from Greenville for $50–60 per person including the meal). Lunch is $6.95, and breakfast, $4.95. (Upstairs rooms tend to have a number

of quilt-covered beds, shared baths, $35 per person, meals included.)
See *Scenic Drives* for toll road fees.

Kineo House (534-8812), Kineo. Open May through October and December through April. Accessible in summer by shuttle boat from Rockwood (see *Bed & Breakfasts*). It would be a shame to spend a few days in the Moosehead area and not explore Kineo with its dramatic walks and hiking trails as well as golf course. Kineo House serves lunch (burgers and sandwiches), has a pleasant pub, and also offers dinner ($9–15) by reservation.

Kokadjo Trading Post (695-3993), Kokadjo. Open 6 AM–11 PM, earlier in hunting season. Fred and Marie Candeloro offer a cozy dining room/ pub room with a large fieldstone fireplace and view of First Roach Pond.

In Greenville

Flatlander's Pub (695-3373), Pritham Avenue, Greenville. Open except Tuesday, 11 AM "'til close." Hamburgers, chicken wings, deep-fried mushrooms, deli sandwiches; beer on tap and house wines; homemade chili, a good pea soup, and pies. Nice atmosphere, the preferred middle-of-town place.

Kelly's Landing (695-4438), Greenville Junction. Open 7 AM–9 PM. A breakfast bar and large salad bar, fried seafood platter, roast chicken, sandwiches. A big, cheerful place with tables on the deck by the lake.

Cabbage Patch (695-2252), Route 6/15, Greenville Junction. Open year-round for dinner. "Early logging atmosphere." A barnboard-sided lounge with lake views. Good for soup and sandwiches, salad bar, house steak, hot dogs, chicken cordon bleu, or whatever your mood fancies; liquor; reasonably priced.

✎ **The Road Kill Cafe** (695-2230), Route 15, Greenville Junction. Open daily 11:30–11:30. The café's subtitle is, "Where the food used to speak for itself." The decor runs from hub caps to license plates, and the menu features potato pelts, a pail o'nightcrawlers, and Route 15 soup *du jour.*

✎ **Red's Lakeside** (695-2527), Pritham Avenue, Greenville. Open year-round with a seasonal lakeside deck. Touristy, but with the only middle-of-town, on-lake dining. Beer, wine, and frozen alcoholic drinks; pizza and sandwiches. A wide choice of dinner entrées. Moderate.

Cafe Catania (695-2440), Greenville Junction. Open for dinner September through June, Wednesday through Saturday; otherwise Thursday through Saturday. A bright Italian place with a big salad bar, prime rib, seafood, Italian specialties.

Auntie M's Restaurant (695-2238), Main Street, Greenville. Open for all three meals but best for breakfast; homemade soups and specials. Caters to truckers, rafters, and kids.

The Indian Store in Greenville

SELECTIVE SHOPPING

Indian Hill Trading Post (695-3376), Greenville. Open daily year-round, Friday until 10 PM.

 The Indian Store (695-3348), corner of Main Street and Pritham Avenue. Since 1929 Ida Faye's store has sold baskets and feathers, candies, souvenirs, firecrackers, and knickknacks of every description. Every inch is filled.

The Corner Shop (695-2142), corner of Maine and Pritham (across from the Indian Store); gifts, books, magazines.

Sunbower Pottery (695-2870), Scammon Road, Greenville, home of the "moose mug"; locally made gifts, artwork.

SPECIAL EVENTS

June to April: **The Ice-Out Contest** offers everyone a chance to guess the exact date. Contact the Moosehead Lake Chamber of Commerce for details (695-3702).

February: **Snowmobile Rally.**

Mid-May through mid-June: **Moosemania** month, sponsored by the chamber of commerce, is big; see "What's Where."

July: **Independence Day** celebrations in Greenville Junction.

August: **Forest Heritage Days.**

September: **The International Seaplane Fly-In Weekend** is held in Greenville (second weekend).

Katahdin Region

Mile-high Mount Katahdin is the centerpiece not only for Baxter State Park but for a surprisingly large area from which it is clearly visible. Like a huge ocean liner in a relatively flat sea of woodland, the massive mountain looms above the open countryside to the east, the direction from which it's most easily accessible.

Though the mountain and park are unquestionably its biggest drawing card, the Katahdin region offers its share of wooded lake country and represents one of the most reasonably priced destinations in Maine for families who want to get away together to hike and fish. Whitewater rafting companies are also based near the Togue Pond Gatehouse to Baxter State Park, handy both to the park and to rafting on the Western Branch of the Penobscot.

Like Acadia National Park, Baxter State Park's acreage was amassed privately and given to the public as a gift. In this case, it was one individual—Governor Percival Baxter—who bought all the land himself, after unsuccessfully attempting to convince the state to do so during his political term. At the time (1931), no one seemed able to conceive why Maine, with all its forest, needed officially to preserve a swatch of woods as wilderness.

Decades of subsequent logging and present concerns for the future of this woodland have heightened the value of Governor Baxter's legacy and his mandate—the reason camping and even admission to the park is strictly limited—to preserve at least this 201,018 acres of Maine's North Woods as wilderness.

The restaurants and beds nearest to Baxter State Park are in Millinocket, a lumbering outpost built by the Great Northern Paper Company around the turn of the century. The town is still centered around the big paper mills and the logging industry that feeds it.

GUIDANCE

The **Baxter State Park** information phone is 723-5140, but it's always busy. Write to park headquarters, 64 Balsam Drive, Millinocket 04462. For details about making reservations, see *Green Space*. The attractive visitors center, which offers picnic tables, rest rooms, and a selection of published as well as free guides to the park, is 1 mile east of Millinocket on Route 11/157.

Millinocket Chamber of Commerce (723-4443), 1029 Central Street, Millinocket 04462. The chamber maintains a seasonal information center on Route 11/157 east of Millinocket; it serves as a year-round source of information about the motels and restaurants that are chamber members.

Northern Katahdin Valley Regional Chamber of Commerce, PO Box 14D, Patten 04765, publishes another brochure focusing on the Patten area and points north and east.

Bowater/Great Northern Paper (723-5131, ext. 1229), One Katahdin Avenue, Millinocket 04462, the largest landowner in this area, maintaining thousands of miles of roads and hundreds of campsites. The company's map/guide to its lands is available at checkpoints on its roads and by writing to the office, attention "Public Relations."

GETTING THERE

The most direct route is I-95 to Exit 56 at Medway (50 miles northeast of Bangor), and 10 miles into Millinocket. From here, it's 18 miles along the Golden Road to the Togue Pond entrance of the park.

GETTING AROUND

Katahdin Air Service Inc. (723-8378), PO Box 171, Millinocket. Available May through November to fly in to remote camps and shuttle in canoes and campers; will also drop hikers at points along the Appalachian Trail. **Scotty's Flying Service** (528-2626) at Shin Pond also serves wilderness camps.

MEDICAL EMERGENCY

Millinocket Regional Hospital (723-5161).

TO SEE

The Katahdin Iron Works. Open May through mid-October, 6 AM–8 PM. Turn at the small sign on Route 11, 5 miles north of Brownville Junction, and go another 6 miles up the gravel road. This state historic site is really not worth the effort unless you plan to continue on down the gravel road to hike in Gulf Hagas or to camp (see *Hiking* and *Campgrounds*). The spot was a sacred place for the Indians, who found their yellow ocher paint here. Then from the 1840s until 1890, an iron works prospered in this remote spot, spawning a village to house its 200 workers and producing 2000 tons of raw iron annually. Guests of The Silver Lake Hotel (1880s–1913) here came on the same narrow-gauge railroad that carried away the iron. All that remains is a big old blast furnace and iron kiln. Tours and books on the iron works are offered by local author and backwoods guide Bill Sawtell (965-3971).

Patten Lumberman's Museum (528-2650), Shin Pond Road (Route 159), Patten. Open Memorial Day through September, Tuesday through Saturday 9–4 and Sunday 11–4; also weekends until Columbus Day. $2.50 per adult, $1.00 per child. The museum, which encompasses more than

4000 displays housed in 10 buildings, was founded in 1962 by bacteriologist Lore Rogers and log driver Caleb Scribner. Exhibits range from giant log haulers to "gum books," the lumberman's scrimshaw: intricately carved boxes in which to keep spruce gum, a popular gift for a sweetheart. There are replicas of logging camps from different periods, dioramas, machinery, and photos, all adding up to a fascinating picture of a vanished way of life. This road leads to the Metagamon Gate, the northern, less trafficked corner of Baxter State Park.

"A.J. Allee" scenic overlook, some 15 miles beyond the Medway exit. The view is of Mount Katahdin rising massively from woods and water.

TO DO

BOAT EXCURSION

Katahdin View Pontoon Boat Rides (723-4225). Seasonal sunrise (6–7:30 AM) and sunset cruises on a 24-foot pontoon boat along Millinocket Lake and into Mud Brook. $10 adults, $7 children 5–12. Departs from Big Moose Cabins, Millinocket.

CANOE RENTALS

Penobscot River Outfitters (746-9349 in Maine, or 1-800-794-5267), Route 157, Medway 04460. Old Town rentals; also specializes in 1- to 7-day canoe trips on the East and West Branches of the Penobscot.

Katahdin Outfitters (723-5700), in Millinocket, offers canoe rentals, trip planning, transport, and shuttle for trips on the Allagash, St. John, and Penobscot.

Canoe rentals are also available in Peaks-Kenny Park (see *Campgrounds.*)

For a more complete list of guide services, contact the **North Maine Woods office** (435-6213) in Ashland.

HIKING

Baxter State Park. Ever since the 1860s—when Henry David Thoreau's account of his 1846 ascent of "Ktaddn" began to circulate—the demanding trails to Maine's highest summit (5267 feet) have been among the most popular in the state. Climbing Katahdin itself is considered a right of passage in Maine and much of New England. The result is a steady stream of humanity up and down the Katahdin trails, while other peaks, such as 3488-foot Doubletop, offer excellent, little-trafficked hiking trails and views of Katahdin to boot. In all, there are 46 mountain peaks and 150 miles of well-marked trails. Allow 3 to 5 days at a campground like Trout Brook Farm Campground in the northern wilderness area of the park, or base yourself at Russell Pond and hike to the Grand Falls and Lookout Ledges. A free "Day Use Hiking Guide" is available from the park headquarters (see *Green Space*).

Gulf Hagas is most easily accessible (3.1 miles) from the Katahdin Iron Works (see *To See*). Billed as the "Grand Canyon of Maine," this 2.5-mile canyon with walls up to 40 feet high was carved by the west branch of the Pleasant River. The approach is through a 35-acre stand of virgin white pines, some more than 130 feet tall, a landmark in their own right (known as "The Hermitage") and preserved by the Nature Conservancy of Maine. The trail then follows the river, along the Appalachian Trail for a ways, but turns off along the rim of the canyon toward dramatic Screw Auger Falls and on through The Jaws to Buttermilk Falls, Stair Falls, and Billings Falls. Allow 6–8 hours for the hike and plan to camp at one of the waterside campsites within the Jo Mary preserve (see *Campgrounds*).

HORSEBACK RIDING
Northern Maine Riding Adventures (564-3451 or 564-2965), Dover-Foxcroft. Judy Cross, a registered Maine guide and skilled rider, offers trail rides ranging from an hour or day to multiday treks in the wilderness area around the Katahdin Iron Works. Inquire about Women's Wilderness Weekends.

WHITEWATER RAFTING
Several whitewater rafting companies maintain bases near the Togue Pond entrance to Baxter State Park; there are mid-May to mid-September departure points for day trips down the West Branch of the Penobscot River through Ripogenus Dam and the Cribworks. **Northern Outdoors** (1-800-765-RAFT), **New England Whitewater** (1-800-766-RAFT), and **Wilderness Expeditions** (1-800-825-WILD) share **The Penobscot Outdoor Center** on Pockwockamus Pond where facilities include a bar, restaurant, hot tub, sauna, canoes, kayaks, and windsurfers; lodging is at campsites and in cabin tents. **Unicorn Rafting** (1-800-UNICORN), based at Big Moose Inn on Millinocket Lake, also offers a 6-day Penobscot expedition tracing Henry David Thoreau's journey in the Maine woods.

CROSS-COUNTRY SKIING AND SNOWSHOEING
Katahdin Country Skis and Sports (723-5839), One Colony Place, Millinocket, offers rental skis; trail maps to over 30 miles of groomed and backcountry trails are available here and from the local chamber. Packages available with Katahdin area B&Bs.

SNOWMOBILING
Snowmobiling is big: The Katahdin region brochure map shows a 350-mile snowmobile system superimposed on it. For details, check with the Katahdin Region Tourism Council (746-5410).

GREEN SPACE

BAXTER STATE PARK
This 201,018-acre park surrounds Mount Katahdin, the highest peak in the state (5267 feet). There are only two entry points: **Togue Pond Gate** near Millinocket, by far the most popular, is open 6 AM–9 PM, May 15 through October 15. **Metagamon Gate,** in the northeast corner of the

The Chimney Pond Trail in Baxter State Park

MAINE OFFICE OF TOURISM

park, is open 6 AM–9 PM. Nonresident vehicles pay an $8 day-use fee at the gate ($25 for the season).

The park is open daily, but note the restricted camping periods and the special-use permits required from December 1 through April 1. Orchids, ferns, alpine flowers, and dozens of other interesting plants here delight botanists. Geologists are intrigued by Baxter's rhyolite, Katahdin granite, and many fossils. Birds and wildlife, of course, also abound. Rental canoes are available at several locations in the park.

Camping is only permitted May 15 to October 15 and December to April 1. As a rule, campsites are booked solid before the season begins. Don't come without a reservation. In all there are 10 widely scattered campgrounds, among which Russell and Chimney Pond near the base of Katahdin are the most popular. Daicey Pond and Kidney Pond each offer traditional cabins with beds, gas lanterns, firewood, and table and chairs ($17 per person per night minimum, $30 for a two-bed cabin, $40 for a three-bed cabin, and $50 for a four-bed; children ages 1–6 are free, 7–16 are $10 per person). Six more campgrounds, accessible by road, offer a mix of bunkhouses, lean-tos, and tent sites. There are two more backcountry, hike-in campgrounds, and beyond that, 25 more single backcountry sites. In 1994, tent and lean-to sites were $6 per person, minimum $12 per site. Space in the bunkhouses was $7 per person.

Summer season reservations (only accepted for the period between May 15 and October 15) must be made in person or by mail with the fee enclosed (check or cash), posted no earlier than December 26 of the year before you are coming (Baxter State Park, 46 Balsam Drive, Millinocket 04462). Send a stamped, self-addressed envelope if you want to receive a confirmation. No refunds.

LODGING

Note: For details about a choice of motels handy to I-95, check with the Millinocket Chamber of Commerce (723-4443).

INNS AND BED & BREAKFASTS

Big Moose Inn (723-8391), Millinocket Lake, Millinocket 04462. Seasonal. A classic old summer inn with 10 guest rooms, cabins, a public dining room; caters to rafters. Moderately priced.

Sweet Lillian B&B (723-4894), Corner of Katahdin and Pine Streets, Millinocket 04462. Donna Cogswell has named this hospitable way station for her mother. Spotlessly clean, comfortable, and friendly: five guest rooms with a common area. Full breakfast included in $25–50.

Katahdin Area Bed & Breakfast (723-5220), 9496 Oxford Street, Millinocket 04462. Rodney and Mary Lou Corriveau offer bright, cheery rooms; $25–50, full breakfast included.

Summit Farm Lodging (365-4236), Route 11, Box 51, Stacyville 04782. This is a 700-acre working farm with a white farmhouse and view of Mount Katahdin. Accommodations include three rooms and kitchen facilities and two apartments, as well as camps. Host Judy Pelletier also drives a schoolbus. Reasonable rates.

Carousel B&B (965-7741), Brownville 04414. Closed when we came through but enthusiastically recommended to us; the most convenient lodging to Gulf Hagas.

REMOTE RUSTIC CAMPS

Katahdin Lake Wilderness Camps, Box 398, Millinocket 04462, at the end of a private, 3½-mile tote trail from Roaring Brook Road in Baxter State Park; it's an hour's walk. Al Cooper will meet you with pack horses, or you can fly in from Millinocket Lake. Ten log cabins (two to seven people per cabin) and a main lodge built on a bluff overlooking the lake; firewood, linens, kerosene lamps, and outhouses go with each cabin, and several also have gas stoves for housekeeping. Sandy beaches. Moderately priced with all meals. Rental boats available.

Bradford Camps (radio phone: 764-6112; winter: 225-3057), Box 499, Patten 04765. Open following ice-out through November. Sited at the Aroostook River's headwaters, Munsungan Lake. Virtually inaccessible by land (unless you want to weather 47 miles on logging roads), this unusually tidy lodge has well-tended lawns and 28 firm beds in comfortable cabins lighted by propane lamps; also five cabins on outlying ponds. $85 per night includes meals, but boat and motor are extra.

CAMPGROUNDS

Jo Mary Multiple Use Forest (695-8135). Open May through October, a 225,000-acre tract of commercial forest stretching almost from Greenville on the west, to the Katahdin Iron Works on the east, and north to Millinocket. Seasonal checkpoints at Katahdin Iron Works and Wilson (Greenville) are open 6 AM–8 PM; off Route 11 south of

Millinocket the gate is also open until 10 PM Friday and Saturday nights.

Gulf Hagas (see *Hiking*), with 50 miles of the Appalachian Trail, 96 lakes, and 125 miles of brooks, streams, and rivers within its boundaries, along with 150 miles of roads over which lumber trucks have rights-of-way. There are over 60 authorized campsites, some on rivers and lakes. The day-use fee (for those between ages 15 and 70) is $4 for residents, $7 for nonresidents, and the camping fee is a flat $4 per person. For reservations (valid only at least a month in advance) write North Maine Woods, Box 382, Ashland 04732.

Peaks-Kenny State Park (564-2003), Route 153, 6 miles from Dover-Foxcroft. Open mid-May through September for camping and for swimming in Sebec Lake.

Mattawamkeag Wilderness Park (947-4585), Mattawamkeag (off Route 2; a half-hour drive from the I-95 Medway exit). Fifty campsites, ten Adirondack shelters, a small store, a recreation building, picnic facilities, 15 miles of hiking trails, and 60 miles of canoeing on the Mattawamkeag River with patches of white water. An 8-mile gravel road leads into the park.

Scraggly Lake Public Lands Management Unit (contact the Bureau of Public Lands, Presque Isle: 764-2033), a 10,014-acre forested preserve laced with ponds and brooks. It has 12 "authorized" campsites (no fire permit needed). Scraggly Lake is good for salmon and brook trout; a half-mile hiking trail loops up Owls Head.

Katahdin Shadows Campground (746-9349 or 1-800-794-KAMP), Route 157, Medway. This is a full-service, family-geared campground with a big playground, a central lodge with a game room and board games, swimming pool, weekend hayrides, athletic fields, free morning coffee, kitchen facilities, tent and hookup sites, and well-designed cabins with kitchen facilities ($35 per couple). Rick LeVasseur also offers canoe and boat rentals, hiking, cross-country skiing, and snowmobiling information. Rabbits everywhere.

(For camping in **Baxter State Park** see *Green Space*.)

WHERE TO EAT

EATING OUT

Big Moose Inn and Restaurant (723-8391), Millinocket Lake, 8 miles west of Millinocket on the Baxter Park road, across from the lake. Open Wednesday through Saturday 6 PM–10 PM. A pleasant Maine woods atmosphere, American cuisine, moderate prices.

Angie's Restaurant (943-7432), Milo. Just in case you happen to be cutting over to the Katahdin Iron Works and Gulf Hagas from I-95 (take the Howland exit and the unnumbered woods road through Medford to Milo)—or for whatever other reason you happen to be in Milo—Angie's (across from the cemetery) is open for all three meals. Great

The Birches Resort in Rockwood

road food, homemade sandwich bread, wooden booths, blue frilly curtains, dinner specials ranging from liver and onions to salmon steak.

River's Edge Restaurant (965-2881), Brownville Junction. Open Tuesday through Saturday, 4–9. Johanna and James McGuinness have created an attractive dining room featuring seafood and pasta dinners. You can also get liver and onions or prime rib.

Penobscot Room (723-4566), Penobscot Avenue, Millinocket. Open for lunch and dinner. George and Bea Simon are third-generation owners. Good for pizza, calzones, fried clams, or prime rib. Children's menu, liquor.

SPECIAL EVENTS

June: Three-day **Katahdin Family Bluegrass Music Festival** (last weekend), Medway.

October: For 3 weeks before Halloween, the scariest, most elaborate **haunted trolley ride** in Maine, sponsored by Jandreau's Greenhouse, Millinocket.

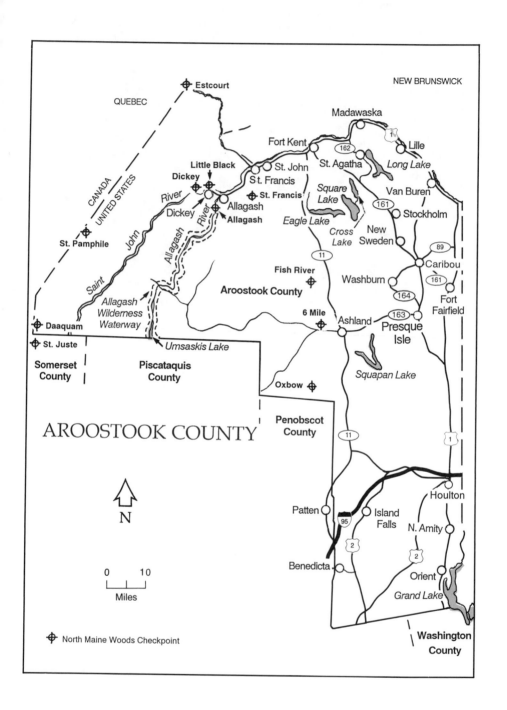

AROOSTOOK COUNTY

Aroostook County

Almost the size of Massachusetts, Aroostook is Maine's largest and least populated county. It's referred to simply as "The County" in Maine, and, contrary to its image as one big potato field, it's as varied as it is vast. Four of Aroostook's 5 million acres are wooded—land that includes many major mountains, most of the Allagash Wilderness Waterway, and more than 1000 lakes.

The Upper St. John Valley at the top of The County, a broad ribbon of river land backed by woodland in the west and by a high, open plateau in the east, has its own distinctly Acadian look, language, and taste. Central Aroostook—the rolling farmland around Fort Fairfield, Presque Isle, and Caribou—is generally equated with the entire county. It, too, has its appeal, especially around Washburn and New Sweden, sites of two of New England's more interesting museums. Houlton, the northern terminus of I-95 and the county seat, is in southern Aroostook, a mix of farmland, lonely woods, and lakes.

"Aroostook" is said to mean "bright," actually the best word I can think of to describe the entire county since the luminosity of its sky—broader than elsewhere in New England—is The County's single most striking characteristic, along with its location. Bounded by Canada on two sides and the North Woods on the third, Aroostook is so far off any tourist route that many New England maps omit it entirely. Maine pundits are fond of noting that Portland is as far from Fort Kent, the northern terminus of Route 1, as it is from New York City.

The conventional loop tour around The County is I-95 to its terminus at Houlton, then Route 1 north to Fort Kent and back down Route 11. We suggest doing it in reverse.

Many visitors actually enter The County in canoes, paddling up the Allagash River that flows north and empties into the St. John River at Allagash, a miniscule hamlet that's become widely known as "Mattagash" to readers of novels (*The Funeral Makers, Once Upon a Time on the Banks,* and *The Weight of Winter*) by Allagash native Cathie Pelletier. Local residents will tell you that the names of Pelletier's characters have been changed only as slightly as that of her town and that the interplay between Catholics and Protestants (descendants of Acadian and Scottish settlers, respectively) chronicled in her books remains very real. From the 1940s to the 1960s French was a forbidden language in local schools, and students were punished for speaking it anywhere on school grounds.

Acadians trace their lineage to French settlers who came to farm and fish in Nova Scotia in the early 1600s and who, in 1755, were forcibly deported by an English governor. This "Grand Derangement," dispersing a population of some 10,000 Acadians, brutally divided families (a tale told by Longfellow in "Evangeline"). Many were returned to France, only to make their way back to a warmer New World (Louisiana), and many were resettled in New Brunswick, from which they were once more dislodged after the Revolution when the government gave their land to American loyalists.

In a meadow overlooking the St. John River behind Madawaska's Tante Blanche Museum, a large marble cross and an outsized wooden sculpture of a *Voyageur* in his canoe mark the spot on which several hundred of these displaced Acadians landed in 1785. They settled both sides of the St. John River, an area known as Mattawaska ("land of the porcupine"). Not until 1842 did the St. John become the formal boundary dividing Canada and Maine.

The 1842 Webster-Asberton Treaty settled the "Aroostook War," a footnote in American history recalled in the 1830s wooden blockhouses at Fort Kent and Fort Fairfield. Until relatively recently this bloodless "war" was the area's chief historic claim, but the valley's distinct Acadian heritage is gaining increasing recognition.

In 1976 a "Village Acadien" consisting of a dozen buildings was assembled just west of Van Buren. It's an interesting enough little museum village, but it only begins to tell the story evinced in the very shape of the St. John Valley towns—the houses strung out like arms from cathedral-sized Catholic churches at their centers.

Aroostook County still produces 1.5 million tons of potatoes a year, but the family farms—once the staple of The County's landscape and social fabric—are fading, replaced by consolidated spreads that grow other crops, notably broccoli, barley, and sugar beets. The family potato farm is already the stuff of museum exhibits. My favorites are in the New Sweden Museum, which commemorates not only family farms but also one of the most interesting immigration stories in American history.

The County is as far removed in time as it is in distance from Maine's more commercialized "Vacationland." You shop in craftspeople's and farmers' homes, ask locally for directions to the best places to walk, ski, and fish, feast on fiddleheads and *ployes* (buckwheat crêpes) rather than lobster. Most visitors, moreover, come in winter—to snowmobile or dogsled. Winter driving, we're told, is less daunting here than elsewhere in the Northeast because, thanks to the region's lowest temperatures, the snow is drier (no ice) as well as more plentiful. Summer temperatures also tend to be cooler than elsewhere, and in early July the potato fields are a spread of pink and white blossoms. Fall colors, which usually peak in the last weeks of September at the end of potato harvest, include reddening barley fields as well as maples.

GUIDANCE

As noted in the introduction, The County divides into three distinct regions. For details about the Upper St. John Valley contact the **Greater Fort Kent Chamber of Commerce** (834-5354), PO Box 430, Fort Kent 04743. A walk-in information center at the blockhouse, staffed by the Boy Scouts, is open seasonally. For central Aroostook contact the **Presque Isle Chamber of Commerce** (764-6561), PO Box 672, Presque Isle 04769; and for southern Aroostook, the **Houlton Chamber of Commerce** (532-4216), 109-B Main Street, Houlton 04730. Request a pamphlet "Guide to 'The County'" from any of the above. The big walk-in information center in The County is maintained by the **Maine Publicity Bureau,** just off I-95 in Houlton (532-6346).

Note the **North Maine Woods** information office on Route 1 in Ashland described in the introduction to this part.

GETTING THERE

By car: I-95 to Benedicta or Sherman Mills, then Route 11 up through Patten, Ashland, and Eagle Lake to Fort Kent, from which you can explore west to Allagash and east along the Upper St. John Valley to St. Agatha and/or Van Buren. Stop at the New Sweden Museum, for a meal in Caribou, and for a final overnight in the Houlton area.

By plane: Regularly scheduled service is limited to **Delta Business Express** (1-800-221-1212), which serves Presque Isle (also see *Bangor*). **Aroostook Aviation Inc.** (543-6334 or 1-800-353-6334), based at the Northern Aroostook Regional Airport in Frenchville, is the prime charter and connector service for the Upper St. John Valley. **Scotty's Flying Service** (528-2626), Patten, is a commercial seaplane operation geared to shuttling canoeists, hunters, and anglers in to remote lakes and put-in places along the St. John, Allagash, and Aroostook Rivers.

By bus: **Cyr Bus Lines** (532-6868), Houlton, runs daily between the Greyhound terminal in Bangor and Caribou, with stops in between.

MEDICAL EMERGENCY

Fort Kent Northern Maine Medical Center (834-3155).

Houlton Regional Hospital (532-9471), 20 Hartford Street, Houlton.

TO SEE

MUSEUMS

(In order of suggested routing.)

See the "Katahdin Region" chapter for details about the **Lumberman's Museum** in Patten.

Fort Kent Historical Society Museum (834-5121), Main and Market Streets. Theoretically open Tuesday through Saturday, 10–4. The former

Camper driving on logging road in northern Maine wilderness

JOSEPH DENNEHY

Bangor & Aroostook Railroad station is filled with local memorabilia.

Madawaska Historic Complex (728-4518), Route 1, Madawaska. Open mid-June through mid-September, Monday through Friday 9:30–4:30, Sunday 1–4:30, and by appointment. The complex includes the Tante Blanche Museum (local memorabilia) and, if you follow the dirt road behind the museum to the river, the 18th-century Albert Homestead, plus the *Voyageur* statue and stone cross described in the introduction to this chapter.

Acadian Village (868-2691 or 868-5404), Route 1, Van Buren. Open June 15 through Labor Day, 12–5, and by appointment. The 16 buildings include a school and store, a barbershop, and a reconstructed, 18th-century log church. $2.50 per adult, $1.25 per child.

St. Agathe Historical Society Museum (543-6364 or 543-6911). The oldest house in this unusually pleasant village on Long Lake, the Pelletier-Marquis home dates just from 1854; it's filled with a sense of the town's unusually rich ethnic and social history.

New Sweden Historical Society Museum (896-3370), just east of Route 161, New Sweden. Open June through Labor Day, Tuesday through Saturday 12–4; Sunday 2–5, and by appointment. Entering the community's reconstructed "Kapitileum" (meetinghouse), you are faced with the imposing bust of William Widgery Thomas, the Portland man sent by President Lincoln to Sweden in 1863 to halt the sale of iron to the Confederacy. Thomas quickly learned Swedish, married two countesses (the second after her sister died), and eventually devoted his sizable energies to establishing a colony of Swedish farmers in Maine. In 1870 the House of Representatives authorized the project, granting 100 acres of woodland to each Swedish family. A pink granite memorial in a pine grove behind the museum complex commemorates the arrival and hardships of those who settled here between 1870 and 1875. Despite the severe climate and thin soil (W.W. Thomas had been struck by the similarities between Sweden and northern Maine), New Sweden prospered, with 1400 immigrants in 1895 and 689 buildings, including three churches, seven general stores, and two railroad stations. New Sweden's annual festivals draw thousands of local descendents. The museum remains a cultural touchstone for Swedes living throughout the Northeast, and the town continues to attract visitors from Sweden, even an occasional immigrant. The museum complex includes hilltop Thomas Park and a picnic area; also an authentic immigrant cottage and restored blacksmith shop.

The Salmon Brook Historical Society (455-4339), Route 164, Washburn. Open summer Sundays 1–4, and by appointment. The pleasant 1850s Benjamin C. Wilder Farmstead and the Aroostook Agricultural Museum (potato harvesting tools and trivia housed in the neighboring barn) offer a sense of life and potato farming in the late 19th century. Washburn's Taterstate Frozen Foods claims to have invented the frozen french fry.

✐ **Nylander Museum** (493-4209), 393 Main Street, Caribou. Open March through May and September through December, Saturday and Sunday 12–4, and June through August, Wednesday through Sunday 1–5. A small but intriguing museum displaying fossils, rocks, minerals, shells, stuffed birds, mounted butterflies, and early human artifacts, most collected by Swedish-born Olof Nylander; also changing exhibits.

Caribou Historical Society (498-2556), Route 1, Caribou. Open June through August, Tuesday through Saturday 10–4, or by appointment. This new log building is filled with local memorabilia from the mid-19th century to the 1930s.

Aroostook County Historical and Art Museum (532-2519), 109 Main Street, Houlton. Open June through September, Monday through Friday 12–4, and by appointment. Same building as the Houlton Area Chamber of Commerce; features local memorabilia.

Webb Museum of Vintage Fashion (862-3797 or 463-2404), Route 2, Island Falls. Open late May to Columbus Day, Monday through Thursday 10–4, and by appointment. $3 adults, $2 seniors, $1 children. This 14-room Victorian-era house is filled with some 6000 articles of clothing amassed by Frances Stratton—hats, jewelry, combs, and mannequines dressed to represent the specific people to whom their outfits once belonged. It's a spooky, fascinating place, chronicling life in a small town as well as what its inhabitants wore from the 1890s to the 1950s. *Note:* This museum can be accessed either from Route 11 (it's 9 miles east of Patten) or from I-95.

Fort Kent Blockhouse Museum, off Route 1. Open Memorial Day through Labor Day, usually 9–dusk, maintained by the town and the local Boy Scout troop. This symbol of the northern terminus of Route 1 is a convincingly ancient, if much restored, two-story, 1830s blockhouse with documents and mementos from the Aroostook War. Be sure to wander down to the Fish River behind the blockhouse, a pleasant walk to picnic and tenting sites. When we visited, a rainbow seemed to underscore the legend that a pot of gold is buried hereabouts.

CHURCHES

As noted in the introduction to this chapter, tall, elaborate, French Canadian–style Catholic churches form the heart of most Upper St. John Valley villages: **Saint Leonard** in Madawaska, **Saint Louis** in Fort Kent (with distinctive open filigree steeples and a fine carillon), **St. David's** in the village of St. David, and **St. Luce** in Frenchville. When the twin-spired wooden church dominating the village of Lille was condemned, it was purchased by local resident Don Cyr, who is converting it into an Acadian cultural center and a setting for concerts and workshops (895-3339).

OTHER ATTRACTIONS

✐ **A.E. Howell Wildlife Conservation Center and Spruce Acres Refuge** (532-6880 or 532-0676), Lycette Road off Route 1, North Amity (14 miles south of Houlton). Open May through November, 9–sunset; $3 adults, free under age 18. Art Howell, one of the best known and respected of Maine's more than 90 wild animal "rehabilitators," nurtures bald eagles, bears, foxes, otters, and many more creatures who have been wounded and are being readied, if possible, for return to the wild. This is a 64-acre wooded area with a picnic area and a pond stocked with fish for children; also a camping area for environmental groups. No dogs please.

New Brunswick Botanical Garden (506-735-3074), Route 2, Saint-Jacques, New Brunswick. Open June through mid-October, daily 9–dusk. More than 50,000 varieties are represented in this spread of flowers, varying with the month.

SCENIC DRIVES

"Flat Mountain." The single most memorable landscape that we found in all Aroostook is easily accessible if you know where to turn. The high plateau is well-named "Flat Mountain" and is just above but invisible from Route 1 east of Fort Kent. Ask locally about the road through the back settlements from Frenchville to St. Agatha, a lake resort with several good restaurants.

Watson Settlement Covered Bridge. Follow Main Street through Houlton's Market Square Historic District (a "Walking Tour Guide" to this area is available from the chamber of commerce) until it turns into Military Street (dating from the Aroostook War). Turn north on Foxcroft Road; in 2 miles note your first view of Mars Hill Mountain (the area's only 1660-foot mountain). The mountain's ownership was disputed in the Aroostook War; it is now a ski area. At roughly 3.5 miles note the road on your left descending to a small iron bridge across the Meduxnekeag River; the covered bridge, built in 1902, is midway down this hill. The road rejoins Route 1 ten minutes north of Houlton.

TO DO

CANOEING

Canoes-R-Us (834-6793), 2 Church Street, Soldier Pond (off Route 11 on the Fish River south of Fort Kent). Canoe rentals and help planning trips from Eagle Lake to Soldier Pond, from Soldier Pond to Fort Kent, and 1- to 3-day camping trips along the Fish River chain.

Allagash Guide Service (398-3418) in Allagash rents paddles and canoes, also offers transport and car pick-up for those canoeing the Allagash Waterway.

Maine Canoe Adventures (398-3191), Route 161, Allagash. Canoe rentals, tenting area, shuttle service.

Cross Rock Inn (398-3191), Route 162, Allagash. Gorman Chamberlain offers 5- to 7-day trips on the St. John and Allagash, also guided trips into the nearby Debouille area departing from his lodge; also offers three guest rooms ($35 double).

(Also see *Canoeing the Allagash* under "What's Where.")

Note: The map/guide to the Allagash and St. John (DeLorme Publishing, $4.95) is useful.

FISHING

The catch is so rich and varied that it is recognized throughout the country. Salmon grow to unusual size, and trout are also large and numerous. The 80-mile Fish River chain of rivers and lakes (Eagle, Long, and Square Lakes) is legendary in fishing circles. Fish strike longer in the season than they do farther south, and fall fishing begins earlier. Contact the Maine Department of Inland Fisheries and Wildlife in Ashland (435-3231, or in-state: 1-800-353-6334).

GOLF

The County's topography lends itself to golf, and the sport is so popular that most towns maintain at least a nine-hole course. The most famous is the 18-hole **Aroostook Valley Country Club,** Fort Fairfield (476-8083), with half its tees split between Canada and Maine. The 18-hole **Jo-Wa Golf Course** (463-2128) in Island Falls and the **Presque Isle Country Club** (764-0439) are also considered above par.

HIKING

See Aroostook State Park and the Debouille area under *Green Space.*

Fish River Falls. Ask locally for directions to the trail that leads from the former Fort Kent airport down along the river, an unusually beautiful trail through pines. Note the swimming holes below the falls. **The Dyke in Fort Kent** is also worth finding: a half-mile walk along the Fish River. The trail up **Mount Carmel** (views up and down the river valley) begins on Route 1 at the state rest area near the Madawaska/Grand Isle town lines.

CROSS-COUNTRY SKIING

The same reliable snow that serves out-of-state snowmobilers allows residents to take advantage of hundreds of miles of trails maintained exclusively for cross-country skiing by local towns and clubs. Any town office or chamber of commerce will steer you to local trails.

SNOWMOBILING

Snowmobiling is the single biggest reason that visitors come to The County (update: 728-7228). For a "Trail Map to Northern Maine" detailing 1600 miles of trails maintained by The County's no less than 42 snowmobile clubs—the "highest rated trail riding in New England"—send $2 to any Aroostook County chamber of commerce (see *Guidance*).

GREEN SPACE

Debouille Management Unit, including Debouille Mountain and several ponds, is a 23,461-acre preserve managed jointly by the state and North Maine Woods (charging gate and camping fees), accessible by gated logging roads from St. Francis and Portage. Campsites are clustered around ponds (good for trout) and near hiking trails leading to the distinctive summit of Debouille Mountain. For details contact the Bureau of Public Lands in Presque Isle (764-2033).

Aroostook State Park (768-8341), marked from Route 1, 4 miles south of Presque Isle. Open May 15 through October 15. A 600-acre park with swimming and picnicking at Echo Lake; also 30 campsites at 1213-foot Quaggy Joe Mountain—which offers hiking trails with views from the north peak across a sea of woodland to Mount Katahdin. Note the monument in the small **Maxie Anderson Memorial Park** next door; a tin replica of the *Double Eagle II* commemorates the 1978 liftoff of the first hot-air balloon to successfully cross the Atlantic.

Allagash Wilderness Waterway (see "What's Where").

LODGING

Given the unusual warmth and hospitality of Aroostook residents, we look forward to the day when more homes and farms will welcome visitors.

BED & BREAKFASTS

Sanctuary (365-4171), Box 38, Benedicta 04733. Not far off I-95 and just over the line in Aroostook County, this 19th-century farmhouse has a very relaxing feel to it. Until relatively recently, this house was a convent for the nuns who taught in the town school. Benedicta was founded by the Catholic diocese of Boston as a community for Irish immigrant potato farmers, and it was slated to be a Catholic college until someone donated the ground that the Holy Cross now stands on in Worcester, Massachusetts. Jack and Sheila Hansen have raised five children here and now offer four guest rooms, all bright and homey, some decorated with Sheila's paintings and macramé. $69.96 double for 2 nights and two full breakfasts. No smoking, pets, or children, please.

Daigle's Bed & Breakfast (834-8503), 96 East Main Street, Fort Kent 04743. This cheery modern house features a sunny, glass-walled, flower-filled dining room in which guests tend to linger over Doris Daigle's generous breakfast. The five guest rooms range from small with shared bath ($45) to a spacious double with twin beds, decorated in red and black with a sumptuous bath, refrigerator, TV, and phone. Guests are also welcome to join Elmer and Doris in the evening for drinks and snacks by the living room fireplace.

Farrell-Michaud Bed & Breakfast (868-5209), 231 Main Street, Van Buren 04785. Open year-round. Sheila Cyr is the gracious host in this very Victorian house with pressed tin walls and ceilings and handsome wood detailing. Rooms are nicely decorated with matched fabrics and paper and antiques, from $39 double with shared bath to $49 for private; $29 single with shared bath.

Rum Rapids Inn (455-8096), Route 164, Crouseville 04738. Not far from Presque Isle, one of the oldest houses in The County (vintage 1839) is set in 15 acres on the Aroostook River. Innkeeper Clifton (Bud) Roudman offers candlelit dinners as well as one room and is happy to help with travel plans. $42.50 double includes a full "Scottish breakfast."

Clarke's Inn (532-0677), Route 1, North Amity. A tidy, attractive B&B 15 miles south of Houlton on Route 1. Hosts Lin and Bev Bubar are the fifth generation of their family to live in this 1830s farmhouse; handy to lakes and the A.E. Howell Wildlife Conservation Center.

Sherman Inn (365-4529 or 1-800-253-4529), Sherman Station 04777. Open year-round. A modern house with four guest rooms (one private bath) sharing an upstairs living room with TV. Modest rates include breakfast, use of swimming pool.

SPORTING CAMPS

Allagash Gardners Sporting Camps (398-3168), Box 127, Allagash 04774. Open May through December. Five tidy camps along a ridge overlooking the confluence of the St. John and Allagash Rivers across the road from Roy and Mande Gardner's welcoming old farmhouse. Bed & breakfast and hiking, hunting, camping, and fishing guide service also offered. $30 double, $100 per week.

Moose Point Camps (435-6156), Portage 04768. Open May 10 to early December. Ten log-hewn camps on the east shore of Fish Lake (5 miles long and connecting with other lakes linked by the Fish River). The central lodge features a library and large stone fireplace as well as a dining room overlooking the lake in which all meals are served (BYOB). The camps are 17 miles from Portage up a paper company road. $280 per person per week or $50 per person per day in spring and summer; ask about children's rates and hunters packages. Boats and canoes available.

Libby Sporting Camps (435-8274), Drawer V, Ashland 04732. Open ice-out through November. One of the original sporting camps, family operated for 100 years. Features hearty meals and guides to take you to 40 lakes and ponds from eight outpost camps. $30 without meals, $70 per person with. Sited at the headwaters of the Aroostook and Allagash Rivers. Boats and seaplane available.

Chiputneticook Sporting Lodge (448-2929), Boundary Road, Orient 04471. Open year-round. Not exactly a sporting camp but, rather, a rustic lodge on East Grand Lake (good for lake trout, salmon, bass), just minutes off Route 1. Host Peter Roach rents rooms in the lodge on a B&B or housekeeping basis.

MOTEL

Long Lake Motor Inn (543-5006), Route 162, St. Agatha 04772. Ken and Arlene Lermon pride themselves on the cleanliness and friendliness of this spanking new motel overlooking Long Lake. $55 for standard room ($45 single), $65 for the suite.

WHERE TO EAT

DINING OUT

Long Lake Sporting Club (543-7584) Sinclair. Open Tuesday through Saturday 5–9, Sunday 12–8, dance floor. Sit down with a drink, order, and then go to your table when it's all ready; seafood specialties. A complete meal for two with drinks averages $30.

Dubois Restaurant (834-6548), 84 West Main Street, Fort Kent. Open except Monday for lunch and dinner. Steaks, seafood, and Italian "cuisine" are the specialties in this flashy, friendly, downtown family restaurant. The menu ranges from $2.50 for a hamburger and fries to $17.75 for blackened prime rib with salad bar. Try the lasagna with sausage, beef, ham, salami, cheese, and sauce. Pizzas and a children's menu also available.

Lakeview Restaurant (543-6331), St. Agatha. Open daily for lunch and dinner. Set on a hilltop with a view off across the lake and valley. Steak and seafood are the specialties. Live entertainment on summer weekends. Entrées average $10.

Jo Hackett's Restaurant & Butcher (496-2501), Route 1 south of Caribou. Open for lunch and dinner. Generally recognized as the best place to eat in central Aroostook, a modern, family-style restaurant specializing in prime beef and fresh fish. Dinner entrées range from "broiled Haddy" ($8.95) to "Broncobuster's Splurge" (a 22-ounce Porterhouse steak, $13.95); the "junior executive" menu includes a "buckaroo's wallet with a cow's blanket" (a cheeseburger; $1.99).

EATING OUT

Lil's (435-6471), Route 1, Ashland. Open 6 AM–8 PM. A counter and orange vinyl booths, homemade bread, pizza, outstanding sandwiches and pies, daily specials.

Ma & Pa's Sunrise Cafe (543-6177), Cleveland Road, St. Agatha. Open daily year-round, 5:30 AM–8 PM. Our favorite kind of eatery: a counter, tables, and a view. Features local items as specials, like chicken stew and *ployes* (buckwheat crêpes).

Doris's Cafe, Fort Kent Mills, open for breakfast and lunch; everything prepared from scratch.

The Dicky Trading Post, Allagash, open 5 AM–7 PM. A combination general store (with stuffed bobcat and lynx), sporting goods shop, and formica-topped coffee shop.

Stan's Grocery, Route 161 north of Jemtland. Home of Stan's 10-cent cup of coffee, to be savored in a back booth of this indescribable store, the center for the surrounding summer community on Madawaska Lake. The pay phone next to the piano is roto-dial.

Elm Tree Diner (532-3181), Bangor Road, Houlton. Open early and late, an outstanding classic diner with everything made from scratch, daily specials.

Traveler's Irving Big Stop (532-2948), North Road, Houlton. Daily specials.

SELECTIVE SHOPPING

Fish River Brand Tackle (834-3951), phone for directions. Tackle made by Don Baker—one of his big metal flashers secured the $10,000 grand

The Can Am Crown dogsled race in Fort Kent

prize in the Lake Champlain Fishing Derby in 1994.

Bouchard Family Farm (834-3237), Route 161, Fort Kent. Stop by the family kitchen and buy a bag of *ploye* mix. *Ployes* are crêpelike pancakes made with buckwheat flour (no eggs, no milk, no sugar, no oil, no cholesterol, no fat—*c'est magnifique*).

Goughan Farms (496-1731), Route 161, Fort Fairfield. Open weekdays 10–5, Sundays 12–5. Pick-your-own strawberries, also a farmstand, animal barn.

SPECIAL EVENTS

Mid-February: **The Can Am Crown,** 250-mile dogsled race, starting and ending at Fort Kent.

June: **Acadian Festival** in Madawaska. The weekend nearest June 21, "Midsommar," is celebrated at Thomas Park in New Sweden with Swedish music, dancing, and food.

July: **Maine Potato Blossom Festival** features 'Roostook River Raft Race and the Festival Parade. **Long Lake Summerfest** (final weekend).

August: **Northern Maine Fair,** Presque Isle.

General Index

Acadia: about, 299-300; information/help, 300-302; restaurants, 322-327; sites/ activities, 302-311, 327-331
Acadia National Park, 28, 308, 310-311
Acadia Repertory Theatre, 328
Acadia Zoological Park, 306
Acadian Village, 487
A.E. Howell Wildlife Conservation Center and Spruce Acres Refuge, 488-489
Agricultural fairs, 13
Air services, 13, 460-461, 475, 485. *See also* Transportation/travel
Air sight-seeing tours: airboat trips, 447; Bar Harbor/Acadia, 306; East Penobscot Bay, 264; Mid-coast, 170; Northern Maine, 463; Washington County/Campobello/St. Andrews, 346, 358; Western Mountains and Lakes, 378, 395, 411. *See also* Ballooning
Airports and airlines, 13
"A.J. Allee" scenic overlook, 476
Allagash Wilderness Waterway, 18, 462
Ames Pond, 290
Amphitheaters, 244
Amusement parks, 13, 41-42, 95, 306
Antiquarian books, 13, 70
Antiques, 13; Kennebec Valley, 445; Mid-coast, 165, 174, 206, 224, 256; South Coast, 70, 91; Western Mountains and Lakes, 389, 406
Appalachian Mountain Club, 17
Apple picking, 14
Aquaboggan Water Park, 94
Aquariums, 14, 94
Arboretums, 440
Arcady Music Festival, 327
Area code, 14
Armrust Hill, 231
Arnold Historical Society Museum, 439
Aroostook County: about, 483-485; information/help, 485; restaurants, 492-493; sites/ activities, 485-491, 493-494
Aroostook County Historical and Art Museum, 488
Aroostook State Park, 491
Art galleries, 14; Bar Harbor/Acadia, 328-329; East Penobscot Bay, 270, 285-286, 294-295; Mid-coast, 150, 174, 187, 193, 206-207, 224, 256; Monhegan Island, 229-230; South Coast, 53, 58, 70-71, 91; Western Mountains and Lakes, 406
Art museums. *See* Museums
Artisans: East Penobscot Bay, 276, 286, 294-295; Mid-coast, 165, 174, 187-188, 207-208, 257; Western Mountains and Lakes, 406. *See also* Crafts
Artisans School, The, 243
Artist's Covered Bridge, 394, 397-398
Asticou Azalea Garden, 303
Asticou Terraces, 303
Atlantic Salmon Information Centre, 368
Attean View, 451
Audubon Society, 112, 127, 196
Augusta: about, 435-436; information/help, 436; restaurants, 442-444; sites/activities, 436-440, 444-445
Automobiles: museums, 58, 304; racing, 95, 375. *See also* Parking. *See also* Scenic drives. *See also* Transportation/travel

Bagaduce Chorale, 285
Bagaduce Lending Library, 278
Bailey Island, 143
Baker Island, 304
Ballooning, 14; Casco Bay, 111, 126-127; Kennebec Valley, 440; Mid-coast, 157
Ballpark, The, 100
Bands. *See* Music and concerts
Bangor: about, 332; information/help, 332-333; restaurants, 336-337; sites/activities, 333-335, 337-338
Bangor Historical Society, 334-335
Bangor Symphony Orchestra, 337
Bar Harbor: about, 299-300; information/ help, 300-302; restaurants, 322-327; sites/ activities, 302-311, 327-331
Bar Harbor Historical Society, 303
Bar Harbor Music Festival, 327
Bar Harbor Oceanarium, 302
Bar Harbor Whale Museum, 303
Barn Gallery, The, 58
Barracks Museum, 357
Barred Island Preserve, 291
Bartlett Maine Estate Winery, 306
Bass Harbor village, 302
Bass Park complex, 337
Bates College, 377
Bates-Morse Mountain Conservation Area, 159
Bath: about, 153-154; information/help, 154-155; restaurants, 163-165; sites/activities, 155-159, 165-166
Baxter Gallery of Portland School of Art, 108
Baxter State Park, 474, 476, 477-478
Bay Chamber Concerts, 255-256
Bay Island Sailing School, 243
Bay View Street Cinema, 256
Beaches and swimming, 14; Bangor, 335; Bar Harbor/Acadia, 310; Casco Bay, 111-112; East Penobscot Bay, 111-112, 274;

Kennebec Valley, 440; Mid-coast, 144-145, 158-159, 178, 196, 218, 241; Northern Maine, 465; South Coast, 43-44, 59-60, 79, 95-96; Washington County/Campobello/St. Andrews, 348, 364; Western Mountains and Lakes, 380-381, 397-398, 413, 424-425
Beals Island, 343
Bed & breakfasts, 15, 20. *See also Lodging Index*
Beech Ridge Motor Speedway, 95
Belfast: about, 261; information/help, 261-262; restaurants, 268-269; sites/activities, 262-265, 270-271
Belfast and Moosehead Lake R.R. Co., 265
Belfast Maskers, The, 270
Belfast Museum, 264
Bethel: about, 391-393; information/help, 393-394; restaurants, 405-406; sites/activities, 394-400, 406-407
Bicycling, 15; Bar Harbor/Acadia, 306; Casco Bay, 110; Mid-coast, 157, 177, 195, 239-240; South Coast, 58, 77; Vinalhaven Island, 231; Western Mountains and Lakes, 395, 424. *See also* Mountain biking
Biddeford Pool East Sanctuary, 79
Birding, 15; Bar Harbor/Acadia, 307; puffin-watching, 29, 234, 346-347; Washington County/Campobello/St. Andrews, 346-347
Blagden Preserve, 305
Blaine House, 437
Blue Hill: about, 277; information/help, 277; restaurants, 283-285; sites/activities, 278-280, 285-287
Blue Hill conservation area, 280
Blue Hill Library, 278
Blueberrying, 16, 77, 344
Boat-building, 16; East Penobscot Bay, 279-280; Mid-coast, 243; Portsmouth Naval Shipyard, 40; South Coast, 78
Boat excursions, 16; airboats, 447; Bangor, 335; Bar Harbor/Acadia, 307-308; Casco Bay, 110-111, 127; East Penobscot Bay, 264, 274, 289-290; Kennebec Valley, 440; Mid-coast, 143-144, 157, 177, 195-196, 215, 240; Northern Maine, 463, 476; South Coast, 43, 59, 78; Washington County/Campobello/St. Andrews, 346-347, 358-359; Western Mountains and Lakes, 378, 412. *See also* Coastal cruises. *See also* Ferries. *See also* Sailing. *See also* Whale-watching
Boat rentals, 16; Bar Harbor/Acadia, 308; Mid-coast, 177, 196; Western Mountains and Lakes, 379, 412. *See also* Canoeing. *See also* Kayaking
Bookstores: antiquarian, 13, 70; Bangor, 338; Bar Harbor/Acadia, 330; East Penobscot Bay, 271, 276, 287; Kennebec Valley, 445;

Mid-coast, 150-151, 224, 257; South Coast, 70, 124; Western Mountains and Lakes, 389, 406
Booth Quarry, 231
Boothbay Harbor: about, 175; information/help, 175-176; restaurants, 184-187; sites/activities, 176-179, 187-188
Boothbay Railway Village, 176
Boothbay Region Art Foundation, 176
Boothbay Region Historical Society Museum, 176
Borestone Mountain Sanctuary, 464
Bowater/Great Northern Paper Co., 475
Bowditch Cemetery, 264
Bowdoin College: Museum of Art, 142; Summer Music Festival, 150
Bowdoinham village, 142
Bradbury Mountain State Park, 128
Breweries and wineries, 306, 431-432
Brick Store Museum, The, 75
Bridges: covered, 19, 394, 489; fireproof wire, 424; toll footbridge, 439
Bridgton Historical Society Museum, 378
British Canal, 274
Brunswick: about, 141; information/help, 141-142; restaurants, 147-149; sites/activities, 142-145, 149-151
Bryant Pond Telephone Museum, 394
Bucksport: about, 261; information/help, 261-262; restaurants, 268-269; sites/activities, 262-265, 270-271
Bucksport Cemetery, 264
Bucksport Historical Society Museum, 263-264
Burnham Tavern, The, 344
Bus tours, 335. *See also* Transportation/travel
Byron village, 410

Calais, 363-366
Camden: about, 235-237; information/help, 237-238; restaurants, 251-255; sites/activities, 238-244, 255-258
Camden Amphitheatre, 244
Camden Civic Theatre, 256
Camden Hills State Park, 243
Camden Yacht Club Sailing Program, 243
Camerata Singers, 256
Camping, 16-17, 478. *See also Lodging Index. See also* Parks and forests
Campobello: information/help, 342; restaurants, 352-355; Roosevelt International Park, 345, 347-348; sites/activities, 343-348, 355-356
Camps, for adults/children, 17. *See also* Learning programs
Canada, New Brunswick/St. Andrews, 366-379
Canoe Factory Outlet Store, Old Town, 338
Canoeing, 17-18; Bar Harbor/Acadia, 308;

Casco Bay, 111, 112, 127; Kennebec Valley, 448; Mid-coast, 157; Northern Maine, 463, 476, 489-490; Washington County/Campobello/St. Andrews, 347, 363-364; Western Mountains and Lakes, 379, 395, 412
Cape Elizabeth village, 106
Cape Porpoise village, 75
Caribou Historical Society, 488
Carousel Music Theater, 187
Carrabassett Valley: about, 421-422; information/help, 422; restaurants, 429-431; sites/activities, 423-427, 431-432
Cascade Water Park, 94
Castine: about, 272-273; information/help, 273; restaurants, 275-276; sites/activities, 273-274, 276
Castine Conservation Commission, 274
Castle Tucker, 169
Celebration Barn Theater, 389
Cemeteries, 113, 264, 344
Center for Furniture Craftsmanship, 243
Center for the Arts at the Chocolate Church, 165
Chair lift rides, 395, 461, 463
Chamber Theatre of Maine, 270
Chapman-Hall House, 194
Cherryfield, 343
Chesuncook Village, 462
Children: camps, 17; museums for, 107, 423, 438. *See also* Family activities. *See also* Learning programs
Children's Discovery Museum, 438
Children's Museum of Maine, 107
Chocolate Church, Center for the Arts at, 165
Christmas wreaths, 356
Churches: Casco Bay, 109; Islesboro Island, 239; Mid-coast, 194-195; Northern Maine, 488; South Coast, 41, 76, 77; World's Smallest, 170
Cinemas. *See* Theaters and cinemas
City Theater, 100
Civil War Monument, 41
Clamming, 18
Coastal cruises, 18-19, 215. *See also* Windjammers
Cobscook Bay, 357-361
Colby College, 437
Cold Comfort Productions, 276
Cole Land Transportation Museum, 334
College of the Atlantic, 302, 327
Colleges and universities: Bangor, 334; Kennebec Valley, 437; Mid-coast, 142; Western Mountains and Lakes, 377
Colonel Black Mansion, 305
Colonial Pemaquid State Historic Site, 192
Columbia Falls, 343
Concerts. *See* Music and concerts

Corea village, 302
Cottage rentals, 19. *See also Lodging Index*
Courthouses, 170
Covered bridges, 19, 394, 489
Crafts, 19; Bar Harbor/Acadia, 328-329; Mid-coast, 150; schools of, 289; South Coast, 53; Western Mountains and Lakes, 389-390, 407. *See also* Artisans
Craig Brook National Fish Hatchery, 264
Cranberry Isles, 304
Criterion Theater, 328
Crockett Cove Woods Preserve, 290-291
Cross-country skiing, 31; Bangor, 335; Bar Harbor/Acadia, 310; Casco Bay, 127; Northern Maine, 465, 477, 490; South Coast, 79, 95; Western Mountains and Lakes, 381, 398, 425
Cross-county skiing: Sunday River, 398
Cruises, coastal. *See* Coastal cruises
Cumberland County Civic Center, 122
Cumston Hall, 439
Curtis Island, 244
Cushing's Landing, 462
Cutler, 345

Damariscotta: about, 189-191; information/help, 191; restaurants, 202-206; sites/activities, 192-197, 206-208
Damariscotta Lake, 195, 196
Damariscove Island, 178
Dance companies. *See* Performing arts
Daniel Marrett House, 377
Dead River Historical Society, 423
Debouille Management Unit, 490-491
Deck House Cabaret Theater, 328
Deep-sea fishing, 19-20; Casco Bay, 111; Mid-coast, 177, 215; South Coast, 78
Deer Isle: about, 288; information/help, 289; restaurants, 293-294; sites/activities, 289-291, 294-296
Deering Oaks Park, 112
DeerTrees Theater, 389
Desert of Maine, 126
Diving/dive shops, 20, 43
Dodge Point Preserve, 197
Dogsledding, 20, 395-396, 426
Downhill skiing, 31; Bangor, 335; Northern Maine, 465; Sugarloaf/USA, 426; Sunday River, 399-400; Western Mountains and Lakes, 381, 398-400, 426
DownRiver Theater Productions, 355
Driving. *See* Automobiles
Dyce's Head Light, 274
Dyer Library, 94

East Quoddy Head Lighthouse, 346
Eastern Cemetery, 113
Eastport, 357-361
Eastport Arts Center, 361

Educational programs. *See* Learning programs; Schools
1893 Columbia Exposition (Chicago), 377
Elizabeth Perkins House, 41
Ellsworth Cinemas, 328
Emergencies: Bangor, 333; Bar Harbor/Acadia, 302; Casco Bay, 106, 126; East Penobscot Bay, 262, 273, 277, 289; Kennebec Valley, 436, 447; Mid-coast, 141-142, 155, 167, 176, 191, 211, 238; Northern Maine, 461, 475, 485; South Coast, 39, 58, 75, 93; Washington County/Campobello/St. Andrews, 342; Western Mountains and Lakes, 375, 394, 410, 422
Emerson-Wilcox House, 41
Evans Notch, 394, 396
Eveleth-Crafts-Sheridan House, 461
Events, annual, 20; Bangor, 338; Bar Harbor/Acadia, 331; Casco Bay, 124; 136; East Penobscot Bay, 271, 276, 287, 296; Kennebec Valley, 445, 453; Mid-coast, 151, 166, 188, 208, 225, 258; Northern Maine, 473, 481, 494; South Coast, 54, 71, 91, 100; Washington County/Campobello/St. Andrews, 356, 362, 366; Western Mountains and Lakes, 390, 407, 420, 432

Factory outlets, 20; canoes (Bangor), 338; Freeport, 133-135; Kennebec Valley, 445; South Coast, 53, 71
Factory tours, 20
Fairs, 13. *See also* Events, annual
Fall foliage, 20
Falmouth village, 106
Family activities, 18, 94-95, 170, 306
Farmers' markets, 20
Farms: bed and breakfasts on, 20; cross-country skiing on, 79, 95; Damariscotta Lake, 196; nature preserves on, 60, 112
Farnsworth Homestead, 212
Farnsworth Museum, The, 223
Fernald's Neck Nature Conservancy Preserve, 244
Ferries, 21; Isle au Haut, 289-290; Islesboro, 238; Matinicus Island, 234; Monhegan Island, 226; North Haven Island, 233; to/from Canada, 20-21, 106, 301; Vinalhaven Island, 230; Washington County/Campobello/St. Andrews, 342, 358-359
Ferry Beach State Park, 95
Festivals, 25-26. *See also* Events, annual
Films. *See* Theaters and cinemas
Fire-fighting museums, 108, 304
Fire permits, 21
Fireproof Wire Bridge, 424
First Parish Church, 41, 109
First Parish Unitarian Church, 77

Fisherman's Museum, 193
Fishing, 21; Bangor, 335; East Penobscot Bay, 274; Kennebec Valley, 440, 448; Mid-coast, 157, 196; Northern Maine, 463, 490; South Coast, 43, 59; Washington County/Campobello/St. Andrews, 347, 364; Western Mountains and Lakes, 379, 396, 412, 424. *See also* Deep-sea fishing
Fishway Viewing Room, 142
"Flat Mountain," 489
Flea markets, 165-166
Flying. *See* Air services
Fore River Sanctuary, 112
Forests. *See* Parks and forests
Fort Allen Park, 113
Fort Baldwin Memorial Park, 159
Fort Edgecomb State Memorial, 170
Fort Foster Park, 44
Fort George, 273
Fort Halifax, 439
Fort Kent Blockhouse Museum, 488
Fort Kent Historical Society Museum, 485, 487
Fort Knox State Park, 263
Fort McClary, 40
Fort O'Brien, 344
Fort Point State Park, 265
Fort Popham Memorial Park, 159
Fort Pownall, 265
Fort Western Museum on the Kennebec, 438
Fort William Henry, 192-193
Fort Williams Park, 107
Forts, 21
Frankfort village, 262
Freeport: about, 125; factory outlets, 133-135; information/help, 125-126; restaurants, 131-133; sites/activities, 126-128
Freeport Balloon Company, 126-127
Frenchboro Historical Society, 304
Friendship Museum, 214
Friendship village, 211
Fryeburg Public Library, 378
Funtown USA/Cascade Water Park, 94

Galleries. *See* Art galleries
Gardens, 244, 303, 489
Gardiner village, 437
Gates House, 344
George Marshall Store, 41
George Tate House, 110
Gilsland Farm Sanctuary, 112
Golf, 21-22; Bangor, 335; Bar Harbor/Acadia, 308; Casco Bay, 127; East Penobscot Bay, 264, 274, 290; Kennebec Valley, 440, 448; Mid-coast, 144, 158, 177, 196, 240; miniature, 59, 94-95, 380; Northern Maine, 463-464, 490; South

Coast, 43, 78, 95; Washington County/ Campobello/St. Andrews, 347, 364, 368; Western Mountains and Lakes, 379, 396, 412, 424
Goose Rocks Beach village, 75
Gorges. *See* Waterfalls and gorges
Grafton Notch State Park, 394, 396
Grand Lake Stream, 363, 364
Grand Theater, The, 328
Great Harbor Collection at the Old Firehouse Museum, 304
Great Wass Island, 343, 347
Grimes Park, 231
Guide services, 22
Guidebooks, 22
Gulf Hagas, 464, 476-477

Hackmatack Playhouse, 52, 69, 90
Hallowell village, 436-437
Hamilton House, 42
Hamilton Sanctuary, 159
Hamlin Memorial Hall, 377
Hampden village, 333
Hancock and Hancock Point village, 302
Harpswells, the: information/help, 141-142; restaurants, 147-149; sites/activities, 142-145, 149-151
Harrington House Museum Store, 135
Harrington Meeting House, 194
Hatcheries, 264, 343, 368, 375
Hayrides, 78
Haystack Mountain School of Crafts, 19, 289
Head Tide Village, 169
Health spas, 32, 426-427
Hearse House, 273
Hendricks Hill Museum, 176
Henry Parsons Park, 79
Hiking/walks, 22-23; Bar Harbor/Acadia, 308-309, 311; Casco Bay, 113; Mid-coast, 240-241; Monhegan Island, 227; Northern Maine, 464, 476-477, 490; South Coast, 45, 61, 79; Vinalhaven Island, 231; Washington County/ Campobello/St. Andrews, 347-348, 359; Western Mountains and Lakes, 379-380, 396, 412, 424
Historic sites/houses, 23; Bangor, 334-335; Bar Harbor/Acadia, 303, 304; Casco Bay, 109-110; East Penobscot Bay, 263-264, 273-274, 278, 289; Kennebec Valley, 437, 438-439, 447; Mid-coast, 156,169-170, 192-195, 211-213; Northern Maine, 461, 475-476, 485, 487-488; South Coast, 40-41, 42-43, 76-77, 94; Washington County/ Campobello/St. Andrews, 343, 367-368; Western Mountains and Lakes, 376, 377-378, 394, 411, 423
Holbrook Island Sanctuary, 280
Holt House, 278

Holt Mill Pond Preserve, 290
Hopalong Cassidy in the Fryeburg Public Library, 378
Horse-drawn tours, 78, 309, 400
Horse racing, 23, 95, 337
Horseback riding, 23; Mid-coast, 177, 196; Northern Maine, 464, 477; South Coast, 43, 78, 95; Western Mountains and Lakes, 380
Hostels, youth/elder, 15, 17
Hot-air ballooning. *See* Ballooning
Hotels. *See Lodging Index*
Houses, historic. *See* Historic sites/houses
Hudson Museum, 334
Hunter Cove Wildlife Sanctuary, 414
Hunting, 23
Huntsman Marine Science Centre, 368
Hurricane Island Outward Bound School, 215-216

Ice skating, 400, 426
Indian Island village, 333
Indians. *See* Native American Information, 23; Bangor, 332-333; Bar Harbor/Acadia, 300-302; Casco Bay, 105; 125-126; East Penobscot Bay, 261-262, 273, 277, 289; Kennebec Valley, 436, 446-447; Mid-coast, 141; 154-155, 167, 175-176, 191, 209, 237-238; Northern Maine, 460, 474-475, 485; South Coast, 39, 57, 74-75, 93; Washington County/Campobello/St. Andrews, 341-342, 357, 362, 367; Western Mountains and Lakes, 374, 393, 409-410, 422
Inns, 23. *See also Lodging Index*
Island Institute, The, 216
Islands, 23-24; Casco Bay, 110-111; Rockland/Thomaston area, 211. *See also specific islands*
Isle au Haut: about, 288; information/help, 289-290; restaurants, 293-294; sites/ activities, 289-291, 294-296
Islesboro Island, 238-239
Islesford Historical Museum, 304

Jackman, 446, 450, 451, 452, 453
Jackson Laboratory, 303
Jefferds Tavern Visitors Center, 40
John Hancock Warehouse and Wharf, 41
John Perkins House, 273
Johnson Hall, 444
Jones Museum of Glass and Ceramics, The, 376-377
Jonesboro, 343-344
Jonesport, 343
Josephine Newman Wildlife Sanctuary, 159
Joshua L. Chamberlain Museum, 143

Katahdin Iron Works, 475

Katahdin Region: about, 474; information/
help, 474-475; restaurants, 480-481; sites/
activities, 475-478, 481
Kayaking: Bar Harbor/Acadia, 308; Mid-
coast, 157; Northern Maine, 465. See also
Sea Kayaking
Kennebec Gorge, 446
Kennebunkport Historical Society, 76
Kennebunks, the: about, 73-74; information/
help, 74-75; restaurants, 87-90; sites/
activities, 75-79, 90-91
Kingfield Historical Society, 423
Kittery: about, 37-39; information/help, 39;
restaurants, 39-52; sites/activities, 39-45,
52-54
Kittery Historical and Naval Museum, 39-40
Kittery Point, 42
Kneisel Hall Chamber Music Festival, 285
Knickerkane Island Park, 179
Knox Hill Museum, 239

Lake Mooselookmeguntic, 412
Lake St. George State Park, 264, 440
Lakes, 24; Bar Harbor/Acadia area, 308;
Calais/St. Croix Valley, 363, 364; Mid-
coast, 195; Washington County/
Campobello/St. Andrews, 348. See also
Beaches and swimming. See also
Moosehead Lake area. See also Rangeley
Lakes Region. See also Sebago-Long
Lakes Region. See also specific lakes
Lakewood Theater, 453
Landing School of Boat Building and Design,
78
Lane's Island Preserve, 231
LARK Society for Chamber Music/Portland
String Quartet, 122
Laudholm Farm, 60-61
Laws/regulations, 21, 25, 367, 478
Learning programs: Acadia National Park,
310-311; Casco Bay, 127; East Penobscot
Bay, 279-280; Mid-coast, 158, 196, 215-
216, 243. See also Schools
Leavitt Fine Arts Theatre, 69
Left Bank Bakery and Cafe, The, 285
Liberty village, 262
Libraries: East Penobscot Bay, 278;
Kennebec Valley, 447; Mid-coast, 211-
212; South Coast, 76-77, 94; Washington
County/Campobello/St.Andrews, 357,
358; Western Mountains and Lakes, 378
Lighthouses, 24-25; Casco Bay, 107-108;
East Penobscot Bay, 274; Mid-coast, 193,
214-215; Monhegan Island, 226;
museums, 214-215; South Coast, 41;
Washington County/Campobello/St.
Andrews, 345, 346
Lily Bay State Park, 461
Lincoln Arts Festival, 187

Lincoln County Courthouse, 170
Lincoln County Museum, 169-170
Lincolnville: about, 235-237; information/
help, 237-238; restaurants, 251-255; sites/
activities, 238-244, 255-258
Litter, 25
L.L. Bean, 127, 133, 134
Llama trekking, 25, 396-397
Lobsters: hatchery, 303; lobstering boat trips,
43; pounds, 25, 100, 186, 205, 223, 255,
326-327; shipping, 25
Locks, boat, 378
Lodging. See Lodging Index
Long Lakes Region. See Sebago-Long Lakes
Region
Louis T. Graves Memorial Library, 76-77
Lower Piscataquis. See Moosehead Lake
area-Lower Piscataquis
Lubec, 345

Machias, 344
Machias Bay Chamber Concerts, 355
Machias Seal Island, 346-347
Machiasport, 344
Madawaska Historic Complex, 487
Maine Aquarium, 94
Maine Audubon Society, 112, 127
Maine Center for the Arts, 337
Maine Coast Artists, 256
Maine Coast Railroad, 170-171
Maine Festival, The, 25-26
Maine Forest and Logging Museum, 334
Maine Maritime Academy, 274
Maine Maritime Museum, 155-156
Maine Masque Theater, 337
Maine Narrow Gauge Railroad Co. &
Museum, 108
Maine Photographic Workshops, 243
Maine Sport Outfitters, 243
Maine State Museum, 437-438
Maine State Music Theater, 149-150
Maine Wild Blueberry Company, 344
Manana Island, 227
Maple sugaring, 26
Margaret Chase Smith Library Center, 447
Marina Deck, 187
Marine Park, 244
Marine science/research facilities, 345, 368
Marshall Point Lighthouse Museum, 214, 215
Mast Landing Sanctuary, 128
Matinicus Island, 211, 233-234
Matthews Museum of Maine Heritage, 214
McClellan Park, 343, 348
Medical emergencies. See Emergencies
Merrill House, 278
Merryspring, 244
Micmac Farm, 344
Milbridge: information/help, 342; restau-
rants, 352-355; sites/activities, 343-348,

355-356
Milbridge Theater, 355
Mini-golf, 59, 94-95, 380
Ministers Island Historic Site, 367
Monasteries, 76, 87
Monhegan Island: about, 211, 225-226; restaurants, 229; sites/activities, 226-227
Monhegan Museum, 226-227
Monmouth Museum, 438-439
Montpelier, 212-213
Moose Point State Park, 265
Moose River Bow Trip, The, 448
Moose-watching, 26, 413, 448, 464
Moosehead Lake area-Lower Piscataquis: about, 459-460; information/help, 460-461; restaurants, 471-472; sites/activities, 461-466
Moosehead Marine Museum, 461
Moosehorn National Wildlife Refuge, 359, 362
"Moosemainea," 26, 464
Moses Mason House, 394
Mount Agamenticus, 44, 61
Mount Blue State Park, 413, 414
Mount Desert Festival of Chamber Music, 327
Mount Desert Historical Society, 304
Mount Desert Oceanarium, 304
Mount Katahdin, 474
Mount Kineo, 461, 464
Mountain biking: Bar Harbor/Acadia, 307; Kennebec Valley, 448; Mid-coast, 240; Northern Maine, 465; South Coast, 43; Western Mountains and Lakes, 395, 424
Movies. *See* Theaters and cinemas
Moxie Falls, 450
Museum at Portland Head Light, The, 107-108
Museum villages, 26, 375-376, 439, 462
Museums, 26-27; about the Arctic, 142; art, 14, 58, 107, 142, 211-212, 488; automobile, 58, 304; Bangor, 334; Bar Harbor/Acadia, 302-303, 304-305; Casco Bay, 107-108; for children, 107, 423, 438; East Penobscot Bay, 262-263, 273; fashion, 488; fire-fighting, 108, 304; fishing industry, 193, 345; forests and logging, 334, 475-476; glass/ceramics, 376-377; Islesboro Island, 238; Kennebec Valley, 437-438; lighthouses, 107-108; marine, 39-40, 155-156, 262-263, 461; Mid-coast, 142-143, 155-156, 169-170, 176, 194, 211-212, 213-214, 223, 239; Monhegan Island, 226-227; Native American, 423; natural history, 302; Northern Maine, 461, 485, 487-488; South Coast, 39-40, 58, 75-76, 94; telephone, 394; transportation, 213-214; trolleys, 75-76; Vinalhaven Island, 231; Washington County/Campobello/St. Andrews, 345, 358, 367-

368; Western Mountains and Lakes, 375-377, 394, 410-411, 423. *See also* Historic sites/houses. *See also* Railroad rides and museums
Music and concerts, 27; Bangor, 337; Bar Harbor/Acadia, 327; Casco Bay, 122-123; East Penobscot Bay, 285; Kennebec Valley, 444; Mid-coast, 149-150, 187, 255-256; Washington County/Campobello/St. Andrews, 355; Western Mountains and Lakes, 389
Music schools, 27
Musical Wonder House, 169
MythWeaver Theater, 270

Naples Historical Society Museum, 378
Naples village, 375
National Audubon Ecology Camp, 196
Native American history/artifacts: Bangor, 333-334; Bar Harbor/Acadia, 303; Kennebec Valley, 447; Kittery and the Yorks, 37; Mid-coast, 193-194; Northern Maine, 475; Washington County/Campobello/St. Andrews, 357-358; Western Mountains and Lakes, 423
Natural History Museum (College of the Atlantic), 302
Nature Conservancy, The, 77
Nature preserves, 27-28; Bar Harbor/Acadia, 305; Casco Bay, 112-113; East Penobscot Bay, 280, 290-291; Mid-coast, 197, 244; Northern Maine, 490-491; South Coast, 60-61, 79, 96; Vinalhaven Island, 231. *See also* Wildlife refuges
Neal Dow Memorial, 109-110
New Brunswick, 366-370
New Brunswick Botanical Gardens, 489
New Harbor village, 192
New Sweden Historical Society Museum, 487
Newcastle: about, 189-191; information/help, 191; restaurants, 202-206; sites/activities, 192-197, 206-208
Nickels-Sortwell House, 169
1910 Farmhouse, 156
Nordica Homestead Museum, 423
Norlands Living History Center, 439
Norridgewock Monument, 447
North Haven Island, 211, 233
North Island Museum, 233
North Woods, 457-458
Northeast Historic Film, 264
Northport village, 262
Norway village, 375
Nott House, 76
Nowetah's American Indian Museum, 423
Nubble Light, 41
Nylander Museum, 488

Oak Street Theater, 123

O'Brien Cemetery, 344
Ocean Adventure, 170
Ocean Park village, 94
Oceanariums, 302, 303, 304
Ogunquit: about, 55-57; information/help,
    57-58; restaurants, 66-69; sites/activities,
    58-61, 69-71
Ogunquit Museum of American Art, 58
Ogunquit Playhouse, 59
Ogunquit Square Theatre, 70
Old Conway House Complex, 239
Old Firehouse Museum, 304
Old Gaol, 40
Old German Church, 194-195
Old Orchard Beach area: about, 92-93;
    information/help, 93; restaurants, 99-100;
    sites/activities, 94-96, 100
Old Orchard Beach Historical Society, 94
Old Rock Schoolhouse, 193
Old Sardine Village Museum, The, 345
Old School House, The, 40
Old Town Museum, 334
Old Town village, 333
Old Walpole Meeting House, 194
Old York Historical Society, 40, 45
Olson House, The, 212
Orchestras. See Music and concerts
Orland village, 262
Orlin Arts Center at Bates College, 377
Orono village, 333
Orrs Island, 143
Outlet stores. See Factory outlets
Outward Bound School, Hurricane Island,
    215-216
Owls Head Light, 214
Owls Head Transportation Museum, 213-214
Oxford Plains Speedway/Dragway, 375

Palace Playland, 95
Park Street Players, 453
Parking: Casco Bay, 106; Mid-coast, 167,
    176, 238; South Coast, 57, 75, 93
Parks and forests, 28; Bar Harbor/Acadia,
    306, 308, 310-311; Casco Bay, 112, 127-
    128; East Penobscot Bay, 263, 264-265,
    274, 290-291; Kennebec Valley, 440;
    Mid-coast, 158-159, 178-179, 218, 243-
    244; Northern Maine, 474, 476, 477-478,
    491; Roosevelt Campobello International,
    345, 347-348; South Coast, 44;
    Vinalhaven Island, 231; Washington
    County/Campobello/St. Andrews, 343;
    Western Mountains and Lakes, 380-381,
    395-396, 413-414. See also Beaches and
    swimming. See also Nature preserves
Parson Fisher House, 278
Parson Smith House, 377
Patte Brook Multiple Use Management
    Demonstration Area, 394

Patten Lumberman's Museum, 475-476
Peabody-Fitch House Museum, 377
Peary-MacMillan Arctic Museum, 142
Pejepscot Historical Society Museum, 142-
    143
Pemaquid: about, 189-191; information/help,
    191; restaurants, 202-206; sites/activities,
    192-197, 206-208
Pemaquid Art Gallery, 193
Pemaquid Point Lighthouse, 193
Penobscot Marine Museum, 262-263
Penobscot Nation Museum, 334
Penobscot Theater, 270, 337
Performing arts: Bangor, 337; Bar Harbor/
    Acadia, 327-328; Casco Bay, 123; East
    Penobscot Bay, 270, 276; Kennebec
    Valley, 444; Mid-coast, 165; 206, 223,
    256; Washington County/Campobello/St.
    Andrews, 361; Western Mountains and
    Lakes, 420. See also Music and concerts.
    See also Theaters and cinemas
Perham's Maine Mineral Store, 29, 380, 397
Perkins Cove village, 58
Perry's Tropical Nut House, 263
Petit Manan National Wildlife Refuge, 343,
    347
Pettengill Farm, 128
Phillips Historical Society, 411
Phillips village, 410
Phippsburg Peninsula, The, 156-157
Photography schools, 70, 243
Picnicking, 197, 218, 348
Pierre Monteux Memorial Concert Hall, 327
Pine Point village, 94
Pine Tree State Arboretum, 440
Plays and playhouses. See Theaters and
    cinemas
Pleasant Mountain, 380, 381
Pleasant Point Reservation, 357-358
Pond Cove village, 106
Population, 28
Porter's Landing village, 126
Portland: about, 103-105; information/help,
    105-106; restaurants, 117-122; sites/
    activities, 107-113, 122-124
Portland Fire Museum, 108
Portland Lyric Theater, 123
Portland Museum of Art, 107
Portland Observatory, 109
Portland Performing Arts Center, 123
Portland Players, 123
Portland Symphony Orchestra, 122
Portsmouth Naval Shipyard, 40
Pottery. See Artisans
Pownalborough Court House, 170
Professional sports, 123
Prospect village, 262
Prouts Neck Cliff Path and Wildlife
    Sanctuary, 112

Puffin-watching, 29, 234, 346-347

Quoddy Tides Foundation Marine Library, 357

Rachel Carson Memorial Salt Pond, 197
Rachel Carson National Wildlife Refuge, 61, 79
Racing, 23, 95, 337, 375
Radio stations, 285
Rafting. *See* Whitewater rafting
Railroad rides and museums, 29; Boothbay Railway Village, 176; East Penobscot Bay, 264-265; Maine Coast, 170-171; Maine Narrow Gauge Railroad Co., 108; Sandy River-Rangeley Lakes RR, 411
Range Pond State Park, 381
Rangeley Friends of the Performing Arts, 420
Rangeley Lake State Park, 413, 414
Rangeley Lakes Region: information/help, 409-410; restaurants, 419-420; sites/ activities, 410-414, 420
Rangeley Lakes Region Historical Society, 411
Rates, 29
Redington Museum and Apothecary, 438
Restaurants——dining out: Bangor, 336-337; Bar Harbor/Acadia, 322-325; Casco Bay, 117-120; 131-132; East Penobscot Bay, 268-269, 275-276, 283-284, 293; Kennebec Valley, 442-443, 452-453; Mid-coast, 147-148, 163-164, 172-173, 184, 202-204, 221, 251-253; Northern Maine, 471, 492-493; Sebago and Long Lakes region, 387-388; South Coast, 49-51, 66-68, 87-89, 99; Washington County/ Campobello/St. Andrews, 352-353, 360, 365-366, 370; Western Mountains and Lakes, 405, 419, 429-430——eating out: Bangor, 337; Bar Harbor/Acadia, 325-327; Casco Bay, 120-122, 132-133; East Penobscot Bay, 269, 276, 284-285, 294; Kennebec Valley, 443-444, 453; Mid-coast, 148-149, 164-165, 173-174, 184-187, 204-206, 222-223, 253-255; Monhegan Island, 229; Northern Maine, 471-472, 480-481, 493; Sebago and Long Lakes region, 388; South Coast, 51-52, 68-69, 89-90, 99-100; Vinalhaven Island, 232; Washington County/Campobello/St. Andrews, 353-355, 360-361, 366, 370; Western Mountains and Lakes, 405-406, 419-420, 430-431
Reversing Falls, 279
Reversing Salt Water Falls, 358
Richmond village, 436
Ripogenus Dam and Gorge, 462
Robert Abbe Museum at Sieur de Monts Spring, 303

Rockhounding, 29, 380, 397
Rockland: information/help, 209-211; restaurants, 221-223; sites/activities, 211-218, 223-225
Rockland Light, 214
Rockport: about, 235-237; information/help, 237-238; restaurants, 251-255; sites/ activities, 238-244, 255-258
Roller skating, 215
Roosevelt Campobello International Park, 345, 347-348
Roque Bluffs State Park, 344, 348
Ross Memorial Museum, 367
Round Pond village, 192
Round Top Center for the Arts, 206
Ruggles House, The, 343

Sabbathday Lake Shaker Community and Museum, 375-376
Saco River, 379
Saddleback Mountain, 413
Sailing, 29-30; Bar Harbor/Acadia, 309-310; Casco Bay, 111; East Penobscot Bay, 278; Mid-coast, 178; schools, 243; South Coast, 59, 78. *See also* Coastal cruises
Sailor's Memorial Museum, 238
Salmon Brook Historical Society, 487
Salome Sellers House, 289
Samoset Memorial, 194
Sandy River-Rangeley Lakes Railroad, 411
Sarah Orne Jewett Birthplace, 42-43
Sayward-Wheeler House, 41
Scarborough Downs, 95
Scarborough Marsh Nature Center, 96, 112
Scenic drives: Mid-coast, 143, 156-157, 195, 239; Northern Maine, 461-462, 476, 489; South Coast, 42, 77; views/overlooks, 451, 476; Western Mountains and Lakes, 394-395, 411
Schoodic Mountain, 309
Schoodic Peninsula, 306
Schoolhouses, 40, 193
Schools: art, 108, 243; boat-building, 78, 243; 279-280; crafts, 19, 289; music, 27; photography, 70, 243; sailing, 78, 243; woodworking, 243. *See also* Learning programs
Screw Auger Falls, 396
Scuba diving, 20, 43
Sea kayaking, 30-31; Casco Bay, 111; East Penobscot Bay, 278-279; Mid-coast, 144, 157, 178, 241
Seacoast Repertory Theatre, 52
Seal Cove Auto Museum, 304
Searsport: about, 261; information/help, 261-262; restaurants, 268-269; sites/activities, 262-265, 270-271
Searsport Historical Society, 264
Seashore Trolley Museum, 75

Sebago Lake State Park, 380-381
Sebago-Long Lakes Region: about, 373-374; information/help, 374-375; restaurants, 387-388; sites/activities, 375-381, 388-390
Sebago-Long Lakes Region Chamber Music Festival, 389
Second Read Bookstore, The, 223
Shaker Village, 375-376
Sheepscot Village, 167, 169
Shell heaps, 193-194
Shelter Institute, 158
Shopping: Bangor, 338; Bar Harbor/Acadia, 328-330; Casco Bay, 123-124; 133-136; East Penobscot Bay, 270-271, 276, 285-287, 294-296; Kennebec Valley, 444-445; Mid-coast, 150, 165-166, 174, 187-188, 206-208, 223-224, 256-258; Monhegan Island, 229-230; North Haven Island, 233; Northern Maine, 473, 493-494; South Coast, 53-54, 70-71, 91; Vinalhaven Island, 233; Washington County/Campobello/St. Andrews, 355-356, 361, 366, 370; Western Mountains and Lakes, 389-390, 406-407, 420, 432. See also Factory outlets
Shore Village Museum, 214, 215
Skating, 215, 400, 426
Skiing: après-ski entertainment, 406, 431; Mid-coast, 242; Western Mountains and Lakes, 413. See also Cross-country skiing. See also Downhill skiing
Skolfield-Whittier House, 143
Skowhegan History House, 447
Skowhegan Indian and Norridgewock Monument, 447
Sleigh rides, 400
Small's Falls, 414
Snow Falls Gorge, 380
Snowmobiling, 31-32; Bar Harbor/Acadia, 310; Kennebec Valley, 450; Northern Maine, 466, 477, 490; Western Mountains and Lakes, 400, 413, 426
Snowshoeing, 477
Songo Locks, 378
South Berwick, 42-43
South Bristol, 192
South Congregational Church, 76
South Freeport village, 126
South Paris village, 375
Spas, health, 32, 426-427
Special events. See Events, annual
Sporting camps, 32. See also Lodging Index
Sports, professional, 123
Spring Point Lighthouse, 108
Spring Point Museum, 107
Squaw Mountain, 461, 463
St. Agathe Historical Society Museum, 487
St. Andrews, 366-370
St. Andrew's Episcopal Church, 194

St. Anthony Monastery and Shrine, 76
St. Croix Island Overlook, 363
St. Croix Valley, 363-366
St. Patrick's Catholic Church, 194
Stanley Museum, 423
Stanwood Homestead Sanctuary and Museum, 305
State Fish Hatchery and Game Farm, 375
State House, 437
State of Maine Building from the 1893 Columbia Exposition in Chicago, 377
State of Maine (ship), 273
State parks. See Parks and forests
State Theater, 122
Step Falls, 396
Steuben, 343
Steve Powell Wildlife Management Area (Swan's Island), 159
Stockton Springs: about, 261; information/help, 261-262; restaurants, 268-269; sites/activities, 262-265, 270-271
Stonington: about, 288; information/help, 289; restaurants, 293-294; sites/activities, 289-291, 294-296
Strand Cinema, The, 223
Sugarloaf/USA, 421, 426, 427, 430-431
Sunday River ski area, 393, 395, 399-400
Surry Opera Company, 285
Swan's Island, 159, 440
Swan's Island Educational Society, 304
Swimming. See Beaches and swimming
Symphonies. See Music and concerts

Taxes, Canadian, 367
Taylor-Barry House, 76
Tenants Harbor village, 211
Tennis: Bar Harbor/Acadia, 310; East Penobscot Bay, 274, 290; Kennebec Valley, 440; Mid-coast, 144, 158, 178, 241; South Coast, 59, 95; Western Mountains and Lakes, 379, 413
Theater at Monmouth, 444
Theater Project of Brunswick, 150
Theaters and cinemas, 32-33; Bangor, 337-338; Bar Harbor/Acadia, 328; Casco Bay, 123; East Penobscot Bay, 264, 270; Kennebec Valley, 444, 453; Mid-coast, 149-150, 187, 206, 223, 244, 256; South Coast, 52, 59, 69-70, 90, 100; Washington County/Campobello/St. Andrews, 355; Western Mountains and Lakes, 388-389
Thomas A. Hill House, 334-335
Thomaston: about, 209; information/help, 209-211; restaurants, 221-223; sites/activities, 211-218, 223-225
Thompson's Ice House, 193
Thuya Garden and Lodge, 303
Time zones, 367
Topsham village, 142

Trails. *See* Hiking/walks
Trains. *See* Railroad rides and museums
Transportation/travel: Bangor, 333; Bar
    Harbor/Acadia, 301-302; Casco Bay, 105-
    106, 126; East Penobscot Bay, 262, 273,
    277, 289; Kennebec Valley, 436; Mid-
    coast, 141, 155, 167, 176, 191, 209, 211,
    238; museums, 213-214, 330; Northern
    Maine, 460-461, 475, 485; South Coast,
    39, 57, 75, 93; turnpike conditions, 26;
    Washington County/Campobello/St.
    Andrews, 342, 362, 367; Western
    Mountains and Lakes, 374-375, 393-394,
    410, 422
Trolley rides and museums, 57, 75-76, 176
Two Lights State Park, 112

Union village, 211
University of Maine, 17, 334, 355
Unusual Cabaret, The, 328
Upper Kennebec Valley: about, 446;
    information/help, 446-447; restaurants,
    452-453; sites/activities, 447-451, 453

Vaughan Woods, 44-45
Vaughns Island Preserve, 79
Vesper Hill Children's Chapel, 239
Victoria Mansion, 109
Villages: Bangor area, 333-334; Bar Harbor/
    Acadia, 302; Boothbay Railway, 176;
    Casco Bay, 106, 126; East Penobscot Bay,
    262; Kennebec Valley, 436; Mid-coast,
    142, 167, 169, 191-192, 211, 238-239;
    South Coast, 58, 75, 94; Western
    Mountains and Lakes, 375, 410. *See also*
    Museum villages
Vinalhaven Historical Society Museum, 231
Vinalhaven Island, 211, 230-232

Wadsworth-Longfellow House, 109
Wagon rides, 464
Waldo Theatre, 206
Waldoboro village, 191
Waldoborough Historical Society Museum,
    194
Walks/walking. *See* Hiking/walks
Waponahki Museum & Resource Center, 357
Warren Island State Park, 244
Washington County, 339-342
Water parks, 94
Waterfalls and gorges, 22, 33; Kennebec
    Valley, 446, 450-451, 451; Washington
    County/Campobello/St. Andrews, 358,
    Western Mountains and Lakes, 380, 396,
    414
Waterville Summer Music Theater, 444
Waterville-Winslow Two Cent bridge, 439
Watson Settlement Covered Bridge, 19, 489
Webb Museum of Vintage Fashion, 488

Wedding Cake House, 76
Weld Historical Society, 411
Weld village, 410
Wells: about, 55-57; information/help, 57-58;
    restaurants, 66-69; sites/activities, 58-61,
    69-71
Wells Auto Museum, 58
Wells National Estuarine Research Reserve
    at Laudholm Farm, 60-61
Wendell Gilley Museum, 304
WERU radio station, 285
West Quoddy Light State Park, 345
West Quoddy Marine Research Station, 345
Western Maine Children's Museum, 423
Whale-watching, 33, 78, 307, 308, 348, 368
White Columns (Nott House), 76
White Mountain National Forest, 396
Whitewater rafting, 33; Kennebec Valley,
    446, 448-450; Northern Maine, 465, 477;
    Western Mountains and Lakes, 425
Wild Gardens of Acadia, 303
Wildlife refuges: East Penobscot Bay, 280;
    Kennebec Valley, 440; Mid-coast, 159;
    Northern Maine, 464, 488-489; South
    Coast, 60-61; Washington County/
    Campobello/St. Andrews, 343, 347, 359;
    Western Mountains and Lakes, 375, 414.
    See also Nature preserves
Wilhelm Reich Museum, 410-411
William A. Farnsworth Library and Art
    Museum, 211-212
Willowbrook at Newfield, 376
Wilson Museum, 273
Windjammers, 34, 216-217, 241-242
Wineries. *See* Breweries and wineries
Winslow Memorial Park, 127
Winterport village, 334
Wiscasset: about, 167; information/help, 167-
    168; restaurants, 172-174; sites/activities,
    169-171, 174
Witch Island, 197
Witherle Woods, 274
Wolfe's Neck Woods State Park, 128
Wooden Boat School, 16, 279-280
Woodstock Historical Society Museum, 394
Woodworking schools, 243
Workshops, 17. *See also* Learning programs.
    See also Schools
World's Smallest Church, 170

Yarmouth village, 106
York Beach Cinema, 52
York Institute Museum, 94
Yorks, the: about, 37-39; information/help,
    39; restaurants, 39-52; sites/activities, 39-
    45, 52-54
York's Wild Kingdom, 41-42

Zoos, 41-42, 306. *See also* Amusement parks

Lodging Index

Abbotts Mill Farm, 403
Acadia, 311-322
Admiral Peary House, 385
Admiral's Inn, The, 64
Aimhi Lodge, 381
Albonegon Inn, 180
Algonquin, The, 368
Allagash Gardners Sporting Camps, 492
Anchor Watch, 182
Anchorage Inn, The, 48
Appalachian Mountain Club campgrounds, 321, 386
Apple Tree B&B, 200
Aroostook County, 491-492
Aspinquid, 62
Asticou Inn, 312
Atlantic Ark Inn, 182
Atlantic Birches Inn, The, 97
Atlantic Oakes By-the-Sea, 320
Atlantic Seal B&B, 130
Attean Lake Resort, 451
Augusta, 441-442
Augustus Bove House, 385

Bagley House Bed & Breakfast, 130
Bailey Inn, The, 171
Bailey Island Motel, 147
Balance Rock Inn By the Sea, 314
Bald Mountain Camps, 417
Bangor, 335-336
Bar Harbor, 311-322
Bar Harbor Inn, 320
Barnswallow B&B, 201
Bass Cottage in the Field, 315
Bass Harbor Inn, 317
Bath, 159-163
Bath Bed & Breakfast, The, 161
Bayley's Camping Resort, 98
Bayview, 313
Beach Farm Inn, 65
Beachfront Condotel, 98
Beachmere, 63
Bear Mountain Inn, 384
Bear Spring Camps, 441
Beaver Cove Camps, 470
Bed & breakfasts: Bar Harbor/Acadia, 312-319; Casco Bay, 114-117, 128-131; East Penobscot Bay, 265-268; 281-283; Kennebec Valley, 441, Mid-coast, 145-147, 160-162, 171-172, 181-183, 199-201, 219-220, 247-250; Monhegan Island, 228; Northern Maine, 467-468, 479, 491-492; South Coast, 47-49, 63-65, 80-86, 96-97; Washington County/Campobello/St.

Andrews, 348-351, 359-360, 364, 369-370; Western Mountains and Lakes, 384-386, 402-403, 415-416, 427-428
Belfast, 265-268
Bell Buoy B&B, The, 48
Belmont, The, 245
Bethel, 400-404
Bethel Inn and Country Club, 400
Bethel Point Bed & Breakfast, 146
Bethel Spa Motel, 404
Big Moose Inn, 479
Birches Resort, The, 468
Black Duck, The, 319
Black Point Inn Resort, 116
Blackberry Inn, The, 248
Blackwoods campgrounds, 321
Blue Harbor House, The, 246
Blue Hill, 280-283
Blue Hill Farm, 281
Blue Hill Inn, 281
Blueberry Patch Inn, 351
Boothbay Harbor, 179-183
Bosebuck Mountain Camps, 418
Bowater/Great Northern Paper campgrounds, 470
Bradford Camps, 479
Bradley Inn, 198
Brannon-Bunker Inn, 199
Breakwater 1904, 313
Breakwater Inn, The, 83
Brewer House, 364
Briar Rose B&B, The, 200
Briarwood Mountain Lodge, 452
Bridge Inn, 293
Broad Bay Inn & Gallery, 200
Brunswick, 145-147
Brunswick, The, 98
Brunswick Bed & Breakfast, 145
Buck's Harbor Inn, 282
Bucksport, 265-268
Bufflehead Cove, 81

Cabot Cove Cottages, 87
Calais, 364-365
Camden, 244-251
Camden Harbour Inn, 246
Camping: Bar Harbor/Acadia, 321; Casco Bay, 131; Kennebec Valley, 442; Northern Maine, 470-471, 479-480; South Coast, 98; Washington County/Campobello/St. Andrews, 352, 360, 365; Western Mountains and Lakes, 386-387, 404, 418
Campobello, 348-352

Camps: Kennebec Valley, 441-442; Northern Maine, 469-470, 479. *See also* Sporting camps
Canterbury Cottage, 315
Canterbury House Bed & Breakfast, 48
Cape Arundel Inn, 85
Cape Neddick House, 49
Cap'n Frost B&B, 220
Captain Butman Homestead, The, 267
Captain Daniel Stone Inn, 145
Captain Drummond House, 160
Captain Fairfield Inn, The, 84
Captain Green Pendleton B&B, 267
Captain Jefferds Inn, The, 80
Captain Lindsey House, The, 219
Captain Lord Mansion, 80
Captain's House, 201
Captain's Quarters Inn and Motel, 291
Carousel B&B, 479
Carrabassett Valley, 427-429
Carriage House, The, 96
Carriage House Inn, 267
Castine, 274-275
Castine Inn, 274
Castle Island Camps, 442
Center Lovell Inn, 383
Chandler River Bed & Breakfast, 350
Chapman Inn, 402
Chebeague Inn By-the-Sea, 115
Chesuncook Lake House, 466
Chetwynd House Inn, 84
Chiputneticook Sporting Lodge, 492
Christie's of South Bay, 350
Claremont, The, 311
Clarke's Inn, 492
Clearwater Sporting Camps, 417
Cliff House, The, 61
Clover Hill Farm, 87
Cobb's Pierce Pond Camps, 451
Cobscook Bay, 359-360
Cobscook Bay State Park, 360
Cod Cove Inn, 172
Colonial Winterport Inn, 336
Colony, The, 80
Condominiums: South Coast, 97-98; Western Mountains and Lakes, 403-404, 417
Cornish Inn, The, 383
Cottage in the Lane Motor Lodge, 65
Cottages: Bar Harbor/Acadia, 319-320; Casco Bay, 117; Kennebec Valley, 441-442; Matinicus Island, 234; Mid-coast, 147, 162, 163, 183, 201-202, 220-221; Monhegan Island, 228-229; South Coast, 65, 97-98; Washington County/Campobello/St. Andrews, 351; Western Mountains and Lakes, 386, 416-417
Country at Heart, 131

Country Club Inn, 415
Country Farm, 97
Cove House Bed & Breakfast, 85
Coveside-Five Islands Bed & Breakfast, 162
Coveside Inn, 198
Craignair Inn, 218
Crescent Lake Cottages, 386
Crocker House Country Inn, 318
Crown 'n' Anchor Inn, 97
Cutty Sark Motel, 49

Daigle's Bed & Breakfast, 491
Damariscotta, 197-202
Damariscotta Lake Farm, 201
Dark Harbor House, 245
Deer Isle, 291-293
Deer Isle Village Inn, 292
Desert of Maine Campgrounds, 131
Devlin House, 467
Diamond Cove, 115
Dockside Guest Quarters, 46
Douglass Place, 402
Driftwood Inn and Cottages, 145
Dunes, 65
Dunes, The, 98

East Wind Inn, 218
Eastland Plaza Hotel, The, 113
Eastport, 359-360
Eden Village Motel and Cottages, 320
Edgecomb Inn, 172
Edgecombe-Coles House, 248
Edgewater Cabins, 320
Edgewater Motel and Cottages, 319
Edwards' Harborside Inn, 47
Efficiencies: Mid-coast, 220-221; Monhegan Island, 228-229
Eggemoggin Reach Bed & Breakfast, 282
1802 House, The, 85
Elizabeth's Bed & Breakfast, 161
Emery's Cottages on the Shore, 319
Emma's Guest House and Cottages, 183
Evans Notch area campgrounds, 404

Fairhaven Inn, 161
Farrell-Michaud Bed & Breakfast, 491
Farrington's, 382
Field View B&B, 403
Five Gables Inn, 181
Flying Cloud, The, 199
Fox Island Inn, 231
Franciscan Guest House, 87
Freeport, 128-131
Friendship By the Sea, 220
Front Porch B&B, The, 162
Frost Pond Camps, 470

Georgia Pacific's campgrounds, 365

Glad II, 162
Glidden House, 200
Goose Cove Lodge, 291
Gosnold Arms, 197
Grand old resorts, 311-312
Grand View, 98
Grant's Kennebago Camps, 418
Green Heron, The, 83
Greenville Inn, 466
Grey Gull, The, 64
Grey Havens, 160
Guest houses: Mid-coast, 162, 183; South
    Coast, 63, 82, 86, 87; Western Mountains
    and Lakes, 404
Gulf Hagas, 480
Gundalow Inn, 45

Hammons House, 402
Hamstead Farm, 336
Harbor Hill, 220
Harborfields, 183
Harbour Cottage Inn, 316
Harbourside Inn, 315
Harpswell Inn, 146
Harpswells, the, 145-147
Harraseeket Inn, 128
Harrison's Pierce Pond Sporting Camps, 451
Hartstone Inn, 247
Hawthorn Inn, 248
Hayes Guest House, The, 63
Henry Point Campground, 352
Herbert, The, 427
Hermit Island, 163
Heron House, The, 317
Herring Cove Provincial Park, 352
Hewnoaks, 386
Hichborn Inn, The, 268
Higgins Beach Inn, 116
High Meadows Bed & Breakfast, 46
High Tide Inn, 250
Highland Mill Inn, 251
Highlawn Bed & Breakfast, 335
Hillside Acres Motor Court, 183
Hinckley's Dreamwood Motor Court, 319
Hiram Alden Inn, 265
Hiram Blake Camp, 280
Hitchcock House, 229
Hodgdon Island Inn, 182
Holbrook House Inn, 315
Holbrook Inn, 129
Holden Homestead, 292
Holidae House, 402
Holiday House, The, 275
Holiday Inn by the Bay, 114
Home-Nest Farm, 441
Home Port Inn, 350
Homeport Inn, 267
Horatio Johnson House, 265

Hostels, 321, 387
Hotel Everett, 114
Hotel Pemaquid, The, 198
Hotels: Bar Harbor/Acadia, 320-321; Casco
    Bay, 113-114; South Coast, 80
Hunter Cover, 416
Hutchins House, 47

Idlease Guest House, 86
Independence Farm, 441
Indian Rocks Camps, 365
Inn at Bath, The, 161
Inn at Bay Ledge, The, 313
Inn at Canoe Point, 312
Inn at Eastport, The, 360
Inn at Ferry Landing, The, 292
Inn at Goose Rocks, The, 86
Inn at Harbor Head, The, 82
Inn at Harmon Park, 47
Inn at Long Lake, The, 385
Inn at Park Spring, The, 114
Inn at Southwest, The, 316
Inn at Sunrise Point, The, 249
Inn by the Sea, 116
Inn on Carleton Street, The, 114
Inn on South Street, 81
Inn on Winter's Hill, 428
Inns: Bar Haror/Acadia, 312-319; Casco Bay,
    114-117, 128; East Penobscot Bay, 265-
    268, 281-283, 291-293; Mid-coast, 145,
    160, 171, 180-181, 197-199, 218-219,
    245-247; Monhegan Island, 227-228;
    Northern Maine, 466-467, 479; South
    Coast, 46-47, 63-65, 80-86, 96-97;
    Washington County/Campobello/St.
    Andrews, 348-351, 359-360; Western
    Mountains and Lakes, 382-384, 400-402,
    415, 427-428
Isaac Randall House, The, 129
Island House, The, 317
Island Inn, 227
Island View Inn, 318
Island View Oceanfront Cottages, 220
Isle au Haut, 291-293

Jackman, 451-452
Jamestown, The, 202
Jed Prouty Tavern, 268
Jefferson House, The, 200
Jeweled Turret Inn, The, 266
Jo Mary Multiple Use Forest, 479
John Peters Inn, 281
Johnson Bed & Breakfast, The, 146
Jonathan's, 182
Jonesport "By The Sea," 350

Katahdin Area Bed & Breakfast, 479
Katahdin Inn, The, 48

Katahdin Lake Wilderness Camps, 479
Katahdin region, 479-480
Katahdin Shadows Campground, 480
Kawanhee Inn, 417
Kedarburn Inn, 383
Keeper's House, The, 292
Keller's, 116
Kendall Tavern Bed & Breakfast, 129
Kennebunkport Inn, 82
Kennebunks, the, 80-87
Kenniston Hill Inn B&B, 182
Kineo House, 467
King's Row Inn, 292
Kingsleigh Inn, 316
Kittery and the Yorks, 45-49
Kylemere House "Crosstrees," 84

Lady and the Loon, The, 147
Lake Brook B&B Guest House, 82
Lake House, 382
Lake St. George State Park, 442
Lake Webb House, 416
Lakeside Inn and Cabins, 365
Lakewood Camps, 418
Lamoine Beach campgrounds, 321
Lamoine House, 318
Lamoine State Park campgrounds, 321
L'Auberge, 401
Lawnmeer Inn, 180
Le Domaine, 318
Ledgelawn Inn, 314
Leen's Lodge, 365
Libby House, 232
Libby Sporting Camps, 492
Lily Bay State Park campgrounds, 470
LimeRock Inn, 220
Lincoln House, 360
Lincolnville, 244-251
Lindenwood Inn, 316
Linekin Bay Resort, 179
Lion's Den, 182
Little Dream, A, 250
Little Island Motel, 147
Little Lyford Pond Camps, 468
Little River Lodge, 350
Littlefield Beaches, 404
Lodge at Camden Hills, The, 250
Lodge at Moosehead, The, 466
Long Lake Motor Inn, 492
Long Lakes region, 381-387
Lord Camden Inn, 251
Lower Piscataquis, 466-471
Lucerne Inn, The, 336
Lumberjack Lodge, 428
Lyman Blair House, 468

Machias Motor Inn, 351
Maine House, The, 404

Maine-lly Llamas Farm, 384
Maine Stay, The, 247
Maine Stay Inn and Cottages, 84
Maison Suisse Inn, The, 315
Mallory's B&B Inn, 415
Manitou Cottage, 467
Manor, The, 275
Manor House Inn, 314
Maple Hill B&B, 130
Maple Hill Farm, 441
Marginal Way House and Motel, 63
Markert House, 200
Marston House, 171
Matinicus Island, 234
Mattawamkeag Wilderness Park, 480
Maynards in Maine, 469
McClellan Park, 352
McKay Lodging, 315
Medawisla, 470
Mermaid, The, 221
Micmac Farm Guest Cabins, 351
Middaugh Bed & Breakfast, 145
Migis Lodge, 381
Milbridge, 348-352
Mill Pond House, 220
Mill Pond Inn, 199
Mira Monte Inn and Suites, 314
Mollyockett Motel, 404
Monhegan House, 228
Monhegan Island, 227-229
Moose Crossing Farm, 386
Moose Point Camps, 492
Moosehead Lake area and Lower
    Piscataquis, 466-471
Mooselookmeguntic House, 416
Morning Dove, 64
Moses Paul Inn, The, 46
Motel East, The, 360
Motels: Bar Harbor/Acadia, 320-321; Casco
    Bay, 131; East Penobscot Bay, 293; Mid-
    coast, 147, 183, 202, 221; Northern
    Maine, 492; South Coast, 65-66, 86-87,
    97-98; Washington County/Campobello/
    St. Andrews, 351, 360, 370; Western
    Mountains and Lakes, 404, 428-429
Motor inns, 62
Mount Blue State Park campgrounds, 418
Mount Desert Island AYH Youth Hostel, 321
Mount Desert Island YWCA, 321
Mountain Road House, 282
Mountain View Cottages, 416
Mrs. G's Bed & Breakfast, 452

Nannau Seaside B&B, 313
Nathaniel Hosmer House, 249
Navigator, The, 221
New Brunswick, 368-370
New Meadows Inn, 163

Newagen Seaside Inn, 179
Newcastle, 197-202
Newcastle Inn, The, 197
Nicholson Inn, 130
Noble House, 384
Norseman, The, 403
North Camps, 416
North Haven Island, 233
Northern Pines, 382
Northern Pride Lodge, 467
Northwoods, 416
Norumbega, 248
Nugent's Chamberlain Lake Camps, 469

Oakland House, 281
Ocean Gate, 180
Ocean House, 218
Ocean Point Inn, 180
Ocean View, The, 85
Ocean View House, 291
Ogunquit and Wells, 61-66
Old Fort Inn, 81
Old Granite Inn, 219
Old Orchard Beach, 96-98
One-Eighty-One Main Street, 129
Outsiders' Inn, The, 219
Owen House, The, 351
Owl and Turtle Harbor View Guest Rooms, The, 250
Oxford House Inn, 382

Packard House, 161
Pansy Patch, 369
Papoose Pond Resort and Campground, 386
Peacock House, 350
Peaks-Kenny State Park, 480
Pemaquid, 197-202
Pentagoet Inn, 275
Penury Hall, 316
Philbrook Farm Inn, 400
Pilgrim's Inn, 292
Pine Hill Inn, The, 63
Pine-Sider Lodge, 403
Pippincott, 369
Pleasant Bay Bed & Breakfast, 349
Point Sebago, 386
Pointy Head Inn and Antiques, 317
Pomegranate Inn, 114
Popham Beach Bed & Breakfast, 161
Porter's Landing B&B, 130
Portland, 113-117
Portland Hall, 114
Portland Regency, 113
Powder Horn, 98
Pres du Port, 291
Pulpit Harbor Inn, 233

Quisisana, 382

Rangeley Inn and Motor Lodge, 415
Rangeley Lake State Park campgrounds, 418
Rangeley Lakes region, 415-418
Resorts: Bar Harbor/Acadia, 311-312; East Penobscot Bay, 291; grand old, 311-312; Mid-coast, 159-160, 179-180, 244-245; South Coast, 61, 62, 80; Washington County/Campobello/St. Andrews, 368-369. *See also* Rustic resorts
Reunion Inn & Grill, 251
Richmond Sauna and Bed and Breakfast, 441
Ricker House, 348
River Port Inn, 428
River View Motel, The, 404
Riverbed, The, 49
Riverside Bed & Breakfast, 350
Riverside Motel, 65
Riverview, 162
Roaring Lion, The, 201
Rock Gardens Inn, 159
Rockland/the Islands, 227-229, 231-232, 233-234
Rockland/Thomaston, 218-221
Rockport, 244-251
Rockwood Cottages, 469
Rose Cottage, 64
Rossmount Inn, The, 368
Rum Rapids Inn, 491
Rustic resorts: East Penobscot Bay, 280-281, 291; Kennebec Valley, 451, Northern Maine, 468-469, 479; Western Mountains and Lakes, 381-382, 417-418

Saddleback Ski and Summer Lake Preserve, 417
Sailmaker's Inn, 182
St. Andrews, 368-370
St. Andrews Motor Inn, 370
St. Croix Valley, 364-365
Salisbury Cove Cottages, 319
Samoset Resort, 244
Samuel Newman House, The, 145
Sanctuary, 491
Sandy Cedar Haven Campground, 131
Sawyer House, 467
Schooners Wharf, 87
Scraggly Lake Public Lands Management Unit, 480
Seafair Inn, 64
Seagull Motor Inn, 65
Seal Cove Farm, 318
Searsport, 265-268
Seaside Inn & Cottages, 86
Seawitch Bed & Breakfast, 183
Sebago, 381-387
Sebago Lake Lodge, 384
Sebago Lake State Park, 386
Sebasco Lodge, 159

Self-service guest houses, 404
Senator, The, 441
Senter Bed & Breakfast, 147
Shawmut Inn, The, 80
Sherman Inn, 492
Shining Sails Guesthouse, 228
Shining Sails Real Estate, 229
Sign of the Owl, 250
Ski lodges, 403-404, 428-429
Sky Lodge Resort, 452
Small Point Bed & Breakfast, 162
Snow Drift Farm Bed & Breakfast, 201
Snowbird Lodge, 385
Sparhawk, 62
Spencer Pond Camps, 470
Spillover Motel, 429
Spinney's Guest House and Cottages, 162
Sporting camps: Kennebec Valley, 451;
   Northern Maine, 492; Western Moun-
   tains and Lakes, 417-418, 429
Sports lodges, 364
Spouter Inn, The, 249
Spruce Point Inn and Lodges, 179
Squire Tarbox Inn, 160, 171
Stacked Arms, The, 171
Stage Neck Inn, 46
Steve Powell Wildlife Management Area
   (Swan Island), 442
Stockton Springs, 265-268
Stonington, 291-293
Sudbury Inn, 402
Sugarloaf, 427-429
Sugarloaf Mountain Hotel, 427
Sugarloaf/USA Inn and Condominiums, 427
Sullivan Harbor Farm, 319
Summerwood Inn, 267
Summit Farm Lodging, 479
Sunday River Inn, 401
Sunday River ski lodges, 403
Sundial Inn, 85
Sundown Lodge and Cottages, 416
Sunset Point Cottages, 416
Swan's Island Vacations, 321
Sweet Lillian B&B, 479

Tarry-a-While, 383
Telemark Inn, 401
Ten Perkins Street, 275
1024 Washington, 162
Thomaston, 218-221
Thompson House and Cottages, 201
Thornhedge Inn, 314
Three Stanley Avenue, 428
Thurston House B&B Inn, 267
Tides, The, 313

Tides Inn By-the-Sea, 85
Tidewater Inn, 232
Tim Pond Wilderness Camps, 429
Todd House, 359
Tolman House Inn, 385
Tomhegan Wilderness Resort, 469
Tootsie's Bed & Breakfast, 349
Trade Winds, 221
Trailing Yew, The, 228
Tribler Cottage, 228
Tuckanuck Lodge, 234
Twin Gables, 249

Union Bluff Hotel, The, 48
Upper Kennebec Valley, 451-452

Vicarage by the Sea, 146
Victorian B&B, 250
View Point, 48
Village Cove Inn, 86
Village Inn, The (Castine), 275
Village Inn, The (Freeport), 131
Vinalhaven Island, 231-232

Wadsworth Blanchard Farm Hostel, 387
Walker Estate, The, 369
Weatherby's, 364
Welby Inn, 83
Welch House, 181
Wells, 61-66
Weskeag Inn, 219
West Branch Ponds Camps, 469
Weston House, 359
Westways, 383
Whaleback Inn, 45
White Barn Inn, 83
White Cedar Inn, 129
White Mountain National Forest camp-
   grounds, 404
Whitehall Inn, 246
Widow's Walk, 428
Willows B&B, The, 48
Windrise Farm, 351
Windward House, 248
Wiscasset, 171-172
Wonder View Inn, 321
Wonderview Motor Village, 66
Wooden Goose Inn, 49

Yachtsman Motor Inn and Marina, 86
Ye Olde Forte Cabins, 201
Ye Olde Perkins Place, 63
York Harbor Inn, 47
Yorks, the, 45-49
Youngtown Inn, 247

Books from The Countryman Press

Explorer's Guides

The alternative to mass-market guides with their homogenized listings. Explorer's Guides focus on independently owned inns, motels, and restaurants, and on family and cultural activities reflecting the character and unique qualities of the area.

Cape Cod and the Islands: An Explorer's Guide Includes Nantucket and Martha's Vineyard, by Kimberly Grant
Connecticut: An Explorer's Guide, by Barnett D. Laschever and Barbara Beeching
Massachusetts: Beyond Boston and Cape Cod, by Christina Tree and William Davis
New Hampshire: An Explorer's Guide Third Edition, by Christina Tree and Peter E. Randall
Rhode Island: An Explorer's Guide, by Phyllis Méras and Tom Gannon
Vermont: An Explorer's Guide Sixth Edition, by Christina Tree and Peter S. Jennison
The Hudson Valley and Catskill Mountains: An Explorer's Guide Second Edition, by Joanne Michaels and Mary-Margaret Barile

A selection of our books about Maine and the Northeast

The Architecture of the Shakers, by Julie Nicoletta
Canoeing Massachusetts, Rhode Island and Connecticut, by Ken Weber
Covered Bridges of Vermont, by Ed Barna
Personal Geography: Almost an Autobiography, by Elizabeth Coatsworth
The New England Herb Gardener, by Patricia Turcotte
Full Duty: Vermonters in the Civil War, by Howard Coffin
Fishing Vermont's Streams and Lakes, by Peter F. Cammann
Fifty Hikes in Northern Maine, by Cloe Caputo
Fifty Hikes in Southern Maine, by John Gibson
25 Bicycle Tours in Maine, by Howard Stone
25 Mountain Bike Tours in Massachusetts, by Robert S. Morse
Walks in Nature's Empire, by Scott Edward Anderson

We offer a variety of fiction and nonfiction, and outdoor recreation guides. Our books are available at bookstores, or they may be ordered directly from the publisher. For ordering information or for a comlete catalog, please contact:

The Countryman Press
c/o W.W. Norton & Company, Inc.
800 Keystone Industrial Park
Scranton, PA 18512
http://web.wwnorton.com